RAF OFFICIAL HIST
Series Editor: Sebastian
ISSN: 1471-5414

THE BATTLE OF BRITAIN

Royal Air Force Official Histories
Series Editor: Sebastian Cox
ISSN: 1471-5414

The intention behind this series is to publish many of the formerly classified studies undertaken by the Air Historical Branch of the Ministry of Defence. These will include both the seminal works produced immediately after the Second World War, and the more recent monographs on post-war RAF policy and operations.

Air Defence of Great Britain T. C. G. James, 2 vols:

Vol I: The Growth of Fighter Command, 1936–1940
Edited and with an Introduction by Sebastian Cox

Vol II: The Battle of Britain
Edited and with an Introduction by Sebastian Cox

Defence Policy and the Royal Air Force 1956–1963, T. C. G. James

Defence Policy and the Royal Air Force 1964–1970, Anthony S. Bennell

THE
BATTLE OF BRITAIN

T. C. G. James

Edited and with an Introduction by
SEBASTIAN COX
Head of the Air Historical Branch, Ministry of Defence, London

FRANK CASS
LONDON • PORTLAND, OR

First published in 2000 in Great Britain by
FRANK CASS PUBLISHERS
Newbury House, 900 Eastern Avenue
London, IG2 7HH

and in the United States of America by
FRANK CASS PUBLISHERS
c/o ISBS, 5804 N.E. Hassalo Street
Portland, Oregon, 97213-3644

Website: www.frankcass.com

British Library Cataloguing in Publication Data

James T. C. G.
The Battle of Britain. – (Royal Air Force official histories)
1. Great Britain. Royal Air Force. Fighter Command – History
2. Britain, Battle of, 1940 3. World War, 1939–1945 – Aerial operations, British
I. Title
940.5'4211

ISBN 0-7146-5123-0 (cloth)
ISBN 0-7146-8149-0 (paper)
ISSN: 1471-5414

Library of Congress Cataloging-in-Publication Data

James, T. C. G.
The battle of Britain/T.C.G. James; edited with an introduction by Sebastian Cox.
p. cm. – (Royal Air Force official histories)
Includes Index.
ISBN 0-7146-5123-0 (cloth) – ISBN 0-7146-8149-0 (pbk.)
1. Britain, Battle of, 1940. 2. Great Britain. Royal Air Force. Fighter Command–History. 3. World War, 1939–1945–Aerial operations, British. I. Cox, Sebastian. II. Title. III. Series.

D756.5.B7 J36 2000
940.54'211–dc21 00-058946

Typeset by The Midlands Book Typesetting Company, Loughborough, Leics.
Printed in Great Britain by Bookcraft (Bath) Ltd, Midsomer Norton, Somerset

CONTENTS

Note:
Detailed lists of contents are given at the beginning of each chapter.

LIST OF ILLUSTRATIONS, MAPS AND CHARTS

MAPS

CHARTS

FOREWORD

Air Chief Marshal Sir Peter Squire KCB DFC AFC FRAeS RAF
Chief of the Air Staff

There are many battles that can clearly be seen to have changed the course of history for an individual nation or nations. Few, however, can be said to have influenced the future direction of mankind in so fundamental a manner as the Battle of Britain. The achievements of Fighter Command in the summer of 1940 not only preserved this nation from invasion, but turned the tide in the larger struggle of humanity and civilisation against the relentless advance of a regime which represented only evil and barbarity. It was the courage and self-sacrifice of those few hundred fighter pilots, who came from many nations in Europe and the Commonwealth as well as our own, sustained by the efforts of many on the ground, which allowed us to enter the new millennium with optimism and hope instead of in subjugation and despair. The sober prose and analytical approach of this volume, written as the Second World War reached a climax, remind us how close the world came to disaster, and how great the debt of gratitude is in both the victorious and vanquished nations.

Ministry of Defence
July 2000

EDITORIAL INTRODUCTION

Sebastian Cox

The Air Historical Branch was originally set up at the end of the First World War to assist in writing the Official History of air operations in 1914–18. This task was completed with the publication of the last of the volumes in the Official History in the mid-1930s, and shortly thereafter the Branch was disestablished. At some point it was decided that the Branch should be reconstituted, and placed under the direction of the formidable Air Ministry Librarian, J. C. Nerney. Nerney set about recruiting historians to assist him in this task, and amongst the first he recruited was a former history teacher, who was then undergoing training as a wireless operator with the RAF. Denis Richards had a first-class honours degree from Cambridge, and had taught history at Manchester Grammar School and Bradfield College. As a result, the Air Ministry swiftly concluded that his talent would better serve his country if he joined the newly resurrected Air Historical Branch, a decision which events were to prove amply justified.[1]

The Branch was formally reinstated in 1941, Denis Richards arrived in early 1942 and was followed later in the year by Cecil James. James, who had been taught by Richards at Manchester Grammar before going up to Cambridge, where he too gained first-class honours in history, joined the Branch when he was invalided out of the Army. Whilst Richards was already busy writing the history of the first of the RAF's major campaign, namely the 1940 campaign in France and Belgium, James was put to work on researching the development of Fighter Command and the United Kingdom air-defence system and the subsequent performance of the organisation during the fighting in 1940.

This study became Volume II of the Air Defence of Great Britain narrative, and concentrated exclusively on the Battle of Britain. The lead-up to the Battle, in the form both of the development of the air-defence system and of Fighter Command's part in the fighting in France, were both covered in the first volume of the same narrative.[2] The research and writing for this volume took place for the most part in 1943 and 1944, and the narrative was based largely on British documentary sources, including the operational records of the squadrons and groups, and of Fighter Command itself. Some use was also made of Air Staff files and appreciations by Air Intelligence. One of the most important sets of documents proved to be the Sector, Group and Command controllers' charts, showing what was known about the strength, height, direction and timing of the *Luftwaffe*'s attacks. Because these have not survived in any comprehensive form, this narrative represents in many ways the only true account based solely on primary records of the successes and failures of the early Chain Home radars and the raid-tracking organisation.

The most obvious lack in the narrative was a comprehensive knowledge of the German side of the Battle. Although a very few records of *Luftflotte* 3 had been captured by the time the narrative was in preparation, they were not comprehensive and could not provide an accurate picture of German intentions. Indeed, even when large quantities of *Luftwaffe* material were captured at the end of the war,

1 On the idiosyncratic recruitment process see Denis Richards, *It Might Have Been Worse – Recollections 1941–1996* (privately published, London, 1998), pp. 17–23.

2 Also to be published in the Whitehall History series as T. C. G. James, *The Growth of Fighter Command 1936–1940* (Frank Cass & Co, London, forthcoming).

there were still many gaps caused by the loss or destruction of records, and it is doubtful whether very many of the necessarily tentative conclusions drawn here would have been significantly altered had they been available earlier. There is, perhaps, a tendency throughout the narrative to credit the Germans with a more comprehensive campaign plan than was actually the case.[3] The German orders of battle included in the appendices were based on intelligence reports which themselves derived from Ultra intelligence gleaned from decrypts of German Enigma traffic. Whilst the listings of units and locations are by and large accurate, the reader should note that the figures given for establishment strength and reserves are just that. In other words, they do *not* represent the actual operational strength of the units at the time, which in most cases would have been lower, often substantially so. It should also be said that the influence of Ultra intelligence on the Battle has been wildly exaggerated by some historians.

On technical aspects, the lack of German documentation led to errors of fact. In particular, the British pilots' habit of consistently mis-identifying German aircraft in the heat of battle is reflected in the text, where there are repeated references to Heinkel He 113 single-engined fighters, and occasional references to Junkers Ju 86s, and other oddities such as Chance-Vought dive-bombers. None of these aircraft types participated in the Battle, and all references to Heinkel He 113s should be taken as referring to Messerschmitt 109s.

Whilst from the British side the narrative may therefore be considered both accurate and comprehensive, indeed more comprehensive than many later accounts, it should nevertheless be read in conjunction with more recent scholarship on German actions and intentions.

The narrative was never intended for publication, but was intended to form an accurate record of events as seen and appreciated at the time. It was also intended to provide the foundation for any later official history which might be written after the war. It was compiled more than half a century ago, and occasionally both its age and its original purpose shows in the writing. It also uses outmoded expressions and vocabulary, as for example in the use of 'RDF', rather than the more modern 'radar'. The first-person plural, as in 'we' and 'our pilots', also reads oddly to the modern historian's eye. Some minor editorial changes have been made here and there to improve the volume's readability for the modern reader, but many of these stylistic devices have been kept in order to retain as much of the flavour and intention of the original as possible.

The footnote references in the volume are also idiosyncratic. This was partly because it was not intended for publication and the sources were often obvious to the insiders for whom it was written, and partly because detailed footnoting was unnecessary for the narrative to serve its purpose. Where original sources are quoted with an Air Historical Branch reference (e.g. AHB IIH/120) the document, if it survives, will now be in the Public Record Office (PRO). The original Air Historical Branch references are listed opposite the document in the Public Record Office class lists, and can also be traced via the Air Historical Branch index cards, copies of which are held on microfilm at the PRO. Where only an original Air Ministry file reference is given (e.g. S.1234), these too, where they survive, can be found in the PRO.

Personalities and personal experiences were never intended to be included in the narrative. It may to some readers become somewhat wearisome as the almost daily accounts of raids, sorties and combats are recited. It is hoped, however, that, to misquote W. S. Gilbert, the narrative, if bald, is convincing: convincing especially in the fortitude of those involved in a battle lasting for more than two months,

3 The author of the Narrative could not know the extent to which the German High Command was divided over the future course of operations at the start of the Battle. The *Kriegsmarine* viewed any attempted landing in Southern or Eastern England as an operation fraught with danger, only to be attempted as a last resort. The *Luftwaffe* was more sanguine about its ability to defeat the RAF, and did not really consider that an opposed landing would be a realistic possibility. Hitler tended to accept Goering's optimistic view of the likely course of the air war, and believed that the quick achievement of air superiority would open up many military and diplomatic possibilities. On German planning see especially Klaus A. Maier, *Germany and the Second World War* (Oxford University Press, Oxford, 1991), Vol. III, pp. 374–83.

with scarcely a day's respite. Little imagination is required to appreciate the strain on pilots, ground staffs, controllers and commanders at all levels. And the stakes were very high.

It is legitimate to ask whether the Narrative served its original purpose in providing the first comprehensive and objective analysis by a historian of the Battle of Britain? Allowing for the understandable weakness of the analysis with regard to Germany, the answer is, surely, unequivocally positive. It is by no means an exaggeration to say that this account provided the firm foundation, directly and indirectly, for much of the subsequent British historiography of the Battle. In particular, it was one of the primary sources, as it had always been intended it should be, for the subsequent Official History. The chapters in the Official History on the Battle of Britain cite the Narrative as a "chief" British source for its account of the Battle, and an analysis of the text makes it obvious that this was so.[4] In addition, the two most detailed and influential books published on the Battle at either end of the decade in the 1960s, which are still widely accepted as being amongst the most authoritative accounts, both clearly drew on the Narrative as a basic source. In particular, Derek Wood and Derek Dempster's classic account in *The Narrow Margin*, reproduces exactly the phasing of the Battle adopted by the Narrative and many of the orders of battle and other detailed statistical information in this volume were reproduced as appendices in the book. The authors' pay fulsome tribute to the assistance they received from the Air Historical Branch, and that clearly extended to sight of this narrative.[5] In similar vein, Francis K. Mason wrote of his indebtedness to the Branch for tolerating his "presence daily for close on twelve months".[6] The influence of the Narrative is equally apparent in such aspects as references to Park's instructions to his controllers, and to the detailed daily accounts of the fighting. There is little doubt that both these impressive histories benefited enormously from the earlier work of Cecil James reproduced here. Both books also deservedly became 'classic' texts on the Battle, on which subsequent historians (including this one) have drawn heavily, and in this way the influence of the Narrative has been felt far beyond the confines of those who have actually read it. The Narrative's influence can also be seen in a later history of the Battle, that by Richard Hough and Denis Richards published to coincide with the fiftieth anniversary.[7] Given Richards's own intimate early connection with the Air Historical Branch, this is hardly surprising, but it bears out the degree to which the Narrative is still, more than half a century on, a key text for any historian who wishes to make a serious study of the Battle.

It would be tedious to review such an extensive text in detail, but there are one or two aspects, apart from the superb general analysis of the fighting, in which the perceptions of its author are sufficiently acute to be worthy of further comment. In particular, the analysis of what has subsequently become known as the 'Big Wing' controversy is both more balanced and more perceptive than much of the ill-informed, tendentious and not infrequently personalised, nonsense which has appeared in print since. Any historian seeking an impartial analysis of the pros and cons of each side of the debate would do well to start with the brief account which appears in Part VII of this volume.

Similarly, the treatment of the vexed question of claims, losses and published figures should be required reading for those of a cynical disposition who believe that in wartime *all* information is subject to official manipulation. The problem of establishing the exact numbers of aircraft lost by each side still taxes us today, even though the most detailed research has been conducted into the matter by historians working in concert across national boundaries. In part, it is simply a problem of definition, as, for example, when an operational aircraft is written off in a landing accident entirely unconnected to enemy action. Although it will probably never be possible to establish the true figure

4 Basil Collier, *The Defence of the United Kingdom* (HMSO, London, 1957 [official edition with unpublished sources]), p. 573, fn. 5 to Ch. XII.
5 Derek Wood and Derek Dempster, *The Narrow Margin* (Hutchinson, London, 1961), *passim*. See especially the authors' acknowledgements.
6 Francis K. Mason, *Battle over Britain* (McWhirter Twins, London, 1960), p. 13.
7 Richard Hough and Denis Richards, *The Battle of Britain: The Jubilee History* (Hodder & Stoughton, London, 1989).

with a mathematician's exactitude, modern research has produced a detailed analysis of losses which is unlikely to be seriously challenged, and which is sufficiently exact for all but the most pedantic soul.[8]

Given both the influence of the Narrative on subsequent studies of the Battle and the quality of much of the analysis, it was felt that it deserved a much wider audience amongst serious historians than it was ever likely to attain from the few copies available to the researcher in the PRO, Air Historical Branch, and the library of the RAF Museum. Hence, the decision to publish it in this the sixtieth anniversary year of the Battle, when its scholarly contribution may serve not only to inform but also to pay tribute to those, mostly young men, who gave their lives.

8 On this aspect see, in particular, the comprehensive day-by-day coverage of the losses on each side recorded in Winston G. Ramsey (ed.), *The Battle of Britain Then And Now* (5th edn, Battle of Britain Prints International, London, 1989).

CHRONOLOGY OF PRINCIPAL EVENTS

1940

10 July	Opening of the preliminary phase of the Battle of Britain: attacks on Channel convoys and south coast ports. Fifty-two operational squadrons in Fighter Command.
13 July	Headquarters, No. 10 Group, opened at Rudloe Manor Wiltshire.
8 August	Beginning of intensive day operations: the second phase of the battle.
12 August	Beginning of heavy attacks against coastal airfields.
19–23 August	Five days' lull in the battle.
24 August	Beginning of heavy attacks against fighter airfields near London: the third phase of the battle. Intensifying of German night attacks.
7 September	First heavy daylight attack on London: the fourth phase of the battle. Beginning of heavy night attacks on the capital. Fifty-seven operational squadrons in Fighter Command.
8 September	Introduction of the Stabilisation Scheme for Fighter Command. Invasion Alert No. 1 in force.
15 September	Heavy daylight attack on London.
17 September	State of Readiness relaxed: Invasion Alert No. 2 introduced.
30 September	Final attack by long-range bombers against London in daylight.
1 October	The fifth phase of the battle begins: fighters and fighter-bombers sweep towards London. Heavy night attacks on London continue.

PREFACE

The following account of the Battle of Britain is very largely one of the operations of Fighter Command. Its chief concern is the phases by which the German offensive developed, how each of these phases was executed and what counteracting policy governed the operations of the fighter squadrons. These are, of course, the most important features of the battle. But there are others which had no little effect on the form that the battle took: the production and repair of aircraft, the training of pilots, signals and telecommunications, maintenance and servicing of squadrons, engine and armament problems, have each a place in any comprehensive narrative of the battle. Nor would such a narrative be complete unless it included more details of the work of Anti-Aircraft and Balloon Commands and the Observer Corps in defence, and of Bomber and Coastal Commands in the counter-offensive, than will be found in the following pages. These aspects have not been forgotten. But it has been found to make for the easier and speedier production of a final narrative if each of them is given separate treatment, the synthesis and co-ordination of the separate accounts representing the last stage of the work. Thus, narratives on Signals, Radar, Flying Training, Armament Development and other technical subjects, and on the work of the Commands associated with Fighter Command are being prepared; and the story of the Battle of Britain will not be complete until such parts of these narratives as are concerned with it have been incorporated in the narrative that follows, which is for this reason an interim account. Indeed, even when this has been done; there is a sense in which the story will not be comprehensive; for the battle could well be made the occasion for a review of the behaviour of the whole community – its morale, its health, its trade and industry – under heavy attack.

The reader should also bear in mind that there is much about the battle that is not yet certain. Details of the scale of the German attack, reliable information of the German targets and authoritative explanations of changes in German policy and intentions are still not available. In particular it is only possible to speculate as to why the Germans abandoned the invasion which they appeared to be preparing.

The records and documents that have served as a basis for the narrative are indicated in detail in the marginal references. Broadly speaking, the accounts of daily operations have been based on the Operations Record Books of Fighter Command, and of the fighter Groups and squadrons, the track charts prepared in the Filter Room at Fighter Command Headquarters, the combat reports of individual pilots and the consolidated combat reports made by squadron intelligence officers, the No. 11 Group Instructions to Controllers, the 'Y' Forms of the Command and Groups and a small number of captured German documents. Air Ministry, Fighter Command and No. 11 and 12 Group secret files, Air Chief Marshal Dowding's correspondence, a few of the Secretary of State's files and the branch folders of the Directorate of Home Operations and such secondary sources as the Commander-in-Chief's despatch and Air Vice-Marshal Park's reports on the fighting have been the foundation of the account of higher policy.

I

INTRODUCTION: THE EFFECT OF THE GERMAN OCCUPATION OF EUROPE ON THE AIR DEFENCE OF GREAT BRITAIN

When in March 1940 the Director of Home Operations had recommended that Fighter Command should be strengthened to sixty squadrons by September, it had been assumed that the Germans would be kept out of France. In those circumstances it was unlikely that the whole of the German bomber force would ever be concentrated against the United Kingdom,[1] or that many regions of the country would ever be attacked except on a light scale. Moreover, it was generally believed that unescorted German bombers attacking Britain by day *en masse* would suffer unacceptable losses. As a result of the fall of France, however, the Germans were free to concentrate on Great Britain; German long-range bombers could reach virtually every part of the country in considerable strength; German fighters and dive-bombers could operate over the Western Approaches from the eighth meridian, and over all England to the south of a line between South Wales and the Humber; and inside that area bombers could be given a fighter escort. At the same time, the occupation of Norway had exposed north-east Scotland, and the naval bases there, to a heavier scale of attack than formerly. In short, the general effect of the German occupation of Western Europe upon the air defence of Great Britain was to extend the area that was open to air bombardment and intensify the scale of attack that was to be expected. The counter-measures that were taken can thus be described under two heads: first, the extension of the air defence system to the newly threatened districts; second, the expansion of the fighter force and the associated defences to meet the increased scale of attack.

I. EFFECT ON SHIPPING IN HOME WATERS

The March review had been chiefly concerned with the need for reinforcing the fighter line at its two extremities, north-east Scotland and south-west England. In each area the Air Staff and Fighter Command were concerned at the growing threat to shipping; and the new situation only heightened their concern. All ocean traffic within four hundred and fifty miles of the coast, all coastal traffic and every important harbour in the United Kingdom, was now open to attack. In particular, the presence of German sea and air units in Brittany was a threat to shipping using the Western Approaches. During June arrangements were therefore made with the Admiralty to route shipping up the west coast of Ireland, through the North Channel and into the Clyde, the Mersey and the ports of South Wales. Only coastal convoys of small ships were to ply between the Bristol Channel and London. This plan was put into effect from 15 July. It simplified the air defence problem to some extent as the Western Approaches could only have been protected if airfields had been available in the south and south-west of Eire, but it did not avoid a major expansion of the air defence system in the south-west and west of England in order to protect the great

1 It should not be forgotten, however, that all estimates of the air defences required by Great Britain had assumed the worst possible case, namely, that the Germans had it in their power to use the whole of the bomber force against this country, at any rate for a short period.

S.3553, Minute 23, DHO-DCAS, 28 June 1940

volume of ocean shipping in the Irish Sea from attacks by aircraft approaching from France. Moreover, in the opinion of the Director of Home Operations, Air Commodore Stevenson, whose duty it was once more to assess what new air defences were required, even this less extensive area could not be defended efficiently unless fighters could operate from stations near Dublin and Wexford. There could be no question, however, of using Eireann bases unless the Germans invaded Ireland, or Great Britain was invited to send forces into the country. All that was done, therefore, was to earmark a certain amount of mobile airfield and signals equipment for speedy use should the Irish situation change. Meantime the Fighter Command system had to be extended to Wales, Lancashire and Northern Ireland. In the south-west the position had to be improved not only in order that fighters there could intercept enemy aircraft on their way north, but so that coastal shipping passing up the English Channel could be protected west of Portland. In Scotland fighters were required near the Clyde, and more strength was needed in the north-east. About this time the first steps were also taken to provide long-range fighters in the Hebrides, but their provision was necessarily some way ahead.

II. EXTENSION OF THE AIR DEFENCE SYSTEM IN THE WEST

With the exception of the last, none of these requirements was altogether novel. All the areas in question had been vulnerable since the outbreak of war, in theory at any rate, i.e. they were within the extreme operational range of the German long-range bomber; and in most cases preliminary measures had been taken for their defence. In the Bristol–Portsmouth area one squadron was already stationed at Filton, primarily to protect the works of the Bristol Aeroplane Company, and new fighter sector stations were being built at Middle Wallop and Colerne. The headquarters of the new fighter Group, No. 10, that was to control the defence of this area, had been under construction since February, and began functioning on 13 July. As for the western defences of the Midlands, the possibility of attacks from that direction had long been appreciated. As early as the summer of 1938 the Air Staff had decided to provide facilities at stations near Chester, Stafford and Birmingham for use by squadrons normally stationed further east at Digby, Wittering and Duxford. Not much progress had been made by the summer of 1940. There was a shortage of airfields in that part of the country, and the intelligence and signals requirements of an effective air defence system were sadly lacking. In the same area, but further to the west, the position was even worse. There were no RAF stations on all the long stretch of coastline between St David's Head and the Great Orme, while such few stations as existed between Liverpool and Carlisle and in Northern Ireland, were in full use by Coastal and Flying Training Commands. It was fortunate that the Germans did not operate in force over the western route to the Midlands and Liverpool, nor harass shipping in the Irish Sea, until the end of August. By that time some progress had been made with the big programme of airfield construction decided on in June and July.

III. THE DEVELOPMENT OF NO. 10 GROUP

For obvious reasons attention was first of all concentrated on south-west England, and early in June the first commander of No. 10 Group, Air Vice-Marshal Sir Quintin Brand, was ordered to reconnoitre the district for suitable fighter aerodromes. West and south-west of Middle Wallop there were no fighter stations, with the exception of Filton, and a paucity of stations of any Command. However, St Eval, Exeter, Pembrey and Warmwell were brought into temporary use by fighter squadrons pending the construction of further aerodromes in the area. By 3 July there were seven fighter squadrons in the area bounded by Milford Haven–Bristol–Southampton–Land's End; a month before there had been one. This rapid expansion was primarily undertaken to provide protection for shipping in the western half of the Channel; and the new stations, especially Middle Wallop and Warmwell, proved of great value during the attacks on coastal shipping in July and early August. It was not until the second week in August, however, that No. 10 Group Headquarters was able to take over control of all the fighter stations in the Group area. Prior to that date Middle Wallop and Warmwell were operated by No. 11 Group. With this extension of the Fighter Command system west of Portsmouth the basic dispositions of the fighter force that was to fight the Battle of Britain were completed.[2]

IV. PARALLEL EXTENSION OF THE RDF CHAIN AND THE OBSERVER CORPS

The formation of new fighter stations in the south-west was necessarily paralleled by the extension of the Observer Corps and the RDF chain in the same area. At the outbreak of war the RDF system extended only as far as the Isle of Wight, but by May 1940 more stations were under construction further west. Two were opened before the end of May and four more in June. On 23 June a temporary filter room began to function at No. 15 Group HQ, Plymouth, but on 30 July the stations were linked to a permanent filter room at No. 10 Group HQ. The stations were much more widely spaced than on the east and south-east coasts, and coverage in the Channel was far from complete.

The complementary expansion of the Observer Corps in this area was ordered early in June and took the form of a new Group in Devonshire, with its Centre at Exeter, and a Sub-Group on the Cornish coast, reporting to a Centre at Truro. The first commenced to operate on 17 July, the second on 2 August. As in the case of the RDF chain the individual observer posts in this area were too widely scattered to admit of accurate reporting.

2 It should not be forgotten that as the great day battles were being fought in south and south-east England new stations and Groups were being organised in the west of England and in Scotland. In brief, the plan of expansion required the formation of two more fighter Groups; No. 9 in north-west England with Headquarters at Preston and No. 14 in north-east Scotland with Headquarters at Inverness. There was no connection between the latter Group and the one which, similarly numbered, had fought in France and Belgium. In addition, No. 13 Group was extended westward to embrace the Clyde and the North Channel, and Ulster was provided with a separate air defence system. But serious operations did not begin in these new areas until the late summer and early autumn of 1940; and their interest belongs rather to the night attack on the great centres of population and to the Battle of the Atlantic than to the Battle of Britain.

V. EXPANSION OF FIGHTER COMMAND

Until the middle of June Fighter Command was working to a programme of sixty squadrons, which were to be formed by September. But this was based on the strategical situation which applied before the collapse of France, and a further expansion of the fighter force was obviously necessary not only in order that the new extensions to the air defence system could be manned, but also to counteract the increase in the potential weight of attack on the country as a whole. The United Kingdom might now be attacked by the whole of the German Air Force, which in June was estimated at nearly 2,000 long-range bombers, 550 dive-bombers, 1,550 heavy and light fighters, and a number of coastal aircraft. Moreover, now that practically all Europe's industrial plants were at Germany's disposal, an accelerated expansion of her Air Force was likely. Adopting the previous Air Staff yardstick for calculating fighter strength[3] DHO estimated that one hundred and twenty fighter squadrons, containing 1,920 first-line aircraft, would be required, which would entail more than doubling the existing fighter force. No price was too high to pay for national security but such an expansion would have completely unbalanced the Metropolitan Air Force as planned, and could only have been achieved at the expense of the bomber programme, which was already behindhand. In any case, the immediate expansion of fighter strength was governed by the available resources of pilots and aircraft; and these were largely committed to the refitting of the squadrons which had suffered in the French campaign. It was therefore recommended by Air Commodore Stevenson that, as an immediate 'stop-gap' measure, ten squadrons should be formed immediately and another ten as soon as possible. By the time that these had been formed ultimate requirements might have been clarified by events.[4]

S.3553, Minute 23

ibid.

VI. EFFECT OF SHORTAGE OF PILOTS

AHB VB/14, Minutes of Meeting 3 July 1940

When, early in July, the DHO's proposal came before the Expansion and Re-equipment Committee of the Air Ministry the supply of fighter aircraft was more satisfactory than at any other time since war had broken out, but there was a notable shortage of pilots; and on that account the proposal was reluctantly turned down. Instead a compromise was arrived at whereby an additional flight of four aircraft was added to all the Hurricane squadrons in the Command, numbering thirty, and to six of the Spitfire squadrons.[5] Extra maintenance staff was added to these squadrons but no more pilots; the intention being that the aircraft should only be used in an emergency, in which case those pilots of the

3 See pp. 98–100, Vol. 1.

4 Ultimate fighter strength would be influenced by a number of factors whose effects could not be estimated with any accuracy until the air battle was joined: 'Our bases, war potential, industry and manpower are concentrated in a relatively small area, encircled by our air defence system. On the other hand, the German areas vulnerable to attack by the British long-range bomber force stretch at present from Narvik to the Pyrenees. Thus, from the German first-line fighter strength, detachments must be made over a wide area to provide protection for important points. In consequence, it may be found, as experience accumulates, that something less than the ultimate standard of fighter strength now contemplated, may suffice.' (DHO-DCAS, S3553 28 June 1940.)

5 This decision affected Coastal Command, for it was DHO's original intention that five of the ten new squadrons should be long-range fighters for shipping protection. It was many months before Coastal Command's requirements for this sort of duty were satisfied.

squadron who would normally be resting or on leave would be called upon to fly them. The arrangement reflected the shortage of fighter pilots, and it was not intended to be permanent. As soon as it was prudent the additional flights were to be withdrawn and amalgamated into new squadrons. By the third week in July the allotment of aircraft and personnel to the thirty six squadrons had been completed.

AHB ID/2/273, Encl 6B

This shortage of pilots was due, firstly, to a more rapid expansion of fighter strength during the first months of war than had been anticipated when the training programme had been provisioned; secondly, to a lower output of fighter pilots than had been expected, owing partly to the bad winter of 1939/40 and partly to the diversion of resources from Operational Training Units to first-line squadrons; thirdly, and most particularly, to the loss of nearly three hundred fighter pilots during the fighting over France.[6] This shortage remained the limiting factor of expansion throughout the period 1 July–30 September, during which time the only new squadrons added to the operational strength of Fighter Command were Canadian, Polish, and Czecho-Slovakian. Consequently, the strength of the Command remained fairly stable throughout the battle at sixty squadrons.

S.65592, Minute, 6 June

The measures that were taken to increase pilot output during June and July chiefly concerned Flying Training Command and will not be examined here.[7] But the earliest important accession of strength, and the more welcome because it came so shortly after the heavy losses in France, was the result of an agreement with the Admiralty for the loan of Fleet Air Arm pilots. The matter was first discussed in the War Cabinet as the Dunkerque evacuation drew to a close; and the Prime Minister instructed the Air and Naval staffs to see whether any naval pilots could be transferred to Fighter Command. He had in mind an allocation of fifty pilots by the end of June. On 6 June the Admiralty issued instructions for the release of forty-five pilots (including seven RAFVR pilots who had been serving with the Fleet Air Arm), half of them trained, half semi-trained. The Air Ministry, however, asked for half the output of the two flying training schools serving the Fleet Air Arm to be allotted to the RAF, beginning with thirty pilots by the end of June. The Admiralty could not agree on the grounds that the casualties amongst their pilots in April and May had been nearly four times as large as postulated and that, in addition, the war with Italy meant more work for the Fleet Air Arm than had been visualised earlier. Thirty more pilots – making sixty-eight naval pilots in all – were loaned during June; but ten were recalled early in July for service in the Mediterranean; and later in the month the First Lord informed the Secretary of State for Air that no further attachments would be possible. The loans, however, were timely and, considering the Admiralty's difficulties, substantial. Casualties among the

Ibid. Alexander-Sinclair, 23 June

6 In May and June pilot casualties in battle and through flying accidents in Fighter Command and the fighter squadrons in France were as follows:

	Killed, Prisoners and Missing	*Wounded and Injured*
May	159	46
June	125	17
Total	284	63

7 See Air Historical Branch narrative on 'Flying Training'. PRO AIR 10/5551.

fifty-eight pilots who served in the RAF were heavy, eighteen being killed during the summer and autumn.

VII. DISTRIBUTION OF THE FIGHTER SQUADRONS

The distribution of the fighter squadrons was on the territorial basis of four fighter Groups. No. 10 Group protected the country to the west and north-west of Portsmouth and the industrial towns of South Wales; its Headquarters were at Rudloe Manor in Wiltshire. No. 11 Group, whose Headquarters were at Uxbridge, covered London, the Thames Estuary and the south coast as far as Portsmouth. No. 12 Group was responsible for the defence of the Midlands and the east coast from Great Yarmouth to Scarborough, and its Headquarters were at Hucknall in Nottinghamshire. No. 13 Group, with Headquarters at Newcastle, protected the industrial areas round the Tyne and Tees, the Forth and Clyde, and the whole of the east coast of Scotland, with the exception of the extreme north, where a separate organisation – though one for which the AOC, No. 13 Group was responsible – based on Wick guarded the approaches to the Orkneys and Shetlands. These four Groups were the foundation of the air defence system.

VIII. ANTI-AIRCRAFT COMMAND

The disposition of these Groups largely dictated the location of the AA corps and divisions with which they necessarily worked in co-operation. The fact that the Headquarters of both Fighter and Anti-Aircraft Commands, as well as those of Balloon Command and the Observer Corps, were adjacent at Stanmore was significant of the close liaison of the two organisations. The higher formations of Anti-Aircraft Command in July 1940, consisted of seven divisions, which were linked to fighter Groups as follows:

5th AA Division, HQ Reading, supported Nos 10 and 11 Groups
1st AA Division, HQ Kensington, supported No. 11 Group.
6th AA Division, HQ Uxbridge*, supported No. 11 Group.
2nd AA Division, HQ Watnall*, supported No. 12 Group.
4th AA Division, HQ Chester, supported Nos 12 & 13 Groups.
7th AA Division, HQ Newcastle*, supported No. 13 Group.
3rd AA Division, HQ Edinburgh, supported No. 13 Group.
*Also Fighter Group Headquarters.

As in the case of Fighter Command, the planned strength of Anti-Aircraft Command postulated a German Air Force based in Germany. A considerable expansion of anti-aircraft strength complementary to that of the fighter force was therefore required in the revolutionary situation in which the country found itself in June 1940. But even by the earlier standard Anti-Aircraft Command had a long way to go before it reached full strength. The last pre-war recommendation had been for the provision of 2,232 heavy and 1,860 light guns whereas on 28 July 1940 the Command held only 1,280 heavy and 517 light

CID 319-A
15 May 1939;
and COS(40) 589

guns.[8] The allocation to London and the Thames Estuary area, for example, included 480 heavy guns, but at the above date only 250 were in position. Portsmouth and Southampton, which should have had 104 heavy guns, could count themselves fortunate to have as many as 87. In the North of England and the Midlands the percentage deficiency was much the same as for London. Liverpool, for example, had only 52 heavy guns instead of 104, Birmingham 63 instead of 120. The light gun position was even worse, chiefly owing to a setback in the Bofors gun programme. Such guns as were available were utilised for the defence of RAF stations, and a few of the more important and vulnerable industrial targets amongst the many hundreds of vital points for which defence were required. The searchlight defences were in better shape, nearly four thousand lights being available, but there was an unilluminated belt of country in the West Midlands, and another to the south of Liverpool. Both gaps were filled by the autumn. Balloon Command had also approached more closely to its planned strength than had the gun defences. At the end of July out of an establishment of 1,870 balloons, 1,466 had been allocated to the various squadrons of the Command.[9] But the air defence system as a whole, more especially the gun defences, showed alarming deficiences. If it had been possible, as the Deputy Chiefs of Staff recommended on 1 June, to devote all new production to ADGB, the position would have improved sooner than it did; but as the defences of the Mediterranean were relatively even weaker than those of the United Kingdom only about 50% of gun production was allotted to the home theatre.[10]

IX. ADDITIONAL AIR DEFENCES APPROVED: CHIEFS OF STAFF REVIEW

Although it was obvious that even the pre-war scale of air defence, much less a new and larger one, would not be completed for many months to come, the Chiefs of Staff gave instructions in July for the air defence position to be reviewed in the light of the new situation. This review was circulated on 16 August and was approved by the Chiefs of Staff on the following day. It remained to a very great extent an ideal that was never realised, and, of course, the provision that it visualised was far larger than the forces that were available during the Battle of Britain. Yet it has a place in the story of that battle for two reasons: first, it shows how wide was the gap between the size of the forces that fought the Battle of Britain and those that the situation actually demanded; and,

COS(40) 632

8 See also Appendix 38.

9 Balloon Command Orders of Battle for July and August are given in Appendices 3 and 13.

10 The following table indicates the main requirements that had to be met, and the proportion of production despatched overseas during the Battle of Britain period.

Holdings of Heavy Anti-Aircraft Guns

	ADGB	*Training*	*Middle East*	*Ports Abroad*
22 June	1,204	55	44	128
31 Oct	1,412	121	124	158

second, it shows how far the Chiefs of Staff were willing to commit the war potential of the country to the production of purely defensive weapons.

The review did not attempt to estimate the full number of fighter squadrons that would be required to defeat the heaviest scale of attack that the Germans could mount. As we have seen, such an estimate had already been made by the Air Staff; and it was, in any case, somewhat academic, as there could be no question of virtually doubling the fighter force until the situation was clarified. But the review did approve those extensions of the air defence system to the West of England and Northern Scotland that have already been noted. It also approved the existing composition of the fighter force, with its emphasis on short-range day fighters such as the Hurricane and Spitfire. Before the end of 1940 the air defence needs of the country had changed, and the cry was for more twin-engined fighters. But it was clearly more prudent, as things stood in the summer of 1940, to expand the strength in terms of Hurricanes and Spitfires. The chief threat to the country's security at that time came from a sustained offensive by day, since only then could the Germans use their own short-range fighters to bring the RAF's to combat.

As for the ground defences, the review based its recommendations on two principles: firstly, that searchlights should be provided for all parts of the country over which the enemy could fly to reach important objectives, provided that their deployment was practicable; secondly, that gun defences were to be allotted to 'all communities of any size engaged in industrial work of national importance'. The following additions in order of priority to the existing searchlight zones were recommended:

1. South Wales
2. Midlands Gap
3. Edinburgh–Tyne corridor
4. Glasgow extension
5. Devon and Cornwall (to Hartland Point)
6. North Lancashire and Barrow
7. Northern Ireland
8. Carlisle district[11]
9. North Wales
10. Aberdeen district
11. Moray Firth
12. Stranraer district
13. Anglesey
14. Devon and Cornwall (to the Lizard)

Eighty-seven extra batteries[12] would be needed for these extensions. Sixty more were approved in order to increase the density of searchlights deployed in gun defended areas, though it was hoped that the radiolocation equipment for the control of gunfire against unseen targets would permit the cancelling of this last

11 Experience showed that extensions 8–14 would not be required, and in January 1941, at the request of the AOC-in-C, Fighter Command, they were deleted.

12 In the first nine months of war all searchlight units had been transferred from the Royal Engineers to the Royal Artillery, and all 'companies' had been renamed 'batteries', the latter containing the same number of lights as the former.

requirement. These additions, plus a small mobile reserve of twelve batteries, entailed an increase of nearly four thousand projectors over and above the five thousand already on establishment.

Extra guns were recommended on a similar large scale. 856 heavy guns were allotted to defend places open to a heavier scale of attack than when their defences had been originally planned, and 672 to towns which previously had been undefended. The chief places in the latter category were the industrial towns within forty miles of Manchester, and towns in the Midlands such as Leicester, Peterborough and Northampton. Over four hundred vulnerable points were added to the list of small targets requiring defence by light guns, and 2,550 40 mm. guns were approved for this purpose. These additions made the total authorised anti-aircraft gun defences of the country 3,744 heavy and 4,410 light guns.[13] The strength of the balloon barrages was also increased. New barrages were planned, chiefly for the protection of ports, harbours and anchorages against minelaying aircraft. Six hundred balloons were to be deployed, making the operational strength of Balloon Command two thousand six hundred balloons, with an equal number in immediate reserve.

It was estimated that Anti-Aircraft Command would probably need five more divisions to absorb the additional weapons that would be issued to it under this programme. In numbers and material it would then be larger than Fighter Command. The Chiefs of Staff thought it proper, therefore, to re-emphasise the paramount importance of Fighter Command in the air defence system. Air defence was to remain the prime responsibility of AOC-in-C, Fighter Command; he must have only a single anti-aircraft commander to deal with; and the territorial organisation of Anti-Aircraft Command must fall into line with that of Fighter Command.

X. SIGNIFICANCE OF THE REVIEW

It would be difficult to imagine a situation, failing the invasion of some part of the British Isles, in which this country could be more seriously threatened, than that in which it was placed in the summer of 1940. The historical importance of the Chiefs of Staff review lies in the fact that, in the situation applying during the Battle of Britain and until Germany attacked in the east, it defined the maximum insurance for the security of the United Kingdom against air attack, relative to the size of the forces arrayed against it. At existing production rates, it would have taken years to complete the plan: e.g. the average monthly additions to Anti-Aircraft Command between June 1940 and February 1941 included only forty heavy anti-aircraft guns. In any case, as the war developed and the threat to this country lessened, it was possible to modify the plan. But it remains a striking example of the extent to which it might have been necessary

13 Some progress had been made by this date in perfecting the Unrotating Projectile (UP) weapon for use against low-flying aircraft, and as a result of the August review an order for eight thousand projectors was placed. As early as June 1940 it had been hoped that some projectors would be available by August, and it was intended to deploy them in defence of aircraft factories, but these hopes were disappointed. At this stage of development there was no means of ensuring the fragmentation of the case of the projectile, and for a time its use was prohibited except for fire to seaward. In July this restriction was removed by the Prime Minister, but the weapon did not become available in time to play any useful part either in the Battle of Britain or in the night offensive of 1940–41.

to use British industry and manpower for the production and manning of weapons useful for little else but defence.

XI. IMPORTANCE OF THE AIRCRAFT INDUSTRY

The immense gap between the number of ground weapons recommended in the review and those that were actually available needs no emphasis. But for the country as a whole the shortage was worsened by the necessity for concentrating on the defence of a particular aspect of industry, the manufacture of aircraft and aero-engines. The importance of protecting the aircraft industry, especially in the early stages of a war with Germany, when she would hold the initiative in the air, had long been realised. Shortly after the outbreak of war Air Chief Marshal Dowding had been instructed to regard this as his most important single task; and the directive was still in force when the campaign in the West began. He had in fact carried out a certain measure of redeployment of ground defences with this purpose in mind in late September 1939. The policy was reaffirmed by the Prime Minister in May, when he gave instructions that 'the utmost available AA strength should be concentrated on the aircraft factories: they are more important than anything else'. On 15 June the Chiefs of Staff asked for details of the redeployment proposed by Air Chief Marshal Dowding; and a day or two later they reminded him of the peculiar importance of the fighter production side of the industry. His first measures entailed withdrawing nearly one hundred and twenty heavy guns from other areas, utilising a regiment of Bofors guns which had returned from Narvik, and distributing them chiefly to the assembly plants in the Thames Valley and Southampton. Forty of the heavy guns were withdrawn from London, a similar number from East Coast and Scottish ports, and the residue from a regiment which had been about to embark for France. In the next two weeks a few guns were taken from new production and allotted to the aircraft factories, and by 7 July the industry was protected by 25% of the heavy guns in Anti Aircraft Command.[14] In addition a number of factories were protected by the Parachute and Cable (PAC) device.[15]

S.4752, Encl 4A, Minute PM – General Ismay, 19 May 1940

COS(40)475

14 On 7 July the close defences of the most important plants included the following equipment:

	HAA Guns	*LAA Guns*	*Balloons*
Derby	36	12	32
Crewe	8	–	32
Kingston	12	–	–
Langley	28	4	24
Brooklands	16	4	–
Brockworth and Cheltenham	36	12	24
Woolston and Eastleigh	51	20	72
Castle Bromwich	21	8	100
Filton	12	8	24
Coventry	40	–	56
Sheffield	24	–	72

For a comprehensive table of heavy AA defences, see Appendix 38.

15 By this, a linear arrangement of rockets, to which light steel cables were attached, was electrically discharged on the approach of a hostile aircraft. The rocket ascended to a height of five or six hundred feet where a parachute, attached to the cable, opened and thus suspended the cable long enough for a curtain to be aligned before the approaching aircraft.

Throughout the Battle of Britain the protection of the aircraft industry remained the chief charge upon Fighter Command. Quite apart from the likelihood of attacks on the industry as part of an independent air offensive against this country, attacks on it on a large scale were expected to form a prelude to invasion, possibly accompanied by an offensive against fighter stations and communications in Kent and Sussex. Only when an invasion expedition was actually launched was Fighter Command to give priority to another task, namely the defence of the naval units that would be attacking the enemy's fleet. Air Chief Marshal Dowding attempted no new employment of his fighter squadrons the better to protect the industry; nor was one possible except the execrable method of continuous patrols over specific factories. The Fighter Command system had been designed to provide air defence for all threatened areas of the United Kingdom, with a particular emphasis on the defence of London. Within each of the fighter Group areas the number of worthwhile targets was so large that to allocate fighter strength to specific objectives would have meant so great a dispersion of squadrons that, unless fighter resources were almost unlimited, there would have been no fighter striking force available to meet what was the greatest aerial threat to the nation's security, attacks by mass formations of enemy bombers; nor would the necessarily small numbers of fighters allocated to particular targets have been capable of withstanding attacks of any size. Guns and balloons, on the other hand, were admirably adapted for close defence; and for this reason redeployment for the defence of the aircraft industry took place in terms of ground defences alone. But this did not in any way relieve the fighter squadrons of responsibility for the defence of the industry. Close defence was at best a deterrent and could never give security. Even if a particular factory or area could have been so heavily defended with ground weapons that attack on it meant virtual suicide, which was certainly not possible in the summer of 1940, the defence problem would not have been solved, for to do that for every vital target in the country would have involved such an immense production of defensive weapons that the war could never have been won. The defence of the aircraft industry, therefore, as of every other branch of the economy of the country, was predominantly the concern of Fighter Command, since only fighters could provide the general cover which would enable industry as a whole to continue working.

COS(40) 593

XII. CONCLUSION

It is apparent from all this that the collapse in France extended and complicated the tasks of the air defence organisation at a time when the weapons available were insufficient, according to the calculations of the Air Staff, to give security even in the more favourable situation that had existed prior to May 1940. The need for extension and expansion also coincided with a period when Fighter Command was re-equipping and re-organising after its serious losses in May and June. Consequently the expansion of the Command's strength that was so clearly called for, was effectively postponed; and no new fighting units were added to the Command between the beginning of July and the end of September, with the exception of one Canadian, one Czech, and two Polish squadrons.

Without Dominion and Allied pilots it would probably have been necessary to 'roll-up' a number of fighter squadrons. As it was, the flow of new pilots during June and early July was insufficient to reinforce all squadrons to full strength; and on 7 July, just before the preliminary operations of the Battle of Britain commenced, the Command had a deficiency of 197 pilots out of an establishment of 1,450. Nevertheless the Command was extended in the south west, a beginning was made in its extension to the West Midlands, Wales, the shores of the North Channel, and also in Scotland, and as a complementary measure the RDF chain and the Observer Corps were expanded in these areas. As for Anti-Aircraft Command, the chief factor governing expansion was gun production, and this was insufficient to make any appreciable difference to the equipment available during the three crucial summer months. All that could be done was to make the best use of strictly limited resources. Here it seemed sound policy to deploy all that could be spared from other areas, up to the very extreme of legitimate risk, in order to protect the aircraft industry. If this could not be kept in continuous and large-scale production, the defeat of the fighter force was only a matter of time. Thus its protection was a matter of particular interest to Fighter Command, as well as to the country at large; and this task had priority over all others that the Command might have to perform. But it would be quite wrong to regard the fighter operations of August and September as a battle fought for the aircraft industry. They were to a great extent dictated by the German Air Force, and Fighter Command fought off their attacks without much thought for nice differences between the probable targets of the enemy formations.

THE AIR DEFENCES OF GREAT BRITAIN
AUGUST 1940

LEGEND

TOWNS •

GROUP HEADQUARTERS ■

SECTOR " ◉

SATELLITES ⊙

GROUP BOUNDARIES – – – –

R·D·F STATIONS •

FIGHTER COMMAND HEADQUARTERS .. ▨

A·A GUNS ■

SECTOR BOUNDARIES ▬

OBSERVER CENTRES ◀

" SECTOR BOUNDARIES

BALLOON BARRAGES ●

SEARCHLIGHT AREAS ▨

SHEET I. S.E. ENGLAND & THE MIDLANDS
 " 2. S.W. " & WALES
 " 3. N.E. " & SHETLAND ISLES
 " 4. S. SCOTLAND & N.E. IRELAND
 " 5. N. " & ORKNEY ISLES

NOTE :– *Changes in the deployment of Anti-Aircraft guns during July-October are given in Appendix 35.*

Scale 1:1,000,000

MILES
10 0 10 20 30 40 50 60 70 80 90 100 110 120 130 140 150

MAP Nº 115 DRAWN & COMPILED AT A·H·B·1.

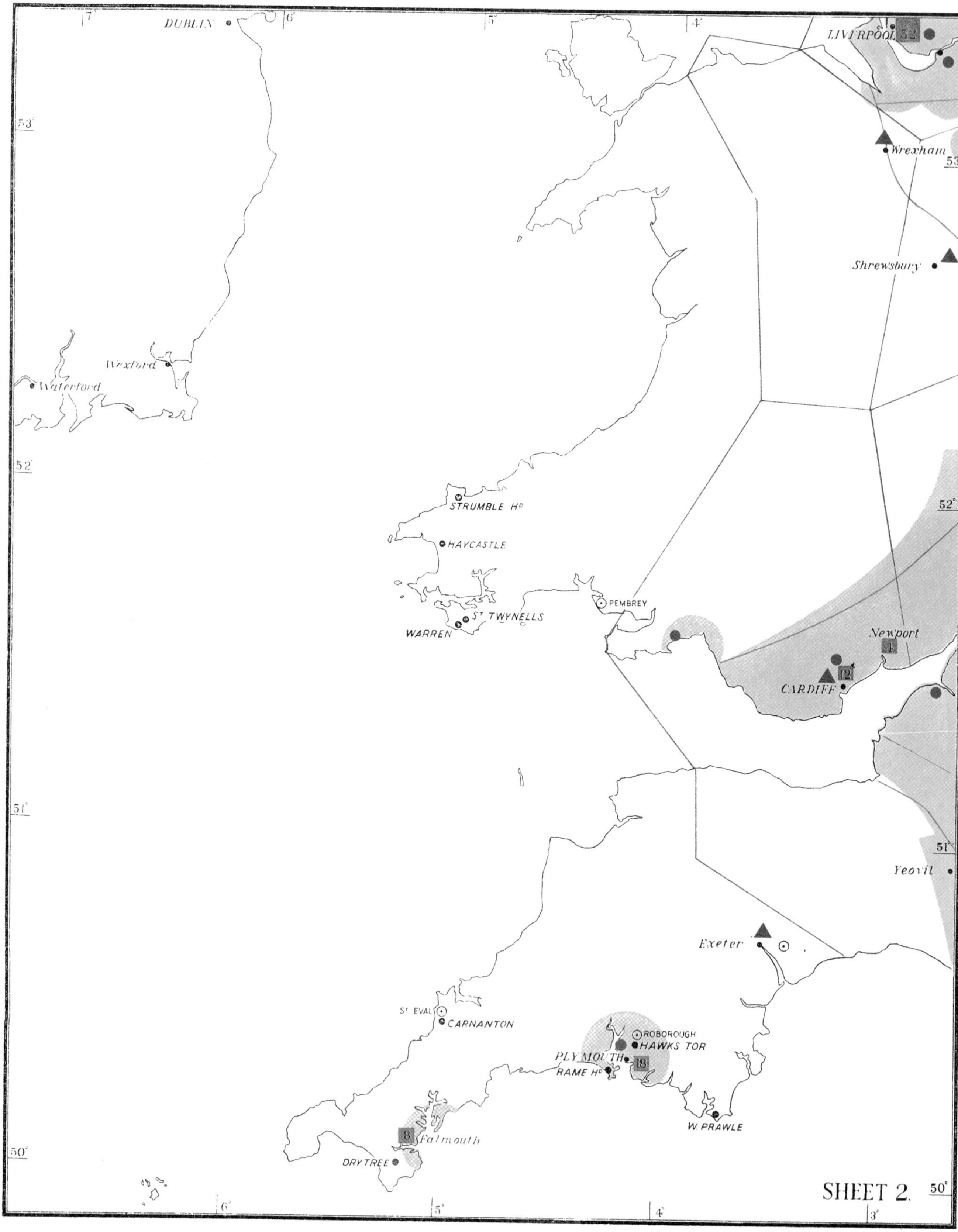

SHEET 2.

MAP No 115 COMPILED & DRAWN AT A.H.B.1

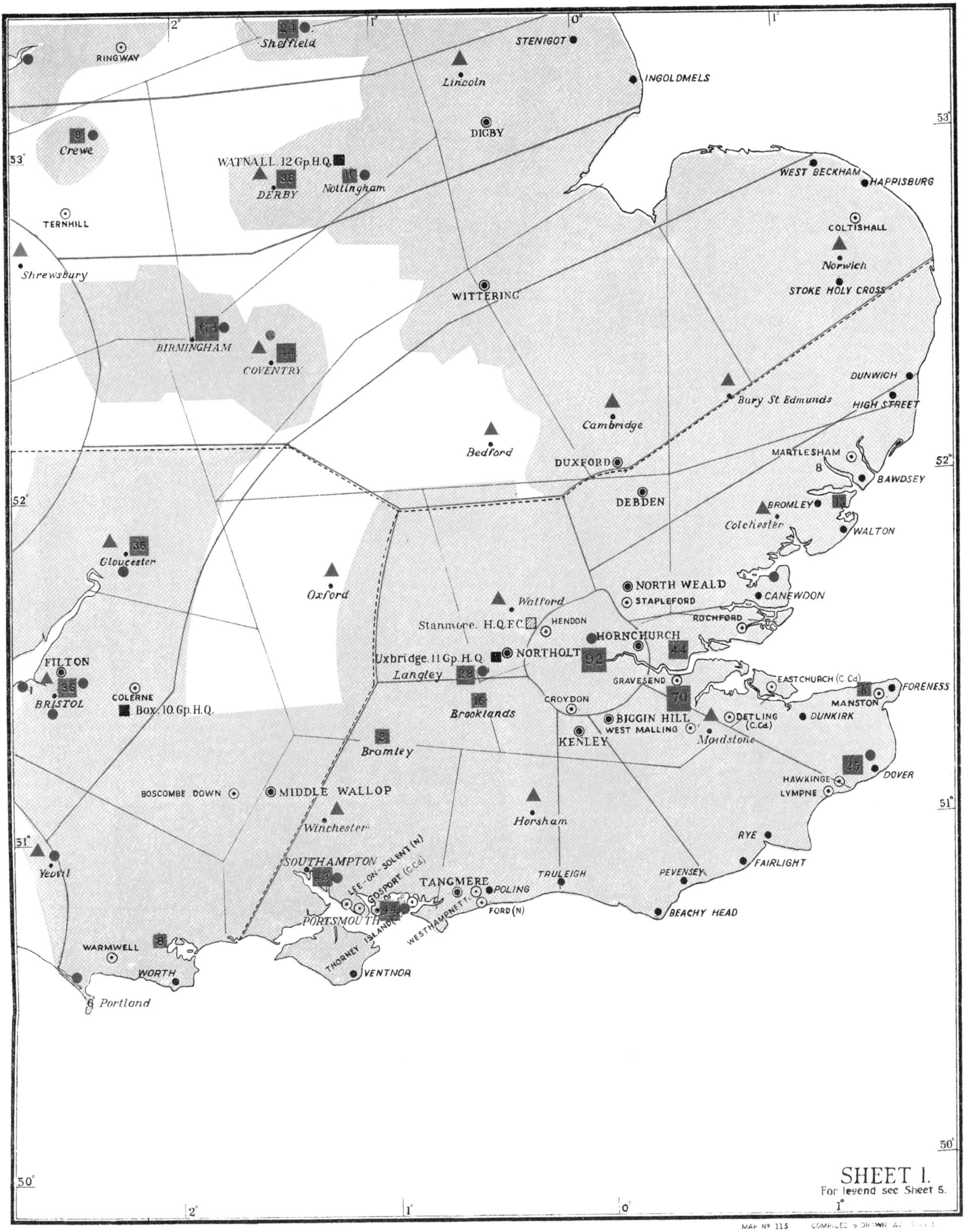

SHEET 1.
For legend see Sheet 5.

MAP No 115 COMPILED & DRAWN AT ...

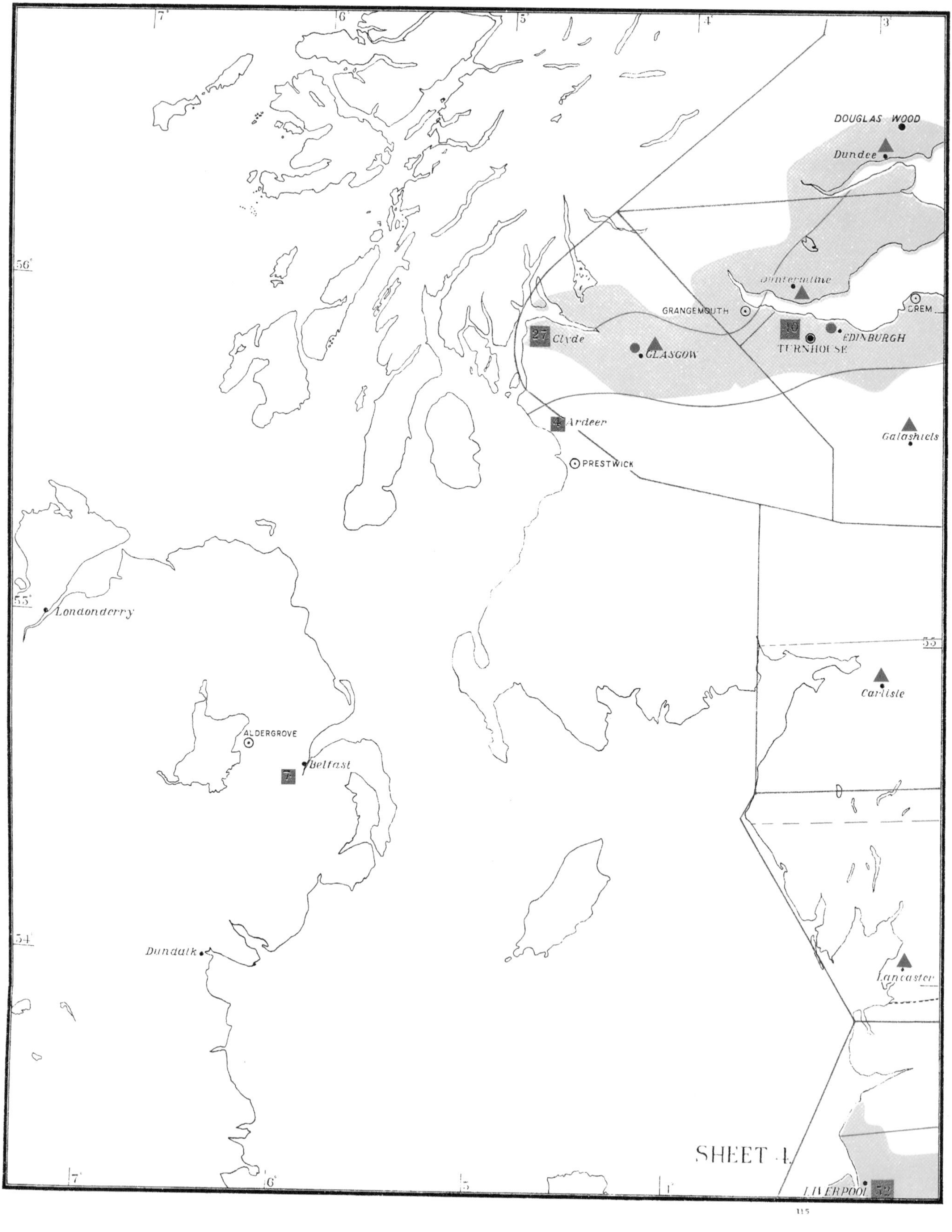
DOUGLAS WOOD
Dundee
Dunfermline
GRANGEMOUTH
CREM
27 Clyde
GLASGOW
10
EDINBURGH
TURNHOUSE
4 Ardeer
PRESTWICK
Galashiels
Londonderry
Carlisle
ALDERGROVE
Belfast
7
Dundalk
Lancaster
LIVERPOOL
52
SHEET 4

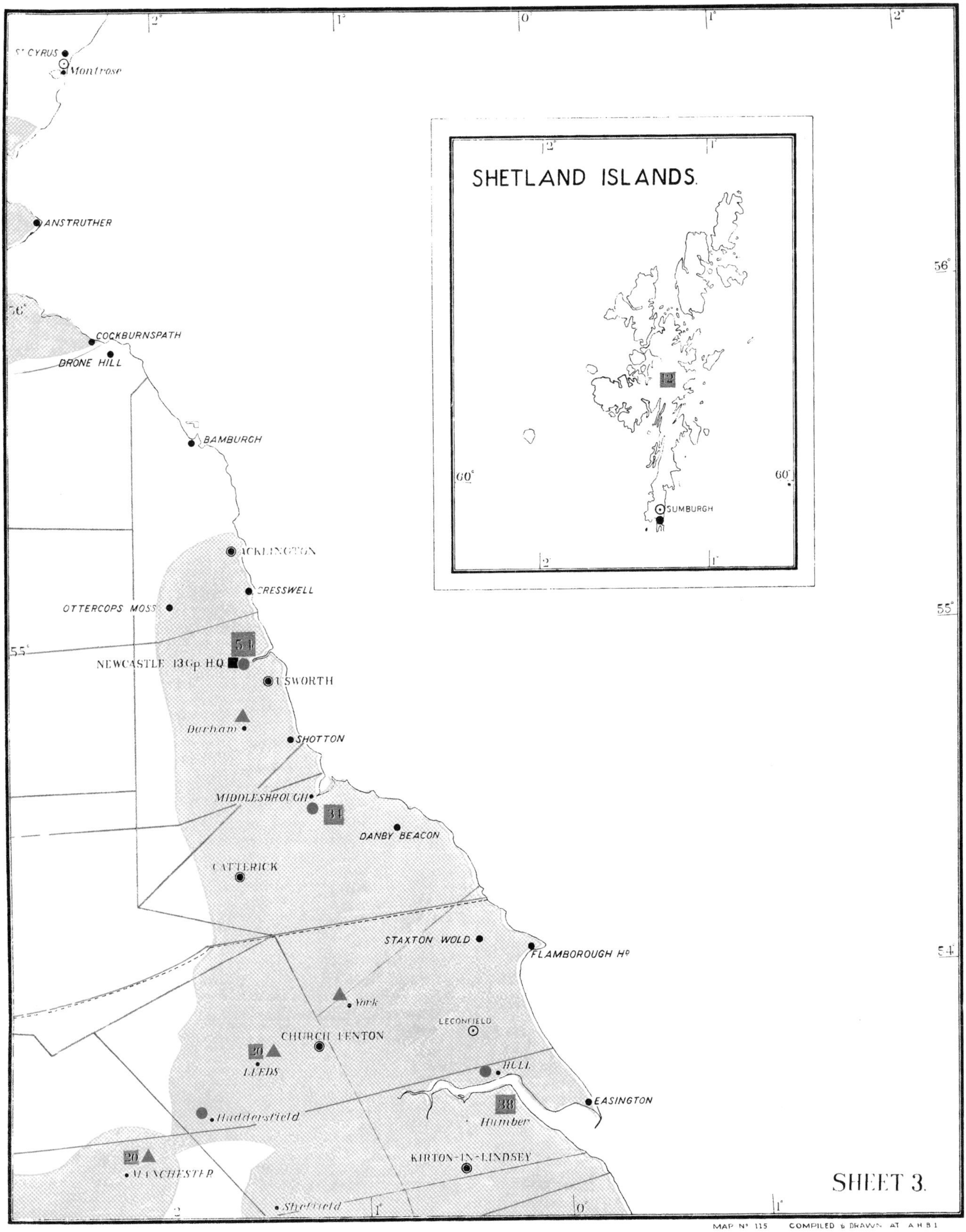
SHETLAND ISLANDS.
SUMBURGH
St CYRUS
Montrose
ANSTRUTHER
COCKBURNSPATH
DRONE HILL
BAMBURGH
ACKLINGTON
CRESSWELL
OTTERCOPS MOSS
NEWCASTLE 13 Gp. H.Q.
USWORTH
Durham
SHOTTON
MIDDLESBROUGH
DANBY BEACON
CATTERICK
STAXTON WOLD
FLAMBOROUGH Hd
York
LECONFIELD
CHURCH FENTON
LEEDS
HULL
EASINGTON
Huddersfield
Humber
KIRTON-IN-LINDSEY
MANCHESTER
Sheffield
SHEET 3.

MAP No 115 COMPILED & DRAWN AT A.H.B.1

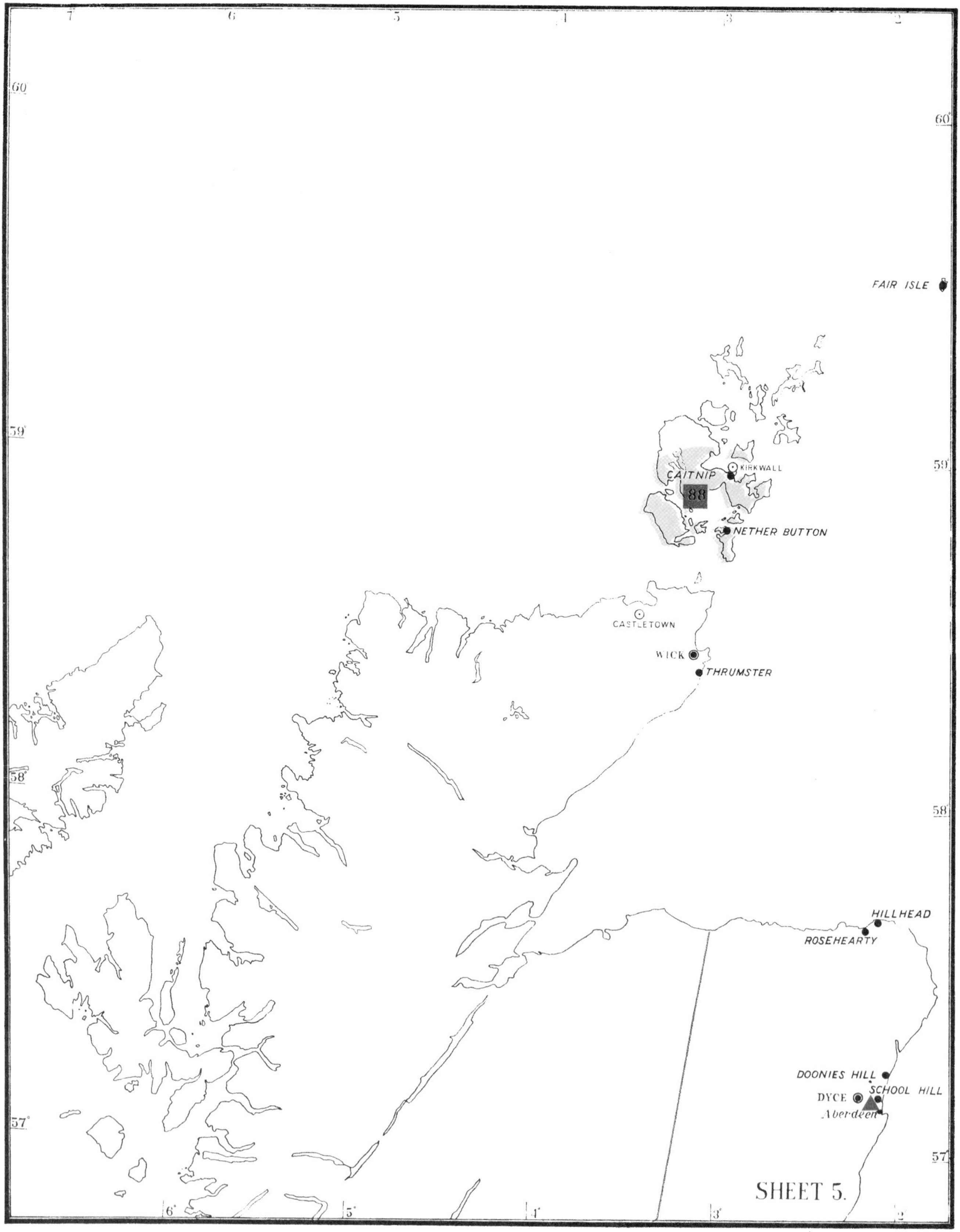
FAIR ISLE
KIRKWALL
CAITNIP
88
NETHER BUTTON
CASTLETOWN
WICK
THRUMSTER
HILLHEAD
ROSEHEARTY
DOONIES HILL
SCHOOL HILL
DYCE
Aberdeen
60°
59°
58°
57°
7
6
5
4
3
2
6°
5°
4°
3°
2

SHEET 5.

M.A.F.
HURRICANES AND SPITFIRES
PRODUCTION, WASTAGE AND NUMBER AVAILABLE FOR IMMEDIATE ISSUE
21 ST. JULY — 26 TH. OCTOBER 1940

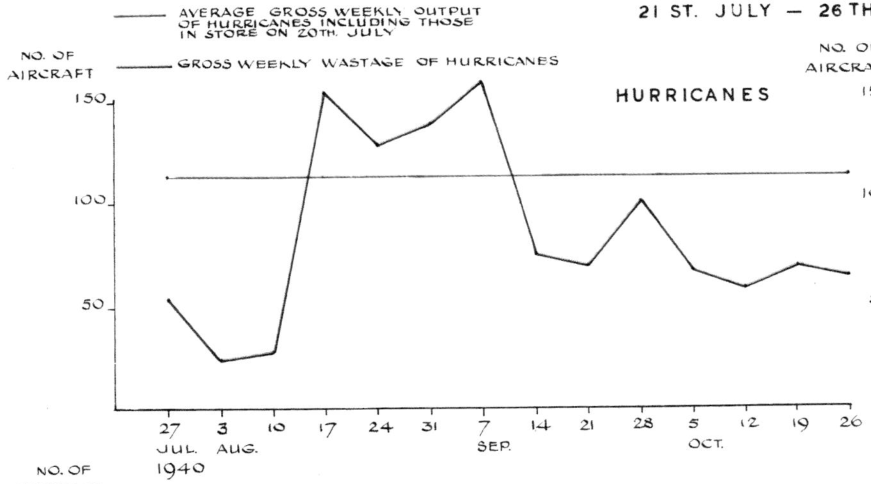

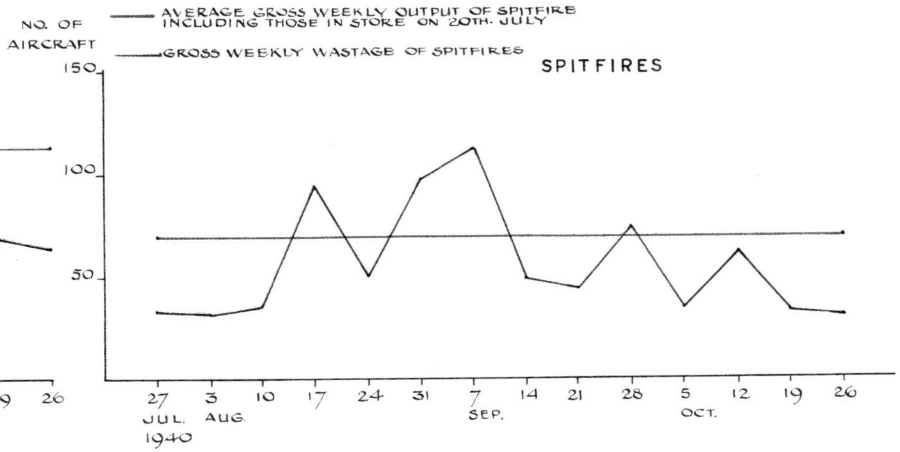

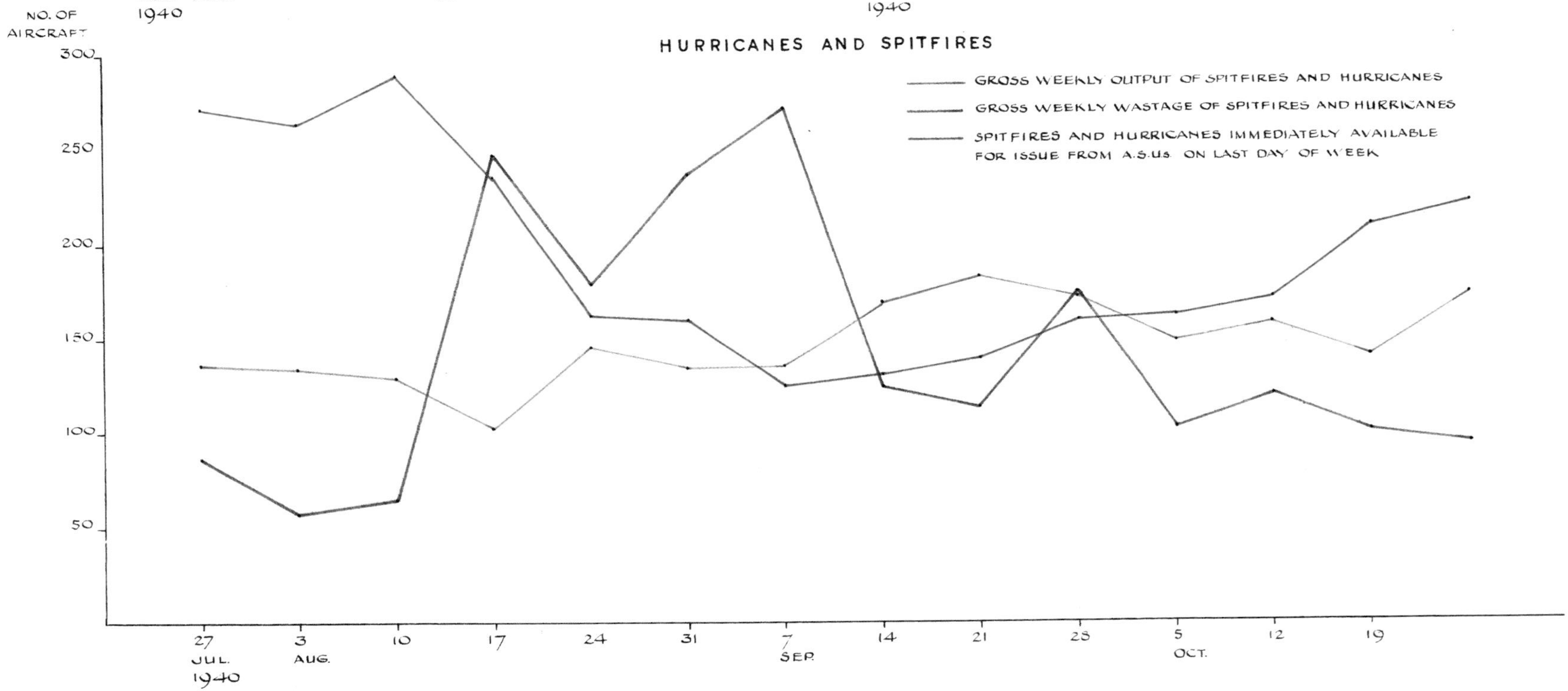

TYPES OF GERMAN AIRCRAFT CLAIMED AS DESTROYED BY FIGHTER COMMAND DURING THE BATTLE OF BRITAIN

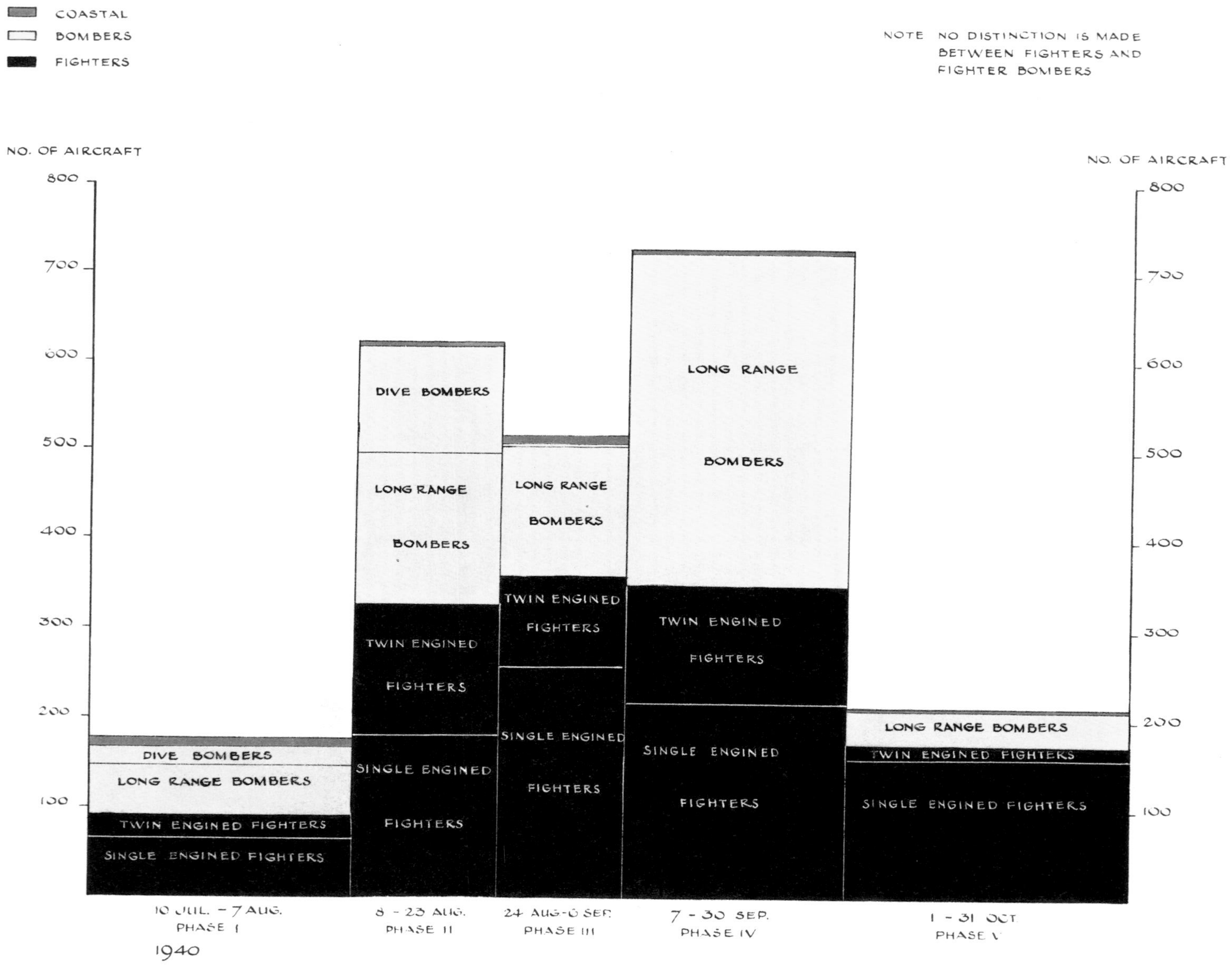

1. Air Chief Marshal Lord Dowding and Air Marshal Sir Trafford Leigh-Mallory at a ceremony to mark the third anniversary of the Battle of Britain, 15 September 1943.

2. The RAF's political and military leaders during the Battle of Britain – the Secretary of State for Air, the Rt Hon. Sir Archibald Sinclair Bt PC CMG MP, and the Chief of the Air Staff, Air Chief Marshal Sir Cyril Newall GCB CMG CBE AM – at a meeting of the Air Council in July 1940.

3. King George VI in conversation with the Air Officer Commanding No. 11 Group Fighter Command, Air Vice-Marshal Keith Park, during a visit to RAF Northolt, 26 September 1940. Very few anti-aircraft weapons, such as the 40mm Bofors AA gun in the background, were available to protect Fighter Command's airfields in the South-East of England during the course of the Battle.

4. Five RAF Fighter Command Pilots, from left to right: Pilot Officer J. L. Allen, Flight-Lieutenant R. R. S. Tuck, Flight-Lieutenant A. C. Deere, Flight-Lieutenant A. G. ('Sailor') Malan and Squadron Leader J. A. Leathart. At a presentation cenemony held at RAF Hornchuch on 27 June 1940, His Majesty King George VI decorated the five pilots; four would survive the Battle of Britain and become outstanding RAF fighter leaders.

5. Squadron Leader E. M. 'Teddy' Donaldson, Officer Commanding No. 151 Squadron, and Wing Commander F. V. Beamish, Station Commander RAF North Weald, June 1940, in front of a Hurricane belonging to No. 151 Squadron. Victor Beamish flew operational sorties with the squadrons based at North Weald whenever possible, claiming two Luftwaffe aircraft destroyed, eight probably destroyed and a further five damaged between 12 July and 30 October 1940. He was killed in action on 28 March 1942 while serving as the Station Commander at RAF Kenley.

6. Flight-Lieutenant I. R. Gleed DFC pointing to his personal mascot ('Figaro the Cat') painted on the side of his Hawker Hurricane, November 1940. Ian 'Widge' Gleed flew with No. 87 Squadron during the Battle of France and subsequently the Battle of Britain, being awarded the DFC in September 1940; he went on to become one of the RAF's most successful fighter leaders prior to his death in action on 16 April 1943.

7. Hawker Hurricane of No. 85 Squadron, October 1940. Although lacking the performance of either the Supermarine Spitfire or the Messerschmitt Bf 109, the Hurricane was rugged, reliable and an excellent gun platform.

8. Pilots of No. 17 Squadron atop one of the squadron's Hawker Hurricanes, RAF Debden. From left to right: Flying Officer D. H. W. Hanson; Flight-Lieutenant W. J. Harper; Flying Officer G. R. Bennette; Pilot Officer L. W. Stevens; Pilot Officer G. E. Pittman; Sergeant G. Griffiths DFM.

9. Pilot Officer L. W. Stevens prepares to take off in a Hawker Hurricane, RAF Debden, September 1940. Leonard Stevens served with No. 17 Squadron throughout the Battle of Britain; he was killed following a mid-air collision while serving with No. 145 Squadron on 30 March 1941.

10. Hawker Hurricanes of No. 85 Squadron, October 1940; heavily committed as part of No. 11 Group during July and August 1940, the squadron transferred to No. 12 Group in September to rest and retrain in the night-fighter role.

11. Hawker Hurricane of No. 615 Squadron landing at RAF Northolt, October 1940.

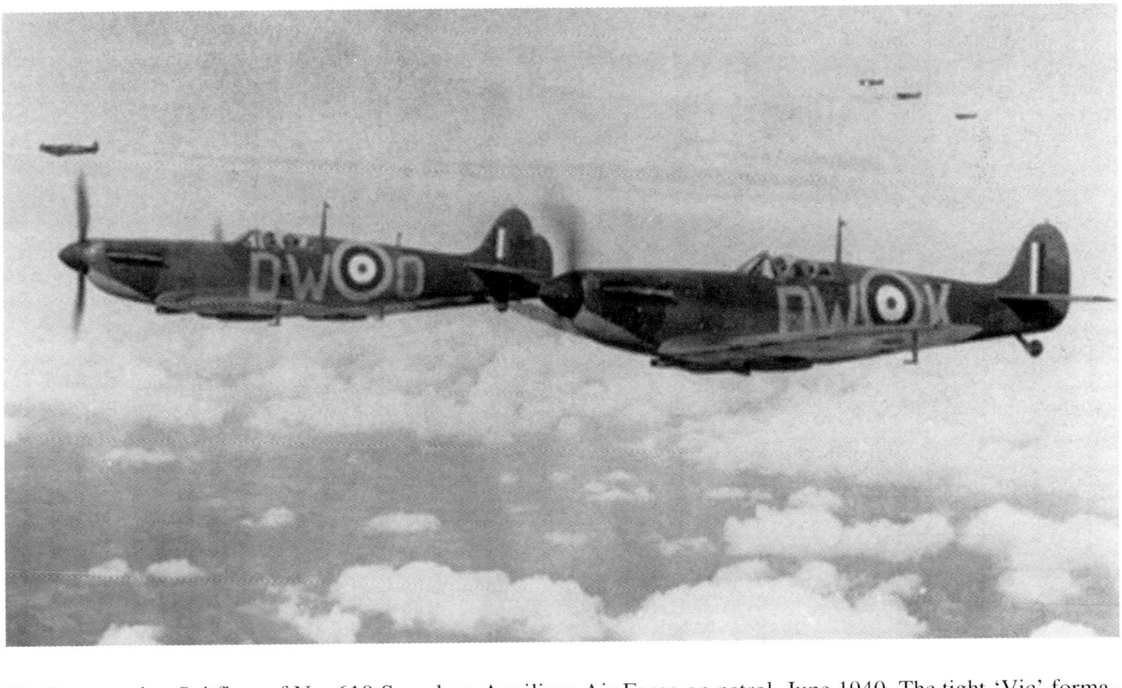

12. Supermarine Spitfires of No. 610 Squadron Auxiliary Air Force on patrol, June 1940. The tight 'Vic' formations flown by RAF fighter squadrons during this period placed them at a severe disadvantage to the Luftwaffe's more fluid tactical formations.

13. Supermarine Spitfire of No. 19 Squadron taking off, October 1940.

14. Test-firing the eight 0.303-inch Browning machine guns of a Supermarine Spitfire I, No. 611 Squadron, January 1940. The rifle-calibre Browning armed virtually all the RAF fighters that participated in the Battle of Britain; however, the Hispano Suiza 20mm cannon had already been selected to supplant the Browning and operational trials with the first cannon-armed Spitfires commenced during the Battle.

15. Armourers re-arming a Supermarine Spitfire of No. 19 Squadron, RAF Fowlmere, October 1940.

16. Wreckage of a Supermarine Spitfire belonging to No. 222 Squadron, destroyed on the ground during the Luftwaffe attack on RAF Hornchurch on 31 August 1940.

17. Boulton Paul Defiants of No. 264 Squadron, August 1940. Although flown with courage and skill, the Defiant's vulnerability led to the withdrawal from daylight operations of the two RAF Fighter Command squadrons equipped with this turret fighter (Nos 141 and 264 Squadrons) in July and August 1940.

18. Underground operations room at HQ Fighter Command, RAF Bentley Priory, June 1941.

19. 'East Coast'-type Chain Home (CH) 'RDF' (radar) station at Poling in Sussex. Although rudimentary by later standards, the CH station network was to afford RAF Fighter Command a vital advantage over the Luftwaffe during the Battle.

20. Barrage balloon of RAF Balloon Command, October 1940.

21. Observer Corps post, September 1940. Observer Corps personnel played a vital role in supplementing the air-defence picture provided by the RAF's radar chain.

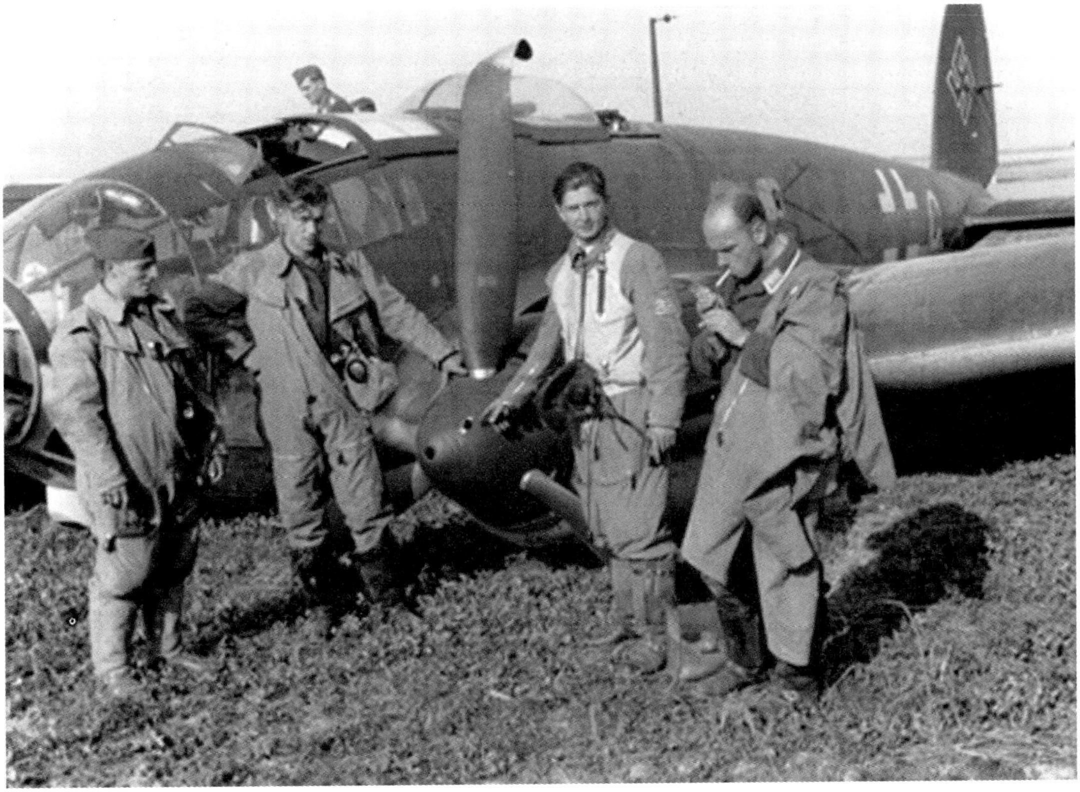

22. Relieved KG53 bomber crew standing next to their Heinkel He 111, which has crash-landed on a Luftwaffe airfield in France following combat damage.

23. Luftwaffe personnel pointing to bullet holes in the tail of a Heinkel He 111.

24. Luftwaffe Messerschmitt Bf 110 twin-engined fighter, framed in a still from a gun camera carried by an RAF fighter.

25. Heinkel He 111 bombers under attack; as seen from the gun camera of an RAF fighter.

26. Heinkel He 111 over the Wapping district of London during the first Luftwaffe mass raid on the capital, 7 September 1940; photographed by a Luftwaffe photographic reconnaissance aircraft.

27. Squadron Leader B. J. E. Lane, Officer Commanding No. 19 Squadron, after returning from an operational sortie, October 1940. Brian ('Sandy') Lane took temporary command of No. 19 Squadron following the death of the Commanding Officer over Dunkirk on 25 May 1940, and resumed command of the squadron on 5 September 1940. He failed to return from a 'rhubarb' sortie while serving as the CO of No. 167 Squadron on 13 December 1942.

28. Flight Sergeant G. C. Unwin of No. 19 Squadron dismounting from the cockpit of his Supermarine Spitfire, October 1940. A pre-war regular, George Unwin was one of the most successful RAF fighter pilots of the Battle of Britain; he was commissioned in the following year, and eventually retired from the RAF with the rank of Wing Commander in 1961.

29. Flight-Lieutenant John A. Kent, RAF flight commander with No. 303 'Warsaw-Kosciuszko' Squadron, flanked by two Polish pilots of the squadron, Flying Officer Zdzislaw Henneberg (left) and Pilot Officer Mirolsaw Feric (right), October 1940. Comprising primarily Polish personnel, No. 303 Squadron was the top-scoring RAF fighter squadron of the Battle of Britain, claiming 117½ victories between 30 August and 11 October 1940.

30. Pilots and other officers of No. 602 (City of Glasgow) Squadron, Auxiliary Air Force, RAF Westhampnett, September 1940. *Standing:* Flying Officer C. B. I. Willey (Medical Officer); Pilot Officer S. N. Rose; Sergeant A. McDowall; Flying Officer J. S. Hart; Flying Officer Graisbrook (Intelligence Officer); Sergeant J. Proctor; Flying Officer Douglas (Adjutant); Sergeant R. F. P. Phillips; Pilot Officer A. Lyall; Sergeant G. A. Whipps; Pilot Officer D. H. Gage; Pilot Officer P. P. C. Barthropp; Lieutenant Taylor (Gunnery Liaison Officer); Pilot Officer H. G. Niven. *Seated*: Flight-Lieutenant C. J. Mount; Flight-Lieutenant R. F. Boyd (with his dog, Max); Squadron Leader A. V. R. Johnstone (Commanding Officer); Squadron Leader J. D. Urie; Flight-Lieutenant D. M. Jack.

II

FIRST PHASE, 10 JULY–7 AUGUST: GERMAN OPERATIONS AGAINST THE UNITED KINGDOM

I. INTRODUCTION[1]

It is not possible to set an exact term to the air operations over this country which are known as the Battle of Britain. Both before and after the period when the fighting was fiercest, operations took place which must be considered, if not in detail, if the great battles of August and September are to be properly understood. An appendix to the despatch of Air Marshal Dowding shows the first phase of the battle as beginning on 10 July and lasting until 25 August, but he admits that there are good grounds for choosing 8 August as its opening day. Certainly it was not until that date that the Germans used the large forces that were to become common place during the following six weeks. Yet the fighting during July and the first week in August cannot be ignored, for, as we shall see, the Germans were already experimenting with the policy that underlay many of their later operations, namely the exhaustion of the British fighter force.

AHB II H1/18, Appendix D

Ibid. paras 11–12

a. Outline of Operations in June

This was certainly not their aim when they operated over this country in June; for practically all sorties over England were made at night. Not until 2 July, i.e. one week after the French armies had stopped fighting, did German squadrons begin regular daylight attacks on targets in this country. Indeed it would have run counter to all that the Germans believed about the concentrated use of air power if, during their land operations in Western Europe, they had diverted any notable proportion of their air forces to attack the United Kingdom.

Consequently, throughout May and the first days of June the people of Britain were disturbed from the air neither by day nor night; and this was the case, with the exception of the nights of 5 and 6 June,[2] until the French request for an armistice on 17 June. The lull was broken on the night of 18 June when bombs were again dropped on and near airfields in Yorkshire, Lincolnshire and Norfolk. Thenceforwards German aircraft were over England on practically every night during the month. On no night were more than seventy[3] aircraft employed, but interceptions of German W/T traffic indicated that no less than six *Kampfgeschwadern* participated in the operations, from which it would appear that the Germans were building up in each a nucleus of crews who were

1 No attempt will be made to include in the body of the narrative exhaustive details of every operation, great and small, that was embarked upon by the German Air Force during this period. To do so would mean a long catalogue of sorties and combats which would only weary the reader without helping him to understand any more clearly the course of events. The story would be incomplete, however, unless the wide geographical and temporal distribution of the German operations was shown, as well as the extensive counter-measures which these forced upon Fighter Command. It has, therefore, been decided to append a series of tables giving such statistical and other information as is necessary for the full scale of the operations to be appreciated. In addition, the fighting over the Channel on a number of days during the period has been treated in considerable detail in order that the defence problem as it appeared to the controllers on the ground and the pilots in the air, should be realised in all its complexity. By these means it is hoped that both clarity and comprehensiveness have been achieved; or, in other words, that the wood can be seen as well as the trees.

2 On each of these two nights about thirty aircraft from *Kampfgeschwadern* 4 and 30 attacked a number of objectives near the East Coast, most of which were bomber airfields, though a few bombs were dropped on a steelworks at Scunthorpe on the night of 6 June. Why the attacks were discontinued it is impossible to say. It is somewhat surprising in view of the fact that neither KG4 nor KG30, which were chiefly stationed in Norway and north-west Germany, appear to have played any part in the French campaign.

3 Except where German records are available it is impossible to give accurate figures of the strength of enemy raids.

experienced in night flying over England. An average of forty fighter sorties was made on each night that the Germans raided in strength, and these were about equally divided between the six Blenheim squadrons and thirty of the single seater squadrons.

In the main the targets attacked were on or near the East coast, but some attention was paid to South Wales, and, towards the end of the month, the route from the Cherbourg peninsular to Merseyside was reconnoitred. The steelworks at Scunthorpe and Middlesbrough, and the Billingham works of Imperial Chemical Industries, were singled out for attack. Aberdeen, Hull, Middlesbrough, and the ports of South Wales, were all bombed, but on so small a scale that it cannot be inferred that the Germans were trying, and failing, to dislocate the work of these ports. Nor can it be inferred that the frequent attacks on the steel industry were part of a plan to cripple that type of war production; for, in that case, the Germans would not only have attacked such works as those of Dorman Long at Middlesbrough, in much greater strength, but they would hardly have briefed pilots to fly over the Midlands, as they obviously did, and neglect the great concentration of industry there.

There was some debate at this period, and no little scorn among the general public, over the high proportion of bombs that fell ineffectively in rural districts seemingly far away from any worthwhile target. But it should not be forgotten that in a country so small and highly developed as England, there are few areas in which valuable targets cannot be found. This is especially so in respect of two important categories of target, communications and airfields. A less accurate bombing of the marshalling yards at March than that of 29/30 June, might well have appeared an indiscriminate and pointless attack to all but those who appreciate the great importance of those particular yards; for they are situated in the heart of an extensive rural district. Similarly, airfields and decoy airfields may well have been the target for bombs that actually fell in open country some distance away. The decoys for the RAF stations at Cottesmore and Dishforth both received salvoes of bombs during June; and it is unlikely that they were the only deceptions that succeeded in their purpose. Here, too, however, the bombing would appear pointless to all except the few who knew of the existence and location of such decoys.

Home Security Daily Appreciation, 25 June

Nevertheless, much of the German bombing was ill-directed, and raises the question, what were the German intentions? One suggestion, which came from the staff officers attached to the Ministry of Home Security, was that some, at least, of the raids were designed not to produce extensive damage, but to enable a timed programme to be worked out in detail as a preliminary to airborne invasion. According to this view, flights were being directed towards, and bombs were being dropped in, open country where parachute troops would be landed. It is doubtful whether this was part of the German plan; but, in any case, the raids were worthwhile to the Germans if only for the effect that they had upon the general economy of the country. From 19–25 June they forced the sounding of air raid sirens in many more districts than the extent of their threat warranted. On 24–25 June, all districts south of a line between Hull and Liverpool were under 'red' warning, though Bristol was the only area where the precaution was really needed. The following night, sirens were sounded in practically all industrial districts except Lancashire, but only in the Potteries were attacks of any consequence carried out. A new policy governing the sounding of sirens was required unless a dozen aircraft were to keep the whole country alert night after night, and one was soon in operation. It needed no reorganisation of the air raid warning system. It was based simply on a greater caution in the despatch of the 'Air Raid Message – Red', except for coastal districts, and a more frequent use of the cautionary 'Yellow' (later 'Purple') message; but its effect was immediately noticeable. On the night of 26 June, Middlesbrough, Norwich, Ipswich and Portsmouth were the only areas under public warning, yet enemy aircraft covered as much of the country as they had done on previous nights. The new policy entailed the danger of bombs falling without warning, as they did in Cardiff on the first night it was applied, but it was a counter to what was doubtless part of the German intentions, a steady sapping of the stamina of the British people. It is relevant that Bomber Command had a plan for the attack of Germany by night, which was intended to dislocate Germany's industry by keeping her industrial districts under air raid warning for most of the hours of darkness. Indeed there was historical justification in the raids on England during the Great War for expecting important results from this policy. It was hoped that a small number of aircraft would suffice to stop night shifts from working, the rest of the population from sleeping, and thus affect industrial output. Those who framed the plan recognised that there must be an offensive element in these operations; and they therefore recommended that at least one objective should be attacked in fair strength every night, altering the areas on successive nights so that the German public would never know if the air raid warning foretold a mere threat or a heavy attack. The main targets were to be self-illuminating, i.e. coke ovens, blast furnaces, port facilities and marshalling yards (where essential lighting had to be displayed for as long as possible).

Plan WA8, AHB IIA/1/9

The German operations over the United Kingdom in June may well have been governed by a similar plan. That of Bomber Command was designed to effect maximum dislocation at minimum cost, and the enemy were doubtless attracted by the same prospect, especially as much of their air force was resting and re-equipping after the French campaign. Moreover the Germans, no less than ourselves, were aware of the effect on industrial output of their attacks in 1915–18. Small numbers of bombers ranging over the whole of this country, keeping the people awake, and attacking, even if the attacks were only small, targets of peculiar importance, or ones easily located at night, were a cheap means of maintaining pressure upon Germany's last enemy until the full weight of her air arm could be used. It was also possible by this means to familiarise a large number of crews with the problems of night flying over England, and to reconnoitre the routes along which aircraft would fly to attack the main centres of population and industry. Whether the Germans were already preparing for the heavy night attacks that commenced in the autumn, it is impossible to say. In any case, these operations are important *per se*, despite the insignificant damage they caused; and their character and purpose must be established, for attacks after the same pattern continued to be made throughout July and August. Not until the last week in August did the Germans cease these light but extensive night raids, attacking during this period practically every industrial district in England and Wales. Such attacks were a nightly background to the great day operations of the first two phases of the Battle of Britain. What precise relationship, if any, existed between the two sorts of operations will be considered later.

b. Outline of Operations, 2–9 July

Home Security War Room, Daily Appreciation

This period was one in which the Germans continued the widespread attacks which they had begun in June, but with the difference that some were made in daylight. The night raids themselves were on a lighter scale than those of June, and only on the night of 8/9 July were more than one hundred HE bombs dropped. Most attention was paid to the South Wales and Bristol area, but all coastal counties south of Tyneside had incidents to report. A number of worthwhile targets were bombed, but in no case was serious damage done. The chief merit of the operations, from the German point of view, was doubtless that they disturbed wide areas of the country at little cost to themselves. We, for our part, still felt that public air raid warnings were being sounded too frequently, and on 6 July the War Cabinet gave instructions that the 'red' warning should be limited, as far as possible, to places where severe attack was expected. The staff at Fighter Command did their best to obey, and the air raid warning officers in the Command Operations Room were informed of the War Cabinet's will. Literal obedience, however, would have meant that warnings would rarely have been sounded, if at all, for on no night during June and July did more than twenty aircraft concentrate on any one region of the country. Moreover, to have ignored the approach even of a single aircraft to targets such as marshalling yards, docks and certain sorts of industry, such as steelworks, at all of which lights would be visible from the air, would have meant jeopardising the lives of the workers there, and those who lived nearby. Consequently, there was no noticeable diminution in the number of public warnings, despite the War Cabinet's instruction.

With a few exceptions, raids in daylight against inland targets during this period were carried out by single aircraft or formations of two or three, but the depth of penetration showed a new determination on the part of the enemy. On 3 July single aircraft flew as far as Berkshire, and successfully bombed White Waltham aerodrome, a Flying Training Command station, and the RAOC depot at Thatcham. On the following afternoon bombs were dropped near the Filton aircraft factory outside Bristol. Two days later barracks at Aldershot were damaged; and on 9 July Boulton and Paul's works at Norwich, Cardiff docks and a RAF station as far afield as Penrhos in Caernarvonshire, were all bombed in daylight. Attacks of this sort were quite novel, and defence against them was not easy.

But the most important feature of the German operations was the effort against shipping in the Channel and against south coast ports. Falmouth, Plymouth, Portland, Weymouth and Dover were all bombed, and there were seven attacks on Channel convoys. Two attacks on Dover, one on Portland and three on convoys were carried out by fifteen to twenty bombers escorted by a similar number of fighters. The results were small enough. Only seven ships were sunk and neither Portland nor Dover harbour had to be closed to shipping but the air fighting which accompanied the attacks promised no easy victory when more intense operations began. Fifteen fighters and twelve pilots were lost by Fighter Command, as against the claim of the confirmed destruction of eleven bombers and thirteen fighters. During all their operations during this period the fighter squadrons claimed the destruction of twenty bombers and thirteen fighters at a cost of seventeen aircraft and fourteen pilots.[4] The effect of the new turn of the German effort on the corresponding effort of the Command was most marked; the number of sorties despatched between 0900 and 1800 hours jumped from ninety-one on 2 July to two hundred and eighty-two on the following day, rising to three hundred and thirty-nine on 8 July.

A number of inferences could fairly be drawn from the German operations in the Channel. Firstly, the Germans were capable of finding and attacking in strength all shipping in the Channel. Secondly, Fighter Command must expect a much higher rate of loss in fighting to protect Channel convoys than it had suffered in its previous operations for home defence. This was made quite clear by the difference between losses sustained north of the Humber, where eight German bombers were destroyed without loss, and those over the Channel, where at least one of our aircraft had been lost for two of the enemy's. Lastly, and quite apart from any casualties that might be suffered, the burden of protecting Channel convoys was likely to be heavy. The number of sorties that the Command sent out on 8 July was well within its capacity, but it had been inspired by, at most, one twentieth of the available German force.

The reaction of Air Chief Marshal Dowding took the typical form of making the best of a situation which he deplored, and, at the same time, presenting his views to the Air Ministry in quite unmistakable terms. Accordingly, during the 2–9 July he carried out a minor redeployment which took the form of moving a number of squadrons to forward airfields on the south coast. No. 79 Squadron moved from Biggin Hill to Hawkinge, No. 65 Squadron from Hornchurch to Manston, and Nos 238 and 501 Squadrons from Middle Wallop to Warmwell, which only came into use by fighters on 5 July. From these stations it was possible for squadrons to move more quickly to the protection of Channel shipping. There had been an analogous move to forward airfields on the east coast in the autumn of 1939 when German attacks on shipping had caused some concern. Also, on 8 July No. 10 Group took over control of the squadrons at Pembrey, St Eval and Exeter, thus relieving No. 11 Group of some of the wide territorial responsibility it had been bearing hitherto. But Air Chief Marshal Dowding gave warning at a conference at his headquarters on 3 July, that if his Command was heavily committed to the defence of targets inland it would be unable to protect coastal convoys. For this reason he looked forward to the time when all ocean convoys for London were passed round the north of Scotland, and the Channel restricted to coastal convoys of small ships, 'so that the South Coast traffic does not very much matter'.[5] A fortnight later he made it clear to the Air Ministry that if he was to undertake to protect shipping efficiently he

AHB IIM/a2/1a

Fighter Command ORB Appendix D5, Dowding – Air Ministry 19 July

4 Those pilots who escaped destruction with their aircraft were not always immediately available for operations. Figures of pilot casualties, including wounded and injured, are given on a monthly basis in Appendix 34.

5 At the moment of writing no figures are available to show what proportion of coastal traffic passed through the Channel between July and October 1940. It may be that it was relatively small, but it was certainly not true of coastal traffic as a whole that it did not very much matter. Between July and October 1940 a monthly average of four million tons of coastal shipping was cleared in the ports of the United Kingdom; and, in general, this sort of sea transport became more important as less ocean-going shipping was sent to east coast ports, and a heavier strain was thrown on the railways radiating from Glasgow, Liverpool and South Wales.

must have more squadrons. He pointed out that recent attacks on shipping were not being made by one or two bombers, as was the case in the previous autumn and winter, but by strong formations of bombers accompanied by fighters. In his opinion three squadrons per sector were needed for no other task than the protection of shipping, if that job was to be done properly. But since the additional squadrons that were needed to make this possible were not available, he felt bound to give notice that he doubted whether it would be possible to give adequate protection to all ships or convoys between Land's End and the Humber.

Ibid.

Lest it should be thought that the Commander-in-Chief was taking too pessimistic a view of the general air defence position, his opinions on another aspect of the fighter problem, namely the defence of our airfields in the south and south-east, are worth noting. At a conference of his Group commanders on 7 July, Air Vice-Marshal Leigh-Mallory, AOC No. 12 Group, expressed the opinion that the enemy would probably concentrate their attacks on these airfields for a week or so as a preliminary to invasion. To this Air Chief Marshal Dowding replied that he only hoped that the Germans would do so, as to spend a week in that way would exhaust the German squadrons before invasion started; while if they spent a month that way their losses would be such that there would be no invasion at all. Interestingly enough, in view of what actually took place, he went on to say that, if the enemy did attack our airfields in strength, the attack would probably only last about twenty-four hours.

AHB IIM/b11/1a

Clearly enough, the Commander-in-Chief did not anticipate defeat, but, equally clearly, he was anxious that his Command should be used in the most economical fashion and under the most favourable circumstances; and he did not consider that either of these conditions applied when his squadrons were used for the protection of shipping. This, we are entitled to say, was his opinion at the beginning of what he himself calls the first phase of the Battle of Britain, during which most of the big engagements were inspired by German attacks on Channel convoys and the corresponding British effort to protect them.

II. DISPOSITIONS AND ORGANISATION OF THE GERMAN AIR FORCE

During the last fortnight in June and the first fortnight in July we discerned much movement by German units, brought about partly by the occupation of newly acquired airfields, and partly by the need for re-equipment, which seems to have entailed the return of many units to Germany. By 15 July, however, the basic deployment of the German Air Force for its offensive against the United Kingdom was virtually complete, and it was possible, therefore, to take stock of the units opposed to us (see Appendix 1).

It should first be explained that the German Air Force was organised in Air Fleets (*Luftflotten*) on a territorial basis. Thus, arrayed against Great Britain by the beginning of July were *Luftflotten 2, 3* and *5*. *Luftflotte 3*, under Generalfeldmarshal Sperrle, was responsible for the operations of all units in the north and west of France; *Luftflotte 2*, under Generalfeldmarshal Kesselring, covered north-east France, Belgium, Holland and north-west Germany; and *Luftflotte 5*, under Generaloberst Stumpff, was located in Denmark and Norway. Each *Luftflotte* was made up of one or more *Fliegerkorps*, the commander of which controlled all units within the area allocated to him.[6] During the Battle of Britain, according to our information, *Luftflotte 3* contained *Fliegerkorps IV* (Generaloberst Keller) in Brittany, *Fliegerkorps VIII* (General der Flieger von Richthofen) in the Cherbourg-Tours area, and *Fliegerkorps V* (General der Flieger von Greim) in the Seine area, but it is not know what were the precise boundaries between them. Under *Luftflotte 2*, were *Fliegerkorps I* (Generaloberst Grauert) in north-east France, and *Fliegerkorps II* (General de Flieger Loërzer) in Belgium. Also under Kesselring's command was *Fliegerkorps IX* (Generalleutnant Coeler) in Holland and North-west Germany, which specialised in minelaying and the reconnaissance and attack of shipping. *Luftflotte 5* contained *Fliegerkorps X* (General der Flieger Geisler).

The operational units of a *Fliegerkorps* were the *Geschwader* and the *Gruppe*. The *Geschwader* normally contained three *Gruppen*, which each contained two to four squadrons of nine aircraft, with an immediate reserve of three. A special headquarters squadron was included in the establishment of a *Geschwader*, and a headquarters flight in that of the *Gruppe*. At full strength, therefore, a *Geschwader* contained one hundred and twenty-six aircraft, including reserves, and a *Gruppe* thirty-nine. *Geschwadern* were only formed for long range bombers (*Kampfgeschwadern*), dive-bombers (*Sturzkampfgeschwadern*), single-engined fighters (*Jagdgeschwadern*), and twin-engined fighters (*Zerstörergeschwadern*). In the case of bomber reconnaissance, army co-operation and coastal formations, the *Gruppe* of three or four squadrons was the normal unit. In addition there were *Lehrgeschwadern* of bombers and fighters. These units were part of a special *Lehr* division, but they carried out operations on the orders of the commander of the *Fliegerkorps* to which they were attached, and thus they were part of the *Luftwaffe's* first-line strength. Their duty was to test all types of aircraft and equipment during active operations, and to report upon any alterations or improvements that might be needed. Officers of high quality were usually drafted to *Lehr* units.

The first point to be noted about the German deployment was that the extensive area which had come into the enemy's hands, had been utilised to broaden the air threat to the United Kingdom. Long range bombers were now stationed as far west as Brittany and as far north as Stavanger, and could reach every part of this country. If they operated over that part of England south of a line from the Bristol Channel to the Wash they could be escorted by single-engined fighters, while north of that line they could be accompanied by the Me 110, whose extreme operational range was reckoned to be nearly five hundred miles. It followed that even if the Germans concentrated their attacks on a restricted area, a minimum fighter defence had to be maintained for areas outside the main zone of operation.

The second important point – obvious from the most cursory study of the German dispositions – was that the enemy had also made use of his new conquests to concentrate by far the highest proportion of his strength in northern France. It was to be expected, therefore, that the heaviest German attacks would

6 It would appear that, under certain circumstances, there was an exception to this principle, as the commanding officer of all fighter units within a *Fliegerkorps* was directly responsible to the *Luftflotte* commander for all fighter operations. How the *Fliegerkorps* commander and the fighter commander exercised their authority in operations involving both bombers and fighters, is not known.

be made across the Channel from that area. But west of the Seine also the Germans boasted no mean strength. Nearly half of their total dive-bomber strength lay in that area, as well as eleven fighter groups and three of long range bombers. The explanation may well have been, as was suggested by the Combined Intelligence Committee on 6 July, that the German Air Force had been assigned two operating areas, to each of which ground forces had also been allotted for the purpose of invasion. The line between the two areas was reckoned to be from Selsey Bill to Halifax in Yorkshire. But this contributed little to solving the immediate problem of dealing with the mass air attacks, which all agreed would be an inescapable and vital preliminary to invasion. All that could be said early in July, after studying the German deployment and such attacks as had already been made, was that the whole of the country was liable to imminent attack, the south coast and Channel shipping most particularly, with a strong possibility of attacks in the Portland area from the concentration of dive-bombers west of the Seine. In other words, the country was on the defensive, the Germans held the initiative, and all that could be done was to be alert to the first signs of a coherent German plan of attack.

AHB IIH1/2, Annex B to Report No. 37

III. CONDITION OF THE GERMAN AIR FORCE

Nor could any reliable assessment be made of the effect of recent fighting on the German Air Force. It had certainly suffered heavily during the French campaign; and early in June there had been indications that bomber units were at three quarter strength, with a serviceability rate of only 50%. But re-equipment had been proceeding steadily since the end of the French fighting, which probably meant that serviceability rates had been improved; and the process was still going on in the middle of July. On the debit side of the German account could be put the fact that many of the airfields in Northern France were unsuitable for the heavier types of German aircraft; and there was also some evidence that, in June at any rate the Germans found it difficult to bring up all the supplies they needed, particularly stocks of bombs, to their newly acquired French bases. On the other hand, there was no evidence of a general shortage of pilots or aircraft; and, altogether, there was no reason to suppose that supply in any form would be a factor limiting the scope of the German operations.

AHB IIH/126, Encl. 19 and 20

IV. DISPOSITIONS OF FIGHTER COMMAND

In view of our ignorance of enemy plans and preparations, other than the general disposition of the German Air Force, it is not surprising that the staff of Fighter Command was concerned to extend and strengthen the fighter force rather than to speculate on where, if at all, the Germans would attack, or on what form the attack would take. It was assumed that an attack would be launched and that it would probably fall heaviest on No. 11 Group area, i.e. on that area on which most care and preparation had been spent since the first days of an organised air defence system. At the same time the extent of the German deployment required a counteracting deployment by which practically all important targets were covered, no matter from what direction the Germans launched their attacks (see Appendix 2).

Thus, in the south-west the recently established No. 10 Group controlled four squadrons at Pembrey, St Eval and Exeter; No. 11 Group defended the area from Southampton to the north bank of the Thames Estuary with twenty-two squadrons; in No. 12 Group area, from Harwich to the Humber, there were fourteen squadrons; and for the defence of the rest of the country, including the industrial districts of the north-east coast and southern Scotland, No. 13 Group had twelve squadrons. Most of this deployment was within the framework of the air defence system as it existed in May 1940. That is to say that all squadrons, with the exception of those in No. 10 Group, were based on established sector stations. It was only in the No. 10 Group area that any improvisation had been necessary and it was there that the defences were weakest; for aircraft operating from Brittany could outflank the squadrons stationed at Pembrey and St Eval, and so approach the Midlands over virtually undefended country. At the other extremity of the fighter line there were even fewer squadrons. Only one Hurricane squadron at Wick, and another at Castletown, assisted by a few Fleet Air Arm aircraft, were available for the defence of Scapa Flow, while a third squadron, with one flight at Montrose and another at Dyce, was responsible for the great stretch of coastline between the Firth of Tay and Aberdeen. However, the long flight over the sea from the nearest German bases in Denmark and Norway encouraged the hope that attacks in this area, while they might be frequent, would not be heavy, the more so since, as we have noted, the German order of battle indicated that the heaviest attacks would be made directly across the Channel. Attention was focussed, therefore, on the No. 11 Group area, and there the position was indeed such as to daunt all but the most stout-hearted, despite the fact that the defences had been long established and were in good order. On 10 July, out of the fifty-two squadrons in Fighter Command that were considered fit for operations, twenty-two were in No. 11 Group. But in northern France there were twelve groups of single and twin-engined fighters, most of which could be used for escorting bombers; and of the latter there were at least thirty groups in the country between Calais, Le Havre and Paris. If these units were up to establishment, no less than one thousand bombers and four hundred fighters directly threatened the No. 11 Group area. It was true, of course, that many of the squadrons outside No. 11 Group – unless they also were heavily committed – could be looked on as a reserve from which to replace tired and depleted squadrons. But it was precisely in this connection that the Germans had one outstanding advantage: they could mass the bulk of their forces against one part of the country, where only a portion of our available fighter force was deployed and, at the same time, by maintaining the threat to other areas, force Fighter Command to keep considerable forces away from the main zone of operations. Fighter Command, in short, was suffering all the disadvantages of being heavily outnumbered. Perhaps the most significant of all gauges of the extent to which our defensive preparations had been outpaced by the swift march of events is that the total fighter force available in July 1940 was one squadron less than that force which, prior to the war, had been reckoned a sufficient defence against the German bomber force *operating unescorted from Germany itself.*

V. OPERATIONS, 10 JULY–7 AUGUST

German operations during the first phase of the battle are best considered under three headings:

i. Daylight attacks on coastal shipping and harbours.

ii. Daylight attacks on inland targets.

iii. Night operations.

a. Attacks on Shipping, 10–11 July

Daily Summary of Naval Events

Practically all losses suffered by both sides resulted from the first type of operations, as only then did the Germans employ large formations. On eleven days during the four-week period convoys were attacked by more than nine German bombers, and in most cases by more than fifteen. In nearly every case the bombers were escorted by at least as many fighters. In addition, there were seventeen reports of attacks on convoys by single enemy aircraft or small formations. With these attacks should be associated the raids that were carried out on harbours on the south, east and Scottish coasts. Of these, only Portsmouth and Portland on 11 July, and Dover on 19, 20 and 29 July were attacked by large formations; but the Orkneys, Peterhead, Aberdeen, Leith, Falmouth, Plymouth and the South Wales ports were also subjected to attacks which, though light, were in some cases frequent.

The distribution of the German effort was orthodox enough, i.e. it followed the pattern that was to be expected in view of the deployment of the German Air Force. Attacks were carried out on shipping as far north as Cape Wrath; and in this area the Orkneys were also bombed. In south-west England daylight attacks were made on shipping in the Bristol Channel, and as far west as a hundred miles off Land's End, where an armed merchant cruiser was attacked on 14 July. It had been manifest from their dispositions that the Germans were capable of reaching out over the whole of the United Kingdom and the neighbouring waters; and incidents such as these were a practical demonstration of their ability. But it was also significant that the only operations of any moment took place between Harwich and Lyme Bay, opposite the massive German concentration in France and the Low Countries. Outside this area no attack on shipping by more than two aircraft was reported, whereas, as we shall shortly see, in some of the attacks in the Straits of Dover as many as one hundred aircraft were employed. This emphasis was reflected in the losses of merchant shipping through air attack. Thus of the nineteen vessels, totalling 41,000 tons, destroyed by aircraft round our coasts, fourteen, totalling 24,000 tons, were sunk in the English Channel. Of the rest, one was sunk in the Thames Estuary, two off the Norfolk coast, one off north-east Scotland, and one off the Hebrides.

The German operations on 10 July began with reconnaissance and meteorological flights along the coast between the Wash and Land's End. These were to be a daily feature of the Battle of Britain, with the results that on most days the first interceptions took place shortly after dawn. On 10 July, for example, a

Dornier 17 was destroyed[7] near Yarmouth at 0520 hours by a Spitfire of No. 66 Squadron. Other enemy aircraft were active about the same time, however, and the Germans doubtless discovered what shipping was moving in this area. Consequently, at 0820 hours a southbound convoy was attacked off Lowestoft, and three hours later, another convoy in the same area was attacked, in each case by two aircraft. Such attacks were in no way unusual. The Germans had begun to make them in October 1939, and had continued throughout the following winter and spring. They were usually carried out by pairs of aircraft, frequently in cloudy weather; and unless a fighter escort was in position over the convoy, the enemy aircraft were not often intercepted. In the first of these attacks on the 10th a section of No. 242 Squadron was patrolling the convoy when two Heinkels appeared. One of the Heinkels was shot down and the convoy steamed on undamaged. But in the second case the convoy was unprotected from the air and a two thousand-ton vessel was sunk.

Just before this incident took place an attack of a different character was launched against a convoy off Margate. It consisted of two Dornier 17s or 215s (it was not an easy matter to distinguish between the two) escorted by no fewer than thirty Me 109s. No serious attack was made on the convoy, which suffered no loss, but confused and inconclusive fighting developed between the escort and some twenty of our own fighters, drawn from the Hornchurch and Biggin Hill sectors. With this exception, the Germans only embarked upon one major operation during the day. This was first detected about 1320 hours when signs of a concentration behind Calais were detected by the RDF stations in Kent. At the time a westbound coastal convoy was off Dover, and six aircraft from No. 32 Squadron had been directed to patrol it. They were in a position when the German formations arrived at 1340–1350 hours, and aircraft from Nos 111, 74, 64 and 56 Squadrons also arrived over the Straits between 1345 and 1400 hours. Our pilots estimated that there were about twenty-four Dorniers at 4,000 feet, twenty Me 110s at 8,000 feet, and twenty Me 109s at a similar interval. From the combat reports it would appear that the ensuing fighting took place chiefly between fighter and fighter, and only one enemy bomber was shot down. But the RAF had solid grounds for satisfaction at the outcome of the fighting. We claimed the certain destruction of seven of the enemy at a cost of one pilot, while the convoy lost only one four hundred-ton ship, a ludicrously small return for so great an effort on the part of the Germans. In terms of shipping destroyed, the enemy had more reason to be satisfied with the achievement of a solitary aircraft which, at the time of the operations in the Straits slipped over from the Brest peninsula and effectively bombed the harbour at Falmouth, sinking one ship of over six thousand tons, and setting on fire two others of seven thousand and six thousand tons respectively, one of which was later abandoned. In this case the 'red' warning was only received two minutes before the aircraft began to bomb, an indication that the newly-formed intelligence organisation in the south-west was not yet working with proper efficiency.

7 Throughout this narrative wherever figures of German aircraft destroyed are given the source is the list of allowable claims compiled at Fighter Command HQ.

These operations, and those on the following day, set the pattern for anti-shipping operations during the whole of this first phase. Those on 11 July were a particularly good example of the methods that the Germans used, and of the difficulties that were forced upon the RAF fighters.

Soon after dawn on the 11th enemy reconnaissance aircraft were active in the eastern and central Channel, the Thames Estuary and off the East Anglian coast, where one, a Do 17, was shot down. Most of those in the Channel were first detected when on a southerly course, and so no RAF fighters were ordered off the ground, although a convoy was moving eastwards across Lyme Bay. The situation remained quiet until 0730 hours, but shortly afterwards two enemy formations were detected off Cherbourg on a northerly course. Three aircraft of No. 501 Squadron, which had taken-off at 0730 hours to patrol their base at Warmwell, were ordered towards the enemy, while 'B' Flight, No. 609 Squadron, was sent up from Warmwell to patrol the convoy. Just before 0800 hours about fifteen miles south of Portland the three aircraft from No. 501 Squadron sighted nine or ten dive-bombers flying at 7,000 feet, with about twenty Me 109s half a mile behind at 12,000 feet. The combat reports of No. 501 Squadron have not been preserved for this particular action, and all that is known for certain is that one of the three aircraft was shot down. When No. 609 Squadron came into action at 0805 hours they found the dive-bombers gliding to attack the convoy. Honours were fairly even in the ensuing combat. Blue section of the flight moved to attack the bombers, while green section acted as rear-guard; not very successfully, however, for the enemy fighters broke through and shot down two of the three Spitfires in blue section as they dived to attack. But one Ju 87 was certainly destroyed, and one of the ships in the convoy was lost. All the enemy aircraft had disappeared by 0820 hours.

During the next two hours the weather deteriorated and there was little activity. At 0945 hours one enemy aircraft was over mid-Somerset on its way north, but no fighters were ordered to intercept it as it had been found best to intercept raids of this kind, which were usually for reconnaissance, on the return journey, when their course showed what part of the French coast they were making for. At 1015 hours 'B' Flight, No. 601 Squadron (Tangmere), destroyed a lone Do 215 off the Isle of Wight. This aircraft was on a westerly course and may perhaps have been searching for the convoy that had been bombed off Portland. Otherwise there was no significant activity.

Just after 1100 hours 'A' Flight, No. 601 Squadron, were ordered up to intercept the reconnaissance aircraft detected earlier. Its mission had apparently been to reconnoitre central and southern Wales. But by this time there were also signs of renewed activity in the central Channel, although the weather was still cloudy, and our fighters were diverted to intercept a raid which was making for Lyme Bay from the direction of Cherbourg. This movement took the flight over Portland, where they sighted an enemy formation of some sixty aircraft; the time, according to our pilots, was between 1130 and 1135 hours.[8] The enemy consisted of about fifteen Ju 87s at 15,000 feet, escorted by thirty to forty

8 No precise explanation of this surprising encounter is possible; all that can be said is that the RDF stations either failed to detect the enemy altogether, or else the RDF operators plotted a major raid as a single aircraft.

twin-engined fighters arranged in five separate 'vic' formations at distances of half a mile to three or four miles behind the dive-bombers.

As soon as the true position was known at No. 10 and 11 Groups, more fighters were sent into the air. Six aircraft from No. 238 Squadron and three aircraft from No. 501 Squadron took off from Warmwell at 1142 and 1150 hours respectively; about the same time three aircraft from No. 87 Squadron and nine from No. 213 Squadron left Exeter; and the remainder of No. 601 Squadron took off from Tangmere at 1155 hours. All these units with the exception of No. 213 Squadron, made contact with the enemy, but none of them were in time to interfere with the bombing of Portland, which took place at 1153 hours. However, it can have afforded the Germans little satisfaction; for there was no damage to the harbour and only one merchant vessel was hit. Credit for this should go to the six aircraft of No. 601 Squadron, and to their good fortune in having the advantages of greater height than the enemy and of being between the enemy and the sun. Thus they were able to dive on the enemy bombers, and inflict serious damage on them, before the escorting fighters could interfere. No Ju 87 was claimed as certainly destroyed, but six were at least damaged by this initial attack.

Daily Summary of Naval Events, 12 July 1940

By the time that the other defending fighters came up the enemy was disengaging, and the ensuing combats were nearly all between fighter and fighter. It was noticed that the rearguard of Me 110s formed a circle, a manoeuvre which was to become familiar to our pilots as one which enemy fighters frequently adopted when they wished to keep the fighting over one spot, in order to allow the bombers to go on to their target, or to withdraw without being interfered with. Our squadrons emerged from the combat convinced that they had found the measure of the Me 110s, and claimed to have destroyed eight of them, losing neither aircraft nor pilots themselves. In addition, the Portland AA gunners claimed to have destroyed three aircraft.

Combat Report of S/Ldr. J S Dewar, No. 87 Squadron

By 1220 hours the battle was over and the enemy aircraft were returning to France. For the next three hours the Channel remained fairly free of enemy movements, though in the Thames Estuary there were one or two light attacks on convoys. Such a lull was not unusual, as for some days enemy operations in the central Channel during the day had chiefly taken place in the morning, and had not recommenced until dusk, when the first of the night raiders began to move across towards the south coast. It was, therefore, an unusual occurrence that, at 1746 hours, a formation of enemy aircraft was located on a northerly course about fifteen miles north of Cherbourg; and No. 601 Squadron, which was patrolling its base at Tangmere at the time, was directed towards the enemy, who came straight across the Channel to the western end of the Isle of Wight. About 1750 hours orders were also given to No. 145 Squadron at Tangmere to intercept the enemy, and twelve Hurricanes took off at 1800 hours. Shortly before that time No. 601 Squadron came in contact with the enemy formation, which was clearly making for Portsmouth, and found that it consisted of twelve Heinkel 111s, escorted by a similar number of Me 110s. The engagement took place at 18,000 feet, one flight attacking the bombers and the other climbing to engage the Me 110s. The latter seem to have made little attempt to protect the Heinkels beyond forming a circle, and a number of the enemy bombers were damaged at a cost of one of our fighters.[9] Nevertheless, practically all the bombers maintained formation; for when No. 145 Squadron came into the fight they found eleven Heinkels flying south, and away from Portsmouth, with only one or two fighters in the vicinity. By then the Heinkels had already bombed Portsmouth, dropping upwards of twenty HE bombs, which, amongst other damage, started a fire at the aircraft factory of the Airspeed Company. No. 145 Squadron, therefore, were not in time to protect the town, but in the running fight which ensued as the Germans retired across the Channel, they claimed to have destroyed three of the Heinkels.

b. Commentary

This marked the end of daylight operations in the Channel on the 11th, and the end of the hardest fighting that Fighter Command had experienced since the fall of France, but it was obviously only the beginning of the German offensive. The fighting on these two days confirmed Air Chief Marshal Dowding's fears that if the Channel convoys became an objective of the German attack an immense burden would be put upon the squadrons on the South Coast. Only small escorts could be provided for the convoys, in which case there was always a danger that an escort might suddenly be overwhelmed by superior numbers; as was the case in the action off Portland on the morning of the 11th. For the operations on both 10 and 11 July showed that while the RDF stations usually detected advancing enemy formations, they could not always do so in time for the controllers at Nos 10 and 11 Groups to put a sufficient fighter force over the target. In the central Channel the Germans could build up their formations outside the effective range of the RDF stations; and, in consequence, enemy formations suddenly appeared on the operations room tables when they were already flying direct to their targets. Furthermore, as there was a time-lag of the order of four minutes between the detection of a raid and its plotting in the operations room either at sector or Group headquarters, the time available for interception was cut down by this amount. Added to this was the need for watching the movements of a raid for some moments as they were plotted, before the controller could decide what squadrons were to deal with it. It was for all these reasons that none of the raids in the central Channel on 11 July was properly countered before the enemy aircraft had released their bombs. In the case of the raid on Portland just before noon the splendid dash of No. 601 Squadron put the dive-bombers off their aim; but the other squadrons that took part in the engagement only arrived when the bombing was over. In the attack on Portsmouth one of the two squadrons which made contact with the enemy only left the ground as bombs were falling on the town.

The tactical situation underlying the fighting further east, over the Straits of Dover, was somewhat different. There, on 10 July, the RDF stations had

9 The claims recorded in the combat reports of the squadron amount to one Heinkel and one Me 110 destroyed and four Heinkels probably destroyed. In the squadron operations record book the result of the same action is given as six Heinkels and one Me 110 probably destroyed, while in the 'Y' Form rendered daily by Fighter Command to Air Ministry it is shown as four Heinkels and one Me 110 destroyed and four unspecified aircraft probably destroyed, which are the figures given in No. 11 Group Operations Record Book, except that there the unspecified aircraft are described as Me 110s. It is not easy to reconcile these various statements after so much time has elapsed, and it appears that it was nobody's duty to do so at the time.

detected the assembling of a large formation over the airfields in the Pas de Calais nearly twenty minutes before it arrived over the Straits and began to bomb a convoy. Yet when the enemy began attacking at 1345 hours only one flight of fighters was actually over the convoy. The four other squadrons that took part in the fight arrived one by one in time only to tackle the enemy's fighters. It would appear that in this particular instance the controller was at fault in not getting his squadrons away earlier. But his duties needed a sense of judgment amounting to an intuition. He dared not send squadrons into the air in any strength when the first signs of a large raid were detected, for, if he did, and the raid turned out to be merely a ruse, the squadrons would probably be returning to refuel when an actual attack developed. The safest method was undoubtedly to reserve the bulk of the fighting force until the enemy aircraft were actually moving towards their target. The danger was that the fighters might arrive too late to intercept the bombers, as was the case in this particular instance.

But if our fighters had not been able to interfere with the enemy's bombers, the latter had made surprisingly little use of their opportunities. One small ship sunk on 10 July, one damaged at Portland and a few French *chasseurs* at Portsmouth on 11 July, was the sum of their successes against shipping. Damage to the town of Portsmouth was slight; the fire at the Airspeed factory was soon extinguished, and production was not affected. In this particular raid it was noticed that the number of HE bombs dropped was small in proportion to the size of the enemy formation; and this phenomenon was frequently observed during the next two months. At the time it was held to be due to the inadequacies of many of the French airfields, which could not be used by fully loaded long range bombers.

There were few remarkable features about the actual fighting, most of which was joined at 10,000–15,000 feet. Our own pilots considered that the Me 110s did not protect their bombers as they ought to have done, and this was certainly the case in the raid on Portsmouth, when No. 145 Squadron found the Heinkels completely unescorted. Nevertheless, most of the combats took place between fighter and fighter for a reason already adduced, namely that most of our aircraft only appeared when the enemy was retiring.

At this time all our aircraft had not yet been fitted with constant speed airscrews, nor were all fighter fuel tanks armoured or encased in self-sealing fabric; and to that extent some of our pilots were handicapped. Fitting parties were travelling round Fighter Command at this time making the necessary alterations to aircraft already in service, while the manufacturers were beginning to produce aircraft in which these two improvements were embodied. The eight .303 guns were usually effective, but there were a few reports – and these from experienced pilots – of bullets striking Do 17s without apparent result. On the whole, however, the fighting revealed no important weaknesses in our fighters, whereas, in the opinion of our own pilots, it had deflated the high reputation of the Me 110.

Certainly, when our claims were balanced against our losses, we enjoyed a handsome margin of superiority. Fighter Command claimed that in the big engagements over the Straits on 10 July and off Portland and Portsmouth on 11 July, fifteen Me 110s seven Heinkels 111s, one Do 17 and one Ju 87 had

Fighter Command 'Y' Forms

certainly been destroyed, at a cost to the Command of four pilots and five aircraft. It was, of course, impossible to check these claims at the time as practically all the fighting had taken place over the sea and concrete evidence of casualties was rarely obtained. On these two days only two German crews were rescued from the Channel, both of them in the Straits on the 10th; and only three enemy aircraft crashed on land, all on the 11th. Two were Me 110s which came down near Portland, the other was a Heinkel 111 which crashed on Selsey beach. This discrepancy between the number of aircraft claimed to have been destroyed, and the number of which definite material evidence of destruction was obtained, applies at all stages of the Battle of Britain;[10] and part of the explanation is undoubtedly that many enemy aircraft fell into the sea. It is more than likely that in these early days of the battle the Germans were more successful than ourselves in rescuing their pilots from the sea. According to information obtained early in July from prisoners who had been employed on this sort of work, a German air/sea rescue organisation had been formed before the Norwegian campaign, and by July contained at least twelve aircraft, most of which, if not all, were Heinkel 59 floatplanes.[11] We, for our part, had no aircraft specially allotted to this task, and such were badly needed. Experience during the first months of war had shown that when aircraft such as the Spitfire and Hurricane alighted on the sea the nose immediately dived vertically under water and the aircraft sank within a few seconds. But it was not until fighting over the Channel became a daily feature of operations that the problems involved in building a rescue service were seriously tackled. On 15 the July Air Ministry informed Fighter Command that arrangements were being made with the Admiralty for motor boat patrols to be carried out close inshore when fighting was taking place, and that, in the meantime, the many small craft round our coasts which the Admiralty controlled – there were over three hundred of them – had been signalled to keep a general watch while the air battle was in progress. The Air Force itself assisted by moving five high speed launches to the No. 11 Group area; one being stationed at Calshot, two at Newhaven and two at Ramsgate. These launches were controlled by Coastal Command, and requests for their assistance could only be sent via the headquarters of the relevant coastal Group, though time was saved by informing the launch station direct that the request was about to be made. But the principal need was aircraft, preferably amphibians or floatplanes, which could both search and rescue, or, alternatively, aircraft which could co-operate with a rescue launch and act as its eyes, so overcoming what was the great disadvantage of the launch, its limited horizon. It was not until early September that arrangements were made for a number of Lysanders to be stationed in Nos 10 and 11 Groups for this sort of duty.

AI 1(K) Reports, Nos 156, 170, 189/1940

Fighter Command ORB Appendix D5

S.5490, DCAS – all Commands 3 September

10 See Appendix 36.

11 One of these aircraft was shot down off Middlesbrough on 1 July, and another off Ramsgate on 9 July. Both were clearly marked with red crosses and were unarmed; and at least one crew was registered with the International Red Cross authorities at Geneva, though all were trained airmen and members of the German Air Force. These men were certainly genuine rescue workers; their aircraft were properly equipped with the necessary medical stores and comforts; and the only evidence we had of improper use was that one had been used for the conveyance of German staff officers. But since they were operating near the coast of Britain and were frequently sighting our convoys, Fighter Command issued orders on 14 July for their destruction when encountered near our territory or shipping; and on 29 July the Government formally protested against the use of the Red Cross symbol for rescue work of this kind.

c. Operations over the Channel, 12 July–7 August

The weather during the rest of July and the first week in August was not good, particularly between 14 and 19 July and 30 July and 7 August. Visibility was frequently as low as two or three miles, with the cloud base at 2,000–3,000 feet. This appears to have governed to some extent the incidence of the German attacks, which were strongest and most frequent during the last fortnight in July.

The period saw some twenty-five raids by formations of more than twelve German aircraft, seven of them in the area of Isle of Wight – Portland, and nearly all the others over or near the Straits of Dover. Only two attacks of any strength were made north of the Thames Estuary, and these will be examined first.

At 0845 hours on 12 July a southbound convoy was passing about fifteen miles east of Aldeburgh on the Suffolk coast when it was attacked by nine or twelve Heinkels (it is impossible to be certain of the figure). Two Hurricanes of No. 17 Squadron (Debden) were patrolling the convoy at the time, but they were not able to protect it from being bombed: and within a few moments a two thousand ton vessel had been sunk. But this was the end of the enemy's success. The two escorting aircraft were joined by a section of Hurricanes from No. 85 Squadron (Martlesham), and together they set about the Heinkels to such good purpose that four were almost certainly shot down. The crews of two of these were later rescued from the sea, and proved to be members of III/KG 53, which we knew to be stationed near Lille.

Daily Summary of Naval Events, 13 July

This attack took place in an area in which the Germans could not escort their bombers by single-engined fighters, and it must have demonstrated conclusively that without some sort of escort bombers would be fortunate to escape without heavy loss. On only one other occasion during July did the Germans launch a similar attack; this was on the 15th when the weather was very cloudy. On that occasion twelve Do 215s[12] swooped swiftly down from the clouds and set two ships on fire before the escort – again consisting of two Hurricanes – could interfere. As quickly as they came the Dorniers retired.

Ibid. 16 July

In the Channel itself the Germans fared better in that while their losses were heavy they at least shot down some of our fighters. In all the major operations over the Channel, i.e. those in which formations of escorted bombers took part, between 10 July and 7 August we lost forty-nine Hurricanes, Spitfires and Defiants, and thirty of our pilots were killed. In the same period and during the same operations, our pilots claimed to have destroyed for certain one hundred and eight enemy aircraft. The Command as a whole, in all operations against the enemy, lost seventy-five aircraft and forty pilots, and claimed to have destroyed one hundred and seventy one German aircraft of all types.

Fighter Command 'Y' Forms

With the exception of the attacks that were made on Dover harbour, all the large enemy raids were directed against shipping in the Channel and the Thames Estuary. They were carried out by all types of German bomber and fighter aircraft, and a great variety of tactics was displayed. Ju 87s were used over the Straits of Dover and further west, as were Dornier 17s and 215s, but Heinkels were confined to operations chiefly in the central Channel. Both Me 109s and

12 This was the report of our pilots. In fact, the aircraft were probably Me 110s from K Gr 210. See note on p. 41.

Consolidated Combat Reports No. 610 Squadron, 24 July

Me 110s were used in each of the main zones of operations. Chance Vought 156 dive-bombers were believed to have taken part in one of the attacks on Dover on 24 July, and though no other evidence was obtained beyond our pilots' reports, it is unlikely that any German aircraft could have been mistaken for this type of machine. A much-publicised fighter, the Heinkel 113, was also reported, but here, too, no concrete evidence was ever discovered. He 59s continued to be used for rescue work, and our pilots continued to shoot them down. Six of them were believed to have been destroyed during the month. The Messerschmitt Jaguar – the Me 110 equipped as a bomber – and the Me 109 fighter-bomber were both employed on a small number of operations.

It is difficult to say what proportion of the German Air Force was involved in the July operations. At the time the figure of 6–10% was advanced, but what was more important was that the Germans were obviously working up all their units to the point where they could be used as a whole against the United Kingdom. During the month all *Kampfgeschwadern*, except KGs 77 and 100, and all bomber reconnaissance *Gruppen* were identified, through wireless interceptions, as taking part in operations against this country. This was partly confirmed through prisoners and wreckage taken from crashed German aircraft. Amongst the thirty-one aircraft which were found between 10 July and 7 August, were represented eight *Kampfgeschwadern*, two *Jagdgeschwadern*, one *Zerstörergeschwader*, and five army co-operation and bomber reconnaissance *Gruppen*. It would appear, therefore, that the July phase was one in which experience of operations against Britain was spread throughout the whole of the German Air Force.

Air Ministry Daily Telegraphic Intelligence Summary, Vol. 1

AI 1 (K) Reports, No. 171-225/1940

The frequent changes in German tactics in the operations over the Channel are probably explained by a policy of training and experiment preparatory to opening a full offensive. From the 12th to the 19th the Germans followed the pattern set in the first two days of the phase, and these we have examined in some detail. On five days out of the eight the Germans operated in strength, launching two or three raids, considerably separated in time, either in the central Channel or the Straits. The targets in every case were convoys, and the German method, having built up a mixed formation of bombers and fighters over the French coast, was to move it quickly to the target, without any attempt at concealment. Then, their bombs having been released, the bombers would retire as quickly as they could, leaving the escort to act as rearguard and fend off the attacks of our fighters. The defending squadrons usually arrived one by one, too late to interfere with the actual bombing, though on two occasions, out of the eight major operations over the Channel during this period, the enemy bombers were successfully engaged as they retired. The relative frequency of combats with bombers and fighters is reflected in our claim to have destroyed fifteen enemy fighters and eight bombers. Certainly, the German fighters showed no unwillingness to fight. On more than one occasion they stayed fighting over the Straits longer than was necessary if they were merely out to protect the retirement of the bombers they had escorted. They normally enjoyed the advantage of height, having usually come over at 10,000–15,000 feet with the bombers five thousand feet below, and our own fighters had usually to climb to engage them. Consequently, the balance sheet of claims and losses was less in favour of the defence than for any corresponding period in the whole phase, and our losses were fifteen aircraft and nine pilots. One engagement in which Fighter Command suffered unusually heavy casualties deserves recording in some detail, as not only does it illustrate the general character of the fighting over the Straits, but it was held at the time to signify the serious limitations of some of Fighter Command's equipment.

Just after noon on 19 July the RDF stations detected signs of a concentration of enemy aircraft over the Pas de Calais. For some time no movement towards the Straits was notified but it would appear that about 1210 hours the enemy must have flown across, for at 1215 hours Ju 87s were reported to be dive-bombing two destroyers in Dover harbour. It was not until 1220 hours that any defending fighters left the ground, and at that time No. 111 Squadron left Hawkinge, to be followed ten minutes later by nine Defiants of No. 141 Squadron. No. 111 Squadron was directed towards Deal at a height of 10,000 feet, and were told to expect enemy bombers. Of these there was no sign but one of the pilots saw a formation of about twenty Me 109s further to the south between Folkestone and Dover. Owing to the failure of the squadron leader to receive the message which was passed to him only one flight of No. 111 Squadron changed course to attack the enemy fighters. These by this time were attacking No. 141 Squadron. The latter had been instructed to fly towards Cap Gris Nez at 5,000 feet but when just south of Folkestone they had been surprised by a squadron of Me 109s which dived down on them out of the sun. Presumably the ensuing fight swung northwards and thus was spotted by No. 111 Squadron. In the first moments of the fight, when the enemy had the advantage of surprise, two Defiants were shot down; and in the subsequent fighting, when conditions were more equal, the inferiority of the turret fighter was sadly exemplified. By attacking from dead astern and below the Me 109s were able to avoid return fire from our air gunners, who were only able to bring their guns to bear as the enemy passed swiftly by on the beam. Only when a Defiant turned inside a Messerschmidt could effective fire be opened, and this happened rarely. No. 111 Squadron, for their part, could not get down to give direct assistance to the Defiants, for there were Me 109s at 10,000–15,000 feet, and it was between those heights that the Hurricanes went into action.

It is impossible to be sure how many German fighters were destroyed. No. 111 Squadron claimed to have shot down three, and the Defiants may have shot down as many as four. But whatever was the score there was only one lesson to be learned, that it was folly to send a turret fighter, such as the Defiant, into action in an area in which it might meet the Me 109. Of the nine Defiants only three returned safely, and of the eighteen pilots and air gunners four pilots were killed and two wounded, and six air gunners were killed. To some extent the heavy losses were due to the initial surprise the enemy achieved, and this in turn was due to the action of the controller in ordering the squadron to fly at a relatively low height, without any overhead protection. Yet Spitfire and Hurricane squadrons had frequently managed to avoid the consequences of being initially surprised. The moral of it all was clear enough, and two days later No. 141 Squadron was moved from the Biggin Hill sector to Prestwick, to be followed on the 24th by the only other Defiant squadron in the Command, No. 264, which was transferred from Duxford to Kirton-in-Lindsey. At neither of the two new stations was there much likelihood of encountering enemy fighters. Only after the heavy fighting in the second week in August did Defiants return to No. 11 Group.

Two other features of this operation bear noticing. The first is the failure of the controller to send squadrons into the air before the bombers appeared. Indeed, the intelligence officer of No. 111 Squadron later reported that two sections of enemy aircraft were seen from the airfield at Hawkinge before the squadron took off. The explanation appears to be that the track of the enemy formation was only one among many that were plotted in the eastern half of the Straits and over the Pas de Calais, and its real significance was detected too late. Secondly, the enemy fighters deliberately waited behind after their bombers had returned in order to engage any of our squadrons that arrived too late to interfere with the bombing.

Consolidated Combat Reports, No. 111 Squadron

This last feature needs to be borne in mind because it apparently conflicts with the subsequent behaviour of the German formations on a number of occasions during the rest of July. On 21 July, for example, an enemy formation assembled over Calais between 0915 and 0930 hours, and by 0940 hours had advanced half-way across the Channel. But between 0922 and 0929 over thirty of our own aircraft, drawn from the Kenley, Hornchurch and Northolt sectors, had taken off, and were patrolling the Straits of Dover when the enemy appeared. The latter, who were about fifty strong, turned back when our fighters were sighted, and although two of our squadrons managed to reach the protective screen of fighters the engagement was not properly joined. About the same time a westbound convoy was off Selsey Bill when an enemy formation approached from the direction of Cherbourg. Here, too, there had been sufficient warning for adequate defending forces to be brought up and two full squadrons and one flight from Tangmere and Warmwell were over the convoy, and again the enemy retired. Later in the day, however, when this same convoy was off the Needles and was being patrolled by a flight from No. 43 Squadron (Tangmere), a heavy attack was pressed home at about 1535 hours by a formation of Dorniers and Me 110 Jaguars protected by Me 109s. Another flight of our fighters, from No. 238 Squadron (Warmwell), was only directed to the convoy after the attack had begun, though it had been in the air since 1505 hours. A flight from No. 609 Squadron (Warmwell), had taken off about the same time and was also directed towards the convoy, but for some reason it failed to intercept. All this can only lead to one conclusion, that the Germans were unwilling to attack when our fighters were already in position in some strength over the target. Later on the same day the Germans were detected concentrating about ten miles north of Cherbourg, and in view of the earlier attack, three flights were despatched to join the nine aircraft that were already patrolling the westbound convoy. Again the enemy avoided combat, approaching within five miles of the convoy and then retiring. On 26 July there were three similar incidents in the Isle of Wight–Portland area. None of the raids approached closer to the coast than five miles, and all appeared to our pilots to set a course for France as soon as our fighters were sighted. The same thing happened in the Straits of Dover about 0900 hours on 5 August.

Fighter Command ORB Form 540

Towards the end of the month a variation of these tactics was adopted by the enemy. This took the form of maintaining strong fighter patrols on the French side of the Channel from Calais to Cherbourg, particularly in the Straits of

Dover. On the evening of 27 July patrols up to fifty aircraft strong were maintained off Calais for over three hours. Occasionally feint attacks were made and the enemy 'trailed his coat' within two or three miles of Dover. About the same time on the following day about fifty aircraft formed up behind Cap Gris Nez at 30,000 feet, and No. 11 Group put six squadrons into the air to meet the expected attack; but none was made. Similar tactics were adopted on 31 July, and again on 5 August.

Fighter Command 'Y' Form, 0900 hours, 29 July

Interspersed with this apparent timorousness were a number of operations in which the Germans showed no distaste for combat. On 20 July at 1300 hours Dover harbour was dive-bombed by Me 110 Jaguars, which dived from 8,000 to 2,000 feet before they released their bombs, whilst their escort of Me 109s stayed at 10,000–15,000 feet in order to dive down on any fighters which moved in to engage the Jaguars. Between 1800 and 1815 hours on the same day a mixed formation of the enemy approached Dover and pressed home an attack on a convoy passing south through the Straits. Three of our squadrons, Nos 32 and 610 from Hawkinge and No. 615 from Kenley, were already over the Straits when the enemy appeared, and they were later joined by No. 65 Squadron from Manston. Consequently, the enemy bombers could only make one swift attack on the convoy before our fighters intervened. The enemy fighters then dived down and confused and bitter fighting ensued, in which we lost three aircraft and one pilot, claiming six fighters, two Jaguars and one Ju 87 in return. There was obviously no disposition on the part of the Germans to shirk combat on this occasion.

Similarly, on 24 and 25 July the Germans launched heavy attacks, both in the Straits and off Portland, regardless of opposition. Those on the 25th are particularly important in that they were the only heavy attacks on Channel shipping during the month which paid a dividend in terms of vessels destroyed and damaged. On that day a westbound convoy was passing through the Straits of Dover between 1200 and 1800 hours. Throughout its passage it was given an escort of fighters, sometimes one flight strong but more often a section, and this was never enough to protect the ships from attack. At least four separate attacks were made, at 1150, 1450, 1630 and 1840 hours, but throughout the day strong enemy fighter patrols were continually over the Straits, and it was almost impossible to pick out from the maze of plots those raids that included bombers. Only on one occasion during the day were our fighters able to engage the dive-bombers before the escort of Me 109s interfered. This was about 1840 hours when nine Hurricanes of No. 56 Squadron (Hornchurch) claimed to have destroyed four Ju 87s. All other combats over the Straits during the day yielded only one more Ju 87, compared with nine Me 109s; our own losses were seven aircraft and five pilots. This disproportion between the enemy's bomber and fighter casualties was due not so much to the protection that the Me 109s afforded the German bombers, as to the failure of Fighter Command to put adequate strength over the Straits when bombing was in progress; the following extracts from squadron combat reports will suffice as examples of this.

Ibid. 1800 hours, 25 July and 0900 hours, 26 July

Consolidated Combat Reports

> Nine Hurricanes of No. 32 Squadron left Biggin Hill at 1200 hours to patrol over Dover where a convoy was proceeding West down Channel. On arrival over Dover at 22,000 feet they saw numerous aircraft

> disappearing in the direction of Boulogne. At 1246 hours they ran into eight Me 109s flying at the same level.
>
> No. 65 Squadron was operating from Manston and at 1210 hours received orders to intercept raiders approaching off Dover. Twelve aircraft took off, arrived over the coast at 14,000 feet, and observed AA fire to the east of them. Then five Me 109 in vic were seen at about 20,000 feet and fearing an attack from above, the squadron broke up and climbed to the attack individually.
>
> No. 111 Squadron were ordered to scramble base at Croydon from 15 minutes available. Squadron were airborne at 1450 hours 14 minutes after order was issued, and were directed to patrol Channel off Dover. Enemy bombers had disappeared when the squadron reached scene of operations, but a number of enemy fighters were seen.

Observations such as these on the situation as our pilots saw it when they reached the Straits can be paralleled from the reports of nearly all the squadrons that participated in the day's fighting. The following extract shows the difficulties under which our men fought on the rare occasions when they were ordered up in time to intercept the German bombers:

> 10 a/c [aircraft] of No. 54 Squadron left Manston 1800 hours and were directed towards e/a [enemy aircraft] bombing ships in mid-Channel ... They sighted 4 Ju 88s at 12,000 feet which were bombing two destroyers. A large number of Ju 87s were approaching from Calais at 5,000 feet to attack the destroyers, and above the Ju 88s and nearer the French coast were circling several layers of Me 109s. Red Section, leading, approached to attack the Ju 88s in echelon to port. Yellow Section climbed slightly above them to act as a guard, and Blue Section were above Yellow Section. Yellow leader saw a number of Me 109s breaking off in threes from their formation, and warned both Red and Blue Sections to break formation. All our a/c managed to evade this attack except P/O Finnie who was shot down. Yellow Section climbed to 18,000 feet in the hope of being able to carry out a surprise attack on the enemy, but each time they approached they were forced to break away without firing as they themselves were being attacked ... No. 54 Squadron were the first to arrive at the scene of conflict and no other friendly fighters were seen until the various sections were returning to Manston.[13]

It was obvious from the day's operations that the Germans had made a great effort to wipe out the convoy, a greater effort, in fact, than on any other day, or against any other convoy, during this phase. It was as if they had determined to make a test case to try and discover what damage could be inflicted in return for

13 Nevertheless, Nos 56, 601 and 610 Squadrons were also over the Straits about this time, and No. 56 Squadron was certainly over the convoy before No. 54 Squadron.

a given effort. One notable feature was the co-operation between the German Navy and the Luftwaffe. Just before 1800 hours a number of E-boats put out from Calais to attack the convoy in conjunction with dive-bombers. Two of the Dover destroyers, HMS *Boreas* and *Brilliant*, supported by two MTBs came across the Channel to engage, and were themselves dive bombed and damaged, though it is not certain whether they were hit by the bombers, by E-boats, or by enemy shore batteries, under whose fire they also came. Their action doubtless saved the convoy from loss, as the slow-moving coastal ships were, if anything, more vulnerable to surface attack than to attack from the air. Altogether, in the course of the air attacks, five ships in the convoy were sunk and five others damaged, of which one had to be beached. Later, in the early morning of 26 July, when the convoy was off Shoreham, it was again attacked, by E-boats, and three more ships were sunk and four damaged.

Cp. Daily Summary of Naval Events and Consolidated Combat Report of No. 54 Squadron

Admiralty Weekly Intelligence Report, 2 August

The operations on the 25th were unique in a number of ways. They were much larger than any others during the month: it was estimated that nearly one hundred and twenty enemy aircraft had taken part in the attacks round about noon, and some sixty to eighty in those in the afternoon and early evening. In addition, between 1130 and 2000 hours the skies over the Straits on the French side were never empty of German fighters. The attacks were also persistent, and showed every sign of being carefully planned, in a degree not previously encountered. And, as a consequence of all this, more important results were achieved than in any previous attacks on a convoy. After this major effort there were no comparable operations until the opening of the main German offensive on 8 August, when, as we shall see, the Germans operated in a very similar fashion.

d. Features of these Operations

At the same time the operations illustrate certain features common to all important operations in the Straits both during this preliminary phase of the battle and that which opened on 8 August. Firstly, The Germans were frequently able to bomb targets in the Straits without being intercepted by our fighters. Secondly, the presence of large covering escorts of fighters made it a perilous business for our fighters to attack such bombers as they saw. Thirdly, the advantages of height and numbers which the German fighters almost invariably enjoyed, placed our own fighters in an inferior tactical position. As to this, there is no doubt that RDF plots at this time were underestimating both the height and the numbers of the German formations. Considerable experience was required before an RDF operator could give a close approximation to the numbers contained in any large formation. Height readings, too, were frequently low, and it was suggested that there was a bias that way in the equipment that was being used. This was not so, but as the Germans were now so near our coasts they were probably approaching in a climb rather than on the level, and this may explain the apparent underestimations of height. Whatever the technical explanation, the fact remains that our squadrons were frequently being ordered to fly at levels well below these of the enemy fighters and, understandably enough, some squadron and flight commanders attempted to redress the balance by

Fighter Command ORB 29 July: Correspondence between AVM Cunningham and AVM Park

Ibid.

adding, without authority, a thousand or two thousand feet to the flying height ordered by the controller on the ground.[14]

But if the enemy's advantage in height can be ascribed to the deficiencies of the RDF system, this was certainly not the explanation for his superiority in numbers. Nor was it an inevitable consequence of the larger forces disposed in the Pas de Calais compared to those available in south-east England. The answer was that the Germans could concentrate before an operation, and we could not – or did not. Our squadrons, nine to twelve aircraft strong, were arriving one by one over the Straits to participate in the fighting, and each often found that it was required to engage enemy fighter formations of *Gruppe* strength, i.e. anything from twenty to thirty aircraft. The Germans were accustomed to using the individual *Gruppe* as a fighting unit, whereas the Fighter Command unit of combat was normally the squadron. It followed, therefore, that unless wings of two or more squadrons could be sent into action as one unit, our pilots would too often find themselves fighting against heavy odds. Yet it is extremely doubtful whether there was any practicable alternative to the use of single squadrons, at any rate in the fighting over the Channel. Our squadrons as we have noted, were rarely arriving at the scene of operations in time to intercept the German bombers; and the position in this respect would have been worse if we had attempted to assemble wing formations. This same question was to bulk larger later in the battle, when the enemy's targets were not in the Channel but inland as far as London. Even then, when there was a little more time to assemble wing formations than was available during the fighting in July, it was rarely practicable to do so, at any rate in No. 11 Group.

Despatch, 'Battle of Britain', paras 198–204

In short, the early fighting over the Channel took place under conditions which were nearly all unfavourable to the defenders. But this itself underlines one more feature of the operations which was as real as those already described, even if it is hardly analysable. This was the willingness of our pilots to accept any odds, and to attack the enemy whenever and wherever possible. The stilted language of the combat reports inadequately reflects the aggressive temper of our pilots, and perhaps only those who have themselves taken part in air battles can fully appreciate the confidence with which sections and flights of our fighters attacked enemy formations of twenty, thirty and more, aircraft strong. It was a weighty asset to balance against those of the enemy.

Before the general effect of the July fighting upon Fighter Command is considered some mention must be made of the German use of fighter bombers. There had been rumours for some time that the Me 110 and Me 109 were being fitted to carry bombs, and early in July German prisoners were interrogated on the subject without much positive information being obtained. The Me 110 – the so-called Jaguar – was the first to put in an appearance. On 20 July three of them were reported to have made a dive bombing attack on Dover harbour between

AI 1(K) Report No. 191/1940

14 E.g. on 29 July S/Ldr H.M. Hood was ordered to lead No. 41 Squadron over Dover at 10,000 feet to intercept a raid which had been detected about 0715 hours. He actually brought his squadron into action at 12,000 feet and found part of the raid a thousand feet below him. However, this advantage of height was short-lived as shortly after the squadron began to attack they were themselves attacked by fighters which dived down on them from about 14,000 feet.

1310 and 1340 hours;[15] No. 32 Squadron (Hawkinge) claimed to have shot one down, but no wreckage was recovered and absolute confirmation was not therefore possible. On the following day No. 238 Squadron (Warmwell) reported that fifteen Me 110s had been intercepted off the Needles whilst dive bombing a convoy, and three days later aircraft of the same type were said to have attacked a convoy off Dungeness. The first time that Me 109s appear to have been used as bombers was on 27 July when six of them took advantage of rainy, cloudly conditions to slip across the Straits and bomb Dover harbour with bombs of approximately 200 lbs weight. Irrefutable evidence that these fighters were being thus employed was not obtained until 14 August in the case of the Me 110, and 18 September in that of the Me 109, when aircraft actually fitted with bomb-carrying gear were shot down over England. Why the Germans had put in hand experiments of this sort it is difficult to say. The decisions could hardly have been taken any later than the collapse of France. It does not necessarily follow that in developing such aircraft the Germans were implicitly confessing that the heavier types of bomber were likely to fail against the air defences of this country. Indeed, they may have been looking forward to the time when their command of the air was so pronounced that all types of aircraft would be able to carry bombs.

Ibid. Nos 255 and 584/1940

VI. MOVES OF FIGHTER SQUADRONS, BALLOONS AND GUNS

The early days of the July offensive seemed to indicate that the south-west area might soon be attacked in strength; and the first movements within Fighter Command during this phase were ordered with this possibility in mind. On 12 July No. 152 Squadron was transferred from Acklington in No. 13 Group to the Middle Wallop sector, and on 18 July a flight of Gladiators, which had been operating at Sumburgh in the Shetlands, was moved to Roborough, near Plymouth. In compensation a Hurricane flight was moved from Wick to Sumburgh. Roborough airfield at this time was not large enough for eight-gun fighters, but it had the merit of being the only available airfield within a short distance of Plymouth, and the Gladiators were intended solely for the direct defence of that place. Further to strengthen this area Air Chief Marshal Dowding decided to withdraw two troops of Bofors guns and four and a half batteries of heavy guns from the aircraft industry, and allot them to the South Wales ports, Falmouth, Plymouth and Portland. Measures were also taken about this time to form a number of new balloon barrages at the ports in the south-west, in South Wales and at Liverpool, but with the exception of a new waterborne barrage in the Mersey none of them were flying before the middle of August. For the same reason – the protection of ports and shipping – July saw the first fighter defences established for the protection of the North

Fighter Command ORB Form 540, Organisation Branch

15 During August evidence was obtained from crashed aircraft which showed conclusively that the first bomber unit to be equipped with Me 110s *Kampfgruppe 210*, was specialiy formed for that purpose some time in June 1940. It carried out its first war flight on 15 July against a convoy off Orfordness, and for the next fortnight was engaged almost every other day in attacking shipping in the Channel. At this period it operated from Denain and St Omer. Then in the second week in August, when attacks on coastal targets and airfields began, the unit appears to have formed the spearhead of numerous attacks on RDF stations and coastal airfields such as Manston and Hawkinge (AI I(K) Reports 268 and 273/1940).

Channel, through which all ocean shipping was directed during the month. On 20 July No. 245 Squadron was moved from Turnhouse to Aldergrove in Northern Ireland, and on the following day No. 141 Squadron was transferred from the Biggin Hill sector to Prestwick. In south-east England, where the battle increasingly concentrated as the month passed by, there was very little reinforcement. No. 604 Squadron was moved from Gravesend to Middle Wallop, where its Blenheims could have more opportunities for intercepting night bombers, and No. 501 Squadron, which was equipped with Hurricanes, took its place. Two new balloon barrages were established in the area, one at Dover and another which, flown from specially equipped drifters, was to accompany convoys passing between the Isle of Wight and Sheerness. The Dover barrage commenced flying at dawn on 31 July, and on the same day one of the balloons was shot down in the first of a long series of attacks. The first Channel convoy to be protected by barrage balloons passed through the Straits on 5 August. German aircraft were over during the day and appeared to show great interest in the new development, but the convoy reached Sheerness during the evening without being seriously attacked.

No. 961 Squadron ORB

VII. USE OF COASTAL AIRFIELDS IN KENT

The German operations, therefore, did not force Air Chief Marshal Dowding to weaken his forces in other parts of the air defence system in order to strengthen the south-east; and he relied on no more than the normal establishment of No. 11 Group for dealing with enemy attacks in that area. There was no criticism of his methods until the end of July. Then, on 29 July, shortly after the heaviest attacks the Germans had so far made on Dover and shipping in the Straits, the Air Ministry informed the Commander-in-Chief that he should make every effort to meet the enemy in the Dover area with superior forces and large formations, and that to effect this more use should be made of airfields near the coast, such as Manston and Hawkinge. We have already taken notice of the problem of engaging the enemy with large formations. As to the question of whether the coastal airfields were being used to full advantage no easy answer is possible. Only one squadron, No. 600 (Blenheim) Squadron, was permanently stationed at Manston, and none at Hawkinge, but both stations were extensively used as satellites to Hornchurch and Biggin Hill. Rochford, near Southend, was also used by Hornchurch squadrons and occasionally, by squadrons from the North Weald sector; and West Malling, near Maidstone, was used by Biggin Hill. On 20 July, for example, No. 32 Squadron flew from Biggin Hill to Hawkinge in the morning, operated from there all day and returned to Biggin Hill in the evening. No. 111 Squadron used Hawkinge throughout the morning and then returned to Kenley. No. 65 Squadron used Manston all day, and returned to its permanent station, Hornchurch, just before dusk. No. 54 Squadron, which was also in the Hornchurch sector, used Manston in the morning and Rochford during the rest of the day. No. 151 Squadron (North Weald) also carried out a patrol from Rochford. On 25 July, when fighting in the Straits was fierce and protracted, No. 111 and No. 257 used Hawkinge during most of the day,

Fighter Command ORB 29 July

See Squadron ORBs

and No. 32 used it in the early morning; Nos 54, 65 and 74 used Manston all day; No. 56 Squadron (North Weald) operated from Rochford from noon; No. 151 Squadron carried out patrols both from Manston and Rochford; and No. 141 Squadron operated from West Malling. After the issue of the Air Ministry directive and before 8 August the only operations comparable to those of 25 July took place on 5 August, and on that day a total of ten squadrons used the three airfields at Hawkinge, Manston and Rochford as their forward bases. This was much the same effort as on 25 July.

It is apparent, therefore, that considerable use was being made of forward airfields; possibly as much as was prudent since they were so open to surprise attacks. But in any case it is doubtful whether the dual problem of timely interception in adequate strength was to be solved simply by the increased use of the stations near the coast. A squadron stationed at Hawkinge could certainly be over the Straits more quickly than if it operated from its parent station at Biggin Hill, Kenley or Northolt, but if it only took-off when the enemy was already advancing across the Straits it would still be too late on most occasions to intercept before the Germans had dropped their bombs.

VIII. SIGNIFICANCE OF THE GERMAN OPERATIONS

Daily Summary of Naval Events, 26 July

But the concern which the Air Staff displayed in this matter signified that the Germans had obtained some success in their Channel operations. It was certainly not to be assessed in terms of shipping destroyed, as over the period as a whole only 24,000 tons of merchant shipping were sunk in the Channel by aircraft; and in the biggest attacks, those of 25 July, the five ships sunk and one beached had only totalled 5,700 tons. Indeed, mine-laying from aircraft at night paid the Germans much better during July than attacks on shipping by day. Between 10 July and 7 August thirteen merchant ships, totalling 38,000 tons, were mined and sunk round the coasts of Britain, most of them by mines laid by enemy aircraft. This was almost as much as was sunk by air attack; and it was obtained at a far smaller cost to the German Air Force.[16]

The main German operations, however, were not to be valued merely on the basis of the shipping destroyed. In the first place, they had forced upon Fighter Command a high scale of defensive effort. Precisely what was the extent of the German effort it is impossible to say; but it is unlikely to have exceeded more than three hundred sorties on any day when serious attacks were launched, with the exception of 25 July when as many as four hundred sorties may have been flown; and on some days it was less than a hundred sorties. Fighter Command, on the other hand, flew approximately 17,500 sorties between 10 July and 7

16 The Germans increased their minelaying effort considerably during the month. On 20 July the Navy exploded more mines than ever before on a single day, only to beat their own record two days later. According to a reliable German document *Fliegerkorps IX*, which specialised in minelaying, claimed to have sunk six ships totalling 40,680 tons and probably sunk two more totalling 8,972 tons in July 1940. It is not known for certain whether *Fliegerkorps IX* was responsible for all German minelaying at this time, but there is fair agreement between these claims and actual sinkings.

Another captured document contains a monthly survey of results achieved against British shipping targets from July 1940 to October 1941. In July 1940 twenty-four British ships, totalling 135,000 tons, were believed to have been destroyed, whereas in fact the losses were nineteen ships totalling 41,000 tons. It is not certain, however, whether the German figures related to the whole German Air Force or only to *Luftflotte 3*.

August, of which only some three hundred were flown at night. The three heaviest days were 25 July, 30 July and 1 August, when 538, 694 and 724 sorties were flown between 0900 and 1800 hours; and the three lightest were 15, 16 and 17 July when in the same nine-hour period 206, 145 and 222 sorties were flown. Much of this effort took the form of routine patrols, particularly for the protection of shipping. The Command provided escorts for a daily average of twelve convoys, and altogether thirty per cent of all sorties were for the escort of shipping about to be attacked, or already being attacked. Most of this routine work was carried out between Start Point and Harwich by sections of three aircraft drawn from the squadrons of Nos 10 and 11 Groups. There was thus this constant diversion of strength from the squadrons which were facing the bulk of the German Air Force.

Secondly, the operations on 25 July had revealed the full extent of the German threat to shipping in the Straits of Dover. Over the whole period such sinkings as the Germans achieved in this area were not unacceptable. Only fourteen ships were sunk by German aircraft in the whole of the Channel; and during the last week in July, which included the day on which attacks were heaviest, one hundred and three ships were conveyed through the Straits of Dover, and only eight were sunk, three of them by E-boats. These eight, however, were all part of one convoy of twenty-one ships which the Germans had obviously set themselves to destroy; and unless future Channel convoys were to move under threat of even heavier casualties a more effective defence in the Dover area was imperative.

Admiralty Weekly Intelligence Report, 2 August

Thirdly, the German operations had underlined the importance of protecting the harbour at Dover and the destroyers and other naval craft based there. It was generally felt that the maintenance of Dover as a base for active naval operations was a vital necessity if any seaborne invasion in this area was to be repelled before it reached our coasts. The damage inflicted on facilities at Dover during July was not serious but two destroyers had been damaged when in harbour there on 19 July, and two had been sunk and four badly damaged during the month while carrying out their duties in the Straits and neighbouring waters. The danger, in short, was that the Navy would be driven from the Straits. Characteristically, the naval authorities emphasised the importance of protecting the Dover base rather than the naval ships at sea, allowing it to be understood that so long as Dover was available HM ships would always operate in the Straits.

COS(40) 235th mtg, 26 July

Ibid. Statement by Admiral Drax, C-in-C, Nore

Certain of the measures that were taken to deal with both problems, that of the convoys and that of the Dover base, have already been mentioned, viz:- the formation of balloon barrages for the defence of Dover and of the convoys using the Straits. In addition, the Admiralty reduced the burden of escort duties in the Straits by ceasing to run outward bound convoys from the North Foreland. From the end of July only Channel convoys of small coastal ships were considered a 'tactical operation' requiring special naval and air dispositions. It was also decided to double the personnel establishment of the anti-aircraft batteries defending Dover, so that the gun defences there could be kept permanently at a high state of readiness. The Air Staff instruction to Fighter Command, urging the operation of more powerful formations in the Dover area, was also part of the arrangements for improving the defences there.

Admiralty Weekly Intelligence Report, 16 August

See S.5135

These measures were essentially precautionary and were intended to counter a situation that was prospective, even imminent, but which had not yet come to pass. They should certainly not be taken to mean that the skies over the Straits of Dover were already regarded as a German preserve. The operations in July were a severe challenge to the Fighter Command system of defence, especially on its intelligence side, and they had not concluded entirely in our favour. But neither had they in that of the Germans, to whom they must have demonstrated that heavy losses would be suffered by any large formations which crossed the Channel and remained to fight. And this was important; for the significance of the July operations lay not only in the degree of success attending Fighter Command's efforts to protect certain ground and sea targets, but also in how it fared in actual combat with the German Air Force. In the absence of reliable German records it is not possible to give an exact ratio of German and British losses, but that alone would not present a true picture. Air supremacy is as much a product of morale as of material strength, and, that being so, Fighter Command had fared well in the July fighting.

IX. STRENGTH OF FIGHTER COMMAND AT THE END OF JULY

Fighter Command ORB, Form 540, Organisation Branch

CSU figures: See AHB VE/1/4

AHB IIH/120, Encl 93, Minute DCAS – AMT, 13 August

Finally, the month had given time for some additions to the strength of the Command. The number of squadrons reckoned fit for operations had risen from fifty two on 10 July to fifty five on 8 August; and there were also, at the latter date, six squadrons under training, including No. 1 (RCAF) Squadron. During the month three new squadrons had been formed, No. 302 (Polish) and No. 310 (Czech) on 14 July, and No. 303 (Polish) on 22 July. There was still a shortage of pilots, amounting to 124 on 3 August, but despite the losses sustained during July which, for the whole Command, were 74 pilots killed, missing and prisoners and 48 wounded and injured, the total pilot strength had risen from 1,259 on 6 July to 1,434 on 3 August. By then the pilot position was considered to have improved sufficiently to allow the period of training at fighter OTUs to be restored from a fortnight to a month, but this was effectively prevented by the heavy fighting which began on 8 August.

III

SECOND PHASE, 8–18 AUGUST

Apart from the actual attack of shipping in the Channel and the North Sea, during July the Germans had carried out extensive reconnaissances round the perimeter of the British Isles; and by the beginning of August they must have known a great deal about the movement of British shipping, where it was most easily found and most vulnerable to attack. And as the German operations as a whole had up to then shown more concern with sea traffic in its widest sense than with any other branch of the British war economy, it is not surprising that the German effort on 8 August, the day popularly regarded as the beginning of the Battle of Britain, should have been directed against shipping in the Channel.

During 6 and 7 August the Germans had operated on only a small scale, and had virtually confined themselves to reconnaissance flights in the Channel and North Sea, minelaying in the Thames Estuary and the Firth of Forth, and some insignificant and apparently haphazard operations at night, including the dropping of leaflets. They made no attempt to interfere with a large westbound Channel convoy which passed through the Straits of Dover on the afternoon of the 7th, but they were not indifferent to its passage, and must have plotted its course accurately; for about 0230 hours on the morning of the 8th it was attacked by E-boats when off Brighton. Three ships were sunk and one damaged, and the destroyer *Bulldog* claimed to have destroyed one E-boat. The convoy was broken up by this attack, and when dawn broke its twenty-seven ships were dispersed in a straggling procession well over ten miles long. Thereafter they were never re-assembled as a whole in a properly organised convoy.

Daily Summary of Naval Events, 8 August

OPERATIONS ON 8 AUGUST IN THE CHANNEL

But not until 0840 hours, when the leading ships were about five miles east of St Catherine's Point, was the convoy further menaced. At that time the RDF stations detected a large force of thirty aircraft or more off Cherbourg; and fifteen minutes later another formation of equal strength was located half way between the mouth of the Seine and Selsey Bill. Both forces were headed straight for the convoy, which was being patrolled by one flight from No. 145 Squadron (Westhampnett). According to one Fighter Command record five squadrons from No. 11 Group and one from No. 10 were despatched to intercept, but this would not appear to be correct. The second flight of No. 145 Squadron was certainly sent off, and it joined the rest of the squadron over the convoy just before 0900 hours. No. 609 Squadron, which took off at 0900 hours from Middle Wallop, was also directed to intercept. But the only other squadrons which were in the air in this area about this time were Nos 615 and 238, which took off at 0915 hours to patrol Shoreham and Middle Wallop respectively.

Fighter Command 'Y' Form, 1800 hours 8 August.

In any case, only No. 145 Squadron actually engaged the enemy. Barely had the two flights joined up in squadron formation when the enemy was sighted. The weather at the time was cloudy down to 2,000 feet, with visibility up to six miles. The original plots of the enemy formations proved to be accurate on this occasion, as there were two separate formations at 14,000 feet each containing about ten Ju 87s protected by twice as many Me 109s.[1] Despite the odds, our squadron attacked and successfully engaged the Ju 87s before the fighter escort intervened. Confused fighting then developed in which, as the squadron intelligence officer put it, 'each pilot was forced to act independently, all Hurricanes engaging an enemy bomber or enemy fighter as opportunity offered'. Two pilots were lost with their aircraft, but six Ju 87s and three Me 109s were claimed as destroyed. And that the convoy was effectively protected is beyond doubt. Some of the dive-bombers jettisoned their bombs some distance away, and no ship was sunk. Indeed some of the ships' crews may never have known that a battle was fought for their protection. The officer in charge of the balloon defences of the convoy makes no mention in his log of any attack at this time, though he wrote, 'Clouds of smoke and spray apparently on our course. Machines have been circling overhead but so high that we can't say definitely whose they are. Presumably ours.' This was an unwitting tribute to the work of No. 145 Squadron.

Consolidated Combat Report.

Balloon Command ORB, Appendix A, August 1940

By 0925 hours the engagement was over, and No. 609 Squadron came on the scene only in time to see the enemy retiring. The action was a splendid example of the ability of a determined squadron, provided it was not in an inferior position to begin with, to throw into confusion a much larger formation of the enemy.

The next enemy move was made in another part of the Channel, over the Straits of Dover. From 0930 until 1030 hours small enemy formations were constantly patrolling over the French side of the Straits, and one of them came over to the Goodwins, only to retire almost immediately. At 1038 hours, however, an enemy force crossed the coast near Dover, but as it was hidden in the clouds the Observer Corps were unable to track its subsequent course. It is more than likely that it steered north-east as No. 65 Squadron, which had been patrolling Manston since 1015 hours, were engaged just before 1100 hours. Unfortunately the combat reports do not appear to have been preserved, and we know nothing about the size and character of the German force. All that is known for certain is that three of our aircraft were shot down and two pilots were killed; and this, coupled with the fact that no bombing was reported from this area at the time, probably means that the enemy consisted simply of fighters.

No sooner had No. 65 Squadron landed than there were unmistakable signs that the Germans would soon be over again. Between 1100 and 1200 hours at least four enemy formations, each between ten and twenty aircraft strong, were detected in the Straits. They appeared to be manoeuvring independently of one another, but as each was too strong to be ignored the controller at No. 11 Group took the precaution of putting patrols over the vulnerable airfields at Manston and Hawkinge. No. 41 Squadron left Hornchurch at 1125 hours to patrol

1 RAF pilots thought they also saw some He 113s, and from this time onwards this type of enemy fighter was frequently reported. Not one was ever shot down over this country, however, and it is doubtful whether any were ever employed. It has been suggested that captured Hurricanes, with German national markings, were occasionally used, and that these may have been mistaken for the He 113. But no such hybrid has ever been discovered, not, at any rate, by the acid test of wreckage found in England; and we can only suppose that the Me 109 from some aspects reminded our men of the silhouettes and models of the He 113, which were all the guidance they had to its actual appearance.

Manston; and No. 64 Squadron, who were using Hawkinge as their forward base, patrolled it from 1120 hours.

Three Germans formations crossed the coast while these squadrons were in the air. One came in near Dungeness at 1125 hours and after making a sweep as far as Maidstone, retired again. Another came in at the North Foreland at 1139 hours and was not subsequently plotted. A third crossed at Pevensey at the same time, and flew along the coast to beyond Beachy Head. This was reported to be fifty aircraft strong, and No. 32 Squadron left Biggin Hill at 1140 hours to intercept it. But they had started too late, and only caught a glimpse of the enemy formation as it left the coast near Brighton.

Enemy formations were still being plotted in the Straits as noon approached. There was a force of at least twenty near the Goodwins, a smaller force near Manston, and two of six aircraft near Calais. All the formations were casting about in such a way that it was exceptionally difficult to divine their intentions. At least two must have crossed the coast about noon; for part of No. 41 Squadron was in action near Manston at that time with a force of fighters; and No. 64 Squadron at the same time was attacked by another fighter formation near Dover. No. 41 Squadron was cruising at 12,000 feet when a suspicious formation of seven aircraft was sighted more than ten thousand feet below. Yellow section was detached to investigate and identified the aircraft as Me 109s. One of the section did not attack owing to trouble with his oxygen supply, but the other two dived on the enemy and achieved a complete surprise. More Me 109s arrived until there were about twenty in all; but in the fight which developed, and which only ended over Calais, our pilots suffered no damage either to themselves or their aircraft, and claimed to have despatched six of the enemy into the sea.[2] No. 64 Squadron was not so successful. They were attracted towards Dover by the smoke from a burning barrage balloon which had been shot down by an enemy fighter, but as they were flying towards the town at 8,000 feet they were attacked by about twenty Me 109s, which dived down on them from 10,000 feet. The engagement was all over in five minutes, two of the enemy being destroyed for one of our own pilots. It was reported that the enemy fighters were very well handled.

Combat Reports of F/Lt Webster and P/O Wallens.

Consolidated Combat Report, No. 64 Sqdn.

While all this had been going on in the Dover area the Germans had been assembling further west for what was to be their biggest operation of the day. At 1210 hours a formation reported as over one hundred strong, was detected about twenty miles north of Cherbourg. It appeared to be making for the west bound convoy, which was between St Catherine's Point and the Needles, and which was being patrolled by six Spitfires of No. 609 Squadron. No. 145 Squadron and one flight of No. 601 Squadron (Tangmere) were also in the air on local patrols, and both were directed towards the convoy. In addition, three more squadrons, No. 257 from Tangmere, No. 238 from Middle Wallop, and No. 213 from Exeter, took off between 1209 and 1215 hours and were directed towards the

2 There were a number of interesting features about this engagement. Pilots reported that while the enemy showed no distaste for the fight they seemed anxious to give battle over the French coast, and with this in mind made all their attacks from west to east. Secondly, the Me 109s were very vulnerable to attack from astern. P/O Wallens used only 389 rounds in accounting for three of the enemy; and it was inferred that this particular formation was unarmoured. It did not follow, however, that the Germans had not realised the need for rear armour. We had in fact already shot down a Me 109 which had an armoured shield and hood fitted for the protection of the pilot's back and head.

convoy. All these squadrons engaged the enemy with the exception of No. 213, who had furthest to fly and arrived too late.

Weather conditions at the time were ideal for the attackers. There was a good deal of cloud about, including one bank at 4,000 feet above the convoy, but otherwise visibility was good. The Germans exploited the conditions, it would appear, by splitting the main formation into two formations of fighters and one of fighters and dive-bombers, the latter about thirty strong. The purely fighter formations circled round east and south of the convoy where the sky was clear, while the escorted bombers dived on the convoy out of the clouds above it. These tactics worked successfully in that only No. 609 Squadron engaged the dive-bombers; and all other defending fighters attacked enemy fighter formations some miles away from the convoy.

As for the actual attack on the convoy, the Germans had obviously given some thought to the problem of overcoming its balloon defences. The plan they adopted was simple enough. Part of the escorting fighters dived down in line astern some distance ahead of the bombers and attempted to shoot down the balloons, and as this was done the dive-bombers came down to attack. The rest of the fighters veered off to the south to protect the bombers as they retired. At least two of the six balloons were shot down and two of the balloon tugs damaged. Four merchant ships, totalling 4,527 tons, were sunk, and six others damaged. No. 609 Squadron, attacking after the bombing was over, claimed to have shot down two of the Ju 87s and three Me 110s at no cost to themselves.

While the German fighter formations succeeded admirably as decoys they fared badly in the fighting. Most of the British squadrons were flying at 15,000 to 25,000 feet, and although this largely accounts for their failure to protect the convoy it was to their advantage when they attacked the German fighters, of which thirteen were claimed as certainly destroyed,[3] at a cost of five pilots and their aircraft.

By 1300 hours the various engagements were over and for the next three hours the Germans launched no major operations. There were some reconnaissance flights in the central Channel towards Weymouth Bay, and some patrolling at flight strength on the French side of the Straits of Dover. But about 1530 hours the situation became more threatening. At that time there were three German formations near Calais, the largest of which was reported as fifteen aircraft strong; and six aircraft of No. 111 Squadron left Hawkinge at 1540 hours to patrol the airfield. Nine minutes later one of the German formations crossed the coast near Dover, but the Observer Corps were not able to follow it owing to the clouds and it was not intercepted.

As in the case of the operations in the early afternoon against the convoy, these enemy manoeuvres in the Straits were doubtless intended to divert attention from the main operations which were about to be launched. These were first detected at 1534 hours in the shape of a force of eighteen or more aircraft flying from the direction of Le Havre towards the convoy, which was east of St

3 One of the German pilots who landed in the Channel after baling out of his aircraft was reported to have put up 'a very vivid bright green smoke signal'. This was one of the first instances to be reported of the use of a chemical substance called 'Fluorescine'. This on contact with water produced a bright green patch on the surface of the sea and thus aided the pilot's rescue. It was adopted by Fighter Command towards the end of August (Fighter Command ORB, Appendix D5, 18 August).

Alban's Head. It was not being escorted at the time but immediate action was taken to protect it; and No. 43 Squadron took off from Tangmere and No. 152 from Warmwell at 1540 hours.[4]

It was hard to say precisely what followed. There were at least two German formations in the Channel at this time, but neither was continuously plotted by the RDF stations, and no enemy movements were tracked between 1600 and 1630 hours, which was when the convoy was being attacked and our own squadrons were in action. Nor is it certain that the main convoy was attacked; for the main German effort was directed against a small number of ships, near St Catherine's Point, which were stragglers from the original convoy and were making for Southampton. But it is certain that there were two main combats, one near St Alban's Head between 1600 and 1615 hours, and one between 1605 and 1630 hours five to ten miles south of St Catherine's Point. Only in the second of these did pilots see any evidence of bombing, so it would appear the Germans missed their objective, which was doubtless the main convoy off St Alban's Head. Enemy aircraft were undoubtedly over these ships, but No. 152 Squadron, who engaged them at 1600 hours, reported that they were all fighters.

The combat off the Isle of Wight took place between No. 43 and No. 145 Squadron, which took off from Westhampnett just before 1600 hours, and an enemy formation about a hundred aircraft strong, some of which were Ju 87s. The dive-bombers were closely escorted by both single and twin-engined fighters, but the lack of flexibility in the formation as much as the determined attack of our fighters hampered their operations, and, despite the immense superiority of the enemy fighters, both squadrons were able to get at the dive-bombers. The fighting was confused and bitter and although the RAF pilots believed they had definitely destroyed six fighters and nine dive-bombers, they themselves lost five pilots and six aircraft, nearly one quarter of their strength. The ships below suffered no casualties, and as far as can be ascertained there was no return in the shape of ships destroyed either off the Isle of Wight or further west for this great effort on the part of the enemy. By 1645 hours the Channel was clear of important enemy movements, and there were no further operations in daylight.

Home Security Intelligence Summary.

During the day the Germans had operated on a large scale only in the Channel. Elsewhere there had been little activity of any sort, and no bombs had been dropped on the mainland. There had been some reconnaissance of shipping in the North Sea, and a single enemy aircraft had attacked a convoy off the Norfolk coast at 1715 hours. In the south-west reconnaissance flights had been carried out as far as South Wales, and at various times during the day the guns at Falmouth, Plymouth, Portland, Bristol and Cardiff had been in action for a few moments against high flying aircraft.

4 This time may not be quite accurate in the case of No. 152 Squadron. The records of this squadron for the whole period of the Battle of Britain are peculiarly badly kept, and it is impossible to reconstruct its activities in any detail.

COMMENTARY

But these raids were obviously of little account compared to the three operations in the central Channel, and those in the Straits of Dover between 1000 hours and noon. As a result of these the Germans had sunk four ships (seven, if those sunk in the small hours by E-boat are included) and damaged six others, some seriously, out of a convoy of thirty one. The total tonnage was but a small percentage of the four million tons that were being cleared monthly in the coastal trade at this time. On the other hand one ship in three had been damaged or sunk, and these were not very attractive odds against being hit to offer to seamen sailing in future Channel convoys. Indeed, if the Germans were aiming at eventually stopping Channel convoys we cannot claim a clear-cut victory on this day.

It is not certain, however, that this was the aim of the German operations. We cannot be sure of what were the German plans until German records become available, but since 8 August was the last day on which the Luftwaffe expended any great effort on attacking convoys a little speculation on the significance of the day's operations, as of those similar if smaller ones which had taken place in July, is perhaps excusable. What is most curious is the disproportion between the size of the German forces and the value and importance of the shipping they attacked. During the months before the opening of the battle in the west the Germans had frequently operated against shipping in the North Sea, and with some success. In every case the attack had been carried out at low level by single bombers or flying boats, or by small formations usually of three aircraft; and by the summer of 1940 certain Heinkel 111 units and coastal units had obtained considerable experience of this sort of work. But during July there had been little activity against shipping in the North Sea. Instead, inflated formations of Ju 87s and Me 100s, whose crews can have had little experience of anti-shipping activities, were used against the small coasters to be found in the Channel, while much fatter prizes were plying up and down the east coast without being disturbed. It would seem, therefore, that if the Germans were aiming primarily at the dislocation of shipping their plan was ill-conceived and badly executed.

But it is at least possible that they were chiefly after other game, namely the fighter force; and that the attacks on shipping, and those on Dover, were intended to bring fighters to battle under conditions which, while bad for the Germans, were also bad for Fighter Command. This would account for the occasional sweeps by purely fighter formations, which were a luxury if shipping alone was the German objective. It may also explain the occasional refusal of the Germans to commit their formations to battle when a strong fighter force was waiting for them. For if the emphasis of the German operations was on the battle in the air rather than in destroying the selected sea or land target there was nothing to be gained by pressing home an attack which might destroy the target but which would mean heavy losses in the air battle. On this theory the Germans were already trying in July and early August to achieve that ascendancy over Fighter Command which they were more obviously pursuing from 12 August onwards. It also implies that the success of their operations is to be assessed not in terms of shipping destroyed but by the relative efforts and casualties of each air force. As to the first the operations on 8 August lead to the same conclusion as those of July, that the Germans were forcing upon Fighter Command a relatively higher rate of effort than they were making themselves. At most three hundred and fifty enemy aircraft had taken part in the Channel operations, against which Nos 10 and 11 Groups had flown over five hundred sorties on interception and convoy patrols. Of the twenty day fighter squadrons between Hornchurch and Exeter, nine had been heavily engaged, five of them once only, three on two occasions, and one (No. 145) on three. The balance sheet of losses showed a claim of thirty-six Me 110s and 109s and seventeen Ju 87s destroyed against a loss to Fighter Command of fifteen pilots and twenty aircraft. How long either side could stand such a casualty rate will be considered when all the major operations up to 19 August have been examined.

OPERATIONS, 8/9–10/11 AUGUST

On the night of 8 August about forty aircraft crossed the coast, most of them coming from the Cherbourg peninsula and keeping to the western half of the country. Birmingham received a few salvoes for the first time, and some bombs were dropped in Birkenhead. There was also a little activity round Norwich and Dover. No military damage was done, and the purpose of the raids appears to have been to harass the civil population.

On the following night activity was again chiefly confined to the west, though there was scattered bombing and leaflet dropping in coastal districts of East Anglia, and the customary incidents on the north-east coast, where the iron works at Skimmingrove was once more hit. Bombs were again dropped in the Liverpool district, and the de Havilland works at Hatfield may have been one of the German targets, as five HE bombs fell nearby just after midnight.

Only about fifteen aircraft crossed the coast on the night of the 10th, and the only incident worth recording was an attack on the Landore viaduct near Swansea, which carries the main GWR line in South Wales. About 18 HE bombs were dropped of which one fell between the metals on the down line causing traffic to be obstructed, but not stopped, for three days.

On each of these three nights the main German activity, however, took the form of minelaying. It is difficult to work out from the operations rooms track charts how many aircraft were employed on this duty, for the individual minelayer frequently stayed for anything up to an hour over one small area off the coast, with the result that the chart frequently displays an intricate series of tracks which might have been made by as many as a dozen aircraft. But it is probable that about fifty aircraft were engaged in minelaying on each of the three nights. All the chief foci of shipping movements received their quota of mines with the exception of the Clyde. The shipping lanes between Harwich and Yarmouth, and off the Kentish coast were more frequently visited than any others.

After their operations on the 8th the Germans operated on only a light scale during daylight on the next two days. Only one enemy aircraft was shot down, a Heinkel 111, which was destroyed by No. 79 Squadron near Sunderland about noon on the 9th. This aircraft had succeeded in bombing the shipyards at Sunderland causing widespread but not serious damage. The only other incident overland on this day was a sharp attack by two Me 109s on the barrage balloons at Dover, but no balloon was destroyed. On the following day only one incident overland was reported, an attack by a single aircraft on West Malling airfield at 0730 hours. Twelve bombs were dropped from a low altitude, causing slight damage to the airmen's quarters and to two aircraft. On both days, however, there were extensive armed shipping reconnaissances, including some in the Irish Sea and off north-west Ireland. In fact it was only from these areas that there came any reports of attacks on shipping. One ship of 900 tons was sunk sixty miles south-west of the Fastnet Rock, two were attacked in St George's Channel, the SS *Warwick Castle* was unsuccessfully bombed when twenty miles west of Achill Head, as was a convoy one hundred and eighty miles west of the Bloody Foreland. All these incidents took place on the 10th, and the last was at the furthest point from enemy-held territory at which shipping had been attacked. If anything was to be learned, therefore, from the German activities in daylight on these two days it was that the prime target was still shipping, and that the scope of the enemy's anti-shipping operations was being widened.[5]

OPERATIONS IN THE CHANNEL AND THAMES ESTUARY, 11 AUGUST

Until 0730 hours on 11 August there was no significant enemy activity, but about that time an aircraft was plotted near a north bound convoy off Southend. Three Hurricanes of No. 56 Squadron were patrolling the convoy and saw nothing suspicious, but this is not surprising as three-quarters of the sky was covered with cloud down to 4,000 feet. It is more than likely, in view of what happened later, that the convoy was spotted and its position reported. Another convoy was south bound off Orfordness at the time, but it had not yet attracted the enemy's attention.

However, it was further south, in the Straits of Dover, that the Germans first brought forces of any size into operation. The RDF stations had detected none of the usual signs that the enemy were assembling when suddenly at 0735 hours they located two formations totalling thirty or more aircraft seven miles east of the South Foreland at 15,000 feet. The only fighters in the air at the time were four Spitfires from No. 64 Squadron (Kenley), and these were ordered towards Dover. In addition, No. 32 Squadron took off from Hawkinge at 0742 hours to patrol the airfield at 15,000 feet, and No. 74 Squadron left Manston at 0749 hours to intercept the enemy formations. But it was already too late, as at 0737 hours what is described as 'a wave of enemy bombers' glided over Dover harbour with their engines shut off and shot down six of the balloons there.

AA Command 'Y' Form, 1800 hours, 11 August, No. 941 Squadron ORB

Other enemy forces were still over the Straits as the squadrons climbed to their patrol heights. There was one about ten miles north-east of the North Foreland moving south, and another in the centre of the Straits. No. 32 Squadron intercepted one at 0805 hours, and No. 74 Squadron another at about the same time. The enemy formations were made up of fighters only, one of twelve Me 109s which approached Dover from the north-east, and the other of similar

5 A German unit, I/KG 40, which was to enjoy considerable success against Atlantic shipping, completed re-equipment with Focke-Wulf Condor aircraft about this time, and was reported on 15 August to have moved from north-west Germany to Bordeaux.

strength, which came from due east. The first was engaged by No. 32 Squadron at a height of 20,000 feet, but the ensuing combat was no more than a skirmish and neither side lost any aircraft. No. 74 Squadron, however, were more heavily engaged. They had climbed to 24,000 feet and being between the enemy and the sun were able to achieve an initial surprise. The squadron were only allowed the claim of one Me 109, but a least six others were probably damaged at the cost of one Spitfire.[6] More than one group of enemy fighters later participated in the fighting, which took place at heights varying between 18,000 and 23,000 feet; and the general picture presented by the pilots' combat reports is of a number of small enemy formations, of *Staffel* strength at most, sweeping over from France as far as Dover, circling the town for a short time and then retiring.

Fighter Command 'Y' Form, 1800 hours 11 August

There was a lull in such harassing tactics from 0830 to 0900 hours, when a force of nine or more aircraft was located in the centre of the Straits, where it remained for the next half hour and was then apparently reinforced. Ten minutes later a new formation of thirty or more aircraft was detected about ten miles to the east of Dover, and another force, of similar strength, was picked up in the Baie de la Seine. The latter was on a course for Portland and events between 0945 and 1015 hours showed that this was the important operation, and that the manoeuvrings in the Straits had been intended to divert attention from its assembling. This was not immediately apparent at the time, of course, and steps were taken to meet the enemy both in the Dover area and in the central Channel. Accordingly, No. 64 Squadron was sent up from Kenley at 0932 hours, No. 74 from Manston at 0950 hours and No. 32 from Biggin Hill at 1100 hours, and all were ordered towards Dover. Further west No. 145 Squadron was sent up from Westhampnett at 0935 hours to patrol Swanage, nine aircraft of No. 1 Squadron left Tangmere at 0945 hours to patrol the coast nearby and at about the same time No. 609 Squadron began to patrol Warmwell.

The squadrons in Kent were first engaged as at about 0951 hours about twenty Me 109s appeared very high over Dover. No. 64 Squadron sighted them but as the squadron were more than nine thousand feet below the enemy it was nearly ten minutes before they were in a position to engage. The enemy were greeted by the Dover guns, however, and the attack which a small number of Me 109s made on the balloon barrage was only half-hearted, and no balloons were lost. By 1000 hours, when Nos 64 and 74 Squadrons came into action, most of the enemy fighters were retiring, and nearly all combats took place against Me 109s which were diving for the French coast.[7] But at least one formation must

6 This combat provided an instance of an apparent enemy casualty which was claimed in all honesty by the pilot concerned, but which was not credited to him in the Fighter Command report on the day's operations. The enemy aircraft was attacked and large pieces were seen to fall away from it, but as the attacking pilot did not see it crash it was at first claimed as only damaged. Later a searchlight site near Deal reported that an Me 109 had been seen to crash a mile off shore at 0808 hours, and believing that the only other squadron in the neighbourhood was No. 64, which had not been engaged, the claim was then altered to a definite destruction. But No. 74 Squadron was also fighting in the area, and the aircraft which crashed was almost certainly a Spitfire flown by P/O Stenson of that squadron, who was forced to bale out, and who, as he parachuted down, saw his aircraft fall into the sea at the time and in the position noted by the searchlight post.

7 Some of the combats in which No. 74 Squadron were engaged took place at 27,000 feet, and the squadron commander, S/Ldr A C Malan, reported that he had the impression that his Spitfire was no better than the Me 109 at that altitude. Interestingly enough, the pilots of this same squadron had reported after their earlier combats over the Straits, that they had easily outfought the Me 109s up to 20,000 feet. This was one of the earliest indications of what was the great merit of the Me 109, and one which the Germans exploited, its excellent performance at altitudes over 25,000 feet compared to that of the Spitfire and Hurricane, especially of the latter.

have remained near Dover, probably at a lower altitude than that at which our squadrons were engaged, as the balloons at Dover were once more attacked at 1015 hours. Again the Dover guns protected the balloon barrage from loss.

By 1020 hours, when No. 32 Squadron arrived over Dover, the series of actions in that area had come to an end, and there was no sign of the enemy. But he was very much in evidence some two hundred miles to the west where Portland was heavily bombed at 1025–1030 hours.

We have already noted the precautions that were taken to deal with the first enemy formation detected in the central Channel. This, however, proved to be only the spearhead of much larger forces, and between 1005 and 1009 hours the following German formations were plotted in the central Channel, all of them on a course for Portland and Swanage:

1. The force originally plotted as it emerged from the Baie de la Seine thirty or more aircraft strong: at 1005 hours this was about thirty miles south of St Catherine's Point.
2. A force of fifty or more aircraft was about fifteen miles north of Cherbourg at 1005 hours.
3. A smaller force, plotted as 'nine plus', was twenty-six miles north-west of Cherbourg at 1009 hours.

The enemy had, therefore, a fair distance to travel before they reached the coast, and the controllers at Nos 10 and 11 Groups had more time than usual to make their dispositions. Furthermore, as there was no convoy in the area at the time it was obvious that the Germans were making for a coastal target, which, from their course, could only be Portland. This simplified the controllers' task, and all the squadrons that they ordered up between 1000 and 1020 hours were directed to patrol the Portland area. At 1000 hours Nos 1, 145 and 609 Squadrons were already in the air, and the following squadrons took off to join them:

Eleven aircraft of No. 601 Squadron from Tangmere at 1000 hours;

Indeterminate number of aircraft from No. 152 Squadron from Warmwell at approximately 1000 hours;

Twelve aircraft of No. 213 Squadron from Exeter at 1009 hours;

Twelve aircraft of No. 238 Squadron from Middle Wallop at 1014 hours;

Seven aircraft of No. 87 Squadron from Exeter at 1015 hours.

The first of our squadrons to make contact with the enemy was No. 609 Squadron, which had been ordered to leave its patrol over Warmwell and intercept enemy aircraft approaching Swanage at 18,000 feet. The enemy, who consisted of about one hundred Me 110s and 109s, proved to be much higher, some as high as 35,000 feet; and they followed their customary practice of keeping the action over one place by moving in tight circular formations. No. 609 Squadron attacked out of the sun, but even though the pilots thought they had destroyed five Me 110s they were unable to make much impression on the enemy.

It was this same German formation with which Nos 601 and 145 Squadrons became engaged some time between 1015 and 1030 hours; No. 145 Squadron came in contact with it almost as soon as No. 609 Squadron. The reports of all three squadrons tally as to the enemy's size, height and tactics, and all found it equally difficult to break up the German formation. Indeed Nos 601 and 145 Squadrons fared badly. They could claim no enemy aircraft definitely destroyed, and between them lost seven pilots and their aircraft.

It is clear from all this that the three squadrons attacked a purely fighter force whose function was doubtless to act as a decoy and thus keep fighters away from the main, bomb-carrying force. The ruse was largely successful, for while the engagement was taking place south of Swanage, the main enemy formation approached Portland some miles to the west. It was reported to consist of an unstated number of long-range bombers (probably no more than twenty, judging by the number of bombs that were dropped), closely escorted by Me 109s, with Me 110s some distance behind. The whole force contained from seventy to a hundred aircraft and flew at varying heights between 10,000 and 15,000 feet. Only one squadron, No. 213, succeeded in intercepting it before it dropped its bombs. This squadron had been ordered to patrol at 10,000 feet, which was considerably lower than the rest of the defending squadrons, and had only just arrived over Portland when they sighted the enemy. An attack was immediately launched against the head of the German formation and some of the bombers were seen to jettison their loads near Portland Bill and wide of any target. Two of the squadron's pilots were killed and one was wounded, but seven enemy bombers and one fighter were believed to have been destroyed.

Yet such was the strength of the enemy that they continued to press on towards Portland. At least seventy bombs were dropped in Portland and about forty in the Chesil Beach–Weymouth area between 1025 and 1035 hours. The railway line at Portland station was blocked, a submarine school was hit, two oil tanks were set on fire, two small destroyers were slightly damaged and there was a good deal of damage to private property. Just after the attack had been delivered No. 238 Squadron came into action between Portland and Weymouth with the main enemy force, as did No. 87 Squadron a few minutes later. Enemy fighters were also engaged by Nos 1 and 152 Squadrons after the bombing had taken place, but none of these squadrons seriously interfered with the German operation. Its failure as a bombing raid – for little serious damage was done – goes to the credit of No. 213 Squadron.

In the various engagements RAF pilots claimed to have destroyed seventeen fighters and nine bombers for certain, and as many more were thought to have been probably destroyed. Two more enemy aircraft were claimed as destroyed by the Portland anti-aircraft gunners, who fired nearly two hundred rounds in the course of the action. There was little direct evidence of the enemy's losses; all that could be ascertained was that the bombers were from KG 54. RAF losses, on the other hand, were higher in proportion to the enemy's than we had come to expect. Eighteen aircraft were destroyed, and five others were too badly damaged to be repaired by the unit, and fifteen pilots were killed and three wounded.

This attack on Portland was the biggest operation of the day, but it was barely over before the Germans renewed their attacks further east. Two east coast convoys, at least one of which had been spotted by the Germans earlier in the morning, were on opposite courses about ten miles south-east of Orfordness when, at 1130 hours, unmistakable signs were received that the Germans were concentrating between Calais and Dunkerque. A section of Hurricanes from No. 85 Squadron (Martlesham) was patrolling the northbound convoy at the time, and shortly after 1130 hours they had a brief skirmish with a single Do 17, which was probably reconnoitring ahead of the main German formation. But not until 1140 hours was it certain that the German objective was the convoys. Only then were the defending fighters sent into the air; and No. 74 Squadron from Manston and No. 17 Squadron from Martlesham took off between 1145 and 1150 hours and were directed towards the convoy. As small enemy forces were still on the eastern side of the Straits of Dover No. 64 Squadron was ordered up from Hawkinge at 1145 hours to patrol the airfield.

The weather off the Suffolk coast was a considerable handicap to the defenders; visibility was good but there was a bank of cloud at 4,000 feet which concealed the approach of the German formation. Consequently, the three Hurricanes of No. 85 Squadron were unable to intervene before the German bombers, of which there were fifteen to twenty, had carried out their attack. Two ships were hit and seriously damaged, the SS *Oil Trader*, a tanker of 5,550 tons, and the SS *Kernwood*, a merchant vessel of 3,800 tons. The German bombers quickly sought the cover of the clouds and the Hurricanes pursued them only to find an escort of fighters of approximately *Gruppe* strength circling above. The three Hurricanes could do little against such superior forces, but by this time, 1205 hours, the other squadrons which had been ordered to the scene were coming into action. Fierce fighting then took place just above the clouds chiefly with the enemy fighters, and although our pilots were allowed to have shot down only four of the enemy for certain, it is probable that heavier losses were inflicted.[8] Three RAF pilots were lost.

By 1210 hours the enemy were retiring to the south-east, and No. 64 Squadron, which was patrolling Hawkinge, was directed to a point north-east of the North Foreland to intercept them. Formations of Me 109s were over the Straits, however, and as the squadron flew north-east it was attacked by a force of similar strength which dived on them from 20,000 feet. Fortunately the Me 109s were seen in time for the squadron to evade the attack, but a fight ensued which made it impossible to carry out the original order to intercept.

During the absence of this squadron from the Dover area the fourth attack of the day was made on the Dover balloons and one of them was destroyed. The precise time of this attack has not been traced, but it was between 1215 and

8 The diary of one of the German pilots taking part in this attack was recovered from his body when he was killed on 15 August. There is no reason to doubt the honesty or the accuracy of the diarist (except where British losses are concerned), and it appears that practically the whole of KGr 210, escorted by fighters from ZG 26, took part in the operation. The bombers started from Calais (Mark) at 1120 hours, formed up with their escort over Gravelines at 1,500 feet, then climbed through the clouds to 11,000 feet and set course for the convoy. Conditions were not considered favourable for attack but an 8,000 ton ship was believed to have been sunk. Two of the writer's *Staffel* were lost in the fighting which followed, and three made forced landings in friendly territory; but what the total German losses were is not stated. ZG 26 claimed to have shot down eight Hurricanes, whereas in fact only one Hurricane and two Spitfires were lost. No traces of the two German pilots named as lost in this operation were ever found by us. (AI1 (K) 273/1940).

1230 hours, and by that time still more operations were about to be launched by the Germans. Unfortunately, not much can be learned from the track charts about the direction of the enemy's attacks or the times at which the first signs of an attack were detected, as few tracks were plotted continuously. Nor are the pilots' reports much help, for the weather was becoming increasingly cloudy, and their impressions of the fighting were more vague then usual. All that is certain is that at least two, and probably three enemy formations, containing both bombers and fighters, crossed the northern entrance to the Straits of Dover between 1245 and 1300 hours. One of them reached the southbound convoy near Clacton at 1250 hours just as three Hurricanes of No. 151 Squadron arrived to patrol it. The enemy force consisted of fifteen Ju 87s protected by twenty Me 109s but rather surprisingly the Germans did not attack the main convoy and concentrated instead on an escort vessel a mile or two away. A few minutes later a formation of Do 215s, protected by Me 109s, was intercepted near the North Foreland by No. 111 Squadron, who had been diverted from a flight from Northolt to the forward base at Hawkinge. At some point in the Thames Estuary No. 56 Squadron also sighted Do 215s about 1300 hours.

No. 151 Squadron ORB

It is a fair inference from the presence of bombers such as the Ju 87 and Do 215 that the Germans intended as serious an attack upon the southbound convoy as that which they had launched against the northbound convoy an hour previously. If so, the attack was a failure. No merchant vessel was sunk: indeed none seem to have been attacked; and only slight damage was caused to a destroyer and to two minesweeping trawlers. Both No. 56 and No. 111 Squadrons were engaged but with little success in terms of enemy aircraft destroyed. No. 111 Squadron lost four of its pilots and aircraft in return for only one Me 109 certainly destroyed; but there is a strong probability that the squadron diverted the German formation from its target, which was presumably the convoy off the Essex coast.

The rest of the day's operations can be quickly described. No. 74 Squadron was in action for the fourth time in seven hours at 1400 hours northeast of Margate, where they came across a small formation of Ju 87s protected by about twenty Me 109s. The squadron leader chose to engage the German fighters and while the action was in progress a destroyer was bombed off the North Foreland. One of the Me 109s was shot down for certain.

Thenceforwards there was no further offensive action in the Straits. One more German aircraft was shot down, a Ju 88 near Thirsk at 1910 hours. An hour earlier No. 242 Squadron engaged a Do 17 during a patrol of the northbound convoy near Yarmouth. Both enemy aircraft were flying alone, and were doubtless reconnoitring east coast shipping. Otherwise there was no significant activity until dark.

SUMMARY

The main German operations on 11 August, therefore, can be categorised thus:

1. The attack on Portland, 1030–1100 hours.
2. The attack on the convoys off Orfordness, 1200–1300 hours.
3. The series of attacks in the Straits of Dover, 0730–1400 hours.

The Portland attack was the first of any serious weight that the Germans had made on a land target since the attacks on Dover in July, but it would be wrong to see in it the beginning of a new policy of attacking objectives inland. It is rather to be interpreted as part of the German policy of dislocating shipping in the Channel and weakening the position of the Navy in those waters. Similarly, the attacks on shipping in the Thames Estuary – the second category into which German operations fall on this day – were in no way inconsistent with the same plan. At the same time the inflated fighter escorts which accompanied the German bombers, as well as the diversionary sweeps by purely fighter formations in the Straits of Dover, indicate that the Germans intended to bring RAF fighters to battle and thus whittle away their strength.

And it must be admitted that British losses on the day were heavier than on any day since the end of the fighting over France; and, what was more important, higher than the current daily rate of fighter pilot replacement.[9] Twenty-five pilots were killed or missing, and twenty-eight aircraft were destroyed. Against this the Command claimed the confirmed destruction of thirty-six German aircraft, of which twenty-one were fighters, and the probable destruction of fifty others. AA Command claimed to have destroyed five of the enemy, and HM trawler *Edwardian* claimed a dive-bomber.

Fighter Command 'Y' Form, 0900 hours, 12 August. Fighter Command ORB Appendix B2, August 1940.

The gross effort of Fighter Command had once more been high. Over four hundred sorties were despatched to intercept enemy raids, nearly two hundred were made for the protection of convoys, and one hundred and fifty sorties were carried out on routine sector patrols. But only one squadron, No. 74, was called upon to fight more than once during the day; and the Command was capable of a higher scale of effort without undue strain. The same could be said for the Germans who had used no more than four hundred aircraft at most.

SUMMARY OF OPERATIONS, 11/12 AUGUST

German aircraft were active over Britain from 2200 hours on the 11th to 0200 hours on the following morning. The principal activity was minelaying, which was suspected in a large number of areas, including Falmouth–Plymouth, the Downs, Flamborough Head, off the west coast in Liverpool Bay and off Barrow-in-Furness. Raids overland were scattered, though more attention was paid to the Bristol Channel area than any other; and 'red' warnings, lasting about two hours in most cases, were given in the northeast region, the Humber area, Norfolk, South Wales and Bristol. Out of some twenty incidents on land five affected railway communications, but otherwise there was no indication of what sort of objective the Germans were attempting to find.[10] There was certainly no sign of an integrated bombing policy governing their operations by night as well as by day.

Home Security Intelligence Summary.

9 See pp. 124–125.

10 A He 111 of II/KG 27 was shot down just after midnight at Sturminster Marshall in Dorset by a Hurricane of No. 87 Squadron. All the crew were captured, and were found to include the commander and second-in-command of the *Gruppe*. The prisoners stated that they had left Dinard to bomb the Bristol Company's works, but that they had attacked 'the harbour at Bristol' instead. Four bombs were in fact dropped in the Long Ashton district about the time that this aircraft was plotted over the city (AI1(K) 240/1940). We now know that six He 111s from II/KG 27 were despatched against targets in the west. Their effort was distributed between Plymouth, Swansea, Cardiff, Bristol and Bournemouth.

OPERATIONS, 12 AUGUST

The early morning of 12 August was hazy, but by nine o'clock the weather was fine and sunny, and remained so for the rest of the day. A fair number of enemy movements were detected between 0500 and 0700 hours but they were all movements by single aircraft that kept well over to the southern side of the Channel. At least one German aircraft must have been operating off the south-east coast for at 0720 hours the destroyer *Witherington* was unsuccessfully bombed some twenty miles south of the Scillies. The RDF cover in this area was poor and it is impossible to reconstruct the movements of this aircraft either before or after the attack. About the same time, however, a German formation, plotted as 'six plus', was detected behind Cap Gris Nez; and a smaller force, 'three plus', was located in the centre of the Straits of Dover. The first was making for Dungeness, and so No. 610 Squadron took off from Hawkinge at 0731 hours to intercept it. About the same time No. 54 Squadron was sent up from Manston to patrol the airfield.

a. In the Dover area, 0800–1000 hours

Neither of the German formations crossed the coast, and it is obvious from what happened later that they were waiting for larger forces to assemble. Indications of this came in at 0744 hours, when a force of at least twenty aircraft was located near Guines and just before 0800 hours when another force of similar strength was detected behind Cap Gris Nez. More defending fighters were sent into the air, and No. 111 Squadron took off from Hawkinge at 0800 hours to patrol it at 10,000 feet.

Not until 0812 hours did the Germans cross the coast, when one of the formations which had originally been detected nearly an hour earlier turned south-west and came in near Romney marshes at 16,000 feet. It was sighted almost at once by No. 610 Squadron, which climbed from 10,000 feet to engage. The enemy proved to be rather stronger than the RDF stations had reported, and consisted of nine bombers in three very tight 'vic' formations escorted by twelve Me 109s. The German fighters dived down as our pilots climbed to intercept and all combats were between fighter and fighter. No great advantage could be claimed by either side.[11] Meantime the enemy bombers broke away and successfully bombed the airfield at Lympne.

The large enemy formations which were detected just before 0800 hours were still over the Straits, and it was with two of these that No. 54 Squadron became engaged at about 0840 hours five miles south of Dover. It had been the intention of the sector controller to use No. 610 Squadron to attack the bombers and No. 54 Squadron the fighters if any attack was made, but in some way the arrangement misfired and No. 54 Squadron climbed to 27,000 feet without seeing

Combat Report, S/Ldr. J. Ellis, No. 610 Squadron.

11 There are baffling inconsistencies between the various reports on the results of this action. All that is certain is that the squadron lost one Spitfire outright and two pilots were slightly wounded. According to the consolidated combat report rendered by the squadron intelligence officer four other Spitfires were so damaged as to be irreparable by the squadron, but no other record mentions this. Two Me 109s were certainly destroyed according to this same document, only one according to the No. 11 Group 'Y' Form, but three according to the Fighter Command 'Y' Form. As one Me 109 was seen to crash in the sea, and another came down at Elham in Kent, at least two would appear to have been destroyed.

anything of the fight in which the other squadron had been engaged. Two raids were visible as the squadron approached Dover, one to the north over the North Foreland, the other south of the town. Owing to a misunderstanding between the squadron commander and one of his section leaders the squadron split up into two, one section turning north towards Manston, the rest going on to the south of Dover. The enemy here consisted of some twenty Me 109s, whereas further north, according to the squadron commander, there were about fifty Dornier bombers escorted by Me 109s. Some time later, when returning after chasing an enemy fighter across the Channel, this same officer came across a formation of twelve Me 110s also going towards England, and shot one of them down into the sea. No bombing was reported in this area between 0800 and 0900 hours, apart from that at Lympne, which can be connected with the large bomber formation seen over the North Foreland, nor did any other officer report the presence of Me 110s. But this is not surprising. On this day, and for some time to come, enemy aircraft, including bombers, were constantly over the Straits even when no bombing operations were impending; and chance encounters with enemy aircraft were frequently reported, especially by pilots who had become separated for their squadron during an engagement.

Combat Report, F/Lt. A.C. Deere, No. 54 Squadron.

Between 0850 and 0930 hours the Germans remained over the Straits, though in reduced numbers, and three squadrons were maintained on patrol, No. 43 Squadron (Tangmere) over the coast nearby, No. 501 Squadron over Hawkinge and No. 65 Squadron (Hornchurch) over Chatham. Two German formations approached the Sussex coast during this period, but no bombing was reported and there were no interceptions.

The next two hours saw one of those rare periods when the Fighter Command system worked inefficiently. Three squadrons were constantly in the air throughout the two hours, one over the Sussex coast and two over the Straits, but although German forces flew over the coast no interceptions were made. A single German aircraft, which was not picked up by the RDF stations, attacked the RDF station at Pevensey at 0932 hours; at 0945 hours the RDF station near Rye was attacked by a formation of six Me 110s from KGr 210;[12] and at much the same time the RDF station near Dover was attacked. The first of these three attacks was successful, and Pevensey was out of action for most of the day; but no vital damage was caused at the other stations and both continued to function. Bombs were also dropped on the north side of Dover town at 0950 hours.

One reason for the failure to intercept any of these attacks was that they took place at approximately the time that the defending squadrons were about to land and their reliefs were preparing to take their places: thus, part of No. 501 Squadron landed at Hawkinge at 0935 hours and the rest of the squadron took off five minutes later; No. 43 Squadron landed at Tangmere at 0940 hours and No. 145 Squadron took off from Westhampnett five minutes later; No. 65 Squadron landed at Manston at 0950 hours and Nos 111 and 615 left Hawkinge

12 The diary of the lieutenant from KGr 210 (see p. 60) again proves helpful. The six aircraft started from Calais at 0915 hours and approached the target at 11,000 feet. They were not interfered with, either by AA or fighters, but their aim was affected by a strong wind from starboard and all the bombs fell wide. They flew home without being followed and landed at 1000 hours. This was the first attack on a ground target carried out by the *Gruppe*.

and Kenley respectively at 0945 hours. Added to this was the difficulty of selecting which formation, amongst the many that were being plotted on the eastern side of the Straits, would actually come across and carry out an attack.

After these attacks the Germans continued to threaten further action. At 1050 hours at least one squadron was in the air behind Cap Gris Nez, and a formation of three or more aircraft cruised to and fro in the central Channel, where a flight from No. 43 Squadron was patrolling Tangmere. Nos 65, 111 and 615 Squadrons were still patrolling in the Straits but the time for the first two to land was not far off; and a further flight of No. 65 Squadron was ordered up from Manston at 1100 hours to protect Hawkinge, while the whole of No. 501 Squadron was sent up from Hawkinge to patrol off the North Foreland. Two coastal convoys were in the Thames Estuary at the time, one about twelve miles east of Foulness, and the other east of Clacton. The latter was being patrolled by three Hurricanes of No. 151 Squadron.

b. In the Thames Estuary, 1100–1145 hours

As the defences were being adjusted the Germans had been reinforcing the formations which had been flying near Calais for some time; and just before 1110 hours a large force, plotted as 'fifty plus', came out into the eastern entrance to the Straits. It came over to the North Foreland and then turned north as though to cross the Thames Estuary; but when it was half way over it began to move backwards and forwards in an east–west direction. As it began this manoeuvre another enemy detachment of twelve or more aircraft was located off the North Foreland at 0815. It moved northwards to join the force already over the estuary and in doing so confirmed what was already suspected, that the two convoys would shortly be attacked. Meanwhile, the two squadrons that were in the air near the Straits, Nos 65 and 501, were ordered northwards, and Nos 54 and 111 Squadrons took off from Manston and Hawkinge to maintain patrols over the Dover area.

At about 1130 hours the Germans began their attacks. The section of No. 151 Squadron sighted about fifteen Ju 87s, escorted by some twenty Me 109s, attacking a ship some distance from the convoy; No. 501 Squadron engaged what was probably the same force some miles north of Margate; and No. 65 Squadron came into action, also about 1130 hours, with a force of twenty Me 109s which were flying at 24,000 feet near the North Foreland. In each case the action was joined some miles to the south-east of both the convoys, and with such success that the enemy never approached within striking distance. As in the operations over Dover earlier in the day the controller aimed at engaging the higher enemy formation with a Spitfire squadron, and the lower with Hurricanes; and on this occasion the plan succeeded. In all, six Ju 87s and four fighters were believed to have been destroyed for a loss of four Hurricanes and one pilot. Two minesweepers were seriously damaged off the North Spit buoy.

Daily summary of Naval Events, 13 August

c. In the Solent 1200–1300 hours

The biggest German operations of the day, which took place in the Solent area, immediately followed the succession of attacks in and near the Straits of Dover, but it is difficult to say whether the earlier operations were preliminary to the later in the sense that they were calculated to assist them. The position, as far as it can be reconstructed, was this: just as our squadrons were engaging the enemy in the mouth of the Thames indications were received that the enemy were about to launch an attack in the central Channel. At 1128 hours two formations of thirty or more aircraft were located near the Cherbourg peninsula, and two smaller forces were moving to and fro off Cherbourg presumably to protect the assembling of other forces some way to the south. A convoy was at this time in Spithead.

By 1140 hours the forces that had been cruising off Cherbourg had disappeared, and two large German formations began to move across the Channel: the westerly one, which at one point was plotted as 'one hundred and fifty plus', headed for the Isle of Wight; and the easterly one, 'thirty plus', headed for Selsey Bill. There were still some German forces in the Straits of Dover and Nos 54 and 111 squadrons were maintained on patrol over Hawkinge and Dungeness.

Further west No. 257 Squadron took off from Northolt at 1140 hours to patrol Tangmere at 15,000 feet; five minutes later No. 266 Squadron took off from Tangmere to patrol their base; and at 1148 hours No. 152 Squadron took off from Warmwell and were directed towards the Isle of Wight. Shortly afterwards the first two squadrons were also ordered to that area, as by 1150 hours it was obvious that the enemy's targets were there, and more squadrons were ordered into the air: at noon No. 609 Squadron went up from Warmwell and No. 213 Squadron from Exeter, and ten minutes later No. 145 Squadron took off from Westhampnett.

But by 1210 hours the Germans had reached their targets – Portsmouth and the RDF station at Ventnor. The convoy in Spithead may also have been an enemy objective, but only light attacks were made on it and no damage was done. There were at least two main German formations: one consisted of about twenty Ju 87s and 88s protected by an undetermined number of Me 109s and 110s; and the other contained Do 17s and 215s, He 111s and Ju 88s at 12,000–15,000 feet, and Me 109s and 110s at heights up to 30,000 feet. This latter force was the largest that the Germans had hitherto launched against this country; and the pilots of No. 266 Squadron, who were in the best position to estimate its size, reckoned that it contained about five hundred aircraft. Its deployment was described thus: 'The enemy bombers were in formations of seven or eight sections in line astern and layered up, defensive circles being frequently seen. Fighters were in echelon astern in sections of five or six.' It is not certain that the larger force was intercepted before it bombed Portsmouth, but the other, whose task was to attack the RDF station at Ventnor, was intercepted by Nos 152 and 609 squadrons just as the bombers commenced to dive on the station from a height of about 10,000 feet. No. 152 Squadron got to the bombers, some of them at any rate, before they released their bombs, while No. 609 Squadron, which was at 20,000 feet, were mainly engaged with the German fighter escort. Even so the station was heavily and accurately bombed.

Consolidated Combat Report. No. 266 Squadron.

Between 1215 and 1230 hours the larger German formation was engaged as it retired by nearly all the squadrons, including two, Nos 43 and 615, which only took off between 1215 and 1220 hours from Tangmere and Kenley respectively.

Fighter Command 'Y' Form, 1800 hours, 12 August

ibid. AA Command

But it must be added that practically all the squadrons had arrived too late to protect Portsmouth, which was bombed between 1205 and 1215 hours. In the series of engagements between individual British squadrons and the retiring German formations RAF pilots claimed to have shot down for certain ten bombers and eleven fighters, while sixteen fighters and ten bombers were thought to have been destroyed. Our own losses were ten pilots and their aircraft. In addition, the Portsmouth anti-aircraft gunners, who fired nearly four hundred rounds between 1204 and 1220 hours, claimed to have shot down five enemy aircraft, and a further two were destroyed by AA fire over the Isle of Wight. The great majority of combats took place over the sea, and direct evidence of destruction was discovered in only seven cases. All these were bombers, and all with one exception were Ju 88s from the first and third *Gruppe* of KG 51, which implies that at least fifty aircraft from this *Geschwader* took part in the operation.[13]

d. In the Dover area, 1215–1315 hours

On this, as on many subsequent occasions, the German commanders succeeded in synchronizing the operations of widely separated forces with considerable accuracy. The attack on Portsmouth succeeded almost immediately the operations against the convoy in the Thames Estuary, and was itself followed by important movements in the Dover area. The track charts prepared in the operations room at Fighter Command headquarters show clearly that by 1220 hours the mass of the forces which attacked Portsmouth were on course for France, and precisely at this time large forces were detected in the Straits; there was a force of twenty or more aircraft off Cap Cris Nez and one of forty or more behind it, while in the next three minutes three smaller forces were located, one twelve miles south of Dungeness, another some way to the south-west, and a third off the eastern entrance to the Straits. The only British squadron in the air in this area was No. 501, which took off from Hawkinge just after 1220 hours to patrol Dover at 7,000 feet.

The later plots of the formations first detected near Dungeness show that both crossed the coast between Rye and Hastings, carried out a swift reconnaissance without being intercepted, and then retired. Not until 1235 hours did the three formations on the east side of the Straits converge and commence to cross, and only then did the No. 11 Group controller order more squadrons into the air: at 1245 hours twelve Spitfires of No. 65 Squadron took off from Manston to intercept the enemy; at the same time No. 56 Squadron took off from Rochford to patrol it; and four minutes later No. 610 Squadron left Biggin Hill to patrol Canterbury and Hawkinge at 20,000 feet.

What followed can be reconstructed in much greater detail than usual. The German force probably contained three separate formations; one of fourteen Me 110s from KGr 210 with a close escort of seven Me 109s from the same unit, one *Gruppe* of Do 17s from KG 3, and about thirty Me 109s from either JG 54 or JG 26, which were intended to cover the bombers' retirement. The objective

13 A German document captured since this estimate was made reveals that sixty-three aircraft from KG 51 took part in the attack. No mention is made of any dive-bomber units, nor is the number of escorting fighters given.

was Manston airfield, and the approach was made at 11,000 feet with KGr 210 in the van. At 1245 hours the first bombs began to fall on the airfield just as No. 65 Squadron was taking off, and with one exception all the aircraft took to the air successfully. No. 510 Squadron came up from the south while the bombing was in progress; but they were unable to interfere and the station was heavily and accurately bombed. As the Germans retired No. 501 Squadron and one section of No. 65 Squadron came into action with the two bomber formations, but despite the fact that the majority of the German fighters arrived too late to take part in the fight RAF pilots could not claim any enemy aircraft as definitely destroyed.[14]

From 1300 to 1345 hours small numbers of enemy aircraft, some of them doubtless on rescue work, were plotted in the central Channel and in the Straits, but there were no indications of a concentration of force. Between 1420 and 1500 hours a force seemed to be assembling behind Cap Gris Nez, and two medium sized formations were plotted off Cherbourg. All these forces dispersed, however, and from 1600–1700 hours the Channel was clearer of enemy aircraft than it had been all day.

e. In the Dover area, 1700–1800 hours

But the Germans were to launch one more big operation before the day was done. Signs of this were received between 1645 and 1722 hours when four formations, two of fifty, one of thirty and one of twenty aircraft were detected. As soon as the first of these forces were detected the No. 11 Group controller took immediate action to protect the airfields in the south-east, being anxious to avoid a repetition of the attack on Manston earlier in the day. Thus, the following forces took off between 1650 and 1710 hours:

9 aircraft of No. 64 Squadron from Hawkinge
12 aircraft of No. 32 Squadron from Hawkinge
4 aircraft of No. 501 Squadron from Gravesend

Each of these forces were ordered to patrol its airfield, and, in addition, Nos 54 and 56 Squadrons were despatched from the Hornchurch sector to patrol the Dover area, and No. 501 Squadron sent up a full squadron formation from Hawkinge at 1725 hours. These five squadrons, totalling fifty-three aircraft, were the defending fighter force.

From the operations room track charts it appeared that two German formations, each of fifty or more aircraft, crossed the coast, one near Dover at 1730 hours, and the other at the North Foreland at 1733 hours. At much the same time a third and smaller force came in at New Romney. No. 56 Squadron and most of No. 54 Squadron engaged the force that came in at the North Foreland, and reported that it consisted of one *Gruppe* of Dornier 17s or 215s at 18,000 feet protected by another *Gruppe* of Me 109s. Both squadrons were able to surprise

14 According to the diarist of KGr 210 all the aircraft of his unit and all the Do 17s returned safely, although his own aircraft at least was so damaged that he was unable to take part in an attack which the *Gruppe* made on Hawkinge later in the day. The Germans believed that they had destroyed three Hurricanes, but in fact only one was lost. (AI1(K) No. 273/1940).

the German formation and both engaged the bombers. An extract from the combat report of No. 56 Squadron illustrates one method of achieving this freedom of action:

Combat Report No. 56 Squadron.

> Attacks were carried out on the rear extreme left hand and right hand section of the bombers from astern and from the quarter by the first three sections of the Hurricanes. The rearmost Hurricane section concentrated on protecting our fighters from an attack by the Me 109s as they carried out their attack on the bombers. They did this by firing at long range in front of the Me 109s as they dived to attack our leading sections ... The Me 109s did not risk running into the tracer which they saw flashing in front of them.

Home Security Daily Intelligence Summary.

The German bombers put up a sturdy defence, and only one was shot down. Nevertheless it can hardly be doubted that the formation was diverted from its objectives The two other German forces found and bombed the airfields at Lympne and Hawkinge, whereas this one, which was certainly making for Manston, the third airfield near the Kentish coast, when it was first attacked, seems to have dropped most of its bombs near two small villages, Bekesbourne and Patrixbourne, five miles south-east of Canterbury, and Manston was left untouched.

The middle of the three German formations was attacked by No. 32 Squadron in a series of combats which ranged over the country between Dover and Whitstable. The enemy were described as about thirty Do 215s at 12,000 feet escorted by thirty Me 109s, i.e. much the same composition as the force which was attacked near the North Foreland. The squadron attacked but were unable to get to the bombers owing to the sharp intervention of the Me 109s and the bombers went on to attack Hawkinge, which was heavily bombed between 1740 and 1745 hours. No. 501 Squadron also engaged this force as it retired. a few of the German fighters took the opportunity to attack the Dover balloons, and one was shot down at about the time Hawkinge was being bombed.

Consolidated Combat Report, No. 64 Squadron.

Home Security Daily intelligence Summary.

The activities of the third German formation, which crossed the coast north of Dungeness, cannot be precisely distinguished from those of the formation that bombed Hawkinge, as some of its aircraft also bombed the airfield there. Like the other two formations it was reported to have consisted of thirty to forty Dornier 215s escorted by a similar number of No. 109s.[15] It was engaged by No. 64 Squadron, but again the German bombers put up a strong defensive fire, and only one was claimed as destroyed. Some of the German bombers may have been diverted, as at 1750 hours about twenty HE bombs fell near the village of Iden two miles north of Rye, but the great majority successfully reached their primary target, the airfield at Lympne, and put down about two hundred bombs upon it.

By 1815 hours this operation, the fifth the Germans had embarked upon during the day, and the fourth in the Thames Estuary–Dover area, was over, and no further activities were reported during the few hours of daylight now left.

15 Only one pilot, F/Lt. Deere of No. 54 Squadron, reported the presence of Me 110s and since it is highly probable that KGr 210 took part in the attack some Me 110s may have been mistaken for Dorniers.

The purpose of the German attacks had been to wreck selected RDF stations on the south and south-east coasts, to make Lympne, Hawkinge and Manston unusable, and to damage Portsmouth dockyard. In addition, the Germans so carefully arranged that the operations in the Thames Estuary, the central Channel and the Dover Straits between 1100 and 1300 hours should follow each other in rapid succession that it seems safe to assume that they were trying to discover whether our fighter squadrons could cover all points between the Solent and the Thames Estuary, and whether a strong defence could be put up against powerful forces operating in rapid succession against widely dispersed objectives.

Certain results of the day's work were probably satisfactory to the Germans. In all their operations, except those against the convoys in the Thames and that in North Kent during the early evening, they had succeeded in reaching their objectives without much interference. They had also kept the air defences constantly on the alert, and forced No. 11 Group alone to make nearly five hundred sorties during the day. Thirteen of the eighteen Spitfire and Hurricane squadrons in the Group had been in action at least once. But the Germans themselves had been at least as busy: the wireless interception service reported that at least nine *Kampfgeschwadern* were in action during the day, and it is probable that certain selected units were being particularly hard worked. We know, for example, that KGr 210 operated during the day on four occasions, on three of them with at least two-thirds of the *Gruppe*. Moreover, no major raid had escaped unscathed. RAF pilots claimed to have shot down thirty-eight German fighters (counting eleven Me 110s as fighters) and nineteen bombers, without taking into account those that were believed to be so badly damaged that they were unlikely to have reached safety; the anti-aircraft gunners also claimed seven fighters and two bombers. British losses amounted to twelve pilots killed and missing and four wounded, twenty-two fighters destroyed and eight badly damaged. However, there was by 12 August insufficient evidence to judge which side was losing most heavily relative to its available strength; the season had barely opened.

No. 11 Group 'Y' Form Part I.

Fighter Command ORB Appendix J.

Fair success attended the German bombing. The RDF station at Ventnor was badly damaged; many buildings were destroyed by fire owing to the lack of water on the site, and on the following day the station was evacuated. Not until 23 August when a station was opened at Bembridge, Isle of Wight, was this gap in the RDF chain replaced. The stations at Pevensey, Rye, Dover and Dunkirk were also damaged but in every case the essential equipment was working by the following day. The injury to the RDF system was, therefore, only temporary.

Fighter Command ORB, Form 540 Signals Branch

As for the three airfields that were attacked, at the end of the day Manston was unserviceable, and Lympne and Hawkinge were unserviceable except for narrow strips. At all three stations considerable damage was done to buildings, hangars, services and communications,[16] but squadrons were operating from both Hawkinge and Manston by the morning of the following day. Lympne was not an operational station, and if it had been wrecked beyond repair the fighter squadrons would hardly have felt its loss; in any case it continued to be used as

16 For a catalogue of attacks upon airfields see Appendix 8.

an emergency landing ground until early in September when it was no longer wanted. The only significant damage caused at Portsmouth was the wrecking of Portsmouth harbour station, but rail traffic to Portsmouth was not interrupted. Altogether, insofar as the results of bombing operations can be assessed on a day to day basis, the Germans had not achieved a degree of success commensurate with their great exertions.

OPERATIONS, 12/13 AUGUST

German night activity on 12 August commenced just before 2230 hours and continued until 0300 hours the next morning. As on the previous night it consisted of minelaying in widely dispersed coastal areas, and scattered raids overland, including light attacks in the Bristol and Cardiff districts. Again it is impossible to perceive any connection between these operations and those which had taken place in daytime, except that they maintained pressure upon the intelligence organisation of the air defence system and, of course, upon the people of Britain. They had little or no effect upon the forces which had been heavily engaged during the day, and were to be similarly engaged on the following day. The Germans did not even attempt to keep RAF pilots from resting, for they confined themselves to the south-west and the east coast, and left practically undisturbed the districts which they had raided during the day.

The anti-aircraft gunners defending Billingham-on-Tees thought that they shot down an enemy aircraft shortly before midnight, but otherwise there was no incident worth recording.

OPERATIONS, 13 AUGUST

a. In the Thames Estuary and near Selsey Bill, 0600–0730 hours

For an hour after dawn on the 13th there were few enemy tracks upon the track charts in the Command operations rooms, and none at all in the eastern and central Channel. The first signs of a concentration, however, came earlier than usual, for between 0530 and 0540 hours two formations of thirty or more aircraft each were located in the Amiens area. For the next half-hour the two forces remained overland, but at 0610 hours they started to move north. Almost simultaneously two more formations were detected; one near Dieppe, which was reported to be one hundred strong, and the other forty or more strong, to the north of Cherbourg. The weather all this time was very cloudy and dull.

The early warning had given the controller adequate time to despatch a fair-sized defending force into the air, and by 0615 hours three full squadrons and detachments from three more were on patrol: No. 151 Squadron (North Weald) was protecting a convoy in the mouth of the Thames; No. 111 Squadron (Croydon) was patrolling Hawkinge; No. 74 Squadron (Hornchurch) was over Manston; and sections from Nos 85, 43 and 238 squadrons were also in the air near their respective bases.

Between 0610 and 0625 hours the German formations came out in the Channel: those in the Baie de la Seine were supported by a force of twelve or more which was detected off Guernsey at 0624 hours; and the two in the Dover Straits steered a northerly course from Cap Gris Nez. Meanwhile the rest of No. 43 Squadron took off from Tangmere to patrol Petworth–Arundel; and at 0630 hours the rest of No. 238 Squadron took off from Warmwell to patrol their base. Further east No. 257 Squadron left Northolt at 0620 hours to patrol Canterbury; and a section of No. 17 Squadron took off from Martlesham five minutes later to patrol the airfield there. But by that time the enemy had approached even closer. One formation was making for Littlehampton, another was near Spithead, and a third was still in the central Channel; in the Straits a large formation was near the North Foreland on a north-westerly course, and another force was following it. More British squadrons were, therefore, sent into the air. To reinforce the defences of the Portland–Littlehampton area No. 601 Squadron took off from Tangmere at 0630 hours, and five to ten minutes later No. 213 Squadron and one flight of No. 87 Squadron took off from Exeter. Three sections of No. 64 Squadron (Kenley) were added to the forces already in the air near the Thames Estuary.

About 0630 hours the squadrons began to come into action. The engagements in northern Kent were slightly earlier than those over the Sussex coast, and will be examined first; but it should be borne in mind that this was the first occasion on which the Germans had simultaneously launched attacks of serious dimensions against two widely separated sections of the coast.

i. *Over the Thames Estuary*

No. 74 Squadron was probably the first to engage the enemy. The latter came up the Thames above the cloud, which was thick between 3,000 and 4,000 feet, and emerged from it near Whitstable only to find our squadron ready for them. The German formation consisted of four sections of Do 17s in line astern, each section containing ten aircraft. There were no enemy fighters to be seen and our squadron singled out the rearmost section of the bombers for attack. Our pilots believed that every Dornier in the section was hit and six were destroyed, so it is unlikely that it went on to its objective. The rest did so, however, and bombed Eastchurch, a Coastal Command station, and Leysdown, a satellite airfield, on the Isle of Sheppey.

Meantime the second German formation had also been intercepted and heavily engaged. It was about the same size and composition as the formation which had preceded it, and it was first spotted by No. 151 Squadron off the North Foreland on a course up the river at 8,000–13,000 feet. Again no fighters were seen, but while the Germans certainly suffered losses,[17] part of the enemy formation continued on its course. Shortly afterwards, however, No. 111 Squadron came into action with the rest of the force, which they described as

17 This was one of the first engagements in which a Fighter Command aircraft equipped with cannon took part. The aircraft, a Hurricane, was fitted with two Hispano-Suiza cannon and was piloted by F/Lt R.L. Smith. He attacked a tight formation of Dorniers from a range of about three hundred yards and one of them burst into flames. In all technical respects the engagement was a success.

two separate formations of ten aircraft each, between Herne Bay and Whitstable. The squadron commander ordered one flight to make a head-on attack on the enemy, while the other flight moved to the enemy's flank to deal with any bomber which failed to keep formation; and these tactics seem to have been highly successful. About this time bombs fell in and near both Herne Bay and Whitstable, where there were no military targets, and no further attacks were carried out on the airfields up the river, one of which was doubtless the German objective. We are, therefore, entitled to say that the attack by the second German formation was a failure.

And together, from our point of view, there was much that was satisfactory about the whole operation in north Kent. Despite the attacks on the previous day the RDF stations had tracked the enemy formations with great accuracy, while the work of the Observer Corps in plotting the enemy formations as they flew up the estuary above the clouds was beyond praise. In the actual combats no British pilots had been killed or wounded and only two fighters had been destroyed, whereas fourteen Dorniers were believed to have been destroyed. The wreckage of three of these was found on land, and there was also direct evidence of two which fell in the sea. All were Dornier 17s from KG2, which was stationed in the Cambrai area; and it is more than likely that most of the *Kampfgeschwader* was detailed for the operation.

The station at Eastchurch, however, was seriously damaged. Over one hundred HE bombs and many incendiaries were dropped; nearly all hangars and building were destroyed, communications and services were affected, and the airfield surface was badly cratered. Even so, it was in use by 1600 hours on the same day. Eastchurch, however, was not a Fighter Command station, from which it might appear to follow that the Germans were ill-advised to attack it when they had not immobilised the regular bases of the Command in the south-east. The station was frequently used by Battle squadrons for attacks upon E-boat bases at Boulogne and Calais, and the German attack may reflect the success of these operations. But it was also housing at the time of the attack Nos 266 and 19 squadrons – the latter of a Spitfire experimentally equipped with 20 mm cannon – which had been loaned to Coastal Command for the support of their operations in the Straits. We do not know whether the Germans were aware of this arrangement, but after the attack both units returned to Fighter Command without having carried out one operation with Coastal Command.

ii. *Near Selsey Bill*

All the time that the operations had been going on in northern Kent the Tangmere squadrons and the squadrons from No. 10 Group had been engaging the enemy forces that had crossed the central Channel from Dieppe and Cherbourg. The easternmost of these formations crossed the coast near Tangmere at about 0635 hours; the second and largest crossed near Portsmouth at 0640 hours, and both flew northwards towards Arundel. The third formation, which was about twenty miles south-west of St Catherine's Point at this time, was not subsequently tracked, and as far as we know took no aggressive action. It may have been a force of fighters which was intended to cover the retirement of the two other formations. Each of the latter contained one *Gruppe* of Ju 88s, escorted by a large undetermined number of Me 109s and 110s. One squadron also thought it saw some Do 215s.

One enemy formation was first engaged at 0640 hours to the south of Tangmere by No. 257 Squadron. The squadron were originally ordered to patrol Canterbury, but were later directed towards Tangmere. The fighting was scrappy and no coherent account of it is possible, but 257's pilots believed they had shot down a Ju 88.

It was probably this same force with which No. 601 Squadron became engaged at 0650 hours over the South Downs west of Arundel. The enemy were still flying northwards at 12,000 feet when the squadron came up, but on being attacked the majority of the bombers sought safety in the clouds, released their bombs and made off south. The squadron succeeded in reaching a small formation of bombers and shot down at least one. Rather to the pilots' surprise the enemy fighters failed to intervene until late in the combat.

This was also the experience of No. 43 Squadron which came into action with the second enemy formation at 0640 hours between Littlehampton and Worthing. The German fighters were so far astern of the bombers that the squadron had virtually a free hand with the Ju 88s, and even when the escorting fighters arrived they seemed to show a most unusual reluctance to engage. In contrast the bombers put up a skilful and determined defence. One more interception was made, by No. 64 Squadron near Chichester as the enemy retired. At least one enemy aircraft was shot down into the sea,[18] but it cannot be said that the action in any war affected the German plan.

Nevertheless, the Germans failed to carry out their plan, partly because of the weather, partly through fighter action. Until some of the records of *Luftflotte* 3 were captured in the summer of 1944 it was impossible to do more than affirm that this was so on the evidence of the ill-directed bombing in the Bordon, Longmore and Liss districts of Hampshire which was all that the Germans achieved. It is now known, however, that the enemy objectives were the RAF stations at Odiham and Farnborough, and neither was attacked. The first was the target of eighteen Ju 88s from II/KG 54, the second of twenty Ju 88s from I/KG 54. Each German force, as we have seen, was escorted by fighters, but in what strength is not known.

b. In the Portland area, 1150–1230 hours

The German retirement had been completed by 0730 hours, and for the next four hours there were no important operations. Indications that another attack was contemplated were received at 1140 hours, when a force of twenty or more aircraft was detected on the eastern edge of the Cherbourg peninsula on a north-westerly course. At 1154 hours when it was about forty-five miles south-west of St Catherine's Point, another formation of twelve or more aircraft was located a little way to the west on a parallel course for Portland. Our pilots were later to confirm these plots, showing that despite the loss of Ventnor the RDF stations

18 This brought our pilots' claims for the whole operation to nine bombers and one fighter. Two Ju 88s from KG 54 were found on land, and one Me 109. No aircraft or bodies were recovered from the sea.

were still capable of accurate plotting for range and bearing in the central Channel.

To guard against this threat the following forces were sent into the air:

No. 238 Squadron from Warmwell at 1150 hours to patrol Portland at 25,000 feet.

No. 601 Squadron from Tangmere at 1155 hours to patrol Swanage at 20,000 feet.

No. 213 Squadron from Exeter at 1158 hours to patrol Portland at 10,000 feet (probably).

The enemy consisted of one purely fighter formation at 20,000 feet, and one of Do 17s and Ju 88s at 15,000 feet protected by fighters. They approached Portland shortly after noon, and enjoyed nearly ten minutes grace before the defending fighters arrived in the area. Yet there was certainly no bombing at the time, and it must be supposed that the purpose of the German operation was simply to sweep the area and bring RAF squadrons to battle.

They succeeded. The defending squadrons came up to the enemy between 1210 and 1220 hours. Nos 601 and 238 squadrons found themselves, for once, well above the German fighters, and in the ensuing fight they claimed to have shot down ten of them at a cost of only one Hurricane. 'B' Flight of No. 213 Squadron ('A' Flight, for some reason, never saw the enemy), which arrived somewhat later, engaged a small number of enemy bombers as they retired, and claimed to have shot one down. Most of these combats took place over the sea, and only one German aircraft, a Me 110, crashed on land; the crew of another Me 110 was rescued from Weymouth Bay.

About an hour after this operation was over the Germans again sent a force, plotted as 'nine plus', into the Portland area, but it was not intercepted and it took no aggressive action. It may well have been searching for aircraft shot down in the sea. The Germans made a practice of following up their big operations in this way, usually employing air-sea rescue float planes, but sometimes operational aircraft.

c. *Between 1530 and 1730 hours*

The early part of the afternoon, however, was free of alarms, and it was not until half past three that there were signs of further enemy concentrations. Between 1527 and 1540 hours three formations, each of thirty or more aircraft, were plotted between St Albans's Head and St Catherine's Point. They constituted a threat to the whole area between Portsmouth, where at the time only one squadron, No. 152 from Warmwell, was on patrol.

Moreover, it soon became evident that a two-pronged attack similar to that of the early morning was being prepared, for at 1539 hours a force of thirty or more aircraft was plotted fifteen miles north of Cap Griz Nez; and a minute later another force of like strength was located five miles to the north and west of the first.

As before it will be necessary to deal separately with events in each area.

i. *In the Solent*

To the west the following squadrons were sent into the air between 1526 and 1555 hours:

> At 1526 hours No. 213 Squadron left Exeter to patrol Portland below cloud base (5,000 feet).
>
> At 1528 hours No. 238 Squadron left Middle Wallop to patrol Portland at 20,000 feet.
>
> At 1530 hours No. 609 Squadron left Middle Wallop to patrol Warmwell at 20,000 feet.
>
> At 1535 hours No. 601 Squadron left Tangmere to patrol Bembridge, Isle of Wight, at cloud base.

In addition, sections from No. 92 Squadron, Pembrey, and No. 43 Squadron, Tangmere, were sent into the air during this period, and were subsequently directed towards the scene of battle.

The first of the German formations came straight across the Channel and reached the Isle of Wight just after 1600 hours. The second was lost by the RDF stations when some thirty miles south of St Catherine's Point, but to judge from what happened later it made its landfall near Portland. A third formation came in a few miles west of St Alban's Head and then followed the coastline towards the Solent, which it reached at 1610 hours.

On reaching the coast the Germans must have detached a number of small forces, for between 1610 hours, when they reached the coast, and 1710 hours, when most of them had recrossed it on their way home, small concentrations of bombs were dropped at widely separated places, including Perham Down (Wilts), Bishops Waltham, Andover, Middle Wallop, Benson and Thorney Island RAF stations, an Australian camp near Stockbridge, and even as for inland as Wroughton, near Swindon. But three formations of considerable strength penetrated inland.

Home Security Daily Intelligence Summary.

Two of these came in near Portland, and at least one was intercepted before it crossed the coast. The squadron concerned was No. 213 which came into action at 1600 hours with a force of fifty mixed Me 109s and 110s some fifteen miles south-west of Portland Bill. No. 152 Squadron also engaged this force somewhere near Portland. Whether the cloudy conditions concealed the presence of bombers, or whether our two squadrons were engaged with an advance guard of fighters is not known, but just after 1600 hours German bombers were certainly in the Portland area, where No. 238 Squadron came across a force of Ju 88s strongly escorted by fighters, and No. 609 Squadron engaged some thirty Ju 87s and about forty fighters. The first of these two forces turned east towards the Solent, but the second pressed on from its crossing point just west of Portland.

No. 238 Squadron were entirely engaged with enemy fighters, and the German bombers were not diverted from their course. It was this force, consisting of nineteen Ju 88s from I/Lehr 1, that attacked Southampton at 1625 hours.

No. 609 Squadron, however, were heavily engaged with Ju 87s. These were flying at 15,000 feet on a northerly course, with fighters some distance behind, but the failure of the escort to carry out its duties is reflected in the pilots' claim to have destroyed nine of the dive-bombers compared to four Me 109s. Only one dive-bomber was actually found on the ground after this engagement, but insofar as no effective and concentrated bombing can be traced to this German formation it would appear that it was disorganised by the attack.

On the other hand, the forces that bombed Southampton at 1625 hours were interfered with hardly at all. The bombing was accurate, several warehouses were set on fire and a cold storage plant was destroyed, but all fires were under control by dusk.

These were the only incidents worth remarking during the whole operation. At none of the airfields that were bombed was the maintenance of operations affected, and only at Andover was there important damage to station buildings. It would appear, therefore, that Southampton was the main objective of the enemy's attack, and such interceptions as took place after 1630 hours are of interest only in that they increased the cost of the operation to the enemy. Between 1630 and 1700 hours No. 601 Squadron and small detachments of Nos 43, 92, 145 and 257 squadrons all engaged the Germans between Portland and Selsey Bill as they retired. Four bombers and five fighters were claimed as destroyed during this series of actions.

Altogether, fourteen bombers and eighteen fighters were believed to have been destroyed for certain, at a cost of three Hurricanes and two pilots. The Southampton anti-aircraft gunners also claimed to have destroyed one enemy aircraft.[19]

ii. *In Northern Kent*

As has been explained, indications of an attack in the Dover and Thames Estuary area were received almost simultaneously with those of an attack in the central Channel. At 1540 hours, when two enemy forces were located in the Straits, three small detachments were patrolling the threatened area: one section of No. 17 Squadron was patrolling a convoy in the Clacton area; two aircraft of No. 1 Squadron, operating from North Weald, were patrolling another convoy off Harwich; and 'A' Flight of No. 65 Squadron from Manston were patrolling Dover, where they were about to be joined by the second flight of the squadron. The weather, which played a big part in the operations, was cloudy at the time, with one bank of cloud from about four thousand to six thousand feet.

Further forces were sent into the air as soon as it was clear that the Germans contemplated an attack:

> At 1545 hours seven aircraft from No. 64 Squadron took off from Kenley and were directed towards the Straits.

19 The gunners stated that this aircraft was a Ju 86, a type which was not infrequently reported as taking part in operations. No aircraft of this type, however, was found on the ground during the battle, nor was there any other reliable evidence that it was ever used.

At 1550 hours No. 56 Squadron took off from Rochford to patrol Manston.

At 1555 hours five aircraft of No. 19 Squadron, operating from Eastchurch, took off to patrol the coast near Martlesham.

One more enemy formation was picked up seven miles south of Dover while these forces were leaving the ground, making three enemy formations in all. Meanwhile one German force steered northwards until it was about fifty miles due east of Sheerness, and then steered west up the estuary; the second came in between Deal and Sandwich at 1545 hours and flew towards Canterbury.

It was probably the formation detected latest with which No. 65 Squadron came into contact over Dover at 1600 hours. It consisted of twenty to thirty Me 109s at 19,000 feet. The squadron was flying at about the same height and engaged the enemy, each section acting independently and attacking in line astern. In the ensuing combats three Me 109s were claimed as destroyed without loss to our squadron, whose pilots got the impression that the German fighters were not anxious to commit themselves to an engagement. Another enemy fighter formation about twenty strong was observed during the fight, and it may be that both these formations had been ordered to protect the retirement of the force that had already crossed the coast.

This formation had steered towards Canterbury, but its subsequent movements are difficult to trace. Doubtless it was this force which carried out an attack on Detling, a Coastal Command station, at 1605 hours. It was reported that the attack was made by Ju 87s and Me 109s. No pilot saw or engaged any of the former type of aircraft so it would appear that the attackers were not intercepted.

No. 53 Sqadron ORB

The force which flew up the estuary turned north and reached Southend at 1600 hours. It then turned south without dropping any bombs, and while on a southerly course was intercepted by No. 56 Squadron. This squadron had originally been ordered to patrol Manston, but was later diverted to Rochford, which was threatened by the enemy's movement northward. Emerging above the clouds at 5,000 feet about two miles east of Rochford our squadron saw an enemy formation some ten thousand feet above them travelling south. It was reported to consist of twelve Heinkel 111s[20] escorted by thirty Me 110s above and behind. In the circumstances there was little chance of reaching the bombers, and what there was dispelled when the Me 110s accepted the squadron's challenge and, by forming the customary defensive circle, kept the ensuing fight over one spot while the Heinkels withdrew. Four Hurricanes were lost in the action but all the pilots were saved, and four Me 110s were claimed as destroyed. In the action near Dover in which No. 65 Squadron was involved three Me 109s were believed to have been destroyed at no cost to the squadron.

The German operation was over by 1630 hours and with the exception of the attack on Detling no important objectives were bombed. It was virtually the last operation which the Germans launched on this day – there was later some shipping reconnaissance off the Norfolk coast – and, as such, the bombing effort in

20 It will appear later that the 'Heinkels' were almost certainly Me 110s.

relation to the forces employed appears suspiciously small. Without doubt the explanation is that of the two bomber formations which the Germans despatched one failed to find its target owing to cloud. The force in question consisted of fifteen Me 110s and four 109s from KGr 210, and their task was to attack Rochford; they were escorted by Me 110s from ZG 26. The cloudy conditions over England seem to have taken the Germans by surprise, and after failing to find Rochford they retired over northern Kent, dropping their bombs blindly near Crundale ten miles south-west of Canterbury. No. 56 Squadron came into action with ZG 26 over the estuary as the Germans flew south.

AI1(K) No. 273/1940

COMMENTARY

Certain things can safely be said about the operations on the 13th. The first is that the Germans had maintained the attack on airfields in the south-west which they had begun the previous day. On the 12th the most easterly of the Kentish airfields had been attacked; and on the 13th the Germans concentrated on two of the second line of airfields in that part of the country. Both were Coastal Command stations not normally used by fighter squadrons, but the Germans may have reasoned that if Hawkinge, Manston and Lympne were neutralised, airfields such as Detling and Eastchurch would rapidly be commissioned for fighter squadrons in order to keep part of the fighter force as far forward as possible. In fact, neither Hawkinge and Manston, nor Detling and Eastchurch, were neutralised as yet, heavy and serious though the attacks on them had been.

Judging by the bombing incidents reported from airfields in Hampshire on the 13th, the Germans many have been trying to widen the scope of their attacks on this type of target; and one may hazard the guess that but for the weather and the action of our squadrons the attacks which were made would have been much heavier.

The second feature of the operations which is worth recording is the two-pronged attacks in the early morning and the early evening. In attacks on previous days during August and in July the Germans had attempted in various ways to weaken the defences in the areas they had selected for attack: notably by maintaining pressure on one area, by threatening attacks which never materialised, and by continuing operations in one area immediately they had ceased in another. How far this new method of simultaneous attacks on separated districts was well conceived, and how far it was successful, is best assessed after further operations of this type, notably those on 15 August, have been considered.

OPERATIONS, 13/14 AUGUST

Activity on the night of 13 August began somewhat earlier than usual, enemy aircraft being detected just before ten o'clock as they moved towards the coast, chiefly from the Cherbourg peninsula but also from Holland, north-west Germany and Norway. As opposed to many previous nights the primary objectives lay inland and minelaying was on a smaller scale than usual, though it was suspected in the Thames and Humber estuaries, off the west coasts of England

Daily Summary of Naval Events, 14 August

and Wales and off Kinnairds Head. In the latter area two attacks on convoys were carried out between 2300 and 0030 hours by single aircraft, but no damage was done.

Overland perhaps half-a-dozen aircraft were active over the coast of north-east Scotland, and a small number of bombs were dropped in Aberdeen, Peterhead and Frazerburgh. The only activity which merits mention, however, was against the Midlands. Between 2300 and 0130 hours about a dozen aircraft operated over the Birmingham area. At 2310 hours the Nuffield works at Castle Bromwich was hit by eleven HE bombs of which five fell inside factory buildings. Casualties were small as the employees had gone to shelter, though the public warning seems not to have been sounded until the attack had begun; but there was serious damage to the offices and tool room of the works, and a gas main was fractured. Incidents continued to be reported from the area for the next two hours, including some from the Castle Bromwich district; and, all told, about forty HE bombs were dropped.

Home Security Situation Report from Birmingham, 0730 hours, 14 August

This attack was the first of any notable dimensions to be made at night against an aircraft factory; and as the Nuffield works was producing Spitfires it represents one of the earliest attempts to maintain pressure by night as well as by day upon Fighter Command and the industry upon which it was based.[21] It is also significant that the attack was almost certainly the work of I/KG 100, one of the few bomber *Gruppen* in the German Air Force which was specially trained for night operations, and one which was to lead many of the heavy night attacks of the autumn and winter of 1940. This unit, which had been based in Norway, had been transferred to Vannes in Brittany shortly before 14 August, and the attack on Castle Bromwich was, so far as we know, the first that it carried out from its new station.

Air Ministry Daily Telegraphic Intelligence Summary.

It was estimated by air intelligence that approximately one hundred enemy aircraft operated against Britain on this night. The operations rooms track charts, however, suggest a figure of between sixty and eighty. This is born out to some extent by the number of HE bombs reported, which was over one hundred and fifty but not more than two hundred. Fighter Command, for its part, made twenty-seven sorties during the night, but no interceptions were made; nor were any claims of destruction made by AA Command. A German airman was captured near Balcombe in Somerset but there was no trace of the aircraft or the rest of the crew. The prisoner was thought to be from I/KG 100, but otherwise nothing was known.

Ibid.

Home Security Daily Appreciation 15 August

21 Captured German documents have revealed that aircraft of *Luftflotte* 3 were being briefed by the beginning of August at the latest to attack aircraft factories, chiefly at night. Between 4 and 23 August the Bristol Co.'s works at Filton was selected for attack on at least eight occasions, but only twice, on the 15th and 23rd, did the Germans succeed in finding and hitting the works. During the same period three attempts were made to bomb the Westland works at Yeovil, two the Rolls Royce works at Crewe, two the works of Leyland Motors in Lancashire and one the Gloster works at Hucclecote. In no case was the attack successful: indeed, only in two of the nine attacks did bombs fall within five miles of the factory, and only once did a German pilot report that he had hit the target. This was the Rolls Royce works at Crewe on the night of the 20th. The pilot was mistaken. In all but two cases the attacks were carried out by single aircraft; the exceptions were those on Hucclecote on the 18/19th and Filton on the 22/23rd, when seven tons and sixteen tons of bombs were aimed at the respective factories.

OPERATIONS, 14 AUGUST

Towards the end of 13 August the intelligence branch of Fighter Command Headquarters estimated that some two thousand German aircraft had operated against this country during the day. This was, of course, an estimate hastily arrived at to meet the demand for a swift summary of the day's operations, and two days later it was reduced by more than a half. But whatever the exact figure it is clear enough that on 14 August the scale of German activity dropped considerably. Only two operations of any magnitude were mounted, neither of which fitted into the pattern which had become familiar. There were also routine weather and shipping reconnaissances, and some reconnaissance before and after the two sets of attacks against land targets.

a. In the Dover area, 1140–1240 hours

The morning was almost over before there were any signs of important enemy movements. Then at 1140 hours, a force of thirty or more was plotted over the Straits of Dover a few miles south-west of Calais. Between 1143 hours and noon three more formations were detected in the Straits each at least twenty aircraft strong. The controller, sent the following squadrons into the air:

> No. 65 Squadron from Manston to patrol the airfield.
>
> No. 615 Squadron from Hawkinge to intercept in the direction of Dover.
>
> No. 151 Squadron (six aircraft only) from Rochford to intercept near the North Foreland.

All three squadrons were airborne by 1155 hours by which time the Germans were obviously about to cross the coast. Accordingly, one more squadron, No. 610, was ordered up from Biggin Hill and directed towards Manston.

At noon one of the German formations crossed the coast at the North Foreland; five minutes later another force crossed just north of Dover and steered towards Manston; and by 1210 hours two more small enemy formations had been plotted in the Straits. The first of the above forces carried out a rapid attack on Manston at 1205 hours. Nine Me 110s from KGr 210 did the bombing and four hangars were either destroyed or damaged. The light AA guns defending the station brought down two of the enemy, but neither No. 65 nor No. 151 Squadron, which were in the vicinity, interfered. No. 65 Squadron, indeed, appears to have been directed away from its patrol of Manston towards Dover just before the station was attacked: one flight returned on hearing over the R/T that Manston was being bombed, but it was too late to intercept. No. 151 Squadron, on the other hand, spotted about fifteen Me 109s at 15,000 feet over Manston; and the squadron attacked them knowing nothing of any other German formation or of the bombing below them. This can quite easily be accounted for by the weather as there was a good deal of cloud (7/10ths) between three thousand and four thousand feet.

At the same time 'A' Flight of No. 610 Squadron fell in with twelve Me 109s over the middle of the Straits, and attacked them. They claimed to have destroyed two Me 109s for certain and damaged others at no cost to themselves, and considering that they were outnumbered by two to one and had to climb to engage the enemy this was no mean achievement. But it is highly probable that the squadron did just what the Germans wished, for this and other German fighter formations were only acting as advance and flank guards for one of the other German forces in the Straits. This force was one of those originally detected at 1140 hours and plotted as 'thirty plus'. Since then it had moved about in the Straits, but at 1220 hours it turned west and made for Folkestone. As it approached, the RDF stations reported that it was much more powerful than had first been imagined, and probably contained one hundred and fifty aircraft. Just before 1230 hours it crossed near Folkestone, where the Observer Corps reported it as one hundred aircraft strong, and flew up the coast towards Dover.

No. 961 Squadron ORB

Its first aggressive action was to detach fighters to attack the balloon barrage at Dover; and about 1230 hours seven of the balloons were shot down. Thenceforward it seems to have done little except carry out a sweep as far inland as Ashford. By 1245 hours it was retiring having done practically no bombing, and certainly none of any importance, for the only incident reported during this period was at St Margarets, where eight HE bombs fell at 1245 hours.

Part of the force, however, may have been detached as the main body approached Folkestone in order to attack the Varne lightship ten miles south-east of the town. 'B' Flight of No. 615 Squadron ('A' Flight having been ordered to patrol Hawkinge) saw the beginning of the attack by nine Ju 87s which were diving down on the ship from 3,000 feet. No German fighters were in the immediate neighbourhood; certainly none interfered with the attack of our pilots who shot down four of the dive-bombers into the sea. But the lightship was hit in the course of these attacks and sank just before one o'clock.

The main enemy force was engaged by two squadrons; No. 160 Squadron as it crossed the coast near Folkestone, and by No. 32 Squadron, which left Biggin Hill for the Dover area at 1227 hours, as it returned. No. 610 Squadron certainly attacked a large force of Ju 87s and fighters but the squadron seems to have been broken up as it climbed to attack, and, in consequence, the pilots' reports vary considerably. One pilot saw only one enemy aircraft, another spoke of approximately three hundred, and another came across fifty Ju 87s. However, virtually every pilot in the squadron engaged the enemy, and four fighters and two bombers were believed to have been destroyed. One of the fighters was reported as a Heinkel 113. No. 32 Squadron's combats were wholly with Me 109s over Dover at 14,000 feet; the enemy fighters were doubtless covering the retirement of the Ju 87s.

The whole operation differed, in some respects, from anything the Germans had previously attempted in this area. Large forces were set in motion, which was nothing new, principally composed of fighters, which was also nothing new, but with a sufficiently large complement of bombers for much more bombing to have taken place than was actually the case. The attack on Manston was carried out by at most a dozen Me 110s, and that on the Varne lightship by an even smaller force. At first sight, therefore, it would appear that the German operation yielded small results in proportion to the total forces employed. And if by it the enemy hoped to bring large fighter forces into the air and inflict losses upon them they had miscalculated. Seven fighter squadrons, all told, were despatched to patrol or to intercept on account of the German moves, but this was not an excessive force. Five of them engaged the enemy at a cost of five aircraft destroyed, two pilots killed and two wounded; and against this the enemy had lost, according to RAF pilots, six bombers and eight fighters, and two Me 110s had been shot down by the Manston gunners. The last two aircraft crashed on land, but otherwise only one Me 109 from I/JG 26 was found.

AI(K) Nos 255, 259/1940.

From 1300–1700 hours the Germans kept forces in the Straits of Dover; but the patrols were never strong, and there was no indication of a new assembly. During this time, however, the enemy made several reconnaissances, of which at least one was doubtless preliminary to the operations that were embarked upon just before 1600 hours. Thus, at 1245 hours a single aircraft crossed the coast near Tangmere and flew towards Kenley; at 1344 hours another aircraft crossed the coast at Beachy Head and flew high over the coast as far as the North Foreland, presumably on a photographic reconnaissance; at 1526 hours an aircraft flew in over St Alban's Head, went inland for some miles and was then lost sight of; and at 1600 and 1619 hours aircraft again came inland over Beachy Head and reconnoitred the country towards Biggin Hill.

b. In the West of England 1530–2100 hours

Towards four o'clock there were indications that the enemy were starting an operation in the central Channel; but just as the operation in the Straits of Dover was peculiar, so the one about to be launched was not of the standard type. For instead of the few, and very large, formations that were usually reported in the central Channel when the *Luftwaffe* were approaching to attack, the RDF stations located a great number of small ones.

Between 1544 and 1605 hours four forces were located off the coast of Normandy as they made for the English coast between St Alban's Head and Selsey Bill. The largest of them was plotted as only nine aircraft, and none were less than fifty miles away, but an attack was clearly impending.

From 1600–1900 hours similar forces continued to be detected as they flew across the Channel and crossed the coast between Selsey Bill and as far west as Start Point; and it is unnecessary to specify each raid. Only one squadron reported a large raid. This was 'B' Flight of No. 87 Squadron which came into contact with a mixed force of about seventy Ju 87s and Me 110s five miles south of Portland at 1730 hours. Otherwise the biggest formation encountered contained only four aircraft.

To counteract this sort of raid the controller at No. 10 Group chiefly sent sections of fighters into the air. Altogether there were eleven combats between our forces and small German formations between 1650 and 2030 hours, representing a high, though indeterminable proportion of interceptions to raids. As a result our pilots claimed to have shot down seven aircraft, all of which were bombers. No less than six were found on the ground, a reflection of the changed location of the battle area from over the sea to overland. Four were from III/KG 27, and one from *Lehr I*, and one from KG 55.[22]

AI1 (K) No. 267/ 1940.

Three aircraft from III/KG 27 had been ordered to carry out an armed reconnaissance as far as Liverpool, and in the course of it two attacked the RAF station at Sealand, near Chester; only one of the three got back to France. Similarly, two out of three aircraft from the same *Gruppe* which set our to bomb Cardiff docks, were shot down.

Ibid.

But in the main the German objectives were airfields – Middle Wallop, Colerne, Cardiff, Kemble, Yeovilton, Andover and Hullavington, as well as Sealand, were all bombed during the evening. Of these the most important, from the point of view of Fighter Command, were Middle Wallop, a sector station, Colerne, a station in No. 41 Group, Maintenance Command and Sealand, where No. 30 Maintenance Unit was located. At Middle Wallop one hangar and certain station offices were destroyed; at Colerne no military damage was caused; and at Sealand, where electricity and water supplies were affected, repairs were made by the following morning, and the maintenance unit put in a full day's work on the 15th. It is true to say, therefore, that the fighter effort was unaffected by these attacks.

In addition, small concentrations of bombs were put down at Bristol, Southampton, Swindon, Newport, and in numerous rural districts. The target in the majority of cases was railway communications, but only at Southampton, where the main line was blocked by debris, was there serious interruption of traffic.

COMMENTARY

It is apparent from these many and widely dispersed incidents – dispersed in time as well as space – that the German operations on this day differed from those that they had previously executed; and it was thought at that time that the German commanders were experimenting with a new method. This is very probably the case. It is now known that seventy one long-range bombers, drawn from I and III/KG 27/55 and I/Lehr 1, were despatched into the west country between 1530 and 2000 hours, and operated in small formations of two and three aircraft against some twenty targets. These aircraft comprised as large a bomber force as the Germans had hitherto mounted in any two of their attacks by large formations. But there was little to show for the new tactics, and on the following day large formations were once more employed.

It is more than likely that the Germans wished to maintain the pressure that they had been exerting continuously since 11 August without running the risk of suffering heavy losses. For they must already have planned the powerful attacks that were to be launched on the 15th. The virtual absence of any activity on the night of the 14th, when the weather was no worse than on many previous nights when the Germans had operated in force, supports the same view.

22 This aircraft crashed near Beachy Head and amongst the crew were the *Geschwader* commander and another senior officer; both were dead. It is almost certain that their objective was the airfields at Netheravon and Upavon (AI1(K) No. 249/1940).

OPERATIONS, 15 AUGUST

The quiet of the night hours continued for some time after dawn on 15 August. Four or five German aircraft were active on reconnaissances between East Anglia and the Bristol Channel, but not until 0900 hours was anything but small formations detected. Then, between 0900 and 1030 hours, there were two reconnaissances to the Dover–Downs area by formations of about six aircraft. Neither was intercepted, though No. 501 Squadron was sent up from Hawkinge, and two likely objects of attack, two convoys off the north shore of the Thames Estuary, were safeguarded.

a. In the Dover area, 1045–1130 hours

These reconnaissances were the prelude to an attack, the first signs of which were received between 1045 and 1110 hours, when a concentration of at least thirty aircraft was plotted as it began to move from the Cap Gris Nez area towards the English coast. Accordingly, in the next quarter of an hour the following British squadrons were ordered into the air:

> No. 501 Squadron from Hawkinge to patrol the airfield at 5,000 feet, and later at 12,000 feet.
>
> No. 54 Squadron from Manston to patrol behind Dover.
>
> No. 56 Squadron from Rochford to patrol Manston.
>
> No. 615 Squadron from Kenley to patrol Dungeness.

The last two squadrons left their airfields at 1120 and 1125 hours respectively and were too late to intercept the Germans, though one flight of No. 615 Squadron had a sharp skirmish with an equal number of Me 109s as the enemy retired. Their movements, therefore, do not concern us.

The Germans came in to the coast just north of Dungeness in two formations at 1129 hours, and then turned north. No. 501 Squadron was correctly informed of their positions and met one formation of twenty or more Ju 87s and about six Me 109s south of Folkestone at 10,000 feet. The squadron wheeled round the enemy formation, got between the Germans and the sun, and attacked the rear echelon of the dive-bombers. Every pilot of 'A' Flight also had some success. Two Hurricanes were lost, one of them being shot down by two Ju 87s which it was attempting to prevent from bombing Hawkinge. This latter airfield, that at Lympne, and Dover itself were the enemy's targets; and the total number of bombs dropped was consistent with the size of the formation reported by No. 501 Squadron.

The second enemy formation was also engaged. No. 54 Squadron had been ordered to patrol behind Dover at 16,000 feet and to engage enemy fighters. Their first action was off Dover where anti-aircraft fire drew their attention to a force of some forty Me 109s. The Germans refused combat, scattered and retired towards France, and only stragglers were engaged. This force may well have been a decoy, for when our squadron had reformed and returned to Dover they found bombing in progress between Dover and Hythe. The enemy force was estimated as forty Ju 87s at about 7,000 feet, escorted by forty He 113 (the pilots were quite certain of the type) at 17,000 feet. The German fighters were circling in fours and fives over their charges, and the Spitfires found great difficulty in breaking these circles and reaching the bombers. Three Ju 87s were thought to have been destroyed, and two Spitfires were lost.

This force put down bombs in Dover, Hythe, Folkestone, and, possibly on Hawkinge. The only serious damage, however, during the whole operation was at Lympne, where services and telecommunications were interrupted, hangars were damaged, the station sick quarters were hit and the oil stores were set on fire. The station was unserviceable for the next two days. Some twelve to eighteen light bombs were also dropped on Hawkinge.

The salient points about the first big operation of the day were thus that the Germans had tried to attack our forward airfields in Kent; that of four British squadrons ordered to intercept two had made effective contact; and that the only serious damage effected was at an airfield of which we made no great use. Five British fighters had been lost, but the Germans had certainly suffered more seriously than this.

The Channel continued to be a scene of some activity during the next two hours, and a number of small formations were plotted. Between 1230 and 1300 hours three squadrons had to be ordered up to insure against the success of a sudden thrust by the enemy. Other aircraft were despatched at about 1320 hours to intercept a reconnaissance aircraft which crossed near Shoreham at 1309 hours and flew over Kenley, Croydon and Northolt towards Stanmore. No attack developed, however, and the next great action of the day was already in progress in an entirely difference area. It is impossible, of course, to say whether these alarums in the south were intended to divert attention from the north. If so, one can only observe that the Germans must have known remarkably little about the air defence organisation.

b. From Tyneside to Flamborough Head, 1230–1345 hours

The attacks which now developed against coastal targets in Yorkshire and Northumberland were the first, and the last, of any strength to be made in that area throughout the Battle of Britain. They deserve, therefore, specially detailed treatment.

The first indication that an attack was projected came at 1208 hours, when a raid of twenty or more aircraft was plotted many miles out to sea, opposite the Firth of Forth. Twenty minutes later a second formation, which had risen to ten or more aircraft by 1236 hours, was also plotted: by this time, too, a third, though smaller formation (of three or more aircraft) was also in evidence. These three raids, pursuing a south-westerly course, all made for the same area on the English coast – that between Acklington and Blyth above Tynemouth – and such of the enemy aircraft as reached it crossed at the same time, a minute or so before 1300 hours. Meanwhile, a different threat developed, for at 1239 hours six or more aircraft (but later plotted as thirty or more) were detected as they made for the coastline nearly a hundred miles south, just below Scarborough. This, in fact, was crossed by enemy aircraft at 1317 hours.

To meet the earlier threat, the following squadrons were ordered up:

> No. 72 Squadron from Acklington at 1215 hours to investigate raid approaching Farne Island.
>
> No. 605 Squadron from Drem at 1218 hours to patrol Acklington–Tyneside.
>
> No. 41 Squadron from Catterick at 1235 hours: the orders are not ascertainable.
>
> No. 79 Squadron from Acklington at 1242 hours to patrol Farne Island.
>
> No. 607 Squadron from Usworth at 1307 hours: the orders are not ascertainable.

No. 72 Squadron at 1245 hours was the first to fall in with the enemy, who were apparently sighted thirty miles east of the Farne Islands, flying due west. The formation was considerably greater than the RDF plots of thirty-three or more aircraft, for the squadron reports tell of approximately one hundred bombers (He 111s). The bombers were reported to be spread over a wide front of ten vics abreast, with three lines of vics astern: Me 110s followed in two waves, three quarters of a mile apart, each wave consisting of thirty six aircraft in vics of six. The bombers were at 18,000 feet, the Me 110s at 19,000 feet and the Spitfires, who were a little to the south, at 22,000 feet. Obviously one squadron, though it might score successes, could not drive back so formidable a force. The Spitfires for the most part attacked the bombers from above and astern, but four of them engaged the Me 110s. They reported that the enemy were apparently taken completely by surprise: some jettisoned their bombs and escaped in cloud, and several were shot down. Some of the Me 110s formed tight circles as evasive tactics, but it was noticed that these aircraft were remarkably impotent. Several of our pilots commented on the absence of return fire, and their view-point may be summed up in the words of one pilot who was engaged with six or seven Me 110s: 'Not once during the engagement did I observe an Me 110 put itself in a position for its rear gunner to fire, nor was any return fire experienced from them. I consider, therefore, that the rear gunner had been sacrificed for an overload of petrol (carried in the bulbous tanks underneath the fuselage?) to obtain the necessary range. Once engaged, the Me 110s left the bombers to their own devices'. Not one of the Spitfires was hit during the engagement.

Combat Report, F/O. Elsdon, No. 72 Squadron

The main enemy force naturally escaped the attentions of No. 72 Squadron, and part now proceeded on a north-westerly, part on a south-westerly course. According to the reports of No. 72 Squadron, they crossed the coast in arrowhead formations of thirty or forty aircraft, but the Me 110s turned back east, and made no attempt to cross the coast at all.

The next squadron to make contact was No. 79 which at 1300 hours intercepted a formation of some sixty bombers and several Me 110s approaching the coast near the Fighter Command sector station at Acklington. This was presumably one part of the force which had been unaffected by No. 72 Squadron's attack. No. 79 Squadron now attacked the Me 110s, which were as yet a few miles from the coast. As a result of these attacks the squadron became split up, but re-formed over Blyth, and were ordered to patrol Usworth at 10,000 feet. They then saw sixty bombers and some Me 110s flying in the direction of Newcastle. They attacked a straggling bomber and the fighters, and noticed that the latter appeared timid, turning away before they reached the coast.

At about the same time (1307 hours onwards), No. 41 Squadron became engaged, but in an area a little further to the south, and mainly overland, for the combat was fought near Bishop Auckland, Durham and Seaham Harbour. They described a massed arrowhead formation of fifty bombers at 18,000 feet followed by a second arrowhead of forty Me 110, a little astern and above. The escort fighters (which were noted as carrying a petrol tank beneath the fuselage) maintained formation when attacked, and the combat finished as a dog-fight with the escort and a few stragglers from the bombers. It is difficult to state whether this formation was that also engaged by No. 79 Squadron, but the similarity in composition suggests that this was so.

No. 607 Squadron was also engaged in the Seaham area from 1315 hours on. They told of a large vic of forty bombers, followed by another vic of about twenty. The Hurricanes attacked in formation, and then individually, on the enemy's rear, claiming large successes for no loss of their own. They noted that such bombing as they saw was from above cloud-level, and apparently indiscriminate – so much so that several pilots had the impression that the enemy was not bombing definite objectives, but was simply testing the strength of opposition.

Finally, part of No. 605 Squadron was also engaged, from 1315 hours onwards. 'B' Flight took off at a slightly different time from 'A' Flight and patrolled north and south of Newcastle. Receiving no further order, 'B' leader kept his flight near to Newcastle, as the most vulnerable point, and at 1310 hours two formations of bombers were seen approaching the town from the south-east. The Hurricanes made a concerted attack on the rear bombers of the first formation, which was described as sixty to seventy strong, and then individual attacks on the second formation, of some twenty aircraft. They considered that they had inflicted heavy damage, at no cost to themselves. The enemy formations engaged were probably those also encountered by No. 607 Squadron.

Piecing together the information thus far, it seems that the large force, estimated at one hundred bombers and seventy fighters, seen by the first squadron (No. 72) out beyond the Farne Islands, had become split into two. Part had then crossed the coast north of the Tyne, being engaged by two squadrons; and the German fighters had turned, or been driven back. The other part, apparently of bombers only, had held a more southerly course, and approached the Tyne from the south-east, being also engaged by two squadrons. The total of enemy aircraft employed in the whole operation was estimated by No. 13 Group as one hundred and thirty to one hundred and forty – rather less than the original estimate of No. 72 Squadron, but sufficiently close where such large numbers are concerned.

It will be remembered that while all this was occurring on the Tyneside area and the Durham coast, a separate attack had been launched a hundred miles further south, crossing the Yorkshire coast some miles below Scarborough at 1317 hours. This, of course, was obviously closely allied with the Tyneside attack, not only in timing, but because part of the new force apparently fanned out north, when the coast was crossed, and made for Tees, Wear and Tyneside. Other elements, however, turned south, and it was these which delivered a sharp attack against Driffield aerodrome. To meet the whole force approaching the Yorkshire coast, the following squadrons were called up:

> No. 616 Squadron from Leconfield at 1300 hours to patrol Hornsea at 2,000 feet.
>
> No. 264 Squadron from Kirton-in-Lindsey at 1305 hours to patrol convoy in the Humber estuary.
>
> No. 73 Squadron from Church Fenton at 1306 hours: 'A' Flight to patrol convoy 'Agent', and 'B' Flight to patrol the airfield.
>
> No. 219 Squadron from Catterick at 1310 hours: the orders are not ascertainable.

No. 616 Squadron was the first to be engaged. While patrolling Hornsea it was directed north and over Flamboro' Head sighted several enemy aircraft, some miles out to sea, and coming in towards the coast. The squadron Operations Record Book also speaks of 'several Me 110s', but there is no mention of these in the various combat reports. The enemy aircraft were apparently not in close formation, for some were flying abreast, some straggling. When attacked they tried to dive into clouds. It seems that the rear-gunner was killed in more than one aircraft by the astern attacks of the Spitfires, for very little return fire was experienced. The action took place some ten miles out to sea, beginning at 1315 hours, and the squadron claimed large successes. Nevertheless, the bulk of the enemy proceeded and, as mentioned above, crossed the coast a few moments afterwards.

Of the other British squadrons ordered up, No. 73 ('A' Flight) was next engaged. When near Hornsea on its duty of convoy patrol, it was diverted to the north and encountered fifty Ju 88s. This was the same force which No. 616 Squadron had just encountered, for the flight came up with the enemy a few miles east of Flamboro' and fought them as they proceeded inland. The Hurricanes got well into the bombers and claimed considerable destruction, but of course were unable to prevent the main part going on and crossing the coast. 'B' Flight, which had been ordered to patrol Church Fenton, was not engaged, nor were the Defiants of No. 264 Squadron, patrolling the convoy at the Humber mouth.

There remained the Blenheims of No. 219 Squadron. These also fell in with the enemy bombers, now described as about forty in number. For the most part they had long and uneventful chases inland, over the coast, and over a hundred miles out again to sea. One Blenheim reckoned to have chased a Ju 88 for 160 miles, never getting closer than 600 yards. Naturally they had not the same chance of inflicting casualties as the Hurricanes or Spitfires, and this squadron was the only one engaged which made no claim of opponents positively destroyed.

Summing up this section of the operation, it will be seen that, of the four squadrons ordered up, two squadrons and one flight made interceptions, but that one of these squadrons was not equipped with aircraft capable of dealing effectively with the German bombers. All the interceptions took place at sea, but our forces were unable to stop the bulk of the enemy crossing the coast.

It now remains to see what damage was inflicted by the raiding forces, first in the Tyneside–Wearside area, and secondly in that area of Yorkshire approached so soon afterwards. In the first area, it may be stated that the military damage was nil, and the industrial damage insignificant. Bombs at Tynemouth nearly all fell into the sea, while the villages round Bishop Auckland, Durham and Seaham Harbour received what must have been the result of extremely inaccurate aiming. The principal damage was at Sunderland, where twenty-four houses were destroyed, and many made uninhabitable. Industrial objectives, however, were not hit at all. No bombs seem to have fallen on Newcastle nor were the airfields of Northumberland and Durham attacked.

Any figures of enemy losses must necessarily be uncertain, but the claims of the British pilots concerned were very large, amounting to over thirty aircraft. In addition to this the Tees guns claimed one victim, the Tyne guns five. Not one of the five squadrons intercepting in this area lost an aircraft, though four were damaged, and two pilots injured. Such were the results of an operation in which the enemy aircraft employed were reckoned to number one hundred and fifty.

Rather better results could be shown by the enemy in the more southerly attack, for here at least, two military objectives were hit. The first was possibly an accident, since some bombs fell near an ammunition dump at Burton Agnes, six miles from Bridlington. Some of the ammunition was ignited, and some army vehicles destroyed. The second was a more serious affair, for at 1330 hours and for some moments afterwards, Driffield was bombed from 500 feet by forces estimated at seventeen to thirty Ju 88s. Over one hundred bombs were dropped and machine-gun attacks were also made. Fires were started, and extensive damage caused to three blocks of buildings (including the AA HQ and the officers' mess) and to four hangars. Seven Whitleys and one Magister were destroyed, and five more Whitleys damaged, though another account mentions ten aircraft destroyed by bombs and fire. Six or seven RAF personnel were killed, and some twenty injured. Apart from this success the German attack had very little to show beyond the usual array of results – houses damaged (in Bridlington), damage to telephone and telegraph wires, bombs on farms, and so on. The British aircraft which were engaged with these forces reported no losses: they claimed that the enemy suffered at least fifteen.

If then, the two series of attacks are considered as parts of the same operation, and a balance sheet is drawn up, the extraordinary paucity of Germans results, with the single exception of the attack on Driffield, is the most prominent feature. Two hundred enemy aircraft,[23] attacking in synchronised waves at

23 The figure of two hundred was the RDF estimate. The Germans probably used most of KG 30, which was normally stationed in the Aalborg area, perhaps two *Gruppen* from KG 26 in the Stavanger area, and, also from Stavanger, the whole of I/ZG 76. Of the seven aircraft that crashed on land during the operation, two Me 110s were from different *Staffeln* of I/ZG 76, three Ju 88s were from different *Gruppen* of KG 30, and two Heinkels were from I and III/KG 26. All this evidence tallies with what we know of the order of battle of the German Air Force, and implies that between one hundred and twenty and one hundred and seventy German aircraft were despatched.

points a hundred miles or so apart, had been able to inflict no damage worth mentioning beyond the destruction of some aerodrome buildings, and a few aircraft on the ground. Seven and a half British squadrons had met them without any loss on our side, and with considerable loss to the Germans: and though the bulk of the bombers had penetrated inland they had been, for the most part, too harried to bomb accurately whatever they were trying to bomb.

What the Germans hoped for by this operation is not precisely known; and until such time as reliable information becomes available we can rest satisfied with the view of Air Chief Marshal Dowding: 'the sustained resistance which they were meeting in South-East England probably led them to believe that Fighter Squadrons had been withdrawn, wholly or in part, from the North in order to meet the attack ... the contrary was soon apparent, and the bombers received such a drubbing that the experiment was not repeated'. It can be added that, judging from the behaviour of the Me 110s, the operation took place at the very extremity of their effective range; from which it followed that, even if the Germans repeated the experiment, our squadrons would be able to devote themselves to destroying what was, after all, the main strength of the *Luftwaffe*, its bombers and bomber crews.

Despatch para. 194 and 195.

One implication of the operation bears remarking. The exceptionally heavy losses of the enemy compared to the infinitesimal ones of the defenders are a justification of the confidence felt by Air Chief Marshal Dowding early in the war when the possibility of attacks by escorted bombers was remote. They also underline the new perils springing from the collapse in Europe which allowed strong German fighter forces to penetrate much of southern England.

c. *In the Dover area and Thames Estuary, 1430–1615 hours*

By 1430 hours the last German aircraft had disappeared from the scene of the attacks in the north, but by that time the third great operation of the day was beginning in the south east.

Between 1414 and 1439 hours the following enemy formations were plotted over or near the Dover Straits:

1414 hours	Nine or more aircraft, becoming thirty or more in the Calais area.
1414 hours	Six or more, becoming fifteen or more near St Omer, and fifty or more as it approached Lympne just before 1530 hours.
1428 hours	Twenty or more north of St Omer, becoming one hundred or more in the Straits, and fifty or more when it crossed the coast at Felixstowe at 1509 hours.
1431 hours	Three or more, becoming thirty or more at 1500 hours when it was approaching the coast near Orfordness.
1439 hours	Three or more and eventually fifty or more when it crossed the coast at Deal at 1508 hours.

To counteract the German movements the controller at No. 11 Group sent no forces into the air until 1430 hours, with the exception of nine aircraft of No. 1 Squadron which left North Weald at 1414 hours to patrol Clacton. And by 1430 hours there was no evidence that any other area than Dover was threatened. Consequently four squadrons, Nos 32, 266, 64 and 151, were sent up between 1430 and 1438 hours to patrol between Manston and Hawkinge. But by 1450 hours two enemy formations were moving across the outer Thames Estuary on a north-westerly course, and orders were given for the protection of the northern shore. Thus, of the eight squadrons that sent forces into the air in the next twenty-five minutes six were directed towards the coasts of Essex and Suffolk. The other two, No. 111 from Croydon and No. 501 from Gravesend, were sent to Beachy Head and Dover respectively. Altogether, the controller called on detachments from thirteen squadrons, which put up forces equivalent to ten and a half full squadrons. If the Germans were as strong as the RDF stations estimated a trial of strength was certainly in prospect.

The sequence of events was now as follows. Two forces of fifty or more enemy aircraft were, as the plots had indicated, moving north across the Thames Estuary, and were (it proved) about to cross the east coast, one near Felixstowe at 1509 hours and the other at Orfordness at much the same time. No. 1 Squadron, patrolling Clacton at 10,000 feet was directed towards the latter force. The Hurricanes were going into line astern to attack some twenty Me 109s when they were themselves attacked and split up by Me 110s. They were then ordered to Harwich, which was reported (wrongly, it would appear) as being bombed, but there is no indication that the Hurricanes fell in with the raiding force. They did, however, came up with the enemy over Martlesham Heath aerodrome, which was being bombed at the time, and some of them came into action, without, however, effectively interfering with the bombing.

The other squadrons ordered to intercept this raid were no more fortunate, for squadrons Nos 19 and 66, and the six Hurricanes of No. 242, all failed to make any contact. It is not possible to ascertain exactly why this was so, but as the aircraft did not take off till 1500 hours, from Duxford and Coltishall some fifty miles away from Martlesham Heath, and as the coast was crossed at about 1510 hours, it is obvious that the fighters had very little time in hand. A few aircraft of No. 17 Squadron, however, were just in time to see their station bombed, and their account throws some light on the whole operation. At 1445 hours six aircraft of No. 17 Squadron were ordered to take off and patrol Martlesham at 3,000 feet, others of the squadron being already employed on convoy duty. One of the sections ordered up, however, was at 30 minutes' notice, and thus only four aircraft actually managed to take off within five minutes, one more becoming airborne some ten minutes later. One of the four aircraft returned, as the pilot found himself unable to keep up with the others, who had apparently received orders to fly out to sea to intercept the approaching enemy. On his way back he saw twenty to thirty Me 109s, and, as a result, the other aircraft, by now twenty miles out to sea, were ordered to intercept this force. They failed and were ordered back to Martlesham where they found Ju 87s and Me 110s dive-bombing the airfield. In the words of some personnel of the searchlight posts 'the first fighter arrived as the last bomber departed'. From this it seems clear that the fighters did not receive orders that would have made interception possible before the bombing of Martlesham.

Further squadrons had, of course, been charged with the duty of intercepting the other enemy formation plotted in to the east coast, that which crossed near Felixstowe and Harwich. These were squadrons No. 32, 266 and 54. The two latter squadrons made no contact. Nos 32 Squadron saw several Me 109s off Harwich, but there is no account of any engagement. Thus, taking the two raids together, of the six British squadrons and two flights ordered to intercept, only one (or possibly two) squadrons and one flight made contact and that for the most part after an important objective had been bombed.

Meanwhile, it will be remembered that other enemy forces were approaching the south-east corner of the country, and that one of these was plotted in over Deal at almost exactly the same moment that the raids were crossing at Felixstowe, Harwich and Orfordness. To meet this threat to the south-east was the special task of squadrons Nos 64, 151, 111 and 501. No. 64 Squadron was first engaged just before 1500 hours with twenty Me 109s which were seen crossing the Straits from south to north near Deal. Both Spitfires and Me 109s were at 22,000 feet but a second group of thirty Me 109s in stepped up vics of five was then seen slightly above the Spitfires. No. 64 Squadron manoeuvred to attack from the sun, and a dog fight followed, in which individual machines were chased to the French coast, and in which both sides seem to have lost two or three aircraft. The combat against large odds could obviously not prevent the bulk of the enemy fighters proceeding on their way and we know that the coast was crossed at Deal at 1508 hours.

Nine aircraft of No. 151 Squadron, when patrolling Deal at 20,000 feet, received an order to descend to 15,000 feet and patrol Dover. They were proceeding to do this when they were attacked at 18,000 feet by Me 109s which were acting as advanced guard to a bomber formation. The latter, protected closely by fighters, approached lower down. The intelligence officer at North Weald wrote of this in his report: 'It is apparent that this tactic on the part of the enemy was successful, since only Me 109s were engaged by our fighters during the whole engagement'. The squadron estimated that, in all, they saw a hundred enemy aircraft. It is difficult to state the exact time at which the squadron was first attacked: combat reports speak of 1530–40 hours, but these relate to claims made against aircraft chased back to France. We know from the RDF plots, however, that fifty or more German aircraft were approaching Lympne at 1526 hours; and this may well have been the formation which No. 151 Squadron saw, but were unable to engage. The same force was probably responsible for the bombing of Folkestone, which took place at 1532 hours.

The next squadron to take up the fight was No. 111, which left Croydon for Beachy Head at 1454 hours, was directed into the Dover area, and was there engaged with enemy forces from 1530 hours onwards. The squadron became split up: two sections fought from Dover north-westwards towards Rochester and the Thames Estuary, attacking a formation of twenty-four Do 215s; one section attacked isolated Do 215s near Westgate; and one section followed Me 109s (variously given as six and sixty) in the direction of

London. The pilots claimed to have destroyed at least two or three of the Dorniers.[24]

There remained the seven Hurricanes of No. 501 Squadron, which did not take off from Gravesend until 1515 hours, two more aircraft following later but being unable to find the rest of the squadron. They were directed to intercept behind Dover, first at 8,000 feet then at 10,000 feet. They were then told by the controller that the enemy was at 3,000–5,000 feet and they consequently dived down over Dover. As they did this, they saw enemy aircraft above them at 15,000 feet and were then aware of what they estimated to be one hundred and fifty Dorniers near Dungeness, flying north-west to cross the coast near Folkestone. The Hurricanes, now at 4,000 feet, consequently climbed until they were a thousand feet above the enemy, and then at about 1530 hours delivered a beam attack on the second wave of bombers. They claimed that they broke the enemy formation, and that they were able to pursue detached aircraft into the Thames Estuary, and to the Maidstone–Chatham area.

From these reports it seems clear that a least two formations crossed the south-east coast, one at 1508 hours, and one at about 1530 hours; and that the three and a half British squadrons were not able to intercept them very successfully. Indeed, the British fighters were very heavily outnumbered wherever they engaged. It will therefore, be of interest to see what damage the Germans succeeded in inflicting, both in the case of these raids which crossed the south-east coast, and in the case of the other raids previously detailed which crossed the coast north of the estuary at approximately the same time.

As for the latter, no significant damage appears to have been inflicted beyond that to Martlesham Heath aerodrome. There are hints in various subsidiary documents that the convoy 'Sollo' off that section of the coast, was attacked, and that Harwich was bombed, but there is neither confirmation nor detail of this in the appropriate reports. At Martlesham Heath, which was apparently attacked in two waves, first at 1515 and then at 1526 hours, two hangars, the officers' mess, and some aircraft were damaged, and telephonic communication very briefly interrupted. Most of this damage was caused by a bomb hitting a bombed-up Battle.

On the other hand, the raids that crossed the south-east coast were more successful. At Folkestone, Sandgate and thereabouts the damage to residential property was serious, but the military or industrial damage apparently nil. A few small bombs fell on the surface of Hawkinge aerodrome without causing serious damage. Bombs also seem to have fallen fairly profusely in rural areas in Kent to no effect, and those which fell at Eastchurch damaged the railway more than the aerodrome. Damage to the surface of this apparently took about two days to repair. At Rochester, however, there was important damage. Between 1540 and 1558 hours dive-bombing by some twenty aircraft succeeded in hitting two aircraft works – Pobjoy's, one-third of which, it was estimated, would be out of production, and Short's, which was temporarily put out of action. In the latter case, where both plant and aircraft under construction were destroyed, it was thought that production would be seriously affected for some time.

24 The squadron losses are variously given: in the ORB as nil; in the patrol report as three damaged, of which two only slightly; in No. 11 Group report to Fighter Command as two lost; in Fighter Command report to Air Ministry as three lost.

Taking both sets of raids – east coast and south-east coast – together, it thus appears that the German operation inflicted little important damage beyond that to the aircraft industry in Rochester. Apparently at least a hundred aircraft were employed in the east coast raids, and something similar for those in the south-east. Thus, an operation which involved some two hundred enemy aircraft, and which penetrated the coastline in force at about four points, could show little result beyond the damage to two aircraft factories, which was, however, admittedly serious. But if the results of the German attacks were hardly proportionate to the effort involved much the same could be said of the defence. The British squadrons had not been fortunate in the orders they received, and few interceptions had been made. Nor had the actual fighting been to their advantage. Nine aircraft had been lost, seven pilots were killed or missing and a further three had been wounded. Against this the Germans were believed to have lost five fighters and three bombers for certain, and possibly two more bombers. The wreckage of two Do 17s from II/KG 3 and one Me 109 from II/JG 51 was found after the battle.

d. Portland–Portsmouth area: 1700–1830 hours

By 1600 hours the Straits of Dover were fairly clear of enemy aircraft, and they remained so for the next two hours. There was, indeed, a respite for the whole country until 1700 hours, when signs were received of an attack in a part of the country which the day's activity had hitherto left undisturbed, the coasts of Hampshire and Dorset. Between 1700 and 1720 hours the RDF stations detected no less than seven strong enemy formations, containing in all two hundred to three hundred aircraft, as they approached the south coast. Approximately half seemed to be making for the Portland area, and the others for the coast between the Needles and Selsey Bill. Most of those aircraft crossed the coast between 1720 and 1740 hours, a feature which should be borne in mind when studying the defensive dispositions taken by the controllers.

The total fighter force despatched was the largest that Fighter Command had yet put into the air to meet a single enemy operation; and it consisted of the following squadrons:

Time of Take-off	*Squadron*	*Orders*
		(where known)
1700	No. 152 Sqdn. (Warmwell)	Intercept raid approaching Portland.
1705 hours	No. 234 Sqdn. (Middle Wallop)	Patrol Swanage,15,000 feet.
1705 hours	No. 601 Sqdn. (Tangmere)	Patrol base, then Tangmere–Selsey.
1705 hours	No. 111 Sqdn. (Croydon)	Patrol Shoreham, 15,000 feet.
1708 hours	No. 43 Sqdn. (Tangmere)	Patrol base, then intercept raid approaching Isle of Wight.

Time of Take-off	*Squadron*	*Orders*
1715 hours	No. 213 Sqdn. (Exeter)	Intercept raid approaching Portland.
1720 hours	No. 249 Sqdn. (Middle Wallop)	One section patrol Ringwood area.
1720	No. 32 Sqdn. (Biggin Hill)	Patrol Horsham, 12,000 ft. then intercept raid off Selsey Bill.
1725 hours	No. 501 Sqdn. (Gravesend)	Patrol Gravesend–south coast.
1725 hours	No. 87 Sqdn. (Exeter)	Intercept raid approaching Portland.
1735 hours	No. 609 Sqdn. (Middle Wallop)	Took-off on warning of approaching aircraft.
1735 hours	No. 604 Sqdn. (Middle Wallop)	Not ascertainable, but probably as for No. 609 Sqdn. above.
1737 hours	No. 1 Sqdn. (Northolt)	Patrol Guildford, then vectored.
1750 hours	No. 602 Sqdn. (Westhampnett)	Patrol behind Tangmere.

Altogether, about one hundred and fifty British aircraft were put up to intercept the various raids which threatened the south coast and its hinterland. Detachments from eight squadrons actually left the ground before the first enemy formation crossed the coast.

The great air battles that resulted were fought principally in two areas – near Portland, and near Portsmouth. Three or four raids totalling over a hundred aircraft, had been plotted as they approached Portland. Nine Spitfires of No. 152 Squadron first came into action with them. Taking off from Warmwell at 1700 hours our pilots had ample time to intercept before the enemy crossed the coast. At 1720 hours they saw a formation of about thirty Ju 87s some five miles south of Portland, at 12,000 feet with an escort of nearly a hundred fighters (in their estimate) stepped up at 14,000 feet (Me 110s) and 16,000 feet (Me 109s). The Spitfires dived out of the sun to attack the dive-bombers, and then climbed to engage the first layer of fighters (Me 110s). One Spitfire was lost (with the pilot saved) and the squadron claimed to have destroyed three fighters and two dive-bombers. Against odds of over ten to one, however, the squadron could hardly break up the enemy formations.

But meanwhile the Hurricanes of No. 213 Squadron had arrived and encountered the same enemy formation. It was by far the squadron's largest combat up to that date, but it was principally with the enemy fighters, for the bombers disappeared 'as soon as the fight started'. Many of the fighters apparently went into a great 'cylindrical wall' which 'it was almost impossible to attack without placing oneself in a vulnerable position'. Some of the dive-bombers were apparently destroyed, but these were stragglers found low-down near the sea. The squadron, which lost one aircraft, put in extremely large claims of successes (including fourteen Me 110s and five Ju 87s definitely destroyed); and the last pilot to take off, who arrived after the combat had started, reported 'burning aircraft falling into the sea south of Portland'.

No. 87 Squadron (also from Exeter) arrived on the scene apparently a little later, but it was obviously with the same enemy formations that they were engaged. They, too, put in much heavier claims than usual – nine fighters and four dive-bombers at a cost of two Hurricanes and one pilot.

The other main area of interception was in the Spithead–Portsmouth –Thorney Island district. Two or three plots suggesting that upwards of two hundred aircraft were approaching this area had appeared, and No. 43 Squadron, from Tangmere, was possibly the first to be engaged. They were patrolling the Isle of Wight when they were told that enemy aircraft were approaching Thorney Island from the south at 14,000 feet. The enemy (estimated at one hundred to two hundred in number) proved to be rather higher, and only one section was able to engage (at 1730 hours) the main body of Ju 88s, above whom were attendant fighters. The Hurricanes lost no aircraft, and claimed one or two successes.

No. 111 Squadron was also engaged with the same force, having been apparently directed to the south-east of Thorney Island from Shoreham. At 15,000 feet they intercepted what they estimated to be a hundred Ju 88s, Me 110s and Me 109s. Some of the Hurricanes apparently held off the fighters, while most of the squadron went for the bombers. The squadron lost one aircraft, but claimed that 'the enemy formation was broken up and diverted'.

No. 32 Squadron (which had taken off from Biggin Hill at 1720 hours) then came up, for at 1745 hours it saw some thirty Ju 88s escorted by about thirty Me 109s crossing the coast near Portsmouth. It engaged the rear Ju 88s, the Me 109s circling above and dropping out one by one to attack the Hurricanes. The squadron's own losses were variously reported as nil and one aircraft: it claimed to have destroyed two or three of the bombers.

At about the same time No. 601 Squadron also met a detachment of the enemy formation, for at 1740 hours it sighted twelve Ju 88s passing towards Portsmouth, with their escort fighters being engaged out to sea. The squadron claimed to have split up the enemy formation by attacks which they made over Bishop's Waltham, but some of the bombers continued inland in the direction of Winchester. Two Hurricanes were lost in the attacks, and the pilots considered that they had destroyed at least twice that number of the enemy.

In addition to these main combats near Portland and Portsmouth, there were subsidiary combats inland. No. 249 Squadron, part of which was patrolling the Ringwood area sighted about forty Ju 88s and Me 110s, and attacked the rear section of the fighters. This was probably a third force which had been plotted as it crossed the coast across Poole Bay. The squadron's own losses are given in most documents as nil, though by Fighter Command as four: they claimed three Me 110s destroyed.

The tail end of the attack was delivered by No. 234 Squadron and No. 609 Squadron. These aircraft were at Middle Wallop, when No. 234 Squadron was ordered to patrol Swanage. This they did for approximately an hour, without seeing enemy aircraft. No. 609 Squadron, or rather eight aircraft of it, took off half an hour later (at 1735 hours) on warning of about fifty Ju 88s and Me 110s approaching the aerodrome. Some of the Spitfires only got into the air as bombs were falling on the station. The Germans seem to have been operating on the same R/T frequency, and communication between pilots and the sector controller was jammed on this account. But some of them managed to attack the enemy, and claimed to have shot down four Me 110s and one Ju 88.

It was probably this same enemy force, now on its return journey, which was fallen in with by No. 234 Squadron, for they saw about fifty bombers and fighters going south-west beyond Swanage. On this occasion the Me 110s protected the bombers successfully. Three Me 110s were destroyed, but four Spitfires were shot down.

Of the remaining British squadrons in the air, No. 501 was not engaged because it maintained its patrol from Gravesend, and was eventually in contact with the next big German operation in that area. No. 604 Squadron (Blenheims), which took off on warning of aircraft approaching Middle Wallop, claimed a victim for one loss on its own part. Only the Hurricanes of No. 1 Squadron and the Spitfires of No. 602 Squadron were unsuccessful in intercepting, at some stage or other, the series of German attacks which has just been described.

It will be seen that most of the interceptions were successful in that they occurred before the coast was crossed, in the Portland and Portsmouth areas. Nevertheless it is apparent that if the enemy forces were indeed so large, very great numbers of aircraft must still have been able to shake off the fighters' attentions, and proceed on their mission. The bombing attacks which resulted were, however, as usual, insignificant. One report speaks of Portsmouth being 'heavily bombed', but the Home Security Summary fails to mention a single bomb having fallen there. Indeed, once again the only significant damage was to an aerodrome, for Middle Wallop received about twenty-eight bombs, which damaged two hangars and five aircraft, and destroyed one more aircraft. Bombs also fell near the Worthy Down naval aerodrome, but failed to achieve any important result. This, then, with a few odd bombs here and there, particularly at Portland, where the W/T station was hit, was the result of an operation in which two or three hundred German aircraft were said to have been employed. The deductions which follow are either that the RAF's pilots won a major victory by turning back the bulk of such forces, or that the German fighters were at enormous strength compared with the bombers, or that the enemy numbers were exaggerated. It is probable that there is truth in each of the contentions. Over the whole operation a total of between thirteen British fighters and six pilots were lost, while RAF claims amounted to over sixty of the enemy destroyed, the majority being fighters. Most of the fighting took place over the sea and only eleven German aircraft crashed on land. The wreckage implied that most of Lehr 1 and ZGs 1 and 76 took part in the operation.[25]

25 The picture of the operation can be filled in to some extent from a captured German map which displays diagrammatically what bomber forces were employed and what targets were reported to have been bombed. The most westerly of the German formations contained forty-seven Ju 87s from I/St KG 1 and II/St KG 2, and had 'military installations' at Portland as its objective. The force which attacked Middle Wallop consisted of twelve Ju 88s from I/Lehr 1. This is quite beyond doubt, yet according to the map the German pilots reported that they had attacked Andover, which lies five miles north-east of Middle Wallop, and had destroyed some hangars there. A third force was employed – the one engaged over the Solent and towards Winchester – the bomber component of which consisted of fifteen Ju 88s from II/Lehr 1. It was clearly disorganised by the attacks of our fighters; seven Ju 88s were shot down and only three succeeded in reaching their target, which was the Fleet Air Arm station at Worthy Down. What fighter forces were employed by the Germans is not known.

e. Against West Malling and Croydon, 1800–1900 hours

The attacks against the south coast were barely over when large forces were again plotted on the French side of the Straits of Dover. The first indications were received at 1753 hours, and new plots continued to come in for the next twenty minutes; and by 1815 hours the position was that some sixty or seventy aircraft were approaching between Dover and Dungeness. Accordingly, between 1818 and 1828 hours the following squadrons were ordered up:

> No. 151 Squadron from Rochford to patrol Manston; later diverted to Dover.
>
> No. 266 Squadron from Manston to patrol it; also diverted to Dover.
>
> No. 615 Squadron from Kenley to patrol Hawkinge.
>
> No. 54 Squadron from Hornchurch to patrol Ashford.

The enemy forces were plotted in to the Folkestone area just after 1830 hours and No. 266 Squadron was early engaged. The eight Spitfires sighted two waves of bombers escorted above by about twelve Me 109s, south-east of Dover, and dived to attack. They were apparently successful in splitting off some bombers, for some of the pilots were afterwards engaged with single Ju 88s. One Spitfire was lost, and some successes claimed. No. 501 Squadron, which had been on patrol from Gravesend for over an hour, also sighted a formation near the coast, at Dungeness. The description of this, however, bears little resemblance to that engaged by No. 266 Squadron; for No. 501 Squadron reported 'two hundred' (!) enemy aircraft, Dorniers, Me 109s and Me 110s. The Hurricanes came up with this force (or some of it), near Gatwick, and attacked a couple of straggling bombers. Me 109s, however, intervened, and the Hurricanes, now short of petrol, had to break off the engagement.

No. 151 Squadron also intercepted enemy forces in the Dover, Folkestone area, but (if the combat reports are accurate) at a later time – 1900 hours. the enemy consisted, moreover, entirely of fighters. If this time of combat is accurate it is very likely that the enemy fighters were covering the retirement of the forces that had penetrated inland. Three of the Hurricanes were destroyed, for no positive success claimed on their part.

Other squadrons engaged the enemy further inland. No. 54 Squadron, after patrolling Ashford, intercepted at Maidstone. It reported two formations, totalling about forty bombers and twenty fighters, some of which were He 113s. The Spitfires attacked the bombers, and though the fighters intervened, the squadron claimed that eventually the enemy turned about and headed back towards the coast. One Spitfires was lost, and possibly one or two of the enemy. A flight of Spitfires of No. 610 Squadron, which had taken off from Biggin Hill on news of the enemy's approach, also intercepted over Maidstone at about 1850 hours. Their version was of fifty bombers escorted by many fighters. The Spitfires reported thus: 'We dived out of the sun at Dorniers, when several Me 109s came down on us.' Their claims of damage inflicted related entirely to Me 109s.

Finally, two more squadrons were engaged at Croydon, which was bombed by the enemy at about 1905 hours. No. 32 Squadron, from Biggin Hill, reported a combat at 1900 hours with twelve to twenty Do 17s and some Me 109s; for no loss to themselves, they claimed the destruction of four bombers and four fighters. No. 111 Squadron, which took off from Croydon on receipt of the warning at 1850 hours, climbed to 5,000 feet and then saw enemy aircraft diving to attack the aerodrome. One section of the Hurricanes attacked from head-on at the bottom of the enemy dive, and the squadron reported that the enemy subsequently formed a defensive circle. In their version, the enemy bombers were Me 110 Jaguars, twelve to fifteen in number, with an escort of Me 109s and He 113s. They claimed several successes against the fighters.[26]

Of the remaining squadrons, a section of Hurricances from Kenley (No. 615 Squadron) saw enemy aircraft near Ashford, but considered them too high and too numerous to engage. Nos 64 and 43 Squadron made no contact. Thus of the ten squadrons which were airborne to intercept these raids, seven were successful in engaging the enemy.

It remains to be seen what damage was caused by the German forces. Damage to residential property occurred in several places, and scattered bombs fell at many places between the coast and the Croydon area. At least eighty bombs fell at West Malling, though by no means all hit the airfield. Some buildings were damaged, and the airfield surface was unserviceable for four days. All the remaining destruction was in the Croydon–Beddington area. Here, the Croydon airfield, attacked by 'minimum of twenty-five to thirty aircraft' including Me 110 bombers, suffered no damage to surface or aircraft, but buildings, including the operations room, were partially destroyed, and some hangars were also hit. The Rollason aircraft factory, and the British NSF factory were severely hit, while damage was also done to the Redwing aircraft factory and the Hatcham Rubber Company. One or two other large buildings were struck, and in all some forty or fifty people were killed, and thirty-five seriously injured.

This operation virtually marked the end of what were by far the heaviest operations the Germans had so far launched in one day. Comment at length on their significance is best left until the operations of this whole phase of German activity – in which attacks on airfields were so obviously important – have been considered.

NIGHT OPERATIONS, 15/16 AUGUST

On the night following the widespread day raids the Germans reverted to the sort of operations which they had carried out two nights earlier, though on a somewhat heavier scale. Up to one hundred aircraft took part, the majority attacking targets inland. Minelaying, however, was carried out in the usual areas, viz: the Dover Straits, the Thames and Humber estuaries, Liverpool bay, and also between the Isle of Wight and Dungeness. Two aircraft, which may

26 There is little doubt, judging from wreckage found in the district, that the attack on Croydon was carried out by KGr 210. The tactics adopted during the attack were typical of this unit, and, if previous operations are any guide, about fifteen Me 110s, escorted by fighters, took part in it. In that case the Germans suffered heavily, for no less than six Me 110s and one Me 109 from this *Gruppe* were found on land after the attack; and its unlikely that this was the sum of their losses.

have been minelaying, were believed to have been destroyed, one by gunfire and the other by a Defiant of No. 264 Squadron over the Humber.

Overland the most obvious concentration was against the Bristol Channel area, where about twenty enemy aircraft operated. Various gun sites at Bristol and Cardiff were intermittently in action from midnight to 0300 hours. Approximately one hundred bombs were dropped in various districts of South Wales, and rather less in the Bristol area. Nowhere was serious damage caused, and only one key point – the Bristol Aeroplane Company at Filton – reported an incident, and this was merely a solitary bomb which did no damage. Birmingham was also raided, however, by aircraft from Brittany, and between midnight and 0200 bombs were reported from seven separate districts of the city. Here, too, only one key point was affected, but in this case the damage was considerable. The works in question was that of Singer Motors at Smallheath, where production was temporarily held up owing to damage to the metal shop.

With the exception of the interception in the Humber area the night fighters – forty-two of which were sent up – had nothing to report.

OPERATIONS, 16 AUGUST

By 0400 hours the country was fairly clear of night raiders, and thenceforwards there was little to report. Not until 0900 hours were there any signs of important German activity, and then they proved to lead to nothing. A number of small formations remained in the Straits, and one force of perhaps six aircraft came over to the Isle of Wight about 1030 hours. This sort of activity quickened after 1100 hours and the enemy reconnoitred behind Portsmouth, in the Thames Valley and in the Kenley area. A convoy which was lying at anchor in the Solent was also inspected by a reconnaissance aircraft. None of these aircraft were engaged, partly because of the weather, which though fine was cloudy, and partly because of the inherent difficulty of intercepting this type of raid.

a. Over Kent and the Thames Estuary

From 1145 hours, however, it was obvious that the Germans were once more preparing to attack in the Dover area; and by noon there were four fairly large formations in the Straits. One of 'thirty plus' was about six miles to the south-west of Cap Gris Nez; another of the same size was four miles to the north-west of the same point; a third of twelve or more aircraft was midway between Dover and Calais; and a fourth of twenty or more aircraft was a few miles east of the South Foreland.

Three full squadrons, Nos 111, 266 and 56, were in the air by this time, respectively patrolling the airfields at Hawkinge, Manston and Rochford; and there were also four small detachments of section strength protecting airfields near London and a convoy off the Essex shore of the Thames Estuary.

These three squadrons were admirably placed for meeting the Germans as soon as they approached our shores, and this is what happened in two cases. One German force came in by way of Dungeness and was almost immediately engaged by No. 111 Squadron. Another came in near the North Foreland and was brought to action by No. 266 Squadron near Canterbury. No. 56 Squadron was not engaged for the simple reason that the Germans kept to the south side of the estuary, while our squadron was maintained on patrol near Rochford.

The force which No. 111 Squadron engaged at approximately 1210 hours consisted of a large, but undetermined number of Do 215s escorted by Me 109s. The squadron commander led two of his sections in a head-on attack against the leading formation of bombers while the other two sections attacked from astern. This part of the enemy force was almost certainly disorganised and broken up by the squadron's attack, and at least one Dornier was chased back to France; but there is nothing to show that the bulk of the enemy force did not continue on its course inland. Indeed, as far as can be ascertained, it was this force which provided the eighteen bombers which carried out an attack on West Malling at 1230 hours. This station was already unserviceable as a result of an attack on the previous day, but the new attack did not materially worsen the position.

The force which No. 266 Squadron engaged between 1220 and 1230 hours consisted simply of Me 109s. There is no doubt, however, that a force of about a dozen Do 215s crossed the coast at about the same time with Tilbury docks as their objective. It is possible that the squadron unwittingly played the German game by engaging the Me 109s. The combat took place at 22,000 feet, and the German bombers probably came in much lower. Certainly when they arrived over Tilbury just after 1230 hours they were at 10,000–12,000 feet.

The damage that they caused was not serious. According to the daily summary circulated by the Ministry of Home Security only five HE bombs were dropped. One medium-sized ship (7,500 tons) and the berth where she lay were damaged.

Meanwhile more British squadrons had been ordered into the air:

> No. 54 Squadron left Hornchurch at 1214 hours to patrol it at 15,000 feet.
>
> No. 64 Squadron left Kenley at 1220 hours and were directed towards Dover.
>
> No. 32 Squadron left Biggin Hill at 1213 hours to patrol Dover area.

The last two squadrons did not make contact with any enemy bombers, and their engagements with small groups of Me 109s over the Straits cannot be said to have influenced the German operations.

No. 54 Squadron was the only one to engage the German bomber formation which carried out the heaviest attack of the period, and that only when the Germans were retiring. The movements of this force were shrouded not in the fog of war but in the mists of the lower Thames. All that we know is that two enemy forces were suddenly detected at 1245 hours well up the Thames east of Tilbury, and neither was plotted for long. Presumably it was one of these forces that bombed Northfleet just before 1300 hours. About fifty bombs were put down; the railway line was damaged, the local paper mill was set on fire, and there was much destruction of domestic property in the town.

As the Germans retired from this attack they were engaged by No. 54 Squadron. First of all some forty Do 215s[27] were seen at 15,000 feet travelling east at their maximum speed. The squadron was a thousand feet higher but as they were about to attack they noticed enemy fighters behind and above the bombers from 19,000 to 25,000 feet. These were circling around and obviously waiting an opportunity to pounce on our pilots as they attacked the bombers. In consequence, most of the ensuing combats were between fighter and fighter, and no Dorniers were claimed as destroyed.

Some of the individual fights in which No. 54 Squadron was engaged, ended over the French Coast, and mark the end of this first big German operation of the day. It was not one which can have given the Germans much satisfaction if ever they learned what results attended their bombing. No great harm had been done to West Malling and virtually none at all at Tilbury docks. Northfleet town had suffered, it was true, but considering its relative insignificance compared to such a target as the nearby Tilbury docks it would appear that the German bomber pilots were badly briefed (which is not likely) or that in the bad conditions of visibility applying at the time Northfleet was bombed in mistake for some other objective, possibly Tilbury itself. The air fighting, however, was not much, if at all, in our favour. Seven British fighters were lost, three pilots being killed and two wounded; and our pilots' claims amounted to nine German aircraft certainly destroyed, of which two were bombers. Of these, one fighter and one bomber crashed on land during the time covered by the various combats.

b. In southern Hampshire and west Sussex, 1245–1400 hours

The attacks in Kent were still under way when once more the enemy launched large forces across the Central Channel. Owing to a fortunately rare aberration in the records it is difficult to reconstruct the first evidence that an attack was about to be made. It is safe to say that the RDF stations must have detected signs of an enemy concentration in the Cherbourg area as early as 1230 hours, for by 1245 hours a much larger force of British fighters was patrolling between Portland and Tangmere than was usual unless a heavy attack was in prospect. Yet the track charts for this period show no enemy movements of any description in the central Channel. Whatever the explanation may be five full squadrons, Nos 1, 43, 213, 152 and 601, were all in the air by 1245 hours, and four of them were heavily engaged within the next twenty minutes.

The attacking forces were in two bodies, one with air establishments near Portsmouth as its objective, while the other made for Tangmere. Both forces contained approximately fifty–sixty Ju 87s heavily escorted by both single and twin-engined fighters. That which came in near Selsey Bill to attack Tangmere was the first to be engaged, but the combat was fought at 20,000 feet between No. 1 Squadron and an unstated number of Me 109s. Only a minute or two later, however, the bombers were engaged, No. 43 Squadron coming into action with

27 We are fully aware of the discrepancy between the reported number of bombs dropped at Northfleet and the size of the enemy force as reported by No. 54 Squadron. Similar discrepancies occur frequently.

a force reported as fifty to one hundred Ju 87s escorted by a small number of fighters. The latter played very little part in the fighting and it is more than likely that No. 1 Squadron had facilitated the task of No. 43 Squadron by diverting some of the German escort from their charges. There ensued a combat in which a heavier toll of enemy aircraft was claimed that in any previous engagement by a single British squadron. No. 43 Squadron had two thousand feet advantage in height over the Ju 87s, which were at 12,000 feet, and the squadron commander led his pilots into a head-on attack which seems to have broken up a great part of the enemy formation. Some of the Ju 87s were seen to jettison their bombs into the sea and others turned back to France. Altogether, thirteen of them were believed to have been destroyed for certain, and four probably destroyed. Two Hurricanes were lost.

Almost as soon as our squadron had finished its attacks No. 601 Squadron came into action with the same formation. The squadron had originally been ordered to patrol Tangmere at 20,000 feet, but had later been ordered towards the raid approaching Selsey with orders to attack the high guard of fighters. Thanks to No. 1 Squadron no fighters were visible, and the squadron commander therefore brought his squadron down on the dive-bombers. He was only just in time for despite the attacks of No. 43 Squadron part of the enemy formation had continued north and was about to bomb Tangmere. Our pilots believed they destroyed seven of the enemy at a cost of only one Hurricane and its pilot. Nevertheless, some of the dive-bombers must have escaped interference for at 1300 hours Tangmere was heavily and accurately bombed. The attack was seen from the nearby airfield at Westhampnett and the CO of No. 602 Squadron, which was stationed there, rushed his whole squadron off the ground, sixteen aircraft in all, partly in order to intercept the enemy, partly in order that his squadron might not be caught on the ground should an attack develop. The squadron managed to destroy a straggling Ju 87, which had probably been disabled as a result of a previous attack, but was too late to make contact with the main enemy body.

Tangmere itself was seriously damaged. All hangars, workshops, station sick quarters, and the officers' mess were destroyed; electricity and water supply was put out of action as was the ground–air R/T. Three Blenheims were completely destroyed, and three more Blenheims and seven Hurricanes were severely damaged. Fortunately, the operations room was one of the few buildings that escaped damaged, and the airfield surface remained serviceable. Consequently, both No. 601 and 43 squadrons continued to use the station: No. 43 Squadron, indeed, made a sortie at flight strength within twenty minutes of the bombardment.

The enemy force which came in further west enjoyed a far easier passage than that which bombed Tangmere. Squadrons Nos 152, 213 and 249 were all in action near the west coast of the Isle of Wight between 1300 and 1340 hours, but in each case with enemy fighters.[28] None of the squadrons reported seeing any dive-bombers, and although this can partly be accounted for by the rather

28 F/Lt. J.B. Nicholson of No. 249 Squadron was awarded the Victoria Cross – the only one to be awarded to a pilot of Fighter Command – for his great bravery during this action in successfully pressing home an attack on a Me 110 despite the fact that his Hurricane was in flames and he himself being severely burned.

hazy conditions there is no doubt that the squadrons were too far west to intercept the bombers, which approached their targets on the east side of the Isle of Wight. These were the RDF station at Ventnor, already badly damaged by an attack on 12 August,[29] the Coastal Command station at Gosport and the Fleet Air Arm station at Lee-on-Solent. The RAF squadrons, it is clear, were also too late to intercept, for the three objectives had all been bombed by 1315 hours. Ventnor RDF station was inoperative before the bombing, though efforts were being made to repair it, and after this latest attack all buildings except two above ground, and those underground, were unusable. Damage at Gosport and Lee-on-Solent to station buildings and hangars was considerable, but as in the case of Tangmere the airfield surfaces were soon serviceable. Neither station, it should be noted, was being used at the time by operational squadrons.

c. 1600–1830 hours

The last enemy aircraft had left Hampshire by 1400 hours, and for two hours there was a lull in German activity. Between 1600 and 1630 hours, however, it became obvious that the Germans were not only about to attack again but that, seemingly, they were going to attempt a dual attack similar to those which they had launched two days previously. The indications that this would happen were as follows:

> At 1609 hours a force of 'thirty plus' was located near St Omer.
>
> At the same time a force half as big was located behind Boulogne.
>
> At 1600 hours a force of 'thirty plus' was located over Dunkerque.

Two minutes late a force of 'twenty plus' was located north of St Omer.

All these formations except one remained overland for the next twenty minutes. The exception was the force first picked up near Dunkerque; and this came out over the sea at 1617 hours and was in mid-Channel at 1629 hours, by which time a small formation was known to be near Dover.

In the central Channel the following forces were located:

> At 1633 hours a force of 'fifty plus' about twenty-five miles north-west of Le Havre.
>
> At 1637 hours a force whose strength was not reported ten miles north-west of Cherbourg.
>
> At 1641 hours a force of 'thirty plus' thirty miles south of St Catherine's Point.

All these forces were flying north.

29 See p. 66.

i. *In northern Kent, Essex and Suffolk*

The German formations that had been detected as they assembled near St Omer and Boulogne consolidated into two formations of fifty or more aircraft each, crossed the Channel on parallel courses and came in near the South Foreland at 1642 hours. The formation first located near Dunkerque remained over the Channel.

Meanwhile some defending squadrons were on the move: No. 165 Squadron had left Kenley and was flying towards Dungeness; No. 65 Squadron from Manston was patrolling Deal; and No. 610 Squadron was patrolling Hawkinge, from which it was operating at the time. In addition, No. 1 Squadron from Northolt was patrolling Guildford, and between 1640 and 1655 hours squadrons Nos 32, 56, 64 and 501 took off and were directed towards north-east Kent.

The first of these units to come into action was No. 65 Squadron which fell in with the more northerly of the two enemy forces at 1640 hours near Deal. It consisted of some sixty bombers (what type they were is not stated, though a phrase in one report implies that they were certainly not Ju 88s) escorted by some two hundred fighters. The squadron commander considered it impossible to attack the bombers, and he led his squadron in a climb to engage the escorting fighters, three of which were claimed as destroyed at a cost of one Hurricane and its pilot.

The southern wing of the enemy's advance was also engaged about this time by No. 32 Squadron which met a large formation of Ju 88s and Me 110s near Sevenoaks at 1650 hours. The squadron carried out a head-on attack and undoubtedly caused some confusion amongst the enemy, but cloudy conditions made it difficult to press home the attack.

Two more enemy formations had been detected by this time. One came in near Dungeness and flew along the coast towards Eastbourne, bombing this town in a somewhat haphazard fashion at 1650 hours. The other was approaching Harwich across the outer Thames Estuary.

The next interception in point of time was by No. 610 Squadron. According to the pilots they came into action at 1700 hours near Dungeness with a force of Ju 88s and Me 109s, fifty aircraft in all. No enemy force of this size was near Dungeness at this time, and it is more likely that the squadron was engaged north of this point with the same force, or part of it, as was engaged by No. 32 Squadron. Owing to bad visibility, however, it was impossible at the time to maintain continuous intelligence of the enemy's movements, and we cannot claim precise accuracy for this reconstruction. The squadron lost one of its Spitfires and claimed no positive successes.

Between 1700 and 1730 hours the force that came in near Harwich was intercepted as it came in by No. 56 Squadron, and as it retired by 'A' Flight of No. 19 Squadron. Its composition was very accurately reported by No. 56 Squadron as twenty-seven Do 17s or 215s and thirty-six Me 109s and He 113s. One interesting feature of the formation was that some of the German fighters were just behind and level with the rear section of the bombers, one of the earliest indications that the Germans were realising the need for closer escorts than they had hitherto provided. The squadron inflicted some damage on the enemy, as did

No. 19 Squadron[30] some twenty minutes later, but the German formation held on its course and operated over southern Suffolk between the two combats.

The only other engagements that took place in the south-east concerned No. 64 Squadron and one section of No. 501 Squadron, both of which appear to have engaged the formations which originally came in near the South Foreland as they retired. Both engagements took place in the region of Maidstone, and no great advantage could be claimed by either side.

This could be said for the operation as a whole. Considering the bad conditions it was indeed surprising that so many squadrons had succeeded in making contact with the enemy; but whereas the clouds had made it difficult for RAF fighters to carry out effective attacks they had equally hampered the enemy in finding his objectives. One of the enemy formations had pressed inland as far as Ware in Hertfordshire, and bombs were dropped there as well as at a number of places in Essex and east Suffolk. But apart from a sharp attack by Me 109s on Manston, and a similar attack on the balloon barrage at Dover, no specific military objectives appear to have been attacked during this period. In view of the attention that the enemy paid to RAF stations earlier in the day, and during this same period further west, it is not extravagantly speculative to suggest that these operations had had airfields such as Kenley, Biggin Hill and North Weald as their principal objectives, but that cloud as much as the attacks of our fighters had effectively saved them from being bombed.

ii. *Between south-west London and the coast*

All this time the Germans had been engaged on an even larger operation further west. The forces that were originally located off the shores of Normandy between 1633 and 1640 hours came steadily across the Channel, and the first of them was near the Isle of Wight by 1650 hours. But the period of warning had been sufficient for a considerable defending force to take the air, and by that same time eight squadrons were covering various points between Portland and Worthing.

Nevertheless, it would appear that three German formations were able to make their landfall without being intercepted. The enemy force was deployed in four formations: one crossed the Isle of Wight at about 1700 hours turned east near Winchester and operated towards Godalming and Haslemere; another came up to Selsey Bill and then turned towards the Isle of Wight; the third crossed just east of Tangmere and flew north-eastwards; and the fourth crossed near Worthing. Only this last force was intercepted as it crossed the coast. No. 615 Squadron fell in with it at 1700 hours and later described it as a large composite formation of He 111s and Me 110s flying at 15,000–18,000 feet. The squadron had originally taken-off to intercept one of the raids further east, but had been diverted as the later threat developed. Having an initial advantage of two thousand feet in height the squadron succeeded in reaching the bombers and

30 'A' Flight of this squadron, consisting of seven Spitfires each armed with two 20 mm cannon, was on its way from Coltishall to Duxford when it was diverted towards Clacton. Most of its combats were with Me 110s (whose presence was not remarked by No. 56 Squadron) and although three of these were believed to have been destroyed at no cost to the flight the cannon gun installations functioned badly. Only two pilots were fortunate enough to have no stoppages, and all were handicapped by the absence of any tracer ammunition. On the other hand, when the 20 mm. guns were fired accurately the effect on the Me 110s was most gratifying.

shooting two of them down before the Me 110s intervened, but the formation flew steadily on northwards.

A little later, and further to the west, No. 1 Squadron engaged the enemy force that had crossed the coast east of Tangmere. The squadron had been ordered to patrol Guildford, then to patrol Portsmouth, and it was while flying south that it sighted the enemy at 18,000 feet over the South Downs. They consisted of He 111s 'in three waves of about forty aircraft each' and were virtually unprotected by fighters, only ten Me 110s being seen. Again losses were inflicted on the enemy, but again the main formation flew on towards the north.

Consolidated Combat Report, No. 1 Squadron

As far as we can judge, these were the only interceptions of the enemy on the inward journey. Further to the west, in the Solent area, Nos 152 and 234 squadrons came into action between 1815 and 1830 hours, but it is obvious that the enemy were retiring. Further north, the Northolt station commander in a Hurricane and another pilot in a Gladiator, enjoyed a brief encounter with a Ju 88. Otherwise no other combats were reported. This implies that some two hundred German bombers were ranging over southern England for at least an hour without being brought to battle. And this was undoubtedly the case.

But once again, the clouds which had hampered the defence hindered the attackers. Bombs fell in the upper Thames valley on the RAF stations at Brize Norton and Harwell, and on two emergency landing grounds; in northern Hampshire at Basingstoke, Farnborough, and in the Borden–Longmore district; and in south-west London suburbs, Wimbledon, Mitcham, Esher, Malden and Combe. At least a dozen villages between the south coast and the Thames had incidents to report. The bombing, in short, was ill-directed and scattered. Certain important objectives, namely Brize Norton, Harwell, and Farnborough airfields were accurately bombed; but in no case were more than nine aircraft used. It may be that small forces were detached from the main German formations for these attacks, it being considered unwise to risk large numbers of aircraft below the cloud base, which was as low as 4,500 feet. Even so more aircraft, forty-six in all, were destroyed by two Ju 88s in the attack on Brize Norton than in any other single attack during the whole of the battle. Three aircraft were also destroyed at Harwell, but the damage at Farnborough was negligible. None of those stations, it should be noted, was used by Fighter Command.

Apart from these attacks the only result achieved was slight and temporary dislocation of railway communications at Basingstoke, Wimbledon and Morden. The significance of the operation, however, lay not in the damage it caused, but in the fact that large formations were able to penetrate so far inland without being effectively interfered with. No less than thirteen of the seventeen available day fighter squadrons in No. 11 Group had sent detachments into the air between 1630 and 1800 hours. Eight of them had made contact with the enemy, which, considering the weather conditions, was not an unsatisfactory proportion. But of the thirteen squadrons eight had been allocated to the operations over the Thames Estuary and northern Kent, leaving a smaller force to deal with what proved to be a heavier attack further west. The lesson to be learned was that No. 11 Group would be hard put to it to withstand heavy attacks launched simultaneously, or nearly so, within the Group boundaries. The difference, it will be noted, between this and previous attacks against the south coast was that the Germans appear to have done little more then demonstrate in the Solent area. By doing so, however, they prevented the squadrons of No. 10 Group from being used further to the north and east. At the same time they brought in their main forces further to the east than usual, while still maintaining large forces in northern Kent. We are not, of course, able to do much more than speculate about German plans, but there is at least a strong probability that by their various moves they intended to create a gap between the two areas of the Solent in the west and the Straits of Dover in the east, through which they might safely pass large forces inland. This, at any rate, was the effect of their operations, and, as we have seen, strong forces were able to penetrate as far as the Thames Valley without heavy loss.

OPERATIONS, 2100 HOURS 16 AUGUST–0600 HOURS 18 AUGUST

Night operations on 16 August were on a much reduced scale, barely a dozen aircraft crossing the coast, most of them coming from the Cherbourg peninsular. A few incidents were reported from South Wales, where two HE bombs fell in the centre of Cardiff. Otherwise such bombs as were dropped fell harmlessly in rural areas. The weather throughout the night was bad for flying, the cloud base being as low as 1,000 feet and extending to most of the country.

The comparative lull, however, somewhat surprisingly continued into the following day when the weather, after the morning haze had disappeared, was generally good. In consequence, the number of sorties carried out by Fighter Command was lower than on any day since 3 August. Less than fifty German aircraft were in action, and those were nearly all on shipping and meteorological reconnaissances. Five small ships were attacked in St George's Channel during the forenoon, and one attack was reported as taking place off Cape Wrath. Only half a dozen aircraft came overland, all of them, it would seem, on reconnaissance. The Solent, the Thames Estuary and London, and, possibly the Welsh Marches were the areas visited. According to the Home Security daily summary of events no incidents were reported, but the Fighter Command report mentions bombs near Hornchurch and Brentwood.

The weather continued fine and on the night of the 17th German activity slightly increased. As before most of it was in the western half of the country, and was the work of aircraft from north-west France which came in over what was already being called the Devonshire Corridor. South Wales, Birmingham and Coventry, and Merseyside, all received small numbers of bombs; but only at Birmingham, where the Brierley Hill goods station was temporarily blocked, and at Liverpool, where there was damage to the Queen's graving dock and other port facilities, was the enemy's marksmanship worth remarking. A small number of aircraft were also over the Thames Valley and the outskirts of London, and incendiary bombs were dropped near Woolwich. In East Anglia there were several instances of the machine-gunning of searchlight sites. Minelaying was suspected off Prawle Point on the Devonshire coast, in the Thames Estuary and off Cromer. One aircraft was shot down off Spurn Head after a long chase from the Liverpool district by a Blenheim of No. 29 Squadron.

OPERATIONS, 18 AUGUST

Enemy activity began shortly after dawn on the 18th, and took the form of shipping and weather reconnaissance over the North Sea by a small number of aircraft. One of these, a Do 17, was engaged and probably shot down at 0720 hours by a flight of No. 257 Squadron which was patrolling a convoy near Harwich. For the next three hours there was little to report, but between 1100 and 1130 hours single enemy aircraft flew over Kent, Sussex, the Thames Estuary and part of Essex. To judge from their tracks they reconnoitred many of the airfields in those areas. Detachments from five squadrons in No. 11 Group took off to intercept, but only one squadron could claim any success. This was No. 54 Squadron which intercepted a Me 110 at 31,000 feet north-east of Manston and destroyed it in a combat which ended at sea level.

a. Against Kenley and Biggin Hill, 1245–1345 hours

Towards the end of this period an enemy formation of twenty or more aircraft was on the move near St Omer, and between 1200 and 1215 hours another force, slightly smaller, was located near St Inglevert. These probably mark the beginning of a concentration for by 1227 hours the two smaller forces had disappeared, to be replaced by one force of 'sixty plus' near St Omer and another of 'twenty-four plus' north of Abbeville. The first of these forces came into the Straits at 1236 hours, flew across and made landfall at the South Foreland at 1249 hours. The other came across at the same time and was plotted in near Beachy Head at 1250 hours.

The first of the defending squadrons were already in the air and preparing to intercept. No. 501 Squadron had taken off from Hawkinge at 1230 hours and was patrolling the Kent coast; and Nos 54 and 56 squadrons had taken off from Manston and North Weald respectively at 1240 hours and had been ordered to patrol in the Canterbury–Manston area. In the next fifteen minutes eight more squadrons were ordered into the air; three from the Biggin Hill sector, two from Kenley, and one each from the Hornchurch, North Weald and Debden sectors. All of them were instructed to patrol airfields, with the exception of No. 65 Squadron which left Rochford at 1250 hours to patrol between Manston and Canterbury.

The northern arm of the German force, that which crossed the coast near the South Foreland, was the first to be engaged. No. 501 Squadron sighted it near Sandwich and reported it as a large force of bombers escorted by twenty or more Me 110s and 109s. The latter prevented attacks from reaching the bombers, and four Hurricanes were shot down at no cost to the Germans. The balance was redressed shortly afterwards by No. 56 Squadron which came upon five Me 110s circling over Ashford at 21,000 feet, and shot them all down. No other enemy aircraft were seen by this squadron, and it must be assumed that most of the enemy formation had continued west towards it target, Biggin Hill. Part of it, however, may have been detached somewhere near Canterbury, for the Observer Corps plotted one force that came in as far as Faversham and then turned south-east at 1300 hours. Moreover No. 65 Squadron when near the north coast of Kent at 1300 hours saw what it described as 'a large force of enemy bombers proceeding south-east', but too far away to intercept. This is difficult to explain, for only at Rye was any bombing reported that could possibly have been the work of this force, and that was on a small scale.

Meanwhile the more southerly of the enemy formations had crossed the coast without being intercepted, and had pressed on across the Weald of Kent towards its objective, which later proved to be the sector station at Kenley. It reached Tonbridge without being interfered with, but there was brought to action at 1300 hours by No. 615 Squadron, which had left Kenley at 1245 hours. The enemy was reported to consist of large numbers of bombers of different types at 10,000 feet–12,000 feet, protected by fighters above and behind at 26,000–30,000 feet. Three pilots were engaged by German fighters, but most combats were with the bombers, four of which were believed to have been shot down; four Hurricanes were lost or badly damaged. About the time of the combat bombs were dropped on Paddock Wood, a small railway junction near Tonbridge, but the great majority of the enemy flew on toward Kenley.

The station was reached about 1310 hours and was attacked almost immediately.[31] Eight Spitfires of No. 64 Squadron had taken off ten minutes earlier, and as the first bombs fell on the airfield they dived down on what was described as a 'straggled formation of He 111s, Ju 88s and Do 17s'. Five of these were believed to have been shot down at a cost of only one Spitfire. No. 111 Squadron also came into action as the attack was taking place. The squadron had first been instructed to patrol Croydon at 20,000 feet, but these orders were changed just before the squadron took off at 1305 hours, and it was directed to Kenley. Its report on the composition of the German force tallies with that of No. 64 Squadron, and likewise it was engaged exclusively with bombers. One Do 17 was also destroyed by PAC rockets, which formed part of the station's ground defences. This was the first aircraft to be brought down by this weapon.

Amongst other damage, all hangars except one were destroyed, the telephone system was disrupted and six Hurricanes of No. 615 Squadron were destroyed or damaged. There were a few craters on the runways, but both Nos 64 and 615 squadrons were able to carry out patrols later in the day. Nevertheless, the effect on communications was such that the sector operations room had to be closed down and the emergency one brought into use. From them on the station only operated two squadrons instead of its normal complement of three.

Ten minutes after the attack on Kenley had finished a small force (presumably a detachment from the main body of the enemy) attacked Croydon, dropping some twenty bombs on the airfield. Rollason's aircraft factory was again hit, but there was no serious damage to the airfield or its facilities.

As a by-product, so to speak, of these two attacks on airfields, numerous incidents affecting domestic property and suburban communications were reported in the Kenley, Croydon and Purley districts.

31 According to the ORB of the station there were two attacks; but only one time of attack, 1310 hours, is mentioned. The daily summary of events complied in the War Room at the Air Ministry gives 1400 hours as the time of the attack, but apart from this all the available evidence goes to show that the bombing had finished well before 1330 hours. The explanation of the entry in the station ORB is that the two attacks were made at much the same time but in different ways, one being a low-level attack by Do 17s, while the other was carried out from a fairly high altitude by He 111s and, possibly, Ju 88s. But this still leaves unexplained the time of attack as given in the AMWR daily summary: see Appendix 8.

While these attacks were being made the force that had crossed the coast near the South Foreland over half an hour previously had not been idle. But it is not possible to give as circumstantial an account of its movements as of those of the force that attacked Kenley. In the first place its course was not continuously plotted by the Observer Corps, probably because there was considerable cloud at about 5,000 feet in the north of Kent. Secondly, there were subsidiary formations moving over the country between Canterbury–Maidstone–Biggin Hill. It is even possible that the force which eventually bombed the RAF station at Biggin Hill was not the one that crossed the coast at the South Foreland. There is some evidence that the forces that bombed Biggin Hill, Kenley and Croydon were all parts of one and the same force, that which crossed the coast near Beachy Head.

All that is certain is that by 1300 hours the controllers on the ground realised that Biggin Hill was menaced; and Nos 32 and 610 Squadrons took off from there at 1300 hours. Both squadrons were ordered to send up every available aircraft and pilot to avoid losses by bombing. No. 610 Squadron were detailed to climb to 30,000 feet to engage enemy fighters, while the Hurricanes of No. 32 Squadron were to attack the bombers.

The plan worked successfully, though the combats of both squadrons were not confined either to bombers or fighter. The enemy formation consisted of some sixty Do 17s and Ju 88s escorted by about forty Me 110s and 109s and both squadrons engaged it before Biggin Hill was reached. The bombers were at 12,000 feet and No. 32 Squadron attacked them head-on. No. 610 Squadron were also able to spare some time for the bombers; and the two squadrons claimed to have destroyed nine bombers and seven fighters. Certainly the interception was responsible for the comparative failure of the attack on the airfield, where no buildings were hit and the landing ground was only lightly cratered.[32] A few incidents were also reported from villages and small towns nearby, notably Oxted and Sevenoaks.

At much the same time as this attack, 1320 hours, West Malling was again bombed. There is no means of tracing the movements of this force, which consisted of Ju 88s, but to judge from the number of isolated plots in this part of Kent between 1300 and 1330 hours it was by no means the only force in the vicinity. Repair work at the airfield was further retarded as a result of this attack, and it was not serviceable again until 20 August. It was not in regular use by Fighter Command at the time.

As the Germans retired at 20,000–22,000 feet, they were engaged by three squadrons. The formation which had attacked Kenley was intercepted by No. 1 and No. 17 Squadron near Dover at 1335 hours. The other enemy force was also intercepted further north by a small detachment of No. 501 Squadron and by No. 266 Squadron. The enemy bombers by this time were not keeping the same disciplined formation as when they had flown inland, but this was offset by the strong rearguards of fighters with which they were protected.

32 The station ORB makes no mention of any attack. This in itself is not significant, for the keeping of records frequently left much to be desired. But as this same station gives very detailed accounts of later attacks it indicates that the attack was only a light one. In his book, *The Royal Air Force in the World War*, Vol. II, p. 200, Captain Norman Macmillan states that the raid caused considerable damage, especially to the block of buildings containing the operations room. This was not so. The operations room was not hit until 31 August.

Fighters Command ORB, Appendix J1.

After all claims had been examined twenty-two bombers and twenty fighters were believed to have been shot down for certain in the whole operation. Of these the wreckage of eight was found on the ground, from which it appeared that most of the bombers used by the Germans were from KGs 1 and 76, which were stationed at various airfields between Paris and Amiens. Such fighters as were found were too badly smashed for their units to be identified.

British losses in aircraft were twelve lost outright, and thirteen so badly damaged that they had to be repaired by Maintenance Command. Four pilots were killed or missing and ten were wounded. The pilot position was now such that any loss not compensated for by a greater loss to the enemy was a blow at Fighter Command where it was most vulnerable. But in this particular operation heavier losses would have been acceptable if they had ensured the continued operation of Biggin Hill and Kenley; and that these two stations remained in action is a measure of the failure of the German attacks.

b. In southern Hampshire, 1400–1530 hours

While these operations had been taking place a few enemy aircraft had been plotted over the central Channel, and some had made swift reconnaissances over southern Hampshire and west Sussex. Just before 1400 hours two Ju 88s had been intercepted by a single Spitfire (nominally returning to Pembrey from Northolt!) near Beachy Head, and one had been shot down. They were probably stragglers from the operations in Kent. On account of these occasional enemy sorties three detachments of fighters had been maintained on patrol between Portland and Selsey Bill between 1300 and 1400 hours. This apart, however, there had been no threat to what, for convenience, can be called the Solent area while the Germans had been operating further east; and when at 1400 hours indications were received that the enemy were about to strike across the central Channel practically all the squadrons from Exeter to Tangmere were ready to take the air.

The signs of a renewed attack were clear enough:

> At 1400 hour a force of ‘eighty plus’ was located twenty miles north of Cherbourg.
>
> At the same time a force of ‘twenty plus’ was located a few miles to the east.
>
> Two minutes late a force of ‘ten plus’ was ten miles north-west of Le Havre.

All three forces were making for the Solent.

No. 601 Squadron was already patrolling Tangmere at 10,000 feet. The following squadrons were also sent up between 1405 and 1420 hours:

> No. 213 Squadron from Exeter at 1407 hours to patrol St Catherine’s Point.
>
> No. 152 Squadron from Warmwell at 1410 hours to patrol Portsmouth.

No. 43 Squadron from Tangmere at 1412 hours to patrol Thorney Island.

No. 602 Squadron from Westhampnett at 1415 hours to patrol base.

No. 234 Squadron from Middle Wallop at 1415 hours to intercept near the Isle of Wight.

The Germans reached the coast between 1422 and 1425 hours. There were two formations of dive-bombers, one of which came in near Selsey Bill, and the other just east of the Isle of Wight. The first was responsible for the bombing of the airfield at Thorney Island, the Fleet Air Arm station at Ford, and the RDF station at Poling. The other had Gosport as its objective. The more westerly of these two forces was intercepted as it flew inland by No. 234 Squadron over Ventnor. But the escorting fighters kept the ensuing combat away from the bombers and the latter passed on without being interfered with.

The force which made its landfall near Selsey was attacked first by nine Hurricanes of No. 43 Squadron, and then by ten Hurricanes of No. 601 Squadron. From the combat reports of these two squadrons it would appear that there were two German formations but if so they were acting in close concert. At any rate just south of Thorney Island No. 43 Squadron came up with forty Ju 87s flying at 10,000 feet with about twenty Me 109s above and behind at 18,000 feet. The latter took little part in the fighting, and No. 43 Squadron, attacking from above and astern, were believed to have shot down eight of the dive-bombers. Nevertheless, it was almost certainly this formation which bombed Thorney Island at 1425 hours.

The engagement in which No. 601 Squadron was involved took place at the same time and in much the same place as that of No. 43 Squadron. The composition of the enemy formation was also similar, the only point of difference being that whereas No. 43 Squadron had virtually escaped interference from the enemy fighters, in the case of No. 601 Squadron the Ju 87s were closely protected by Me 109s on each flank. This was one of the first occasions on which the Germans adopted this method of protection. But even though pilots found that their attacks were much hampered, they claimed to have shot down six dive-bombers and three fighters at a cost of three Hurricanes. Despite the difference between the reports of the two squadrons on the German tactics it seems clear enough that they engaged the same force.

As the engagement came to an end the enemy bombers split into two formations, one making for Thorney Island and the other for Ford. As they approached the latter station No. 602 Squadron, which had taken off from Westhampnett at 1415 hours and had been patrolling its base, came into action. This squadron, like No. 43, reported that the fighter escort was considerably higher than the dive-bombers. These were attacked from astern by one flight, while the other climbed to meet the fighters. Six Ju 87s and two Me 109s were claimed as destroyed, and the pilots believed that they had disorganised to some extent the attack on the airfield. They said, however, that only one of two waves of dive-bombers manoeuvred to attack the airfield; and it is probable that the other went east to attack Poling, which was bombed at 1245 hours.

The progress of events, therefore, can be reconstructed as follows. One formation had flown over the Isle of Wight and bombed Gosport at 1430 hours. The German fighters had kept No. 234 Squadron from intercepting the bombers. Another, and larger formation came in near Selsey Bill and was engaged by No. 43 Squadron and then by No. 601 Squadron. Despite its losses part of it went on to bomb the airfield on Thorney Island and part went east to Ford. As the attack on the latter station developed No. 602 Squadron came into action; and almost simultaneously a further split took place in the enemy force, part of which continued east and attacked the RDF station at Poling.

A graphic and detailed account of the bombing of the Coastal Command station at Gosport is recorded in the Operations Record Book of the station (see Appendix 8). The attack was the work of twenty-one Ju 87s which approached from the south-west in three groups at 4,000–5,000 feet. Heavy damage was inflicted; some twenty buildings were destroyed or damaged and four aircraft were destroyed and seven damaged. Rather surprisingly it was only after the bomb attacks that some Me 109s appeared and began to attack the Portsmouth balloon barrage. Fifteen balloons were shot down.

At Thorney Island thirty-five HE bombs and a number of incendiaries were dropped; two hangars were hit and three aircraft were destroyed. At Ford a hangar, the equipment stores and workshops were heavily damaged. Neither of these stations were under the control of Fighter Command, nor were they ever used, except in an emergency, by fighter aircraft.

The attack on Poling, in contrast, was a blow directly aimed at the Fighter Command system, and was the more dangerous since the station at Ventnor had already been wrecked. Approximately ninety bombs were dropped and the station was badly damaged. Emergency equipment was installed but it could no longer give comprehensive and reliable information of enemy movements. Air Vice-Marshal Park warned his controllers to this effect on 25 August.[33]

No. 11 Group Instructions to Controllers, No. 4

This marked the end of the German operations in this part of the country. The formations that had operated east of Portsmouth were not further engaged, but the force that attacked Gosport was intercepted as it retired over the Isle of Wight by No. 152 Squadron at 1445 hours. No. 213 Squadron was also in action a few minutes later in the same area with a rearguard of Me 109s. Neither squadron arrived in time to interfere with the bombing, but they at least helped to increase the cost of the operation to the enemy. This, pilots were confident, was a high one. No less than thirty Ju 87s were believed to have been destroyed, and thirteen Me 109s; two Ju 87s were claimed by the anti-aircraft gunners. Five of our own fighters were destroyed and two badly damaged; two pilots were killed and four were wounded. From wreckage found after the battle it appears that I and II/St KG 77 had provided the dive-bombers and JGs 2, 27 and 52 the fighters.

By 1500 hours the operations room tables showed no movements in the central Channel, and once more the focus of enemy operations was switched to the Dover area. Small formations had been plotted in the Straits while the attacks near Portsmouth had been taking place. Between 1428 and 1435 hours

33 This implies that the station remained in action, but according to the records of the Signals branch at Fighter Command Headquarters it was out of action for the remainder of the month.

one of them had made a brief sweep over the country between the North Foreland and Dover; and at 1445 hours a force of some twenty aircraft was located in the middle of the Straits where it remained for the next twenty minutes. During that time no enemy force was plotted over eastern Kent; nevertheless at 1530 hours[34] a force of fighters (reported as twelve He 113s) appeared suddenly over Manston and machine-gunned it, destroying two Spitfires of No. 54 Squadron. About the same time one of the Dover balloons was shot down by fighters. But with this exception there was a lull over the Channel between 1500 and 1630 hours.

c. In the Thames Estuary area, 1630–1800 hours

Between 1630 and 1700 hours there were signs of an impending attack, but they displayed themselves in a somewhat slower succession than usual. This, it will appear later, greatly affected the outcome of the operation.

> At 1620 hours a force of 'twenty plus' was detected between St Omer and Boulogne.
>
> At 1635 hours a considerable force of unstated numbers was detected south of Cap Gris Nez.
>
> At 1650 hours a force of 'fifty plus' was detected near Lille.

The usual arrangements were made to protect the forward airfields in Kent. Thus, No. 501 Squadron patrolled Hawkinge from 1650 hours and No. 54 Squadron patrolled Manston from 1700 hours.

By 1710 hours it was abundantly clear that the three enemy forces would operate against targets on both sides of the estuary. One force was about twenty miles east of the Barrow Deep lightship on a westerly course; another was making for the North Foreland from the east; and a third was over the eastern entrance to the Straits on a north-westerly course for the Essex coast.

It was chiefly on the strength of this information that all the squadrons that later engaged the enemy were ordered into the air. They took off as follows:

> No. 56 Squadron from Rochford at 1705 hours to intercept the force approaching the Blackwater.
>
> No. 257 Squadron from Martlesham at 1705 hours to return to Debden, but later diverted to patrol Canterbury at 12,000 feet.
>
> No. 32 Squadron from Biggin Hill at 1720 hours to intercept north of Canterbury.

34 This is the time given in the station ORB, which ought to be the authority on the subject. The Air Ministry War Room summary, however, gives the time of attack as one hour later. If this should happen to be correct, the attack was doubtless carried out by the force that came in at the North Foreland at 1428 hours.

No. 46 Squadron, reinforcing from Digby, from Duxford at 1725 hours to patrol North Weald.

No. 85 Squadron from Debden at 1730 hours to patrol it.

No. 151 Squadron from North Weald at 1730 hours to patrol it.

No. 1 Squadron from Northolt at 1745 hours to intercept near Southend.

In addition, six other No. 11 Group squadrons[35] sent detachments into the air between 1715 and 1745 hours. Most of them were maintained on security patrols over airfields south and west of the estuary; and only one of them sighted the enemy.

One of the German formations crossed the coast just south of the North Foreland and flew north towards the estuary, while the two northerly columns came in, one near the Blackwater and the other between Shoeburyness and the Crouch at much the same time, 1732 hours. Thanks to the early warning of the operation each force was engaged before it crossed the coast.

That to the south was engaged by Nos 32 and 501 Squadrons in an action which began just north of Margate and continued almost to Chatham, for although the Germans were heavily engaged they continued to press on up the river. Both squadrons reported that the enemy consisted of fifty Do 17s and 215s escorted by thirty Me 109s. The seven Hurricanes of No. 501 Squadron were the first to attack, and they found the escorting fighters very quick to intervene. No. 32 Squadron had a similar experience a few minutes later and further up the river. Consequently, nearly all combats were with Me 109s and the bombers flew on parallel to the south shore of the estuary. Then, just before they reached Gillingham and Chatham they wheeled round and began to retire on a course a little to the south of the one they followed as they came in. Whether they feared to go on without their fighter escort, which had been scattered by the attacks of our fighters, whether they were diverted by the Thames and Medway barrage, which fired on them as they approached Chatham, or whether they had failed to find their target, the reason for the retirement is not known. All that can be said with certainty is that they did no serious damage. The only bombs dropped in this part of Kent fell near the hamlets of Upchurch and Lower Halstow, some five miles east of Gillingham. Small salvoes at Whitstable (1755 hours) and Deal (1800 hours) may also have been dropped by the enemy as they retired.

Two series of actions were fought with the enemy forces that crossed the Essex coast: one as they approached the coast, and the other in the Chelmsford area. The more northerly of the two enemy formations was first engaged by No. 54 Squadron. This squadron had been patrolling Manston but was directed across the estuary to intercept. Just south of Clacton they came up with the enemy force which, they reported later, consisted of 'large herringbone formation of about fifty bombers (He 111s and Do 17s) in tight vics line astern, escorted on either side by a similar formation of Me 110s flying at the same level as the bombers, and also escorted by Me 110s flying above and behind'.

35 One of them was No. 1 (RCAF) Squadron, which was stationed at Northolt. This was its first day of active operations.

One section of the Spitfires attacked the main formation, while the remaining sections climbed to attack the high escort, which was three thousand feet higher and immediately below the cloud base at 16,000 feet. Most of the combats, therefore, were with Me 110s, three of which were believed to have been destroyed; and the main formation carried on and made towards Chelmsford.

About the same time, 1730 hours, No. 56 Squadron and, a moment or two later, No. 257 Squadron came into action further south. It is difficult to specify the precise point on the coast at which the enemy force made its landfall. Combats took place as far north as West Mersea and as far south as Shoeburyness. But as the AA guns at Rochford were in action against a large enemy formation it seems likely that they came in between Shoeburyness and Foulness Island. It is equally difficult to be precise about the size of the enemy force. No. 56 Squadron reported that it contained about 'two hundred plus' He 111s and Do 17s with a hundred or so Me 110s and Me 109s. No. 257 Squadron, on the other hand, reported only some fifty bombers (including a small number of Ju 87s) and made no mention of a close escort of fighters. They also reported seeing a Hurricane squadron (which could only have been No. 257) attack the bombers head-on, whereas that squadron says nothing of such tactics.

The essentials of the action, however, seem to be clear. No. 56 Squadron was the first to be engaged; and most of its individual fights were with Me 110s for, as in the case of the enemy forces further north, the bombers were closely escorted. Another part of the same force was attacked by No. 257 Squadron and as most of the escorting fighters were engaged with No. 56 Squadron they were able to reach the bombers. A third party to the attack of the enemy was the AA guns between Rochford and the coast; and between them the fighters and guns effectively countered the German attack. According to No. 257 Squadron many of the German bombers turned south-west on being attacked, and some of them jettisoned their bombs; while some of the pilots of No. 56 Squadron whose combats had carried them south, reported that a large formation of enemy bombers turned round when met with heavy anti-aircraft fire from the Rochford district. There was certainly no attempt on the part of the enemy to press on inland either to Rochford or other RAF stations further west and north-west, and there is a strong presumption that it was this type of target that the Germans were interested in. The only concentration of bombs was put down on Shoeburyness. Here there were important military establishments, but it is doubtful whether they constituted the primary target of the German force.

Nor is there much doubt that the attack further north was frustrated. Only No. 56 Squadron had engaged the enemy force as it crossed the coast, but three other squadrons were directed to intercept it as it continued towards Chelmsford. Two of these and one section of the third came into action between Chelmsford and the coast. It is almost unbelievable in view of the odds involved that the enemy forces were turned back, but by the acid test of bombs dropped that would seem to have been the case. The only bombs that can possibly have been dropped by this particular force were reported to have fallen at Burnham-on-Crouch (1735 hours), and Southminster (1755 hours), and these amounted to no more than a dozen in number. Yet it is clear enough that very large numbers of enemy bombers were over this part of the country. No. 85 Squadron reported that 'the enemy raid consisted of a number of aircraft estimated at between one hundred and fifty and two hundred machines ... They were approaching in very high vic formation, stepped-up from 10,000 to 18,000 feet. The lower advance tier comprised Ju 87s followed by He 111s 2,000 feet higher, and higher were Ju 88s and Me 110s at approximately 15,000 feet, with Me 109s at approximately 17,000 feet'. No. 151 Squadron likewise reported that the enemy force was in four groups, but it made no mention of Ju 87s. The one section of No. 46 Squadron which came into action simply reported 'large formations of enemy aircraft'. This great force was engaged by a total of twenty-eight Hurricanes, and, it would appear, was checked by them and forced to retreat.[36]

By 1800 hours all enemy tracks plotted on the operations rooms tables were directed east and south-east. No. 1 Squadron enjoyed a brief skirmish with a dozen Me 109s south of Southend, but otherwise there was nothing to report. The whole operation can hardly have gratified the enemy. If, as we believe, airfields on both sides of the Thames were the German objectives then the attacks failed to achieve anything. At Shoeburyness many houses were damaged, a signal box wrecked and part of the railway line damaged, but this was not a very large return for an operation in which about one hundred bombers participated. Nor did the losses sustained by the defending squadrons afford the enemy much compensation. Nine Hurricanes had been destroyed; three pilots had been killed, and three wounded. Thirty-six German aircraft were claimed, ten being bombers. Most of the fighting took place over the sea and only four fighters and two bombers were found on land. Two of the fighters were from II/ZG 26; the bombers were from III/KG 53.

With this attack the main German operations came to an end, as did what has been commonly recognised in this country as the second phase of the Battle of Britain.

COMMENTARY ON OPERATIONS FROM 8–18 AUGUST

When the operations on 18 August were completed the Germans attempted nothing upon an equal scale until six days later; and when they began again they chiefly attacked targets well inland, whereas up to 18 August their objectives had been mostly near the coast. It is for both these reasons – the lull as well as the changed direction of later attacks – that this day is commonly considered to mark the end of one phase of the Battle of Britain, a phase which had begun ten days before; and for our purpose the notion is acceptable. It is acceptable, however, simply because these ten days mark the first period of intensive fighter operations. We cannot yet be sure that they represent a phase of German activity. It may well be found that not 8 August but 12 or 13 August was the date on which the commanders of the *Luftwaffe* reckoned that the great offensive began. Nor can we be sure that 18 August was held by them to be the end of one period or the beginning of a new one. The weather between 18 and 24 August was not good, and it may have been on that account, rather than that they were gathering their strength for a fresh onslaught, that the Germans did not

36 The other sections failed to hear an order, addressed to them over the R/T, by the Squadron commander, owing to heavy interference by the Germans over which conversations between the enemy pilots could be plainly heard.

operate in force. In short it is too early to dogmatise on the course of this great and crucial battle. However, in that the period 8–18 August indicated fairly clearly the dangers with which Fighter Command had to contend and what general aims the *Luftwaffe* was pursuing, it bears a measure of analysis.

I. SUPERIOR NUMBERS OF THE ENEMY

In the first place it should be recalled that the situation in which the country found itself on the eve of the battle, and throughout its course, was one that required much stronger air defences then were actually available. The point has already been stressed in these pages, but at the risk of stating the obvious its most important repercussion on the fighting of this, and every other phase of the battle must be emphasised. It was that on virtually every occasion that the Germans operated in force they grossly outnumbered the defending squadrons. There were not sufficient forces available for a reserve of fighters, a *masse de manoeuvre*, to be keep back and used only when the direction and strength of the enemy's attack were known. Instead the concentrated formations of German bombers and fighters were being met by squadrons containing no more than twelve, and frequently fewer aircraft. It was rarely, therefore, that the Germans failed to reach their targets, provided that the state of the weather was fair. Nor is the relative strength of the opposing forces employed in one operation an adequate gauge of the odds involved. For whereas as many as seventy or eighty British fighters might engage enemy formations totalling anything from one hundred to three hundred aircraft, the *individual* fighter squadrons, since they normally came into action independently of each other, were engaging up to ten times their number of the enemy.

The problem of overcoming this inferiority was harder to solve owing to the comparatively short warning of attack that was usually obtained, particularly in eastern Kent; for this meant that there was rarely time for more than one squadron to be formed into a fighting formation before the Germans were overland. The general plan of employment was to send half the available squadrons, including the Spitfire squadrons, against the enemy fighters, and the remainder against the bombers; and on a number of occasions, as the controller had planned, one squadron attacked the bombers at much the same time as another engaged the fighters. But in every such case each squadron operated as an independent unit. Longer warning would have enabled pairs of squadrons to be grouped together as one fighting formation; and later in the battle, when the Germans were regularly penetrating well inland, this was sometimes effected. It was impossible, however, as a regular tactic when the Germans were attacking fringe targets, as they did during this phase of operations. The whole position would have been much easier, of course, if additional squadrons had been stationed in the south and south-east; for strong standing patrols (alien though these were to the Fighter Command technique of interception) could then have been maintained. But this brings us full circle to the basic and inescapable fact of numerical weakness.

AHB IIM/b11/1a, Report by AVM Park

II. GERMAN ADVANTAGE IN HEIGHT

In addition to being outnumbered our squadrons were frequently required to fight under that most serious of disadvantages, an initial inferior height. The point is so important that it is worth illustrating at some length. (See Table below.)

TABLE ILLUSTRATING THE ADVANTAGE IN HEIGHT NORMALLY HELD BY GERMAN FORMATIONS, 8–18 AUGUST

Date	*Squadron*	*Area where engagement began*	
8th August	64	Dover	The squadron was attacked by an echelon of about twenty Me 109s from 2,000 feet 'above them and astern.'
"	152	Swanage	Blue and Green sections were attacked by twenty or more Me 109s 'from above.'
11th August	601	Swanage	When the squadron fell in with the enemy, the enemy fighters were well above them.
"	45	Swanage	The Me 110s were in large formations, from 30,000 ft downwards; and pilots were attacked while climbing.
"	213	Portland	The squadron was at the same height as the enemy bombers; but as they engaged them, they discovered that a large force of enemy fighters was well above them.
"	64	Dover	The squadron, which was only eight aircraft strong, fell in with about twenty Me 109s which were five thousand feet above the squadron.
"	64	Dover	When the squadron's second engagement began, the enemy fighters were 8,000 ft above the squadron.
"	609	Swanage	The enemy were stepped up from 15,000 to 30,000 ft and the squadron climbed to attack them.
12th August	610	New Romney	The enemy bombers were 6,000 feet above the squadron when action was joined; and the enemy fighters were above the bombers.
"	65	Eastern Kent	The largest formation of enemy fighters that was sighted was about 15,000 feet above the squadron.
"	64	Dungeness	The squadron were at about the same height as the lowest tier of enemy fighters; but large numbers of Me 109s were stepped up above them.
"	501	Hawkinge	The squadron was at 7,000 feet, attempting to defend Hawkings aerodrome: the enemy fighters were 'at various heights from 10,000 feet down'.
12th August	152	St Catherine's Bay, Isle of Wight	As the squadron went in to attack the bombers, it was discovered that enemy fighters were 'hovering at two to three thousand feet above'.
13th August	257	Tangmere	The squadron was at 12,000 feet: the enemy at 18,000 feet when action was joined.
"	43	Worthing	The enemy fighters dived onto the squadron, when it came up to the bombers.
"	74	Portland	The squadron was at 16,000 feet, and the enemy fighters at 25,000 feet, when action was joined.
15th August	54	Dover	The squadron was preparing to attack a force of dive-bombers at 7,000 feet, but were prevented by a force of He 113s [sic] at 17,000 feet and 19,000 feet.
"	1	Martlesham	The enemy fighters were 5,000 feet above the squadron when they were first sighted.
"	17	Martlesham	The squadron was defending Martlesham and were not all at the same height: three formations of Me 109s were well above some sections of the squadron.
"	501	Maidstone, Rochester	The squadron climbed to attack the enemy bombers.

Table Continued

"	152	South of Portland	The squadron was below both the bombers and the fighters when action was joined.
"	43	Thorney Island	The enemy aircraft were one thousand feet above the squadron.
16th August	266	Canterbury	The squadron was at 20,000 feet: the enemy were at 22,000 feet when action was joined.
"	64	Hawkinge	The squadron was at 21,000 feet and was approaching a group of enemy fighters that was slightly below it, when they fell in with another group of enemy fighters that was 3,000 feet above.
"	1	Selsey Bill	The enemy fighters dived down on the squadron.
"	43	Beachy Head	The squadron was at 12,000 feet and the enemy at 14,000 feet when action was joined.
"	65	Straits of Dover	The squadron climbed to attack the enemy's fighters.
16th August	56	Eastchurch	The squadron was at 10,000 feet; the enemy bombers were at 14,000 to 15,000 feet, and the enemy fighters were about 5,000 feet above their bombers.
"	234	South of the Isle of Wight	The squadron was at 16,000 feet when action was joined.
18th August	1	Northolt	The squadron was patrolling base at 10,000 feet: the enemy were at 19,000 feet when sighted.
"	56	West Mersea	Red section climbed to attack the enemy fighters.
"	65	between Canterbury and Manston	The squadron was at 4,000 feet: the enemy, when sighted, were at 20,000 feet.
"	234	between the Isle of Wight and Southampton	The squadron was approaching Southampton at 12,000 feet when they sighted 20 Me 109s at 16,000 feet.

Thus, on at least thirty-three occasions the enemy enjoyed the double advantage of height and numbers. The reasons for it are not far to seek. The RDF stations on the south and south-east coasts were certainly detecting the approach of the enemy, and were succeeding in distinguishing between large and small formations. But they frequently failed to make any estimate of height, and where one was made it was usually an under-estimate. Secondly, the marks of Spitfire and Hurricane in service at the time took between eighteen and twenty one minutes to reach 25,000 feet, by which time high-flying enemy fighters were usually waiting for them. Thirdly, a controller's orders necessarily took into account the state of the sky; for he could not take the risk of sending his squadrons so high that a German formation could slip underneath them under the cover of low cloud. The protection of Manston and Hawkinge in particular demanded that a least one flight should patrol each airfield below the lowest clouds when an attack threatened; and on 23 August the No. 11 Group controllers were instructed to this effect.

No. 11 Group Instructions to Controller, No. 2

TABLES ILLUSTRATING THE OPERATIONAL WORK OF FIGHTER COMMAND DURING 8–18 AUGUST

Table I: Sorties and Engagements by Squadrons and Sectors in No. 10 and 11 Groups on days of major operations.

Group and Sector	*Sqdn.*	*8th Aug*		*11th Aug*		*12th Aug*		*13th Aug*		*15th Aug*		*16th Aug*		*18th Aug*	
		S.	E.	S.	E.	S.	E.	S.	E.	S.	E.	S.	E.	S.	E.
No. 10 Group															
Pembrey	92	6	0	14	0	9	0	26	1	33	0	12	0	11	
St Eval	234	9	1	22	0	15	1	8	0	–	–	–	–	–	1
	238	–	–	–	–	–	–	–	–	3	0	9	0	7	0
Filton	87	11	0	8	1	15	0	19	1	23	2	23	0	18	0
	213	27	1	24	1	27	1	50	2	19	1	24	1	22	0
Middle Wallop	238	37	1	15	1	20	0	43	3	–	–	–	–	–	–
	609	49	2	35	1	12	1	51	1	11	2	27	0	23	0
No records available	152	–	1	–	1	–	1	–	2	–	0	–	1	–	1
	604	–	–	3	0	1	0	7	0	8	0	5	0	0	0
	234	–	–	–	–	–	–	–	–	35	1	22	1	25	1
	249	–	–	–	–	–	–	–	–	30	1	32	1	24	0
	Total	139	(23)	121	(17)	99	(14)	204	(29)	162	(20)	154	(19)	130	(18)
No. 11 Group															
Tangmere	43	24	1	56	0	54	1	22	2	36	1	34	1	63	1
	145	39	3	16	1	23	1	9	1	–	–	–	–	–	–
	601	47	1	11	1	20	0	60	2	31	1	48	2	28	1
	266	–	–	0	0	12	1	0	0	–	–	–	–	–	–
	602	–	–	–	–	–	–	–	–	19	1	33	3	29	1
Northolt	1	5	0	15	1	57	0	38	0	44	1	35	1	24	2
	257	14	1	0	0	26	1	21	1	15	1	–	–	–	–
Kenley	64	23	2	29	2	8	1	16	1	32	1	19	2	16	1
	111	18	0	12	1	48	0	12	1	40	3	28	1	20	1
	615	26	0	15	0	24	1	18	0	19	1	30	1	15	1
Biggin Hill	32	12	0	24	2	24	1	51	0	29	3	40	2	22	2
	501	14	0	20	0	66	3	0	0	68	3	34	1	57	3
	610	12	1	12	1	12	1	0	0	8	1	12	1	15	1
Hornchurch	41	13	1	–	–	–	–	–	–	–	–	–	–	–	–
	54	13	0	6	0	46	2	10	0	41	2	9	1	48	2
	65	12	1	41	0	53	1	11	1	30	0	24	1	29	1
	74	6	0	43	4	0	0	21	1	–	–	–	–	–	–
	266	–	–	–	–	–	–	–	–	23	3	10	1	10	1
North Weald	56	9	0	18	1	21	1	11	1	23	0	38	1	32	2
	151	13	0	9	1	16	1	12	1	34	2	26	0	31	1
Debden	17	31	1	15	1	0	0	27	0	42	1	43	0	33	1
	257	–	–	–	–	–	–	–	–	–	–	8	0	35	2
	Total	331	(18)	342	(21)	510	(32)	339	(23)	534	(31)	471	(28)	508	(30)

Notes:
1. S = Sorties
   E = Engagements
2. No. 10 Group figures exclude sorties made by No. 247 Squadron for the local defence of Plymouth.
3. Figures in brackets shown average sorties per squadron.

III. OPERATIONAL EFFORT OF FIGHTER COMMAND

The burden of operations during the period is best illustrated statistically (see Tables below and page 123) though perhaps only those who have themselves been concerned in the routine of refuelling, rearming and maintaining aircraft during active operations can fully appreciate what such figure of sorties mean in terms of human effect and fatigue. The quantitative difference between the effort of No. 10 and No. 11 Groups compared to that of No. 12 and No. 13 is obvious enough, but even more emphatic is the difference in the character of their operations. With the exception of the operations on 15 August neither of the northern Groups had been required to deal with any major German attacks; and the sorties that were made by No. 12 Group contained a higher proportion of convoy patrols than was the case in the two southern Groups.[37] In short, the heavy fighting of the period fell on the shoulders of approximately half the squadrons in the Command, disposed in two of the four Groups. On this account it is proper to enquire how far the two southern Groups were reinforced.

IV. REINFORCEMENT POLICY OF THE COMMAND

On the morning of 8 August there were twenty-one squadrons in No. 11 Group, eight and a half in No. 10 and twenty-six and a half in Nos 12 and 13.[38] During the next week the respective Group strengths remained the same except that No. 249 Squadron was moved down to the Middle Wallop sector from No. 12 Group. During the next three days three new squadrons became fit for operations. They were Nos 1 (RCAF), 302 (Polish) and 310 (Czech); the first of these came under No. 11 Group, the others under No. 12. It is apparent, therefore, that any notable addition to the strength of the squadrons in the south could only have been at the expense of the defences in the Midlands, the North of England and Scotland.

TABLES ILLUSTRATING THE OPERATIONAL WORK OF FIGHTER COMMAND DURING 8–18 AUGUST

Table II: Comparative burden of operations

Date	*Number of Squadrons Operating*				*Total Operational Sorties in Daylight*				*Daily Sorties for Protection of Convoys*			
	10 Grp	11 Grp	12 Grp	13 Grp	10 Grp	11 Grp	12 Grp	13 Grp	10 Grp	11 Grp	12 Grp	13 Grp
August 8	7	18	9	7	160	317	117	27	47	81	99	8
" 11	8	18	10	5	142	342	165	30	0	78	101	6
" 12	8	18	6	3	124	510	82	16	6	91	51	14
" 13	8	18	5	6	223	339	102	36	0	85	28	0
" 15	9	17	9	12	183	534	109	148	12	57	66	3
" 16	9	17	8	4	175	471	118	12	9	57	9	0
" 18	9	17	6	4	148	508	93	17	0	37	9	10

37 Early in August Coastal Command took over responsibility for the protection of all convoys outside the area Start Point to Flamboro' Head. The chief effect of this was to reduce the burden of No. 13 Group, which was, in any case, the quietest in Fighter Command.

38 The 'half-squadrons' were No. 247 at Roborough and No. 3 at Wick, each of which mustered one flight for operations.

Such a policy was not adopted, and, in the opinion of Air Chief Marshal Dowding, there were some weighty objections to it. In the first place the German offensive, which he considered would be maintained for some time, had only just begun; and while the squadrons in the zone of operations were outnumbered they were not being outfought, nor were the Germans causing unacceptable damage on the ground. Therefore, it seemed to him better to maintain No. 11 Group at a strength of some twenty squadrons by exchanging squadrons that were tired and depleted for fresh squadrons from quiet sectors, than to reduce his reserve of fresh squadrons by moving some of them into the areas most heavily and frequently attacked.[39] He was not to know how long the battle might last or to what extent he might need the squadrons in No. 12 and No. 13 Groups. Events were to prove, indeed, that he was to need every one of them. Nor was he to know that the raid of 15 August was the first and last against any other area than that covered by Nos 10 and 11 Groups. That raid, it was true, had seemed to him to be a failure; but there could be no guarantee, even if the Germans agreed with him, that similar attacks would not be made in the future. At any rate, the risk of weakening the quieter Groups was not worth running unless the position in the south could be saved by no other means; and there was as yet no danger of that. Meantime a policy of replacement rather than one of reinforcement was pursued, and the following exchanges were effected as a result of fighting during the ten days:

13 August. No. 145 Squadron, Westhampnett, for No. 602 Squadron, Drem.

14 August. No. 74 Squadron, Hornchurch, for No. 266 Squadron, Wittering (this squadron had also been in No. 11 Group since 9 August).

19 August. No. 64 Squadron, Kenley, for No. 616 Squadron, Leconfield.
No. 111 Squadron, Croydon, for No. 85 Squadron, Debden.
No. 601 Squadron, Tangmere, for No. 17 Squadron, Debden.

22 August. No. 266 Squadron, Hornchurch, for No. 264 Squadron, Kirton-in-Lindsey.

The six squadrons thus moved to quieter sectors, had lost forty-four pilots killed and between fifteen and twenty wounded in the course of the ten-day period; which, at an average strength of twenty pilots, amounted to a loss of fifty per cent.

39 It is open to question whether it was practicable, with the R/T facilities available at the time, to operate more than three or four squadrons from one sector. If not, this was another objection to increasing the number of squadrons in No. 11 Group to more than twenty-four at the most.

V. EFFECT OF THE PHASE ON THE STRENGTH OF THE COMMAND

Altogether, between 8 and 18 August ninety-four pilots were killed or missing, and some sixty more or less seriously wounded. In the same period 54 Spitfires and 121 Hurricanes were made 'Category 3', i.e., they were lost outright or so badly damaged that they were beyond repair. In addition, 40 Spitfires and 25 Hurricanes became 'Category 2', i.e., they could not be repaired by the unit. Approximately thirty Spitfires and Hurricanes had also been destroyed or damaged on the ground by enemy action.[40]

Aircraft losses were being met and were no longer the primary problem that they had been in May and early June. That is not to say that the Aircraft Storage Units were meeting with ease all the demands that were made upon them; it will be shown in another narrative what difficulties had to be overcome in order to maintain a flow of aircraft to the operational squadrons. But day to day demands were being met without exhausting the number of aircraft immediately available for issue. Thus on 9 August there were 289 Spitfires and Hurricanes ready for immediate issue from the ASUs; a week later there were 235; and on 23 August there were 161. Over the same period the number of new aircraft being prepared for issue fell from 235 to 166. Clearly enough losses were more than output; but the margin in hand added to output was sufficient to maintain the Command at full strength for some two months, provided the rate of loss did not rise.

AHB VD/13/1

The pilot position, on the other hand, gave rise to much anxiety. When heavy fighting began on 8 August the Command was in process of making good the losses it had suffered in May and June, but it was still one hundred and sixty pilots short of establishment. There was, moreover, a further gap between the number of squadron pilots fit for operations and those still under training though nominally on the strength of a squadron. Thus by 17 August the average pilot strength of the Hurricanes and Spitfires squadrons was nineteen, of whom sixteen were operational in the Hurricane squadrons, and seventeen to eighteen in the Spitfire squadrons. The total deficiency in the day fighting squadrons was, therefore, nearly three hundred and fifty pilots, making the *effective* strength of the Command between nine hundred and one thousand pilots compared to an establishment of between thirteen hundred and fourteen hundred.

AHB IIH/120, Encl.92, Minute ACAS(G) – DHO, 12 August

As early as 12 August No. 11 Group requested Fighter Command to replace some of their recent casualties by experienced pilots from other Groups. Air Chief Marshal Dowding, however, stood by his policy of removing squadrons that had received heavy punishment and replacing them by complete Squadrons from quieter sectors. But it was obvious that the German offensive had started and that for some time to come there would be an extensive drain on fighter strength which could not be met by the normal output from the Flying Training Schools and Operational Training Units. He therefore suggested to the Air Staff that the experienced pilots of the Battle squadrons in Bomber Command should be regarded as a reserve behind the fighter squadrons. He assumed that this type of aircraft would rarely be used on active operations, whereas their best men would be of great value in Fighter Command, after a short conversion course at

Ibid.

40 The precise figures for this category for the period 8–18 August cannot be ascertained. For the period 15–21 August there were fifteen Hurricanes and Spitfires destroyed out right, and seventeen badly damaged (Fighter Command ORB, Appendix J1).

Ibid. Encl. 93, Minute, DCAS – AMT, 13 August

an OTU The objections to this move were firstly that while the Battle squadrons were only in limited use at the time they would be very valuable for attacking invading forces; secondly, that as soon as possible they were to be re-armed with a better type of bomber, and if their most experienced pilots were withdrawn the expansion of the bomber force would be retarded.

There then arose the question of increasing the output from OTUs. Less than eighty Spitfire and Hurricane pilots were expected to be produced before 24 August, and these would meet less than half the casualties that would certainly be incurred if the current scale of fighting continued. The only other sources of supply that could be quickly tapped were Allied pilots and pilots in other Commands of the Metropolitan Air Force.

On 17 August at the Air Ministry the whole position was examined by the Expansion and Re-equipment Policy Committee. There it was agreed that the immediate needs of Fighter Command should be met as quickly as possible; the problem was to effect this without delaying unduly the expansion of other arms of the Air Force. The measures that were decided upon were of two sorts. First, the next courses at the three Fighter Command OTUs were to be filled to capacity by calling upon Allied pilots and specially selected Group II British pilots, i.e. pilots who would normally have passed from a Service Flying Training School to Bomber or Coastal Command. These courses were to last only a fortnight. Second, five volunteers were called for from each of four Bomber Command Battle Squadrons, and three from each of eleven Lysander squadrons in No. 22 Group.[41] How far these measures succeeded in maintaining and increasing the strength of the Command as they were intended to do will be considered when the next phase of heavy fighting is reviewed.

Ibid.

These decisions were taken in order to maintain the strength of the fighter squadrons then in being. But in that they entailed the increased use of Allied pilots they created a problem which was only solved by the somewhat inconsistent method of forming still more squadrons. Air Chief Marshal Dowding has freely admitted that he was dubious at first of the fighting value of pilots who were, after all, the survivors of defeated air forces; and when it was decided to make sure use of them he favoured forming them into their own national squadrons rather than mixing them with British and Dominion pilots in RAF squadrons. But there was a more specific and weighty objection to diluting British units, namely that language difficulties hampered operational efficiency, and more so in Fighter Command, where so much depended on the efficient use of R/T, than in any other branch of the service. When to this was added the understandable pressure from Allied governments for the formation of national squadrons the case for separate units was a strong one.

Despatch, para. 164

The matter was reviewed by the Expansion and Re-equipment Policy Committee on the same day as it considered what immediate measures should be taken for improving the pilot position. There was no disagreement over the principle of forming separate units of Allied pilots, but certain members of the committee doubted whether the time was ripe for such squadrons to be formed

41 A number of army co-operation pilots had been transferred to Fighter Command towards the end of July, but the precise number is not known. The thirty-three volunteers obtained from army co-operation squadrons under the decision of 17 August were given an intensive six-day course at No. 7 OTU, Hawarden, commencing on 22 August.

ERP Meeting, 17 August.

over and above the three already in being. In the opinion of AMSO, who was supported by AMT, to form new fighter squadrons would inevitably mean a diversion of resources from the overdue expansion of the bomber force without the compensating advantage of an immediate addition to the strength of Fighter Command; for if pilots were formed into new squadrons instead of being posted to squadrons already in being it would be some weeks before they could be in the line of battle. Their formation would also mean that more calls would be made on the Hurricane reserves (Air Chief Marshal Dowding was opposed to equipping Allied squadrons with Spitfires), which had already fallen by seventy aircraft since the start of heavy fighting.

The resultant decisions of the committee sought to compromise between this point of view and those of Air Chief Marshal Dowding, who was anxious to augment the first-line strength of Fighter Command, and of the Polish and Czechoslovak governments, who were eager for the formation of squadrons manned by their own nationals. Thus it was decided to form one more Czechoslovak and three more Polish squadrons; but in order to reduce the drain on Hurricane resources these were at first allotted only enough aircraft to maintain a single flight. Each squadron was to be at half-strength in pilots, but would have a complete ground staff. In addition, in order not to burden the overloaded OTU capacity with pilots who would not be flying in operational squadrons for some time, it was agreed that all pilots posted to the new squadrons would carry out their operational training there. Under such conditions it was many weeks before the new units entered the line of battle; none of them, in fact, was operational before the end of September.

It is apparent from these various measures that the first ten days of heavy fighting had underlined the main weakness of Fighter Command. Nor could the output of pilots be expected to improve until the end of the next series of OTU courses, i.e. between 31 August and 15 September, while the new squadrons that it had been decided to form could not influence the battle unless it lasted for at least six weeks. Inevitably the question arises, had this weakening of the Command been counter-balanced by the losses suffered by the Germans?

VI. GERMAN LOSSES

Fighter Command ORB, Appendix J.

Here it is necessary to draw a distinction between what was known and believed at the time and what has since been discovered. According to the claims that were made by individual pilots in their combat reports, and by anti-aircraft gun sites, and which were sanctioned by Fighter and Anti-Aircraft Commands, 508 German aircraft had certainly been destroyed by our fighters and 88 by anti-aircraft guns between 8 and 18 August. If these claims were accurate then our own losses, even taking into account the disparity between the two forces, were offset by those of the enemy. In the very nature of things these figures could not be checked before they were passed on every evening *via* the press and the BBC to the general public, in whose minds they undoubtedly represented the strict mathematical truth. Nor can it be doubted that they were also deemed to be accurate by the pilots of Fighter Command – a circumstance which helped them to bear their own losses the more cheerfully. Air Chief Marshal Dowding

Despatch, para. 113.

himself has described the claims as 'an honest approximation' and early in the battle he protested to the Secretary of State for Air against their presentation as a verified and verifiable figure. On the other hand he was no less outspoken against anything that cast doubt upon his pilots' veracity.

Yet the fact remained that between the pilots' claims and the number of enemy aircraft found after a battle there was an immense gap which was not entirely to be explained by the fact that most combats took place over the sea. What was obviously needed was an independent examination of the whole question, and one was begun by a section (AI3 (b)) of the Air Intelligence branch at the Air Ministry; but its first reports were not available until 19 September. Until then all that was positively known was that whereas some six hundred German aircraft were claimed as destroyed between 8 and 18 August the wreckage of only one hundred and four was actually discovered. If the first figure was not to be trusted as a guide to German casualties the second was even less reliable; for the Germans themselves admitted twice that number of losses.[42] The success or failure of air operations such as those of the Battle is, however, not only to be judged by relative losses in aircraft. Another standard, and one more easily applied whilst operations are in progress, is the damage caused by bombing relative to what the Germans intended and the scale of the German effort. This leads us to consider the general pattern of German attacks during this early phase of the battle.

VII. STATE OF THE GERMAN AIR FORCE

In the opinion of the Air Intelligence branch the German Air Force was not in a position early in August to begin and maintain even for one month what was described as 'a maximal attack'. Estimates of the stocks of fuel, bombs and ammunition which such an attack would require were worked out, and it was concluded that the Germans had not yet had sufficient time to accumulate them. Airfield construction and extension was still going on in northern France in order to provide all the bases that such an enterprise would require. Bomber aircraft were still being fitted with new equipment, especially armour plating, to meet the different conditions of air warfare over Britain. Some re-equipment with new aircraft was still going on, and not all units were yet up to establishment in aircraft. For all these reasons it was believed that the full weight of the German Air Force could not yet be launched against us. It was also thought that the full onslaught would precede the airborne and sea-borne invasion which the Germans were thought to be planning, but which was not yet ready to move. In short, the crisis in affairs had not been reached when in the second week of August the Germans began their attacks.

AHB ID/2/2 280.

Combined Intelligence Committee, Report No. 71, 9 August.

42 Between 8 and 21 August the Germans admitted the loss of 209 aircraft. For a more detailed examination of this whole question of claims and casualties see Appendix 36.

VIII. GERMAN OBJECTIVES AND TARGETS

Yet it was against the background of invasion that the Germans' attacks were necessarily interpreted and analysed. Their main targets were as follows:

8 August	South coast convoy.
11 August	Portland: Dover: Thames Estuary Shipping.
12 August	RAF stations at Manston, Lympne and Hawkinge: RDF stations at Ventnor, Pevensey, Rye and Dunkirk: Portsmouth town and harbour.
13 August	RAF stations at Eastchurch and Detling: Army camps at Borden and Longmore: Southampton docks and various RAF stations in Hampshire.
14 August	RAF stations at Manston, Middle Wallop, Colerne, Cardiff, Kemble, Andover, Sealand and Hullavington, and FAA station at Yeovilton: communications between Bristol and Portland.
15 August	RAF stations at Hawkinge, Lympne, Eastchurch, Martlesham, West Malling, Croydon, Middle Wallop and Driffield (Yorks): North-east coast: Kent coast towns: Aircraft works at Rochester and Croydon.
16 August	RAF stations at West Malling, Tangmere, Gosport, Brize Norton, Harwell, Farnborough and FAA station at Lee-on-Solent: RDF station at Ventnor: south-west London suburbs.
18 August	RAF stations at Kenley, Biggin Hill, Croydon, West Malling, Gosport, Thorney Island and FAA station at Ford: RDF station at Poling: Shoeburyness.

In addition, as the day-to-day narrative has shown, small concentrations of bombs were dropped on numerous rural districts of southern England; and insofar as these were part of any consistent plan they seem to have been directed against railway communications.

Clearly enough, however, the Germans' chief targets were RAF stations between Middle Wallop in the west and Manston in the east. It is on this account that 12 August is held to be the beginning of this phase of operations rather than 8 August, which is more properly considered the last day of that phase of German activity which had begun on 10 July and which was chiefly directed against Channel shipping. Most of the heavy attacks from 12 August onwards were against airfields on or near the south and south-east coasts, viz: Lee-on-Solent, Gosport, Tangmere, Ford, Lympne, Hawkinge and Manston; Eastchurch, on the Isle of Sheppey might also be included in this category. A number of airfields outside the coastal strip were also attached, e.g. Middle

Wallop, Farnborough, Kenley, Croydon, Biggin Hill and West Malling; and of the occasional attacks on airfields well inland or in the north those against Sealand, Driffield and Brize Norton were the most serious.

See A.M. Weekly Intelligence Summary, Home Security Daily Appreciation and CIC Reports.

No special significance was attached to these attacks at the time beyond the fact that they marked the opening of a general offensive against the Royal Air Force, and against Fighter Command in particular. Nor was there perhaps any need for a deeper analysis. It was the policy of all Commands to maintain airfields in operation as long as possible and, if that became impossible, to continue to assist the Army to defend them against seaborne or airborne attack; and as the Germans had not yet compelled the evacuation of any airfield their attacks could be considered to have failed and the general position remained satisfactory.

See Minutes of Fighter Command Conference, 3 July.

But the German attacks could not be disregarded. They had underlined the danger to aircraft on the ground and it became a point of honour with controllers to despatch every available fighter into the air whenever attack threatened a station. For the same reason the extra flight which had been allotted to all Hurricane and six Spitfire squadrons was withdrawn during the last week in August at the request of Fighter Command.

S.3553. Encl.2A.

The attacks also inspired much criticism of the arrangements which had been made for filling-up craters on landing grounds.[43] Both the AOC-in-C and the AOC No. 11 Group have recorded their opinion that these were inadequate, while the Prime Minister himself protested against what he regarded as the feeble efforts that were made to repair the damage caused at Manston by the attack on 12 August. During this first period of the battle, however, no fighter station with the exception of West Malling, was out of action for more than twenty-four hours; and in the case of the bombing of Manston on the 12th a landing strip was available within one hour of the attack. It was not this type of damage, not damage to hangars, which was to prove most dangerous but damage to operations rooms and telecommunications, of which there was little during these first ten days except at Kenley on the 18th.

Despatch, para. 137. AHB IIM/b11/1a, Encl. 2.

AHB ID/2/153, Encl. 1.

The distribution of the German attacks was somewhat peculiar. In the first place they were by no means concentrated upon Fighter Command stations. Every airfield within five miles of the coast between the Solent and the Thames Estuary was attacked irrespective of its function. As heavy attacks, indeed, were made on the Coastal Command station and the Fleet Air Arm station at Ford as on either of the forward airfields used by Fighter Command at Hawkinge and Manston. Similarly Eastchurch and Detling were severely bombed, though neither was normally used by fighter squadrons. Secondly, there was a seeming

43 The organisation for airfield repair was primarily the responsibility of the Air Ministry Works Directorate. At this time the first line of defence, so to speak, consisted of detachments of Royal Engineers, usually sixty strong, which were stationed at over twenty stations south of the Thames and as far west as Middle Wallop. Then there were twenty seven Works Repair depots in various parts of the country so located as to be central to a group of airfields. The number of men in each varied from fifty to two hundred; and reserves of equipment, including bulldozers, excavators, mobile generating plants, petrol and water pumps, and some electrical repair equipment were held at these depots. Stocks of hard core, clinkers and ashes had been laid down at all stations prior to the battle, but they proved insufficient to deal with a major attack.

The maintenance and repair of telecommunications was the business of the GPO, assisted in many cases by the Royal Corps of Signals. The GPO had set up a special organisation (GPO (War Group)) prior to the war to deal with the interruption of communications; and liaison officers had been appointed to Command and Group headquarters. At all sector stations in No. 11 Group, GPO maintenance staff were continuously in attendance.

dissipation of German effort, particularly on 13, 14 and 16 August against RAF stations which were many miles away from the main zone of battle. Even the effective attack on Brize Norton – which can well be interpreted as an attack on the training organisation of the Air Force at a time when its maintenance and expansion were more than usually important – affected Bomber rather than Fighter Command, for all the pilots trained there were in Group II and all the aircraft destroyed were Airspeed Oxfords which were not used for training fighter pilots.[44] The attack on Sealand may also have been intended to interfere with fighter pilot training, as well as with the output of aircraft from the Aircraft Storage Unit there. But it is clearly impossible to square every attack on an RAF station during this period with a policy of attacking Fighter Command to the exclusion of other arms of the Air Force. Precisely what was the German policy is not at the moment known, but no harm will be done by drawing a number of inferences from the facts as set out above.

In their attacks on airfields the Germans may have had three objects in view: first, the neutralisation of coastal airfields in Hampshire, Sussex and Kent; second, the denial of alternative airfields in the general area of southern England to Fighter Command; and third, by spreading their attacks over a wide area of the country to underline the extent of their threat and thus prohibit a concentration of fighter strength in the area between the Solent and the Thames. As to the first of these, the motive that springs obviously to mind is that the Germans were hoping to be able to use one or more abandoned airfields for future airborne landings, but they may also have been intending to deny the use of any forward airfields to Fighter Command.

S.5293, Encl. 4A DCAS – Dowding, 24 June

If the second inference is correct the Germans had not misappreciated the situation. As early as 24 June it had been decided to safeguard the fighter defences as far as possible by arranging alternative airfields and landing grounds for each sector in Fighter Command. What the Air Staff and Fighter Command had in mind was the possibility of evacuation because of invasion rather than through bombing; consequently the alternative airfields were well inland.[45] It is unlikely that the Germans knew the details of the scheme; and, in

44 If this attack was intended to interfere with fighter pilot training – and there can be no proof of this until German records are examined – then the Germans may have been working on out-of date intelligence, as until the end of June one-third of the output from Brize Norton consisted of Group I, i.e. single-engined aircraft pilots.

45 By direct arrangement with other Commands Fighter Command obtained the use of some thirty airfields. Each fighter sector thus had one or more airfields, other that its own satellites, from which it could operate if compelled to evacuate its usual station. It was intended that the scheme should be able to come into operation at very short notice; the evacuated squadrons relying for maintenance and servicing on a small party from the squadron assisted by such personnel as could be spared by their hosts. The majority of the squadron ground staff would stay on at the parent station to defend it. This also entailed laying down supplies of ammunition and fuel at the alternative airfields, but owing to a shortage of equipment, especially petrol bowsers, little was effected in this respect during the three months of the battle. The scheme affected all fighter Groups, and the alternatives for the south and south-east sectors are given below.

Station	*Alternative Airfields*	*Controlled by*
Filton	Hullavington	Flying Training Command
Middle Wallop	Upavon	Flying Training Command
Tangmere	Odiham	No. 22 Group
Northolt	Benson and Abingdon	Bomber Command
Kenley	Worthy Down	Admiralty
Biggin Hill	Heathrow	Bomber Command
Hornchurch	Hatfield	No. 22 Group
North Weald	Henlow and Cranfield	Flying Training Command

fact, only one of the emergency stations was bombed during the period under review.

The third aim behind the German attacks is one that can be substantiated by reference to other aspects of German operations. It has frequently been remarked in these pages that the collapse of France at once made it possible for the Germans to extend as well as to intensify the scale of attack against these islands; and the counter-measures that were taken correspondingly took the form of strengthening the air defences of the country and extending them to areas which had previously been defended only lightly, if at all. Such operations as those by single aircraft or small formations against Sealand and South Wales on 14 August, those against shipping in the North Sea, St George's Channel and the North Channel, and, above all, those against the north-east and Yorkshire coasts on 15 August, emphasised how wide was the area open to attack, and confirmed the need for the expansion in the north-west and in Scotland that had been decided on in June and July. Yet it should not be forgotten that the Fighter Command system had been designed to cope with attacks against widely separated sections of the perimeter of Britain. Each of the four fighter Groups was capable of operating independently within its own area, and simultaneously with the others. The danger that was apprehended, therefore, was not that the Germans would be constantly attacking different areas of the country, but that as much strength as they could muster would be continuously against one of the four Group areas, or an even more restricted locality, with the intention of creating suitable conditions for an invasion. Thus, speaking in July of what tactics the Germans might be expected to employ, Air Chief Marshal Dowding said: 'The two main alternatives are, in principle, that the enemy will try from the very beginning a battering-ram attack on a certain locality, concentrating all his strength and all his air and sea effort on the one place, trying to batter down opposition; or he might do what he had done more or less all along, attack on a wide front, not knowing where he is going to break through by taking advantage of every opportunity, pouring in through any gap he makes … This [latter] form of attack would be very convenient for us from the air point of view, because we are already dispersed all along the coast and we could bring our maximum forces to bear in countering the attack; whereas, supporting it was all concentrated on the south-east coast of Kent, we could not deploy more than a fraction of our forces at one time'.

Fighter Command Conference, 3 July

These remarks are not precisely relevant to the operations between 8 and 18 August as the AOC-in-C, was thinking of combined, rather than exclusively air operations; but they exemplify his views on which of two forms of air attack was most to be feared. The Germans, it is clear, had adopted neither the one nor the other. That is not to say, however, that their attacks were governed by an unsatisfactory compromise. If, on the one hand, they had not yet taken the form with which our defences would find it most difficult to deal, on the other the battle had patently not yet reached its climax. Moreover, by the scope of the attacks, German air power had been carried over most of the country either by day or night; and at the same time at least some of the large formations which had been launched against the south coast had been able to penetrate as far as London. Certainly it could not be inferred at the time – nor was it – that the Germans were unaware of the most effective way in which to employ their great forces. Indeed, even though the Germans were not yet operating at full strength the squadrons in No. 11 Group had been considerably extended, and this was obviously one of the German aims.

For although it is not possible, as we have seen, to interpret all the German attacks as part of an offensive against Fighter Command, it is equally clear that much of their effort was intended to weaken No. 11 Group. The attacks on Lympne, Hawkinge and Manston and, later in the period, on Tangmere, Kenley, Croydon and Biggin Hill were all part of this policy, and with them must be coupled the attacks on the RDF system in the south and south-east. At least two of the three RDF stations most heavily attacked – Ventnor, Poling and Rye – continued to observe, though with emergency equipment; and throughout the period no major attack was undetected. Their estimates of height and numbers, however, were still suspect.

IX. GERMAN TACTICS

The bomber formations employed in the larger attacks were rarely more than *Gruppe* strength, though occasionally two *Gruppen* were employed in one and the same force (e.g. the attack on Portland 15 August). This we now know for certain, and it accounts for the low tonnage of bombs dropped relative to the size of the forces that were believed at the time to have been employed. Unfortunately, without reliable figures of the size of German fighter escorts it is impossible to assess the accuracy of the pilots' estimates of enemy numbers. It is clear, however, that in nearly all the German attacks the escorting fighters outnumbered the bombers.

The average height at which the bombers flew was 11,000–18,000 feet, with escorts behind and above up to heights of 25,000 feet. This, it has already been noted, placed the defending fighters at a disadvantage on many occasions. But there was one compensation, that in the early stages of a combat attacks were frequently pressed home against the German bombers before their escort was able to interfere. By the 16th the Germans had learned the obvious lesson, and on that day our pilots reported for the first time that enemy bombers were protected by fighters flying ahead and on the flank at the same level. These tactics were repeated on the 18th and were continued after heavy attacks recommenced on 24 August. Consequently, Air Vice-Marshal Park gave instructions that the practice of sending one squadron to engage the high-flying fighters and another to attack the bombers would be discontinued, and all forces would be despatched against the bombers.

No. 11 Group Instructions to Controllers, No.4, 25 August

Against the German fighters our own pilots had little to fear, although by this date many Me 109s and 110s were fitted with rear armour. The German practice of forming a defensive circle was frequently encountered, and it was difficult to break into the circle without being attacked by superior numbers. But the large fighter formations which the Germans launched in support of a major bombing raid were unwieldy and suffered heavily. Where opposing forces were more equal the ratio of losses was not so much in the defenders' favour. Moreover, most fighter combats took place at medium altitude where the high-flying qualities of both types of Messerschmidt fighters were not given full scope; and this remained the case until later in the battle when the enemy bombers came in at higher altitudes.

The long-range bombers proved more difficult to destroy, and it would appear that the two months' lull after the collapse in France had been utilised for equipping these aircraft with more and heavier armour. In consequence, deflection shooting, beam attacks and head-on attacks were increasingly used to supplement the standard attacks from astern. Head-on attacks by other than single aircraft were discouraged by Air Chief Marshal Dowding, chiefly on the grounds that once an attack had been made the fighter would be so far behind the enemy that a second attack would usually be impossible. He visualised its usefulness against large and comparatively slow-moving bomber formations, and it was chiefly against this type of target that the head-on attack was most successfully used (e.g. the attack by No. 151 Squadron over the Thames Estuary, 13 August).

S.1965, encl. 29A, Dowding – Air Ministry, 1 August

There was one type of German attack which our pilots believed they had regularly punished severely. This was a medium-altitude approach by Ju 87 formations culminating in a dive attack. Heavy claims for the destruction of this aircraft were made, especially on the 15th and 18th; and as no more Ju 87s were reported before 7 September it seems reasonable to infer that the dive-bomber units were suffering too heavily to be kept in the battle. We are the more entitled to say this since Ju 87s were responsible for the successful series of attacks against airfields and RDF stations in Hampshire, and the Germans would be aware of it.

X. CONCLUSION

But on the whole there is not yet sufficient information of German intentions for this first phase of the battle to be reckoned a positive victory for either side, tempting though it is to infer from the five days' comparative lull which followed it that the Germans had suffered a setback. We can say, however, that the *Luftwaffe* had suffered more severely than Fighter Command, and that it had not obtained a sufficient return in targets damaged or destroyed to compensate it for its losses. On the other hand it had so far used barely one-third of its available strength in the west. Fighter Command, for its part, had lost pilots it could ill-afford; and the grim prospect of the fighter force slowly wasting away through lack of pilots was already apparent after little more than one week's intensive fighting.

IV

THIRD PHASE, 24 AUGUST–6 SEPTEMBER

INTRODUCTION, OPERATIONS, 19–23 AUGUST

The Germans launched no operations comparable to those of 11–18 August until 24 August, and the scale of enemy activity fell sharply away during the intervening five days. This comparative lull could not be put down to any regrouping of German forces, for as far as we knew *Luftwaffe* dispositions remained unchanged. The only explanation that was advanced at the time was that previous activity had overstrained the *Luftwaffe* organisation in northern France, which was believed still to be inadequate to sustain heavy operations for periods longer than a week. Even now no authoritative explanation can be given. It may be that the weather, which was unfavourable for large operations and suitable for harassing attacks by small formations, weighed with the Germans as much as any other factor.

i. By Day

The only large formations to approach the coast during the five days came over the Dover–North Foreland area on the afternoon of the 20th and again on the evening of the 22nd. Both forces were reported to be over one hundred aircraft strong, and their object appears to have been simply to sweep the skies over the Straits, though on each occasion a small number of fighters and fighter-bombers carried out a swift attack on Manston. After the second attack No. 600 Squadron, which was the only unit permanently stationed there, was moved to Hornchurch, but the airfield continued to be used as a forward base chiefly by squadrons from the Hornchurch sector.

19–23 August

Otherwise German activity in daylight took the form of scattered attacks by small formations against targets in many areas of the country, though chiefly south of the line Bristol Channel – the Wash; and on no day were more than sixty aircraft estimated to have been employed. Two of these attacks met with a degree of success which stands out in marked contrast to the paltry results which had frequently attended larger raids. On the afternoon of the 19th a single aircraft bombed the oil storage depot at Llanreath, Pembroke, causing a fire which burned for a week and destroyed ten out of fifteen oil tanks. Two days later an attack was made on a naval training establishment, HMS *Royal Arthur*, near Skegness, where some nine hundred small huts were demolished or damaged. Most of the attacks, however, were directed against RAF stations and railway communications, and no major incidents were reported.

There was a quickening in the attack of shipping during this period, and some twenty attacks were reported, chiefly in the south-west and in St George's Channel, where the cruiser *Manchester* was unsuccessfully attacked on the 21st. All those carried out by day, however, were the work of single aircraft, and the Germans showed no inclination to resume the heavy attacks on coastal shipping that they had launched in July and early August. One of the few convoys that had been routed through the Straits since 8 August was virtually unmolested from the air as it made the passage on 21 and 22 August. Instead it was left to the coastal batteries which the enemy had emplaced near Cap Gris Nez. One hundred and twenty rounds were fired at the convoy between 0930 and 1215 hours on the 22nd, but no ship was hit.

The interception of these small and scattered raids was not easy, especially as the prevalence of cloud throughout the period assisted evasion. It involved, too, a higher scale of effort for the defenders than for the Germans, and on no day were the total operational sorties of Fighter Command less than four hundred. Nevertheless, forty-five enemy aircraft were believed to have been destroyed by fighters during the day, and six by anti-aircraft fire, four of the latter in the attacks in east Kent on the 22nd. Wreckage or prisoners were obtained from twelve aircraft, all of which were bombers, in itself a reflection of the altered character of the German operations. Seventeen British fighters, including two destroyed on the ground at Manston, but only six pilots, were lost.

ii. By Night

The scale of enemy activity at night was largely dictated by the weather. Between seventy and one hundred aircraft were believed to have operated on the nights of the 18th and 19th, but less than twenty on each of the two following nights when high winds and low clouds made flying difficult over the whole country. Over two hundred aircraft were estimated to have come over on the night of the 22nd/23rd, and over one hundred the next night, when the weather had improved a good deal.

All regions in England and Wales reported incidents at one time or another during the six nights, but the emphasis of attack was on the Midlands, South Wales and the south-west. Without comprehensive information of the German targets it is unwise to deliver any judgement upon the accuracy of the bombing, but if important industrial and commercial establishments, focal points of communications, and RAF stations were their objectives – and one would expect this to have been so – they achieved only trifling material success. At Derby on the night of the 19th some forty HE bombs were dropped and the railway was damaged; on the 22nd/23rd an ammunition train standing in a siding near Aldershot was attacked and some of the ammunition was destroyed; on the same night incidents affecting property and public services were reported from some London suburbs, Harrow, Wembley, Willesden, Edmonton and Walthamstow. Further west a fairly heavy attack was carried out on the Filton aircraft works, sixteen tons of bombs being dropped, affecting production at No. 4 Factory; and on the following night aircraft of KGr 100 once more demonstrated their ability to find and bomb the Castle Bromwich district of Birmingham, where a power house and a river bridge were seriously damaged. Otherwise, the bombing resulted in the now customary catalogue of rural incidents, entailing little loss of life and no military damage.[1]

1 One other night operation by the Germans deserves recording as it was one of a type that could not be countered by Fighter Command as it was then constituted and equipped. It was an attack on an outward bound convoy off the Moray Firth shortly before midnight on the 23rd. The defence consisted entirely of the AA guns of the merchant ships and their escorts, as it had been agreed some time before that it was a waste of effort to despatch fighters to protect shipping at sea at night. The attack, which was carried out by torpedo-carrying aircraft of KG 30, met with some success. Two merchant vessels totalling 11,700 tons were sunk, and one of 10,000 tons was set on fire and had to beached near Kirkwall.

But if the night attacks seemed to us to have failed, it was not due to the active defences of Fighter and AA Command. Three aircraft were claimed by the latter, but no positive confirmation was obtained; while out of one hundred and sixty night fighters sorties only one resulted in a definite engagement, and then the pilot could not claim a certain success.

OPERATIONS, 24 AUGUST

After the early morning haze had disappeared the weather on the 24th was fine and visibility was good until noon, especially in the southern counties. In the afternoon more cloud came up from the south-west and operations were affected to some extent.

The first signs of enemy activity were detected between Norwich and the Norfolk coast at 0750 hours, when a small force, which had been missed by the RDF stations, was picked up by the Observer Corps. A few minutes later this force dropped some twenty HE bombs just west of the harbour at Great Yarmouth, which was very probably the German objective. Public services were affected, but all damage was repaired within twenty-four hours. A section of Spitfires from No. 66 Squadron, Coltishall, was sent into the air, but the enemy was not sighted.

a. Over East Kent and the Thames Estuary

i. 0800–0915 hours

About the same time as this small raid was detected two forces of some strength were located behind Cap Griz Nez, and as usual squadrons were immediately despatched to patrol the forward airfields: Hawkinge, Manston, Rochford and Martlesham were each protected. Shortly before 0815 hours two separate forces were plotted as they crossed the coast, one near Winchelsea and the other near Folkestone. By that time more enemy formations were detected over the Straits but for the time being none showed any disposition to cross the coast. Nevertheless, more British squadrons were ordered off the ground: No. 615 Squadron, Kenley, No. 501 Squadron, Gravesend, and No. 56 Squadron, North Weald, all took off between 0815 and 0830 hours, thus forming a second line of defence if the enemy should try to break through to the sector stations in Surrey, Kent and Essex. With these latest additions the defending force amounted to six full squadrons and two flights.

There then occurred one of those fortunately rare operations when the Germans seem to have operated over south-east England much as they pleased without being brought to action except by the smallest of fighter detachments. Between 0813 and 0900 hours five enemy forces, none of which was reported to consist of less than twenty aircraft, were plotted as they crossed the coast at different points between Hastings and the North Foreland. Yet only two British pilots engaged the enemy, one from No. 85 Squadron, the other from No. 610. Both actions took place near Ramsgate with the force that originally crossed the coast near Folkestone, and which later reconnoitred the coast as far north as

Manston. One of the pilots reported that he had attacked twenty – thirty Ju 88s, while the other engaged a single Me 109 which had become detached from a larger formation. With the exception of the guns at Dover, which fired sixty rounds between 0810 and 0848 hours at various formations of Me 109s, these were the only engagements. Fortunately (though somewhat surprisingly in view of the reported presence of bombers) the enemy merely carried out reconnaissances. One force reconnoitred the southern bank of the Thames Estuary as far as Chatham, another force was in the same area and went as far west as Woolwich; a third flew over the country from Hastings to the south-east of Biggin Hill; a fourth, as we have noted, covered the east coast of Kent; and a fifth, which came in west of Dungeness, was plotted as far as Ashford where its track was lost. The detailed orders which were given to the defending squadrons have not been preserved, so it is impossible to explain the failure to intercept. Much may have been due to the morning haze which had not yet dispersed.

ii. 1000–1045 hours

By 0925 hours the last reconnaissance aircraft had recrossed the coast and no enemy movements were plotted over the country. But activity was still taking place on the eastern side of the Straits; and towards 1000 hours it quickened. There were then three forces of between ten and twenty aircraft over the French coast between Boulogne and Dunkerque, and two small detachments were manoeuvring over the Straits. On the British side two of the squadrons that had taken off earlier, No. 501 and No. 54, were still in the air and could remain on patrol until 1100 hours. They were reinforced by a flight of No. 151 Squadron from Rochford, and eight aircraft of No. 85 Squadron from Rochford.

By 1020 hours the Germans had completed their preliminary moves, and two formations crossed the coast just before 1025 hours, one near Hythe and the other between Folkestone and Dover. The latter force was heavily engaged between 1025 and 1030 hours by the Dover AA gunners, who reported that there were about thirty Ju 88s protected by Me 109s. This tallied with what our own fighters reported shortly afterwards. No. 54 Squadron was engaged by enemy fighters at 20,000 feet some miles north of Dover, and consequently was unable to engage the Ju 88s, which passed inland towards Canterbury. Without loss to itself the squadron shot down two Me 110s and one Me 109 into the sea.

The second German formation also flew north after it crossed the coast, and was engaged by No. 501 Squadron. It was similar in numbers to the first force, but the fighter escort was entirely of Me 109s and the bombers were Do 215s. Again the German fighters effectively protected their charges. No sooner had the squadron commenced to attack the rearmost section of the bombers, when it was itself attacked from each flank. Honours were even in the ensuing fight, one of each side being lost.

Once more the virtual absence of bombing in the area over which the enemy are known to have been flying makes these operations remarkable. The only bombs reported were a small number which fell near no obvious target to the south-east of Canterbury; not a large return for an operation in which some fifty German bombers are believed to have participated.

iii. 1115–1145 hours

Only half an hour elapsed after the Germans had finished their previous operation before they attacked once more; and on this occasion the defences were outwitted. Strong enemy formations had been plotted over the Straits since before 1100 hours without making any threatening move. The defensive dispositions – as was the normal procedure – took the form of maintaining patrols over Hawkinge, Manston and Rochford; and Dover was also being protected. By 1120 hours, when it became clear that the Germans in the Straits were moving west, a Hornchurch squadron was sent off to reinforce the patrol over Manston, and a further squadron was sent off from Rochford to take the place of No. 151 Squadron, which had been directed south towards the enemy. The latter came straight across the Straits in three forces; the two flanking formations being composed of fighters and the centre one of bombers. No. 151 Squadron ran into the northerly force of fighters near Manston and never saw any enemy bombers, while No. 610 Squadron, which had been directed north from Dover was also exclusively engaged with fighters south of Ramsgate. Meanwhile the main German force skirted Dover, came up to Ramsgate from the south and bombed the town and civil airport heavily. Between 1130 and 1135 hours it was heavily engaged by the Dover gunners, who reported that it contained over twenty He 111s; but otherwise it was unmolested. Some sixty bombs were dropped at Ramsgate airport, which was not used by the RAF, and about one hundred and fifty on the town, where extensive damage was caused: the number of bombs indicates a larger force than that which was reported. By 1140 hours the attack was over, and five minutes later the south-east was quite clear of the enemy.

iv. 1230–1315 hours

But as before during the morning there was no clear gap between the end of one attack and the beginning of another. The threat of attack was maintained by a continuous procession of small formations in the Straits; and the controllers at No. 11 Group had little warning before the enemy had effected a concentration and were on a course for the coast of England. This was the state of affairs at 1230 hours, shortly before the Germans launched their most serious attack of the morning. There were then five enemy formations plotted within fifty miles of Dover:

> One of 'twelve plus' behind Cap Gris Nez.
> One of 'twenty plus' just to the westward.
> One of 'six plus' off Dunkerque.
> One of the same size eight miles south-east of Dover.
> One of 'eighteen plus' to the east of Boulogne.

Two British squadrons were in the air at the time: No. 264 were patrolling Manston but were just about to land; No. 501 Squadron had just taken off from Gravesend to patrol Hawkinge; and, in addition, detachments from Nos 43 and 111 were patrolling Tangmere and Martlesham respectively. Also, No. 65 Squadron was ordered up from Rochford to take the place of No. 264 Squadron, but it did not take-off until 1250 hours and was too late to take part in the subsequent fighting.

Between 1245 and 1250 hours three German forces moved west and crossed the coast, two near Deal, and one near Dover. Two of them, it is clear, were mere diversions, and having crossed the coast and penetrated inland a short distance they then turned east and retired towards France. One was fired on by the Dover guns at 1250 hours, but neither was engaged by fighters. The main body, which crossed at Deal, consisted of about twenty Ju 88s protected by a similar number of fighters, and it steered north towards Manston.

There, three of the four sections of No. 264 Squadron had just landed and were about to refuel while the fourth kept guard over the airfield, but the aircraft on the ground took to the air again when warning of attack was received. They had barely taken off when the Ju 88s appeared and dived down on the station, and the Defiants were unable to interfere with the bombing. No. 501 Squadron likewise were too far from the enemy to intercept before the attack was carried out. Both squadrons, however, took up position to attack the enemy as they retired. No. 264 Squadron managed to carry out a number of individual beam attacks before they were engaged by the escorting fighters, and at a cost of three Defiants and their crews they claimed two bombers and one fighter. No. 501 had a free hand with the bombers for some minutes thanks to No. 264, and they believed that they shot down three before the enemy fighters came up. One of these was also destroyed, the whole action costing the squadron neither aircraft nor pilots.

Manston itself was badly damaged. The living quarters were wrecked, all communications were cut, and a large number of unexploded bombs made it unusable. All administrative staff were permanently evacuated, and only such staff as were required for defence and for servicing of aircraft when the airfield was once more fit for operations were left behind.

v. 1515–1630 hours

After this attack was over the Germans adhered to their procedure of maintaining formations over the Straits in such strength that we were unable to decide whether or not an attack was imminent, the more so as occasional feint attacks were made by fighter formations, two of which crossed the coast and remained overland for a few minutes in the period between 1300 and 1500 hours. Consequently, nearly one hundred sorties were flown by No. 11 Group in these two hours; but only one engagement was reported, between No. 32 Squadron and twelve Me 109s at 20,000 feet over Dover.

This state of suspense continued until 1515 hours when it became clear that the enemy was again about to move. Four forces, amounting in all to over fifty aircraft, were plotted on the eastern side of the Channel between Boulogne and Dunkerque. On the British side, No. 32 Squadron was returning to Hawkinge after its combat over Dover; No. 54 Squadron was patrolling Hornchurch and had an hour's petrol left; No. 65 Squadron was near Dover, having been in the air since 1455 hours; No. 501 Squadron was patrolling Hawkinge; and No. 615 Squadron was on patrol near Kenley.

By 1530 hours the German movements had resolved themselves into two main threats: one from a force of 'thirty plus' that was approaching Dungeness, the other from a somewhat larger force which was coming in near the North Foreland on a course for the Essex coast. In addition, two medium-sized forces were over the middle of the Straits. Both came over Kent between 1550 and 1615 hours to act as rearguards for the formations which penetrated inland.

The southerly arm of the enemy's attack was spotted first by No. 501 Squadron near Lympne. It consisted of about thirty Ju 88s with a fighter escort; and the whole formation made for London at 13,000 feet. Our squadron came into action in the Maidstone–Gravesend area about 1540 hours, having first carefully positioned themselves with the sun at their backs. The enemy escort, however, also circled round into the sun, and the majority of the fights were between fighters. Meanwhile the bombers pressed on across the river to their objective, which was the sector station at Hornchurch, and were not again engaged except by the AA guns near Hornchurch until they had carried out their attack. No. 610 Squadron saw them when they were some miles south-east of Hornchurch, but the German fighters occupied their attention. The attack proved a failure because of the heavy AA fire to which the formation was subjected. Over one hundred bombs were dropped, but only six fell within the station.

Seven Defiants of No. 264 were about to take-off from Hornchurch when the enemy arrived, and not all of them were airborne before the bombs began to fall; but they succeeded in reaching the enemy as they retired, and found that most of the protecting fighters had disappeared. Employing over-taking attacks on the Ju 88s, thus allowing the rear-gunner to fire back into the cockpits of the enemy, they claimed to have shot down four of them at a cost of only one Defiant. The remainder of the enemy continued to retire towards the northern tip of Kent, and were speeded on their way by the Thames and Medway guns.

But while this attack on Hornchurch had been taking place operations comparable in size had been going on further north and east. The enemy were first engaged by No. 65 Squadron near the North Foreland as they made for the northern shore of the estuary. The combat was with some forty enemy fighters but bombers were also seen flying on a north-westerly course.[2] No. 54 Squadron was also in action with enemy fighters in this area, and despite the fact that the squadron reported the time of the engagement to be 1510 hours it was probably with the same force engaged by No. 65 Squadron about 1535 hours.

The mass of the enemy formation continued its flight across the estuary and made landfall near Shoeburyness. Part of the force was sighted by No. 615 Squadron who reported that it consisted of fifteen He 111s at 13,000 feet escorted by a number of Me 109s behind and above. AA fire interfered with the squadron's attack but they managed to get to the bombers and shoot at least one of them down. Shortly afterwards, and further to the east, No. 151 Squadron came across a much larger force of thirty to fifty Do 215s and He 111s, accompanied by about one hundred Me 109s and 110s, the whole formation flying at 15,000 feet above the clouds. No 110s were flying on the same level as the bombers, and the squadron found it difficult to make a concerted attack. Before the engagement was over the enemy came down through the thin cloud and bombed North Weald from about 13,000 feet.

2 The Home Security daily summary mentions a further attack on Manston at 1539 hours, which was approximately the time that this force of bombers was seen. No mention is made of such an attack, however, in the ORB of Manston station, nor in the Fighter Command 'Y' Form for this period.

One other squadron, No. 111, may have succeeded in intercepting the enemy before this attack was made. They were certainly in action near North Weald about the time of the attack, but in any case they reported that they were unable to press home their attacks owing to the interference of the enemy fighters.

North Weald was more seriously bombed than Hornchurch. The ground staff reported a force of exactly the same composition as the one that No. 151 Squadron had encountered. It put down between one hundred and fifty and two hundred bombs, damaging the residential parts of the station and the power house very severely. Few of the bombs hit the landing area, however, and communications were soon in order. In consequence the station remained serviceable.

As far as can be ascertained the Hornchurch raid was attacked by only two squadrons before the station was attacked; while that on North Weald was intercepted by three. But as the enemy retired more squadrons came up to the outer estuary and northern Kent, most of them having taken off after 1530 hours. No. 19 Squadron left Duxford at 1535 hours and came up with the enemy over the estuary. No. 56 Squadron did not leave Rochford until after 1600 hours and was in action over Foulness Island both with He 111s and Me 109s, all of which were flying east. No. 32 Squadron left Hawkinge at 1549 hours and met fifteen Me 109s at 10,000 feet off Folkestone. Part of No. 54 Squadron, which had remained over northern Kent after its earlier combat, came across fifty Me 109s near Herne Bay which were travelling west to meet a retiring force of some fifty enemy bombers. All these combats, therefore, though they meant additional loss to the enemy, had no effect on the main object of the German operation.

Altogether, ten bombers and eleven fighters were believed to have been destroyed by fighters, and two aircraft were claimed by the AA gunners. Of the five He 111s from which wreckage was obtained all were from KG 53, and four, if not five, from its third *Gruppe*. Four Me 109s were also found, but only one could be identified: it was from II/JG 51. Eight British fighters were lost, but only three pilots were killed or wounded.

b. In the Solent Area

By 1630 hours the skies over Kent and the Thames Estuary were clear and remained so for the rest of the daylight hours, except for one or two reconnaissance aircraft. For eight hours the area had either been attacked, or was under the threat of attack, and five large operations had been launched against it. But outside the south-east there had been no large raids. Single aircraft had been active in the North Sea, St George's Channel and in the extreme south-west, where three or four aircraft had reconnoitred and attacked the Scilly Isles. In addition, the RAF station at St Eval was attacked early in the afternoon. Otherwise there was nothing to report.

i. 1545–1645 hours

About 1545 hours, however, the first signs of an impending major raid other than in the south-east were received. A force of 'fifty plus' was located just north of Cherbourg, and two others of twelve aircraft or more were somewhat to the south-west. The main force came straight across the Channel and at 1610 hours was about thirty-five miles south-east of St Catherine's Point. There were indications, though not very clear ones, that three smaller formations were also in that area. But by that time certain counter-measures had been taken:

> At 1555 hours No. 17 Squadron took off from Tangmere to patrol base at 15,000 feet.
>
> At the same time five aircraft of No. 43 Squadron took off from Tangmere, but their orders are not known.
>
> Between 1600 and 1610 hours No. 234 Squadron took off from Middle Wallop and were ordered towards the Isle of Wight.
>
> Between 1605 and 1610 hours No. 609 Squadron took off from Middle Wallop and were ordered to patrol St Catherine's Point at 10,000 feet.
>
> At 1610 hours 'B' Flight No. 249 Squadron, took off from Boscombe Down to patrol between Portsmouth and the Isle of Wight.

In addition, precautions were taken to protect the fighter stations at Exeter and St Eval.

After 1615 hours the information provided by the RDF stations deteriorated, and what had previously been a single large formation supported by two or three smaller forces was reported as no less than seven medium-sized forces. It is clear, however, that there was in fact only one bombing formation, and that such other forces as were present were flanking and escorting formations of fighters. The main force skirted the east coast of the Isle of Wight and made for Portsmouth at about 16,000 feet, and was not engaged by fighters. The only British squadron to sight any bombers was No. 609 Squadron which, in its own rueful words, 'found themselves 5,000 feet below a large formation of bombers and fighters, right in the middle of our own AA fire and down-sun'. In this position they were attacked from above by the escorting enemy fighters, and reckoned themselves fortunate to escape with only two aircraft damaged. They were unable, in these circumstances, to interfere with the enemy bombers which went on to bomb Portsmouth town and dockyard between 1625 and 1630 hours. As a result, the railway between Southsea and Portsmouth harbour was blocked, a railway signal box was destroyed, and there was, according to the Ministry of Home Security, 'widespread damage in the Northern and Southern divisions of the town'. Nevertheless, the attacking force can have been barely a *Gruppe* strong, for only some thirty-five HE bombs were dropped.

After the bombing both No. 234 Squadron and No. 249 Squadron engaged formations of the enemy. The first came into action with a force of Me 109s and 110s at 17,000 feet near the southern end of the Isle of Wight. No great advantage accrued to either side. No. 249 Squadron also engaged a returning detachment of single-engined and twin-engined fighters. The action was not fully joined as the Germans were too far above for an effective attack to be made. One section of No. 17 Squadron, which had been patrolling Tangmere, also engaged a lone He 111 as it returned to France.

Thus ended the last major operation which the Germans launched on this day. Their results are chiefly to be judged by the damage inflicted to the No. 11 Group stations north of the river and in east Kent. From the British point of view they were not wholly unsatisfactory. Manston had been severely and accurately bombed as a culmination of a number of lighter attacks; and its days of usefulness were numbered. North Weald had also been heavily hit for the first time, though operations were able to continue. Hornchurch, on the other hand had escaped the worst results of as heavy an attack as had been launched against North Weald. What was a less satisfactory feature was the low proportion of squadrons despatched that succeeded in reaching the German formations before their attack was delivered. It was as a result of this, and other, failures that Air Vice-Marshal Park decided that the advantages to be gained from breaking R/T silence in order to report the numbers and position of the enemy outweighed the possibility of thereby losing the advantage of surprise. The new system came into operation on the 27th, when formation leaders began the practice of reporting to the controller the strength, height, course and approximate position of the enemy as soon as they were sighted.

No. 11 Group Instruction to Controllers, No. 6, 26 August.

NIGHT OPERATIONS, 24/25 AUGUST

There was a slight intensification of German activity on the night of 24 August compared to what had gone before; but in most respects it was typical of the enemy's night activity during the whole of July and most of August. Targets continued to be sought over wide areas of the country; and although there was some concentration on South Wales, the Birmingham district and Teeside, there was nothing approaching what the Germans themselves considered a major attack, for which their standard was a minimum of one hundred tons of bombs. The first attack of such dimensions either by night or day against any British target was not launched until the night of 28 August. It has been decided, therefore, to select the night of the 24th for a more detailed review than has previously been given to a single night's operations, so that the reader may realise what was entailed in these early night attacks.

The first raids were detected off Yorkshire and Lincolnshire and off the Cherbourg peninsula before darkness had fallen. All of them, like most of the night raids at this time, consisted of a single aircraft, and they were the first of a stream which was to fly over most of England and Wales before dawn. The majority operating north of a line from the Wash–Cardigan Bay came in from the North Sea; those active south of that line chiefly came from Brittany. It will be convenient on this account to consider first the German operations against southern England and Wales.

a. In South-West England, South Wales and the Midlands

i. Offensive Operations

Four raids had been picked up off the Cherbourg peninsula between 2048 and 2116 hours. One of them was lost as it approached Lyme Bay, but the others, without any of the feints and diversions which were such a feature of day operations at this time, came straight across the Channel, made their landfall at different points of the Dorset coast and continued towards Bristol and South Wales. Otherwise, the operations room plotted no enemy aircraft in the southern half of England.

However, German aircraft were certainly over South Wales, for St Athan RAF station was bombed at 2100 hours, and bombs fell at different points between Swansea and Cardiff during the next twenty minutes.[3] Thirty-four bombs were dropped at St Athan and it was made temporarily unserviceable. It was not used by operational squadrons but experimental work on RDF was carried out there.

In the next hour other aircraft crossed the coast of Dorset on their way north to Bristol and the Midlands. At 2215 hours three raids were within forty miles of Birmingham; another had just left the Bristol area on a northerly course; and four raids were crossing Dorset and Somerset on a course for Bristol. The total number of aircraft involved was barely a dozen, including the elusive raids in the Cardiff district. Those flying north retained their bombs, but those operating round Cardiff and Bristol put down a small number, most of which fell in rural districts. South Wales again boasted the most serious incident when, at 2210 hours, bombs hit the railway embankment at Penarth, near Cardiff, derailed a train and blocked the line to the west.

From 2300 hours the Germans switched their attentions from the southwest to the Midlands. Their aircraft continued to be plotted over Cardiff and Bristol as they flew to the Midlands or returned (which accounts for the activity of the AA guns at these two places) but there was less than half-a-dozen incidents reported there during the rest of the night.

Bombing in the Birmingham area did not begin until midnight, for the first aircraft from Brittany had flown over the Midlands and confined their activities to Lancashire. It is doubtful whether more than six aircraft attacked the city, but incidents were reported from midnight to 0130 hours, most of them, as usual, in the Castle Bromwich district. The Nuffield works, the Moss Gear Company and Fort Dunlop were all affected but there was little damage to plant and equipment. A small number of bombs were dropped in Sutton Coldfield between 0200 and 0230 hours, but otherwise Birmingham was not further molested.

After 0200 hours the Germans continued to operate over the southwestern quarter of England, but few incidents were reported. The most notable (and thus a measure of the significance of the rest) occurred at Poole at 0400 hours when a single aircraft, which had not been detected by the RDF stations or the Observer Corps, dropped a few bombs and caused some damage to property.

ii. Defensive Operations

The responsibility for the defence of this area rested primarily with No. 10 Group. On this night only eight fighter sorties were made against the thirty to forty enemy aircraft which crossed over the Group's territory. It is impossible

3 The Cardiff AA guns went into action at 2107 hours and remained in action, firing at frequent intervals, for the next five hours. It was not until midnight, however, that the Fighter Command tracks charts shewed any enemy activity in this neighbourhood. The fact that the RDF and Observer Corps system had only recently been extended to this area seems hardly a sufficient explanation.

to relate any of these sorties to particular raids, but there were at least two aircraft patrolling the corridor from the Devon and Dorset coasts to the Bristol Channel, along which the Germans flew, during the peak period of enemy activity, 2100 to 0100 hours. The squadrons providing the aircraft were No. 604 (Blenheims) Middle Wallop, No. 92 (Spitfires), Bilbury (Glos), and No. 247 (Gladiators), Roborough. However, no fighter sighted or engaged an enemy aircraft, and the Germans operated unhindered except for searchlights and AA fire from gun defended areas. Guns were in action as follows:

Place	*Time*	*Height of Enemy*	*Type of Fire*
Cardiff	2107–0206 hrs	10,000–23,000 feet	GL barrages
Bristol	2250–2253 hrs	14,000 feet	Direct fire at illuminated target
Birmingham	0035 hrs	–	GL barrages
	0155 hrs	19,000 feet	
	0208 hrs	10,000 feet	
Coventry	0116	–	Direct fire at concentration of searchlight beams
Portland	0131	12,000 feet	Direct fire at illuminated target.
Swansea	0153	15,000	GL barrages

The Swansea gunners believed that an aircraft exploded in mid-air as a result of their fire. Otherwise, no claims were made.

b. In Southern England and the London Area

i. Before Midnight

Apart from some slight activity in the Norwich district and near Chelmsford between 2200 and 2230 hours, and some activity off Aldeburgh by three or four aircraft which may have been mine-laying, such German aircraft as came over the eastern half of southern England confined themselves to Greater London. Of the first four aircraft to do so two came into the Thames Estuary from the direction of Dunkerque, and two between Beachy Head and Dungeness from the direction of the Somme. Most of the raiders that followed likewise came in by one of these two routes.

The first bombs to be reported fell in Islington, Tottenham and Millwall between 2320 and 2340 hours; and at Millwall serious fires broke out in the dock area. But raiding did not develop on any notable scale. In the hour before midnight about fifteen German aircraft were over southeast England, including the London area, but their actively hostile acts were very few. Apart from those at Millwall the only incidents worth noting were at Feltham, where damage was caused to the RASC depot, and at Esher where damage to property blocked the Portsmouth road.

ii. After Midnight

After midnight enemy activity quickened. In the first half-hour four raids were detected as they approached the coast near Beachy Head, and one aircraft was over the London area. It was this aircraft which dropped the first bombs to fall on the City of London since 1918: they caused a fire in Fore Street and London Wall to which two hundred pumps were called. Several unexploded bombs were also reported and part of the area was evacuated until midday on the 25th.

Meanwhile, another aircraft was plotted by the Observer Corps on an extensive flight around London and the Home Counties, which was typical of many made at this time. It embraced Heston, Northolt, Maidenhead, Radlett, the line of the Thames from Richmond to Gravesend, and Maidstone, where it was last plotted at 0118 hours. Another in contrast, came in at Dungeness at 0030 hours, flew direct to the river at Tilbury, turned west and operated over the East End for the next twenty minutes.

During this period bombs were reported from numerous districts in east London, including Stepney, Bethnal Green, East Ham and Leyton. A delayed-action bomb, dropped about this time, exploded an hour later at Walthamstow and completely blocked the LNER track there. There was a similar incident at Coulsdon, near Kenley airfield, at 0030 hours. The only other damage caused in the London area was the work of two aircraft at most, which dropped bombs in the East End between 0300 and 0330 hours. A large fire broke out at Dundee Wharf, Stepney; and railway bridges in Finsbury and Bethnal Green were damaged. In the latter district, about a hundred people were rendered homeless. Otherwise, there were no serious incidents; though unexploded bombs caused much inconvenience. This may have been deliberate policy on the part of the Germans: no more than fifteen aircraft were over the London area during the night and rather less over the rest of the south-east, yet the Ministry of Home Security reported on the evening of the 25th that there were still about fifty unexploded bombs to be dealt with in Surrey alone.

Most of the aircraft that came in over the coast of Sussex came north to the London area even though some of them turned west and reconnoitred the Thames Valley. It is highly probable that some of the German crews had been briefed to attack any of the important group of airfields in the Abingdon–Oxford district, but no incidents were reported. The only airfields in the south and south-east which may have been the object of an attack were West Malling and Detling, where bombs fell a quarter of an hour after midnight. The bombs fell in open fields and no damage was done.

iii. Defensive Operations

The responsibility for the defence of the eastern half of southern England lay with No. 11 Group and, to a lesser extent, No. 12 Group. The former contained two night fighter squadrons, No. 600 in the Hornchurch sector and No. 25 in the North Weald sector; in No. 12 Group was No. 23 Squadron which operated from Wittering, near Peterborough. The three squadrons were equipped with

Blenheims Mk I. In addition a small number of single-seater fighters could be called upon at night.[4]

Altogether, there were eighteen fighter sorties in the area between 2230 and 0330 hours. Nearly all were carried out by Blenheims, the exceptions being two Hurricane sorties by No. 615 Squadron and one by No. 43 Squadron. Only one of these aircraft, a Hurricane of No. 615 Squadron, sighted and engaged the enemy. The pilot's report illustrates a number of features of a successful, searchlight-aided interception:

Combat Report, F/Lt Sanders

> I took off from Kenley at 0010 hours on 25.8.40 to intercept e/a in sector. I climbed above the clouds and toured the South coast waiting for the searchlights to expose an enemy aircraft. Soon I spotted a He 111 miles away and proceeded to intercept. When low enough I lowered undercarriage to produce drag to avoid colliding with e/a. Four short bursts, of about three seconds each, set both engines on fire; he half-rolled and dived over the vertical probably in sea. The rear gunner put in some effective fire at me, damaging my port wing slightly; he seemed to fire with four guns. Attacks were from astern below, firing 15° up to 8,000 feet.

Almost immediately after this attack this same pilot saw another Heinkel illuminated by the searchlights. He succeeded in reaching it and damaging it, but he did not claim to have destroyed it. A survivor was rescued from the first Heinkel. The aircraft was from III/KG 55 and had left Villacoublay with orders to reconnoitre RAF stations in the Thames Valley with Harwell as the primary objective. It was on its inward journey when attacked.

The AA guns in the southeast did little. The Slough guns fired some twenty rounds between 2342 and 0023 hours, and the Dover and Bramley guns fired a few rounds. The guns of the Inner Artillery Zone, however, had held their fire.

c. *In the North of England*

The operations rooms tables showed little activity at dusk north of the Wash. One raid came overland at Skegness at 2147 hours and dropped a few bombs in rural districts of Lincolnshire; and at least two others were approaching the Yorkshire coast. One of them had been detected off the Texel at 2100 hours and it was plotted continuously until it made landfall near Flamborough Head at 2235 hours. This was a more than usually efficient piece of tracking, but the standard of RDF performance on the east coast was a high one, raids being consistently detected at ranges of sixty miles.

i. *In Lancashire*

After 2200 hours activity quickened, not so much in the east, where only two aircraft crossed the coast, as in Lancashire, where five aircraft arrived in the first half-hour. These aircraft had originally been detected off the Cherbourg

4 We do not know exactly how many 'day' fighters could be called upon for night operations. The question of reducing the night commitments of the day squadrons was raised at a conference held at No. 11 Group on 30 August, when it was decided to reduce the night state in each sector to one section at fifteen minutes available. This suggests a previous state of one section at readiness. This decision applied only to No. 11 Group.

peninsula between 2045 and 2115 hours. They had flown steadily northward over Bristol and the Welsh border, reaching their target area about 2220 hours. They dropped few bombs – the only ones reported in the area fell at St Helens at 2320 hours – but every district of any industrial importance between the Mersey and the Pennines, the Cheshire plain and the Lake District, was visited in the course of the next hour. The virtual absence of bombing in the region, and the deliberate and detailed attention which it clearly received, point unmistakably to a grand night reconnaissance of the Mersey distribution centre and the industrial area further east.

ii. In Yorkshire and the North-East

a. Midnight–0230 hours

It was not until shortly after midnight that activity developed overland in the east. Single aircraft were over Teeside, over the West Riding and over the Humber estuary, but few bombs were dropped. Some fell in the residential districts of Hull between 0110 and 0150 hours; others were dropped on the Bomber Command station at Driffield at 0107 hours. The aircraft responsible for the latter attack came in at Flamborough Head at 0045 hours, flew due west to Dishforth, doubled back to Driffield, bombed it and went straight out to sea. Twelve bombs were dropped, the sergeants' mess was destroyed and there was some damage to services.[5]

Between 0100 and 0130 hours a number of aircraft were plotted off the Yorkshire coast, and while some may have been mine-laying at least two were steering direct for the Tyne. One aircraft which had first been detected off Flamborough Head at 0040 hours, and had since been plotted in the hills south of Middlesbrough, came north and dropped bombs on different parts of Teeside between 0145 and 0200 hours. These bombs which fell in Middlesbrough and West Hartlepool only damaged house property, but bombs dropped on the ICI works at Billingham seriously damaged a nitrate acid plant. Half an hour later another aircraft dropped bombs on Eston and Grangetown, near Middlesbrough, causing serious damage to houses and public services at the second of these two places.[6]

Between 0200 and 0230 hours a small number of bombs were dropped on Tyneside. One of the two aircraft responsible had been flying over the area for at least half an hour before it dropped its bombs. These chiefly damaged house property at Wallsend but one delayed-action bomb fell in the shipyard of Swan and Hunter, the Admiralty contractors. Its presence was unknown until 1425 hours on the following day, when it exploded. The Regional Controller at Newcastle reported that production would not be affected, but another Home Security report speaks of serious damage to machinery. The other aircraft operating in the locality caused the most serious incident of the night affecting the

5 Driffield was in a very exposed position within a few miles of the coast and after this attack it was decided to reduce it temporarily to a 'care and maintenance' basis. The squadrons there left on the 26th and 28th August.

6 The activities of the aircraft responsible for these incidents are typical of many raids during this period. The aircraft was first detected off the Tyne on a southerly course at 0145 hours, and after operating for some time over the Cleveland Hills it turned north and dropped bombs at Eston and Grangetown. Twenty-three bombs were released, of which at least twelve were HE, from which it might be supposed that its full load of bombs had been discharged. However, the aircraft then flew steadily up the coast until it reached the Firth of Forth at 0320 hours and on its return journey south it appears to have dropped six HE bombs near Berwick, causing traffic on the Great North Road to be diverted at this point for the next four days. It continued southward along the coast, was engaged by the Tyne guns at 0356 hours, and arrived back at the Tees five minutes later. Soon afterwards its track was lost as it returned home on a south-easterly course.

general public. It dropped its bombs at South Shields at 0215 hours: a gas works, all types of public services and much house property were damaged, and nearly two hundred people were made homeless. This was the only period of the night in which bombs were dropped on Tyneside. The neighbouring Fighter Command station at Acklington was attacked about 0230 hours by a raid which had been operating over the sea off Alnwick for an hour. Six bombs were dropped, but only two fell near the station.

During this activity operations continued further south. Three aircraft had operated between Hull and Leeds, and a few bombs had been put down, again in residential districts of Hull. Two aircraft were active over the Humber estuary and may have been mine-laying. It is likely, however, that it was one of these aircraft that dropped bombs at Immingham at 0300 hours, when some damage was done to a power-house and to a number of feeder lines at the LNER sidings.

b. 0230–0430 hours

About 0200 hours the Germans extended their activities to the Firth of Forth. One raid, detected twenty miles east of St Abbs Head, came in at 0220 hours, operated over the country between Berwick and the Forth, but dropped no bombs. In addition, two raids were plotted making for the Tay. One of these was lost, but the other turned south at Fifeness at 0300 hours, and, flying ten miles out to sea and parallel to the coast, came steadily south until it reached Seaham Harbour at about 0345 hours. It then came inland and reconnoitred the country between Consett and the Cleveland Hills.

Another aircraft came in at the Tees at 0300 hours, remained over the Middlesbrough area for twenty minutes, and by 0330 hours had crossed the coast on its return journey. In that time, however, it had dropped bombs in West Hartlepool, destroying one foundry, damaging others, and stopping production for some days at a steel mill.

South of Flamborough Head, during this same period, there were four reports of bombing. One raid which had escaped detection until it was over the West Riding, dropped bombs at Leeds and Rotherham between 0310 and 0320 hours, but at neither place was there damage of any importance. Then, between 0320 and 0335 hours, there was considerable damage to property at Cottingham and Hedon, near Hull. The oil storage farm at Hedon was doubtless the target.

All told, the Germans sent about fifty aircraft into the country north of the Wash. Most of these had approached from the North Sea, but a few came overland over the length of England. With the exception of the reconnaissance in the Lancashire area the operations had been confined to the country east of the Pennines. Many bombs fell harmlessly in rural districts, but in smaller proportion to the total number of bombs dropped than was the case in southern England. The more industrialised character of the region, and the fact that three of the main target areas – Hull, Teeside and Tyneside – are close to the sea would account for this. The largest number of bombs in any one district of the country – about twenty in all – had been put down between Stockton and Middlesbrough, a district whose industrial importance needs no emphasis. Yet the operations in the north show as clearly as those further south that the Germans had not yet begun to attack the industry of the country on any significant scale. They were concerned to harass and reconnoitre large areas of the country, rather than to select and destroy specific target areas.

iii. Defensive Operations
No. 12 Group and No. 13 Group were affected by the raids in the north. Six Blenheim sorties were made by No. 29 Squadron from Digby and seven Hurricane sorties by No. 73 Squadron from Leconfield. In No. 13 Group four sorties were made by No. 219 Squadron, No. 605 Squadron and No. 141 Squadron. Enemy aircraft were sighted twice: once near Harrogate about 0020 hours by a Blenheim of No. 219 Squadron, and once over the Humber about 0120 hours by a Blenheim of No. 29 Squadron. In the second case the enemy aircraft, an He 111, was illuminated by the searchlights at 8,000 feet, and the ensuing combat seemed entirely successful to our pilot. This particular aircraft had been plotted for over on hour, and was on its way its way over Hull towards the coast when it was attacked. The combat was an instance of an AI-equipped fighter using the older technique of co-operation with the searchlights to effect a successful interception.

As for the AA guns, the AA Command reported guns in action on one occasion only, at Tyneside at 0356 hours. This is hardly credible; certainly not to a Hurricane pilot of No. 73 Squadron who reported that he was illuminated by searchlights and shot down by AA fire about 0125 hours near Beverley despite the fact that he flashed the correct recognition signals. Such incidents were not uncommon at this time; and they emphasised the need for some dependable means of recognition between the various parts of the night defence system.

However, the general ineffectiveness of the defences, both on the ground and in the air, needs no underlining. The scattered and seemingly aimless nature of the German operations complicated the defensive problem, but it was shortly to be demonstrated – if, indeed, demonstration was necessary – that the available technique was inadequate even when the Germans concentrated on a limited target area for an extended period.

OPERATIONS, 25 AUGUST

Apart from a low cloud base at 2,000–4,000 feet the weather over England on the 25th was fair, but it was not until early evening that the Germans embarked upon any large scale operations. During the day the usual reconnaissance aircraft were reported overland and round the coast. A single Do 17 attacked Plymouth in the morning: three aircraft attacked the Scilly Isles during the afternoon and hit the RAF W/T station there, as well as some civilian property: in the evening an He 111 made an attempt on the oil farm at Pembroke, where the fires started by an attack on the 19th had not yet been extinguished.

i. 1645–1830 hours

At sea, five ships were attacked in St George's Channel; one small vessel was sunk and another set on fire. One of the German aircraft was shot down off Linney Head shortly after 1800 hours.

a. In the Portland area

About 1640 hours, however, the first signs were detected of what was to prove the only bombing raid of any size launched during the day. Off St Malo a large raid of '100 plus' was picked up as it moved north-west up the Cherbourg peninsula. When it was some twenty miles north of Cherbourg the RDF stations reported that its strength had fallen to some thirty aircraft, but the explanation of this, it appeared later, was that the original force had split into a number of smaller formations following closely upon each other. There were three of these, each containing about thirty aircraft, on a direct course for Portland, and a fourth of about the same size was some miles to the west. This latter force later penetrated as far inland as Yeovil, but it appears to have dropped no bombs and was probably a fighter formation protecting the main body further east from flanking attacks from that direction.

At 1700 hours the main enemy body was still some thirty miles south-south-west of Portland, but the unusually long range of the initial RDF detection had given the No. 10 Group controller ample time to make his dispositions; and the following squadrons were either in the air or about to take off:

> No. 17 Squadron from Tangmere at 1650 hours to patrol base at 15,000 feet.
>
> No. 152 Squadron from Warmwell at 1657 hours to patrol west of Portland at 17,000 feet.
>
> No. 609 Squadron from Middle Wallop at 1700 hours to patrol base at 15,000 feet.
>
> No. 602 Squadron from Westhampnett at 1704 hours to intercept in the Portland area.
>
> No. 213 Squadron from Exeter at 1705 hours to patrol Warmwell at 22,000 feet.
>
> No. 87 Squadron from Exeter at 1710 hours to intercept in the Portland area.
>
> No. 234 Squadron from Middle Wallop at 1715 hours to patrol base. (This squadron was maintained on patrol over Middle Wallop and took no further part in the operations).

It is clear enough that the controller's chief concern was to protect the fighter stations within the area threatened by the enemy's advance. Warmwell, Tangmere and Middle Wallop were each patrolled by at least one squadron. For the same reason all squadrons were ordered to take off at the utmost available strength, and four did so at more than twelve aircraft strong.

By 1715 hours, however, it seemed to him to be safe to redispose his forces. No. 17 Squadron was called off its Tangmere patrol and directed towards Portland; similarly, No. 213 Squadron was called off its Warmwell patrol and sent in the same direction; and No. 609 Squadron was ordered to take its place over Warmwell at 20,000 feet.

The enemy force approached Portland at 1720 hours (the AA gunners there were in action from 1722–1724 hours) by which time it was once more a large formation of over one hundred aircraft. It is impossible to state its exact composition: both Ju 88s and Do 17s were reported, as well as escorting Me 109s and 110s; but judging by the number of bombs that were put down, and by the size of the force normally employed in this part of the Channel; it is unlikely that there was more than one *Gruppe* of bombers and possibly two of fighters.

The first British squadron to come into action was No. 213, followed a few moments later by No. 87, though neither remarked the other's presence. No. 152 Squadron, which was also in the area, was, surprisingly, not engaged until after the German bombers had reached their target. No. 213 Squadron was chiefly engaged with enemy fighters between 15,000 and 20,000 feet, and the German formation as a whole continued on its northerly course. Part of No. 87 Squadron, however, succeeded in reaching the bombers. The squadron intelligence officer describes their tactics with an admirable brevity: 'B' Flight went for Ju 88s and the Me 110s went for 'B' Flight. 'A' Flight then attacked the Me 110s. Our pilots noticed that some of the Me 110s discharged red Verey lights, presumably to call down the high escort of Me 109s. The latter did in fact come down and join in the fighting, while the bombers continued to press on inland to their objective which proved to be the fighter station at Warmwell.

This they reached and bombed between 1725 and 1730 hours, but not before one more British squadron, No. 609, had come into action. They came across twelve Ju 88s, protected by thirty to forty Me 110s, flying west towards Warmwell, but all combats were with Me 110s and later on, when the fighting ranged over a wide area, with Me 109s. It was undoubtedly this force of Ju 88s that bombed Warmwell. Twenty to thirty bombs were put down; two hangars were damaged, the station sick quarters were burnt out, and communications were disorganised until midday on the 26th. After the bombing the rest of the defending squadrons came up with the enemy. Virtually all combats were with the enemy fighters.

There is little doubt that the German incursion had the bombing of Warmwell as its sole objective, that strong opposition was expected and, therefore, the small bomber force was heavily protected by fighters. Consequently, whereas the defending pilots claimed only four bombers destroyed they claimed no less than thirty-six fighters. They themselves lost eleven aircraft and three others badly damaged, but only eight pilots were killed or wounded. The only information that could be gained from wreckage found after the battle was that the Me 110s had been from I/ZG2.

b. In the Straits of Dover, 1755–1900 hours

By 1740 hours all German aircraft in the central Channel were on southerly courses, but already forces further east were assembling for another move against the Channel coast. No signs of this were detected from the British side until 1755 hours when a force of 'thirty plus' was picked up inland from Cap Gris Nez. Little defensive action was taken except to despatch a section of

No. 32 Squadron to protect Hawkinge against low-flying attacks, as it was clear that the process of concentration was still going on. In the next twenty-five minutes four more formations were picked up in the Pas de Calais, and all of them eventually merged into one large force of '100 plus' which commenced to move across the Straits shortly after 1820 hours. The Germans had made little effort to conceal the move, and the controller at No. 11 Group must have been fully aware that an attack was imminent from 1810 hours onwards. What is surprising is not only that he delayed sending up any British squadrons until 1820 hours, but that even so they were in time to intercept the Germans.

Three squadrons were ordered up to patrol between Deal and Dover, which was the only area the enemy had so far threatened. They were No. 32 Squadron from Hawkinge, No. 616 Squadron from Kenley and No. 54 Squadron from Rochford; and all took off between 1820 and 1823 hours.

The German formation came slowly across the Straits making for a point just south of Dover. It was first sighted at 14,000 feet by No. 32 Squadron who reported that it consisted of about twelve Do 215s escorted by about thirty-six Me 109s. This was later confirmed by No. 616 Squadron. The enemy seemed to make no effort to cross the land and circled round over the Channel until attacked at 1850 hours. In the fight with No. 32 Squadron both sides lost two aircraft.[7] No. 54 Squadron was in action at the same time and place with a formation of Me 109s. When No. 616 Squadron arrived the enemy were retiring towards France, but combat was joined and one of the Dorniers was shot down into the sea.

With the exception of a clash between No. 610 Squadron, which left Biggin Hill at 1852 hours, and a small formation of Me 109s over Dover at 25,000 feet, this was the end of an operation which can perhaps best be described as a 'trailing of the coat'. The individual actions were brief but fierce. Seven German aircraft were claimed, of which two were Dorniers, seven British fighters were lost or were made unserviceable, and four pilots became casualties.

Of the day as a whole it could be said that the Germans had failed to maintain the previous day's scale of operations either because they did not consider the weather to be suitable for large-scale attacks, or because they were preparing for the heavy onslaught of the following day.

OPERATIONS, 26 AUGUST[8]

A total of five reconnaissance aircraft were plotted over southern England during the first five hours daylight on the 26th. One of them attacked the bomber airfield at Harwell at 1103 hours, but otherwise there was no bombing. It was not until 1130 hours that any signs of a major attack were detected. On

7 One of the pilots of this squadron owed his life to the chemical 'Fluorescine' with which the pilots of the Command had recently been issued. He was forced to bale out over the sea and was immersed for over an hour before being rescued. The naval launch was guided to him by another pilot from the squadron who could plainly see the vivid green stains caused by the chemical, though it was invisible to the crew of the launch. As far as is known this was the first occasion on which this device was instrumental in saving the life of a British pilot.

8 For night operations 25/26 August to 6/7 September see pp. 208–215.

this occasion the German operation developed exceptionally swiftly, for barely a quarter of an hour elapsed between the first indications of an attack and the bombing of Folkestone, which was the first German objective on this day.

a. Over East Kent and the Thames Estuary, 1135–1340 hours

Warning of what was to prove a long drawn-out operation was first obtained when a force of 'thirty plus' was detected behind Gap Gris Nez as a few moments afterwards a force of 'nine plus' was picked up a few miles to the south, and a third of 'twenty plus' at 1139 hours in the same area. All three were steering towards Dover where the only British force in the air was 'B' Flight of No. 616 Squadron, Kenley, which was trying to intercept the He 111 which had bombed Harwell. Within the next six minutes, however, the following squadrons took off:

> No. 65 from North Weald to patrol Maidstone at 12,000 feet; then diverted to patrol Hawkinge at 15,000 feet.
>
> No. 610 from Hawkinge to intercept near Dover.
>
> No. 264 from Hornchurch to patrol Dover.
>
> No. 54 from Rochford to patrol Manston at 22,000 feet.
>
> No. 616, 'A' Flight, from Kenley to intercept near Dover.

The controller had reacted very quickly to the German move, yet not quickly enough; for the enemy crossed the Straits and bombed the Folkestone area at 1153 hours, escaping interception except for No. 616 Squadron. Nor did the latter engage the main German force: they came upon eight Me 109s which were bombing Folkestone from 5,000 feet, but by then the main body was retiring northwards. The German target appears to have been the military camps and coast defences between Shorncliffe and Folkestone, and the military damage was insignificant.

Between 1200 and 1210 hours the rest of the defending squadrons came into action chiefly between Dover and Deal, and probably with the retiring enemy. It is impossible to be certain of this as other German formations were being plotted in the Straits at this time, at least two of which crossed the coast. These were considered to be a second wave of attack; and the controller sent up forces further west to protect Kenley, Croydon, Biggin Hill and Gravesend. Moreover, 'free-lance' formations of German fighters were certainly in the area. One of them surprised 'B' Flight of No. 616 Squadron near Deal just before noon; and another attacked the Dover balloons at 1220 hours, shooting down three of them.

However, both No. 264 Squadron and No. 56 Squadron sighted a formation of twelve Do 17s near Deal before noon. It was flying at 13,000 feet and was protected by thirty to fifty Me 109s. The seven Defiants of the first squadron succeeded in getting at the bombers and claimed to have shot down six of them, though the Me 109s harassed them continuously. Three of the Defiants were shot down, but matters might have gone even worse with them if No. 56 Squadron had not appeared and closed with the German fighters, shooting down three of them. The only other action was one between No. 54 Squadron and various small formations of Me 109s at 25,000 feet north of Deal; but this was simply a clash which did not influence the main German operation.

All the squadrons that had been put into the air had engaged the enemy; and this was no small tribute to the efficiency of the Fighter Command technique of interception; for the cloudy weather made the tracking of the enemy forces very difficult. But in the next stage of the operations it was the Germans who could claim a tactical success. This was achieved by sending over a second wave of attacking formations which operated overland while the British squadrons that had already been engaged were returning to refuel and re-arm, and before their places had been taken by other fighter squadrons. Thus at approximately 1230 hours Broadstairs was bombed by a small force of unknown composition which was not intercepted. Thirty-two HE bombs were put down, but, fortunately, most of them fell on the foreshore and little damage was done. Then just after 1300 hours, by which time all the British squadrons that had been in action earlier had landed, another force came in near Ramsgate and dropped bombs. But again no military damage was caused, the bombs falling near the small village of Minster. At least two fighter detachments were in the air further west, but none was directed towards the Straits. Similarly, there was no interception of yet another small enemy formation which must have come inland shortly after 1300 hours, and which dropped over thirty bombs on Brentwood at 1340 hours. In this case, indeed, there was a complete failure to detect and track the enemy.

This was the last incident in an operation which had lasted in all quite two hours. Its one unsatisfactory feature from the British point of view was that two or three small forces had evaded the defences, but this was hardly surprising in view of the cloudy weather and of the proximity of the enemy to eastern Kent. Otherwise, the Germans appeared to have achieved little. Their bombing had met with virtually no success, while to the best of our belief, German losses in aircraft were slightly heavier than British, even though they had succeeded in surprising No. 616 Squadron and shooting down seven out of twelve Spitfires. British claims amounted to nine fighters and seven bombers. Fourteen British fighters were destroyed, and six pilots were killed, missing or wounded. It is known that aircraft from III/KG 3 and I/JG 52 took part in the operation.

b. Over the Thames Estuary and Southern Essex, 1430–1545 hours

There was barely an hour's pause before the Germans once more returned to the attack in force, and again their zone of operations was the south-east.

The German assembly area was Dunkerque where three forces of approximately sixty, twenty and twelve aircraft respectively were detected between 1430 and 1443 hours. By 1450 hours these forces were over the eastern approaches to the Straits of Dover and were apparently making for the Thames Estuary.

The following British forces were ordered up:

> No. 501 Squadron from Hawkinge at 1425 hours to patrol base.
>
> No. 65 Squadron from Rochford at 1438 hours to intercept north of Manston.
>
> No. 615 Squadron from Kenley at 1445 hours to intercept in the same area.
>
> No. 1 (RCAF) Squadron from North Weald at 1445 hours: its orders are not known.
>
> No. 85 Squadron from Croydon at 1450 hours to patrol base: shortly afterwards they were ordered towards Maidstone.

Shortly before 1500 hours the position was that two enemy formations were crossing the north-east corner of Kent; two others were some distance to the north and north-east; and another was about to cross near Hythe. All these forces were flying north-west.

The magnitude of the threat was now clear, and not only were more squadrons sent up by No. 11 Group but No. 12 Group was requested to provide protection for the northerly airfields in No. 11 Group. Thus,

> No. 111 Squadron left Martlesham at 1500 hours and was ordered towards Chelmsford.
>
> No. 56 Squadron left North Weald at 1502 hours to patrol Colchester at 15,000 feet.
>
> No. 19 Squadron and No. 310 (Czech) Squadron left Duxford between 1510 and 1515 hours to patrol Debden and North Weald respectively.
>
> No. 54 Squadron left Hornchurch at 1510 hours to patrol Manston.

But before the last of these squadrons had left the ground the first combats were in progress. At 1500 hours No. 615 Squadron came into action over Whitstable with a fighter formation which was probably acting as flank guard to one of the forces further north. The squadron was at 19,000 feet, one thousand feet higher than the enemy, and between the enemy and the sun; and their initial attack was a surprise. Nevertheless, the action was fiercely fought out, four Me 109s being destroyed at a cost of three Hurricanes.

From then onwards the defending squadrons were continually in action at various points between the Isle of Sheppey and Colchester, and it is impossible to be certain of the order in which engagements occurred. It is fairly clear, however, that the most southerly of the enemy formations was engaged on its inward journey by No. 85 Squadron; the middle force was also engaged before it reached its target by No. 65 Squadron; and the most northerly force, which eventually attacked Debden, was attacked before it did so by No. 56 Squadron and No. 111 Squadron. All other combats took place with a retiring enemy.

No. 85 Squadron engaged the force that had crossed near Hythe over the Isle of Sheppey at approximately 1515 hours. The enemy were fifteen Do 215s at 15,000 feet escorted by about thirty Me 109s between 20,000 and 25,000 feet. The squadron carried out a head-on attack on the Dorniers and forced the leading section to break away and turn for home. They were followed by the Hurricanes and three of them were shot down. The majority of the enemy held on their course, which was taking them towards north-east London; and it was probably for this reason that the escorting fighters chose not to remain behind to protect the bombers threatened by No. 85 Squadron. These as they retired jettisoned bombs near Eastchurch, Detling and Maidstone. The main formation was no more successful. There is little doubt that the airfield at Hornchurch was its objective, but not one bomb fell there. Indeed, Hornchurch town was hit and although public services were affected and the railway between Hornchurch and Elm Bank was cut the damage was not comparable to what the Germans had intended.

The second of the German formations crossed the land at the mouth of the Blackwater and then flew north-west. As it approached the coast it was sighted by No. 65 Squadron who reported that it consisted of thirty bombers in two large vics at 20,000 feet escorted by a similar number of Me 110s above. Our squadron had to climb to attack, one flight making a flank attack on the bombers, the other engaging the fighters. Two separate combats developed as the Me 110s formed defensive circles and the Do 17s maintained their formation and brought cross fire to bear. Two of the bombers were brought down but there is nothing to show that the formation was diverted. Yet the fact remains that it failed, no less than that engaged by No. 85 Squadron, to find its target. The only bombs that can be traced to it fell at Brentwood, and it is unlikely that this was the target. It is much more probable that Hornchurch, North Weald and Debden were the objectives of the whole operation, and that the force in question failed to attack the second of these. Part of it was engaged near North Weald, probably after it had dropped its bombs, by No. 1 (RCAF) Squadron, who had the good fortune to find it unescorted by fighters. Two of the Dorniers were destroyed.

The third German force was more successful. It crossed the coast near Maldon where it was sighted by No. 111 Squadron who described it as containing about fifty Do 17s escorted by about one hundred Me 110s and 109s. This was probably an exaggerated estimate: No. 56 Squadron sighted the same force when it was ten miles south-west of Colchester and reckoned that it consisted of fifteen to twenty bombers escorted by about fifty fighters. What is certain is that the German bombers were heavily escorted, that neither of our squadrons were able to penetrate to them, and that while the fighter combats were taking place the German bombers went on to attack Debden.

They were not further interfered with,[9] except by the ground defences at the station, and dropped approximately one hundred bombs. Electricity and water

9 No. 19 Squadron had been despatched from Duxford in No. 12 Group to protect Debden but it failed to intercept the enemy. The explanation offered by the Squadron is that the attack took place from below cloud while they were patrolling above it. This is not so: the Germans approached the airfield above the clouds, which were from 5,000–7,000 feet, and then glided through them to attack. The failure of No. 12 Group squadrons on this and on a subsequent occasion to protect No. 11 Group stations was later advanced by No. 11 Group as a reason for taking over the control of all No. 12 Group squadrons which were sent in as reinforcements. On this occasion, however, the failure appears to have been due chiefly to the time of take-off: No. 19 Squadron only left Duxford at 1510 to 1515 hours and Debden was being bombed at 1520 hours. This implies that No. 11 Group delayed too long in requesting assistance.

supplies were damaged; the sergeants' mess, the MT shed and the equipment stores were all hit; and there were several craters on the landing area when the attack was over. Nevertheless, there was no vital damage to the station as a base for fighter operations, and it remained in service.

The enemy bombers were not to escape unscathed. They were attacked as they retired by No. 310 (Czech) Squadron which had originally been ordered to protect North Weald but was diverted to the Debden raid. One of the Dorniers was destroyed and one of the small number of fighters which had succeeded in maintaining the escort, but three Hurricanes were lost.[10]

On the whole the operation had issued in favour of the defenders, though it is impossible to say how far the failure of two of the German formations to find their targets was due to weather, and how far to the action of the British fighters. What is certain is that a three-fold attack, designed to strike each of the sector stations in No. 11 Group north of the Thames, succeeded in striking only one.

The ratio of interceptions to sorties was also gratifying, seven out of nine squadrons having made contact with the enemy. The claims of our pilots amounted to six bombers and eight fighters destroyed; and three more were claimed by AA Command, two of them by the LAA gunners at Debden. Fourteen Hurricanes were made Category 3, but only four pilots were casualties. The wreckage of ten German aircraft was found after the battle, a higher proportion than usual. Five were Do 17s from I and III/KG 2; there were two Me 109s from I/JG 52 and one from an unknown Gruppe of JG 70; two were Me 110s, one of which could not be identified; the other was from I/ZG 1

c. *Over the Solent, 1600–1700 hours*

As the operations over Essex were coming to a close the Germans had already begun assembling further west for an attack across the central Channel. The Solent area had already been reconnoitred by two separate aircraft earlier in the afternoon, and it was there that Germans intended their blow to fall.

At 1600 hours a force reported as '100 plus' was detected sixty miles out on a course for Portsmouth. Simultaneously a force of 'thirty plus' was picked-up some miles to the west off Cherbourg, and ten minutes later a similar force was detected in the same area by which time the other formations were about thirty miles off the Isle of Wight.

Few British fighters were in the air at the time, and the No. 10 Group and No. 11 Group controllers set the following squadrons in motion:

No. 11 Group	No. 43 Squadron from Tangmere at 1605 hours to patrol base at 15,000 feet.
	No. 615 Squadron from Kenley at 1610 hours to intercept in the Portsmouth area.

10 The squadron intelligence officer's report indicates why this combat was not more successful: 'All aircraft were equipped with H/F excepting S/Ldr Blackwood's, who was using VHF. Consequently it was impossible for the CO to issue any order to the other pilots, and, further, as VHF was used by the Sector Controller, pilots were unaware of any signals from the ground.'

No. 602 Squadron from Westhampnett at 1613 hours with the same orders.

No. 10 Group No. 234 Squadron from Middle Wallop at 1610 hours to patrol Swanage.

No. 249 Squadron from Boscombe Down at 1615 hours to patrol Isle of Wight at 25,000 feet.

No. 213 Squadron from Exeter at 1620 hours to patrol Warmwell at 25,000 feet.

No. 609 Squadron from Middle Wallop at 1625 hours to patrol Portsmouth at 15,000 feet.

By the time the last of these squadrons had left the ground the first combats were taking place, and as the main German attack was put in east of the Isle of Wight only No. 234 of the No. 10 Group squadrons engaged the enemy.

At 1620 hours the enemy was advancing on the Solent on a twenty-mile front. One formation of 'twenty plus' was approaching Swanage followed some twenty miles behind by another force of much the same size; while further east a force of '100 plus' was approaching Selsey Bill. This force was also being followed by a formation of 'twenty plus'. Events were to show that the formations to the west and behind the main body were fighter forces whose duty was to protect the western flank of the largest formation and cover its retirement. It is significant that the Germans rarely troubled to protect the right flank of any force attacking across the Channel, as it was a relatively simple matter to pin down the squadrons in Kent and Surrey by a demonstration if not an actual attack in the Straits.

On this occasion, however, two of the Tangmere squadrons and one Kenley squadron were sufficient to inflict what seemed at the time, and still seems, a heavy defeat on the Germans. As the main force approached Selsey Bill it was sighted by No. 602 Squadron and No. 43 Squadron, who were acting independently. All that is established from their reports is that the enemy consisted of a mixed bomber formation of fifty aircraft flying at 15,000 feet protected by anything up to one hundred Me 109s and 110s about five thousand feet higher.

No. 43 Squadron was the first to attack, followed a moment or two later by No. 602. A head-on attack was delivered and while this did not force the enemy aircraft to break formation many of them jettisoned their bombs in the sea near Hayling Island. Verey lights were fired to bring down the escorting fighters and thenceforwards the pilots of the squadron were involved in individual combats. But by then No. 602 Squadron had taken up the attack. They had climbed to 17,000 feet to the west of the enemy to get the advantage of both height and sun; and as they dived down they saw the main formation split in two, part making for the south-west, part for the south-east. This is not borne out by the tracks of the enemy recorded in the Fighter Command Filter Room, which show that the enemy continued to come in-land, although a split quite certainly took place.

Over Portsmouth itself No. 615 Squadron went into action at about 1630 hours. There were still many fighters protecting the German bombers, of which the squadron saw two formations of fifteen Heinkels, and it was chiefly with them that the squadron was in combat. Part of the squadron failed to engage the enemy; instead, they carried out an attack – happily it was broken off in time – on a formation of Blenheims which they had failed to identify.

Meanwhile, further to the west No. 234 Squadron had engaged two formations of Me 109s, containing eight and thirty aircraft respectively. The squadrons succeeded in surprising the smaller of the two forces; and in the ensuing fight, in which some of the larger formation joined, they claimed to have shot down six at no cost to themselves. Part of the enemy force, however, swept in as far as Southampton, where the guns were in action from 1625 to 1633 hours.

This was virtually the end of an operation in which the Germans achieved singularly little compared to the effort that was made. Fort Cumberland was hit, and a small fire was started at a gas works; but most of the bombs fell harmlessly on Hayling Island and in Langstone harbour. There is little doubt that the timely interception off Selsey Bill saved Portsmouth town and dockyard from what might well have been a most damaging attack.

The claims of the defenders were not remarkably large; they were six bombers and seven fighters. Against this five fighters were lost and five pilots were wounded. The success of the defence, therefore, is to be put down rather to the timing of the attack and the determination with which it was executed than to the casualties that were inflicted.

Only three German bombers, all He 111s from I and II/KG 55, and one fighter, the unit not being identifiable, crashed on land. Others undoubtedly crashed in the sea; for about 1900 hours an He 59 was intercepted just south of the Isle of Wight on its way back to France by 'B' Flight of No. 602 Squadron. The enemy aircraft fought back but the issue was hardly in doubt, and it was destroyed. These rescue aircraft were usually escorted by fighters, but none were protecting this particular aircraft although Me 109s were in the area.

Thus ended the day which can hardly have given the Germans much cause for satisfaction, if they knew what paltry results had attended their bombing. Of the three attacks only part of one – that against Debden – had achieved any success. On the debit side of the British account could be put a higher loss in fighters proportionate to those of the enemy than we had come to expect. Thirty-two Hurricanes and Spitfires were lost against just over fifty of the enemy. Fortunately only sixteen pilots were killed, wounded or missing, though even this loss, sustained daily, meant further inroads into the Command's capital in trained pilots.

OPERATIONS, 27 AUGUST

The day following their intensive operations on 24 August the Germans launched only one attack of sizeable dimensions; and similarly the activity of the 26th was followed by one of the quietest days since the beginning of the month. Fewer than fifty aircraft operated against the country, and only four bombing incidents were reported by the Ministry of Home Security. No attacks on shipping were notified, but German aircraft were known to have shadowed east coast convoys. There were a number of interceptions of reconnaissance aircraft, four of which were destroyed.

The weather over Britain was mainly fair, except in the Midlands where there was low cloud and some rain; and it would appear that the Germans were preparing for the attacks that they launched on the night of the 27th and during the following day.

OPERATIONS, 28 AUGUST

Two reconnaissances overland, in the Solent area and in the south-east, began the German operations on the 28th. In each of them particular attention appeared to be paid to the chain of RDF stations on the coast, but as this type of target was not seriously attacked either on this day or, indeed, during the rest of the battle, the probability is that the enemy were investigating the progress of the coast defence works.

i. Against Eastchurch, 0830–0915 hours

The first signs that the Germans projected something other than activity by single aircraft were received early in the day, for between 0819 and 0835 hours one formation of 'twenty plus', one of 'three plus' and one of 'twelve plus' were detected between the mouth of the Somme and Cap Gris Nez. The No. 11 Group controller quickly appreciated the threat and ordered up the following forces:

> No. 79 Squadron from Biggin Hill at 0825 hours to patrol its forward base at Hawkinge.
>
> No. 264 Squadron from Rochford at 0835 hours to patrol Dover.
>
> No. 615 Squadron from Kenley at 0835 hours: the squadron was ordered towards the Straits.

These precautions were taken none too soon, for within fifteen minutes of the third German force being detached the enemy were crossing the coast. The force of 'twenty plus' crossed between Folkestone and Dover at 0845 hours, and that of 'twelve plus' between Dover and Deal at the same time. Shortly afterwards, two more British squadrons were sent into the air to act as a second 'line of defence: No. 501 Squadron went up from Gravesend to patrol Canterbury at 15,000 feet and No. 616 from Kenley to patrol Tenterden. This last squadron was the only one of the five sent up which did not engage the enemy, whose line of advance proved to be to the north-east.

The two German forces that had crossed at different points of the coast joined up north of Dover and flew on towards their target, which was the RAF station at Eastchurch. No. 79 Squadron was the first to sight the enemy; and it reported a mixed force of He 111s and Me 109s at about 16,000 feet, a thousand feet higher than the British squadron. The ensuing engagement followed the standard pattern of most initial combats between a small defending and a large attacking force. The Hurricanes were forced to climb to engage the enemy and just as they had succeeded in making an attack from the rear upon the bombers they were themselves overwhelmed by the German fighters and after a short time were forced to break off the struggle. But they had made things easier for No. 264 Squadron which next took up the attack. They were able to reach the Heinkels, of which there were about twenty, and destroy one of them. The enemy fighters were still in great strength, however, and hotly engaged the Defiants, which, as usual, lost heavily, two being destroyed and four badly damaged.[11]

All this time the German formation had pressed on to the north-east and fighting was still going on when No. 615 Squadron, followed shortly by No. 501 Squadron, came into action in the Faversham–Canterbury district. No. 615 Squadron believed that the enemy bombers were Do 17s and not Heinkels as previously reported; but such contradictions were a common feature of the fighting. The experience of this squadron was similar to that of No. 79: two pilots succeeded in reaching the bombers and shot one of them down; but otherwise all the fighting was with the escorting fighters which again intervened very sharply. No. 501 Squadron chose to go to the aid of the Hurricanes rather than to attack the bombers, and they also were wholly engaged with Me 109s. By this time the latter, who had been defending their charges with great vigour, must have been feeling the effects of the constant fighting in which they had been involved since crossing the coast, and three were claimed as shot down at no cost to No. 501 Squadron. This was some return for the losses suffered by No. 79 and No. 264 squadrons; but the action enabled the bombers to complete the last stage of their flight and bomb Eastchurch which they reached at approximately 0900 hours, detailed results of the attack are lacking but it was not without success. The landing ground was so damaged that it was only usable for restricted day flying: two Battles were destroyed on the ground and two more damaged.

The retirement was first due east and then south-east. First the Manston and then the Dover guns went into action against the returning enemy. There was no further interception by fighters.

Thus ended a swift attack which had turned out well for the Germans, thanks chiefly to the fighter escort. Two German bombers and three fighters were believed to have been destroyed. It is not known what unit the bombers were drawn from, but the fighters were from JG 51 and I/JG 26. Eight British fighters were destroyed and six pilots killed or wounded. The one puzzling feature is that the Germans should have deemed it worthwhile bombing this particular station.

11 Within a day or two Air Chief Marshal Dowding finally decided to use the Defiant henceforth primarily for night fighting (Fighter Command ORB, Form 540, 31 August, 1940).

ii. Against Rochford, 1200–1315 hours

A peculiarity of the first attack had been that some He 59 air-sea rescue aircraft, escorted by fighters, had appeared over the Straits whilst it was in progress, and had remained there for some time after it was over. One was still about shortly after 1100 hours and was shot down by a section of No. 79 Squadron. Otherwise there was no activity other than routine patrolling during the rest of the morning.

About noon, however, the strength of the German patrols on the French side of the Straits increased. No. 11 Group therefore ordered a patrol over Hawkinge by one flight of No. 79 Squadron and one over Manston by No. 54 Squadron. In addition, No. 615 Squadron left Kenley at 1210 hours with instructions to patrol Tenterden.

As this squadron left the ground it became evident that an attack was indeed imminent. Between 1215 and 1225 hours three fairly large formations were located between Boulogne and Dunkerque. The most southerly crossed the Straits shortly before 1230 hours and came overland at Dungeness. The other two formed into one force and began to move towards the North Foreland at 1225 hours crossing there ten minutes later.

The following squadrons were therefore ordered into the air:

> No. 603 Squadron from Hornchurch at 1227 hours for what is described as 'a defensive patrol'.
>
> No. 1 Squadron from Northolt to patrol Hornchurch–Rochford.
>
> In addition, squadrons at North Weald, Kenley and Gravesend were sent up to protect their bases.

The German force which crossed at Dungeness was engaged by No. 615 Squadron near Tenterden. It was a fighter formation of about thirty Me 109s but despite its great numerical superiority it evaded combat and flew on towards Maidstone. Here it turned and made for France. Its task was doubtless to cover the flank of the force that crossed near the North Foreland. Throughout the next half hour small fighter forces were over Dover, also attempting to divert some of the defending forces from the main attack.

The force detailed to carry this out consisted of twenty-seven Do 17s from II/KG 3, protected by a similar number of Me 109s. He 113s were also reported amongst the escort. They were first engaged by No. 54 Squadron which was patrolling Manston at 30,000 feet. The squadron split into widely spaced sections and dived down on the bombers in the hope of breaking up the whole formation. One Do 17 was shot down into the sea, but otherwise all combats were with fighters and the bombers flew on up the estuary. They held to this course until they reached the Isle of Sheppey, when they turned north and made for Rochford which they were approaching shortly before 1300 hours. There they were engaged by No. 1 Squadron which carried out a diving head-on attack, succeeding thereby in forcing the leading section of Dorniers to break away. Most of the enemy maintained their course, however, and bombed the airfield at Rochford from 18,000 feet. No. 264 Squadron was stationed there and had barely obtained permission to take-off before the bombs began to fall. The station appears to have suffered only slightly, and it remained serviceable.[12]

The enemy then made for home across the estuary: and it seems safe to say that all the Germans had undertaken since noon had been done to bomb this airfield. No. 603 Squadron engaged a formation of fighters near Canterbury shortly after 1300 hours, but this hardly influenced the operation.

Five bombers and three fighters were believed to have been destroyed, of which one bomber and two fighters crashed on land. Three RAF aircraft were lost, but no pilots.

iii. Over Eastern Kent, 1530–1900 hours

The Germans took no further offensive action until shortly after 1530 hours. Then there began a series of attacks which differed sharply from the previous operations on this day, and indeed from anything the Germans had previously attempted during the whole course of the battle. They took the form of a number of sweeps by purely fighter formations. These were so arranged that there was no period between the start of the attacks at 1530 hours and their close just over four hours later when British squadrons were not engaged in interception patrols. No purpose would be served in enumerating the German sorties or those of the defence, but seven British squadrons were in action during the period, most of them in bitterly fought struggles at high altitudes (18,000–25,000 feet) with forces of Me 109s varying from twelve to thirty aircraft strong.

As we do not know for certain what the Germans had in mind by departing from their usual methods it is only safe to say that these sweeps at least succeeded in weakening the Command just prior to the opening of a series of attacks more continuously sustained than at any other phase of the battle. The losses suffered by the Command were not heavy: nine fighters had been lost and the enemy, our pilots believed, had lost thirteen; but this loss, coming at the end of a day on which twenty British fighters were destroyed in all, was not to be lightly regarded.[13] Moreover, the Germans had not operated in great strength during the day.

OPERATIONS, 29 AND 30 AUGUST

i. 29 August

29 August was another of the quiet days which the Germans had been observing alternately with days of sharper activity since 24 August. A number of formations crossed the coast of Kent shortly after 1500 hours and penetrated as far as

12 No ORB was kept by this station, and the only report of the damage caused by this attack comes from the intelligence summary of the Ministry of Home Security: this states that '60 HE and several IB fell, setting fire temporarily to some of the aerodrome buildings'.

13 The relative increase in British casualties was generally held to be due to the employment of new squadrons with little experience of engagements with German fighters, to the increasing proportion of fresh pilots and to the better armament and armour of the German bombers. There was a feeling among the sector commanders in No. 11 Group that some of these disadvantages could be overcome, a. if larger fighter formations were used and, b. if experienced pilots were posted to No. 11 Group squadrons when the pilot strength of any of the latter fell to fifteen (see pp. 222–227).

Westerham and Maidstone but only a very small number of bombers was included: and the operation lasted barely an hour. Between 1800 and 1900 hours there were a few fighter sweeps behind Dover, but if these were similar in form they were very different in degree from the long drawn-out sweeps of the previous evening. In all nine fighters were lost by each side.

ii. 30 August

On the 30th, however, the Germans once more launched large-scale attacks at different times during the day. These displayed one novel feature of the operations on the 28th that has not so far been remarked; namely that activity was entirely directed against south-east England instead of being varied, as it had been on most days prior to the 28th, with an attack in force across the central Channel. In other words the enemy was concentrating upon the defences of No. 11 Group even more than before.[14]

The first few hours of daylight were notable for the lengths to which the Germans went to simulate an attack. A number of patrols were put up over the eastern side of the Straits shortly before 0800 hours culminating in an advance towards Dover by one force of 'twenty plus' and another of 'twelve plus'. The controller at No. 11 Group was not impressed and only one section was sent up. Again, between 0915 and 0930 hours three small enemy forces were located as they moved over the Straits, and two British squadrons were ordered to patrol Hawkinge and Rochford respectively; but still no enemy aircraft crossed the coast. Indications of an assembly continued to come in, but it was not until 1030 hours that the position warranted the despatch of any squadrons additional to those patrolling the coastal airfields.

a. Against Biggin Hill, 1030–1215 hours

By that time three forces of about twenty aircraft were near Calais and one of 'fifty plus' was over Tramecourt. Here was an unmistakable threat and, in fact, as the first defending squadrons left the ground the enemy began to move towards the coast. The first British forces that were set in motion were as follows:

No. 501 Squadron from Hawkinge at 1025 hours to patrol base.

No. 1 Squadron from Northolt at 1030 hours: their orders are unknown and they did not engage the enemy.

14 It is perhaps unwarrantable to deduce from this that the Germans were feeling the strain of continuous operations and had therefore decided to concentrate their efforts against the area where success had most to commend it. Yet it was not until 9 September that any serious attack was made by day upon targets in the Solent area; and in fact from 25 August the long-range bomber resources of *Luftflotte* 3 were largely employed firstly in the heavier night attacks which began on that date against towns in the western half of England, and secondly, from 7 September, in the night attacks on London. This meant that some of the fighter units of *Luftflotte* 3 were released from the escort duties on which they had been employed earlier in August in the central Channel; and it is known from wreckage found in south-east England that *Luftflotte* 3 fighters from Brittany were used over Kent from 25 August. These units - I, II, III/JG 53 - remained formally based in Brittany, but whether aircraft returned there at the end of a day or were lodged further east is not known. What is certain is that from the last week in August practically all available German fighters were concentrated between the Seine and Dunkerque.

No. 603 Squadron from Hornchurch at 1035 hours to patrol Canterbury.

No. 85 Squadron from Croydon at 1036 hours: they were directed towards Dover.

No. 56 Squadron from North Weald at 1040 hours: their orders are unknown and they did not engage the enemy.

No. 610 Squadron from Biggin Hill at 1045 hours: they were directed towards Dover.

The remainder of No. 501 Squadron left Hawkinge at 1050 hours to patrol it, the others having been directed towards Dungeness.

The weather at the time was fine, with visibility excellent though there was some cloud between 5,000–7,000 feet.

After the last of three squadrons had left the ground a new force of over fifty aircraft was located behind Cap Gris Nez. At the same time, 1100 hours, the force that had been detected over Tramecourt steered towards Dungeness. Further British forces were therefore sent into the air:

No. 253 Squadron from Kenley at 1055 hours to patrol Maidstone.

No. 151 Squadron from Stapleford at 1100 hours: their orders are unknown.

No. 234 Squadron ('B' Flight) from Middle Wallop in No. 10 Group at 1105 hours to patrol Northolt.

The first German force to cross the coast came in at Dungeness at 1103 hours and flew towards Tonbridge. Within a few minutes it had been intercepted by No. 85 Squadron who reported that it consisted of about fifty He 111s at 16,000 feet with numerous escorting fighters still higher. The squadron commander led his formation inland until he could carry out a head-on attack on the bombers from out of the sun. This he did and apparently with striking success, for the squadron were agreed that the bomber formation was effectively dispersed. Certainly the track charts compiled in the Filter Room at Fighter Command Headquarters show a number of small formations in this area after the combat had taken place, whereas the main enemy formations was not plotted after 1110 hours, which was the time of the engagement. Bombs fell near the village of Smarden and in the wooded country south-west of Ashford about this time; and it is hardly to be doubted that they were jettisoned by German aircraft that were in trouble.

Meanwhile a second wave of aircraft consisting of two or three separate formations was approaching the coast between Dungeness and Dover. Only one of these formations contained bombers and it was first engaged to the north-east of Dungeness at 1120 hours by No. 501 Squadron, who reported that there were some sixty bombers, both Heinkels and Dorniers, at 15,000 feet, with about twenty Me 109s at the same height and a large force of Me 110s still higher. Shortly after No. 501 Squadron opened the engagement No. 610 and one flight of No. 603 Squadron came into action, the latter entirely with Me 110s. At least five bombers were believed to have been shot down at a cost of only one Spitfire, but the main body of the German force continued to fly on towards south-east London. Further north No. 151 Squadron were also in action about this time but with a force entirely composed of fighters. Unfortunately the tracking of the enemy formations at this time was hampered by a layer of cloud at 6,000–8,000 feet, and few tracks were clearly established. For the next half-hour German forces were being intermittently reported over all the country between Biggin Hill, Beachy Head and Dungeness; and we have no means of telling whether there was a number of small enemy forces operating in that area or whether these isolated pilots were all that was known of two or three fairly large formations.

At any rate as the force engaged near the coast pressed on towards the capital other enemy forces were being detected as they made for the coast of Kent. Accordingly the following squadrons were ordered into the air:

No. 222 from Hornchurch at 1110 hours to patrol Gravesend.

No. 54 from Rochford at 1115 hours to patrol Billericay at 20,000 feet.

By 1120 hours it was obvious to the controller that the Biggin Hill-Kenley airfields were threatened. He therefore brought back No. 253 Squadron from the patrol over Maidstone to protect Kenley, and sent up the rest of the squadron to join them, as well as part of No. 616 Squadron which was also stationed there: this made twenty-seven aircraft in all. No. 79 Squadron was ordered up from Biggin Hill at 1130 hours to patrol it, while five minutes earlier No. 19 Squadron left Duxford in No. 12 Group with instructions also to patrol Biggin Hill.

By 1130 hours the first bombs were being reported. They fell in the Chislehurst, Bromley and Orpington districts, and continued to fall there until shortly after 1142 hours. It is almost certain that they came from bombers which were part of the force that had crossed near Dungeness at 1103 hours and had been engaged subsequently by No. 85 Squadron. They did little damage, and as we can safely assume that the Germans had something else in view than the wrecking of suburban house property it would appear that the aircraft concerned had failed to find their targets.

At 1140 hours an enemy force was located for the first time as it flew up the Thames Estuary near the Isle of Sheppey. By then the force originally engaged by Nos 501, 610 and 603 squadrons was approaching Redhill. It was near that place that the next engagement took place when just before 1145 hours No. 253 Squadron, having been ordered south, met a force of twenty-seven bombers and some thirty escorting fighters. No. 79 Squadron had also left their patrol over Biggin Hill to meet this threat. Between the two squadrons serious losses were believed to have been inflicted on the Germans, amounting in all to six He 111s and three Me 110s, at a cost of four Hurricanes; and as shortly after the engagement began bombs fell in the Dorking–Leatherhead district it is obvious that some of the enemy bombers were forced to release their bombs. Moreover, it is impossible to trace any further bombing to this particular German formation. It is possible, therefore, that the whole enemy formation was diverted from its target.

But it was only one part of the force that had crossed the coast shortly after 1120 hours: and while this engagement had been going on Biggin Hill, to the north-east, was being bombed by a force that was not intercepted, at any rate not during the later stages of its advance. It was this force that was engaged about noon by No. 616 Squadron, who reported that it consisted of twelve to eighteen Do 17s and an escort of Me 109s. The enemy were travelling east when first seen, in other words they were returning home.

There is no mention of the strength of the bombing force in the records of the Biggin Hill station. Nor is much recorded there about the results of the attack. The surface of the landing area was damaged, but remained serviceable; and the squadrons that were based there operated from it during the remainder of the day.

By noon the operation was over, although isolated plots of German forces continued to come in from the Observer Corps both north and south of the Thames until 1230 hours; and about noon No. 43 Squadron had a brief skirmish with a retiring force of fighters near Brighton. No further bombs were reported, however, and by 1300 hours the south-east was virtually clear of the enemy and was to remain so for another two hours.

The success of this operation from the German point of view is largely judged by the results achieved by the bombing in relation to the forces employed and the losses sustained. As to the first there is little doubt that the damage done at Biggin Hill was an insufficient return for the efforts of, as we believed, at least sixty bombers and more than that number of fighters; and from a study of British records it seems certain that at least one of the German bomber formations failed to find its target. German losses, moreover, were believed to be heavy: fourteen bombers and thirteen fighters were claimed as destroyed. British losses were eight aircraft and five pilots. The claims could not be confirmed, which is not surprising as much of the fighting in the early stages of the operation was over or near the sea. Wreckage was recovered from six enemy aircraft: four were He 111s from IV/KG 1, and two were Me 109s from units that could not be identified.

iii. Against Luton, Detling and Biggin Hill, 1515 to 1815 hours

For two hours after 1300 hours there was a lull in operations, but shortly before three o'clock in the afternoon a long drawn-out operation began that threw no little strain on the defending squadrons. It opened with the simulation of an attack between 1440 and 1500 hours which persuaded the controller to send six squadrons into the air between 1500 and 1530 hours. All that happened, however, was that a small force of bombers lightly attacked Lympne just after 1500 hours, and two fighter forces swept inland as far as Redhill and then came out by Beachy Head. Two British squadrons made contact with forces of Me 109s: one of them, No. 616, saw a small force of bombers but at such a distance that it could not be identified much less attacked. In any case, the squadron became involved with a force of enemy fighters that was guarding the retiring bombers. Doubtless the Germans hoped by these incursions to force a number of defending squadrons into the air for so long that they would be about to land to refuel when more important operations began, as they did an hour later. Four of the six squadrons, in fact, were ordered to take-off again within twenty minutes of landing. On the other hand, a fifth, No. 222, was found to be admirably placed to attack the first wave of the main German advance.

Just after 1540 hours German formations, three in all, moved north-north-west across the Kent coast near Dover, while other formations, small in size, were located in the central part of the Straits. In short a threat was developing both over the estuary and further south. But it was not until 1555 hours that British squadrons began to leave the ground; and this is surprising as only No. 222 Squadron were in a position to intercept in north-east Kent. They were in action shortly after 1600 hours near Canterbury with twenty-five He 111s and a similar number of Me 110s, which were flying north. The odds on this occasion were too great and two Spitfires were destroyed.

By that time, however, other squadrons were moving into position:

> At 1555 hours No. 603 left Hornchurch to patrol Manston.
>
> At 1600 hours No. 501 left Gravesend to patrol Gravesend-Chatham.
>
> At 1605 hours No. 151 left Stapleford to patrol a convoy near the North Foreland.

Ten minutes later No. 616 Squadron left Kenley to intercept an enemy raid near Eastchurch, and No. 303 Squadron left Northolt with the singular aim of carrying out an interception exercise with a Blenheim squadron near St Albans.

a. Against Luton

By 1615 hours it was clear that the enemy were intent on operating north of the estuary; and in the next fifteen minutes two more squadrons took off to intercept in that area. But there were at least two other enemy formations over eastern Kent, with still more forming up further east. Consequently the controllers did not commit all their available squadrons to meet what might prove, and did in fact prove, to be only the first wave of a lengthy attack.

Part of the force – or an auxiliary to it – that had been engaged by No. 222 Squadron was further engaged over the estuary by No. 603 Squadron at about 1620 hours. The enemy proved to be a large formation of Me 109s and no bombers were seen; and the action had little or no effect on the bombing that followed. This took place first at some scattered points of little importance in Essex; Billericay, Hadleigh and South Benfleet being affected; and an attack by No. 151 Squadron north-west of the Isle of Sheppey explains this seemingly peculiar choice of targets. The squadron reported that it had succeeded in attacking one of three formations of twenty bombers before their escorting fighters could interfere, and forced most of them to jettison their bombs. But by 1645 hours, the rest of the enemy had flown as far north and west as Bedfordshire where they attacked Luton. The Vauxhall motor works was hit, the experimental building being badly damaged and fifty employees killed; and bombs also fell on the civil airport and on houses in the town. This was a different sort of target to that which the Germans had recently been attacking; and while this particular works was important it may be found that the vital Skefco ballbearing works was in fact the enemy's objective.

Three more squadrons, including two from No. 12 Group, took off about the time that Luton was being attacked; and two of them, Nos 242 and 253, with four squadrons that had taken off earlier, succeeded in engaging the Germans as they retired to the south-east. Ten enemy bombers and thirteen fighters were claimed as destroyed for a loss of five of our own fighters.

b. Against Detling

The Germans had been at some pains to protect this first attack from interference by sending fighters into eastern Kent as well as into the areas in which bombing actually took place. A few isolated plots of some of these formations were still coming in from the Observer Corps at 1710 hours, and by that time the second wave of the enemy's attack was approaching. The first indications of this were received at 1700 hours when the RDF stations detected a force of 'fifty plus' approaching from the direction of Cap Gris Nez. It remained over the Straits but it was no rearguard formation; for it was rare that these covering forces exceeded a dozen aircraft. At 1715 hours, however, a force of twenty or more aircraft was located about ten miles east of Dungeness, and after crossing the coast at Folkestone it flew towards Chatham. One flight of No. 222 Squadron was sent off to intercept it. The enemy were attacked as they came in by No. 43 Squadron who had originally taken off to patrol Beachy Head while the Germans had been operating over Essex and Hertfordshire. The squadron reported twenty Do 17s at 18,000 feet protected by a similar number of fighters behind them and at the same height, with a further fighter force some two thousand feet above. Our pilots managed to attack from above and out of the sun but there was little loss to either side in the succeeding fight.

Henceforth the German movements are quite clear. The enemy force reached Chatham just before 1740 hours, turned south-east and then bombed the Coastal Command station at Detling without being further interfered with. The number of bombs put down was not large (forty to fifty) but the attack was accurate and the airfield was made unserviceable until 0900 hours the next day. The neighbouring village of Thurnham received about a dozen bombs that were presumably intended for the station.

When Detling was attacked ten fighter squadrons were returning to their bases after the previous operations; and this goes far to explain why there was only one interception. About the same time as the attack was carried out another enemy formation, about whose movements we know nothing, penetrated into the London area and dropped a small number of bombs on Lambeth.

From the initial detection to the enemy's retirement across the Kent coast the whole operation lasted barely half an hour; and it was followed by another that was executed almost as swiftly.

c. Against Biggin Hill

At 1750 hours there were three large and two large and two small forces moving about over the Straits of Dover. Five minutes later one of the larger forces – it was plotted as twenty or more aircraft – suddenly swung west and crossed the coast near Dover and steered towards the Isle of Sheppey. Almost simultaneously the controller at No. 11 Group ordered No. 501 Squadron to patrol Hawkinge and No. 616 Squadron to patrol Kenley. Only the second of these squadrons might have intercepted the enemy who were moving very quickly; for on reaching Sheppey they flew straight towards Biggin Hill and bombed it from a low altitude at about 1810 hours. Six aircraft from No. 79 Squadron took off just before the attack and succeeded in engaging the enemy, who were a composite force of about thirty aircraft, as they retired; and No. 222 Squadron also engaged them nearer the coast. One Me 109 was destroyed but four of our own aircraft were lost. Three other squadrons were sent up to engage the raid but none made contact either with the main force or with a covering force that crossed the coast near Hythe at about 1820 hours. By 1830 hours the skies over the south-east were almost clear of German movements.

The number of bombs dropped on Biggin Hill was less than twenty, but the attack was one of the most successful that the Germans had so far made against a Fighter Command station. The workshops, MT yard, equipment and barrack stores, armoury, meteorological office and NAAFI institute were wrecked; power, gas and water mains were severed and all telephone communications on the northern side of the station were cut, thirty-nine officers and men were killed and twenty-six wounded.

The main German operations on this day ended with this attack. From the enemy's point of view it was a good end to what they probably considered a good day. The morning operations, it is true, had been effectively checked, but the three main targets of the evening attacks, Luton, Detling and Biggin Hill, had each been reached and accurately bombed. German losses for the whole day were believed to be high: sixty-three aircraft of which just over half were fighters. But our own losses, bearing in mind the comparative strengths of the contestants, were equally, if no more heavy. Twenty-six fighters were destroyed and seven badly damaged; fourteen fighter pilots were killed or wounded. In addition to the aircraft from IV/KG 1 that were discovered on land after the morning operations, the wreckage of aircraft from each *Geschwader* of KG 53 and from II/KG 3 was found after the evening attacks. Fighters from at least two *Geschwadern* of Me 109s and two of Me 110s also operated during the evening.

OPERATIONS, 31 AUGUST

The day came up fine and cloudless, with a slight haze up to 7,000 feet; and the enemy's patrols were over the Pas de Calais and the Straits of Dover soon after six o'clock. At 0730 hours there were indications that an attack was impending and three squadrons, Nos 1, 253 and 501, at once took off to patrol the Kent and Essex coasts.

As the last of these squadrons took off at 0740 hours the signs that the Germans were concentrating became very strong, and ten minutes later there were four formations, sixty aircraft in all, on the move between Cap Gris Nez and Dunkerque: two of them were twenty or more aircraft strong. Eight Hurricanes from No. 151 Squadron now took off from Stapleford Tawney and were directed towards Deal and Dover (0750) hours. A few moments later, one of the formations in the Straits came over at Dover and made a wide circuit over northern and central Kent. As this force was sweeping the country between Ramsgate and Westgate, it was brought to action by No. 151 Squadron. The enemy were a fighter force of about thirty Me 109s, and were flying at about twenty thousand feet: No. 151 squadron became very scattered after action was joined but suffered no loss. The enemy continued his sweep over the country between Ashford and the northern coast of Kent, and then steered for the eastern end of Sheppey.

The easternmost of the formations that were located just before 0800 hours was now crossing the outer estuary: the course upon which it was moving indicated clearly that an attack north of the Thames was intended, probably against the sector stations there. Another German formation now crossed the Straits, came in by way of Dover, and steered for the estuary across north-eastern Kent; and simultaneously a new formation was located just off Dover. It skirted the coast between the South and the North Foreland and then steered north-west towards Southend.

i. Against Debden, 0815–0900 hours

At 0812 hours the formation that was leading the advance towards Essex was very near the coast, and was brought to action by No. 1 Squadron, which had taken off from Northolt at 0735 hours. According to the pilots, the enemy were in far greater strength than the RDF had indicated – one hundred bombers and Me 110s. The bombers were in groups of fifteen and were flying in very close formation from 12,000–18,000 feet: the fighters were moving freely between the bombers in groups of five or more. The squadron attempted to attack the bombers from ahead; but the enemy fighters intervened before the attack could be delivered. The German formation held straight on towards the country between Great Dunmow and Bishop Stortford.

While this engagement was being fought out, nine Hurricanes from No. 111 Squadron took off from Debden and twelve Spitfires from No. 19 Squadron took off from Duxford to patrol between Duxford and Debden. As they did so, yet another enemy force was located, in the middle of the Straits, without any previous indications of its presence being received: it steered north-west, and followed the other across the estuary. The second German formation in the estuary now came in by way of Southend. As it did so five aircraft from No. 56 Squadron took off from North Weald and were directed towards Colchester (0820 hours); seven Spitfires from No. 222 Squadron took off from Rochford; nine Hurricanes from No. 257 Squadron took off from Martlesham; and eleven Hurricanes from No. 601 Squadron took off from Debden to patrol it (0820–0825 hours). The large composite force that had been engaged by No. 1 Squadron was now south-east of Debden; while the force that had been engaged by No. 151 Squadron was coming out into the estuary near Sheppey (0829 hours).

No. 111 Squadron now engaged the force that had recently crossed the land at Southend. The squadron, which had taken off from Debden at 0810 hours, was south of Brentwood. The approaching enemy consisted of about thirty Do 17s from 10,000–15,000 feet, with some forty Me 110s either side of the bombers and slightly above them: ten thousand feet above all, there was a high guard of Me 109s. Notwithstanding the great odds, the squadron contrived to attack a section of bombers and to force several more to jettison their bombs. At least one enemy bomber and one fighter were destroyed for one of our own aircraft; but the German formation held on its course towards Debden.

Shortly after this action was over, the force that came in at 0812 hours, and which had manoeuvred over the country near Great Dunmow after its action with No. 1 Squadron, bombed the sector station at Debden. The bombing force was made up of Do 17s and the attack was made while the bombers were on a north-westerly course. About one hundred HE bombs were put down; the sick quarters and a barrack block were hit, and other buildings were damaged: the operations room and its communications were, however, untouched, and the station was still usable. The German force was not interfered with during the attack, which is rather remarkable as No. 601 Squadron took off at 0825 hours to patrol it; and No. 19 Squadron, from No. 12 Group, had been patrolling between Duxford and Debden since 0815 hours. The force that carried out this attack appears to have been on a course for home about 0840 hours. The force that followed it in was then over the country between Colchester and Chelmsford, and was being engaged by No. 56 Squadron.

Although the Germans contrived to reach their principal target, and to bomb it without being seriously interfered with, they were fiercely attacked during their retirement, by No. 601 Squadron between Stradishall and Colchester, by No. 19 Squadron south of Colchester, by No. 257 Squadron between Chelmsford and Clacton and by No. 111 Squadron (for the second time that morning) near Clacton. Every German aircraft that was brought down – and in all eight were claimed – was an Me 110; and as ten British fighters were shot down it can be said that the enemy fighters had protected their bombers successfully.

But equally it can be said that at least one part of the German operation had gone awry. At different times between 0820 and 0850 hours bombs were dropped in eight villages to the south of Cambridge and near the sector station at Duxford. It would follow from this that the Germans sent into this part of the country a formation of bombers additional to the one that bombed Debden. This was not intercepted as far as we know but the bombs that it dropped did no damage. It is admittedly an assumption that its target was Duxford, but it is a fairly safe one. In addition, bombs fell at the same time on Colchester and Maldon, and on Saffron Walden and two nearby villages.

While these operations has been taking place north of the Thames strong forces of enemy fighters had been over eastern Kent. Their object was doubtless to divert some of the defending squadrons away from the bombers further north but in addition the Dover balloon barrage was attacked, and in no uncertain fashion: every balloon – twenty-three in all – was shot down by a small force of about six Me 109s two of which were claimed as destroyed by Bofors guns and one by rifle fire from balloon operators. Fighter formations continued to be plotted in the area until 0930 hours, and three squadrons, Nos 1 (RCAF), 79 and 603, were in action.

Even before the last of the German forces had recrossed the coast there were signs that the Germans were still assembling in the Pas de Calais, and at 0950 hours, matters were in this position. Since 0900 hours nine separate formations had been located in the Straits, or just behind Cap Gris Nez. Some had been lost, a few minutes after they have been detected; but there was still a threatening collection of forces on the operations room tables. On the British side, four of the squadrons that had taken off during the last operation had recently landed: one was just returning, the remainder were again in the air patrolling Debden.

Soon afterwards, the northernmost of the German forces in the Straits came rapidly over, crossed the coast at Folkestone, and steered north-west towards Chatham (0957 hours). Eight Hurricanes of No. 151 Squadron took off from Stapleford; and a few moments later, twelve Hurricanes from No. 17 Squadron took off from Debden (1000 hours to 1005 hours): as they did so, the force that had come in by way of Hythe passed rapidly over the airfield at Detling and machine-gunned it. The Observer Corps were not able to discover what course the Germans followed afterwards; but it does not appear that they were brought to action.

During and after this sudden irruption, the Germans continued to assemble; and just before 1030 hours there were four considerable formations over the Straits, of which three came over and crossed at Dover steering north-west (1027 to 1030 hours). This was the third attack that the enemy launched during the morning; and, when they crossed the coast:

> No. 17 and No. 601 squadrons (Debden) were just returning to their base.
>
> Sections from No. 111 Squadron (Debden) and No. 501 Squadron (Gravesend) were just taking off on local patrol.
>
> No. 151 Squadron (Stapleford) was in the air, with enough petrol to remain there for three-quarters of an hour.

ii. Against Eastchurch, 1015–1045 hours

The right wing of the three enemy formations was engaged by No. 151 Squadron as it flew over Canterbury: the pilots estimated that the enemy were about sixty strong – thirty Do 17s and Ju 88s with as many Me 109s. The enemy continued on their north-westerly course, and the engagement ended over the estuary: a convoy was, at that time coming up the river, and although the enemy aimed a few bombs at it, they did not deliver a methodical attack, and flew on towards Southend.

It would appear as though the central enemy formation had been ordered to deliver the attack for which the operation was planned; for it was over Sheppey Island at about 1030 hours, and it then bombed Eastchurch. Very little had been recorded about the attack, but it is certain that it did little damage: the airfield surface was broken in several places but it remained serviceable.

Ten minutes after this attack was over, the three German formations that had come in to deliver it were operating over the country between Southend and Colchester. At 1045 hours they were beginning to make for their home bases, and about ten minutes later all had left the coast. The controller only sent two sections and one flight into the air by way of reinforcement to those that were already there and they were not in time to bring the enemy to action.

iii. Against Croydon and Hornchurch, 1230–1330 hours

The signs that an attack was impending neither increased nor decreased during the next half hour. At 1230 hours, however, two forces were making for the coast; they crossed near Folkestone at 1234 and 1238 hours, and steered towards Biggin Hill and Kenley. Even before the Germans crossed, twelve Hurricanes from No. 79 Squadron took off from Croydon to patrol it; and as the enemy came in, seven Hurricanes from No. 253 Squadron took off from Kenley (1235 hours); six Hurricanes from No. 253 Squadron took off from Kenley (1235 hours); six Hurricanes from No. 17 Squadron took off from Debden (1235 hours); twelve Spitfires from No. 603 Squadron took off from Hornchurch (1240 hours); ten Spitfires from No. 616 Squadron took off from Kenley to patrol it (1248 hours); twelve Hurricanes from No. 85 Squadron took off from Kenley to intercept (1250 hours); and seven Hurricanes from No. 501 Squadron and twelve Hurricanes from No. 601 Squadron took off from Gravesend to patrol Colchester (1255 hours). During the time when our squadrons were thus concentrating, two more German formations were located in the Straits: one of them was fifty, the other twenty or more aircraft strong.

The forces that had crossed near Folkestone advanced without deviation across Kent and Surrey and were approaching Croydon at 1250 hours. No. 79 Squadron, which was patrolling there, engaged them before any bombs had been dropped. They reported that there were about forty Ju 88s with an escort of Me 109s, and that the latter seriously interfered with their attack on the bombers. A detachment from the enemy force (probably Me 110s of KGr 210) attacked the airfield itself, where there was only slight damage; and the rest concentrated on the industrial premises nearby, particularly the Rollason aircraft works, where damage was severe. Even so, the amount of bombing was light in relation to the size of the force reported by No. 79 squadron.

During their return the German formations were briefly engaged by No. 253 Squadron, between Kenley and Biggin Hill, and near Tunbridge Wells by No. 85 Squadron. As they did so, another of the German forces in the Straits came in over Dungeness at 1310 hours, and they turned north following two more forces which had crossed at 1300 hours near Dover and had also steered towards the estuary.

By this time, however, more forces had been sent into the air, and the second part of the German operation was well forward. While Croydon was being bombed, nine Hurricanes from No. 1 Squadron took off from Northolt to patrol the sector; nine Hurricanes from No. 151 Squadron took off from Stapleford; and twelve Hurricanes from No. 310 Squadron (Duxford) took off to patrol North Weald (1300 hours).

When the last of these squadrons took off, the German force that crossed at Dover were coming into the estuary near Sheppey. The enemy came up the Thames as far as Tilbury, and then steered for Hornchurch. So far it had been unhindered, but as it approached the airfield it was engaged by Nos 151, 501, 310 and 601 Squadrons. The reports from the four squadrons state that the enemy force was about fifty aircraft strong, and that it was made up of Do 17s, Me 109s and 110s. No. 501 Squadron also stated that a large part of the enemy force turned back and steered for the sea near Colchester; and this is substantiated by the tracings from the operations room tables, which show eastgoing enemy tracks at about this time. It appears certain, however, that the enemy's move to the east was a device of their fighter squadrons to draw RAF fighters away from the Dornier bombers, and to leave them free to do their work. The stratagem succeeded; for, while three of the four British squadrons were engaging the enemy fighters, thirty Dornier bombers (approximately the number that the pilots believed to be present when action was first joined) having shaken off an attack by No. 310 Squadron appeared over Hornchurch and bombed it. The whole of II/KG 3 took part and one hundred bombs were put down but with very little result: three Spitfires from No. 54 Squadron were destroyed; the power cable to the station was cut and emergency equipment had to be brought into operation; but the station continued to operate its full complement of squadrons.

The enemy retired across the estuary in three groups: the two advanced ones were between the North Foreland and Southend at 1330 hours; and the third operated over North Weald and Hornchurch until about 1340 hours, without, however, renewing the attack. This force was lightly engaged by No. 603 Squadron; but as only one brief report from one pilot has survived, nothing positive can be said about the action or its consequences.

It should be added, for it illustrates how determined the Germans then were to attack airfields and nothing else, that there was practically no subsidiary bombing during this long operation: two or three bombs were put down on Whitstable while the German formations were moving across north-east Kent, and two more fell on Thameshaven during the retirement, but that was all.

Between 1400 and 1500 hours the enemy reconnoitred the country between Colchester and Swanton Morley; but for several hours there were no signs that the Germans were re-assembling. Between 1645 and 1651 hours, however, reconnaissance planes came in over the northern side of the estuary: one of them turned north and inspected the country between Duxford and Debden; the other flew over Hornchurch, west London, and the country between Kenley and Tangmere. A few moments later indications began to be received that the Germans were concentrating again.

iv. Against Maidstone, East London and Biggin Hill, 1715–1845 hours

At 1700 hours a force whose strength could not be estimated was located off Calais; and a few moments afterwards, a formation of twenty or more aircraft was detected near St Omer. Thereafter new forces were located in rapid succession and by 1730 hours seven formations had been picked up by the RDF stations. Four of these were believed to be about sixty aircraft strong in all; and the remaining three, whose strength could not be exactly estimated, probably brought the total number of enemy aircraft that were on the move to about one hundred. At the time, one flight of No. 79 Squadron was in the air on a local flight from Biggin Hill to Croydon: it was directed towards the Straits to meet the enemy. The following squadrons were also ordered up to intercept the enemy near the coast:

No. 54 Squadron from Hornchurch at 1705 hours to patrol Manston.

No. 85 Squadron from Croydon at 1710 hours to patrol Hawkinge.

No. 222 Squadron from Rochford at 1725 hours to patrol Canterbury.

All these squadrons engaged the first of the enemy forces, which crossed between Dungeness and Folkestone about 1725 hours and flew towards Maidstone. They were some thirty Do 17s at 16,000 feet accompanied by about a hundred Me 109s and 110s; and all combats took place between Maidstone and Purfleet. Only No. 85 Squadron succeeded in engaging the bombers, yet it would appear that some of the bombers were induced either to jettison their bombs or to select other than their primary targets. Thus, twenty-five to thirty bombs were dropped near the railway junction at Maidstone about 1800 hours; a little later houses were damaged at Rochester by a small number of bombs; at 1808 hours the railway track between Dartford and Crayford was damaged by bombs; and bombs also fell at Hornchurch and Rainham shortly after 1800 hours. It is almost certain that the sector station at Hornchurch was the German objective; and as observers there reported that the force that bombed the airfield was thirty aircraft strong the enemy undoubtedly succeeding in reaching the target. But as this force was the only one, as far as we know, that was operating over northern Kent and the estuary at the time it would appear that some of the formation had released their bombs before Hornchurch was reached. At any rate the effective damage there was very slight and none of the airfield buildings was hit. No. 603 Squadron took off from the station shortly before the attack. It made contact with the enemy, but with a pure fighter formation.

As this force had been moving inland other German formations had been plotted as they approached the coast; and shortly before 1800 hours there were two formations over southern Kent on a course for Biggin Hill and Kenley. Numerous British squadrons were, however, already in the air:

At 1733 hours No. 1 (RCAF) Squadron left Northolt:
(their precise orders are unknown but they engaged the enemy near the estuary: probably their action was with the force that bombed Hornchurch, but as it retired).

At 1740 hours No. 17 Squadron left Tangmere: their orders are also unknown.

At 1744 hours 'A' Flight of No. 616 Squadron left Kenley to patrol base.

At 1745 hours No. 72 Squadron left Biggin Hill and was directed towards Dungeness; and at the same time one flight of No. 79 Squadron took off from the same station to protect it.

A 1750 hours 'B' Flight, No. 501 Squadron, left Gravesend.

No. 1 Squadron left Northolt and No. 253 Squadron left Kenley, all to protect their bases; and two squadrons (Nos 242 and 611) came in from No. 12 Group to protect Hornchurch and North Weald.

As the Germans approached London still more squadrons were sent up at or about 1800 hours:

> No. 257 Squadron from Martlesham to patrol it.
>
> No. 609 Squadron ('A' Flight) from Middle Wallop in No. 10 Group to patrol Windsor at 15,000 feet.
>
> No. 602 Squadron from Westhampnett to patrol Biggin Hill–Gravesend at 20,000 feet.
>
> No. 303 Squadron from Northolt to intercept near Biggin Hill.

This was a large force, and four squadrons succeeded in intercepting the Germans before they reached their target. No. 72 Squadron first engaged them near Dungeness, No. 17 took up the attack nearer Maidstone, No. 602 were in action in the same area, while No. 79 made contact near Biggin Hill itself. There were two distinct impressions of the enemy's composition: some pilots saw two forces of bombers, each of twenty-five to thirty aircraft; others saw only one bomber formation of about thirty aircraft. However, as only one force attacked Biggin Hill and there was otherwise no bombing in the country over which the enemy flew, it can be taken that there was only one German formation.[15]

It is quite clear from the combat reports of the British squadrons that the enemy were not diverted from their course by their attacks. Only two bombers were claimed as destroyed; and one squadron in particular, No. 602, remarked the effectiveness of the escorting enemy fighters. In this case six of the squadron's Spitfires climbed to engage the German fighters while the other six attacked the bombers; but the enemy were too numerous to be contained in this way and with one exception the squadron engaged Me 109s.

It is not surprising, therefore, that the German bombers succeeded in making an accurate attack on Biggin Hill. Approximately one hundred bombs were dropped; the operations room block was hit and set on fire and an emergency room outside the station had to be brought into use; telephone communications were badly damaged; the officers' mess was made virtually unusable; and a number of other buildings and hangars were destroyed. In consequence of this attack and that of the previous day the number of squadrons that were stationed there had to be reduced: No. 72 Squadron, which had only arrived that day from Acklington, was sent to Croydon; and thenceforward only one squadron used the station. Moreover, as a centre for the control of squadrons operating within the sector the efficiency of the station was much affected: in the words of the No. 11 Group commander, 'Only one squadron could operate from there, and the remaining two squadrons had to be placed under the control of adjacent sectors for over a week.'

Report on Operations, 8 August–10 Septermber

The cost to the Germans of what had been the most successful attack they had so far made against a sector station was increased as they retired when one flight

15 A Do 17 from I/KG 76 was brought down just before 1900 hours near Dungeness and was probably part of the force that bombed Biggin Hill. There is no proof of this, however: it may have been one of the force that had operated further north against Hornchurch.

of No. 303 (Polish) Squadron came up with them east of Biggin Hill. 'A' Flight attacked out of the sun and undoubtedly succeeded in surprising the fighter escort, six of whom were believed to have been destroyed. The German bombers once more escaped without loss.

With the attack on Biggin Hill the main German operations on this day were over, but enemy fighter forces continued to operate over the Straits. On the credit side of the British account was a combat between nine Hurricanes of No. 85 Squadron, who were in action for the third time during the day, and a similar number of Me 109s. The latter were caught over Dover from sunward and four were believed destroyed at no cost to No. 85. Against this the Germans could count a second successful attack on the Dover balloon barrage. Eighteen balloons had been raised since the morning attack, but fourteen were destroyed in an attack at 1922 hours. This spectacular incident brought the day's operations to a close.

OPERATIONS, 1 SEPTEMBER

i. Introduction

From the renewal of intensive attacks on 24 August to the last day of the month the Germans had set out to cause as much damage to airfields as possible. With the exception of two attacks on Portsmouth on the 24th and 26th and that against Luton on the 30th all the main German targets had been RAF stations; and in all this type of target was bombed fifteen times by formations of some twenty or more bombers. Moreover, this obvious concentration of effort was more precisely directed than that of the period 8–18 August. For whereas stations of all commands had then been attacked, the last week in August saw the Germans concentrate on the stations of Fighter Command and in particular the airfields near London. Thus, eleven of the fifteen attacks[16] were against No. 11 Group stations; one was against Warmwell, the most easterly station in No. 10 Group; and three were against Eastchurch and Detling, both of which were Coastal Command stations. All these attacks, including those against Eastchurch and Detling, can be seen as part of the execution of a plan for clearing the way from the Kent coast to the capital.

And already after one week the German efforts were beginning to show a dividend. Manston was no longer being used and Kenley and Biggin Hill were not working at full strength. If the Germans knew this they would start on their September operations with fair hopes of neutralising the defences of the south-east; for while no sector station had yet been rendered inoperative all in that area were working under difficulties; and the cumulative effect of further damage could reasonably be expected at least to reduce the efficiency of the fighter force, and at best to frustrate it altogether. It is against this background that we must place the operations from the first day of September to the sixth.

16 'Attacks' here refer to raids where the Germans actually located and hit their targets. If ever comprehensive German records are open to scrutiny it will almost certainly be found that a number of raids against RAF stations went astray.

ii. *Against Targets near Thames Estuary, 1030–1130 hours*

There was some photographic reconnaissance over the Sussex coast soon after daylight on the 1st but no attacks of any moment threatened until shortly after 1000 hours. At that time the sky was clear and the day warm and sunny; and it remained so.

When indications began to come in from the RDF stations that the Germans were assembling, two squadrons were sent forward to patrol the east coast of Kent:

> At 1023 hours No. 222 Squadron left Rochford to patrol Manston.
>
> At 1028 hours No. 616 Squadron left Kenley to patrol Hawkinge.

Two German forces, each plotted as 'fifty plus', came across the Straits and crossed the coast at 1045 hours, one near Dover and the other near Deal. The more southerly force was quickly engaged by seven aircraft of No. 616 Squadron (the rest of the pilots failed to hear the order to climb and intercept); and our pilots reported a formation of enemy bombers already on their way inland and a force of thirty Me 109s. All combats were with the latter force which was scattered by the attacks of our squadron; and the enemy bombers, being unwilling presumably to press on without a fighter escort, were seen to swing round and return to France. There is no confirmation of this from the track charts, which do not record the enemy's course at all clearly; but as all the bombing that took place in the next half hour is traceable to the force that crossed near Deal, it may well be that the attack further south was checked by this small British force.

As this action took place and as the second German force advanced north-west from Deal more fighter squadrons were sent into the air:

> At 1040 hours No. 54 Squadron left Rochford to intercept the enemy as they approached across northern Kent.
>
> At 1045 hours No. 1 Squadron left Northolt to patrol it: shortly afterwards it was towards Maidstone.
>
> At the same time No. 72 Squadron left Croydon (where it had been transferred after the previous day's attack on Biggin Hill) and was also ordered in the same direction.

The first contact with the enemy was made by No. 222 Squadron, who were engaged with Me 109s in the neighbourhood of Canterbury. There was then an interval before further fighters came into action, and between 1100 and 1115 hours the Germans advanced up the estuary, penetrating as far as Hornchurch. During this period six more British squadrons were sent up, most of them to protect their bases. The one exception, No. 85 Squadron, which was ordered from Croydon towards Dover, where a small German force had been plotted, was the only one of this batch of squadrons to intercept the enemy.

All the combats after 1100 hours were with a retiring enemy. In other words, except for the brief skirmish with No. 222 Squadron the Germans were not interfered with until after they had dropped their bombs. But they took little advantage of their freedom. The biggest concentration of bombs was at Tilbury where Harland and Wolff's works, the railway station and a number of dockside buildings were hit. Most bombs, however, fell in numerous small places near the Thames: Gill, Grave, Stockbury, Upnor, Chattenden and, finally, Hornchurch were all lightly bombed between 1115 and 1135 hours. One of our squadrons reported that the Germans were being heavily and accurately attacked by AA fire when they were near Hornchurch; and this may have been the explanation for the badly directed bombing. No claims of destruction were made by the gunners of the Thames and Medway barrage.

However, the Germans were not to escape without loss. There was a brief skirmish between some of No. 54 Squadron and six He 111s escorted by a small number of Me 109s. This took place near Maidstone, and one bomber was destroyed. In the same area No. 72 Squadron intercepted thirty to forty Do 17s on a south-easterly course heavily escorted by fighters. The squadron, in its first engagement in No. 11 Group after some time near Newcastle, fared badly: three Spitfires were shot down at a cost to the enemy of two fighters and possibly one bomber. No. 1 Squadron also saw some escorted enemy bombers between Maidstone and the coast, and shot down four Me 109s. No. 85 Squadron's engagement was with a small number of Me 109s that carried out an attack on the barrage balloons at Dover at 1130 hours.

In sum, there was nothing conclusive about the operation. The Germans had been able to approach their target area little hindered by RAF fighters. On the other hand, they had not succeeded in causing serious damage. It is surprising that such a target as Tilbury was attacked at a time when so much of the enemy's effort was concentrated against RAF stations. When the account of the attack can be completed from German records it will probably be found that the Germans failed to find their primary targets.

All we know for certain about the German units participating is that at least some of the fighters were from III/JG 52.

iii. Against Biggin Hill and Kenley, 1330–1445 hours

Between the end of their first attack on this day and the beginning of the second the Germans sent a small number of reconnaissance aircraft into the Thames Estuary area. Two or three were active just before the second attack showed signs of developing. Consequently, at 1330 hours two British squadrons were over eastern Kent, No. 72 Squadron near Dover and No. 222 Squadron further north. Shortly before that time a force of 'twelve plus' had been detected over the middle of the Straits, and another of 'thirty plus' behind Cap Gris Nez. Both of them were flying west; and further squadrons were sent up on the British side:

> At 1330 hours No. 253 Squadron left Kenley and after a few minutes was despatched towards Dungeness.
>
> At 1340 hours No. 54 Squadron left Hornchurch to patrol Canterbury at 20,000 feet.

At the same time No. 85 Squadron left Croydon to intercept in the Tunbridge Wells area for which the enemy was making by that time.

The first enemy force to cross the coast was the one originally plotted as 'twelve plus'; and it came in at Dungeness at 1340 hours and steered towards Tunbridge. Shortly afterwards, it was engaged by No. 72 Squadron who reported it to be considerably stronger than the RDF stations had indicated; there were about forty Do 17s and He 111s and rather more Me 109s and 110s. The combats ranged over the country between Dungeness, Tunbridge Wells and Ashford; and although the squadron managed to make their opening attack against the bombers they were afterwards entirely engaged with enemy fighters. Considering the disparity in numbers the squadron could congratulate themselves on escaping without loss: they claimed to have destroyed two Me 110s. The Germans were not diverted from their course by this engagement, and by 1350 hours they were approaching Biggin Hill. Meanwhile, another enemy force, which the Observer Corps reported as one hundred aircraft strong, came in over Hythe.

Two things were now clear: first, that the first enemy force threatened Biggin Hill and the other airfields south of London; and, second, that either a second attacking force or a strong rearguard was approaching. The following defensive dispositions were then made:

At 1400 hours No. 1 (RCAF) Squadron left Northolt to intercept near Biggin Hill.

At the same time No. 79 Squadron left Biggin Hill to patrol it; and No. 616 Squadron left Kenley to patrol its base there.

At 1405 hours No. 303 (Polish) Squadron left Northolt to patrol it.

At 1410 hours No. 501 Squadron left Gravesend to patrol between there and Maidstone.

The orders to the first three of the above squadrons were probably given no later than 1350 hours, but even so they were given too late. For at 1400 hours a force of bombers appeared over Biggin Hill and bombed it from about 15,000 feet: No. 79 Squadron had barely taken off before the first bombs fell.

This squadron, No. 85 Squadron, No. 1 (RCAF) and No. 54 all made contact with the enemy only after the attack was over. It is not certain, however that all were engaged with the same force; it is clear that at least one detachment from the original force that crossed near Dungeness broke away and attacked the Kenley district. Probably its objective was the airfield there, but no damage was done: bombs fell on the nearby Guards' depot at Caterham, and in the Addington and Coulsdon districts. This force was engaged by No. 616 Squadron near Maidstone after a long chase from Kenley.

The attack against Biggin Hill was more accurate, though a large number of bombs fell to the west of the base; and it showed how dangerous the cumulative effects of bombing could be. The station had been attacked three times recently; and those buildings that had been left standing were very unsafe. After this attack, practically all equipment had to be removed into the open or away from the station lest a further attack should bring down the buildings.

As these attacks had been taking place in Surrey the German forces that had crossed the coast near Hythe were moving steadily towards Tunbridge Wells. It was in that area that No. 253 Squadron entered upon a remarkably successful action. The enemy were reported to consist of some fifty Do 17s and He 111s at 15,000 feet escorted by up to one hundred fighters ranged at varying heights up to 22,000 feet. The nine Hurricanes succeeded in getting between the main formation and the sun and they dived down on the bombers in echelon formation. Our pilots considered the attack a success, and although the German fighters intervened and made impossible the detailed observation of results the enemy were afterwards seen to have broken formation. No. 501 Squadron joined in the later stages of the combat but they were entirely engaged with Me 110s.

It is almost incredible that so small a force should have checked so great a number of the enemy. Yet the fact remains that about the time that the action took place bombs fell near Tunbridge Wells, Tenterden, Kemsing and Southborough, far away from any targets of importance.

On the whole, therefore, the operations had turned out a defensive success. Only at Biggin Hill was there serious damage, and even so the same degree of serviceability was maintained there. Nine fighters had been destroyed and three badly damaged; and eight pilots were killed or wounded. Against this was a claim of eight bombers and five fighters.

iv. Other Operations

By 1500 hours the enemy's main operations on this day had come to an end, somewhat earlier than usual. Henceforth, only one brief combat was reported. But the squadrons of No. 11 Group were not allowed a respite from at least the routine of take-offs and sorties; for the Germans continued to send patrols over the eastern side of the Straits of Dover; and, to ensure keeping the defences at readiness, they varied these tactics with a small number of fighter-bomber raids against fringe targets. Thus, the RDF station at Dunkirk, near the North Foreland, and the airfields at Lympne and Hawkinge were lightly attacked during the afternoon and early evening. In addition, one raid came in as far as Detling and dropped a small number of bombs there, causing some damage to communications.

These attacks were no great menace to the defence system in the south-east, but they were a reminder, if one was necessary, that the German Air Force was very close to our shores and could dictate the scale of defensive operations.

OPERATIONS, 2 SEPTEMBER

i. Against Thames Estuary Targets and Lympne, 0715–0845 hours

As early as 0715 hours the Germans showed signs of preparing for a strong attack, and by 0730 hours two medium-sized forces were over the middle of the

Straits and a small one was off the North Foreland. For the time being they remained there; but they constituted an obvious threat and counteracting forces were accordingly sent into the air on the British side:

> At 0720 hours No. 249 Squadron left North Weald to patrol Rochford at 15,000 feet: later it was sent towards Folkestone.
>
> At 0725 hours No. 253 Squadron left Kenley to patrol Hawkinge.
>
> At 0728 hours No. 603 Squadron left Hornchurch to patrol the estuary (the exact position of the patrol is not known).
>
> At 0730 hours No. 501 Squadron left Gravesend and was ordered towards Dungeness.
>
> At 0740 hours No. 54 Squadron left Rochford and was ordered towards Chatham.
>
> At 0745 hours No. 72 Squadron left Croydon and was ordered towards Maidstone at 15,000 feet.

In addition, five squadrons (including one from No. 12 Group) were sent up on close patrols of airfields in No. 11 Group; but as the Germans advanced only as far as Rochester none of them took part in the fighting.

Not until 0740 hours did the Germans cross the coast, and thanks to this delay five British squadrons were able to intercept before the Germans reached their targets. Two enemy columns crossed between Dover and Folkestone, and a third and smaller one further north. All made for the Gravesend–Chatham area. Unfortunately, it is impossible to be precise about their subsequent movements; for the day, after dawning fine, had become cloudy and the sky was overcast at 3,000 feet. In consequence, the Observer Corps were unable to give a coherent track of the enemy's course.

It is fairly safe to say, however, that there were two main enemy forces, each consisting of about one Gruppe of bombers, of which III/KG 3 was one, and an escort of fighters provided by ZG 26 and JG 51. No. 253 Squadron was the first to make contact. They were flying at 20,000 feet north of Dover when they sighted a formation of twenty to thirty bombers escorted by a similar number of fighters at 17,000 feet about ten miles south of the North Foreland. The squadron began a shallow dive attack on the bombers but they could not press it home owing to the intervention of the enemy fighters. The Germans continued to fly up the estuary until they were near Chatham. Here they were heavily engaged by the anti-aircraft gunners and were forced to turn inland, where they were attacked by No. 54 Squadron, whose attention had been drawn by the anti-aircraft fire. But once more the German fighters protected their bombers successfully; and with one exception all the pilots reported combats with Me 109s. It was probably this force that dropped about fifty bombs at Rochester at about 0810 hours; for it was about that time that the Sheerness and Chatham guns were in action. The only damage that was caused was to house property.

Meantime, the second German force, which had crossed the coast near Folkestone, had been flying across Kent towards the estuary. It consisted of about twenty Do 17s with an escort of Me 109s and 110s (some pilots thought they also saw some He 111s); and it was almost continually engaged between the coast and the Maidstone area by Nos 501, 72 and 249 Squadrons, which, however, fought independently of one another. As in the encounters further north the German fighters fought well and eight Hurricanes were shot down. But two German bombers and some fighters were believed to have been destroyed; and that a number of bombs fell at the time of these actions in rural districts near Canterbury and Maidstone implies that some of the enemy bombers were forced to jettison their loads. Furthermore, when the Germans reached their targets their bombing was inaccurate: a dozen bombs fell on the outskirts of the fighter station at Gravesend, and a similar number in and near Chatham; but in neither case was any serious damage caused.

As the enemy retired No. 603 Squadron came into action with the escorting fighters near Canterbury, and in a sharply fought action three Me 109s were claimed as destroyed without loss to our squadron. Otherwise, there were no further actions. The Germans, however, took advantage of the concentration against northern Kent to put in a swift attack against Lympne shortly after 0830 hours. About thirty bombs were dropped, most of them falling outside the airfield boundaries; and the station remained serviceable in its limited use as an emergency landing ground.

ii. Against Eastchurch and Detling, 1200–1315 hours

For well over three hours there was a respite from further attacks. Not until shortly before noon did the Germans once more begin to mass over the Straits. By 1215 hours they had completed their concentrations; and five minutes later a force of between thirty and fifty aircraft came in at Hythe and flew towards Chatham by way of Ashford. Ten minutes later three forces totalling over one hundred aircraft converged on Dover and also made towards Chatham; while at the same time a further force of some forty aircraft came into the Thames Estuary over the North Foreland. These moves were countered by the despatch of eleven squadrons between 1205 and 1230 hours. Six of these were sent up to patrol sector stations north of the estuary; for it was that area that seemed chiefly to be threatened, especially as the enemy force that had come in near the North Foreland made for the Essex coast. The rest of the defending squadrons were sent forward to intercept in the area Maidstone–Chatham–Rochford: two of them, Nos 46 and 111, had orders to join up over Rochford. Between 1240 and 1300 hours, by which time the bulk of the enemy forces were near the Isle of Sheppey, six more British squadrons took off: four remained over their bases but two, No. 501 from Gravesend and No. 43, from Tangmere were ordered towards Maidstone.

About 1245 hours, No. 72 Squadron came into action. It had taken off from Croydon at 1206 hours to patrol behind Dover but it came into contact near Herne Bay with what was probably the right wing of the forces that had advanced from the direction of Hythe. There were between twenty and thirty Do 17s flying high (20,000 feet) with Me 109s to one flank and Me 110s astern and on the other flank. Attacking in a steep dive the squadron succeeded in reaching the bombers and claimed casualties, but the enemy fighters intervened and the squadron became very much dispersed.[17]

It can only have been a short time afterwards that No. 603 Squadron came into action somewhere near Chatham with this same German force. The RAF pilots believed that they destroyed two of the escorting fighters and one of the Do 17s at no cost to themselves; but it is clear from what happened later that the German formation maintained its course towards its target.

No. 111 Squadron then made contact with a second part of the force that originally came in over Hythe. This squadron had joined forces with No. 46 over Rochford and had followed it south. But for some reason that is not clear only No. 111 Squadron came into action. The enemy were flying westwards up the estuary and consisted of about twenty He 111s at 15,000 feet escorted by Me 109s and 110s, but the latter were at first hidden from No. 111 Squadron by cloud. At least one section of the Hurricanes succeeded in reaching the bombers by means of a head-on attack, and one He 111 was seen to crash into the sea. Most combats, however, were with Me 110s.

By 1305 hours both German forces had succeeded in shaking themselves free of opposition, and each approached their targets without further trouble. The first attacked Eastchurch at 1310 hours; while the second bombed Detling five minutes later. At Eastchurch great damage was done, for a dump of 350 and 250 lb bombs was hit and the airfield surface nearby was badly cratered. In addition, the administrative buildings were wholly, and the station sick quarters, partly wrecked; the water supply and sewage system was broken; teleprinter and telephone services were cut; and five aircraft were destroyed.

As for the Detling attack, all we know is that it was carried out by about thirty aircraft, that a hangar was badly damaged and that the airfield was unserviceable for about three hours.

The Germans retired from these attacks part by way of the estuary and part by Dungeness. Some of the latter were engaged by No. 43 Squadron between Maidstone and the coast in an action entirely fought out between fighters with equal loss to both sides. Another fighter formation had come in at Hythe at 1310 hours, presumably to cover the retirement, but it was not intercepted. The force that had come in at the North Foreland at the beginning of the operation had doubtless also been intended to cover the flank of the attacking force. It had flown as far as Foulness Island and had not been brought to action.

The operation had been well planned and its objectives had been reached and attacked: but once more it is worth noting that if the effort had been expended with like results against any two stations in No. 11 Group its effect would have been more embarrassing to the defences. The German fighters had carried out their task especially well: they were chiefly drawn from I/ZG 2 and II/JG 2.

17 According to the ORB of this squadron four of the nine Spitfires were destroyed at a cost to the enemy of three Me 110s destroyed and two Do 17s probably destroyed. According to the Fighter Command records, which should be authoritative, three Do 17s and two Me 110s were shot down at a cost of one Spitfire destroyed and two badly damaged. The detailed losses do not perhaps matter so much as that at least one-third of the attacking force became casualties.

iii. Against Eastchurch, Hornchurch and Thames Estuary Targets, 1545–1700 hours

The first indications that the Germans were concentrating again were received about 1545 hours; and fifteen minutes later it was obvious that another major attack was in prospect. At 1615 hours three different forces crossed the coast between Deal and Dungeness and spread out fanwise over Kent. Two of them were tracked continuously by the Observer Corps as they flew to their targets, which were Hornchurch and Eastchurch stations. The third lost its identity shortly after crossing the coast; but, as will be shown, it certainly contained some bombers and was responsible for a number of incidents in northern Kent.

The British squadrons that took off prior to the Germans crossing the coast were as follows:

> At 1555 hours No. 240 Squadron from North Weald to patrol Rochford.
>
> At the same time No. 72 Squadron from Hawkinge to patrol Dungeness at 10,000 feet.
>
> At 1600 hours No. 85Squadron from Croydon: its orders are unknown and it did not make contact with the enemy.
>
> At the same time No. 222 Squadron from Hornchurch to patrol Canterbury.
>
> At 1604 hours No. 603 Squadron from Hornchurch to patrol base.
>
> At 1615 hours No. 253 Squadron from Kenley to patrol near Maidstone.
>
> No. 616 Squadron from Kenley to patrol base: No. 242 Squadron from Duxford to patrol what the squadron ORB describes as the 'London area': it did not make contact with the enemy.

The most southerly of the three enemy forces crossed the coast at Dungeness; the centre one near Deal; and the northernmost one near the North Foreland. The first of these was sighted by No. 72 Squadron when it was still a few miles out over the Channel; and our pilots reported that it consisted of Do 17s protected by Me 110s and 109s, but did not specify in what numbers: the enemy were flying north-west. The British squadron formed line astern and attacked the Me 110s from above and behind. None of the enemy was claimed as destroyed; but it was reported that 'the enemy turned to starboard and headed for France'. It is possible that a section of the German force did indeed retreat; but there is no doubt that the main body continued inland. It passed close to Biggin Hill and Hornchurch and continued north until it was about five miles south of North Weald. It then turned south and shortly afterwards arrived over Hornchurch and bombed the sector station there. During this time there was no interception of this force until either just before or just after Hornchurch was bombed. This was the work of No. 603 Squadron who were over their base at 23,000 feet when they saw below them 'a large solid triangle of about fifty bombers' and a similar number of fighters between 15,000–20,000 feet. The squadron dived to attack and were entirely engaged with German fighters.

The bombing was on a large scale. Approximately one hundred bombs were put down; but they were badly aimed. Only six fell on the airfield and no serious damage was done. Afterwards some portion of the German forces returned by way of Essex and the estuary; and No. 54 Squadron engaged it between Hornchurch and the east coast of Kent. The greater part, however, came out by way of central Kent; and at least four squadrons made contact during this retirement.

It is possible that some of the enemy bombers had retained their loads; for about twenty-five bombs fell on Maidstone about the time that returning forces were over that district. It is more likely, however, that this was the work of part of the force that had come in at Deal and which had flown towards the Chatham–Rochester district without being intercepted. A number of places in northern Kent received salvoes of bombs from this force between 1630 and 1650 hours: the most noteworthy incident was at Rochester where bombs hit the drawing office of the Short works. Then, shortly before 1700 hours over twenty HE bombs fell in and around Ashford. This sort of bombing usually implies either a failure to find the primary target or the jettisoning of bombs owing to interference by the defending forces. The first alternative is more likely in this case as, as far as we know, there was no engagement in the areas concerned.

The only other interception during this phase of the operations was of the most northerly enemy force by No. 249 Squadron over the estuary. This engagement was almost wholly with enemy fighters; and the German bombers flew on up the river without being interfered with. They were comparatively small in number – twelve in all – but they carried out yet another accurate and damaging attack on the Coastal Command station at Eastchurch. Eight large craters were made in the airfield; one of the few remaining hangars was wrecked and a number of station roads were blocked. As a result of this and previous attacks the administrative staff and the medical services of the station were removed to quarters outside the camp.

iv. Against Eastchurch and the East Kent coast, 1700–1745 hours

Barely had the forces responsible for these attacks crossed the coast on their return journey than other attacks were threatened. A number of British squadrons, which had taken off towards the end of the first phase of the operations, were still in the air:

> No. 46 Squadron was patrolling between North Weald and the Thames.
>
> No. 72 Squadron (for the second time in two hours) was patrolling in the Dover area.

To these were added the following forces:

> At 1720 hours No. 303 Squadron from Northolt to intercept in the Chatham district: No. 257 Squadron from Martlesham to patrol East Mersea.
>
> At 1725 hours No. 85 Squadron from Croydon: their orders are unknown and they did not intercept the enemy.

By the time these last three squadrons had taken off a hostile formation, plotted as 'twenty plus', had emerged from the forces that the Germans had maintained over the central Channel and was making for the North Foreland. At the same time a number of small enemy detachments crossed the Kent coast, but only stayed overland for a few moments before retiring. One of them dropped a few bombs on the inner harbour at Folkestone at 1735 hours.

Four British squadrons were ordered towards the Chatham area to engage the force of 'twenty plus'; and it was first intercepted near Herne Bay by a flight of No. 72 Squadron, who were in action for the fourth time that day. Anti-aircraft fire first drew the pilots' attention to the enemy, who consisted of about twenty Do 17s and some fifty Me 109s and 110s.

The attack was carried out from above and astern and out of the sun, but despite these advantages it was impossible to penetrate to the bombers. Shortly afterwards No. 46 Squadron also attacked the same force and succeeded in reaching the bombers and damaging two of them. The enemy were able to reach their target – once more it was Eastchurch – but no record was kept of the size and effects of the attack. After it, No. 303 (Polish) and No. 257 Squadrons engaged the German fighters, with no advantage to either side.[18]

Thus ended a day of hard fighting with few consolations possible to the British. Losses in fighter aircraft were high; thirty-one were destroyed or badly damaged. Fortunately, only ten pilots were killed or seriously wounded. German losses were relatively low – forty-three aircraft being claimed as certainly destroyed – and the wreckage of only eleven fighters and one bomber was found after the battle. However, only at Eastchurch had the Germans achieved anything worth while.

OPERATIONS, 3 SEPTEMBER

i. Against North Weald and Eastern Kent, 1100–1115 hours

The only attack of notable size that the Germans launched on this day was first detected at about 0945 hours when there was a suspicious number of enemy formations over the Straits and the Pas de Calais. Three British squadrons were over northern Kent and the Thames Estuary at the time, there having been a few reconnaissance aircraft over southeast England shortly after 0900 hours.

By ten o'clock two forces of 'fifty plus' were emerging from the Straits and making for the Essex coast; a third, which was still over the land near Le Touquet, was also flying north; and a fourth was still moving backwards and forwards over the middle of the Straits. By that time the following British squadrons were on patrol or were flying towards their patrol area:

18 No. 257 Squadron delayed attacking a fighter formation for some moments being under the impression that the aircraft were friendly. In fact, they were Me 109s, but with the tips of their wings painted white to give then an elliptical appearance, doubtless to trick our pilots. Whether this practice explains the numerous reports early in the battle that the Germans were using captured Hurricanes is open to doubt. Air Chief Marshal Dowding is personally convinced that such aircraft, with British markings, were used during July, but that their use was dropped early in August owing to the confusion it caused amongst German pilots and anti-aircraft crews. There is no irrefutable evidence that this was the practice of the enemy even for a short time.

No. 222 Squadron between Hornchurch and Eastchurch.

No. 46 Squadron over Rochford.

No. 501 Squadron over Detling.

No. 310 Squadron (Czech) from No.12 Group between Hornchurch and North Weald.

No. 603 Squadron over Manston.

No. 257 Squadron over the coast between the rivers Crouch and Blackwater:

No. 17 Squadron in the same area.

In short, by 1015 hours the estuary towns and the sector stations north of the Thames were well protected against attack from the south-east. During the next fifteen minutes and whilst the main German forces were still approaching closer to the Essex coast, three more squadrons took off:

No. 1 Squadron from Northolt to intercept in the Maidstone district.

No. 54 Squadron from Hornchurch to patrol base.

No. 19 Squadron from Duxford in No. 12 Group to patrol Duxford–Debden.

As early as 1015 hours the first engagement with the enemy had taken place. It was between No. 257 Squadron and what was probably an advance guard of fighters. The first bombers were not sighted until 1025 hours, when No. 46 Squadron made contact near Southend with a formation of Do 17s and Ju 88s and the usual fighter escort. At about the same time, if not a little earlier, No. 603 Squadron sighted a force of six Do 17s protected by twelve Me 109s over Manston at 20,000 feet: the ensuring fight was entirely between our Spitfires and the Me 109s. The main enemy force, however, was that engaged by No. 46 Squadron. There were between thirty and fifty Dorniers and Junkers flying in vics and in line astern at 15,000 feet. Enemy fighters were disposed on the starboard flank of the bomber formation and astern up to about 17,000 feet. One flight of the Hurricanes attacked the bombers while the other attempted to contain the fighters; but as was to be expected the majority of combats were with the enemy fighters. Two or three Do 17s were detached from the main body, however, and forced to jettison their bombs, which fell near Billericay.

At this time (1025–1030 hours) it was impossible to forecast what was the German target; for their course was taking them midway between Hornchurch and North Weald. However, after approaching close to the former station, where they were sighted by No. 54 Squadron, who were protecting it, they swung north and made for North Weald, which by this time had been cleared of aircraft as far as possible; one section of Blenheims from No. 25 Squadron even took off to defend the base. During the next ten minutes No. 310 (Czech) Squadron engaged some of the Me 110s that were escorting the German bombers; but otherwise the enemy were not intercepted again until they had dropped their bombs on North Weald.

Twenty-five to thirty Do 17s appeared over the station and well over one hundred bombs were dropped. The MT yard was damaged and several lorries were set on fire; and two hangars were also left burning: all but one of the telephone lines to the Observer Corps were cut; the internal broadcasting was wrecked; and the main store was badly damaged. Most of the bombs however, fell in the south and south-west corners of the airfield; and although these made many craters the landing area was serviceable for day flying. The most satisfactory feature of the attack was that a bomb which hit the roof of the new operations room failed to penetrate or do any damage.

Only after the attack were there any further engagements. Two of the three Blenheims of No. 25 Squadron were shot down; which is hardly surprising. No. 19 Squadron, on the other hand, who had been ordered south from their Debden patrol, claimed at least two Me 110s destroyed at no cost to themselves. This squadron reported that there were between fifty and sixty bombers protected by one hundred fighters, mainly Me 110s, and that they were retiring to the south-east. This implies that only a portion of the main German body had bombed North Weald, and this may well have been the case; for there were also bombs reported from numerous rural districts in Essex, especially in the neighbourhood of Epping and Harlow. Nos 17 and 54 Squadrons also succeeded in intercepting during the retirement; and at the cost of one Hurricane they claimed the destruction of five of the enemy.

As this main thrust had been taking place north of the Thames there had been slight activity in eastern and northern Kent. German forces, chiefly composed of fighters, started to cross the land shortly before 1100 hours, i.e. when the retirement from the attack on North Weald had just begun; and they were doubtless intended to create a diversion from that move. However, no British squadrons north of the river were ordered south to deal with these attacks, which were left to No. 1 Squadron and No. 303 (Polish) Squadron.

Altogether, RAF pilots claimed the destruction of seven bombers and sixteen fighters, but only one bomber and five fighters were found on the ground after the battle. The bomber was a Do 17 from II/KG 2, the whole of which had been briefed to attack North Weald, and the fighters were Me 110s from I/ZG 2 and II/ZG 26. RAF casualties were fifteen aircraft destroyed and four badly damaged, and thirteen pilots killed, missing or wounded. This was a higher relative casualty rate than Fighter Command could afford; but this was not the most unsatisfactory feature of the operation. This was that the Germans had broken through to their chief objective with few losses, and bombed it accurately even though, thanks to the ampler warning than usual, ten British squadrons had been over Essex while the Germans were still advancing. Moreover, the weather throughout the attack was excellent and the Germans had no clouds to hide their movements; and in fact all the RAF squadrons intercepted, though half only did so as the Germans retired. But their engagement took place independently of each other; and at no time were the escorting German fighters called upon to deal with the attack of more than a squadron of RAF fighters.

ii. In the afternoon

The rest of the operations on this day need little more than a passing mention. Between 1400 and 1600 hours the Germans simulated another attack against the sector stations guarding London. Over one hundred enemy aircraft crossed the coast between Dungeness and the North Foreland and penetrated as far as Tilbury. A correspondingly large force of defending fighters, twelve squadrons in all, was despatched but there were only two skirmishes, each with enemy fighters. West Malling was lightly bombed but the object of the operation seems simply to have been to maintain pressure upon the squadrons of No. 11 Group. And to the extent that our pilots were forced to take off to little or no purpose the object was attained: almost as much flying was carried out by No. 11 Group on the 3rd (404 sorties) as on the previous day (568 sorties) when there had been three major bombing raids.

OPERATIONS, 4 SEPTEMBER

Two main attacks were launched on this day by the Germans; and as usual both were against the south-east. The second was over by 1430 hours, however, and thenceforwards the day was quiet. Both of them took place in fine sunny weather that offered no special advantage to either side.

i. Against Bradwell and Eastchurch 0830–1015 hours

Signs of the first attack were initially received shortly after 0830 hours when a force of 'twenty plus' was plotted behind Cap Gris Nez. At the time, seven Hurricanes of No. 111 Squadron were patrolling east of Folkestone from Hawkinge; and No. 66 Squadron was immediately despatched from Kenley to patrol in the same area. During the next fifteen minutes, another German force was located just north of Calais, while a third force near Creçy also appeared on the operations rooms tables. Two more squadrons were accordingly ordered into the air: No. 222 from Rochford to patrol Canterbury and No. 46 from North Weald to patrol Rochford.

Shortly after 0800 hours the force that had been located near Creçy approached the coast near Folkestone and was engaged almost at once by No. 111 Squadron. There were a number of formations of Me 109s which far outnumbered the tiny British force. Nevertheless, the squadron carried the attack to the enemy, engaging one of the German formations in a head-on attack. Immediately, other enemy fighters converged, and as a result three of the eight Hurricanes were shot down and one badly damaged: the maximum German losses were five Me 109s. During and after the action the enemy flew towards Tunbridge Wells.

At 0910 hours two more enemy formations crossed the coast in quick succession north of Dungeness and steered north. One of them was sighted while it was still over eastern Kent by No. 66 Squadron who, however, were unable to carry out an attack until the estuary had been reached. There were about twenty Do 17s in the enemy force, but the squadron only succeeded in attacking the German fighters.

All this time, and it was now 0920 hours, there had been no certainty that any German bombers other than those in the force over the estuary, had crossed the coast. The Observer Corps were plotting the enemy's tracks with fair continuity, but they were unable to distinguish the types of aircraft employed owing to the height (20,000 feet) at which the enemy were flying. The controller at No. 11 Group, therefore, held his hand until he knew more of what objectives, if any, the Germans seemed likely to attack; and while he sent up squadrons from Westhampnett, Northolt, Biggin Hill, Gravesend and North Weald between 0900 and 0920 hours, he ordered them all to patrol close to their bases. Moreover, there were isolated plots of enemy aircraft coming in from the country east of Biggin Hill, as well as more reliable tracks from the forces further east; and at the same time more enemy forces were being located: one was suddenly picked up overland south of Sheppey and another was plotted east of Deal on a northerly course. This latter formation flew as far as the North Foreland, then turned east and then south; so that it was very doubtful what it intended. Altogether, there was much that was incoherent about the position as it was after 0920 hours; and doubtless this is the explanation for the failure to intercept the enemy during the next quarter of an hour, although reports of bombs were coming in from different places on both sides of the estuary.

The first bombs fell at the RAF station at Bradwell on the Essex coast and were dropped by the force, or part of it, that had been attacked by No. 66 Squadron. Thirty bombs were put down but little damage was done. The Germans must either have failed to identify their target or they mis-apprehended the importance of the place; for it was not being used for operations at this date. After the attack the enemy force appears either to have scattered or to have dropped bombs at random as it passed north: Barling, Haybridge, Canewdon (where there was an RDF station) and Maldon all received small and ill-directed salvoes of bombs. Ten minutes later the force that had behaved so confusingly near the North Foreland came in near Dover and shortly afterwards dropped about thirty bombs on Lympne. Most of them fell outside the airfield and it remained serviceable.

Five more British squadrons took off between 0925 and 0930 hours, but still no interceptions took place and still bombs were being dropped. Between 0935 and 0940 hours sixteen HE bombs fell in and around Canterbury; and three small villages nearby also reported incidents at the same time. A most puzzling operation came to an end shortly after 1000 hours when some eighteen bombers attacked Eastchurch, damaging the runway in one part and also the ration stores. The force responsible for this attack crossed the coast between Folkestone and Dungeness and steered towards the Isle of Sheppey. Its track, on the inward journey at any rate, was closely followed; which makes it difficult to understand why no interception was effected. No less than thirteen squadrons had been despatched from No. 11 Group between 0830 and 0930 hours of which only two had been so directed that they sighted and engaged the enemy.

ii. Against Brooklands, Eastchurch and Targets in Northern Kent, 1230–1400 hours

The next attack that the Germans launched was a more serious affair, and happily more effectively countered, than that of the morning. The first warning of it was received at 1230 hours when a force of 'twenty plus' was plotted near the enemy base at Norrent Fontes and two smaller formations near Calais. No. 66 Squadron had just taken off from Hawkinge to patrol Dover; and during the next fifteen minutes No. 222 squadron left Rochford to patrol Canterbury and No. 602 Squadron left Westhampnett to patrol Beachy Head.

By 1250 hours the force that had first been detected was reported to be at least one hundred aircraft strong; and a new formation, of 'fifty plus', was plotted off Boulogne on a course down Channel. No. 1 (RCAF), No. 72 and No. 234 squadrons now took off (the last at only flight strength): the first two were kept patrolling their bases for the time being, but the No. 10 Group squadron was ordered to patrol Tangmere at 12,000 feet.

The first enemy force to cross the coast was not one of those that had been located during the previous half hour; for it had suddenly been detected shortly before 1300 hours when it was a few miles south of Dungeness. It was estimated as fifty or more aircraft and having crossed the coast near Hastings it operated towards Tunbridge Wells. The majority of the defending forces were despatched between 1300 and 1315 hours. The first of them, taking off at 1300 hours, were:

> No. 19 and No. 73 squadrons from Duxford in No. 12 Group to patrol North Weald and Hornchurch.
>
> No. 43 Squadron from Tangmere to intercept the raid coming down Channel.
>
> No. 249 Squadron from North Weald to patrol it.

By 1300 hours the position was fairly clear. There was one force flying down Channel in the direction of Beachy Head: one force was overland in west Kent: the large force that had been detected originally near Norrent Fontes was about to cross the land at Folkestone: a force of 'twelve plus' was also about to cross at Rye: finally a force of 'twenty plus' was about fifteen miles from Littlehampton on a northerly course.

First, the force flying down Channel: this was brought to action south of Beachy Head by No. 602 Squadron who reported about forty Do 17s at 17,000 feet preceded by fifteen to twenty Me 110s at the same altitude. The squadron commander ordered line astern prior to attacking the rear of the bomber formation; but the Me 110s swept round to the rear and the Spitfires were obliged to engage them while the enemy bombers continued west.

What can only have been the same force was next attacked at 1310 hours near Littlehampton by the six Spitfires of No. 234 Squadron; but its composition was reported differently than by No. 602; for it had been transformed into one group of fifteen Me 110s and another of fifty Me 110s in the middle of which were two shallow vics of Do 17s. No. 43 Squadron also attacked this force. Both squadrons made large claims: No. 234 believed that it had destroyed fourteen Me 110s and 1 Do 17; and when the individual combat reports were examined at Fighter Command Headquarters all but one were allowed: No. 43 Squadron claimed six Me 110s destroyed. Most of the Do 17s, however, as we shall see later, flew on northwards, though after passing Horsham their track was lost. Some of the escorting Me 110s were further engaged at 1320 hours by No. 1 (RCAF) Squadron which had been ordered south from Northolt.

Meantime, fighting was taking place further east. No. 66 Squadron was the first to come into action in this area. As has been said, the squadron was patrolling near Dover when the enemy were preparing to attack; but the large enemy forces that crossed between Rye and Folkestone slipped past the squadron, which was then directed westwards. At 1310 hours the squadron was near Maidstone when it sighted a force of twelve He 111s and forty to fifty Me 109s on a north-westerly course. The squadron moved in to attack but was itself surprised by a force of Me 109s which dived down on them out of the sun. Five of our Spitfires were shot down at little cost to the enemy.

The He 111s continued towards Gravesend; and No. 501 Squadron, which was stationed there, had barely left the airfield before it was bombed. However, no bombs hit the station, which thus maintained an immunity the more remarkable as Eastchurch and Detling in the same district had been so heavily attacked. No. 501 Squadron sighted the Heinkels but were too late to engage them. About the time of the attack No. 222 Squadron engaged some of the escorting Me 109s over Maidstone: otherwise this force was not further intercepted.

A second enemy formation was also over northern Kent at this time, having approached from the direction of Tunbridge Wells. It had been attacked by No. 72 Squadron in that area just before 1320 hours; and our pilots reported that it consisted of Me 110s and (somewhat surprisingly) Ju 86s, in all about thirty aircraft. Three of the bombers were claimed as shot down but no wreckage was found afterwards from which it could be confirmed that the Germans were using this obsolescent aircraft.

At any rate most of this force pressed on northwards and bombed in the neighbourhood of Chatham. Bombs were reported from Chatham itself, from Walderslade and from Rochester, where Pobjoy's aircraft factory was hit, although not seriously. Afterwards the enemy crossed the river and returned by way of southern Essex: they were not further intercepted.

At 1324 hours a force was suddenly detected to the south of Dover: it came straight in and steered towards the Isle of Sheppey. Simultaneously, the most serious incident of the whole operation occurred well to the west at the Vickers aircraft factory at Brooklands. The attack was carried out by the force that had been engaged over the Sussex coast by Nos 234 and 43 Squadrons. No air-raid warning was sounded at the factory until after the attack and casualties were very heavy: forty-seven workers were killed and nearly two hundred seriously injured. No. 1 Squadron from Northolt was supposedly patrolling Brooklands at the time, but it appears not to have seen the enemy much less engaged them. No. 253 Squadron, however, sighted them as they were about to bomb the factory, describing the force as twenty 'Me Jaguars'. It is more than likely that this interception saved the factory from a more destructive attack; for the enemy formation was undoubtedly broken up by the squadron and only six bombs hit the works. A number of incendiary bombs fell three miles away at Chertsey.

After the bombing the Germans made off first to the west and later south, making for the coast near Worthing. As they retired they were engaged by one section of No. 602 Squadron near Arundel; by No. 43 Squadron (for the second time) near Worthing; and by No. 601 Squadron, also near Worthing. Four

German aircraft were seen to crash into the sea, and three on land during these engagements.

One peculiarity was that Do 17s were once more reported amongst the enemy aircraft: yet as far as we know the only bombing that had taken place in the country over which this force had operated had been the work of Me 110s, and all the aircraft that crashed on land in the area were Me 110s. In default of any other explanation it can only be suggested that the pilots had been misled by the similarities between the two types; but this is advanced with some diffidence as the pilots of no less than four squadrons were sure that there were Do 17s amongst the enemy.

The whole of this complicated operation (and all important operations on this day) came to an end at 1345 hours when the force that had crossed at Dover twenty-one minutes earlier bombed the already battered Eastchurch. It came as far west as Dartford, then turned due east and bombed Eastchurch as it returned to France. A few craters were blown in the landing area and two huts and two Battles were damaged. This force was not intercepted.

Apart from the incidents at Vickers' works the German bombers had little to show for their efforts. But the operation as a whole demonstrated how difficult it was to engage effectively every enemy force that penetrated inland when more than one formation was attacking over a wide area. The success of the raid on Brooklands was accountable chiefly to the inability of the raid intelligence system to cope with more than five or six simultaneous raids: when questioned about this particular attack Air Chief Marshal Dowding admitted that at about 1310 hours the operations rooms tables were almost at saturation point. It should be noted, however, that Fighter Command had never claimed that all raids would be intercepted.

On the other side of the balance sheet could be reckoned the very heavy casualties that had been incurred by the enemy in flying so long and so far to reach their target at Brooklands. Thirty-two Me 110s and four Do 17s were claimed as destroyed by our pilots at a cost to themselves of only four fighters destroyed or badly damaged. Three bombers and seven fighters were claimed in the fighting over northern Kent at a cost of eleven of our own aircraft. Twelve Me 110s, nine of them from the formations that took part in the Brooklands attack, were found on the ground after the operation. Five separate *Gruppen* were represented amongst them, indicating that probably one hundred Me 110s were despatched.

OPERATIONS, 5 SEPTEMBER

i. Against Biggin Hill, 0945–1115 hours

Two major attacks were launched by the enemy on the 5th. The first was in most respects similar to the attacks on airfields that had been taking place for over two weeks; and no lengthy description is necessary, the more so as the operation was conducted in such a way that it is next to impossible to specify how many separate forces were engaged or what targets were attacked by what force. For whereas the enemy aircraft taking part crossed the coast almost simultaneously in two large and coherent formations, when they reached the neighbourhood of

Maidstone they split up into a number of small forces whose tracks were not continuously plotted by the Observer Corps.

The two forces crossed the coast at Dungeness at 0945 hours and set a north-westerly course. As they came in, part was engaged by No. 501 Squadron which had taken off from Gravesend at 0910 hours and sighted the enemy while patrolling between Canterbury and the coast. There were thirty Do 17s and seventy fighters at 20,000 feet; and 501 Squadron were entirely engaged with the fighters. A second German force of equal strength was attacked half way between Romney and Maidstone by No. 41 Squadron who had left Hornchurch at 0915 hours with orders to patrol Canterbury. They had subsequently been directed south when the German formations were seen to be making landfall at Dungeness. The squadron were flying very high (27,000 feet) and one flight was able to break through the escorting fighters and damage two of the bombers. As usual, however, the subsequent fights were exclusively with the enemy fighters. None of our aircraft were lost whereas two Me 109s of II/JG 3 crashed between Ashford and Maidstone.

From 0955 hours onwards the picture of the enemy's movements, which had been clear so far, becomes blurred; and all that can be described is the bombing that took place and such actions as the defending squadrons were engaged in.

One fairly large force of bombers appeared over Biggin Hill shortly after 1000 hours and aimed bombs at the station; but all fell wide. One flight of No. 79 Squadron took off shortly before the attack and succeeded in damaging a straggling Dornier. At the same time bombs were reported from various places in Kent: Westerham, Wilmington, Horton Kirby all received small salvoes. Somewhat later, at 1015 hours, Bromley and Bexley were lightly bombed and the main line between Charing Cross and the coast was blocked by a salvo of bombs at Chislehurst. Bombs continued to be reported from the outer south-eastern suburbs of London until 1045 hours; and about that time bombs fell near Tonbridge.

While the Germans were over north-west and northern Kent three more British squadrons made interception. No. 111 Squadron engaged some forty Do 17s escorted by Me 109s near Biggin Hill and reported that the Germans turned to the south-east when attacked; No. 19 Squadron, which had been ordered from No.12 Group to patrol Hornchurch, came across the river and attacked a force of forty Do 17s and a similar number of Me 109s which were retiring east near Chatham; twenty Do 17s with a fighter escort were attacked by No. 603 Squadron nearer the coast. It is more than likely that each of these squadrons attacked the same force, or part of it. In all these engagements casualties on both sides were light: nine fighters were claimed as destroyed by our pilots and five Spitfires and Hurricanes were lost.

It is difficult to understand what the Germans hoped to achieve by these operations. The number of bombs dropped was not commensurate with the size of the bomber forces – at least sixty aircraft – that it is believed were employed. Moreover, small detachments from the main body had flown as far west as Guildford and as far north as the borders of Norfolk; which were surely dangerous gestures unless the aircraft concerned were intended to divert attention from a serious attack in the Biggin Hill area. One deduction, of course, is that such an attack was indeed planned but misfired. However, as the German commanders must already have decided to bring the long succession of attacks against airfields to a close, it is possible that they intended simply a reconnaissance in force of the approaches to London as a preliminary to the attacks on the capital that began two days later. Nothing much could be learned at the time from wreckage found on the ground after the battle: five Me 109s from four different *Gruppen* were discovered.

ii. Against Thameshaven and Detling, 1430–1630 hours

There were no indications until early afternoon that the Germans were again concentrating for an attack; but shortly after 1400 hours there were more enemy patrols over the Straits of Dover than was usual; and No. 72 Squadron was ordered from Croydon to patrol Hawkinge at 25,000 feet. Shortly afterwards, No. 222 Squadron was ordered from Rochford to patrol Maidstone. The majority of the squadron was refuelling at the time and only one section was able to carry out the order. About 1430 hours a small force of Me 109s came in near Dover and flew north-east towards Maidstone but after a clash with No. 72 Squadron it retired. One Me 109 was shot down and crashed near Detling but its unit could not be identified: three Spitfires were destroyed.

The squadrons in the air were reinforced between 1430 and 1440 hours:

> No. 17 Squadron left Debden to patrol Colchester: after ten minutes it was ordered to patrol Hornchurch.
>
> No. 249 Squadron left North Weald to patrol Rochford at 20,000 feet: ten minutes later No. 46 Squadron left North Weald to join it.
>
> No. 501 Squadron left Gravesend to patrol Maidstone at 15,000 feet.
>
> No. 66 Squadron left Kenley to patrol it.
>
> No. 303 Squadron left Northolt and after various orders was sent towards Chatham.

By 1440 hours one enemy force was in the central Channel between Boulogne and Dungeness: two formations were near Cap Gris Nez and were joined at 1450 hours by another force that had first been located near St Omer; and all three formations flew towards the coast of Kent. According to the RDF assessment there were about one hundred and ninety aircraft in the four German forces.

On the British side more squadrons took off between 1445 and 1505 hours:

> No. 234 Squadron from Middle Wallop in No. 10 Group to patrol Kenley at 20,000 feet.
>
> No. 310 Squadron from Duxford in No. 12 Group to patrol North Weald at 15,000 feet.
>
> No. 253 Squadron from Kenley to patrol Maidstone.

No. 601 Squadron from Tangmere: its orders are not known and it was not engaged with the enemy.

No. 73 Squadron from Castle Camps to patrol Gravesend.

No. 41 Squadron from Hornchurch to patrol Thameshaven–Gravesend.

No. 43 Squadron from Tangmere to patrol Biggin Hill at 20,000 feet.

The majority of these squadrons engaged the enemy and constituted the striking force of the defence for this particular operation. But in addition every other single-seater squadron in No. 11 Group was ordered into the air, most of them to protect the airfields at which they were stationed.

At 1456 hours three enemy formations crossed the coast near Dover. One of them came only a mile or two inland before turning back over the Straits; a second flew towards Herne Bay; and a third made for south London. Five minutes later a force plotted as 'twenty plus' came in at the North Foreland and took up position on the right flank of the force approaching the Thames Estuary. Part of this force, if not the whole of it, was engaged by No. 303 (Polish) Squadron south of Thameshaven at 1505 hours. There were fifteen Ju 88s at 15,000 feet with escorting Me 109s above and around them. The squadron had the advantage of height and its leader ordered one flight to engage the fighters while the remaining section went for the bombers. The tactics were successful up to a point: three Ju 88s were believed to have been destroyed but in the later stages of the action the nine Hurricanes were almost overwhelmed by the German fighters; and our pilots reckoned themselves fortunate to escape at a cost of only one aircraft. No. 222 Squadron were also in action at about the same time and in the same area; but there were no bombers among their opponents, who were almost certainly the flanking force of fighters that had flown in near the North Foreland.

These actions did not prevent the Germans from attacking their target which was the oil farm at Thameshaven. Eight tanks and a refinery were hit and there was serious damage to one of the wharves: all fires were out before dawn on the following day.

After the attack the Germans continued west for a little time and then turned north and east. A few bombs, chiefly incendiaries, were dropped on three or four villages along their route. Nos 46 and 249 squadrons engaged them near Southend, causing casualties amongst the escorting Me 109s.[19] No. 73 Squadron, who were attracted towards Thameshaven by AA fire, also came into action over the estuary shortly after Thameshaven had been bombed. The Squadron succeeded in attacking the rear-most formation of bombers (which they identified correctly as He 111s) without being interfered with by the escorting fighters who were already engaged with No. 249 and No. 46 Squadrons. However, the limitations of an eastern attack against heavily armoured and stoutly defended bombers were well exemplified: three Hurricanes were

19 One of the pilots of No. 46 Squadron was flying an experimental four cannon Hurricane. He reported that one Me 109 completely disintegrated under his fire.

destroyed and three damaged at a maximum cost to the Germans of two Heinkels.

As this force of Heinkels had bombed Thameshaven, the formations that had advanced on parallel lines further west and south, swung round to the north and east and retired down the estuary and across northern Kent. It is now clear that these were entirely fighter forces intended to protect the one formation of bombers that the Germans appear to have despatched; and it was chiefly with fighters that the combats that RAF pilots engaged in between 1520 and 1540 hours, were conducted. Unless a further bomber force was despatched (and of this there was certainly no evidence in the bomb incidents that were reported) well over one hundred fighters must have been sent over to protect, either closely or at a distance, no more than thirty bombers.

There was in fact one more bombing raid, but it was carried out by a force of Me 109s. These came in near Pegwell Bay at 1546 hours and flew west as far as Maidstone where they turned and bombed Detling at 1600 hours. Only a few bombs were dropped and the station was only slightly damaged. The Germans had probably calculated that our squadrons would be returning to rearm and refuel after the earlier fighting; and most of them were. Nevertheless, No. 43 Squadron came up with the enemy force near Maidstone before Detling was attacked. There were thirty to forty Me 109s and our squadron was unable to prevent those that were carrying bombs from breaking away and going on to their target. With this attack the German operations came to an end.

The enemy's attacks on this day were peculiar in that very little bombing was done notwithstanding that large bomber forces were reported to have been employed. If the combat reports of British pilots were the sole criterion it would follow that some of the enemy bomber formations were unable to find their targets, and therefore returned to France with their loads. But it is more likely that a high proportion of the German forces were fighters; and this is reflected both in the wreckage that was found on the ground and in the high casualties that the British squadrons suffered relative to those of the enemy. Five aircraft were discovered after the morning attack: all were Me 109s. Five were found after those of the afternoon and early evening: four were Me 109s and one was an He 111 from III/KG 53, the *Gruppe* that carried out the attack on Thamesaven. British claims for the whole day, including two He 111s and two Me 109s claimed by the gunners of the Thames and Medway zones during the attack on Thameshaven and one Me 109 by the Bofors gunners at Dover during an attack on the balloons at 1030 hours, were thirty-four fighters and ten bombers destroyed. British losses were twenty-three fighters destroyed and seven badly damaged; and eleven pilots were killed and eight wounded.

OPERATIONS, 6 SEPTEMBER

The salient features of the attacks on the 5th were repeated the following day. On three occasions the Germans sent over two hundred or more aircraft; and each time few bombs were dropped. Correspondingly, most combats were with fighters and only seven were believed to have been destroyed compared with over forty fighters. The German aircraft that crashed on land reflected this proportion; for there were only three bombers – one Ju 88 from II/KG 76, one Me 110 from KGr 210 and one He 111 from I/KG 53 – whereas there were fourteen fighters, amongst which at least ten different *Gruppen* were represented. When more precise information becomes available it will probably be found that the proportion of fighters to bombers was about 4:1. Certain it is that the proportion had not been so high before the operations on the 4th; but that the number of bombers employed should have fallen away at this stage is not surprising in view of the heavy calls that the Germans made on their bomber units on 7 September and the succeeding days and nights.

As far as Fighter Command was concerned the burden of defence remained the same. That few bombers were being employed was not fully appreciated until after an attack; and the controller had to assume the presence of bombers until he knew the contrary. Thus, on 6 September, seventeen squadrons were sent up to meet the attack that was launched between 0830 and 1000 hours; nineteen squadrons to meet the attack of 1230–1400 hours; and fourteen squadrons to meet that of 1715–1845 hours.

i. Against Hawkers', Weybridge and targets in Kent, 0830–1000 hours

More bombers took part in the first German attack than in either of the other two. The operation began about 0815 hours when there were clear indications that the enemy were concentrating near Calais; and at 0836 hours a raid of 'fifty plus' came in over Hythe at 20,000 feet. It was followed at short intervals by five further raids: these came in at Hythe, Sandwich, Dover, Ramsgate and New Romney, the biggest being plotted as 'seventy-five plus' and the smallest as 'twelve plus'. Four of these forces made towards Maidstone but the one that came in over New Romney flew west towards Hailsham where it was engaged by No. 234 Squadron who had come in from No. 10 Group at 0837 hours to patrol south-east of Brooklands. The enemy force consisted of about fourteen Do 17s escorted by about thirty Me 109s. Fighter Command pilots were confident that they inflicted exceptionally heavy casualties, amounting to at least eight fighters destroyed and four bombers damaged; and as the enemy's track was lost about the time of the attack and no bombs can be traced to this force it is probable that the enemy were forced to turn back from whatever was their objective.

The forces that had converged upon Maidstone contained two formations of bombers. The first consisted of an unknown number of Me 110s from KGr 210 whose task was to bomb the Hawker aircraft works at Weybridge. They were not engaged until 0925 hours when they were preparing to carry out their attack. Nor were they attacked in great strength; for only one pilot of No. 1 Squadron, who had dropped out of his formation, and a few pilots of No. 601 Squadron came into action. Nevertheless, the German bombers were very much hindered: there was only slight damage to the factory, most of the bombs falling wide.

The second enemy bomber formation operated further east; but it is impossible to do more than speculate about its target. It was strongly attacked on its inward journey between Maidstone and the Croydon district by four British squadrons; which probably explains why bombs fell at different points in the Oxted–Caterham area while these engagements were in progress. Some of these bombs fell on stretches of railway line; and near Oxted and at Warlingham the Southern Railway lines were blocked. It will be surprising, however, if German records reveal that communications were the primary target on this occasion. It is more likely that Biggin Hill or Kenley was the main objective but that the attack was frustrated.

Certainly the Germans put no little effort into the operation. The squadron commander of No. 303 (Polish) Squadron reported afterwards that he had never seen so large a formation: 'It covered an area twenty miles by five. There were many big planes, Dorniers, He 111s and some four-engined. There were the usual Me 110s among them, and formations of Me 109s up to 25,000 feet. There were fully 300 to 400 enemy aircraft.' This squadron was forced to attack climbing and in consequence lost five aircraft. No. 111 Squadron, however, put in a head-on attack on a formation of Ju 88s near Kenley and compelled them to retreat. No. 1 Squadron also enjoyed much success against Ju 88s and Me 109s which were part of the large force encountered by 303 Squadron. Six more squadrons engaged the Germans, but only as they retired to the south-east, making eleven squadrons who carried out interceptions out of seventeen despatched; and as by the acid test of bombs dropped the Germans succeeded in achieving so little despite the strong forces employed, it can be said that the attack was a failure.

ii. Against Targets on the East Coast of Kent, 1230–1400 hours

The same test cannot be applied to the attack that developed early in the afternoon; for it is very doubtful whether more than fifteen to twenty bombers were employed. Yet a big attack was simulated and big defending forces were despatched, including the first of the Duxford wing formations. Four raids, totalling over one hundred aircraft, came in between Dover and Dungeness at 20,000 feet between 1243 and 1257 hours and, as in the morning attack, made for Maidstone. Another raid of '100 plus' came in at Hythe and then split up; and it is certain that this was an offensive sweep of Me 109s. The plotting of all three raids overland was very confused; but enemy aircraft were seen over a wide area, from Redhill and Cuckfield to Hornchurch and Brentwood.

Only one British squadron got a clear view of enemy bombers, which were sighted over the north Kent coast. It was there, in the Rochester–Chatham district, that a small number of bombs fell on Pobjoy's aircraft factory and the nearby airport; and a small fire was caused at the works. About the same time a salvo of bombs fell in the opposite corner of Kent near Dymchurch: the RAF emergency landing ground at Littlestone was probably the enemy's target.

All combats with the enemy were with Me 109s. Seven of the No. 11 Group squadrons made contact; all of them east of a line from Beachy Head–Maidstone. Only three British fighters were destroyed and a like number of Me 109s. Once again a German operation must be summed up, until evidence to the contrary is available, as an offensive sweep designed to maintain pressure upon the defences of the south-east, and at the same time permit economy in the employment of bombers.

iii. Against Thameshaven, 1715–1845 hours

In the evening attack, however, one *Gruppe* (I/KG 53) of long-range bombers was certainly employed, reaching its target and bombing it successfully. The bulk of the German forces crossed the coast flying very high between Dover and Dungeness shortly after 1730 hours, and for the third time that day flew towards Maidstone. There were over one hundred aircraft in the various formations. Some ten minutes later a force of fifty plus came up the Thames Estuary without crossing the coast at any point.

The forces south of the river were an elaborate diversion in aid of this last formation which, at 1800 hours, bombed the oil installations at Thameshaven. A wing composed of No. 46 and No. 249 Squadron had been sent up from North Weald twenty minutes earlier to patrol Rochford at 20,000 feet, but they arrived too late to interfere with the bombing. This was heavy and accurate: the Shell-Mex refinery was gutted by fire, and serious fires were caused at three oil wharves. They burned all through the night, when they were further attacked, and were still burning when the heavy attacks of the evening of the next day were launched.

The force of Heinkels that carried out this attack was not intercepted; and with one exception the three squadrons that did succeed in engaging the enemy were in action to the west of Thameshaven with Me 109s. The exception was a combat between the North Weald sector commander, Wing Commander F V Beamish, who was flying alone, and six Ju 87s which were flying at 7,000–8,000 feet over Thameshaven after the main attack had been delivered. Two of the dive-bombers were shot down into the sea. The North Weald wing was in the area at the time but it was flying at 20,000 feet and failed to see the German formation, which was also obscured by the smoke from the blazing oil tanks. It is unlikely that so experienced a pilot wrongly identified the enemy aircraft; and if he was correct, this was the first occasion since 18 August that this type had been used.[20]

After the Thameshaven attack small formations of fighters continued to be plotted, though not continuously, over eastern Kent as well as over the Straits of Dover. There were no further interceptions, however, and no more bombs were reported. Thus ended the last day of a long drawn out phase of the battle and one clearly distinguishable from the phase that followed it not by reason of a lull in large-scale attacks similar to that which followed the period 8–18 August, but because the character of the operations that began on the evening of 7 September was markedly different from anything that the Germans had previously attempted.

NIGHT OPERATIONS, 25/26 AUGUST–6/7 SEPTEMBER

i. Introduction

The great operations which the Germans launched by day from 25 August–6 September were clearly calculated to destroy the fighting strength of Fighter Command by attacking its ground organisation and by bringing it to battle under conditions of great numerical inferiority. Over the same period the Germans intensified their night operations, but not with the same object as

20 See also p. 219.

governed their attacks by day. It is clear that there was no direct connection between the target policy dictating the day attacks – which was to destroy the airfields covering London – and that applied at night – which entailed a general attack upon the economy of the country coupled with the attack of specific industrial districts. The tracing of a more indirect relation must needs wait until the documents of German strategy are open to examination. One conjecture may be permitted: the Germans may well have believed that the British will to resist could best be broken by making the weight of their air arm felt as widely as possibly by night while clearing the way to a grand assault on the capital by day. As for the answers to the associated questions, what place, if any, had the Germans' night attacks in the preparations for invasion, and were these night attacks well conceived? Speculation would be unprofitable.

ii. Character of the German Attacks

The character of the night attacks changed somewhat during the last week in August. Previously the attacks on any one night had ranged over wide areas of the country, and the bomb tonnage dropped in relation to the number of aircraft which were estimated to have been employed was small. A measure of concentration against particular regions of the country had been noticeable, but no single urban area had suffered on any one night from the attacks of more than twenty aircraft. Commencing on the 25th, however, the German night operations were concentrated against a few target areas, and the weight of the attack was increased. From that date until 7 September, when the night attack of London began, a few cities received the main weight of attack on each night. They were as follows:

iii. Areas chiefly attacked

August	25/26	Birmingham and Coventry:
	26/27	Birmingham and Coventry: Plymouth
	27/28	Birmingham and Coventry: Portsmouth
	28/29	Merseyside
	29/30	Merseyside
	30/31	Merseyside
Aug 31	/Sept 1	Merseyside: West Riding
September	1/2	Swansea and Bristol
	2/3	No concentration
	3/4	Merseyside
	4/5	Merseyside: Bristol
	5/6	Merseyside
	6/7	Greater London

iv. Attacks on Merseyside

The four attacks on Merseyside at the end of August were intended by the Germans to be the first major attacks launched against the United Kingdom, their standard for a major attack being a minimum weight of one hundred tons of HE bombs.[21] Approximately one hundred aircraft were sent against Merseyside on the first of the four nights; while on the next three nights 137, 109 and 107 aircraft were believed by the Germans to have bombed the area. In fact, as we shall see later, many of the German pilots failed altogether to find the Mersey. Those were the only major attacks that the Germans launched until those of 7 September against the capital. In the other concentrated night attacks between thirty and sixty aircraft took part, each aircraft dropping approximately one ton of bombs.

v. *Relative failure of the Attacks*

But it cannot be too strongly emphasised that the extent to which German night bombing policy has changed was not fully appreciated at the time in Britain. That a heavier weight of attack was being brought to bear upon industrial and commercial targets was realised, but not that Merseyside had been the object of four successive attacks of the dimensions that we have already noted. On the day following the first of the big attacks on Merseyside the staff officers of the Ministry of Home Security summarised the night's activity as follows: 'Activity was very heavy, the Midlands being the main objective.' Of the next night they said: 'The areas mainly attacked were the Tyne and Hartlepool, South Wales, Liverpool and Manchester. No serious damage was done'; and of the night of the 30th: 'Considerable bombing occurred in London and the Midlands; Manchester, Wrexham, Derby and Nottingham being mainly affected.' Fighter Command and AA Command, having detailed information of the tracks of the enemy, were aware that the main stream of German aircraft had flowed towards the north-west; but they were not aware that on these nights quite half of the German effort had been directed against Merseyside. Nor was this due to any deficiency on the part of the defences. The explanation is simple enough: it is that a large proportion of the German aircraft had failed to find the target, even if that is understood as an area within ten miles of the centre of Liverpool. How large this proportion was will never be known, but that the attacks were a failure can be amply demonstrated, especially for the second and third nights.

Home Security Daily Appreciation

It is not clear from the German documents now in British custody whether the number of aircraft shown as participating in these two attacks were those that were originally directed against Merseyside, or those whose crews reported that they had actually bombed that area. In other words, we cannot yet be sure

21 It is now known from captured German documents that 103 tons of HE and 6,800 incendiaries were aimed at the Liverpool area on the night of the 28th. On the two succeeding nights the figures were 130 tons and 11,200 incendiaries, and 127 tons and 8,100 incendiaries.

The units taking part on each night were drawn exclusively from *Luftflotte 3*. Their precise identity on the first night is not known; but on the second all *Gruppen* of KG 27, 51, 55 and Lehr 1, KGr 100, 606 and 806 were involved. I/KG 40 also despatched three of its small complement of FW 200s; which seems a wasteful use of a unit specially trained in the attack of shipping. Exactly the same units less one *Gruppe* on the 31st took part in the attack on the following two nights, each providing much the same number of aircraft. KGr 100, which was to lead many of the large raids of the autumn and winter, was not in the vanguard of either the attack of the 29th or that of the following night. Both were begun by KGr 606 and 806.

The forces used in these attacks probably represented the maximum which *Luftflotte 3* could raise at night at this time without making a special effort; and it is significant that its daylight activities during this period were on a very small scale.

whether the failure of many of the German crews to find the target area was realised by them or not. But that many did fail to clear. On the 29th bombs fell to the east of Liverpool, in Widnes, St Helens, and Wigan and to the south in rural districts of Cheshire. In Merseyside proper there was some desultory bombing, chiefly with incendiaries, near the Rootes aircraft factory at Speke, in Halewood and Netherton, at Ellesmere Port and Stanlow, where four oil tanks were hit; and in all barely fifty tons of bombs were dropped compared to the one hundred and thirty tons the Germans believed they had dropped. Part of the German load fell in places far to the south of the Mersey, which can, at best, only have provided targets of opportunity to enemy crews who had failed to find Merseyside. Thus, the small numbers of bombs which fell at Wrexham, Stoke-on-Trent, Bridgnorth and Ledbury were almost certainly dropped by aircraft whose primary target was Liverpool.

The same features are apparent on this same night in other parts of the country; for while the main weight of the German operations was directed against the north-west, all regions of the United Kingdom, with the exception of Northern Ireland, reported raids. The Germans knew these as 'dislocation raids' (*Störangriffe*) whereby aircraft operated over important industrial areas of the country, interfering with night work and the sleep of day workers as much by the threat of their presence as by the damage they caused.

Six aircraft attacked targets in the Portland–Portsmouth area, five attacked Bristol, eight South Wales and about twelve Yorkshire and the north-east coast. Nearly all bombs, however, fell harmlessly in open country, the most important exceptions being in South Wales, where two railway lines had temporarily to be closed, and Hull, where a salvo fell in the dock area.

The same wide dispersion of effort occupied in the attack of 30/31st on Merseyside, when some forty tons of bombs were dropped on Liverpool, Birkenhead and adjacent suburbs. None fell in the dock areas and most incidents affected suburban property, particularly in Wallasey, Blundellsands, Seaforth and Hightown. The only important undertaking that was damaged was the Port Sunlight works of Unilever. Outside the area bombs fell at Queensferry, where the airfield at Sealand may have been the objective, at Frodsham and Malpas in Cheshire and at Whitchurch, Salop. All these should have fallen on Liverpool and the immediate district. Some attention was also paid to a woodland fire which had been started by incendiaries near Wrexham on the previous night.

Much more success attended the attack of the 31st. The commercial centre of the city was located and over one hundred and sixty fires were started, all but two being out by morning. The Custom House was badly damaged and a small number of bombs fell in the docks. Across the river about thirty bombs fell in Birkenhead. But again a number of the enemy dropped their bombs far away from the Mersey. St Helens, Shrewsbury, Whitchurch and a number of rural districts in Flintshire all reported small numbers of bombs. Yet according to the German records only two aircraft attacked targets in all the long corridor between the Severn and the Mersey.

The general picture that emerges, therefore, from the German operations against Merseyside on these four consecutive nights is of aircraft operating individually over the blacked-out north-west, with pilots and navigators rarely aware of their precise position. Even when the Liverpool area was reached accurate bombing was beyond the majority of the crews; some of whom were forced to seek secondary targets elsewhere. There is little doubt that river mist and industrial haze combined to make the area a difficult one to attack; and it was unpopular with German pilots for this reason. In sum, it can be said with confidence that the attacks failed to produce results at all commensurate with the forces employed.

vi. Other German attacks

a. Against Towns

Bristol, Leeds, Swansea, Birmingham and Coventry also reported serious incidents during this period. The most important were at Swansea on the night of 1 September where much property was destroyed, some flour mills were badly damaged and eight thousand tons of wheat were lost, and at Birmingham which was attacked on every night during the period and in fair strength on the first three nights.[22] Here two sections of the BSA (Small Arms) works were gutted, the BSA (Tools) factory was seriously damaged, and the James Cycle Company and seven other engineering works were affected.

One feature of the German operations was their effect upon the air raid warning system. Many industrial districts were kept under 'red' warning for long periods, even though they were only lightly attacked, if at all. On the night of 31 August, for example, when the scale of activity was low, and when such as there was chiefly directed against Merseyside and the West Riding, the following ports and industrial towns were under public warning:

District	*Duration of Warning*	*District*	*Duration of Warning*
Liverpool	6 hours	Coventry	5 hours
Manchester	4 hours	Leicester	2 hours
South Wales	4 hours	Derby	2 hours
Portsmouth	5 hours	Humber	5 hours
London (Central)	6 hours	West Riding	2 hours
Norwich	5 hours	Middlesbrough	4 hours
Birmingham	5 hours	Newcastle	2½ hours

It is difficult to say what effect these long 'alerts' had upon production. The production of certain basic materials, such as iron ore, steel ingots and castings, and coal, fell during the July quarter compared with the previous one. However, other factors besides night bombing would have to be taken into account before

22 The German estimate of less than one hundred tons of HE dropped on Birmingham during August seems to us to be too low. On the Birmingham and Coventry district they believed that nearly one hundred and seventy tons were dropped; and it is possible that some of the weight assigned to Coventry fell on Birmingham. Unfortunately, it is not possible to check the German figures for these early months as no adequate organisation for the plotting of bombs and subsequent analysis was yet in being.

A little under thirty tons of the German effort was aimed at the Nuffield works at Castle Bromwich on the nights of the 23rd, 24th and 26th, but nothing like this weight of bombs fell on the factory.

any authoritative explanation of this fall could be made. But what can be said with safety is that part of the German plan was to affect production and civilian morale by forcing the frequent sounding of public warnings. For the same reason, so the officers of the Ministry of Home Security maintained, a large proportion of the bombs dropped were of the delayed-action variety.

b. Against Communications and Vulnerable Points

The officials of the same department also saw clear evidence of an attack on communications in the Merseyside and Bristol Channel areas; and they reported that 'unless an improvement is effected in the black-out of the railways, serious damage to communications will occur'. The figures given below,[23] however, show that the sort of bombing the Germans employed during this period had little effect on railway traffic. They reveal instead that the concentrated attack of the London area was far more effective than the previous widespread operations. As for attacks on specific industrial and commercial targets especially important to the war economy the Germans secured few successes. The raids on Birmingham included aircraft whose crews had been specially briefed to attack the Castle Bromwich district, and in particular the Nuffield aircraft works. At the latter, one large shop was put out of action for a week and the long succession of raids materially increased absenteeism,[24] but the total effect was less than had been feared.

On the night of 1 September, however, the Germans succeeded in finding and hitting one of the most important oil targets in the country, the great refineries at Llandarcy, near Swansea. Five tanks were ignited but, fortunately, the Admiralty tanks were not affected. Whether this success was an accidental by-product of the attack on Swansea itself which was made on this night, or whether the target was deliberately selected for attack, we cannot say. It is surprising that on the following night, when the tanks were still blazing, the attack was only followed up to the paltry extent of four HE bombs, none of which hit the vulnerable area.

vii. Attacks on Airfields

Over the whole period there were only six reports of bombs on RAF stations, and in each case the attack was by a single aircraft. Yet it is certain that many more attacks than these were made. On one night alone, that of the 26th, and in the western half of the country only, the enemy attempted to hit six airfields – Worthy Down, Boscombe Down, Witney, Brize Norton, Filton and St Eval. In four cases the German pilots were not sure that they had succeeded in bombing

23 The coaching mileage of the four main companies rather than the freight returns is the better index of the effect of bombing, as passengers traffic over a period is governed by a precise schedule. The drop in the four weeks following 7 September, particularly on the Southern Railway, contrasts sharply with the insignificant variation of the preceding months.

COACHING TRAFFIC BY THOUSAND MILES

Four Weeks Ending	*LMS*	*LNER*	*GWR*	*SR*
13 July	1347	996	632	867
10 August	1351	981	613	863
7 September	1349	977	614	847
5 October	1298	937	619	677

24 This aspect is being covered by the historical section of the Ministry of Aircraft Production.

the target, but Brize Norton and St Eval were believed to have been hit, the latter with especial severity. In fact neither place was hit.

St Eval owed its escape to the success of the decoy airfield which had been constructed near the station proper. About 2115 hours an aircraft from KGr 806 set fire to the dummy flare path; and aircraft from the same *Gruppe* kept up the 'attack' until the early hours of the morning, practically the whole unit taking part. Morning found over sixty craters on the heathland on which the decoy was sited, but St Eval itself was untouched.

Decoys of this sort enjoyed considerable success during the month. The Air Ministry department responsible for camouflage and deception reported that whereas only two dummy airfields were attacked by day in August, twenty-nine attacks were made at night. We are not entitled to say, therefore, that the Germans made no attempt to maintain at night, the offensive against airfields that they were prosecuting so vigorously during the day; but airfields in general were attacked rather than fighter airfields in particular.

viii. Defensive Measures

But if the passive defences had proved their worth the active defences had little to show for their efforts. An average of barely thirty sorties was made each night between 25 August and 6 September, and only two aircraft were claimed as destroyed by fighters. The burden of defence was chiefly sustained by AA Command, but they too had few positive successes to claim. Altogether, against the sort of operations launched at night prior to 7 September the defences of the country were ineffective.[25]

ix. Summary

After the last three nights in August German night activity slackened, and only on the night of 4 September were more than two hundred aircraft over the country, while on the 6th less than one hundred were in action. The reduction was doubtless demanded by the preparations needed for the attack on London which was to open in earnest on the 7th. Yet it is clear that the night attacks of the last week in August and the first in September represent a second stage in the development of the German night offensive, and in its intensifying. The first stage had taken the form of widespread operations designed to reconnoitre the whole country, to interrupt its work and sleep, and place a general strain upon its economy; and to familiarise crews with the appearance of the country and its defences. The third stage was to see the concentration of the great majority of enemy aircraft available for night bombing against the one target area of London. In between comes the stage just considered, when a measure of concentration is clearly discernible but when harassing attacks against widely

25 See Air Historical Branch narrative on 'The Night Air Defence of Great Britain'. It can be mentioned here, however, that Air Chief Marshal Dowding was so alarmed at the failure of the night fighters to intercept and by the ability, as it seemed to him, of the German night bombers to navigate to the immediate vicinity of important industrial targets, that during August he pressed the Air Ministry to agree to a wholesale jamming of all radio aids to navigation even though it would entail hindering the night operations of Bomber Command.

separated regions were also maintained by a sizeable proportion of the forces employed.

COMMENTARY ON THIRD PHASE, 24 AUGUST–6 SEPTEMBER

i. Introduction

The various phases into which the Battle of Britain can conveniently be divided, without straining the facts for the sake of symmetry, relate to significant alterations in the German plan of attack rather than to important changes in the scheme of defence. The reason is obvious enough: the battle was one in which the initiative lay in the hands of the Germans; and while the defenders could, and did match move with countermove, the character of their measures was largely dictated by those of their opponents. This, as we shall see, remained the case even when, thanks to the achievements of the defence, the Germans ceased their most dangerous forms of attack – their onslaughts by day against the airfields guarding London and against the capital itself – and initiated the fighter-bomber sweeps. Thus in surveying and commenting upon the operations between 24 August and 6 September it is necessary first to see what plan had governed the German offensive.

But here a difficulty at once becomes apparent: it is that there is not yet sufficiently reliable and comprehensive information from the German side to enable the narrator to state with authority precisely what the Germans intended. It is especially difficult to trace a connection between the air operations and any timetable or plans for the invasion of this country that may have been prepared. In the absence of such information, what is at best an 'intelligence appreciation', based on an incomplete picture of events, is all that is possible, or, indeed, permissible; and a good deal of conjecture cannot be avoided. Yet this deficiency has one important merit: the reader will be presented with very little more than the information that was available during the battle to the British commanders. He should not, therefore, fall into the error of being wise after the event.

ii. Concentration against Fighter Airfields

a. Number and Distribution of Attacks

In the first place, however, it is beyond argument that during this third phase the Germans were seeking ends different from those of the preceding fortnight. From 24 August onwards their attacks were almost exclusively directed against airfields in south-east England, and Fighter Command airfields in particular, whereas previously their taste in targets had been more catholic. Insofar as they had attacked airfields during the first three weeks of August they had seemingly considered the proximity of these to the coast rather than the Command of the Royal Air Force that controlled them. Only on the last day of the phase, and immediately prior to a five-day lull in large-scale attacks, had they attacked any of the fighter sector stations near London.

The extent to which the Germans concentrated, from 24 August, upon attacking the south-east is best expressed arithmetically. During the next fourteen days thirty-three heavy attacks were made by day upon British targets; and by this is meant attacks in which a force of at least twenty German bombers found, bombed and hit a military or para-military target. Of the dozen or so attacks (it is impossible to be sure of the exact figures) that went astray, the majority were probably directed against airfields.[26] Of these thirty-three, twenty-four were against airfields east of a line from Lyme Regis–Great Yarmouth. One only of the No. 10 Group stations was seriously attacked – Warmwell on the 25th. Otherwise, the Germans concentrated on airfields within the area defended by No. 11 Group. Biggin Hill was hit four times, Hornchurch four times, Debden twice and North Weald twice. These were four of the six sector stations that closely defended London. A fifth – Kenley – escaped a heavy attack but it is almost certain that at least one was directed against it. In any case, it had suffered heavily in the attack of 18 August. The sixth – Northolt – was not attacked; or, if it was, it was not hit. Other airfields in No. 11 Group that were attacked in strength were Croydon, Gravesend and Rochford. Hawkinge and Manston, in contrast to the earlier phase of the battle, were virtually ignored; and the Germans must have been aware that Manston was not being used, except for emergency landings, and Hawkinge used much less than when Dover and convoys in the Straits were being regularly attacked.

But when there was such an obvious concentration against fighter airfields it is strange that the Germans made more attacks – seven in all – against Eastchurch, a station controlled by Coastal Command and never used by fighters except in emergency, than against any other airfield in the south-east. Detling, another Coastal Command station in northern Kent, was also attacked on two occasions. There are numerous explanations for this seeming waste of effort: the German intelligence service may have mistaken the function of Eastchurch and believed it in use by fighters; or German pilots may have bombed it on some occasions under the impression that it was the fighter station at Gravesend; or – and this is the explanation that commends itself to the narrator – it may have been a convenient secondary target when weather or the defending fighters frustrated the bombing of the prime objective.

Few attacks were made on other types of target. During the first three days of the period Portsmouth was attacked twice. During the next eight, Luton and Tilbury were each attacked once. During the last three, Brooklands was attacked once (a second attack miscarried) and Thameshaven twice. Together these attacks amounted to a small proportion only of the whole German effort in daylight.

b. Weight and effect of Attacks

What weight of bombs was dropped during the period under review is not precisely known. What is certain, however, is that a far larger tonnage was dropped on airfields than on any other type of target attacked during the day. In fact, during August nearly one half of the two thousand five hundred tons that

26 E.g. 26 August, 1430–1545 hours, 31 August, 0815–0900 hours.

the Germans dropped on this country *in all attacks* was aimed at airfields; and of this approximately half was dropped during the last week of the month.

The individual attacks were comparatively light. Most of them were carried out by formations of between twenty and thirty aircraft, each of which carried approximately one ton of bombs. Bombs of medium-calibre, i.e. 250 and 500 lbs were chiefly used, and with two or three exceptions, e.g. Kenley on the 18th and Biggin Hill on the 30th, the attacks were made from heights between 12,000 and 18,000 feet. They were most effective against wooden buildings; but steel framed hangers stood up well to anything except a direct hit. Similarly, only when direct hits were made on trench shelters, as happened at Biggin Hill on the 31st, were casualties high. Few aircraft were destroyed (see Appendix 34, Table III), thanks to a policy of wide dispersal; but in any case the Germans attacked airfields not so much to destroy aircraft, or even to render areas unserviceable, but to destroy the nodal points of communication and control in the complex intelligence system that was, and will always be, the foundation of an effective air defence. Thus, it was damage to operation rooms and telecommunications rather than to landing grounds and hangars that most interfered with the proper working of No. 11 Group. Kenley and, later, Biggin Hill operations rooms were put out of action and forced to move to emergency rooms which had been prepared beforehand but which were neither sufficiently large to contain all the staff required nor equipped with the full scale of landlines to enable three squadrons to be controlled. A beginning was made, therefore, towards the end of August, in building alternative operations rooms, fully equipped in all respects, within five miles of each sector station. Meantime, each sector prepared its existing emergency room for immediate used when required.

Even when operations rooms luckily escaped serious damage, as at North Weald on 3 September, important operational landlines were frequently, and internal communications invariably, severed. The work of repairing the first was carried out by the GPO (War Group), while that of repairing station lines was chiefly done by station signals sections and the Royal Corps of Signals. Their work was such that even where, as at Biggin Hill, it became impossible to operate the normal complement of squadrons from the parent station, operational control was retained by the sector operations room through landlines connected to satellite stations by way of the neighbouring sector station at Kenley.

IIG/S493, 12 Sept 1940, paras 36–41

It is, of course, difficult to say how long this sort of improvisation could have continued or how far it affected the efficiency of the defence. Air Vice-Marshal Park is explicit on the latter question: 'Contrary to general belief and official reports, the enemy's bombing attack by day did extensive damage to five of our forward aerodromes, and also to six of our seven sector stations.[27] … There was a critical period between 28 August and 5 September when the damage to sector stations and our ground organisation was having a serious effect on the fighting efficiency of the fighter squadrons, who could not be given the same good technical and administrative service as previously. As a result of an immense amount of hard work day and night on the part of Group staff and personnel at

27 The forward airfields were Lympne, Hawkinge, Manston, Rochford and Martlesham: the sector station that was not hit in any big raid was Northolt.

sector stations and satellite aerodromes, the critical period was tided over, without any interruption in the operations of our fighter squadrons. The absence of many essential telephone lines, the use of scratch equipment in emergency operations rooms, and the general dislocation of ground organisation, was seriously felt for about a week in the handling of squadrons by day to meet the enemy's massed attacks, which were continued without the former occasional break of a day … Had the enemy continued his heavy attacks against (Biggin Hill and) the adjacent sectors and knocked out their operations rooms or telephone communications, the fighter defences of London would have been in a perilous state during the last critical phase when heavy attacks have been directed against the capital … Fortunately, the enemy switched his raids from aerodromes on to industrial and other objectives, and gave a short respite during which the station organisation at bombed aerodromes was completely reorganised.' And there the matter must needs be left; for as the attacks were not continued nobody can say whether the defenders would have continued to improvise successfully and thus maintained an effective defence.

iii. Relation between the Attacks on Airfields and an Intended Invasion

a. The Switch to the Attack of London

When, in the above report, Air Vice-Marshal Park spoke of the switch 'to industrial and other objectives', he was thinking of the attacks that were made during the last three days of the phase against the aircraft industry in the Weybridge and Rochester districts and against the oil depot at Thameshaven. But the narrative of operations for 4, 5 and 6 September has shown that there is strong evidence that the Germans did attempt attacks against Kenley and Biggin Hill on these three days, only to fail. It may well be that the Germans intended to keep up the attack on these two most important stations guarding London until the last moment before their great stroke at the capital on the 7th. The fact remains that at a time when the defenders were at last feeling the effects of the cumulative damage to their system, the Germans stopped attacking airfields and instead attacked London. During the coming month no attempt was to be made to maintain pressure upon the sector stations of Fighter Command. Few attacks were made upon them, even by single aircraft. The Germans were to concentrate as wholeheartedly on attacking London as they had previously upon attacking airfields.

b. The Progress of Preparations for Invasion

Such a fundamental change of plan demands an explanation; and an authoritative one can only be made when the relevant German records are examined. It is unlikely, however, that the change was due to despair of ever achieving important results from the attack of airfields. It is much more likely that the reasons were either political or were connected with preparations for invasion. As to the first of these, German diplomacy had been active during the summer months in stabilising the territorial and political situations in central Europe and the Balkans; and the Vienna Award of 30 August had registered German supremacy in this region. In the conquered countries of western Europe great efforts were made to erect a facade of co-operation with the occupying power.

All this underlined, on the one hand the isolation into which the British Commonwealth had been forced, on the other the almost unparalleled hegemony that Germany had achieved in Europe. It would be well, therefore, until more is known of German policy, to bear in mind the possibility that the attack on London, combined with the preparations for invasion that seemed to be in hand, was intended to force the British government to negotiate.

At the same time it seemed that invasion was both likely and practicable and that the most suitable conditions would apply during the middle fortnight in September. Both the attacks on the airfields in the south-east and the switch to the attack of London on 7 September can be squared with such a hypothesis. During the last week in August and the first in September the inter-service committee that was co-ordinating and analysing all intelligence on German preparations for invasion was regularly reporting significant air and sea dispositions. Not all their reports indicated either that invasion was imminent or even that invasion was being prepared. On 23 August it was reported that, 'no serious threat of invasion yet exists from the Netherlands, France or south-west Norwegian ports'. A fortnight later the position was summarised as follows: 'There is little evidence other than the movement of small craft towards the Channel ports to show that preparations for invasion are more advanced than they have been for some time.' But the activities of the German Air Force, having been so clearly designed to weaken the defences of south-east England, could be interpreted as the execution of the preliminary stages of a plan to invade in that area. Moreover, on 2 September AI3 (b) reported that an important concentration of dive-bomber and fighter units was taking place in the area Somme–Amiens–Bethune–Dunkerque. Eight dive-bomber *Gruppen* and five fighter *Gruppen* which had been stationed along the north coast of France and in Denmark, were to move into the area bordering the Straits of Dover, making a total force there of ten dive-bomber and twelve fighter *Gruppen*. It was also reported that four *Gruppen* of long-range bombers, previously in Holland, Denmark and Norway, were moving to Belgian stations. Some of the most experienced pilots in the German Air Force in the attack of ports and shipping were amongst the latter units. As for the concentration of dive-bombers, it was no more than obvious caution to deduce that they were to be re-employed on a large scale in preparation for, or as an accompaniment to, invasion. On 6 September there was an isolated report that this type of aircraft was once more being used against us: a flight of them was sighted during the evening attack against Thameshaven. On the same day the moves of the long range bombers were confirmed; and that fighters from the *Luftflotte* 3 area operated against the south-east during September is known from aircraft shot down over this country. The position, therefore, on the 6th was that while nothing definite could be concluded from the dispositions and movement of shipping in western Europe, the distribution of the German Air Force and, above all, its operations during the previous fortnight, pointed unmistakably to the maintenance and intensifying of the offensive against south-east England. Then on the 6th a photographic reconnaissance was flown as a result of which Invasion Alert No. 2 – i.e. attack to be regarded as probable within the next three days – was introduced. The reconnaissance showed between six hundred and seven hundred self-propelled barges, each between 120 and 150 feet long, in or near Le Havre,

CIC Report No. 85 – Annex A

Ibid. No. 99 – Annex A

AHB IIH/126 Encl 32, Minute Inglis – PS to CAS

CIC Report No. 100, 7 September

Boulogne, Calais, Dunkerque, Ostend and Bruges. About one-third were at Ostend. Barges had been seen on many previous reconnaissances but usually in and near Antwerp and Flushing; and the movement westwards of such large numbers suggested an early date for invasion, since they would not be moved unnecessarily early to positions so exposed to bombing. In addition, those barges that were photographed while at sea were moving in divisions of three and their station keeping was excellent; which indicated that they were manned by trained and disciplined crews, possibly provided by the German Navy. It was concluded, therefore, that invasion by self-propelled barges could be attempted at a very early date. Whether they would carry the main expedition was doubtful. This was expected to come from Hamburg or the Baltic, where the necessary merchant shipping was known to be available. Up to the 7th, no evidence that an expedition was being embarked there had been obtained. But it was an irruption from this area that was felt to be the greatest danger; and the continuous reconnaissance of the Heligoland Bight and the Skagerrak was necessary in order to give early warning of the attack and some much-needed indication of where it would fall. In short, even when these barge movements had been reported, there was much that was uncertain about German intentions.

c. German Night Attacks: Attacks on Shipping: Mine-laying

This was so even as far as German air operations were concerned. For while the day raids clearly indicated at least an intensified air attack in the south-east, if not an actual invasion in that area, the night attacks seemed to point to a long offensive against British industry and trade. The raids against Merseyside, South Wales and the Midlands occupied most of the bomber resources of *Luftflotte* 3, which indeed dropped a greater weight of bombs by night upon industrial targets than was dropped by *Luftflotte* 2 against military targets in the south-east. Thus a large proportion of the available German bomber force was taken out of the daylight battle. *Luftflotte* 3 only began heavy attacks in daylight in the last week in September when it used one *Geschwader* and two *Gruppen* in a series of attacks on the aircraft industry. Its participation in attacks on the 'invasion front' was limited to night attacks on London from 7 September onwards.

The phase was notable also for the reduction in the scale of German mine-laying and anti-shipping activity. Attacks continued to be made by Fw 200s against Atlantic shipping off the north-west coast of Ireland; and off Kinnaird Head KGs 26 and 30 continued to carry out torpedo and bombing attacks on convoys after dark. These two units and a small number of *Gruppen* of coastal aircraft were also employed in minelaying but not to the same extent as in July. There is some evidence that pilots, crews and aircraft from coastal units were being transferred at this time to the German air-sea rescue service; and two coastal units *Gruppen* 606 and 806, that had been employed over the North Sea until the spring, had been re-equipped with long-range bombers. Both were employed in this role as early as the last week in August.[28] The attacks on

28 The Germans may have been to some pains to conceal this conversion. Both units are known to have led the early night attacks against Merseyside and were particularly well trained in navigation. But AI3(b) had no knowledge of these activities and continued to locate them in north-west Germany, whereas in fact they were in Brittany.

Channel shipping that had been so frequent in July and early August virtually ceased, and where made were only the work of single aircraft. Dover, too, the attack of which had earlier caused so much concern, was never attacked in force: the attacks that were made on the Dover balloon barrage were as much a sport as part of a serious military operation. Nor was any attempt made to drive the light forces of the Navy from the Straits; and this, it might have been thought, was an essential preliminary to invasion in that area. This general reduction in activity against maritime targets is reflected in the German claims for the month. *Fliegerkorps* IX, which was chiefly responsible for minelaying, claimed to have sunk or damaged some seven thousand tons of shipping compared to seventy thousand in July. Their September claims were also low – thirteen thousand tons – whereas in October, when minelaying was once more on a large scale, the figures jumped to over sixty thousand tons. Another reliable document gives the claims of *Luftflotte* 3 of shipping sunk or damaged by bombing. For July ninety ships, totalling over three hundred thousand tons, are claimed: for August and for September, less than a third of this amount. Altogether, there was a remarkable singleness of purpose about the daylight attacks during this phase. Very little effort was spared for targets other than airfields or for regions other than the south-east.

iv. Methods of Attack

By concentrating their efforts the Germans were forced to modify the means whereby they attempted to conceal the direction and timing of attack. Earlier in the month they had sought on more than one occasion to achieve surprise by the wide spatial distribution of their attacks: the operations on 14 August in the west of England and on 15 August in the north-east exemplify this method. But different tactics had to be used when the targets to be attacked lay within the comparatively small area of Beachy Head–Guildford–Saffron Walden–North Foreland.

The changes were rung on a number of stratagems. Throughout a day in which heavy attacks were made at intervals, activity over the Straits of Dover was constant; and the operations rooms tables would show a maze of plots in that area out of which would suddenly emerge anything from three to six formations heading for the coast of Kent. The length of warning was, consequently, normally short – of the order of twenty minutes prior to the enemy crossing the coast. It is interesting, however, that the Germans made no attempt to interfere with the observations of the RDF chain by bombing important stations, as they had done earlier in the month. Occasionally, stations reported what appeared to be deliberately jamming; but on the whole little was done to add to the problems of the defence by hampering the warning system.

To the continuous threat of attack was added the difficulty of identifying the bombing formations among the forces that came inland. The Germans rarely attacked more than two targets in any one operation; but it was equally rare for less than four formations to be employed, two being forces of fighters only whose duty was to sweep ahead of the bombing formation or to protect its flanks. In addition, fighter formations often came overland towards the end of an attack in order to cover the retirement. It was to assist in identifying bomber

No. 11 Group Instruction to Controllers, No. 6

as opposed to fighter formations that sighting reports were introduced on 27 August. The bomber formations were normally closely protected by fighters both on the flanks and behind: very rarely was there the 5,000 feet gap between bombers and escort that had been so common in earlier fighting. The bombers flew at 16,000–20,000 feet, coming down to 12,000–15,000 feet to attack their target. Bombs were usually released by the whole formation on a signal from the leader. Frequently, screens of fighters at altitudes of 20,000 feet and over were met with.

Towards the end of the period bomber formations pressed inland to targets in the Weybridge area even though not closely escorted; but there is good reason to believe that the aircraft were from the specially trained fighter-bomber unit, KGr 210. Usually, the escorting fighters did all they could to maintain some protection for the bombers.

v. The Tactics of the Defence

When, towards the end of the previous phase, the Germans had begun to escort their bombers more closely, Air Vice-Marshal Park had instructed his controllers to despatch both Hurricane and Spitfire squadrons to meet bombing raids, whereas previously the Spitfires had been engaging chiefly the high flying fighter escorts. But in this third phase, when our squadrons had to contend with high screens of fighters as well as the close escort of the bombers and the bombers themselves, he returned to the previous system and instructed his controllers to send Spitfire squadrons to engage the highest fighters and Hurricanes to attack the bombers and their escort. Frequently, however, Spitfire squadrons were called upon for the latter task and Hurricanes for the former, much depending on the state of readiness at the time an attack developed. But as for most of the phase the defending squadrons were flying and fighting singly, only too often the units of combat were a British squadron of twelve aircraft at most and a German formation of twenty to forty bombers and up to one hundred fighters. Some British squadron commanders attempted to contain the enemy escort with one flight, and with the other attack the bombers; but time after time, as the narrative has shown, there were sufficient German fighters to engage both British flights. Other commanders abandoned the usual methods of attack from astern and adopted head-on attacks, having in mind the breaking up of the opposing bomber formation before the enemy fighters could intervene. Previously this sort of attack had not received the official approval of the Commander-in-Chief, though he was well aware that it was sometimes being used. But on 25 August he urged its use whenever there was opportunity as a means of counteracting the armour plate which was being fitted to German fighters as well as to bombers. Nor is there much doubt that this was a type of attack that the German bomber crews feared.

Signal C 82, Dowding-Group Commanders

vi. Lessons of the Fighting: The Case for Larger Fighter Formations

It is not surprising that considering the phase as a whole the fighting was not so much in favour of the defenders as that of the previous phase. The ratio of claims of German aircraft certainly destroyed to the number of British fighters destroyed fell from 3 : 1 for the phase 8–18 August to 2 : 1 for that from 24 August to 6 September. The more effective participation of the German fighters was even more strikingly reflected in losses; for whereas during the previous phase twice as many bombers as fighters crashed in England, during the phase under review there were only two bombers for every five fighters. The implication was obvious enough: the ratio of losses would not improve for the defence unless the German attacks weakened or unless they could be met in greater strength.

There was a feeling general throughout No. 11 Group that everything should be done to put more aircraft into one fighting formation and that if this meant sending squadrons into the Group from quieter sectors, then these should be sent. This is quite clear from the minutes of a conference that was held at No. 11 Group Headquarters on 30 August. First, it was suggested that the strength of sector patrols be increased so that the enemy might be engaged over the coast by two squadrons or more, thus easing the task of the squadrons that took off only when warning of a raid had been received. This would have required either an increase in the state of preparedness when squadrons were on the ground or an increase in the number of squadrons in the Group. The first was undesirable as heavy demands were already being made on squadrons: the second was impossible in view of the Commander-in-Chief's policy of maintaining No. 11 Group at a strength of three day fighter squadrons in each sector, and no more. The North Weald Commander then suggested that two squadrons in one sector, should be at readiness at the same time so that they could take off and come into action together. This, too, was turned down, though the Group commander was clearly sympathetic to the idea of larger formations *if there was time to assemble them*. But formations of two squadrons took longer to climb to a fighting height than a single squadron; and this delay could not be accepted when it was proving difficult enough to intercept with single squadrons before the enemy had reached their targets. Moreover, such an innovation would mean that two squadrons would be immobilised on the ground at one station and thus exposed to destruction. Air Vice-Marshal Park agreed, however, that the time had come for larger formations to be used; and instructions were given that, whenever time allowed, squadrons from adjacent sectors should be ordered to a rendezvous prior to being directed together towards the enemy. The policy was applied for the first time on 2 September but not until the second week in September did it become the rule rather than the exception.

The arguments that had been advanced formerly against the use of formations of more than one squadron had been based on the short interval between the initial warning of attack and the dropping of bombs. They were unanswerable during the first two phases of the battle when most of the enemy's targets were in the Channel or on the coast: unanswerable, at any rate, if, as was commonly accepted, it was the prime task of the fighters to prevent the enemy reaching and attacking their objectives. During the third phase, however, the German targets lay further inland; and while warning was still being received only a short time before the coast was crossed, the defending squadrons had a better chance than in the earlier operations to reach fighting height before the target area was reached. It was chiefly for this reason that our pilots were not fighting under the grave disadvantage of an initial inferior height as frequently as earlier in August.

Furthermore, the No. 11 Group squadrons were able to concentrate almost entirely upon the task of meeting the enemy's large-scale attacks. From 30 August the burdensome duty of providing close escorts for convoys was excused them. The change of emphasis of the German offensive, the flying of kite balloons for the protection of the convoys and the more elaborate measures that were being taken by the Navy whenever convoys were passing through south-eastern waters were all good reasons for relieving the Group of what had been a difficult and unprofitable task. Further relief, in an indirect form, was afforded by systematising the arrangements for the despatch of reinforcements from the adjacent Groups whenever the south-east was threatened by a heavy attack, for which the standard was more than one hundred and fifty enemy aircraft. No. 10 Group agreed to send up to two squadrons to patrol the Maidenhead–Brooklands–Guildford area: these squadrons came under the operational control of No. 11 Group. The reinforcements from No. 12 Group were to patrol the sector stations in No. 11 Group north of the Thames, thus allowing No. 11 Group squadrons that would otherwise have been kept over these bases for their protection to be sent to the main area of combat: these reinforcements remained under the control of the Duxford sector in No. 12 Group.

The arrangements applied throughout the phase under review; and their effect was to increase the size of the forces in No. 11 Group that could be sent to intercept the main body of the enemy. Unfortunately, it is impossible to say how the larger formations that thus became possible would have fared against the type of attack that was launched during the third phase; for it was not until the Germans had switched to the attack of London that pairs of squadrons operated together as a matter of course. This, indeed, was a point on which Air Vice-Marshal Park was criticised when, later in the battle, the controversy over the use of wing formations reached the stage of an Air Staff enquiry. Most of the questions that then arose are more properly discussed after the September operations have been described. But this at least is clear from the operations of the third phase, that while a succession of attacks by individual squadrons sometimes thwarted an enemy attack, more often the Germans were able to fight their way through to their target and at the same time inflict dangerously heavy losses on the defenders.

vii. British Losses and their Effect on Fighter Command

It is the losses of Fighter Command rather than any other effect of the fighting that stamp the phase as the most critical of the whole battle. Spitfire and Hurricane losses, including flying accidents, for the fortnight 23 August–6 September totalled 295 totally destroyed and 171 badly damaged (Category 2). Gross output for the same period, including Category 2 aircraft that had been repaired, amounted to 269 Hurricanes and Spitfires; and although the needs of the fighting squadrons were being met it was only by expending reserves that had been built up during quiet periods. That the supply of aircraft never became a factor limiting the scale of operations was due to a great extent to the aircraft industry, to Maintenance Command and the Ministry of Aircraft Production. But is was also due to the lower rate of casualties after 7 September; which in itself emphasises the bitterness of the fighting during the previous fortnight.

As in the previous phase, however, it was the supply of pilots that caused most concern. During the fortnight, 103 pilots were killed or missing and 128 were wounded. Not all the latter were permanently lost to the Command but the total wastage amounted to nearly 120 pilots a week out of a fighting strength of just under a thousand. This would have been an extremely serious rate of loss even if replacements had been forthcoming; for the loss was in battle experience and fighting skill, and not in pilots only. In this respect it is significant that fresh squadrons coming into No. 11 Group from quieter Groups often lost more heavily than tired squadrons that had been stationed in the south-east for some time. Thus, No. 616 Squadron lost five pilots and twelve aircraft between 25 August, when it came into No. 11 Group, and 2 September, when it returned to No. 12 Group; No. 603 Squadron lost seven pilots and sixteen aircraft between 28 August and 6 September; and No. 253 Squadron lost nine pilots and thirteen aircraft between 30 August and 6 September. Of the more experienced squadrons, No. 54, which was relieved on 3 September, had lost nine aircraft but only one pilot since 24 August; and No. 501, which was in the Biggin Hill sector for the whole phase, lost only nine aircraft and four pilots. Much depended on what sector a squadron was operating in. Two of the squadrons stationed at Tangmere, which was a comparatively quiet sector, lost only two pilots during the whole fortnight.

But casualties were the more serious in that replacements were no longer arriving in sufficient numbers to maintain the strength of the fighting squadrons. The measures that had been taken earlier in the month (see pp. 124–125) to increase the output of pilots had hardly begun to show results. For the whole of August, only some two hundred and sixty fighter pilots had been produced by the OTUs;[29] and these additions were outweighed by casualties, which amounted to just over three hundred. The Command was steadily wasting away. On 1 September there were fifty-three Spitfire and Hurricane squadrons (including part squadrons) that were reckoned fit for operations, though these included squadrons refitting and reforming in quiet sectors of the line after a period of operations in No. 11 Group. At an establishment of 26 pilots in each squadron (which was the optimum establishment during intensive operations) their total strength should have been 1,378 pilots. In fact, they mustered 1,023 pilots, including pilots on leave. Nor does this indicate the full extent of the deficiency; for some 160 pilots were 'non-operational', the majority because they had reached a sufficiently high standard of training. There was, therefore, an average deficiency of about ten operational pilots in each squadron. It was not allowed to be so high in the squadrons of No. 11 Group; these averaged 19 operational pilots. On the other hand, there were few squadrons outside the Group that could be regarded as fresh and complete squadrons to take the place of any battle-weary units in the south-east that needed to be relieved. In the words of Air Chief Marshal Dowding: 'By the beginning of September the incidence of casualties became so serious that a fresh squadron would become depleted and

29 It has proved unexpectedly difficult to discover the exact output, chiefly because pilots from other Commands and Allied pilots, in addition to the normal flow of pilots from Flying Training Schools, were being passed through OTUs, most of them taking conversion courses of varying length, of which there are few detailed records. (See Air Historical Branch narrative on Flying Training.)

exhausted before any of the resting and reforming squadrons was ready to take its place'.

Until the first week in September the Commander-in-Chief had maintained his policy of exchanging tired squadrons in No. 11 Group for rested squadrons from the quieter sectors. It was not a policy that was universally approved. Very early in the fighting Air Vice-Marshal Park had asked for trained and experienced pilots to be posted into his Group to maintain his squadrons at full strength and on 30 August he again asked that this should be done whenever a squadron was reduced to fifteen pilots. One of his sector commanders, Group Captain Bouchier, suggested that more squadrons should be stationed in the Group; and that this should be effected by using the pilots and ground staff of each of the squadrons in No. 13 Group as a basis for the formation of two squadrons. Quite apart from the difficulty of providing additional aircraft and tradesmen, many of whom, in particular armourers and wireless mechanics, were in short supply, it is difficult to see how such a move could have improved the pilot position, which was the most pressing problem; and the suggestion was not taken up by the Group commander.

However, a change became inevitable as the first week in September saw no slackening in the rate of casualties. No less than twenty-one squadrons moved into or out of No. 11 Group between 24 August and 6 September; and two more squadrons Nos 1 (RCAF) and 303 (Polish) had become operational since the end of the second phase and were stationed in the Group. These frequent changes were a heavy burden upon the station organisation of the Command and upon the limited resources of transport aircraft and motor transport that were available; and it was usual for only a skeleton squadron – pilots, aircraft and a limited number of ground staff – to be moved.[30] This might have been supportable so long as the squadrons that could be called on as replacements were up to strength and fit to fight. But by 6 September all Spitfire or Hurricane squadrons that could be used in the south-east were either serving in No. 11 Group or the flanking Duxford and Middle Wallop sectors, or had served there in the last month; and the broad position was that no fresh squadrons could be found as replacements for battered units. A new system was inevitable; and the decision to introduce one was taken on 8 September.

viii. The Stabilisation Scheme

It was known as the 'stabilisation scheme' and it bears some examination here, even though it was tested during the fighting of September and October, in that it was a direct effect of the heavy casualties of 24 August–6 September. It entailed dividing the day fighter squadrons of the Command into three categories. 'A'

30 The number of maintenance staff that was moved depended on the length of time that the squadron was likely to operate at the station to which it was moving. If this was for two or three weeks, sixty to seventy men were moved: if for a few days, the move was entirely by air and the number of tradesmen was limited to two per aircraft. Early in the battle a transport flight (No. 271) was put under Fighter Command. It was stationed at Doncaster, which was a convenient centre for the traffic between Nos 11 and 13 Groups. In addition, DH 86 aircraft were allotted to the three southern Groups. Early in August, however, the Air Ministry centralised the control of transport aircraft in order to ensure their maximum use; and Fighter Command had then to apply direct to Air Ministry when aircraft were required for a move. The AOA at Fighter Command, Air Vice-Marshal H.R. Nichol, has testified to the promptness with which all his requests were met. MT companies were also established to facilitate squadron moves. They were located at Darlington, Cambridge and Ightham (Kent).

class squadrons, which were stationed in No. 11 Group and the Middle Wallop and Duxford sectors; 'B' class squadrons, most of which were in Nos 10 and 12 Groups; 'C' class squadrons, which were in all Groups except No. 11, but mostly in No. 13 (and in Nos 9 and 14 when these were formed). The first were to be kept up to strength in fully trained pilots who were chiefly drawn from 'C' squadrons. The latter were allowed only a small number of experienced fighter pilots – usually five or six. They spent most of their time training pilots fresh from OTUs or pilots experienced on other types of aircraft than fighters, but they were reckoned capable of tackling any raids on their sectors, most of which were too remote for enemy fighters to reach. The 'B' squadrons – of which there were only five when the scheme was introduced – were also kept at operational strength and were intended to relieve any 'A' squadrons that needed to be replaced entire. Most of the 'B' squadrons were in No. 10 Group.

The scheme had obvious merits. It avoided the over-frequent moves that the previous policy had necessitated; and squadrons whose pilots and ground staffs had been divorced could be reassembled. It relieved squadrons that were engrossed in the London battle from any responsibility for training and also added to the insufficient capacity of the Operational Training Units. It also concealed to some extent the wastage that was taking place in the Command. But it also had some less obvious drawbacks. It condemned a large number of 'C' squadrons to the unenviable task of training new pilots only to have them posted away to 'A' or 'B' squadrons as soon as they had become efficient. It meant, too, that the only element of elasticity in the Command was represented by the few 'B' squadrons; and 'A' squadrons were consequently kept in the south-east longer than their welfare demanded. It is difficult to see how its advantages could have been obtained in any other way without accepting the same, or worse, disadvantages; but this is not to say that it was admired or liked. In the words of Air Chief Marshal Dowding: 'The stabilisation of squadrons in the line and the creation of class "C" squadrons was a desperate expedient forced upon me by the heavy losses to which the squadrons were being subjected.'

Dowding–US of S 15 November 1940.

ix. German Losses

The remarks that were made when reviewing the second phase of the battle on the size and effect of German losses apply with equal force to the third phase. That is to say that nothing was known for certain about the German casualty rate or the effects that it was having upon the German Air Force as a whole. Indeed, judging from the age and service of prisoners the Germans had not so acute a pilot problem as had Fighter Command. Virtually all pilots who were made prisoner had been trained in peacetime and had an average service of four years in the case of bomber pilots and three in that of fighter pilots. On the other hand, when reviewing the battle as a whole, the Air Ministry interrogation officers believed they saw more definite signs of nervous strain and low morale amongst prisoners taken during the third phase than amongst those captured later in September, when there was a feeling of confidence in the coming invasion and an expectation of early release, or in October, when morale was, to quote the report, 'uninspired and stolid'.

AHB 1D/2/200 Encl 3c

x. Preparations for Further Attacks

But there was nothing to indicate that the German offensive would shortly weaken. Everything that was known about enemy movements indicated rather the reverse; and while the third phase was still being fought out preparations were made for meeting an intensified offensive. All sector and squadron commanders were warned on 3 September of the significant concentration of fighters and dive-bombers in north-east France and were told that the next two weeks would probably see an attempt at invasion, for which the control of the air over south-east England would be vital to the enemy. Part of the immediate German effort, it was believed, would be directed against the aircraft industry in the Thames Valley and at Southampton, where such fighter aircraft production as was within easy reach of France, was situated; the German intention being to do what the attack on airfields alone had outwardly failed to do – materially reduce the scale of fighter defence. The attacks on the Brooklands–Weybridge area on 4 and 6 September indicated that this policy was already being carried out; and on 5 September Air Chief Marshal Dowding directed that the factories in the two areas should be given maximum fighter cover during the next week. It was accordingly arranged that No. 10 Group should send three or four squadrons to reinforce the Tangmere squadrons whenever a strong attack was made across the central Channel towards the Solent. The Kingston, Slough and Brooklands factories were in a less exposed position than those at Southampton and were indirectly covered by all the No. 11 Group squadrons. The only provision that was made for their direct protection was to alter slightly the patrol lines that were manned by the two squadrons which came in from No. 10 Group whenever a heavy attack was made south of the Thames. If called upon, these squadrons were to patrol Brooklands–Croydon and Brooklands–Windsor.

No. 11 Group Instruction to Controllers, No. 10.

But any attacks that might be made against aircraft factories in the latter area would only be a part of the general offensive that the Germans were expected to maintain and intensify against the south-east and the approaches to London; and it was supposed that RDF stations, airfields and communications, as well as aircraft factories, would be the chief targets. There was no prior knowledge, it should be noted, of the switch to the attack of London itself that the Germans were about to make. Air Vice-Marshal Park's preparations for meeting the prospective German onslaught were these.

Ibid. Nos 10 and 12.

In the first place, he was satisfied that the German bombers were sometimes reaching their targets without being attacked, or only lightly attacked, because the controllers at Sector operations rooms were ordering many squadrons to fly too high. Having been much impressed by the regularity with which the enemy had enjoyed the advantage of height during the earlier operations, the controllers had, so to speak, made too large a correction: 'When Group order a squadron to 16,000 feet, Sector Controller, in his superior knowledge, adds one or two thousand, and the squadron adds on another two, in the vain hope that they will not have any fighters above them.' As a result, some enemy formations had slipped underneath our fighters without being intercepted until after they had reached and bombed their objective.

The controllers were, therefore, to apply certain principles when meeting a heavy attack. The main German attack was to be met by as strong a defending force as possible between the coast and the line of sector station. If time permitted squadrons were to be put into the battle in pairs; this applied also to the Hawkinge and Rochford squadrons who were to be ordered to join up over Canterbury. Spitfire squadrons were to engage the enemy's high fighter screen at 20,000 feet, or more: Hurricanes, because of their inferior performance, were to be ordered to 16,000 feet to meet the German bomber formations. A maximum of two squadrons was to protect the stations at Kenley, Croydon and Biggin Hill; and the airfields west and south-west of London would be covered by the No. 10 Group squadrons patrolling in the Brooklands district. North of the Thames, the fighter airfields were to be protected until No. 12 Group squadrons flew south to take over this duty; but immediately these reinforcements arrived the No. 11 Group squadrons were to be ordered to the main battle. Requests for assistance from No. 12 Group were to be despatched through the controller at the Fighter Command operations room.

These arrangements were to receive their first test on 7 September.

V

FOURTH PHASE, 7–30 SEPTEMBER

OPERATIONS, 7 SEPTEMBER

1.

The German operations on this day have generally and rightly been regarded as the beginning of the attack on London. The reasons are obvious enough. Not only were virtually all enemy operations against the United Kingdom concentrated against the capital between 1700 and 1800 hours, but they were followed up by the largest concentrated night attack the Germans had thus far launched,[1] and one which proved only the beginning of a night offensive that continued for over two months.

There is some reason to believe that the Germans put into the day and night attack the highest proportion of their bomber force in the west that could be spared, always bearing in mind the necessity of maintaining the offensive day by day. Certainly, there was peculiarly little activity on the 7th directed against the United Kingdom until the forces selected for the attacks on London began to assemble between 1530 and 1600 hours; and on the two previous days only a small number of bombers had been employed. There was some reconnaissance off the east coast and overland during the morning, including one flight over the Midlands, Manchester, Liverpool and Cardiff by a single Ju 88; and there was also a demonstration in east Kent between 1100 and 1130 hours by some fifty fighters, during which a dozen Me 109 fighter-bombers lightly attacked Hawkinge. One of the reconnaissance aircraft, a Ju 88 from 1/123, crashed into a mountain in mid-Wales; one Do 17 was brought down on Walcheren after a long chase by a section of No. 266 Squadron; one Me 110, probably on photographic reconnaissance, was destroyed south of the Isle of Wight by a section of No. 602 Squadron; but otherwise there was nothing to report.

AI1(K) 455/1940.

2. *Attack on London – Phase 1: First Signs of Attack and Defensive Counter-Measures*

A swift incursion near New Romney at 1545 hours by one of the small formations that were constantly patrolling the Straits was a prelude to the German preparations for their major attack. Ten minutes later the first of three forces of over fifteen aircraft that were detected before 1615 hours was located behind Cap Gris Nez. Another was detected a little later ten miles out from Dunkerque on a course for the Thames estuary, and the third was picked up between Boulogne and St Omer on a westerly course. The reaction of No. 11 Group was to send three individual squadrons towards north-eastern Kent and the estuary, while a wing of two squadrons was sent into the air and retained near London. Thus, No. 253 Squadron, Kenley was directed towards Thameshaven; No. 504 Squadron, Hendon, was ordered to patrol Canterbury; No. 249 Squadron, North Weald, was ordered to patrol Maidstone at 15,000 feet; and two Northolt squadrons, No. 1 and No. 303 (Polish) joined up at 20,000 feet and moved round

1 This was shared in by units of *Luftflotte 3*, which provided no bombers for the day attack. We know for certain that out of two hundred and fifty aircraft which were over London at night one hundred and seventy-four were from *Luftflotte 3*.

London to the north and east. All these squadrons took off at approximately 1620 hours.

At that time a German force of 'twenty plus' was detected off Dunkerque: it came straight across the northern entrance to the Straits of Dover, and with one other force constituted the northern arm of the German attack. But it must be understood that it was extremely difficult for the controllers on the ground to appreciate the position clearly. The Germans went to considerable lengths to conceal both the direction of their attack for as long as possible, and which formations would execute it. Four other forces were located between 1630 and 1637 hours: a small force of 'six plus' fifteen miles east of Beachy Head; an even smaller force just south of Dover; one of 'twenty plus' ten miles south-east of Dungeness; and one of unknown size which was not detected until it was crossing the coast at New Romney at 1637 hours. By that time it was obvious that the enemy was about to attack on a wide front from Beachy Head to the North Foreland and that there would be at least four formations to contend with.

The following British squadrons were ordered into the air:

9 Hurricanes from No. 43 Squadron, Tangmere, to patrol Beachy Head.
9 Hurricanes from No. 111 Squadron, Croydon, to patrol Maidstone.
6 Hurricanes from No. 79 Squadron, Biggin Hill, to patrol base.
12 Hurricanes from No. 501 Squadron, Gravesend, to patrol base.

All these detachments took off between 1635 hours and 1640 hours.

As the last of them took off, a force of twenty or more aircraft (which had been picked up originally behind Boulogne) crossed at Folkestone, making the second German force over Kent. To these was added a third of fifty or more aircraft, which the Observer Corps reported near Hythe on a north-westerly course; and there was another force about to cross between Dover and Deal. It did so at 1645 hours and steered west.

Nine of the No. 11 Group squadrons now had detachments in the air, and to them were now added No. 603 Squadron, which took off at 1645 hours to patrol its base at Hornchurch, and 'A' Flight of No. 66 Squadron, which went up to patrol its base at Kenley. More than half the strength of the Group had now been despatched and combat had not yet been joined. Yet the potential magnitude of the German threat must have been appreciated by 1630 hours at the latest, and a request sent to No. 12 Group through Fighter Command for help in protecting the airfields north of the Thames; for at 1645 hours a wing of three squadrons (Nos 19, 242 and 310) from No. 12 Group left Duxford to patrol North Weald. During the next ten minutes detachments took off from Hornchurch, Martlesham and Castle Camps (a satellite in the Debden sector) to patrol in the Chelmsford–Hornchurch area until the arrival of the Duxford wing freed some of them for action further south. Three more forces were sent up at 1700 hours: No. 1 (RCAF) Squadron, Croydon, to patrol its base; one flight of No. 72 Squadron, also from Croydon, which was directed towards the Thames estuary; and one from No. 46 Squadron, Stapleford Tawney (a satellite in the North Weald sector), which was ordered to patrol North Weald. This completed the defending force until the reinforcements from the Solent area, which had already been requested, began to arrive at about 1730 hours.

Attack on London – Phase II: The First Combats; the Bombing of Woolwich.

No less than twenty-one detachments had been sent into the air between 1620 and 1700 hours, most of them to patrol airfields near London; and it is this which partly explains why no combats had yet taken place although strong German forces had crossed the coast as early as 1640 hours. But it was also partly due to the slow progress of most of the German forces of which only one, which was near Rochester, was further west than a line from Canterbury–Ashford–Tenterden. It is impossible to be certain of this, however, for the tracking of the enemy forces, despite the clear weather, left much to be desired. Throughout the operation enemy tracks were disappearing and reappearing with disconcerting frequency; and to the extent that this narrative is incoherent it only reflects the situation as it appeared to those who were controlling the defence at the time.

About 1700 hours the battle began in earnest. One large German force, which from later reports probably consisted of about eighty bombers in three formations of equal strength each escorted by fighters, was in the neighbourhood of Rochester on an westerly course. As it passed up the river the Thames and Medway guns opened fire, the commencement of a period of intense action that was to last over an hour. It is impossible to say whether this force was attacked by fighters at this time. Both No. 501 Squadron and No. 249 Squadron were in the neighbourhood and were certainly in action at some indeterminate time between 1700 and 1720 hours; but nothing is known for certain. The only fact of which we can be reasonably sure is that at 1715 hours bombs began to fall on Woolwich. It is not even proven, though it is likely, that this attack was carried out by the force that was near Rochester at 1700 hours.

Three targets at Woolwich – the Arsenal, Harland and Wolff's works, and that of Siemens – were all hit and heavily damaged. The German bombers could thus far, therefore, congratulate themselves on a successful attack; for even if it is the case that Nos 501 and 249 Squadrons intercepted them before they reached their target they had not been diverted. But their immunity did not last much longer. Most if not all of the force retired to the north and east, and was engaged on the way by at least seven squadrons. One of the first British formations to attack was the pair of Northolt squadrons, No. 1 and No. 303 (Polish). They were flying at 24,000 feet (somewhat higher than the height to which they had been ordered) when they came upon about forty Do 215s flying northwards. Most of the German rearguard was already engaged with a British squadron (probably No. 603 Squadron from Hornchurch); and what was left was drawn off by No. 1 Squadron which attacked first, leaving the field clear for the Polish squadron. The bomber formation had already been loosened, so pilots reported, by AA fire; and when, just before the squadron attacked, the Dorniers turned east, the whole squadron were able to dive down on them in line abreast from out of the sun. No less than eleven bombers were claimed as destroyed.

The Duxford wing was also in action in this area shortly afterwards against part of the same force. The enemy were sighted to the east of North Weald at approximately 1725 hours, and consisted of some seventy to ninety aircraft at 20,000 feet. The bombers were flying in tight box formation with Me 110s circling round and Me 109s five thousand feet above. Our squadrons were five thousand feet below the enemy (though like No. 303 Squadron, they were flying higher than they had been ordered) and their climb to attack lost them the advantage of surprise. Consequently, the majority of combats were with the escorting fighters. Nevertheless, eighteen of the enemy were believed to have been destroyed at a cost of four aircraft and one pilot. No. 73 Squadron from the North Weald sector also took part in the later stages of the action; its pilots' combats ranging from Billericay in Essex to the neighbourhood of Canterbury. Similarly, No. 504 Squadron engaged retiring forces of both He 111s and Do 215s in a series of combats which began north-east of Hornchurch and ended in the neighbourhood of Manston.

Attack on London – Phase III: Approach of the Second Wave

Combats as satisfactory in outcome as these cannot be ignored; but the fact remains not only that they were with enemy formations which had dropped their bombs, but that bomb-carrying formations were bombing London or approaching to bomb it while one-third of the fighter forces in the air were thus engaged. At least two formations were operating over East London; for bombs fell before 1730 hours on the oil tank farm at Thameshaven and on the dock areas on the north bank of the river at West Ham. One of these forces was engaged by No. 253 Squadron near Thameshaven; but the squadron's reports make it clear that the enemy were retiring.

However, these forces were of little consequence compared to those which were being detected from 1715 hours as they approached the coast. Three formations, each of twenty aircraft or more, were plotted in the Straits at that time, and all crossed the coast between Hythe and Dover before 1720 hours and flew towards London. It was obvious, moreover, that the German concentration was still continuing; for at 1718 hours a large force of fifty or more aircraft was located behind Cap Gris Nez, while five minutes later another formation of unknown strength was suddenly detected a few miles off Dungeness. Both these forces crossed the coast soon afterwards; the first near Folkestone, and the other near Hythe.

Though there is much that is uncertain about the German movements it would appear that this second series of attacks converged upon London from three points of the coast: at least one formation crossed near Hastings; at least one near Folkestone; and at least two crossed near Deal and advanced up the estuary. Each prong of the attack was engaged shortly after it crossed the coast.

At 1730 hours No. 602 Squadron, which was patrolling between Beachy Head and Mayfield at 15,000 feet, saw twenty-eight Do 17s at 18,000 feet flying north-west. An attack was carried out on the rear section of the enemy formation but before our squadron could break away they were themselves attacked by German fighters which had not been spotted previously. Two Spitfires were destroyed for one Do 17 and two Messerschmitts. The squadron also saw two more formations of bombers advancing along the same line. These on reaching the Thames to the south-west of London turned north and east and then made their bombing run over East London.

The forces that crossed near Folkestone were first engaged by No. 43 Squadron which was nine Hurricanes strong. A formation of some twenty Do 215s was sighted as it crossed the coast at 15,000 feet: Me 109s were in close support, and also stepped up above the bombers to 25,000 feet. One section of Hurricanes climbed to attack the fighters while the others engaged the bombers, but the enemy fighters, who were in overwhelming strength, dictated the unequal combat. Three of the Hurricanes were lost for one Me 109. The bombers, in the circumstances, were not diverted from their course.

Shortly before they went in to attack, No. 43 Squadron saw two more formations of the enemy further north on a course up the estuary. It was probably one of these forces that was engaged by No. 257 Squadron between Sheppey and Rochester at about 1730 hours. The Squadron had originally been sent up to patrol Chelmsford, but had been directed across the river. The enemy consisted of forty–fifty bombers flying at the same level, with Me 109s circling round them at 18,000–20,000 feet. One section of Hurricanes succeeded in making a head-on attack on the port section of the bomber formation, but with little effect. Most combats, in fact, were with the German fighters and went against 257 Squadron, two of whom were lost. Some of the squadron pilots stayed in the air until German bombers returned from the East End, and then carried out individual attacks with some success.

The same formation of the enemy may have been engaged a little further west by No. 46 Squadron, which was in action near Thameshaven at approximately 1740 hours, but it was not diverted from its course. Only one other squadron engaged the Germans before they reached their targets: this was No. 609 Squadron which had been sent in from No. 10 Group to patrol between Brooklands and Windsor at 10,000 feet. It was about 1750 hours that the squadron saw a large formation over London surrounded by AA fire. Some very confused fighting developed but it is clear enough that some at least of the German bombers had not dropped their bombs when they were attacked; for more than one pilot reported that they dropped them indiscriminately as they were pursued across London.

Attack on London – Phase IV: The Bombing of the East End

The main weight of the German attack fell on the capital between 1745 and 1810 hours, after which there were very few incidents until the first of the night raiders arrived. A number of enemy forces were plotted after 1740 hours as they approached the coast, but these were probably fighter formations which were acting as rearguards to the retirement of the main forces. Most of the bombs fell on the Commercial Docks, the Millwall Docks, West Ham and Barking, but in addition there was heavy damage at Purfleet, Grays Thurrock and Thameshaven, chiefly to oil storage tanks. At all these places tremendous fires were started, which served as a guide to the large forces that attacked during the night. In addition, the Vicker's works at Crayford was hit; Brentwood was also bombed; and in London itself there were incidents as far north as Tottenham and as far south as Croydon. But the German targets were clearly distributed amongst the riverside boroughs east of the City; and it was there that the heaviest damage was caused to domestic, commercial and industrial property. The last attack was carried out shortly after 1800 hours; and whereas some of the German targets on this day, notably oil farms and docks, were of obvious military importance, on this occasion the bombing affected some of the poorest and most crowded districts in London. Heavy concentrations of bombs fell in East Ham, West Ham, Silvertown, Barking and nearby districts, blasting and burning dozens of working-class streets.[2]

Phase V – The German Retirement

This was the last episode in the enemy's long operation: indeed, the German formations were already retiring when this final attack was delivered. Four British squadrons came into action during this period: No. 234 Squadron from No. 10 Group fought a number of actions between London and Brighton; No. 46 Squadron engaged part of the forces that had been attacking Thameshaven; part of No. 249 Squadron, having taken off for the second time since the attack started, engaged part of a force that was retiring to the north-east; and No. 1 Squadron, which also took off immediately after rearming and refuelling after its previous sortie, succeeded in engaging returning German bombers east of London, though with doubtful success. By 1830 hours, the Germans had cleared the coast and the attack on London was over.

Commentary

The whole operation presents a number of remarkable features. The first and most obvious is that the Germans had struck their first heavy blow at London; they had reached the capital in daylight, and they had bombed it successfully.[3] It is, of course, difficult to assess what damage was caused in isolation from what was effected in succeeding attacks; for the daylight operations of the 7th do not, in one sense, constitute a battle, but only the opening of a battle which was to continue over many days and nights. The very least that can be said, however, is that London could not lightly suffer many more attacks of the same weight and accuracy,

Second, a much higher proportion of the defending squadrons had made contact with the enemy formations than had been the case in the earlier and different type of operations against dispersed targets. No less than twenty-one out of twenty-three squadrons despatched engaged the enemy, two of them on two occasions. The reason is not far to seek. It was simply that the Germans were converging upon one target area for an hour and a half, and made no attempt to evade interception once the coast had been crossed.

Third, the plan which Air Vice-Marshal Park had devised to meet just such an operation as this, and which has already been outlined,[4] seems not to have succeeded; in one of its most important particulars it was hardly attempted. He had intended that the mass of the defending squadrons should meet the advancing enemy between the coast and the sector stations near London. This was certainly not achieved in respect of the first wave of German attack, only part of which was engaged, and then by no more than two squadrons, before it

2 A more precise catalogue of the damage caused and its effects on production and morale has its place rather in the history of the civil departments than here. Its immediate military significance was that it facilitated the work of the night bombers.
3 The Germans reckoned that 316 tons (metric) of HE bombs and 12,800 incendiaries were dropped.
4 See pp. 228–229.

reached the Woolwich area and began to bomb. As for the second wave, three British squadrons certainly engaged the enemy formations before they were within striking distance of London, and one other squadron engaged near London but before the enemy had dropped his bombs; but these could not be reckoned the mass of the defending force, and it is not surprising that, despite the gallantry and determination of the pilots' attacks, the German bombers were not diverted. In any case by the time that the second wave arrived over London twelve British squadrons had already been in action, most of them with a retiring enemy, and were either scattered or were returning to their bases, or both. These squadrons included both the Duxford and the Northolt wings. As we have seen, two of the squadrons that succeeded in engaging the second wave were in action for the second time within an hour. In short, the major part of the defensive effort was employed between 1700 and 1730 hours against the first and less important of the German attacks.

That such squadrons as succeeded in intercepting the Germans on their inward journey were not able to check or disperse them is not surprising in view of the immense disparity in numbers. Inevitably this prompts the question, what had happened to the No. 11 Group plan of operating squadrons in pairs rather than individually? The answer appears to be that it was not applied, except in the case of the Northolt squadrons. We can only suppose that the controller at No. 11 Group considered that there was not sufficient time to assemble pairs of squadrons since from 1640 hours onwards German formations were crossing the coast in a steady stream, demanding interception at the earliest possible moment. Yet he must have given orders for the Northolt squadrons to operate as a pair as early as 1620 hours, for five minutes later both squadrons had left the ground with instructions to join up at 20,000 feet.

The failure, for whatever reason, to employ strong formations of fighters threw into prominence the fourth feature of the operations, which was the high degree of fighter protection given to the German bombers. Large fighter escorts had been encountered earlier in the battle, but squadrons had not previously reported with such unanimity such numbers of fighters, nor such difficulty in reaching the German bombers. Only one squadron, No. 303 (Polish), enjoyed the opportunity of attacking a formation of German bombers without being seriously interfered with by the escorting fighters. Its success, as the squadron commander emphasised, was due in the first place to the action of No. 603 Squadron and No. 1 Squadron in drawing off most of the escorting fighters. If such striking successes were not guaranteed by large formations of defending fighters (the Duxford wing, for example, was unable to neutralise the enemy fighters protecting the bomber formation which it singled out for attack) the experiences of squadrons that went into action alone on this day indicated that they would rarely be achieved in any other way. Apart from the actions in which Northolt and Duxford squadrons took part only eleven bombers were claimed as destroyed compared to twenty-five fighters; including those two actions, twenty-nine bombers and forty-three fighters were claimed. The wreckage of enemy aircraft found after the fighting also reflected its character to some extent. Only two bombers were found compared to fourteen fighters. The bombers were from II/KG 53 and I/KG 76, but it is quite certain that more than two *Gruppen* of long-range bombers took part in the attack: the weight of bombs dropped indicates that at least three complete *Geschwadern* were employed. On the other hand, five *Gruppen* of single-engined fighters and two of twin-engined were identified amongst the fourteen fighters. It is not known, however, how many of these aircraft were destroyed by the AA gunners who claimed no less than twenty-three aircraft.

The high ratio of British losses to claims of enemy aircraft destroyed is accountable to the strength of the German fighters rather than to any improved defensive methods on the part of the German bombers. Twenty-eight RAF fighters were destroyed and sixteen badly damaged; twelve pilots were killed and five seriously wounded. There was thus no reduction in the excess of casualties over the output of trained fighter pilots; and it was on the following day that Air Chief Marshal Dowding reluctantly put into operation the scheme for the grading of his squadrons.[5]

NIGHT OPERATIONS, 7/8 SEPTEMBER

i. Against the London area

As the Germans returned to France after the evening raids on the capital many large fires were raging in the London dock area, and in the oil depots at the mouth of the Thames. The biggest were at the Surrey Commercial Docks, the East India and Royal Albert Docks, Woolwich Arsenal, Barking, Shellhaven, Thameshaven and the Anglo-American oil works at Purfleet. The fire services had little more than two hours in which to extinguish these fires before darkness fell. This was beyond their powers, and the blazing targets of the day were a guide to the German bombers at night.

This is not to say that the night attacks were swiftly organised to take advantage of the situation created by the attacks of the early evening. The speed with which the night bombers took over the offensive from those which had operated by day, and the size of the night's operation, both point to a plan which would have been put into operation whatever had been the result of the earlier raids. In fact, this is the first night on which the Germans carried out attacks clearly integrated with their efforts during the day. Not all their effort was directed against the capital. The Wash and the north-west were also visited. But only about thirty aircraft operated against targets other than London.[6]

It is worth while considering in some detail the first enemy raids to reach London after 2000 hours. In the first place, no attempt was made to intercept them, even though darkness had not settled in; in the second, they set the pattern for the rest of the night's activity.

The RDF stations in the south detected three raids ten to fifteen miles north of Cap D'Antifer between 2008 and 2014 hours, all of them on a northerly course. Two of the raids were estimated as thirty aircraft, the remaining one as six, and all were thought to be flying at about 15,000. This original estimate of strength proved to be excessive, and when the three raids crossed the coast, as they did

5 See pp. 226–227.

6 Of the 188 aircraft that were despatched from *Luftflotte* 3 only fourteen were briefed to attack targets other than London.

just west of Beachy Head between 2022 and 2034 hours, their joint strength was reckoned to be some forty aircraft. But this, in turn, was probably an over-estimate, and it is unlikely, judging by the later courses of these raids, and by the extent of the bombing when they were over the London area, that they mustered twenty aircraft. RDF estimates of enemy strength were never exact at the best of times; and, moreover, on this particular day, the stations in the south and south-east seem not to have been working well; for they ceased estimating the strength of enemy formations from 1720 to 1900 hours.

But this hardly explains why no squadrons were detailed to engage these raids. The only fighter aircraft airborne between 2022, when the raids made their landfall, and 2035 hours, when bombs again began to fall on London, were two Hurricanes from No. 213 Squadron, Tangemere, which appear to have been patrolling near their sector station, but which were not directed to intercept.

The German aircraft flew steadily on to London, dropped bombs chiefly in Battersea, Hammersmith and Paddington, turned round to the south-west, and eventually went out by way of Selsey Bill. Some of them probably dropped their bombs without being hindered by AA fire; for, according to the AA Command 'Y' Form for this period, the guns of the Inner Artillery Zone only began their night's activity at 2100 hours, twenty-five minutes after the first bombs began to fall in Battersea.

The long procession of raids had now begun. Unlike those so far described, they were mostly of single aircraft, but they followed the same route. They came in between Dungeness and Brighton, and, having carried out their tasks, they either flew on over London and left England over the East Anglian coast, or they came south-west and left England by way of the Solent and Selsey Bill.[7]

The majority of the defensive night fighter sorties took place before midnight. Two Blenheims of No 25 Squadron, Martlesham, patrolled near North Weald from 2050 to 2350 hours, but neither had anything to report. Two more AI-equipped aircraft from the Fighter Interception Unit patrolled during the night without success. The unit record states, somewhat sourly, 'Numerous AI contacts were obtained but constant interference from undirected AA fire and searchlights prevented success'. One of these aircraft was one of the eagerly awaited Beaufighters.

After midnight only one patrol was made in the 11 Group area. Again it was by No. 25 Squadron and again without success. But the procession of enemy aircraft continued, most of them following similar routes to their predecessors, i.e. Beachy Head–Biggin Hill–London, and thence south-west and out near the Solent, or east by way of the coast between Foulness and Great Yarmouth. Activity continues until 0345 hours. After that time only one aircraft crossed the south coast on a northerly course. The usual photographic reconnaissance aircraft flew over London between 0705 and 0715 hours.

7 The extent to which the Germans used this route is indicated by the fact that, although there was no bombing in the area, the Solent guns were almost continuously in action from 2320 to 0315 hours.

ii. Night Fighter Activity

The weakness of the defensive fighter effort is obvious enough. To some extent it was due to the strain put on the single-seater fighter squadrons by the evening attack. The squadrons that had been heavily engaged with the enemy could not be expected to operate at night, the more so as every pilot needed all the rest he could obtain before facing the renewed onslaughts which were sure to made on succeeding days. Yet five of the single-seater squadrons in No. 11 Group had not been called upon during the 7th for anything but routine patrols. It is surprising, therefore, that only two sorties were made by a single-seater squadron, No. 213, especially as the Group Commander intended, while giving the bulk of the night work to the Blenheim squadrons, to have one section of single-seater fighters available within each sector. This made a total of twenty-one aircraft of that type which could be called on at night. Moreover, No. 600 Squadron, one of the two twin-engined squadrons which Air Vice-Marshal Park intended to utilise to the full, was unable to make a single sortie during the night; for the smoke from the extensive fires in East London so obscured visibility over Hornchurch that aircraft could not take-off. All this meant that the German bombers attacked London unimpeded by fighter action.

iii. AA Defence

The AA gunners were more active and were rewarded by the only aircraft which was shot down during the night. In the Thames and Medway area there were 120 heavy guns, but many of the German bombers were too far to the west to be engaged by the guns on the South Bank of the river, while those across the river were mostly in action against enemy aircraft which had dropped their bombs and were returning over the Essex coast. Much of the work, therefore, fell on the gunners of the Inner Artillery Zone who were in action from 2105 to 0300 hours. The volume of fire was restricted owing to a prohibition on barrage shoots; and targets were engaged by individual sites when illuminated or when GL date was obtained.

Moreover, the number of guns available was far below establishment, which for the Greater London area was 450 heavy guns. The various AA requirements which had arisen since the outbreak of war had all been partially met by a reduction in the London defences, until only 92 heavy guns were deployed in the Inner Artillery Zone on the night of the 7th. Fifty more were sited for the defence of the aircraft industry in the Weybridge–Slough district. The whole metropolitan area, therefore, including the Thames and Medway zones, was deficient by nearly two hundred guns. During the succeeding three days the position was to be much improved at the expense of other defended areas.[8]

iv. Accuracy of the German Attack

The immensity of London, its nearness to the German bases and, above all, the fires already burning before nightfall, all facilitated accurate navigation; and

8 See Appendix 35.

there was nothing like the dissipation of effort which had attended the attacks on Merseyside at the end of August. Within the LCC [London County Council] area the riverside boroughs east of the City were chiefly affected, as was to be expected, but virtually all districts reported bombs. Railway communications were hit at a number of points.

The Germans estimated that they had dropped 333 tons (metric) of HE and over 13,000 incendiaries on the capital. This was slightly more than in the attacks earlier in the day. Less than ten per cent of this weight of bombs fell outside an area within ten miles of Charing Cross; and to this extent the attack was accurate. But as no comprehensive bomb analyses were made until early in October it is impossible to say what proportion of the German attack fell in the docks area which, presumably, were a special target.

v. German Operations Against the rest of the Country

Over the eastern half of England enemy activity was very slight, and only four incidents were reported north of the Wash; in the west there were only two. It is now known, however, that fourteen aircraft were despatched by *Luftflotte* 3 on dislocation raids *(Storangriffe)* to Falmouth, Plymouth, South Wales, the Solent and Brighton, the Midlands and Lancashire. Six out of ten aircraft from III/KG 27 had Liverpool as their primary target, but no bombs were reported from Merseyside on this night. Two aircraft flew as far north as Cockermouth and Barrow-in-Furness, and one came in at Lyme Bay and flew north-east over the length of England, crossing the coast near Newcastle.

These few raids were sufficiently threatening to force the sounding of sirens in Bristol (4½ hours), Cardiff (4½ hours), Manchester (4 hours), Liverpool (4½ hours) and the Humber area (4½ hours), so they were not fruitless. Nevertheless, it is surprising that so few bombs were dropped.

Commentary

As the first of the heavy night attacks on London that of the 7th is of obvious importance. Moreover, in conjunction with the earlier attacks on the same day it constituted the heaviest single attack which the capital was to suffer until the spring of 1941. But whereas the day battle was one in which Fighter Command was the chief contestant, that at night was sustained by AA Command and the civil defence services. At this stage the contribution of Fighter Command and the government departments on which it was based was more in preparation for night battles to come than participation in those that were actually taking place. There is, therefore, very little to say about the work of the Command on this and on succeeding nights.[9]

From the Air Force point of view the significance of the attack lay chiefly in its confirmation of the change in German policy which had announced itself earlier in the evening, and which had been expected for some days. The Battle of London had begun. The night attack had been the more heavy and accurate because of the success of that by day. Yet events were to show that this was the first and last time that the capital had to endure a heavy blow by day followed by

9 For an appreciation of the night attacks during the remainder of September see pp. 292–293.

one equally heavy the same night. Only two of the twenty-four major attacks which were made on London during the month took place in daylight, representing only five hundred out of over five thousand tons of bombs aimed at the city. In view of the success of the 7 September attack the question arises, why did the Germans virtually cease their daylight attacks on London? An answer can only be given after the rest of the September daylight operations have been reviewed.

OPERATIONS, 8–10 SEPTEMBER

i. General

During the three days following 7 September the Germans mounted one attack by about one hundred aircraft on the 8th and one by a somewhat larger force on the 9th. Otherwise the only activity by day took the form of occasional sorties across the Channel coast by small numbers of fighters, some photographic reconnaissance overland and a small number of attacks on shipping at sea by single aircraft. Fw 200s of I/KG 40 operated daily to the north and west of Ireland and attacked ships shortly after dawn on the 8th and 10th. On the 8th a convoy was attacked without success in St. George's Channel. But altogether there was a general reduction of daytime activity compared to the first week of the month. The night attacks on the capital continued in strength, but here also the weight of attack on each night was only two-thirds of that on the 7th. Except on the 10th the weather cannot be held accountable for this decrease in activity.

ii. Over northern Kent and the Thames Estuary, 8th September

The attack on the 8th took place shortly before noon. It was preceded by a suspicious increase in the strength of the patrols that the enemy had been maintaining over the Straits of Dover during the morning; and to deal with the move that was obviously about to take place ten squadrons from No. 11 Group were ordered into the air, most of them to protect the sector stations near London. The enemy movements resolved themselves into three separate raids. One came in near Dungeness just after 1130 hours, made a sweep as far as Ashford and then turned east and passed over the coast of Dover. Shortly afterwards, a second formation flew in at Dover and dropped a small number of bombs causing damage to houses near St Margaret's Bay.

Both incursions may have been intended to divert attention from the main attack by the third of the German forces. This was made by a formation which crossed the coast near Ramsgate about noon. It had been continuously plotted since 1135 hours and was reported as 'fifty plus'. As it flew westwards parallel to the estuary it continued to be plotted although there was a good deal of cloud at 5,000–6,000 feet. For this reason it is impossible to ascertain exactly where our squadrons came into action or in what order.

No. 46 Squadron came across the enemy somewhere between Maidstone and the Isle of Sheppey and reported that they consisted of about thirty Dorniers at

15,000 feet protected by twenty Me 110s which were circling five thousand feet above the bombers. No. 605 Squadron also observed the same tactics on the part of the Me 110s, but they saw in addition one formation of Me 109s below the bombers and another some five miles behind. No. 46 Squadron, for its part, was hotly engaged by Me 109s when it attempted to reach the bombers and five of the twelve Hurricanes were destroyed or badly damaged for one Dornier and one Me 109; and it would appear that the German force was not checked by this attack. The squadron pilots said nothing in their combat reports about AA activity, but it was about the time that the squadron was engaged, 1215–1220 hours, that the guns of the Thames and Medway zone came into action. It was their efforts, coupled with those of No. 605 Squadron, which was the next British squadron to come into action,[10] which effectively checked the German advance. As our squadron approached the enemy somewhere in the Maidstone–Gravesend area they saw at least one bomber shot down by AA fire; and it was probably to escape further fire that the German formation swung south-west. It did this just as No. 605 Squadron were about to launch a beam attack, and at least one of the British pilots held on his course and made a head-on attack, while others attacked the left flank of the enemy.

Judging by the bombing on the ground and the track charts it seems certain that it was in this area that the Germans decided to call off the attack and make for home. Various small forces broke away from the main force and made off, some going north and east, others south-west and east. Bombs were dropped near Dartford, West Malling, Wrotham and Sevenoaks, indicating jettisoning or attempts to hit railway communications; and the Germans, it should be noted, to the best of our knowledge never used forces such as were employed on this day to sever communications.

Shortly after these actions had been joined another force of about fifteen aircraft came across the Straits and crossed the coast near Dover. About 1230 hours No. 41 Squadron and No. 501 Squadron each had a sharp skirmish with Me 109s in that area. It is more than likely, therefore, that this force was a fighter formation acting as rear-guard to the forces further inland.

Whether, as a prisoner stated, the objective of the attack was the 'Thames Docks', we cannot say for certain. But that the operation was a failure is clear enough. A whole *Gruppe*, II/KG 2, heavily escorted by fighters, had been employed, but no target of military importance had been attacked and such damage to telephone and telegraph services as was caused by the scattered bombing was repaired within twenty-four hours.

AI1(K) No 485/1940

iii. Over northern Kent and SW London Suburbs, 9 September

The next major operation on which the Germans embarked also seemed to us to have failed. Large forces were sent over, including many bombers: indeed there was an impression at the time that the proportion of bombers was higher than usual. Yet the damage on the ground was light and scattered, and no obvious

10 The ORB of this squadron states that at the beginning of the patrol the squadron joined up with eight Hurricanes of No. 253 Squadron. The latter squadron, however, says nothing of any combat on this day. What probably happened, therefore, was that No. 253 remained on patrol over Croydon and Kenley while No. 605 was directed towards northern Kent to intercept.

Fighter Command 'Y' Form, 2100 hours, 9 September

military target was hit.[11] Moreover, the German formations failed to display their usual determination to press on to their targets despite interception: signals instructing formation leaders to break off the attack if strong opposition was met were intercepted.

The exact pattern of the operation cannot be reconstructed. At least six enemy forces crossed the coast between the North Foreland and Beachy Head between 1655 and 1700 hours, but not all of them were continuously plotted; for there was much cloud (7/10ths) between 6,000 and 7,000 feet although visibility above cloud was good. The main attack, however, was made in two waves: one came in between the North Foreland and Dover at 1655 hours, and the other between Beachy Head and Dungeness twenty minutes later; but there were also a number of fighter forces ranging ahead and to the flanks of the main formation. While it will be convenient to describe the operation in terms of these two waves, this will inevitably mean a simplification of events; for there were enemy forces over east Sussex and Kent whose movements are inextricably hidden in the fog of war.

a. The Attack on Canterbury, 1655–1720 hours

The strength of the German patrols over the Straits had been increasing since 1605 hours and half an hour later formations of over twenty aircraft were being plotted. By 1650 hours six raids of an average strength of thirty aircraft were over the northern part of the Straits and off Calais, and four of them were moving towards northern Kent and the Thames estuary. The first defensive moves had been taken as early as 1630 hours when No. 92 Squadron went up from Biggin Hill to patrol Canterbury; and between 1645 and 1655 hours seven more detachments took off and moved towards the threatened area:

> No. 41 Squadron from Hornchurch to patrol Maidstone.
>
> No. 46 Squadron and No. 249 Squadron from North Weald to patrol Rochford.[12]
>
> No. 501 Squadron from Gravesend to patrol Canterbury at 25,000 feet.
>
> No. 66 Squadron from Kenley to patrol Maidstone at 20,000 feet
>
> No. 257 Squadron from Martlesham to patrol West Mersea.
>
> No. 603 Squadron from Hornchurch: their orders are unknown.
>
> No. 605 Squadron from Croydon to patrol Maidstone at 15,000 feet.

Meantime, heavy attacks were being threatened further south where large formations were moving from the Pas de Calais towards Sussex; and shortly

11 That the attack on Canterbury was intended to damage the operational control and administration of the troops in South-East Command is a possibility that should be borne in mind.

12 This was an application of Air Vice-Marshal Park's policy of operating squadrons in pairs whenever possible. These two squadrons, however, were maintained on patrol over Rochford throughout the operation.

after 1645 hours No. 11 Group requested reinforcements from both the flanking Groups. Consequently, as the squadrons in northern Kent were coming into action other squadrons from the Group were moving to the hinterland of Beachy Head and Dungeness to intercept the second German attack, while squadrons from No. 10 Group and No. 12 Group came in to protect the aircraft factories in the Thames Valley and the sector stations north of the Thames.

Of the squadrons that were despatched to meet the northern attack four were only taking-off when the enemy were crossing the coast; and the first shock of attack fell upon Nos 41 and 92 squadrons. Little is known of the composition of the enemy force: both squadrons simply reported a large formation of bombers escorted by Me 109s. No. 41 Squadron were attacking the bombers between Canterbury and Maidstone when No. 92 Squadron came up; and the latter engaged about twelve Me 109s. No. 501 Squadron were also in the neighbourhood, but only one pilot glimpsed the enemy: it is probable that the height at which the squadron was patrolling, 25,000 feet, was too high and the enemy slipped underneath them.

What happened after these initial engagements is obscure. No. 605 and No. 603 squadrons both engaged an enemy formation of some twenty He 111s protected by fighters. In the case of the first squadron the action began near Farnborough, Kent and ended near Farnborough, Hampshire; and No. 603 Squadron, which had taken off from Hornchurch, reported combats as far west as Horsham. No. 66 Squadron, on the other hand, engaged part of the original force near Maidstone and reported that it was flying north-west. Moreover, approximately fifty bombs fell at Canterbury at 1715 hours, having been dropped by the German forces about the time that No. 41 Squadron came into action. The Home Security reports also mention incidents in rural districts of Kent, but do not specify them. From all this seemingly disconnected evidence it would appear likely that there were either two German forces, one of which dropped bombs on Canterbury and then steered east, the other going on towards London, or that the original force was split by the attacks of our fighters in the Canterbury–Maidstone area. All that can be said with safety is that up to 1720 hours the only bombing of any moment had taken place at Canterbury. After that time the only incidents that could possibly have been the work of the northern arm of the German attack took place at West Ham at 1738 hours; they were unimportant.

So far, therefore, of the six squadrons that had been ordered to northern Kent to intercept five had made contact with the enemy. They claimed seven bombers and nine fighters destroyed at a cost of five aircraft to themselves.

b. Over Sussex and South-West London

While this confused fighting had been taking place the No. 11 Group controller had been making the necessary dispositions to counter the second wave of the enemy's attack, which by 1710 hours was approaching Beachy Head. The squadrons that he ordered up were as follows:

No. 607 from Tangmere at 1700 hours to patrol Mayfield at 15,000 feet.

No. 602 from Westhampnett at 1704 hours with the same orders.

> No. 17 from Tangmere at 1705 hours to patrol base.
>
> No. 1 (RCAF) and No. 303 (Polish) from Northolt at 1720 hours to join up over base.
>
> Duxford wing (Nos. 242, 310 (Czech) and 19 squadrons) left at 1700 hours to patrol North Weald.

No. 609 Squadron from No. 10 Group was on its way to patrol Brooklands-Guildford by 1705 hours, and one section of No. 234 Squadron, Middle Wallop, patrolled Brooklands below cloud level. At 1735 hours, when the enemy had already crossed the coast, No. 229 Squadron was sent up to protect Northolt, and No. 72 Squadron to protect Biggin Hill.

At 1720 hours the main German force crossed the coast and flew steadily inland for twenty miles before being intercepted in the Mayfield district by No. 607 and No. 602 squadrons. The enemy consisted of thirty to forty Dorniers in vic formation at 16,000 feet, with a smaller box formation of more bombers, including He 111s some distance behind. There were many fighters about but none seemed to be escorting the bombers closely. No. 607 Squadron who were taking part in their first big battle after a long stay in No. 13 Group, first engaged the enemy. They succeeded in getting above the German formation and dived down upon it; but matters went ill with the squadron who lost four Hurricanes for only one Dornier. However, they succeeded in forcing one section of Dorniers to break away and two aircraft were destroyed by No. 602 Squadron. The main body of the enemy continued on a north-westerly course towards Brooklands.

The next actions concerned No. 253 Squadron and the Duxford wing; and although for the sake of symmetry it is tempting to assume that these forces took over the fight from No. 607 and No. 602 squadrons there are a number of points which cannot be reconciled with such a reconstruction. In the first place, No 253 Squadron engaged a force of thirty-four Ju 88s (the pilots were quite sure of this figure) which approached Kenley from the east; and if the squadrons in action near Mayfield had reported correctly this was an entirely different formation. The Duxford wing seems to have engaged yet another force. Its leader sighted an enemy force fifteen to twenty miles to the south-west when he was near Hornchurch, which would place the enemy in the Biggin Hill-Kenley area. When eventually the wing closed with the enemy 'over the south-western suburbs of London' they reported two large rectangular formations of sixty aircraft each, which was a much larger force than anything which had been reported previously. Nevertheless, the number of bomb incidents during the time the enemy were over south and south-west London was far smaller than was to be expected if there were three large German forces. In the absence of any certain information a mere catalogue of engagements is all that is possible.

The first to follow those that had taken place near Mayfield was between No. 253 Squadron and the Ju 88s which we now know were part of KG 30. The British squadron climbed into the sun, then turned east and dived down on the starboard beam of the bomber formation. Five were believed to have been shot down, and the formation was broken up, many aircraft jettisoning bombs as they fled southwards. A second attack was impossible as Me 109s came down in answer to a Verey signal from the bombers, but the squadron had sharply checked the enemy. Three aircraft of this *Geschwader* were found on the ground well south of the area where combat was first joined. The unit was one of those which had come south from Denmark and Norway earlier in the month.

The Duxford wing also broke up at least one of the two bomber formations which it encountered. Similar tactics were adopted to those of the 7th: No. 19 Squadron (which had lately exchanged its cannon Spitfires for the normal type) climbed to engage the enemy fighters while the Hurricanes went for the bombers. There were too many Me 109s for one squadron to contain and both the Hurricane squadrons fought numerous combats with fighters. Even so, many of the bombers jettisoned their bombs; and the track charts indicate clearly that one part of the force made off to the south-west by way of Kenley, while the others escaped round north London. The final actions were between the Northolt wing and scattered formations of the enemy, all of them on a southerly course. The wing had taken off too late to intercept the enemy on their inward flight.

c. Summary

At the time that the Duxford wing and No. 253 Squadron were in action, 1745–1800 hours, small packets of bombs were dropping in southern suburbs of the capital. Kingston, Barnes, Richmond, Epsom, Walden, Purley, Surbiton and Norbiton all had incidents to report; and nearer the centre of London bombs fell in Wandsworth, Lambeth, Fulham and Chelsea. This was not the sort of bombing associated with an aimed and deliberate attack such as that against the riverside boroughs on the evening of the 7th; and it is this feature more than any other which justifies the view that the attack was a failure; for it is beyond doubt that the German targets were within the London area. At least four long-range bomber *Gruppen*, four of single-seater fighters and two of twin-engined fighters took part in the operation. This was a force capable of striking the capital a very heavy blow, but it was barely one third the size of the force that attacked two days before.

As on the 7th the proportion of interceptions to sorties was high. A total of twenty-two squadrons and parts of squadrons, was sent off in the south and south-east during the operation. Of these six were maintained on security patrols over airfields or on set patrol lines and were given no opportunity of engaging the enemy. Of the rest fifteen out of sixteen came into action.

Twenty fighters were destroyed outright during the fighting, and six more were badly damaged; five pilots were killed or missing and nine were wounded. Forty-eight German aircraft, twenty of which were bombers, were claimed as destroyed by fighters, and six by AA fire. Eighteen of these crashed on land or close inshore.

If, therefore, as we believe, the Germans attempted on the evening of the 9th a further stroke against the capital they must have been grievously disappointed at the result.

OPERATIONS, 11 SEPTEMBER

The relative calm of 10 September continued until well into the afternoon of the following day: not until 1450 hours was there any sign of a big attack. Then in quick succession formations of 'twenty plus' and 'twelve plus' were located south of Cap Gris Nez. Both came across the Straits between 1500 and 1510 hours and crossed the coast near Folkstone. They flew west for a time, then north to Maidstone and finally out by the North Foreland. No bombs were dropped; and the operation was undoubtedly a feint attack intended to divert defending squadrons from the larger forces which, from 1500 hours, were assembling in the Pas de Calais. It proved a failure, however, for it was not intercepted, chiefly because it was carried out so swiftly that few British squadrons were in the air before the raiders had re-crossed the coast.

The Germans may also have intended to draw off some of the defending squadrons from the usual avenues of approach to London by mounting an attack in the central Channel. Preparations for this were detected off the mouth of the Seine and off Cherbourg between 1520 and 1545 hours, the period in which the main concentration was being effected further north. It was left to the Tangmere squadrons to deal with, and did not affect the attack on the capital. It will be considered in detail after the main attack has been described.

i. Against London, 1530–1700 hours

The information received from the RDF stations between 1500 and 1520 hours pointed to a big attack across the Straits; and the following squadrons were sent up to intercept between the coast and the line of sector stations near London:

At 1510 hours	No. 46 from Stapleford No. 504 from Hendon	to join up over North Weald; thence to patrol Gravesend at 15,000 feet.
At 1515 hours	No. 253 from Kenley No. 501 from Kenley	Both were directed towards Maidstone[13]
	No. 41 from Hornchurch No. 603 from Hornchurch	to patrol Maidstone: their orders are unknown.
At 1520 hours	No. 92 from Biggin Hill	to patrol Maidstone

As these squadrons were climbing to their patrol lines the German movement began to take shape. Two formations – one of 'fifty plus' and one of 'one hundred plus' were approaching the coast near the South Foreland at 1535 hours, while one of 'fifty plus was between Folkestone and Dover ten minutes later. This distinction between a northern and southern arm of attack was maintained throughout the advance; and such other formations as were occasionally plotted were purely fighter formations. Except for these two forces the Germans did not despatch any bomber formations as far as we know. Each contained at least two *Gruppen* of long-range bombers; those in the north being I and II/KG 1, while

13 According to the ORB of No. 501 Squadron they took off 'in company with No. 253 Squadron to patrol Maidstone', but there is no other evidence that the two units operated together. Their combat reports indicate that they operated independently: they do not appear even to have been in action in the same area.

further south were I and II/KG 26. All these units, however, were equipped with He 111s, and as more than one British squadron reported the presence of other types of bomber it is unlikely that these were the whole of the bomber forces employed. It is not yet known what fighter units participated. Only three of the eleven aircraft that crashed on land were fighters. They were all from JG 51.

a. The Advance in the North

The larger of the two main forces, that further north, was the first to be attacked. Nos 46, 504, 92 and 253 squadrons had been directed towards the Dover area when it became clear that the enemy would cross in that neighbourhood, and all were in action between 1545 and 1600 hours, during which time the fight swung north towards Gravesend. Their reports are consistent on one point, that there were between thirty and forty bombers escorted by upwards of thirty Me 109s and 110s, but there was no agreement over the type of bomber. Some pilots reported that the formation contained only He 111s; others were sure that there were only Do 215s; still others that both types were present. The point cannot be resolved solely from British sources.

It is fairly certain, however, that the enemy formation was flying between 15,000 and 18,000 feet and that there were protecting fighters both in advance and in the rear of the bombers and slightly higher. Nevertheless, each British squadron succeeded in carrying out a beam attack upon the bombers before the German fighters intervened. Indeed the chief features of the engagement were first that the German fighters showed less than their usual determination to protect the bombers and, second, that none of the British squadrons reported the presence of any other friendly fighters, although four squadrons were in action with the same enemy formation within a period of a quarter of an hour or less. In all, RAF squadrons claimed ten bombers and two fighters at a cost of five aircraft.

As far as can be ascertained each of the four squadrons had been in action against only one, and that the smaller, of the two formations that composed the northern force. Henceforth, however, other squadrons were almost continually engaging the enemy between Maidstone and the south-east suburbs of London; and it is impossible to distinguish which enemy force was attacked by the individual squadrons. The second batch of squadrons to be sent up to engage the enemy's more northerly forces, was made up thus:

> No. 72 Squadron from Croydon at 1525 hours to patrol base at 15,000 feet: they were then directed towards Gravesend.
>
> No. 249 Squadron from North Weald at 1525 hours to patrol the river east of London docks.
>
> No. 222 Squadron from Hornchurch at 1528 hours to patrol base at 15,000 feet.
>
> At 1530 hours the Duxford wing from No. 12 Group left to patrol Hornchurch-North Weald.
>
> No. 66 Squadron from Gravesend at 1535 hours 'to intercept a raid approaching from the south-east'.

> Nos 17 and 73 Squadrons from Debden at 1545 hours to patrol Rochford at 15,000 feet.
>
> No. 605 Squadron from Croydon at 1545 hours to patrol base at 15,000 feet: they were then directed towards the east.
>
> No. 257 Squadron from Martlesham at 1545 hours to patrol North Weald at 15,000 feet. (They were kept on patrol in this area and were the only squadron despatched that did not engage the enemy.)

No. 72 Squadron encountered a formation of sixty Do 17s and He 111s protected by fighters, near Maidstone: bursts of AA fire from the Thames and Medway guns first drew the attention of our fighters. The German force was flying north-west at 21,000 feet but the British squadron climbed above and carried out an effective attack on the port side of the formation. Four of the bombers were believed to have been destroyed. It was about this time, 1530–1545 hours, that bombs were dropped in rural districts of Kent to the north-west of Maidstone. They were probably jettisoned by some of the bombers in this particular enemy force. Further north and east a small number of bombs were dropped on the Isle of Grain at 1540 hours.

No. 222 Squadron from Hornchurch was also in action before 1545 hours, but seemingly with another force; for they reported a formation of He 111s and Ju 88s, with the usual fighter protection, at 24,000 feet (one of the highest altitudes at which formations of bombers had so far been seen). Again the squadron got above the enemy and dived down on the rear section of bombers, claiming three of them as destroyed at no cost to themselves. Some of the German bombers were certainly turned back as two of them crashed near the coast between Hastings and Dungeness. No. 605 Squadron then came into action, probably with the same force as had been engaged by No. 72 Squadron. The pilots experienced little interference from the escorting fighters and were convinced that they forced at least a part of the German force to retire.

It is fairly safe to say that by 1600 hours neither of the two formations that made up the northern arm of the enemy attack had escaped interception. At this stage the Duxford wing came into action. It had been arranged that the two leading squadrons (No. 19/266 and No. 611) should engage enemy fighters leaving No. 74 Squadron free to attack the bombers. The plan was not entirely successful, partly because there were too many enemy fighters, and partly because the leading squadrons did not concentrate on the fighter escort. No. 19 Squadron, in fact, started the action by carrying out a head-on attack on the leading formation of Heinkels. No. 611 Squadron opened with an attack on a formation of Me 110s, but as was to be expected as soon as the action began each pilot attacked the most favourable target irrespective of type.

The German force that was engaged bore some resemblance to that engaged earlier by No. 222 Squadron. There were two *Gruppen* of bombers, each escorted by fighters, flying at 21,000–24,000 feet. AA fire first attracted the attention of the wing leader, for which he was duly grateful; but fire continued even after the action was joined and two British fighters were hit. The claims of the wing were very large, and amounted to nineteen aircraft, seven of which were bombers, at a cost of only three of their own aircraft. What was almost as important was that part of the German force was turned away to the south-west and is unlikely to have reached its target.

But it is quite certain that a good proportion of these northerly forces reached the dock area, which was one of the German targets; for at 1620 hours No. 249 Squadron encountered 'a large compact vic of fifty He 111s at 19,000 feet' over the London docks. Bombs were being dropped as the squadron came up and shortly afterwards the enemy made off to the south-east. The British pilots remarked with no little pleasure the very small fighter escort; and as they were flying ten thousand feet above the bombers the fighters were unmolested in their first attacks. No. 501 Squadron, who were surprised by enemy fighters, also saw a bomber formation making for the river.

Most of the bombs that fell on London during the attack fell between 1610 and 1630 hours, beginning at Woolwich in the east and ending near Paddington. Half a dozen districts were involved – Lewisham, Deptford, Bermondsey, Islington and Paddington – and there was some evidence that the Germans had been attempting to hit railway communications as well as docks. But there was nothing like the concentration of bombs that had fallen during the attack of the 7th, and the total weight dropped was under one hundred tons.

The German operations were not finished when these bombs had been dropped; the retirement had still to be carried out; and it was harassed by three more British squadrons. Two of these, No. 17 and No. 73, formed a wing, and they came across about twelve Me 110s flying east near Herne Bay at 10,000 feet, destroying two of them. This was doubtless a formation which had either completed its escort duties or had lost its bombers owing to a previous combat. By 1715 hours, however, the skies over northern Kent and the capital were virtually clear of the enemy.

b. The Advance further South

The German forces that came overland near the South Foreland, and whose activities have now been sufficiently reviewed, were followed by another force that crossed the coast near Dungeness and steered towards Tunbridge Wells. Fifteen squadrons had already been despatched to deal with the forces nearer the river when the second threat developed and only four squadrons, one of them a reinforcement from No. 10 Group, were available to meet it. They took off as follows:

> No. 303 Squadron (Polish) } from Northolt at 1530 hours to patrol in
> No. 229 Squadron } the Biggin Hill area.
>
> No. 238 Squadron from Middle Wallop at 1530 hours to patrol Brooklands–Weybridge below cloud.
>
> No. 1 Squadron (RCAF) from Northolt at 1540 hours: their orders are unknown.

The Germans advanced unopposed until they reached the neighbourhood of Reigate where they were sighted by the Northolt wing at about 1610 hours.

There were two formations of bombers flying at 20,000 feet, one containing He 111s and, possibly, Do 17s[14] and the other Ju 88s. There was a gap of four to five miles between the two and each had its allotment of protecting fighters. Both the Northolt squadrons attacked the leading force; No. 229 attacked the leading vic of Heinkels head on, while the Polish squadron came round and attacked the middle and rear sections. The tactics were abundantly justified. The leading vic of the enemy turned back and flew south before it had been attacked, and the rest of the formation appeared to be broken up by subsequent attacks. Large quantities of bombs were reported to have been jettisoned; and there was certainly no bombing further north during the next fifteen minutes that could have been the work of this formation. Moreover, No. 1 (RCAF) Squadron was engaged in this area about this time with He 111s which were on a southerly course. These may have been retiring from the engagements further north and east; but it is more likely that they were retreating after the actions near Reigate.

The second enemy force, however, pressed on towards London, only to be intercepted by No. 238 Squadron somewhere between Brooklands and Croydon. The squadron inflicted some damage on the enemy but failed to turn the formation – there were about thirty bombers – from their course; and it participated in the bombing of London between 1620 and 1630 hours. Its movements after 1630 hours are uncertain, but it does not appear to have been intercepted on its return journey.

ii. Against Southampton, 1545–1630 hours

The emergence of two raids from the Cherbourg peninsula and the Seine at much the same time as German formations were moving across the Straits of Dover indicates that the enemy hoped to contain the Tangmere and Middle Wallop squadrons by this threat to the Solent; and in fact the Tangmere squadrons took no part in the battle further east and only one Middle Wallop squadron was sent into the London area. In fact, the raid was left entirely to the Tangmere squadrons to deal with.

The squadrons in question, Nos 213, 602 and 607, were ordered up between 1540 and 1550 hours. For the time being they were maintained on patrol over the airfield but at 1550 hours the first two were directed towards Selsey Bill, where the two enemy forces seemed likely to converge, while No. 607 remained to protect Tangmere. No. 602 Squadron had been instructed to tackle the German fighters and No. 213 the bombers, and together they flew out to sea to meet the attack, No. 602 in front and slightly the higher of the two.

The enemy were sighted about five miles east-south-east of Selsey Bill just before 1610 hours. At first only about twenty Do 17s or Me 110 bombers (pilots were not sure which) protected by a similar number of Me 110 fighters could be seen, but soon a formation of Me 109s was observed about twelve

14 No. 229 Squadron reported only He 111s, but the Polish squadron saw Do 17s also and claimed to have shot down three aircraft of this type. However, the bombers that crashed on land during the battle were without exception He 111s. The day was notable for the number of reports of unusual aircraft. Two pilots in different squadrons thought they saw a Ju 52 another reported a Ju 86 and a fourth reported 'several very large aircraft escorted by strong contingents of fighters'.

miles behind the rest of the German forces. It would appear from this that the synchronization of the German attack was not all it was intended to be.

Both British squadrons attacked from the west and, selecting their respective opponents, dived down on the enemy, who were at 15,000 feet, before the Me 109s arrived. The Me 110s adopted their usual tactics of forming a defensive circle and although the fight tended to move towards the coast it did so only slowly; and all the aircraft that our pilots claimed to have destroyed, fell into the sea.

The interception had been timely and the attack itself not unsuccessful; for at least seven of the enemy were believed to have been destroyed at a cost of one Spitfire and two Hurricanes. Nevertheless, it is fairly certain that very shortly after the action had been joined some, if not all, of the German bombers had broken away, gone on across the coast and behind Portsmouth towards Southampton. The guns there were in action from 1613–1618 hours, and at 1615 hours what were described locally as 'six dive-bombers' attacked the Cunliffe Owen aircraft works at Woolston.[15] A fire was started in a recent extension to the factory but it was soon extinguished and there was no damage to plant. More serious was the loss of life amongst the workers, forty-one of whom were killed.

Just after 1630 hours the Solent was clear of the enemy, and from then on there was little to report. There were one or two threatening moves by what turned out to be purely fighter formations between 1800 and 1830 hours near Dover; and two squadrons were brought into No. 11 Group from No. 12 Group to protect two of the sector stations near London. However, no attack developed.

iii. Summary

That the German operations since 1500 hours, including the diversionary attack on Southampton, had been intended to strike a powerful blow at London is scarcely to be doubted; but the damage that was caused was slight and scattered. There was no single incident in the metropolitan area that is worth remarking here; certainly there was nothing comparable to what had been achieved during the evening attack of the 7th or on any of the nights since that date. The aircraft losses that had been suffered in repelling the attack were not small – twenty-four fighters were destroyed and nine badly damaged – but only eleven pilots were killed and four wounded. What the precise German losses were is not known, but the claims included fifty bombers and thirty fighters destroyed. This was a significant ratio and confirmed our pilots' impressions that the German fighters were not in such strength as earlier in the battle, nor were they as determined to protect their charges. The AA gunners of the IAZ and the Thames and Medway zones also claimed the destruction of six aircraft: only sixteen guns in the IAZ had gone into action, an indication of the German failure to penetrate into London proper.

Looking back it can now be seen that the whole operation displayed some of the earliest signs of a weakening in the German day offensive. Indeed it may well be found when more German records are open to examination that this day

15 The German target was actually the Supermarine works. According to German records, just over eleven tons of bombs were dropped.

marked the beginning of a new policy – the attack on aircraft factories in the south and south-west – that was soon to demand more of the *Luftwaffe's* energies in daytime than the attack on London. Whether this be so or not, it can fairly be said that the second of the two attacks that had been launched against London by day since the 7th had failed like the first to do anything like the damage commensurate with the forces employed.

OPERATIONS, 12–14 SEPTEMBER

a. 12 and 13 September

A marked deterioration in the weather on 12 and 13 September gave the defences a respite from large-scale attacks, but on both days the Germans took advantage of the cloudy conditions to send single aircraft deeper into the country than was usual in daytime. Air Ministry buildings at Harrogate, an aluminium works at Banbury and the railway junction at Reading were attacked by single aircraft on the 12th, and at the last two places railway traffic was affected. On the 13th there was rather more of the same sort of activity, commencing with the first incidents to be reported in Ulster where a few bombs were dropped by a Fw 200 of I/KG 40 which was looking for shipping in Belfast Lough. Most bombing, however, took place in and near London. Hornchurch was attacked at 1017 hours by a single He 111 but there was no important damage to the airfield. Buckingham Palace, the Admiralty and the War Office were slightly damaged in the morning; and in the evening two or three raiders attempted without success to hit St Pancras and Marylebone stations. Minor bombing was reported from a large number of London districts, and probably between fifteen and twenty aircraft succeeded in reaching the capital. Only a few interceptions were effected, but Fighter Command was compensated by two of its easiest days since the beginning of July.

b. 14 September

i. General

Similar armed reconnaissance to those of the 12th and 13th were all that the enemy embarked upon in the morning and early afternoon of the 14th. There were incidents in Essex and east and south-east London in the morning; and in the afternoon Norfolk and Suffolk, and coastal districts in Sussex and Hampshire, including Southampton, were attacked by single aircraft. There was one serious incident as far north as Warrington where the works' canteen of the Thames Board Paper Mills was hit at 1700 hours.

Weather conditions were rather better than on two previous days, although there was still a good deal of cloud between 5,000 and 10,000 feet, and the number of interceptions was correspondingly greater. Four of them were carried out by No. 74 Squadron at various points between Ipswich and Great Yarmouth; and there were also six combats between Swanage and Beachy Head.

ii. Against London, 1515–1900 hours

During this period there were two distinct enemy attacks, in each of which some two hundred enemy aircraft took part. A small force of Dorniers was employed in the first attack (1515–1630 hours) but only three were sighted, each flying alone. The number of bombs dropped was very small; and none was reported during the second attack. Both attacks, therefore were demonstrations in force by the German fighters; and their chief interest lies in the foretaste they gave of the type of operation that was to become so common in October.

a. 1515–1630 hours

From 1500 hours onwards German formations were plotted over and behind Calais as they concentrated prior to moving west across the Straits. These preliminary movements took quite twenty minutes, probably because the enemy leaders wanted to reach 20,000 feet before commencing the attack; and the first of the German forces did not cross the coast until 1530 hours. Four separate formations then crossed between Dover and Ramsgate during the next fifteen minutes and two near Beachy Head. All advanced at least as far as a line Biggin Hill–Tilbury, but two advanced as far as the Inner Artillery Zone, which they reached shortly before 1600 hours. All the bombs that were to fall on London during this and the succeeding attack fell between 1600 and 1605 hours in Camberwell, Battersea and Chelsea. Battersea power station was hit and a gasometer in the same borough; and the line from Victoria to Clapham Junction was damaged. Between ten and fifteen bombs were dropped.

By 1615 hours all enemy aircraft were on east or south-easterly courses; and by 1630 hours the whole operation was over, having lasted barely an hour. The speed of the attack, the height (20,000 feet) at which most of the enemy operated and the fact that the first British squadron did not take off until only five minutes before the Germans crossed the coast, sufficiently account for the failure of the great majority of the defending squadrons to intercept; for of twenty squadrons and wing formations despatched only four made contact with the enemy. In three cases the combats were mere skirmishes with small fighter formations over the estuary. The exception was an action between Nos 222 and 603 Squadrons, who were operating from the Hornchurch sector as a wing, and a large but unspecified number of Me 109s between Canterbury and Dungeness. The wing was flying at 24,000 feet but the bulk of the Me 109s were even higher; and our squadrons had to form a protective circle and climb to the attack. Somewhat surprisingly they were not themselves attacked while carrying out this manoeuvre and they were able to take the fight to the enemy. At no cost to themselves they shot down four Me 109s. Two of these crashed on land, one of them proving to be from 1/JG 77.

b. 1745–1900 hours

The proportion of interceptions to take-offs during the next German attack was higher, the explanation being that eight defending squadrons were airborne within five minutes of the enemy crossing the coast, as compared to only two squadrons during the previous attack. All interceptions – six in all – were the work of these first squadrons.

The operation had many features in common with the previous one. It was carried out at 20,000 feet and higher, by five separate formations, three of which flew as far as Biggin Hill–Chatham; the others flew on, one to the west of Kenley, the second over London.

All combats took place over northern and eastern Kent. The Hornchurch wing again engaged large forces of Me 109s between Canterbury and Dungeness. Another wing (No. 504 from Hendon and No. 46 from Stapleford Tawney) joined up over Maidstone and shortly afterwards engaged two separate formations of twenty and seventy Me 109s. A further force of sixty Me 109s was seen nearby. Nos 41, 66, 72 and 92 Squadrons were likewise engaged chiefly with Me 109s between Tilbury and the North Foreland. Some pilots reported that the Germans were using He 113s, which were painted the same shade of blue as our own fighters, and that this caused no little confusion of identity. Henceforward reports of He 113s were to become more frequent.

By 1900 hours the last of the German fighters had departed after an operation for which neither side had much to show in the way of casualties: eleven British fighters were lost and much the same number of German. It was probably sufficient justification for the German operations that twice within two hours they had forced No. 11 Group to despatch most of its available squadrons and even to call on No. 12 Group for assistance: all this to meet a threat which was hardly a threat at all to targets on land.

OPERATIONS, 15 SEPTEMBER

At dawn on Sunday the 15th the weather was fine and visibility was good; but as the morning wore on cloud steadily formed over south-east England until by the middle of the afternoon there was thick cloud (8/10th–10/10ths) at 4,000–6,000 feet.

There was some reconnaissance over the west and north-west between 0900 and 1100 hours, while in the south-west an He 111 was shot down off Bolt Head shortly after nine o'clock. In the south-east there was nothing significant until 1000 hours when there was an increase in the number of patrols that the Germans were maintaining over the Straits of Dover. At 1040 hours two of these came overland at Dover and Ramsgate, only to return east almost immediately. By 1100 hours it was obvious from the forces that were massing near Calais that a big attack was imminent; and a large force of British squadrons was sent into the air in the next twenty-five minutes.

i. Against London, 1130–1245 hours

a. The German Assembly and the first British Moves

It was a further half hour, however, before the first of the enemy forces crossed the coast of Kent; and the success that the RAF squadrons later enjoyed was not least due to the unusually long interval between the first warning of attack and the enemy's advance. The controller at No. 11 Group not only had sufficient time to couple ten squadrons into wings, he was able also to bring in reinforcements from the adjacent Groups before the first German force crossed the Coast: in particular the Duxford wing was airborne at 1125 hours whereas the enemy did not cross until 1133 hours.

The squadrons that were ordered up at this stage were as follows:

> At 1105 hours No. 72 and No. 92 squadrons from Biggin Hill to patrol Canterbury at 25,000 feet.
>
> At 1115 hours No. 229 and No. 303 (Polish) squadrons from Northolt to patrol Biggin Hill at 15,000 feet.
>
> At 1115 hours No. 253 and No. 501 squadrons from Kenley to patrol Maidstone at 15,000 feet.
>
> At 1115 hours No. 17 and No. 73 squadrons from Debden to patrol Chelmsford at 15,000 feet.
>
> At 1120 hours No. 504 Squadron from Hendon and No. 257 Squadron from Martlesham to meet over North Weald at 15,000 feet and then patrol Maidstone.
>
> At 1120 hours No. 603 Squadron from Hornchurch to patrol Dover at 25,000 feet.
>
> At 1120 hours No. 609 Squadron from Middle Wallop (No. 10 Group) to patrol Brooklands–Windsor at 15,000 feet.
>
> At 1125 hours Nos 242, 19, 302 (Polish) 310 (Czech) and 611 squadrons from Duxford (No. 12 Group) to patrol Hornchurch: the wing flew at 25,000 feet.

b. The German Advance (I)

The great majority of the German forces crossed the coast between Dover and Ramsgate between 1133 and 1140 hours. They were arrayed in three columns which flew north to begin with, then turned south-west for Maidstone, where they spread out before flying over the London area. It is as near certain as is possible in the absence of the relevant German records that the number of bombers employed was not more than forty and may have been as few as twenty: most of III/KG 76 was certainly in action and in addition there may have been some aircraft drawn from I/KG 76. As for the fighters, we know positively that at least two complete *Gruppen* took part in the close escort of the bombers; but there were certainly others over the south-east at the same time.

Within a few moments of crossing the coast, the main enemy body was brought to action, first by the Biggin Hill squadrons – Nos 72 and 92. Our force was between Canterbury and the coast when they sighted the approaching enemy who were described by No. 72 Squadron as a formation of Do 17s at 22,000 feet with an escort of Me 109s below them. No. 92 Squadron, however (and this illustrates how varied are impressions gained in this type of warfare) reported that the bombers were at 15,000 feet with Me 109s above them. The facts probably were that the escorting fighters were ranged on the same level and above the bombers. Each British squadron was armed with Spitfires and carrying out their instructions to clear the way for later attacks by Hurricane squadrons upon the German bombers, each opened the engagement with the escorting fighters. No. 603, another Spitfire squadron, who were over north-east Kent about this time, also engaged high-flying Me 109s.

Not all the escorting fighters were diverted by these attacks; for when the next British squadrons – Nos 253 and 501 – came into action they reported that there were about twenty Do 17s at 17,000 feet and above them an escort of fifty fighters, including He 113s. Both squadrons carried out head-on attacks in a shallow climb on the leading section of the enemy formation; and between them they claimed to have destroyed at least three bombers and two fighters. This engagement began about 1145 hours in the Maidstone area.

c. Despatch of Further British Squadrons
By that time the last of the defending squadrons that was to take part in the battle had left the ground. Altogether, six squadrons had been ordered up since the Germans had first crossed the coast. They were:

> At 1135 hours No. 249 Squadron and No. 46 Squadron from North Weald: they were ordered towards South London.
>
> At 1140 hours No. 1 Squadron (RCAF) from Northolt and No. 605 Squadron from Croydon to join up over Kenley at 15,000 feet.
>
> At 1140 hours No. 41 Squadron from Hornchurch to patrol Gravesend at 20,000 feet.
>
> At 1142 hours No. 66 Squadron from Gravesend to intercept the approaching enemy.

d. The German Advance (II)
After the combats over Maidstone the enemy was further engaged by Nos 41 and 66 Squadrons, operating independently of one another, south-west of Gravesend. No. 66 attacked the bombers and shot down at least one Do 17, but No. 41 were entirely engaged with Me 109s, which dived down and prevented an attack on the bombers.

The main battle, however, took place further to the north-west and began as the Germans approached south-east London. It was opened by Nos 257 and 504 Squadrons who had been ordered towards London from their rendezvous over North Weald. Just after noon they sighted over south London what they described as: 'A square formation of twenty-five Do 17s and 215s in five lines of five aircraft in line abreast, all at 18,000 feet, with escorting yellow-nosed Me 109s at 23,000 feet.' This was undoubtedly the identical force that had been so heavily and continuously engaged since crossing the coast.

Both squadrons attacked the bombers from the starboard quarter and experienced surprisingly little interference from the enemy fighters; which feature was also remarked by the other squadrons that were in action during the next twenty minutes. It is clear from their combat reports that shortly after the engagement opened, Hurricanes and Spitfires from the Duxford wing also joined in the fighting. Both these formations arrived over south London between 1205 and 1215 hours.

The North Weald squadrons sighted a formation of Heinkels, which was engaged by a few of their pilots. Otherwise most combats were with the self same formation of Dorniers and their escorting fighters as had been engaged so often already. Similarly, the Duxford squadrons were in action with the same force. The leader of this wing was forced to delay his attack until the No. 11 Group fighters had cleared away. Then as arranged, he led his three Hurricane Squadrons against the bombers while his two Spitfire squadrons went for the enemy fighters. Most of the latter, it was reported, broke away and climbed towards the south-east, leaving the fighters a free hand with the Dorniers. Nor is there much doubt that many bombers were destroyed. The total claims of the four No. 11 Group squadrons – Nos 257, 504, 249 and 46 – that took part in this engagement amounted to seven Dorniers destroyed and a number damaged at a cost of two Hurricanes. The Duxford wing claimed to have destroyed no less than nineteen bombers and seven fighters.

e. *The Bombing of London*

Most of the bombs that fell on London during this attack fell in the ten minutes after noon. Some pilots of No. 504 Squadron reported that high-level bombing was taking place as they attacked the enemy formation: No. 249 Squadron also reported that one flight of Dorniers broke away from the main body and dived down through the clouds as though to find their targets. In short, the bombing took place during the first few minutes of the engagement over south London. It achieved very little: an electricity station at Beckenham was hit; house property was damaged in Lewisham, Battersea, Camberwell and Lambeth; two bridges between Clapham Junction and Victoria were hit; and one unexploded bomb fell on the lawn outside Buckingham Palace. The number of bombs dropped indicated a force of about thirty bombers at the very outside.

f. *The Retirement*

The remaining enemy bombers retired first to the west until they were somewhere near Brooklands and then to the south. Some of the German fighters, however, returned by way of the estuary and north-east Kent. On both routes the enemy were brought to action. No. 609 Squadron engaged two formations of fifteen Do 17s, escorted by Me 109s and 110s, near Brooklands at 1215 hours. No. 605 Squadron engaged the same formation further south, and No. 1 (RCAF) Squadron were in action with Me 109s in the same area. Further east, the Northolt squadrons met formations of fighters returning east.

g. *Summary*

That this attack was roughly handled is obvious enough. The early warning of the German concentration enabled large defending forces to be set in motion, which, as it turned out, were overwhelmingly stronger than those of the enemy. On their way inland the German formations had to withstand the attacks of four separate pairs of No. 11 Group squadrons and then the powerful blow dealt by the Duxford wing; and in addition three more No. 11 Group Squadrons – Nos 603, 41 and 66 – flying alone, engaged part of the escorting fighters on the way in. During the German retirement four more British squadrons made interceptions.

That the claims of pilots were excessive is equally obvious; but this was unavoidable when as many as half a dozen British fighters had engaged, often unknown to one another, one and the same victim. The probability is that about ten bombers and twice as many fighters were destroyed at a cost of fourteen fighters destroyed and five badly damaged: only seven British pilots were killed or missing, and four wounded.

ii. Against London, 1345–1530 hours

a. The German Assembly and the first British Moves

Signs that the Germans were once more concentrating, and again in the Calais-Boulogne area were received shortly after 1345 hours. None of the enemy formations began to move west until 1405 hours, by which time twelve British squadrons were already in the air:

> At 1400 hours No. 222 and No. 603 squadrons from Hornchurch sector took off to patrol Sheerness at 20,000 feet.
>
> At 1400 hours No. 17 and No. 257 squadrons from the Debden sector took off to meet over Chelmsford at 15,000 feet.
>
> At 1400 hours No. 249 Squadron from North Weald and No. 504 Squadron from Hendon took off to meet over Hornchurch at 15,000 feet.
>
> At 1400 hours No. 605 Squadron from Croydon and No. 501 Squadron from Kenley took off to meet over Kenley at 5,000 feet.
>
> At 1405 hours No. 92 Squadron took off from Biggin Hill to meet No. 41 Squadron over Hornchurch at 20,000 feet.
>
> At 1405 hours No. 229 and No. 1 (RCAF) squadrons took off from Northolt to patrol base.

b. The Beginning of the German Advance

At 1405 hours three German forces left the Calais area and moved west, crossing the coast between Dungeness and Dover between 1415 and 1420 hours and advancing on parallel lines towards Tenterden and Maidstone. There were over one hundred and fifty aircraft in these three formations according to the RDF observers. The Observer Corps could not confirm or amend this estimate; for there was so much cloud that they were unable to keep continuous track of the German formations, much less estimate their size. Between 1420 and 1435 hours five smaller forces totalling some ninety aircraft crossed in the same area and flew after the first formations. These were probably purely fighter formations.

By 1415 hours most of the British squadrons that were to engage the enemy had taken off; not with as much time to spare as in the morning attack but, as we shall see, sufficiently early for the majority of them to intercept before the Germans reached London. These squadrons were as follows:

> At 1410 hours No. 41 Squadron from Hornchurch to patrol base at 25,000 feet.
>
> At 1410 hours No. 46 Squadron from Stapleford Tawney: they were ordered towards the London docks.
>
> At 1410 hours No. 66 Squadron from Gravesend and No. 72 Squadron from Biggin Hill to meet over Biggin Hill at 20,000 feet.
>
> At 1410 hours No. 73 Squadron ('B' Flight only) from Castle Camps to patrol Maidstone at 15,000 feet.
>
> At 1415 hours No. 253 Squadron from Kenley to patrol base at 15,000 feet.
>
> At 1415 hours No. 607 and No. 213 squadrons from Tangmere to patrol Biggin Hill–Kenley at 15,000 feet.
>
> At 1415 hours the Duxford wing (Nos 242, 19, 302 (Polish) 310 (Czech) and 611 squadrons) to patrol Hornchurch at 25,000 feet.
>
> At 1415 hours No. 238 Squadron from Middle Wallop to patrol base: then ordered to the Brooklands–Kenley line.

The exact number of bombers employed by the Germans is not known: but judging from their own claim to have dropped some one hundred and thirty tons of bombs during this attack and from RAF pilots' estimates of their numbers, one hundred to one hundred and twenty were used. There is a rough confirmation of this from the wreckage that was found on the ground after the battle, amongst which bombers from six different *Gruppen* were identified: usually the Germans employed about two-thirds of the first-line strength of a *Gruppe* in a major attack.

The enemy crossed the coast in three large bodies before 1420 hours: the aircraft that crossed the coast after that time were chiefly fighters. One force – the most southerly one – which set a course from Dungeness towards Tenterden was composed of Dorniers 17s; the centre one – which flew on a roughly parallel course from Folkestone towards Maidstone – was a mixed body of He 111s and Dorniers; while the most northerly force, which flew from Dover towards Gravesend, was composed chiefly of He 111s. Each bomber formation was escorted by a similar number of fighters; but there were also purely fighter formations ranging over the south-east during the operation, which brought the fighter:bomber ratio to something like 2:1. Even so, this was a smaller proportion than was normally employed; which was reflected by the number of crashed enemy aircraft, sixteen bombers and only eight fighters, found after the fighting.

The three formations advanced over a front of less than thirty miles; and it is impossible to describe the fighting in terms of attacks on each of the main forces; for some British squadrons attacked more than one bomber formation. However, the first attack was made by the Hornchurch squadrons who made contact with the enemy south of Canterbury. The German bombers were flying very high (22,000 feet) with Me 109s below and 110s above. Our fighters attacked the bombers but were themselves attacked by superior numbers of Me 109s, and although only two British pilots became casualties they were not able to check the enemy's advance. At least one pilot saw two formations of Do 17s, forty aircraft in all, flying inland apparently unescorted.

The next attack was the work of five Hurricanes of No. 73 Squadron. They reported a large diamond shaped formation of about fifty Dorniers and Heinkels and fifty Me 110s at 15,000 feet near Maidstone. No attempt was made by the German fighters to baulk this small formation – possibly it was deemed to small – and all of them attacked bombers, three of which were damaged.

So far the northerly German forces had advanced without meeting very heavy opposition; but from Dartford to London they were constantly attacked. First by Nos 66 and 72 squadrons; then by Nos 504 and 249; next by the Debden and Kenley squadrons; and finally by Nos 92 and 41 squadrons and by the Duxford wing. By the time that these last forces came into action, 1450 hours, some, if not all, of the German bombers had dropped their bombs; for bombs were reported from numerous districts west of Dartford after 1435 hours.

By that time, too, the most southerly of the three enemy bomber formations was approaching south London. It had been engaged in the Edenbridge area by Nos 213 and 607 squadrons, which were diverted to intercept while on their way north to patrol Biggin Hill. These squadrons reported a formation larger than those further north: eighty Do 17s (and possibly some Ju 88s) in two formations of forty at 13,000 feet. The only enemy fighters that were seen were some Me 109s about five miles to the east which made no attempt to interfere. No. 213 Squadron attacked one Dornier formation head-on, while No. 607 attacked from the starboard quarter. Great destruction was claimed – amounting to at least six Dorniers – and a number of bombers were seen to jettison their bombs and return east. However, most of the enemy continued inland and were over south London before 1500 hours.

Attacks by our squadrons and the bombing of the metropolitan area were going on simultaneously from 1450–1515 hours. Ten squadrons from No. 11 Group and the Duxford wing were all in action during these twenty minutes, most of them with the forces that had advanced from Maidstone. Those that came in further west were also engaged over London, but they had enjoyed an easy passage since their interception by the Tangmere squadrons. The Northolt station commander, who took off alone at 1440 hours, carried out a head-on attack on part of this force and reported that he turned a portion back; but most of it was unmolested until it was over the city.

There then took place a series of actions more successful for the defenders even than those of the morning. With the exception of the Duxford wing and the Debden squadrons our pilots remarked the comparatively few fighters that were present and of the seeming timorousness of those that were. The Duxford wing, however, which was still climbing when it first sighted the enemy over south-east London, was forced to change its planned tactics as a result of enemy fighters attacking the three Hurricane squadrons; and instead of the latter attacking the bombers, the two Spitfire squadrons took over this task, while the Hurricanes fought the fighters – indeed they had no choice in the matter.

Including the actions further east and south, pilots claimed to have destroyed fifty-nine bombers and twenty-one fighters: their own losses were eleven aircraft destroyed and nine badly damaged. Casualties in pilots were remarkably low, four being killed or missing and five wounded.

c. The Bombing of London

But in contrast to their attack at noon the enemy had at least something to show for their bombing. A large number of riverside boroughs reported incidents, most of them the result of bombs that fell between 1445 and 1515 hours. The most serious incidents were at Littleborough near Dartford, where an electric power station received three direct hits; at East Ham, where a telephone exchange was put out of action and a gas holder was destroyed; at West Ham, where an electricity transformer sub-station was completely destroyed and the adjacent generating station heavily damaged; and at Erith, where an oil works was hit and set on fire. Railway communications were damaged at West Ham and at Penge. However, there was nothing like the damage caused by the raid of the 7th, when nearly three times the tonnage was dropped and when the damage was concentrated on a smaller area. For this reason, if the weight of bombs dropped is to be reckoned an index of the German offensive, it is wrong to speak of this day either as the culmination of the attacks on London or as the crisis in the battle as a whole.

d. The German Retirement

As after the morning attack, some of the German forces retired first to the west and then south, others by way of the estuary and northern Kent. Along the latter route No. 303 (Polish) Squadron engaged a force of Dorniers protected by fighters, claiming three Dorniers and two Messerschmitts at a cost of two Hurricanes. Further west the two Middle Wallop squadrons and No. 602 Squadron from Westhampnett came into action, each chiefly with bombers. At little cost to themselves they claimed seven bombers and two fighters, thus making the total claims for the operation, including those of the gunners of the IAZ and the Thames and Medway zones seventy-seven bombers and twenty-nine fighters. Again it must be recorded that the actual German losses are unlikely to have been so large. Twenty-four enemy aircraft crashed on land, and though these alone represented losses twice as heavy as our own, they are themselves only a proportion of what the Germans lost. What that loss was precisely we do not know.

e. Summary

The success of the defenders in the morning attack was largely due, we have said, to the unusually long warning of attack that was received. To some extent this was true also of the second attack; for before the Germans had crossed the coast eleven British squadrons had taken off. A similar number of defending squadrons, however, only took off after the advance inland had begun; and while most of these were in time to intercept before the enemy had swung round after bombing the capital, few of them managed to come into action before the

German bombers had released their loads. South London, in short, was a fighting area and bombing area at much the same time. If the Germans had advanced with their customary directness, it is almost certain that they would have been retiring before the mass of the defending squadrons had overtaken them and brought them to action. As it was, their leading formations took over half an hour to fly the sixty miles between the coast and the outskirts of London; and this was largely accountable to the unwieldiness of the German formations, which might have been acceptable if powerful fighter escorts had been used, but which, in their absence, served only to multiply the targets of the defending fighters.

iii. Against Portland, 1500–1545 hours

The German operations were not over when the second attack on the capital had been repelled. A sortie across the central Channel was undertaken just as the climax of the attack on London was reached; for at 1455 hours a force that was plotted as 'six plus' flew north from the Cherbourg peninsula towards Portland. Whether it was intended to divert the Middle Wallop squadrons from the battle further east is not known. If it was; it was an ill-timed move as Nos 238 and 609 Squadrons had already been transferred to the control of No. 11 Group.

The threat was left to No. 152 Squadron to deal with. It is not known at what time they left their base at Warmwell but they failed to intercept before the German force had dropped its bombs on the harbour at Portland. The enemy had come straight across the Channel to St Alban's Head and there turned west, arriving over Portland at 1530 hours. They proved to be stronger than the RDF stations had indicated; for there were at least twenty He 111s and no fighters.

The attack was carried out very swiftly and only one of the Portland gun sites came into action. Fortunately, little damage was done. House property was damaged near the Verne citadel; some unexploded bombs forced the evacuation of a few streets; there was a certain amount of damage to telephone cables; and there were incidents in the dockyard which the naval authorities reported as insignificant.

The enemy force did not escape unscathed. No. 152 Squadron succeeded in closing with it five miles south-east of Portland Bill as it retired; and at least one Heinkel was destroyed.

iv. Against Southampton, 1740–1815 hours

There was one more noteworthy operation before the Germans ceased their attacks for the day. At 1740 hours a raid of 'twenty plus' was picked up just north of the Cherbourg Peninsula. It made across the central Channel for the Isle of Wight and at 1750 hours was three miles south-west of St Catherine's Point. By then Nos 213 and 602 Squadrons were patrolling near Tangmere, where they were kept for the duration of the raid. No. 607 Squadron, also from Tangmere, was flying from its base to Southampton at 15,000 feet; and No. 609 Squadron was on its way from Middle Wallop to patrol Portsmouth. At 1800 hours, by which time the German operation was virtually over, the British dispositions were completed when No. 238 Squadron took off from Middle Wallop to patrol it.

The enemy's target was the Supermarine aircraft works at Woolston; and they arrived near it at 1755 hours. They were engaged by the Southampton guns throughout the attack, which was over a minute or two after 1800 hours. But not until the German retirement was well under way did any British squadron come into action.

Fortunately, the Germans failed to hit the Supermarine works. There was severe damage to property in the Woolston district; a number of gas and water mains were cut; and there was slight damage at the works of J I Thorneycroft, the shipbuilding firm. According to German records, between ten and eleven tons (Metric) of bombs were dropped; sufficient, if they had hit the works, to retard seriously the production of Spitfires.

Both Nos 609 and 607 squadrons engaged the Germans south-west of the Needles, reporting that there were thirty to forty Me 110s and about fifteen Do 17s. The number of bombers was probably rather lower judging by the weight of bombs that was dropped. Each squadron succeeded in reaching the Dorniers and each claimed to have shot two down into the sea; so the Germans did not carry out the attack without loss. The fact remains that they had succeeded in penetrating well up the Solent and carrying out an attack that came perilously near to success without being attacked on the inward journey. The RDF stations were certainly not to blame; for they had given warning of the approach quite twenty minutes before bombs began to fall on Woolston. The fault was rather with the controllers at No. 10 Group and No. 11 Group who were too late in ordering the defending squadrons to the Southampton district.

With the interception near London just before seven o'clock of two Heinkels that were doubtless reconnoitring the damage that had been done in the earlier raid, the day's operations came to an end. The claims of the fighter squadrons totalled one hundred and seventy-four aircraft destroyed, making a grand total, with the claim of the anti-aircraft gunners, of one hundred and eighty-five, of which one hundred and twenty-seven were bombers. It is chiefly on account of these claims, which were the highest made by Fighter Command, that 15 September has been observed as a day symbolical of the achievement of the Command over the four months of battle, July to October. Whether it was a day from which the Germans expected any specially fruitful results or whether it occupied any unique place in their plan of action is somewhat doubtful. In any case, a consideration of the significance of this day for the phase of the battle of which it was only a part must wait until further operations in September have been described.

OPERATIONS, 16 AND 17 SEPTEMBER

It is impossible to be certain whether the operations of 15 September had any effect upon the policy of the German commanders; for the weather on the two following days was sufficient explanation for the reduced scale of enemy activity. There was a good deal of cloud at low altitudes on both days, while on the 17th a strong wind at times reached gale force.

On the 16th about one hundred enemy aircraft came over the coast of Kent soon after 0730 hours; but no attack developed. Later in the day, single aircraft were active over widely separated regions of the country taking advantage of cloud to penetrate well inland. Most of them, however, flew towards the London area above cloud; and bombs were reported in the afternoon from eight districts of south and south-east London.

On the 17th the enemy's activity took a similar form. One Ju 88 came as far north as Merseyside to attack, without success, Rootes' aircraft factory at Speke. But most of the German sorties were made between 1500 and 1600 hours when about one hundred and fifty enemy aircraft in nine separate formations swept in as far as the Rochester district. A heavy attack seemed to be beginning and twenty squadrons from No. 11 Group and the customary reinforcements from the adjacent Groups were sent into the air. Six No. 11 Group squadrons intercepted over northern Kent and all reported meeting only enemy fighters. Casualties were light on both sides and no bombs were dropped.

OPERATIONS, 18 SEPTEMBER

With the return to finer weather on the 18th, the Germans again operated in some strength against targets in Kent. Three attacks were carried out in the morning, early afternoon and early evening. In no case did the Germans penetrate to London; and what little evidence there is concerning their targets indicates that these were all in towns on the shores of the Thames estuary.

i. Against Tilbury, 0915–1010 hours

The first attack was first detected at 0910 hours when the enemy were still concentrating their forces over the eastern side of the Straits of Dover. But it was over twenty minutes before the first German formation crossed the coast; and by then twelve squadrons had taken off from stations in No. 11 Group. Landfall was made between Hythe and Sandwich by three of the German formations and near the North Foreland by a fourth; and all advanced towards the Rochester area.

Their advance, and such bombing as they were to undertake, was completed by ten o'clock; and immediately they began to retire. It was for this reason, coupled with the fact that most of the German forces consisted of fighters flying at 20,000 feet and over, that only six of the defending squadrons were able to intercept despite the adequate warning that had been received. This was a sample of an interception problem that was to become increasingly acute.

Only one of the British pilots reported sighting any enemy aircraft other than fighters. The exception was a pilot of No. 92 Squadron who had lost his squadron and who attacked a single Do 17, escorted by three Me 109s travelling west over northern Kent. But as Tilbury was bombed by more than one aircraft – the local anti-aircraft gunners reported an indeterminate number of Heinkels – just after 0950 hours, the enemy bombers obviously evaded interception. However, their bombing was inaccurate: the docks were not hit and damage was confined to houses.

None of the German fighters was claimed as certainly destroyed whereas five of our own fighters were shot down. It was possibly with this aim in view rather than the destruction of targets on land that the attack was launched. Its smallness in comparison with the attacks of the 15th and even more so of the 7th needs no comment.

ii. Against the Chatham district, 1220–1330 hours

The Germans again concentrated near Calais shortly after noon; and the first British forces began to patrol at 1220 hours. Not until between 1230 and 1240 hours did the bulk of the attacking forces cross the coast, by which time ten defending formations including a wing of three squadrons from Debden, the Duxford wing and four pairs of squadrons from sectors in No. 11 Group – had been despatched to patrol in northern Kent and southern Essex.

Five enemy raids were plotted as they crossed the coast between Dover and the North Foreland: four flew north to Whitstable and then due west; but one, which was plotted as 'one hundred plus' came towards Maidstone, turned north-east for Sheerness and then returned via Dover. This last force was almost certainly entirely composed of fighters; and such bombers as the Germans employed were amongst the aircraft that flew due west over the south side of the Thames estuary.

Only the first British squadrons to take off – Nos 249 and 46, who had left North Weald together at 1220 hours to patrol Gravesend at 20,000 feet – succeeded in engaging enemy bombers, and only three more squadrons were able to get to grips with the German fighters; for, as in the earlier raid, the enemy came in high and fast and carried out their attack within twenty minutes of crossing the coast. But the one interception of the German bombers was enough to put them off their aim. The North Weald squadrons sighted a force of about fifteen bombers, with a fighter escort, at about 18,000 feet east of Gillingham. A head-on attack was made, under the direction of the leader of No. 249 Squadron, as the quickest way to break the enemy formation; and while it is not certain that this was achieved, it is clear that the Germans were not allowed to bomb accurately. All their bombs fell in or near Gillingham, well to the east of the complex of naval targets in the Chatham–Rochester area. The anti-aircraft gunners also played a useful part in repelling the attack: 227 rounds were fired by the Thames and Medway guns on the south side of the river, between 1246 and 1301 hours, by which time the German force had swung round to the east.

During this action and the fighter v fighter engagements that took place, six RAF fighters were lost as against a claim of four of the enemy: three enemy bombers were damaged. Only one of the two Me 109s that crashed on land could be identified: it was one of a formation of eight aircraft from JG 27. In addition, No. 303 (Polish) Squadron shot down a Do 17 from 4/Ob d L that was on a photographic reconnaissance flight.

iii. Against Tilbury and Targets in the Medway, 1600–1745 hours

The third and last of the German attacks in the south-east on this day was also the largest. It fell into two phases: a swift attack between 1600 and 1630 hours against oil installations at Port Victoria in the Medway and one against Tilbury beginning shortly before 1700 hours and ending about three-quarters of an hour later.

Very little is known of the first attack. A force plotted as 'one hundred plus' came in at the North Foreland at 1600 hours and flew due west as far as Gravesend, where it turned round and returned on its own tracks. The first British squadrons to be sent up only left at 1555 hours and none of them intercepted the German force; and apart from a few rounds fired by the Medway guns at 1610 hours against a group of fighters there was no opposition to the attack. There was little damage at Port Victoria: one Admiralty tank was hit but the fire was soon under control.

But the defending forces that had taken off too late to check this swift incursion were in good time to meet the second German attack. Moreover, there had been no slackening of enemy activity over the Straits of Dover and behind Calais when the retirement from the Medway attack had been under way; and in consequence the Duxford wing, which had taken off at 1615 hours, remained on patrol between Hornchurch and Thameshaven. This wing, No. 41 Squadron and Nos 92 and 66 Squadrons, were the only British forces to engage the enemy out of a total of sixteen squadrons despatched.

The German attack began at 1645 hours when a force of forty fighters crossed the coast near Deal and made for the Maidstone district. Nos 92 and 66 Squadrons, who were patrolling at 20,000 feet south of Maidstone, were attracted to the enemy by anti-aircraft fire from the direction of the estuary; but after a short encounter the German fighters withdrew towards the outer estuary. One of them came down in east Kent after this fight.

Meantime, the main German forces had been concentrating across the Straits and at 1715 hours four groups of aircraft, some two hundred aircraft in all, crossed the Kent coast between Dover and the North Foreland. Only one of these included bombers; and only this group moved west, the rest remaining over east Kent. Within a few minutes three Spitfires of No. 92 Squadron and some of No. 66, intercepted a formation of eighteen Ju 88s with no escorting fighters visible. At least three of the enemy bombers were believed to have been shot down; and this is so, for aircraft were afterwards found at the places where RAF pilots reported them to have crashed. But this was only part, though the most important part, of the formations which composed the advancing enemy force; and despite these pilots' successful encounter the group was once more coherently formed when the Duxford wing and No. 41 Squadron sighted it near Gravesend a few minutes later.

The Duxford squadrons (Nos 242, 302 (Polish), 310 (Czech) 19 and 611) were patrolling at over 20,000 feet, where there was cloud, when anti-aircraft fire was seen to the south across the estuary at 1730 hours. One of the Spitfire squadrons, No. 611, remained on patrol above the clouds; the rest of the wing descended to investigate, and between Gravesend and Tilbury found two German formations flying west at about 16,000 feet. The reports of the individual squadrons are not consistent concerning the composition of the German force. Dorniers, Ju 88s and He 111s were reported to have been shot down; but only aircraft of the latter type were found on the ground after the attack. Some squadrons saw no fighters whereas others reported seeing fighters and destroying them; but none were found after the battle. All that is certain is that there were at least eighteen Ju 88s from III/KG 77 in the German force: there may have been more, including some Do 17s, for this *Gruppe* was re-equipping from Dorniers to Junkers at the time and the process was possibly not complete. There were probably some fighters present; for it is unlikely that the Germans would have risked a long range bomber formation without a close escort.

At any rate, the enemy bombers were roughly treated. Each squadron of the wing successively attacked the right flank or rear of one or other of the German formations; and only a few of the enemy were able to attack what we know to have been their primary target, the docks at Tilbury. Bombs fell here at 1720 hours; but all near the centre of the town, not one striking the docks. In addition, bombs fell on the southern shore of the estuary and as far east as Southend. Most if not all of these were released by aircraft in trouble.

The claims of the Duxford squadrons in this engagement were eighteen Dorniers, eight Ju 88s, three Heinkels (one shared with No. 66 Squadron) and one Me 110 as well as a number of bombers and fighters claimed as probably destroyed or damaged. The fact that all the aircraft that crashed in this country during the engagement, or were recovered later from the sea, were Ju 88s from II/KG 77 implies that these claims were exaggerated; for the long arm of coincidence is hardly likely to have stretched out to select one type of aircraft from one formation out of such a diversity of choices. There were six of these aircraft from a formation originally about eighteen strong; and while these losses alone represented an unacceptable casualty rate they are unlikely to have been the only ones.

The operation, in short, was a failure, as, indeed, were the day's operations as a whole, judged by the damage that the Germans had caused to their chosen targets. Nor was the total weight of the German attack to be compared with that of three days previously; and as we shall see, the weight of the attack was not increased for the next week, we are entitled to say that the Germans either could not afford the casualties that they had suffered during the early part of the month or that they had decided to wear down the British fighter force by what were essentially offensive fighter sweeps. Either case implies the breakdown of the attempt to bomb London heavily and persistently by day.

OPERATIONS, 19–24 SEPTEMBER

i. General

On the 19th the Germans once more returned to the attacks by single aircraft against different regions of the country as well as against London, and the occasional sweeps by fighter forces as far as the outskirts of the capital, that had been the chief features of their operations on 16 and 17 September; and these remained their tactics until the 25th. The weather may well have been responsible for this comparative lull, at any rate until the 23rd; for it was uniformly bad, with the cloud base frequently as low as 2,000 feet. Significantly, activity was heavier on the 23rd, when the weather improved, than on any of the previous four days; but it again took the form of fighter sweeps over the south-east. The improvement continued on the following day when activity was again fairly heavy. The only bombing raids by day of any consequence during this period took place on this day. One was against Supermarine's works at Woolston, when, according to German records, just under twenty-five tons (metric) were dropped, indicating that a force of twenty aircraft at most was employed. On the same day a force of similar strength bombed Tilbury about nine o'clock in the morning, and another, also about twenty aircraft strong, attacked coastal targets in Kent shortly before noon. Altogether, by the 24th the curve of enemy activity had risen once more to the level of the 18th; but this did not mean that Fighter Command was once more fighting with all its strength.

ii. *Targets attacked*

The majority of incidents during these few days occurred in suburbs of south and south-east London, which reported incidents on every day except the 23rd, and in the coastal towns of Sussex and Kent. The biggest attack on any of the latter was at Eastbourne on the 23rd, when approximately thirty bombs were dropped. Little important damage was caused in this or any other attacks. The RAF stations at Lyneham, near Swindon, and Middle Wallop were lightly attacked on the 19th and 21st respectively; but here again there was no damage that could not be made good in a few hours. Except for the raids on the 24th, the only incident that deserves more than passing mention was an attack on Hawkers' factory at Weybridge at half-past eight in the morning on the 21st. According to the Ministry of Home Security, three aircraft carried out the attack, according to Anti-Aircraft Command, only one. Six bombs were dropped and all hit the factory. Three failed to explode, however, and such damage as was caused did not affect production. There was similarly little result from the heavier attack on the Supermarine works on the 24th. Damage to the factory was slight but one bomb hit a factory air raid shelter, killing twenty-four workers and injuring over seventy. During the attack on Tilbury on the same day the training ship *Cornwall* was sunk. The third attack that the Germans launched on the 24th probably failed to find its target; for bombs were dropped at a number of places in eastern Kent of which only Lympne had any military importance.

MHS Daily Intell. Summary.
AA Command 'Y' Form.

iii. *Scale of Defensive Activity: German and British Casualties*

Thus the damage that was caused by the Germans during these six days was practically negligible. Nevertheless, only on two of them had the fighter squadrons in the south a rest from intensive flying. For while few bombs were dropped, the operations room's table frequently showed strong enemy forces sweeping over the Kent coast towards London; and the same forces of fighters had to be sent into the air as when a major bombing raid was in progress. For example, the Command made as many sorties on the 23rd, when the Germans launched little except fighter sweeps, as on the famous 15th. These sweeps were never intercepted by more than three or four of the twenty squadrons that were frequently sent up to meet them. Fair warning of their approach was being obtained from the RDF stations; warnings that rarely gave less than ten minutes notice before the Germans crossed the coast. More often they were about twenty minutes long. But the RDF stations – so at least both the Commander-in-Chief and

Air Vice-Marshal Park complained – were not giving sufficiently precise information either of plan position, numbers or height for interception to be certain. Nor was it possible to distinguish between fighters and bombers. The tracking of these sweeps after they had crossed the coast was also bad; for the Observer Corps could not be expected to see through thick cloud to the 20,000–30,000 feet at which the German fighters were flying. Interceptions were accordingly rare; and when they took place our fighters were frequently at a disadvantage as they were often still climbing to reach the enemy's height. Moreover, at altitudes over 25,000 feet the Me 109 was decidedly a more effective aircraft than the Hurricane, and little if any inferior to the Spitfire. All these factors mean that the ratio of casualties was very little in favour of the defenders. Over the six day period twenty-two British fighters were destroyed, the majority in combats in which our pilots claimed the destruction of seventeen enemy fighters. In addition, twelve enemy bombers were believed to have been destroyed. As early as the second week in September No. 11 Group had taken the first steps towards counteracting the enemy's tactics by despatching single reconnaissance aircraft from the Spitfire squadrons at Hornchurch and Biggin Hill to patrol at maximum height on the usual enemy routes across the coast. Having located advancing German formations they then reported back to the sector controller on the numbers, compositions, route and altitude of the German force. So far, however, this valuable information had usually failed to reach the Group operations room in time to be effective. During the third week in September, therefore, it was decided to ask Air Ministry for a special flight of Spitfires to be formed for this sort of reconnaissance and to be attached to the Biggin Hill sector. The aircraft were to be fitted with VHF R/T and would be in direct communication with the Group operations room. However, instructions for the formation of this flight – No. 421 – were not given until the last day of the month.

S 6402 Encl 1 A

OPERATIONS, 25 SEPTEMBER

i. Over Kent and Sussex

The weather continued to improve during the night of the 24th, and on the following day conditions were no worse than on many previous days when the Germans had sent large formations to attack targets in or near London. Activity in this area, however, merely took the form of flights by aircraft flying singly or in pairs: no bomber formations and no fighter sweeps were reported. Bombs in small numbers fell chiefly in coastal districts; Brighton, Hastings, Margate and Broadstairs all reporting salvoes of bombs at different times between noon and three o'clock. During the same period, two Dorniers and two Me 110s, each flying alone, were intercepted over the country between Tangmere and Tunbridge Wells; and at least one Me 110 was shot down at no cost to us. Otherwise there was little to report from this part of the country.

ii. Against Portland and the Bristol Aircraft Works, 1115–1215 hours

What made the day remarkable was an attack by the whole of KG 55 against the Bristol Company's works at Bristol. This was the first occasion on which so large a force had been despatched against any target well inland, except for the attacks in the south-east.

The advancing German force was picked up at 1110 hours, when it was already about thirty miles north of the Cherbourg peninsula on a course for Portland; and to a great extent this late warning dictated the form of the operation. Two squadrons were sent up within five minutes: No. 609 from Middle Wallop to patrol Portland at 15,000 feet and No. 152 from Warmwell, also to patrol Portland. The second squadron, however, did not operate as one unit: two aircraft were already on patrol when the enemy raid was identified, and the rest of the squadron took off in sections and pairs of sections, each of which flew and fought independently.

Neither of these squadrons took off in time to intercept the enemy before they crossed the coast; which they did at 1124 hours a few miles to the west of Portland. At this time they consisted of three *Gruppen* of He 111 from KG 55 – about seventy aircraft in all – an unknown number of Me 110 fighter-bombers from K Gr 210 and escorting Me 110s and Me 109s. The fighter-bombers did not carry on to Bristol but swung away from the main body and attacked Portland. The target was the naval oil depot but little damage was done except for the fracturing of the water main from the mainland to the naval base. This would have had serious effects if fires had been started by further attacks, but none were made.

Meantime, the He 111s and Me 110s – the Me 109s did not go far inland – flew inland on a course that would take them a few miles west of Yeovil. More British forces were now in the air:

> Three Hurricanes of No. 601 Squadron left Exeter at 1120 hours to patrol Portland Bill at 15,000 feet: on their way they were diverted to patrol Yeovil.
>
> No. 238 Squadron left Middle Wallop at 1125 hours to patrol 10 miles south of Yeovil at 15,000 feet.

It is fairly clear that until a short time after 1130 hours the controller at No. 10 Group thought that Yeovil, where there was the Westland aircraft factory, was the German target. The four British squadrons were all ordered towards that area, only to find that the Germans had passed it and were forging ahead towards the Bristol Channel. For three of the four squadrons this meant a stern chase, which had to be successful if the enemy were to be intercepted before reaching Bristol, which was obviously their objective; for there were no fighters ahead of the Germans.[16] Two or three Spitfires of No. 152 Squadron succeeded in closing with the Germans between Yeovil and Bristol and carried out head-on attacks against the leading sections of bombers, but without effect. No. 609 Squadron also reported that they overtook the enemy just south of Bristol; but it is clear from their combat reports that most of them were in action against a retiring enemy. Anti-aircraft fire was bursting near the Germans as our pilots

16 A fighter squadron was stationed at Filton for a short time after the withdrawal from France. Early in July, however, it was transferred owing to the demand for squadrons for the fighting further east and south.

overhauled them, indicating that the interception took place very close to the city.

The Me 110s, which were from ZG 26 had closely escorted the Heinkels until near Weston-super-Mare. There, the main body turned west and flew towards the Bristol Company's works at Filton, and, after bombing them, retired by way of Colerne and Frome. Some of the fighters, however, flew as far north as Chepstow before retiring, while others turned south before reaching Bristol and acted as advance guard to the retiring bombers.

The whole of the *Geschwader* appears to have bombed as one, from a height of about 12,000 feet shortly after 1145 hours and eighty tons of bombs were dropped. Damage was severe, especially at the Rodney works, where complete aircraft were assembled and tested prior to delivery; and it was not until the middle of October that output was normal again. The public air raid warning had been sounded at 1128 hours and the majority of the workers had taken cover in trench shelters. But a number of these suffered direct hits, and eighty-two people were killed and over one hundred and seventy injured. Nearby railways were blocked in three places; and there were numerous craters and unexploded bombs on the Filton airfield. It remained serviceable but communications with No. 10 Group Headquarters were destroyed and the station commander was given independent control of the Bristol and Gloucester defences.

One of the attacking bombers was shot down by anti-aircraft fire before it reached its target, but otherwise the Germans suffered no casualties until they were on their homeward journey. Then they were under continuous attack from Bristol to the coast. No. 609 Squadron was the first in action, followed closely by No. 238. Both were chiefly engaged with He 111s (though there were the usual reports of Do 17s and Ju 88s, neither of which types were amongst the enemy force). The three Hurricanes of No. 601 Squadron, having waited near Frome for the enemy's return attacked a force of about fifteen Me 110s, in the area; and nearer the coast No. 152 Squadron joined in the attacks on the German bombers. Altogether, three fighters, fourteen bombers and two unidentified aircraft were claimed as destroyed at the small cost of three Spitfires and one Hurricane. Only three of the enemy were reported to have crashed in the sea. Nevertheless, the wreckage of only four bombers and one fighter was found on land after the fighting.

iii. Against Plymouth, 1615–1645 hours

An attack on the harbour at Plymouth at 1640 hours by about a dozen Ju 88s was the only other noteworthy German operation on this day. It was intercepted by one flight of No. 601 Squadron, but whether before or after the Germans had dropped their bombs is not certain. At any rate, the attack did little damage: an oil pipe was broken and there was minor damage to a crane, one of the jetties and a carriage shed.

However, it served to underline the danger of increasingly heavy attacks in an area that had been virtually untroubled by day since the end of August. Fighter Command's immediate reaction was to despatch No. 504 Squadron on the following day from Hendon to Filton, with the special duty of protecting the aircraft works. It was a timely move, as the events of the 27th were to show.

OPERATIONS, 26 SEPTEMBER

i. General

Again on the following day the one attack of any moment that the Germans launched was against the British aircraft industry. This time it was the factories of the Vickers-Supermarine group at Woolston that were bombed. Otherwise, German activity over England took the form of reconnaissance flights and harassing attacks mostly by single aircraft. During the morning there was an attack on the Skinningrove iron works on the north-east coast. Only three bombs were dropped but all hit the works; and the management estimated that as a result the production of pig iron would be reduced by about one-third. In the late afternoon single aircraft penetrated as far as Coventry and dropped bombs on the works of the Standard Motor Company. Three large workshops and the roofs of the machine shop and one or two other buildings were damaged.

There was no effect on the assembly of aircraft but armoured car production was slightly retarded. In the south-east there was a series of incidents between 1430 and 1730 hours. Coastal towns were again the chief target, and the Chatham district was also lightly attacked, Shorts' aircraft works being the target. There were only three interceptions in this area.

ii. Against Southampton, 1600–1700 hours

The first warning that a big attack was threatened against the Solent area was received at 1602 hours when a raid of 'fifty plus' was plotted about forty miles south-west of the Needles. In the next fifteen minutes two more raids were picked up in the same area, one of 'twenty plus' at 1610 hours and one of 'thirty-five plus' at 1616 hours. All were on courses that would take them a few miles west of the Isle of Wight; and it was difficult to be sure of their target.

Consequently, while five squadrons were sent up from the nearest fighter airfields to Southampton sufficiently early to have been over the city before the enemy appeared, none of them were; for each was kept over its base for some time until the controllers were sure of the German objective. The squadrons that were despatched immediately the German attack threatened were as follows:

> No. 152 Squadron from Warmwell to patrol base.
>
> No. 609 Squadron from Middle Wallop to patrol base at 20,000 feet.
>
> No. 602 Squadron from Westhampnett to patrol base at 10,000 feet and join up with No. 607 Squadron from Tangmere, who also took off shortly after 1600 hours, and No. 213 Squadron from Tangmere, who, however, did not take off until 1610 hours.

In addition, two Northolt squadrons – Nos 229 and 303 (Polish) – left at 1603 hours: their initial orders were to patrol Guildford at 12,000 feet.

By 1615 hours, by which time the leading German force was only a few miles south-west of the Needles, further dispositions had been made. No. 238 Squadron left Middle Wallop to take the place of No. 609, and the latter were directed to patrol Bournemouth at 20,000 feet, No. 213 Squadron left Tangmere to join the other squadrons from the sector; but each was ordered west to patrol Portsmouth, and the wing never operated as one formation. The Northolt squadrons were also ordered to the Portsmouth area, No. 152 Squadron, however, was still maintained on patrol over Warmwell.

The enemy forces crossed the coast near the Needles between 1618 and 1625 hours and flew towards Southampton. Some of the Solent guns were in action as the Germans passed overhead at about 15,000 feet but otherwise the main body of the enemy was not engaged before Woolston had been bombed. This was carried out – so ground observers reported – by two waves of bombers at 14,000–16,000 feet, and, in addition, two dive-bombing attacks were made. The latter were made by Me 110s from KGr 210. The attack lasted less than fifteen minutes and was over by 1645 hours. Judging from the weight of the bombs that the Germans claim to have dropped – 67.5 tons (metric) – between fifty and sixty bombers were employed; and this confirms the reports of the British squadrons that sighted the enemy.

By 1630 hours all the defending squadrons had been directed towards the Solent, and four of them came into action near Southampton. No. 609 Squadron had seen the enemy force a few miles south of the Needles on its inward journey but an attack on the bombers was baulked by a formation of a dozen Me 109s. It was only when the Germans were retiring that the squadron's pilots were able to engage the bombers. No. 602 Squadron, while flying near Southampton, also saw the enemy approach their target and reported a force of between thirty and forty bombers, but no fighters. As his original orders had been to attack German fighters only, the squadron commander asked the Tangmere controller for permission to attack; but according to the records of the squadron, this was refused. The enemy fighters were being engaged by No. 238 Squadron over the Isle of Wight when No. 602 sighted the bombers.

The Northolt squadrons, having come south-west at full speed from their Guildford patrol, arrived in time to see the bombing of Woolston and they could only attack as the Germans retired to the south. Combats continued until well south of the Isle of Wight, the rest of the Tangmere squadrons and No. 152 Squadron joining in as the enemy went south over Southampton Water. Some pilots only broke off their attacks when they were over the Cherbourg peninsula.

Heavy casualties were believed to have been inflicted on the Germans, amounting to fifteen He 111s and Ju 88s and sixteen fighters. Most of these were seen to crash in the sea and only two Me 110s from ZG 26 were found on land. It was this *Geschwader* that provided the escort for the attack on Filton on the previous day. An hour after the attack another enemy aircraft crashed two miles off the Needles, having been shot down by three Hurricanes of No. 607 Squadron. It had been sent over to photograph the damage at Woolston. Our casualties were very light: six aircraft and two pilots were lost.

But the Germans had struck almost as severe a blow at the British aircraft industry as on the previous day at Filton. The northern part of the Supermarine works was extensively damaged; two workshops received direct hits and production was completely stopped; and over thirty people were killed. At the Southampton docks, a warehouse filled with grain was totally destroyed. The gasworks on Marine Parade was also damaged; one gasholder was set on fire and burned until the following morning; and gas supply was not normal for a few days. This made the third attack that the Germans had launched in strength against the aircraft industry since 23 August.

OPERATIONS, 27 SEPTEMBER

It will almost certainly be found when the relevant German records are available that a fourth attack against the same branch of the British economy was attempted on the 27th. A fair-sized force certainly approached the Bristol works only to be checked by RAF fighters. But the day as a whole contrasts sharply with those that immediately preceded it; for attacks were once more made against London that compare with those of the 15th.

i. Against London, 0845–1015 hours

The usual maze of plots in the Straits of Dover and the Pas de Calais was showing on the operations rooms' tables by 0830 hours; and three minutes later a stick of four bombs fell on the harbour at Dover. But not until 0850 hours did any British squadrons leave the ground, by which time three enemy formations, totalling some fifty aircraft, were approaching Dungeness. The squadrons that were assembled were:

> Nos 213 and 602 squadrons from Tangmere to patrol over the Mayfield district.
>
> Nos 303 (Polish) and 1 (RCAF) squadrons from Northolt to join up over their base.
>
> Nos 46 and 249 squadrons from North Weald to patrol Rochford at 20,000 feet.
>
> Nos 92 and 72 squadrons from Biggin Hill to patrol Maidstone at 25,000 feet.

The first German forces crossed the coast near Dungeness shortly before nine o'clock and flew towards Tunbridge Wells. The Observer Corps reported that they were flying at 20,000 feet. In the next twenty minutes at least three more formations came in over southern Kent, some aircraft flying no further than a line from Maidstone–Tonbridge, others following up the first forces, which came in as far as Kenley and South London. From the times at which enemy aircraft later crashed on land it would appear that most, if not all, of the bombers that the enemy despatched were in this second wave.

By 0910 hours the Northolt squadrons, like the Tangmere formation, had been ordered towards Mayfield to meet the advancing enemy; the North Weald squadrons were flying south across the Thames in execution of an order to sweep the area Maidstone–Dungeness; and more British squadrons had been ordered into the air. These were:

> At 0900 hours Nos 253 and 501 squadrons from Kenley to patrol Biggin Hill at 15,000 feet.
>
> At 0905 hours Nos 17 and 73 squadrons from Debden to patrol Hornchurch–North Weald at 12,000 feet.

Between 0910 and 1920 hours the Duxford wing, consisting of Nos 242, 310 (Czech), 19 and 616 squadrons, was also preparing to patrol. It later operated over east Kent,[17] but by the time it reached its patrol height the enemy had retired.

The first combats took place shortly after nine o'clock. No. 1 (RCAF) and No. 303 (Polish) squadrons met about twenty Ju 88s escorted by some sixty Me 109s a few miles south of Gatwick. The Canadians led the formation and its commander succeeded in reaching the rearmost sections of the bombers in an attack from astern; and from then on the majority of the pilots were able to engage the bombers. As the fight continued about forty Me 110s appeared and formed their usual defensive circle; and this force was engaged by the Tangmere and North Weald squadrons during the next fifteen minutes.

The same formation of Ju 88s was next attacked further to the north by the Biggin Hill squadrons who reported that it was flying at 15,000 feet. A head-on attack was made, led by No. 92 squadron, and some of the bombers were forced to break formation.

But in addition to the Ju 88s another force of bombers, consisting of Me 110s from Lehr 1, was also in action. Some of them had been engaged in the actions near Gatwick and Redhill in which the Northolt and Tangmere squadrons were involved. They were further attacked by Nos 501 and 253 squadrons who, after shaking off a surprise attack by a small number of Me 109s, met them about six miles south-west of Kenley. No. 605 Squadron, who had taken off from Croydon at 0920 hours, also joined in this fight, in which the Me 110s once more formed their wide defensive circle. This manoeuvre was reported for the third time further west, near Maidstone, by the Debden squadrons who in company with No. 66 Squadron from Gravesend, attacked thirty Me 110s.

This series of combats was spread over forty minutes, between 0905 and 0945 hours; and there is no doubt that many of the enemy bombers were forced to turn back from London, which we know was their objective. Even if the attack had been a complete success the weight of bombs dropped would have been fairly small; for no more than twenty Ju 88s and an even smaller number of Me 110 bombers were employed. As it was, there were few incidents. Most of them occurred in Lambeth at various times between 0925 and 0950 hours. Nineteen people were killed when a factory shelter near Clapham Road was hit; and a main sewer was breached. The Southern Railway line between Brixton and Loughborough Junction was damaged. In Battersea there was considerable damage to the weighbridge and the Albert yard.

As was the case on the 15th when a large numbers of RAF fighters engaged enemy formations at much the same time and in the same area, the claims of enemy aircraft destroyed were certainly inflated, though to what extent is uncertain. Altogether, fifty-three aircraft were claimed as destroyed two of them by anti-aircraft fire: twenty-six were Me 110s, eight Dornier 17s or 215s, seven Me 109s, five Ju 88s and five He 111s. Where Dorniers were claimed, the pilot

17 The arrangements for the operation of the No. 12 Group reinforcements were that the Duxford wing would normally patrol in the neighbourhood of Hornchurch; and according to the records of No. 19 Squadron this particular patrol was actually made in that district. However, the ORB of No. 242 Squadron, who led the patrol, states that the wing operated between Dover and Dungeness at 25,000 feet; and this was almost certainly the case. No. 11 Group were complaining at this time that the Duxford wing did not always patrol where requested; and in this instance their complaint seems to have been warranted. For a fuller consideration of the operations of the Duxford wing see pp. 324–325.

had probably mis-identified a Me 110; where Heinkels, a Ju 88. Twelve British fighters were lost and nine badly damaged; but only nine pilots were killed or missing. The German losses represented by aircraft that crashed in England – and the total enemy losses were certainly more than these – were considerably more serious than our own. Seven Me 110s four Ju 88s and one Me 109 crashed on land during the battle. The Ju 88s were all from I/KG 77; the Me 110s were from Lehr 1 and Zg 76; and the Me 109 was from II/JG 27.

ii. Against Bristol, 1100–1215 hours

The last of the forces that had operated against London had recrossed the coast by 1015 hours, and for three quarters of an hour there was little activity. Then, at 1104 hours, the RDF stations detected two forces of 'twenty plus' just north of Cherbourg. In the next twenty minutes these forces merged into one as they crossed the central Channel. Until about 1115 hours the enemy's course still implied an attack in the Solent area, and No. 56 Squadron was diverted, while climbing to patrol Middle Wallop, to patrol the Isle of Wight. But at 1120 hours the German force turned north-west and crossed the coast near St Alban's Head, passing high above No. 609 Squadron who were climbing to their patrol over Bournemouth. Both squadrons were then committed to the chase.

A detachment of the German force turned back near Frome, and No. 609 Squadron engaged it between there and the coast. It consisted entirely of Me 110s. No. 56 Squadron were also engaged with Me 110s in this area. The two Hurricanes of No. 238 Squadron, however, caught up with the main body of the enemy about ten miles south of Bristol and reported a force of He 111s at 15,000 feet with Me 110s some distance behind at 20,000 feet. Later, during the retirement, another squadron reported forty Ju 88s. But the most reliable evidence concerning the composition of the force that actually reached Bristol comes from No. 504 Squadron, which had been stationed at Filton less than twenty-four hours. They had taken off at 1125 hours to patrol the Bristol area, but five minutes later were warned that an enemy force was approaching at 20,000 feet. In fact, a mixed force of Me 110 bombers and fighters was sighted coming up from the south at 10,000 feet, and the squadron intercepted before Filton was reached. Individual attacks were carried out against the enemy formation and at least part of it was seen to swing round and return to the south-east. Certainly, there was very little damage either to the station at Filton or to the aircraft factory; and the work of the squadron and the Bristol anti-aircraft guns, which were in action from 1137 to 1139 hours, undoubtedly saved these targets from a further damaging attack.

The only other squadron to engage the enemy was No. 152, who had taken off from Warmwell at 1135 hours to intercept during the German retirement. It was this force that reported seeing Ju 88s; but it was unable to close with them as it was itself attacked near the coast by Me 109s which had remained over southern Dorset to cover the retirement from Bristol. Other German formations were plotted north of Cherbourg between 1140 hours and midday: these also were doubtless covering the retirement.

British losses in this series of actions were only two aircraft and one pilot. British claims amounted to fifteen Me 110s, two Me 109s, and one Do 17; but unless a force of long range bombers was despatched that failed to find the target and returned with all its bombs, it is certain that the German forces were drawn from the Me 110s of KGr 210 and those of ZG 26, and some Me 109s from an unknown unit. Eight German aircraft crashed on land and all were from these two units; and as some of the fighting took place over the sea we can be sure that the ratio of casualties was heavily in the British favour. More important even than this was the fact that the enemy had been prevented from bombing the chosen target.

iii. Against London, 1115–1230 hours

As has already been mentioned, shortly after the Germans attacked to the west of the Isle of Wight they threatened also the No. 11 Group area. There was longer warning of this attack than of the previous one against the south-east; and six British squadrons took off between 1115 and 1130 hours, although it was not until 1135 hours that the first German forces crossed the Kentish coast. This they did between Dungeness and Dover, flying very high towards Maidstone. There were estimated to be some two hundred aircraft in this attack. By 1150 hours there were numerous plots in the Maidstone area, but by that time nine more squadrons from No. 11 Group were in the air and the Duxford wing had left ten minutes before to patrol the Hornchurch district.

Most of the German aircraft, after reaching the Maidstone area, stayed there for some time. One formation, however, was plotted from Maidstone to Chatham whence it returned by way of the estuary. Another flew on as far as south London, which it reached shortly after noon (some of the IAZ guns were firing at 1206 hours) and then returned by Redhill and Shoreham. By 1215 hours a general retirement was under way; most of the enemy going out between Folkestone and Deal.

Thus the focus of the German operation was over Maidstone and it was between there and the coast that the majority of the defending squadrons came into action. Ten of the No. 11 Group squadrons were engaged, all with one exception with Me 109s and 110s, mostly the former, in combats that started at altitudes of 20,000 feet and over. Most of the enemy fighters were in loose formations of between six and twelve aircraft.

The exception was No. 501 Squadron, which had been one of the first squadrons to take off, having left Kenley to patrol Maidstone at 1115 hours. They reported a formation of eighteen Do 17s approaching the town from the south-east at 18,000 feet at approximately 1150 hours. About fifty Me 109s were closely escorting the bombers, so closely that they succeeded in frustrating a head-on attack that our squadron tried to make by diving over and ahead of the formation of Dorniers. Most combats were with these enemy fighters. It is possible, however, that the Germans were persuaded by this attack to release their bombs on a secondary target; for about midday thirty to forty HE bombs and a number of incendiaries fell on Maidstone. On the other hand, this may have been the original German objective. Certainly the bombing was accurate and concentrated. The railway station was hit; some sidings were damaged; and one bomb hit the high level bridge, a railway key point.

But there were other bombers among the enemy forces; for a small number of bombs fell in London south of the Thames shortly after noon. The precise number is not known: it was certainly small but important damage was caused to communications. All lines on the south-east section of the South Railway out of Victoria were blocked, chiefly through the presence of an unexploded bomb at Grosvenor Road. Railway lines were also blocked in the Loughborough Junction and Herne Hill districts.

Only one British formation, other than No. 501 Squadron, sighted German bombers: this was the Duxford wing. The aircraft that they saw were probably those that had penetrated to London, although, if that is the case, the Observer Corps had failed to plot them; for the only aircraft that were plotted over London retired to the west and south, whereas the No. 12 Group squadrons were in action between Canterbury and the coast. In any case, it is impossible to reconstruct the wing's engagement with any precision. It is fairly clear that it opened with an attack from 25,000 feet on a group of enemy fighters circling at 23,000 feet over Canterbury. No. 19 Squadron, however, also saw what they described as 'about twenty enemy bombers 10,000 feet below and to the south of them'; but they attacked Me 109s as was their usual function as a Spitfire squadron in the Duxford wing. No. 310 (Czech) Squadron, in the same wing, also saw a number of bombers far below them; and one of the Czech pilots attacked what he reported as a Do 17. It would appear, therefore, that such few bombers as the Germans employed were flying well below the covering fighters, hoping in this way to slip past the defending squadrons. All the aircraft that were claimed as destroyed were either Me 109s or 110s. Four Me 109s fell on land and were identified as coming from II/JG 27 and II/JG 52. Five British fighters were lost.

iv. Against London, 1445–1600 hours

Signs that yet another attack was likely to be launched across the Straits of Dover were first received about 1445 hours, when two formations of 'twenty plus' were plotted near Calais. For some minutes there was no movement towards the coast of Kent, but a number of British squadrons were ordered up at 1450 hours:

> No. 1 (RCAF) and No. 229 squadrons left Northolt to patrol base at 15,000 feet.
>
> No. 249 and No. 46 squadrons from North Weald to patrol Hornchurch at 20,000 feet.
>
> No. 92 Squadron from Biggin Hill and No. 66 Squadron from Gravesend to join up over Biggin Hill and patrol Maidstone at 20,000 feet.

Shortly after 1500 hours a formation of about forty enemy aircraft crossed the coast between Dover and Dungeness flying at 19,000 feet. Five minutes later another formation of similar size, flying at no more than 12,000 feet, crossed in the same place. Both forces flew towards Maidstone. Their crossing was the signal for the bulk of the defending forces to be sent into the air. In all, fifteen squadrons were sent up from No. 11 Group. The three Debden squadrons were sent to patrol Maidstone as a wing, and three Tangmere squadrons to patrol

Horsham. The rest were kept over the country between Croydon and Hornchurch until the direction of the German advance was more certain. In addition, the Duxford wing took off at 1515 hours for the third time during the day, but by the time it had reached the estuary most of the enemy were retiring and it failed to intercept.

Both enemy forces, on reaching the Maidstone area, flew towards Dartford and then in the direction of Biggin Hill; and it was near the estuary that at least one of them was brought to action, first by the North Weald squadrons. At 1520 hours their leader sighted a force of ten to twelve Ju 88s flying very fast up the estuary at 18,000 feet, with a large escort of Me 109s above and behind from 20,000–25,000 feet. He decided against a concentrated attack by the whole British formation, but the individual attacks forced a melee in which the Biggin Hill squadrons joined. All our pilots got the impression that the enemy bombers were broken by these attacks; No. 249 Squadron reported that not one escaped. Some were certainly chased back to the coast and four certainly crashed on land; but five or six carried on and were seen near Biggin Hill by the Northolt squadrons, who also reported a second formation of Ju 88s about twelve aircraft strong.

It is not clear from the reports of the Northolt squadrons whether some of the German bombers were returning from London or were still flying north when they were attacked. Two points are, however, quite clear: first, that a few bombers did break through and bomb the capital; second, that the enemy were much disorganised by our attacks. Lambeth, Camberwell and Wandsworth reported bombs about 1530 hours and for the third time during the day there was damage to the Southern Railway near Brixton. But there was no sign of the concentrated bombing of a limited area that we had come to associate with a methodical and unhampered attack. And as for the disruption of the German bombing formations, it is probable that these were drawn from two *Gruppen* of KG 77, the *Geschwader* that had provided the bombers for attack before noon; and Ju 88s from both were found on land after the attack. As they retired the individual aircraft relied on their own speed and evasive tactics to escape attack; the formations as such being broken. Nos 303 (Polish), 72 and 605 squadrons all succeeded in intercepting individual bombers or pairs of bombers as the retirement took place. Otherwise, the defending squadrons were engaged near the coasts of West Sussex and Kent with small formations of Me 109s that came over at about 1530 hours to cover the retirement.

v. Summary

The enemy's major operations for the day were completed by this attack on London. They can have given them little satisfaction, if they knew the truth. Not one of the four attacks had been successful. In the morning and evening raids against London the bombing forces had been intercepted on their inward journey; some had been destroyed and some had been turned back; and such as got through were too few to deal a heavy blow. In the midday attack a small number of bombers appear to have reached the capital without being intercepted; but we shall probably find that most of the bombers that were despatched failed to get through and their bombs were dropped on a secondary target, Maidstone. As for the Filton raid, the Germans had achieved nothing, thanks chiefly to the squadron newly stationed at Filton.[18]

And if it was their aim rather to inflict casualties on Fighter Command than to destroy targets on land, they can have been no more satisfied; not at any rate, if they believed the Air Ministry casualty figures. For they would know that twenty-eight British aircraft had been lost, but only nineteen pilots; whereas their own casualties were probably three times as big. Moreover, their losses had been suffered in the type of medium-altitude bombing raid that had been so successful earlier in September when mounted on a large scale. It is not, therefore, surprising that, except for a somewhat half-hearted effort on 30 September, henceforth their attacks chiefly took the form of high-altitude fighter and fighter-bomber sweeps.

OPERATIONS, 28 AND 29 SEPTEMBER

Visibility remained good throughout 28 September but there was cloud (6/10th) at 1,000–3,000 feet. On the following day the weather worsened and there was light rain in the south-east until the middle of the afternoon. On neither day was there much enemy activity.

On the 28th two sweeps were made towards London, one at ten o'clock and the other early in the afternoon. Both were made at heights of 20,000 feet and over; and although more than twenty squadrons were despatched on each occasion by Nos 11 and 12 Groups, only five squadrons intercepted each attack. All combats were with Me 109s, which were usually higher than our own fighters when first sighted and in a strong position for attack. Consequently, the fighting went in the enemy's favour, ten British fighters being lost at a maximum cost to the enemy of six Me 109s. The second of the two sweeps crossed the coast of Kent three-quarters of an hour before an advance was made across the central Channel towards the Solent by about fifty Me 110s and 109s, and it may have been intended to clear the way for an attack against either Portsmouth or Southampton. However, three squadrons intercepted between the Isle of Wight and Selsey Bill. No bombs were dropped on land, but according to the Observer Corps bombs were seen to be jettisoned in the sea. Finally, a small number of bombers were active over Kent and Sussex coasts between 1730 and 1800 hours. A section of Hurricanes sighted and damaged a Ju 88 off Eastbourne: but otherwise the Germans were not intercepted. Eastbourne, Hastings and Ramsgate each received salvoes of bombs.

On the 29th similar sharp but light attacks were made on coastal districts in East Anglia as well as the south-east. In addition, one raid of about fifty aircraft came inland as far as the Weybridge district, which was reached at 1640 hours,

18 It is worth making an attempt here to refute the criticism that was made at the time, and will doubtless be made again, of the Fighter Command policy of refusing to provide squadrons for the close and specific defence of certain vital objectives, a policy which would appear to be sufficiently answered by the success of No. 504 Squadron in repelling the attack on Bristol. There was, however, a world of difference between stationing units near an isolated industrial area, such as Bristol, or an even more isolated military objective, such as Scapa, and allotting squadrons to the defence of particular targets in an area such as London or the Midlands, where there was a multitude of targets. Moreover, the squadron at Filton, while in an excellent position to intercept an attack upon the local aircraft industry, was not confined to that task. It could join the other squadrons of No. 10 Group in defending targets further south; and it did in fact do so during the attack on Yeovil on 30 September.

and a few bombs were reported from Weybridge Heath. Two squadrons intercepted enemy aircraft during the raid; but in each case only Me 109s were seen. A southbound coastal convoy was twice attacked by single aircraft, once off Harwich in the early afternoon and once in the Thames Estuary at 1630 hours. No damage was done. This was one of the Command's lightest days for over a week.

OPERATIONS, 30 SEPTEMBER

The weather improved in the south and south-east on the 30th, though there was still a good deal of cloud about; and the Germans took the opportunity to launch a series of attacks that forced upon Fighter Command its heaviest day's activity during the whole of September.

i. Against London, 0900–1030 hours

Two or three enemy aircraft, operating singly, were over the south-east between 0800 and 0900 hours and bombs were reported at Ealing Common, near Woolwich Arsenal and on the coast at Bexhill. Then at 0855 hours formations of 'twelve plus' and 'fifty plus'were located only a few miles east of Dungeness. These came inland at nine o'clock and flew towards Biggin Hill. The first British squadrons only took off as the enemy crossed the coast and owing to the unusually late warning only two of them intercepted.

According to the Observer Corps plots, the German forces split into a number of small formations, some flying over Kenley and Biggin Hill, others sweeping west as far as Farnborough and then south. These latter forces – or some of them –attacked the Northolt formations – Nos 1 (RCAF) and 229 squadrons – but even the approximate area of combat is not known. About fifty Me 109s in small groups were seen and two Hurricanes were shot down and five damaged. No claims were made by the British squadrons but two Me 109s crashed near Hayward's Heath at the time of the combat. One of these may have been shot down by the only other squadron to make contact with the enemy. This was No. 66 Squadron, who engaged a small force of Me 109s near Tenterden.

The only bombs that were reported between 0900 and 1000 hours fell near the RAF station at Odiham and at Portslade near Brighton. But the purpose of the attack may have been to clear the way for a further raid that came in between Hastings and Dungeness at 1005 hours. This was made up of about sixty aircraft in four formations. At the time, most of the nineteen squadrons that had taken off to meet the previous raid were returning to their bases, and No. 11 Group had only one squadron immediately ready to intercept and two more available in five minutes. Fortunately, nothing serious developed. The Germans flew in as far as Biggin Hill and then returned towards Beachy Head; and it was in that area only that bombs were dropped. Bexhill and Hastings both reported considerable damage to property and public services from bombs that fell there at 1030 hours. According to Fighter Command records two squadrons succeeded in engaging some part of these forces; but there is no confirmation of this from any combat reports.

ii. *Fighter Sweep over Hampshire, 1045–1130 hours*

Altogether, little is known about these first operations over the south-east; and, therefore, not much can be said of what the Germans intended by them. The next important raid, however, can be more accurately described; for we know something of its purpose and composition from German sources. It took place west of the Solent shortly after eleven o'clock. Ample warning was received from the RDF stations, which picked up two raids, each of 'fifty plus', just north of the Cherbourg peninsula at 1045 hours. The enemy came steadily across the central Channel and at 1100 hours were still thirty miles south of Weymouth Bay. Two British squadrons took off at that time: No. 56 from Boscombe Down to patrol Warmwell at 22,000 and No. 609 from Middle Wallop to patrol Southampton at 20,000. At 1110 hours, when the enemy were about to cross the coast west of St Alban's Head, No. 238 Squadron took off from Middle Wallop to patrol Bournemouth. Nothing was yet known about the German forces or their probable objective; and No. 504 Squadron was also ordered up about this time to guard against an attack on Filton. In fact the German force consisted entirely of fighters. There were forty-four Me 110s from ZG 26 and sixty Me 109s from JGs 2 and 53 – the accuracy of the RDF estimate is worth noting – and their purpose was simply to bring our own fighters to battle.

After crossing the coast the Germans flew north towards Dorchester where No. 56 Squadron sighted them. The Squadron was at 16,000 feet, and climbing, and the enemy at 20,000 feet, but the squadron commander gained sufficient height to lead the squadron into a head-on attack on the leading Me 110s. The clash was brief. One Hurricane was lost and one Me 110 damaged.

The Germans then moved south-east and were west of the Needles when No. 609 Squadron sighted them. The enemy were circling at the time but no attack was made immediately as the squadron commander thought that enemy bombers might be coming in later; but when the Germans retired south he decided to engage. The squadron had a slight advantage in height and surprised a small formation of Me 109s, three of which were seen to crash in the sea. There were no British losses; and this action brought the operation to an end.

iii. *Against London, 1300–1415 hours*

Much more intense fighting occurred during the next attack, which was against the London area. Warning of it was short; and the first British squadrons to take off only did so at 1300 hours. They were the Biggin Hill and Hornchurch Spitfire squadrons who were now being despatched to 30,000 feet, immediately a raid threatened, to meet the highest enemy fighters. Behind them Hurricane squadrons were sent up in pairs or wings to engage any bomber formations, with fighters closely escorting, that the enemy might send over. Thus,

> At 1300 hours Nos 41 and 222 squadrons left Hornchurch to patrol Chatham–Rochford at 30,000 feet: No. 603 left Hornchurch to patrol Maidstone at 30,000 feet: Nos 92, 72 and 66 left Biggin Hill and

> Gravesend to meet over Biggin Hill and then patrol Maidstone at 30,000 feet.
>
> At 1305 hours Nos 1 (RCAF), 229 and 303 (Polish) squadrons left Northolt to patrol base at 15,000 feet: Nos 253 and 501 left Kenley to patrol Sevenoaks at 20,000 feet: No. 605 left Croydon to patrol base.

Five minutes after the Germans crossed the coast the North Weald squadrons – Nos 249 and 46 – came south to patrol Hornchurch at 20,000 feet.

About one hundred and fifty enemy aircraft crossed the coast on a front from Rye to Folkestone and flew towards Biggin Hill and Kenley; and it was around this district that the German operation pivoted. From there about thirty aircraft flew west to the Thames Valley; others flew east to Dartford and Chatham; and a few flew into the IAZ, only to return almost at once having dropped no bombs. These were fighters only, as were those that operated near the estuary.

The advancing Germans were first sighted shortly after they had crossed the Kent coast by a pilot of No. 41 Squadron who had climbed independently to reconnoitre and report on the enemy's strength. He barely had time to report a dozen twin-engined aircraft and fifty to sixty Me 109s before he was attacked by fighters and forced to abandon his reconnaissance. No further actions took place until the Germans had penetrated as far as Tonbridge. When in quick succession No. 603 Squadron, then the Hornchurch and Biggin Hill formations, sighted and engaged the enemy. The majority of the combats were with fighters; but it is clear that there was also a formation of about twenty bombers – probably Dornier 17s – and that it flew towards Kingston-on-Thames. There was, however, a good deal of cloud at 6,000 feet and our pilots could not be sure where they came into action.

All the bombing took place between 1340 and 1350 hours. There were incidents at Walton-on-Thames, Staines and Southall; but the biggest concentration of bombs fell at Greenford near the RAF station at Northolt. According to the Ministry of Home Security approximately one hundred bombs were dropped. This was a larger number than in any daylight raid in the south-east since 15 September. No military damage was caused but much surburban property was destroyed. It was believed at the time that the probable German objective, which clearly they had failed to hit, was one or other of the aircraft factories in the Weybridge–Brentford–Slough area; and this may well be the case.

The number of bombs that was dropped was consistent with a force of about twenty bombers: and a force of this size was engaged by the Northolt squadrons and by No. 501 Squadron, who had failed to make rendezvous with No. 253 Squadron, as it retired towards Beachy Head. Each squadron reported a close escort of Me 109s and most of the combats were with these fighters. Two bombers were believed to have been destroyed and at least twelve Me 109s at a cost of four British fighters. German losses are likely to have been at least these; for eleven fighters crashed on land. No less that eight fighter *Gruppen* were identified amongst the wreckage, implying that possible as many as one hundred and fifty fighters were employed in the operation compared to some twenty bombers. Nevertheless, the operation had failed. No important targets had been hit and British casualties were at most one-third of the enemy's.

iv. 1545–1715 hours

Between 1600 and 1715 hours the Germans operated in very great strength against widely separated sections of the coast. They opened with an attack across the Kent coast by about one hundred and eighty aircraft; and at the same time a feint attack was made by a dozen aircraft against the Solent area preparatory to an attack twenty minutes later against Yeovil by a force of one hundred and fifty. These last two operations were controlled by *Luftflotte* 3 and the feint towards Southampton was probably designed to relieve the attack that was later made against Yeovil rather than that in the south-east. At the same time it effectively prevented the use of the Tangmere squadrons against the German forces to the east. However, as we shall see, much the most important attack was that against Yeovil; and the Tangmere squadrons played no small part in the defence that was put up against it.

a. Against London, 1545–1715 hours

While the aircraft that participated in the attack against the London area were overland longer than those that operated west of the Solent they were the earliest to move against us, and for that reason their operations will be described first.

In many respects the operation was similar to that earlier in the afternoon. The main body of the enemy moved towards Biggin Hill, where most of them turned west towards the Thames Valley. As before, the bombers failed to find their objective (there was still much cloud at about 6,000 feet) and no serious damage was done. There was, however, even shorter warning than before; and the first of the defending squadrons only left the ground as the Germans crossed the coast. They were Nos 603 and 41 squadrons from Hornchurch and their orders were to patrol Maidstone at 25,000 feet. Shortly afterwards, the controller realised that they would be in grave danger of being attacked while climbing; he therefore ordered them to reach their operating height over their own base.

The next British squadrons to take off did not do so until 1615 hours, by which time the first of the German forces were near Tonbridge. The defending squadrons were:

> Nos 66, 72 and 92 to patrol Biggin Hill at 25,000 feet: No. 72 was late in taking off and did not join up with the others.
>
> Nos 1 (RCAF), 303 (Polish) and 229 to patrol Northolt at 20,000 feet.

The chief burden of the combat fell upon the Hornchurch and Northolt squadrons, especially the latter. The former were ordered west from Hornchurch and came upon a large number of fighters, including He 113s, near Biggin Hill. No bombers were reported and while none of our own fighters were lost the enemy's losses were only two at the most. By the time that this combat was joined (1635 hours) the main enemy force was approaching Brooklands where it was sighted by the Northolt wing. Our pilots reported about eighteen bombers flying at 17,000 feet, with a large number of Me 109s on each flank and behind the bombers and some 2,000 feet above them. No. 1 (RCAF) Squadron, who were leading the wing, were about to attack the fighters, as had been arranged, when they were themselves attacked by Me 109s. The Polish squadron were also unable to reach the bombers before being attacked; and although No. 229 succeeded in doing so they lost three Hurricanes without any certain loss to the enemy. However, these were the only British casualties during the whole of the operation.

The Germans continued to press on to the north-west and were sighted at 1645 hours near Windsor by the Northolt station Commander. He had taken off 'to watch the Northolt Wing in action' and was flying at 20,000 feet when he saw the whole enemy formation approaching from the south. One attack was made head-on against the bombers and a second from below; shortly afterwards the whole force was seen to swing to the south. As it retired, No. 72 Squadron came into action with a flanking force of fighters near Biggin Hill; more German fighters were engaged near the coast by the other Biggin Hill squadrons; and one pilot of No. 501 Squadron, who had been unable to maintain formation, engaged a solitary Ju 88 that was already damaged, and shot it down. This was the only bomber that was claimed as destroyed. It crashed near Gatwick and proved to be a Ju 88 from 1/KG 77.

These interceptions meant that only the Kenley and North Weald squadrons, who had not taken off until 1640 hours, had failed to engage some part of the German forces. Two Duxford squadrons came south at 1650 hours to patrol Hornchurch but they were never in a position to intercept.

Only eight Me 109s were claimed as destroyed in addition to the one Ju 88, and five crashed on land. They were from JGs 26, 27 and 52; which confirmed that, as in the previous attack against the same area, the Germans had used powerful forces of fighters to protect less than one *Gruppe* of bombers.

And, again as in the previous attack, the bombers despite this strong protection, had failed to hit any worthwhile target. For with the exception of a stick of bombs that fell near Manston about the time that the first enemy forces came inland, the only bombs that were reported fell near Marlow a few minutes after the Northolt squadrons had come into action and about the time that the Northolt station commander had carried out his single-handed attack. About seventy bombs were dropped, most of them falling in marshy ground and doing no damage.

b. Feint Attack towards Southampton, 1545–1615 hours

As part of the operation that reached its climax in the Yeovil district shortly after 1630 hours, the Germans launched a feint attack (*Scheinangriff*) by eleven Ju 88s of I/KG 51 towards Southampton. The force was plotted at 1545 hours when it was about fifty miles south of the Needles and one Tangmere squadron, No. 602, went up two minutes later with orders to patrol Selsey Bill at 15,000 feet. On the way it was diverted to patrol Bembridge in the Isle of Wight, and while at 13,000 feet five miles east of Bembridge, the formation of Ju 88s was sighted as it approached from the south a thousand feet lower than the British squadron. There were no enemy fighters present, and it is almost certain that none were despatched. The squadron commander ordered individual attacks on the enemy aircraft, four of which were believed to have been shot down at a cost of one Spitfire. Certainly the enemy penetrated only a short distance inland before retiring rapidly to France. No bombs were dropped on land.

c. Against Yeovil, 1545–1700 hours

This action over the Isle of Wight was fought at about 1615 hours, by which time the main German force was halfway across the central Channel on a course for Portland Bill. The first measures to meet it were taken at 1600 hours when No. 238 Squadron took off from Middle Wallop to patrol Swanage at 15,000 feet. In the next fifteen minutes as the German force steadily approached Portland the following squadrons were ordered to take off:

No. 56 Squadron from Boscombe Down to patrol Portland at 22,000 feet.

No. 609 Squadron from Middle Wallop to patrol Portland at 22,000 feet.

No. 213 Squadron from Tangmere to patrol Portland at 15,000 feet

No. 607 Squadron from Tangmere to patrol base at 15,000 feet; later ordered to Portland.

No. 152 Squadron from Warmwell to patrol at 22,000 feet.

No 87 Squadron ('B' Flight) from Exeter to patrol Portland at 22,000 feet.

One more British squadron, No. 504 was later to take off with orders to patrol the Portland area. It left Filton at 1625 hours.

By that time the first combats had taken place. No. 238 Squadron were informed that the enemy were approaching Portland and after climbing for some miles to the west they sighted them at about 1620 hours some twenty miles south of Portland. The combat reports do not precisely describe the German force, but we know now that it consisted of about fifty[19] He 111s from KG 55 with an escort of forty Me 110s from ZG 26 and fifty-two Me 109s from JGs 2 and 53. The defending squadrons were between the Germans and the sun, and also had about 3,000 feet advantage in height, and their attack was very successful. They claimed to have shot down two Heinkels and two Me 110s at no cost to themselves.

Then in quick succession, Nos 152 and 56 Squadrons and the six Hurricanes of No. 87 Squadron engaged the enemy force near and over Portland. The actions took place between 1630 and 1640 hours. Four British fighters were lost but two bombers and two fighters were claimed. Some of the German bombers certainly broke formation and returned to France. Others were hurried away to the west; and bombs fell near Bridport about 1645 hours many miles away from the target area at Yeovil.

The main enemy body, however, pressed inland and was next engaged near Yeovil by No. 609 Squadron. Again no great losses were inflicted but while attacks were taking place the whole German formation released its bombs. Thereafter the two Tangmere squadrons engaged fifteen Me 110s to the south-east of

19 According to the German document giving the units participating in the raid, there were four Heinkels from the *Stabstaffel* of KG 55, sixteen Heinkels from *Gruppe I* and twenty-three from *Gruppe II*. These figures, however, are wrongly added in the digest of the raid, which states that fifty-three Heinkels took part and dropped 63¼ tons (metric) of bombs. Moreover, in another document emanating from the Intelligence branch at the headquarters of *Luftflotte 3*, the weight of bombs dropped is given as 88¼ tons (metric), which indicates a force of about seventy bombers.

Yeovil; while No. 504 Squadron caught the Heinkels over Weymouth Bay and claimed the destruction of two. These interceptions brought the British claims to nine fighters and seven bombers destroyed; but as most of the fighting took place over the sea only one enemy aircraft – an Me 109 from II/JG 2 – was found on land after the battle. British losses were proportionately heavier than usual: seven aircraft were destroyed and three badly damaged but only three pilots were lost.

But where so large a force of bombers was employed the success or failure of the attack is to be judged chiefly by reference to damage caused to the chosen objective; and in this case the target had not been hit. The Germans had intended to strike just such a blow against the Westland aircraft works at Yeovil as they had successfully launched against the Bristol Company's works five days previously. But all their bombs fell to the east of the target, mostly on the small town of Sherborne, where there was much damage to domestic property. In addition the main line of the Great Western Railway was blocked between Yeovil and Sherborne, and traffic had to be diverted temporarily through Westbury and Bridgewater. The German pilots certainly aimed at the Westland factory; but it is not possible to say at the moment how far their failure to hit it was due to our fighters, to cloud or to the deficiencies of their bombing technique. No comparable attack was launched in later operations in this area. Henceforth the bomber strength of *Luftflotte 3* was entirely reserved for night attacks.

With this attack the German operations for the day and the month were virtually over.

COMMENTARY ON FOURTH PHASE, 7–30 SEPTEMBER

i. Scale and Direction of the German Attacks

In the review of the operations between 24 August and 6 September it was pointed out that early in September there were two strong indications that the Germans would shortly intensify their offensive, particularly against south-east England. First, according to reliable intelligence (which was later confirmed) the Germans were concentrating much of their dive-bomber and fighter strength in north-east France; and, in addition, most of the small number of long-range bomber *Gruppen* that were not already stationed in France and the Low Countries were moving there from Denmark and Norway. Second, what all were agreed was the most suitable period for invasion was approaching; and that the Germans were likely to take advantage of it was indicated both by photographic reconnaissance and by the consensus of reports from secret sources.

And certainly by one index – that of the weight of bombs dropped – the Germans increased the scale of their attack after the first week of September. It appears from reliable German documents that three and a half times the tonnage dropped on the whole country during August fell on it in September. Furthermore, there had been the anticipated concentration against the south-east; for of the nine thousand tons of HE bombs[20] that the Germans had aimed at Great Britain during September six thousand five hundred had been released in attacks

20 See Appendix 32 for the precise tonnages that the Germans claim to have dropped.

on London; and nine thousand five hundred of the twelve thousand incendiary containers that had fallen had also been aimed at the same target. In fact, the increase in the total tonnage dropped as compared to August was entirely accounted for by the attacks on London, which had suffered very little prior to 7 September.

Another and no less significant change, even though no comparable weight of bombs was involved, was reflected in the difference between the scale of attacks on airfields during the two months. Over one thousand tons had been dropped on this type of target in August, but less than one-third of this in September. Probably some proportion of the tonnage dropped on secondary targets (*Ausweichziele*), especially at night, was also aimed at airfields; but it is beyond argument that they were no longer the primary objectives that they had been in the third phase. The majority of such attacks as were made on them were the work of single aircraft.

Of the other categories of target, *Ausweichziele* had received eleven hundred tons of bombs compared to four hundred in August. There is nothing to show what sort of target was classed in this fashion, nor on what days and nights secondary targets were perforce attacked because the primary target could not be found. But there is good reason to believe that the remarkably high tonnage that was thus dropped was at least partly due to the failure of the German bombers to penetrate to London in daylight, particularly on the 9th, 11th and 27th. As for target areas in other regions than the south-east, Merseyside was frequently raided at night during the month; but no attacks were made on the area comparable to those that had been launched during the last week in August. A typical attack was that of the 18th/19th when twenty-three Do 17s and He 111s from K Gr 606 and II/KG 27 were employed. Birmingham and Coventry were very lightly attacked, less than fifty tons being dropped during the month. Southampton and Bristol, on the other hand, each received over one hundred tons, which were chiefly dropped in the attacks on the aircraft factories at Woolston and Filton.

ii. Importance of the Night Attacks

Yet despite the heavier weight of attack the month had not taxed Fighter Command as much as had been expected; for most of the German bombs had fallen at night, both in the London area and elsewhere in the country. The attack on London, in particular, had been a night attack. Only on two nights after 7 September – the 12th/13th and 14th/15th – did the Germans fail to send at least one hundred bombers against London; and the nightly average was over two hundred. Conversely, only on the 7th and 15th had more than one hundred bombers attacked London by day. About three hundred were employed on the 7th and just over one hundred on the 15th. The tonnage dropped by night was, correspondingly, far higher than that dropped in daytime. At the very most the latter was barely one thousand tons; at the very least the former was five thousand five hundred tons.

Now this was a significant development; for what had caused so much concern towards the end of the third phase had been the prospect of intensified attacks *in daylight* that would not only mean heavy damage to ground targets but the continuance of the high casualty rate amongst fighter pilots. The expectation was not entirely belied by events. The great attack of 7 September was only a surprise in that London proper was heavily attacked for the first time: its scale and intensity were only what was to be expected. Nor, having shown their hand, was it surprising that the Germans followed up the day attack by one of similar scale at night, though the fact that the 8th was a day of recuperation indicated that a special effort had been made on the 7th that was beyond the daily capacity of the German Air Force. On the 9th, and again on the 11th, there was heavy fighting over the south-east, from the 12th to the 14th the weather was bad; and the German effort by night as well as during the daytime dropped to its lowest level for the whole month. On the 15th the weather improved and London was again heavily attacked by day. Thereafter, the bombing attacks by day in the south-east continued to be made but they were comparable neither with those of the 15th, much less the 7th, nor even with the attacks on airfields during the third phase. Instead, such heavy attacks as were made by day were on the 25th against Filton, on the 26th against Woolston and on the 30th against Yeovil. Meantime, however, every night saw between one hundred and fifty and three hundred long-range bombers launched against London. It is broadly the case, therefore, that by the middle of the month the German daylight offensive had lost much of its dangerousness.

iii. Effect on Aircraft and Pilot Casualties

Except on the 7th and 15th and to some extent on the 9th, 11th, 27th and 30th, Fighter Command was not required to deal with the sort of attacks that would have tested it most – attacks by heavily escorted bomber formations against targets well inland. Consequently, its casualty rate both in aircraft and pilots fell appreciably. It remained high for the period 7–15 September, fell during the next week, only to rise in the last five days of the month. But in the whole three week phase only 258 Hurricanes and Spitfires were destroyed compared to 295 in the previous fortnight. Output at a figure of just over five hundred aircraft, including repaired aircraft, was once more ahead of wastage.[21] Pilot casualties showed a comparable decrease. During the three weeks 119 pilots were killed or missing and 101 wounded, giving a total wastage of some eighty pilots a week, only two-thirds of that during the previous phase. We shall see that the casualty rate was still higher than the Command could afford; but that it should have fallen at all was an index that the fighting was no longer as desperate as in late August and early September.

iv. Relation between the German Attacks and an Intended Invasion

In sum, it would appear that during these three weeks the Germans had not endeavoured as strenuously as in the previous two to break the power of Fighter Command. The weight of their attack had indeed shown a more than threefold increase; but it had been directed neither at the ground organisation of the Command – its airfields and system of warning and communication – nor at its strength in the air; for the Germans must have known that while they themselves

21 See Appendix 33, Table 1.

would suffer less by attacking at night rather than during the day, the casualties of the opposing fighters would be no less light. And as it seemed to us that the enemy would do all they could to destroy or neutralise Fighter Command before an invasion was attempted, it is clearly necessary to see, first to what extent they were still preparing an expedition, second how far an invasion was served by the air attacks that were actually launched.

a. The Progress of Preparations for Invasion

German preparations were adjudged sufficiently complete by the evening of the 7th to permit an immediate invasion. German cargo ships were reliably reported to have left Stettin, Lubeck and Kiel for the Dutch coast during the last week in August; and much activity was reported from other ports in north and north-west Germany. Barge movements from the Scheldt towards Calais and Boulogne were still taking place. The largest concentrations were at Calais, Dunkerque, Ostend and Flushing, where there were between five hundred and six hundred small craft. West of Boulogne no significant volume of shipping appeared to have been collected. The report of the Combined Intelligence Committee covering the situation up to noon on 8 September summarised it as follows: 'Conditions of weather, moon and tide, offensive action by the GAF, and movements of barges and small craft, all combine to make immediate attempt at invasion likely. The reported activities in North German ports are such as have often been forecast as the likely preliminary. The decision to invade and the timing, however, will probably still depend on the results estimated by the enemy to have been achieved in the air.' Already, on the evening of the 7th, immediately after the heavy attack on London, the armed forces and such other departments as needed to be advised, had been put under 'Alert No. 1', which signified that attack was regarded as imminent and likely to occur within the next twelve hours.

CIC Report No 101.

Home Forces GHQ Combined Ops Room, Form 540.

Until the 17th the danger was still considered acute and this highest degree of preparedness remained in force. Up to the 11th most of the information that pointed to early invasion concerned the movements of the German Air Force and of shipping. Then on the 11th and 12th reliable reports of a different kind were received. First, Gestapo detachments, specially trained for work in England, were believed to have arrived at Ostend on 11 September; second, leave for the German Army was stopped as from the same date; third, German Air Force port embarkation officers were known to have been appointed at Calais, Dunkerque, Ostend and Antwerp. It was true that stoppages of leave had previously occurred since the end of June and that embarkation officers might have been required to improve normal supply arrangements. But the information was consistent with the moves of shipping in the Channel; and there could be no question of relaxing precautions. On 12 September the Combined Intelligence Committee reported, 'that an expedition may be launched at any time now ... It is, however, still possible that the loading of many of the ships has yet to be fully completed, and that the 'Zero Hour' may not, therefore, be immediate.' During the next two days fewer movements of shipping were spotted in the Channel, which might have meant that preparations were nearing completion.

CIC Report No 105.

Ibid.

Preparations, or seeming preparations, continued to be reported after 15 September. But from 19 September to the end of the month no major changes

CIC Report No 112.

in the situation were reported; and at the former date it was reckoned that there were 240 merchant ships between Brest and Delfzyl with a maximum carrying capacity of 400,000 tons, to which could be added a barge capacity of 500,000 tons.[22] Between Bayonne and Brest there were about one hundred ships of over one hundred tons. This capacity was ample for the purpose of invasion; but as there had been no positive signs of any forward movement of troops to fill and utilise it, the state of readiness was slightly relaxed on the evening of the 17th and 'Alert No. 2' (attack probable within three days) was reintroduced.

b. *Effect of the Attack on London*

All this time the attack of London had been going on, chiefly at night. The attack of the dock areas on the evening and during the night of the 7th was difficult to reconcile with a pre-invasion policy; but serious interference with road and rail communications was also caused, which, if deliberate, showed an intention of hampering communications between London and the south-east coast. This sort of damage continued after the 7th. From the evening of the 8th to the morning of the 15th seventy-eight direct hits were obtained on railway lines within ten miles of Charing Cross. The effects were thus summarised by the Ministry of Home Security:

i. South of the Thames so many lines have been immobilised as seriously to impede passenger traffic.

ii. North and South of the Thames, damage to link lines for the North and South transfer of goods traffic has caused considerable congestion, and much traffic is held up on the Northern lines.

iii. The frequency of Red Warnings adds to the congestion and delay in the marshalling yards.

CIC Report No 107, 14 September.

The Combined Intelligence Committee commented: 'The selection of targets for attack was evidence of a thorough and carefully thought out plan. There is insufficient evidence, however, to show whether it was designed for its nuisance value by the disruption of passenger traffic and of the transit of goods for industrial purposes, or whether it was definitely intended as a prelude to invasion … All that can be said is that the effect was serious, and would undoubtedly add to our difficulties if attempted invasion were to follow before repairs are complete or congestion was relieved.' Congestion was in fact so bad that on 11 September there were 5,000–6,000 railway wagons waiting north of the Thames for

22 The concentrations of barges merited close study; for there was positive evidence that they were connected with the invasion. In the first place, they were chiefly located at ports which were most convenient for invasion but not, with the exception of Antwerp, for trade. Then, on the occasions when they had been seen under way, their skilful handling suggested that naval crews had been put aboard. There was also evidence that barges were being modified to take 88 mm guns, anti-tank guns and tanks. The fact that major movement of barges from the 'Scheldt' towards the Channel ports had taken place a few days before the most favourable dates for invasion was perhaps the best evidence of all that they were to be used for this purpose. On the other hand, they were berthed in groups instead of being dispersed for security against bombing, nor were any signs observed that they had been loaded or unloaded. For the latter reason, it was unlikely that they were being used to ease the strain on railway communications between Germany and France and Belgium. It was suggested, and with some reason, that they might have been a *ruse de guerre*, deliberately concentrated in the Channel ports in order to draw the fire of our bombers from targets in Germany proper and also divert our attentions from an invasion operation that was being prepared in some other quarter.

forwarding to the Southern Railway. Normally between fifty and sixty trains were forwarded daily to the Southern Railway from the Great Northern section of the LNER. During the second week in September only four were being passed.

But it is very doubtful whether we were justified in assuming that all this was the result of a deliberate plan. This may have been the case as far as the daylight attacks were concerned but most of the bombing had taken place in darkness; and there was no direct evidence that the German pilots were singling out communications from the great mass that is London. After the doubling of the gun strength of the Inner Artillery Zone, a process which had been completed by the 11th, the Germans were bombing from 15,000 feet and over, and while from such altitudes they could perhaps identify and bomb the railway terminals near the Thames they could hardly have selected stretches of line in the suburbs for attack. Yet these were hit very frequently;[23] and a glance at a railway map of London will show that the network of communications might well be often hit even by indiscriminate bombing. However, we are in no position to say that the switch to night bombing proves that the Germans were no more interested in communications than any other class of target. Nor does it follow that the attack of London was not part of a pre-invasion bombing policy.

v. Methods of Attack and Defence

a. By Day

During the third phase the Germans had never allowed their attacks to become stereotyped but usually they had launched about three heavy attacks a day at intervals of about three hours. The attacks developed quickly and were carried out quickly. On most occasions there was little more than an hour and a quarter between the detection of the first enemy forces and their retirement across the coast. It was this sort of attack that Air Vice-Marshal Park had in mind when on 5 September he had instructed his controllers to build up a strong defending force as quickly as possible to meet the enemy's advance between the coast and the sector stations near London. Only if time permitted were squadrons to be grouped in pairs.

The attack of 7 September, however, was not comparable to those that the Germans had previously launched. Warning of it was short but it continued for two hours; and at least two waves of bombing formations are known to have been employed. These forces converged upon London and were therefore less difficult to intercept than when the German targets had been the comparatively widely separated sector stations in Surrey, Kent and Essex. In these circumstances it was important to keep back a proportion of the defending squadrons to meet the second wave of the enemy's advance; which the controllers were not successful in achieving during the attack of the 7th. The German bombers were prepared, if necessary, to fight their way through to the capital; and their comparatively slow advance was protected by very large fighter forces.

23 The Germans by this date were using the *Knickebein* technique of navigation, by which they could guarantee to reach a target area of limited dimensions, provided the transmissions were not interfered with. But this was little or no help to an observer who was under orders to bomb a small and specific target.

Consequently, the larger the defending formations the better their chance of reaching the bombers and checking their advance. This had always been so but under the changed conditions it was now practicable in that once it was established that the target was London itself the problem of intercepting the large converging forces was not a difficult one.

No. 11 Group Instructions to Controllers, No. 16

The reaction to this change in German methods was registered in an instruction that was circulated to the No. 11 Group controllers on 11 September. By this the plan of defence was to despatch squadrons 'at readiness' in pairs to meet the first wave of the enemy; Spitfires were to engage the high fighter screen and Hurricanes the bombers and close escort. Squadrons available in fifteen minutes were to be brought to readiness and then despatched in pairs to meet the second wave. Squadrons available in thirty minutes were to be brought to readiness and then despatched to protect sector stations or aircraft factories or to reinforce squadrons already in the air. If, however, there was a third wave the squadrons from adjacent sectors were to be paired and despatched to meet it. By keeping the Biggin Hill and Hornchurch sectors equipped exclusively with Spitfires Air Vice-Marshal Park ensured that squadrons paired in this way were capable of performing the same function.

No. 11 Group Instructions to Controllers, No. 18

It was not to be expected that the new scheme would work smoothly as soon as it was introduced; and on the 16th Air Vice-Marshal Park made the following criticisms:

i. Individual squadrons were sometimes failing to rendezvous as detailed.

ii. Individual squadrons had been detailed to big raids.

iii. Pairs of squadrons had been placed on patrol too far forward and too low and had been exposed to attack by enemy fighters.

iv. Individual squadrons had been given a rendezvous so far forward that they were meeting the enemy before joining the second squadron.

v. Preliminary sweeps of fighters had on occasion drawn up nearly all the Group prematurely.

But with the exception of the last, most of these defects could be, and were, rectified fairly easily; and on the 15th, in clear weather and against attacks similar to those of the 7th in execution if not in size, the new methods worked well, particularly against the morning attack.

Thereafter the Germans altered their tactics. Only in the raids against aircraft factories in the south and south-west was a force of more than fifty bombers ventured in a single daylight attack. Pressure upon the day fighter squadrons in the south-east and upon the air defence system as a whole was maintained chiefly by operations in which high-flying fighter formations far outnumbered the bombers. The operations in this area on 30 September are a good example of the sort of forces employed and the type of target that was attacked. By these means the enemy forced No. 11 Group to exert as high a scale of effort, judged by the sorties that were flown, as on days when much larger numbers of bombers were used; and the defensive plan had to be changed to meet the new conditions.

Part of the problem for the defenders was accountable to the cloudy weather which had been experienced on many days during September and which would become normal as winter approached; for this meant that it was difficult for the Observer Corps to furnish accurate reports of enemy movements, the more so as most of the German fighters were flying at over 20,000 feet. A beginning was made, therefore, in the use of reconnaissance fighters to supplement RDF information and give more precise warning of what sort of forces were approaching; and a special reconnaissance flight, No. 421, equipped with Spitfires, began to form at Gravesend on the last day of the month. This was the first attempt that had been made since RDF was introduced to obtain warning of the enemy's approach by other than mechanical means. In addition, Air Vice-Marshal Park decided that the new situation demanded a less strict control of the squadrons in the air by the operations rooms on the ground. The sector controllers were no longer receiving sufficiently accurate information of the enemy movements to direct their squadrons with confidence towards a German formation. They were frequently forced to give a series of instructions to squadron commanders instead of the two or three brief and clear orders that were all that were required when the technique of ground control worked as it should. Instead, the AOC decided in favour of definite day patrol lines which would be taken up by the first squadrons despatched on the approach of a large raid. The task of the sector controller was then confined to keeping those squadrons on their respective patrol lines and giving them such information as he had about the attack; the squadron commander was then largely responsible for searching for and locating the enemy. However, when in good weather clear tracks of a German formation were being received in the operations rooms, the squadron or pair of squadrons was despatched direct to intercept it. During October this plan was to be extended. Squadrons were then despatched to man patrol lines in the Maidstone area even when there was no definite sign that an attack was imminent; which was a departure from one of the principles of the Fighter Command system – that squadrons only took off to intercept when warning of attack was received – that was unavoidable owing to the unreliability of RDF observations of high-altitude raids.

Altogether, the harassing attacks that the Germans launched after 15 September were a severe test for the squadrons of No. 11 Group, even though the rate of casualties dropped sharply. Fifteen to twenty squadrons were regularly being despatched to meet enemy attacks in which bombers played a very small part. This in itself entailed some waste of defensive effort; but in addition only five or six of these squadrons usually succeeded in engaging the enemy. The German fighters normally had an advantage of height over the defenders; and relative British casualties were higher even than in the bitter battles of the third phase. The innovations that were made, therefore, were intended to improve the fighting chances of our squadrons by giving them time to reach altitudes of 20,000–25,000 feet before the enemy arrived. But although Air Vice-Marshal Park had always emphasised that one squadron could climb more quickly than two or more, he impressed on his controllers the importance of

No. 11 Group Instructions to Controllers, No. 24, 4 October

operating pairs of squadrons unless it was clear that only a single squadron could reach the enemy's height in time to intercept before bombs were dropped; and he informed all squadrons that they would only be ordered to operate alone during a large attack if otherwise the enemy would reach their targets unmolested. This was consistent with his point of view throughout the battle regarding the optimum size of fighter formation, a question that must now be examined in some detail.

During the third phase of the battle, when reinforcements from No. 12 Group were regularly coming into No. 11 Group to patrol the sector stations north of the Thames, Air Vice-Marshal Leigh-Mallory had been convinced that the large German formations would be more successfully engaged by wings of three squadrons than by the successive attacks of single squadrons or even pairs of squadrons. He was entirely responsible for the form that his reinforcements took and for their operational control though not for their patrol line; and from 6 September these almost invariably consisted of wings of three to five squadrons, which operated under the control of the Duxford sector. They were led on all occasions but one by S/Ldr D R S Bader of No. 242 Squadron. Seven times in September the wing came into contact with large German formations; and large numbers of enemy aircraft were believed to have been destroyed at little cost to the British squadrons. Some eighty bombers and sixty fighters were claimed as certainly destroyed at the expense of twenty British fighters destroyed, nine pilots killed or missing and six wounded – a most satisfactory balance sheet. It was chiefly to examine how far these claims were due to the employment of such large formations that the Air Staff held an enquiry during the second week in October.

But another issue was involved. Air Vice-Marshal Park had never been satisfied with the arrangements for reinforcements from No. 12 Group. He complained that twice during the last week in August sector stations had been heavily bombed when No. 12 Group squadrons were supposed to be patrolling them; and on 27 August the controllers at No. 11 Group were instructed to pass all requests for No. 12 Group squadrons through the Command Controller so as to ensure that the reinforcements patrolled where requested. Later on, when the Duxford wing was regularly operating in No. 11 Group, he again complained that it frequently came far to the south-east of the patrol line Hornchurch–North Weald that it was supposed to man. The issue in this case was how and by what Group the Duxford wing was best controlled.

Ibid No 7.

Unfortunately, what should have been an enquiry became a controversy, with both sides seeming at times to impugn each other's good faith. There is no point in cataloguing all the various debating points that were made.[24] What is more important is to examine what contribution the Duxford wing made to the defence of London, what light was thrown on the optimum size of defending

24 Two examples will suffice to illustrate how each side tended to exaggerate its case. Air Vice-Marshal Leigh-Mallory in a letter to Air Chief Marshal Dowding on 9 October said, in rebuttal of the criticism that his squadrons had twice failed to protect No. 11 Group stations in Essex, that 'on no occasion when the Duxford wing has been operating have either Hornchurch, North Weald or Debden been bombed'. This was perfectly true, for the simple reason that the Germans neither attempted or intended to attack these stations during the period in question. Air Vice-Marshal Park, on the other hand, exaggerated when he claimed that attacks by single fighters had been known to break up large formations of the enemy.

formation, and what arrangements were made to ensure the better functioning of reinforcements between the two Groups.

The immense claims of the Duxford wing were never queried by Air Vice-Marshal Park; but he was at pains to point out that the wing usually came into action with outgoing raids which had been engaged previously by No. 11 Group squadrons and were therefore more sensitive to attack. In fact, the wing certainly engaged incoming raids on at least two, and possibly three, of the seven occasions on which it made contact with the enemy in September. It was true, however, of the combats in which the wing claimed its most striking successes – those of the 15th and 18th – that No. 11 Group squadrons had already engaged the enemy. But the question obviously arises, had No. 11 Group made its requests sufficiently early for No. 12 Group squadrons to intercept before the Germans reached the London area?

This is a difficult question to answer as there appear to be no records of the exact times at which requests were made. It is not even certain at what times the wing left Duxford; for the record books of the constituent squadrons give times of take-off which sometimes differ by as much as fifteen minutes. However, No. 11 Group only requested assistance when at least one hundred and fifty aircraft were approaching the Group area; and as the weight of attack was not known until ten to fifteen minutes before the coast was actually crossed, it is not surprising that the first enemy forces were usually overland before the Duxford squadrons took off. Anticipatory action on the part of No. 12 Group was rarely possible; for under the existing system it was not told when raids were building up over the French coast. Eventually, RDF plots as far south as the line Dungeness–Cap Griz Nez were 'told' to No. 12 Group from Fighter Command Headquarters; but this amendment was not introduced until 24 October. Consequently, the wing intercepted either when an enemy attack was long drawn out (e.g. 7 and 15 September) or when rather longer warning than usual was received (e.g. 18 September). Against the swiftly executed, high altitude attacks of late September and October it had little or no success; and it is probably the case that even a single reinforcing squadron would rarely have intercepted this type of attack, much less a wing of four or five squadrons.

But the successes of the Duxford wing were the more emphatic, coming as they did after a phase in which British casualties had been so high; and some amongst the Air Staff drew the conclusion that the tactics that No. 11 Group had pursued in the third phase and, to a lesser extent, in the fourth phase, were outmoded and that large formations should be made the rule. An Air Staff Note of 14 October recommended that the minimum size of units for the engagement of large enemy formations should be the wing of three squadrons; and this was formally laid down at the conclusion of meeting held at the Air Ministry on 17 October.

11G/S486/1, Encl. 48, Appendix 1

Ibid. Encl. 52B

The fact was that this had never really been questioned. Neither Air Chief Marshal Dowding, who, it should be noted, inclined to the No. 11 Group point of view, nor Air Vice-Marshal Park, were opposed in principle to wing formations. Air Vice-Marshal Park had begun to pair his squadrons and, later in September, use his Tangmere, Northolt and Debden squadrons in wings of three, shortly after the Germans began to use heavier formations and to penetrate regularly into the London area. In the fighting over Dunkerque he had also

Dowding – US of S 15 November

employed wings of three and four squadrons. But his contention was that their use was essentially a matter of the time available and that until the lengthy attacks on London began on 7 September only single squadrons could be used unless the enemy were only to be engaged after they had attacked their targets. And in this he was surely right so long as the forces at his disposal allowed him no *masse de manoeuvre*.

It was in providing the latter that No. 12 Group contributed to the battle for London. The Duxford squadrons were located within easy reach of London and yet were outside the main battle area, and when, as on the 7th and 15th, they met enemy formations that were suffering the strain of a long flight and of a number of previous combats, their striking power was highly effective. The pity was that not until the battle was over were adequate arrangements made for the control of their operations in the No. 11 Group area. The controller at No. 11 Group was never certain where the Duxford wing was operating, and while it is difficult to criticise the wing leader for flying towards the battle it confused the Observer Corps and the whole raid intelligence system when a large formation, nominally patrolling in the Hornchurch area, operated south of the Thames. From 24 October, however, it was arranged that No. 12 Group should be given information of enemy raids over the Straits, and that the Hornchurch sector should 'fix' the position of the wing when it was patrolling.[25]

b. By Night[26]

With the exception of the regular but small-scale, attacks on Merseyside and a number of dislocation raids, rarely by more than twenty aircraft each night, the German night attacks were concentrated on London. Usually they commenced about 2000 hours, the first of the raiders having approached during dusk, and continued until between three and five o'clock the following morning. The comparatively light attacks of the 12th–14th and the 20th–22nd were called off because of the weather shortly after midnight. The main stream of aircraft came in from the south and returned the same way, the Solent, Beachy Head and Dungeness being the usual points of entrance and exit. But a proportion went out over Essex and the East Anglian coast; and on a few nights the main attack came from this direction.

The devices and techniques that were eventually to improve the efficiency of the night fighter were still in an experimental stage or had only just come into service. Moreover, the expansive effort of the Command had largely been in terms of single-seater fighters; and in September there were only the same six twin-engined night fighter squadrons as had been formed prior to the outbreak of war. To these had been added two Defiant squadrons. Few calls, however, could be made upon the Spitfire and Hurricane squadrons in view of the continuing battle by day. Thus, Air Chief Marshal Dowding was forced to concentrate most of the night fighting squadrons for the night defence of London to an extent that he had never done for the day battle. By 11 September four of the six

25 For the precise arrangements that were made see Appendix 22, No. 11 Group Instructions to Controllers, No. 35.

26 For a detailed survey see Air Historical Branch narrative on 'Night Air Defence of Great Britain'.

Blenheim squadrons, two flights of the two Defiant squadrons and the Fighter Interception Unit were in No. 11 Group and the Middle Wallop sector. Even so the nightly fighter effort averaged only fifty to sixty unsuccessful sorties. On the experimental side, the main contribution of the Command was to make the Kenley sector a testing ground for the new marks of AI, GL, and SLC that were coming into service and for new methods of searchlight and fighter co-operation.

But because of the shortage of suitable aircraft and the deficiencies of night fighting technique the defence of London was largely the concern of Anti-aircraft Command and the Civil Defence services. But the former was little nearer than Fighter Command to finding an answer to the night bomber. The doubling of the gun strength of the Inner Artillery Zone and unrestricted barrage fire made a joyful noise for the comfort of Londoners and doubtless affected the weight of bombs dropped in the centre of the capital; but there was little return in the way of enemy aircraft destroyed. Consequently, the month saw a quickening of the tempo of research and experiment in the problems of night defence and the creation of a number of reviewing bodies, notably a War Cabinet committee under the chairmanship of the Prime Minister. For the time being, however, no day fighter squadrons were transferred to night work.

And as the Germans were unable (or if they were they did not choose) to mount day and night offensives of equal violence, their concentration on night bombing relieved the pressure on Fighter Command. For the direct effect of the night raids was small. They meant that operations rooms personnel were rarely free from intensive work; there was some extra strain on day fighter pilots stationed near London; and an occasional bomb or parachute mine hit the London sector stations. But the overall casualty rate, which was the gravest of the Command's problems, fell, just at the time when relief was most needed.

vi. Pilot Position in Fighter Command

For the best that could be said of the pilot position in September was that it was getting no worse. On 16 September there were 984 pilots in the Spitfire and Hurricane squadrons, a deficiency of nearly two hundred on an establishment of twenty-two pilots per squadron. But again it must be emphasised that this did not reveal the full extent of the deficiency; for nearly one third of the Command consisted of 'C' squadrons containing approximately one hundred and fifty semi-trained pilots. The 'A' and 'B' squadrons on the same date averaged twenty pilots, including those on leave. There was, therefore, still the dual problem, first, of bringing the Command up to establishment, and, second, of training all its pilots to the requisite standard of efficiency. Both problems were best answered by creating adequate capacity in the Operational Training Units for sufficient and sufficiently-trained pilots to pass to the operational squadrons. For the time being, however, the 'C' squadrons had to assist the OTUs in solving the problem of training but they could do little to make up quantitative deficiencies.

This could only be achieved by accelerating output from the Flying Training Schools and to the extent that this fell short of the Command's needs, by transfers from other Commands. In mid-September the immediate numerical requirements were one hundred pilots each week to replace wastage and 198 pilots to bring Fighter Command, including the night fighting squadrons, up to establishment; and at a meeting held under the Vice-Chief of the Air Staff on 18 September the following measures were agreed upon. Four hundred British and eighty Allied pilots would be found for Fighter Command from the output of the Flying Training Schools and from the pools of Allied pilots. The first of these would enter the Command on 21 September. In addition, a dozen pilots from Battle squadrons in Bomber Command would be posted to 'C' squadrons for training, thus by-passing the usual OTU stage. Those, with approximately one hundred and thirty pilots that were expected to come into the Command between 21 and 25 September, would substantially meet the Command's requirements. The extent to which the fighter squadrons were still dictating the expansion of the Royal Air Force as a whole is apparent from the fact that the four hundred British pilots that were to be posted to Fighter Command represented a little over two-thirds of the total output of the Flying Training Schools for the period 21 September–19 October.

vii. German Losses: Possible Significance

There was still no direct evidence of the extent to which the shortage of pilots was parallelled on the German side. The first analysis of claims by AI3(b) was circulated on 19 September and thereafter weekly. From this all that was certain was that the Germans had lost at least 531 aircraft between 22 August and 25 September out of a force of fifteen hundred to two thousand bombers and about two thousand fighters: not a prohibitive rate of loss. On the other hand, the switch to the attack of London by night implied the defeat of the heavy daylight raids; for there was good reason to believe that provided their casualties were not unacceptably high the Germans would have preferred to maintain their offensive by day. And as the second half of September showed no sign of its renewal it seemed fairly certain that the immediate and most obvious perils of the defeat of the day fighter force and a consequential invasion had been overcome: certainly, the Spitfire and Hurricane squadrons, while reduced in strength, were very far from being a beaten force

VI

FIFTH PHASE: THE DECLINE OF THE BATTLE

I. INTRODUCTION

Those tendencies in the German operations that had arisen during the latter part of September continued and were intensified in October. That is to say that the main weight of the German effort continued to be applied at night, chiefly against London but also against Liverpool and the Midlands; during the day fighter and fighter-bomber sweeps were made towards London and harassing attacks, usually by single bombers, were carried out against important targets near London, in the Midlands and as far north as the Preston district. Attacks on shipping were the work, as in September, of single aircraft. On the invasion front preparations still seemed to be going ahead. But there was no alarm comparable to that of the second week in September; indeed, such diplomatic evidence as was received indicated that no expedition would be launched until the spring of 1941. In short, there is no clear dividing line between what for convenience have been termed Phases IV and V of the battle. The attack on London, as a daylight operation, declined after 15 September, though it did not fade away altogether: at night it continued with increased force throughout October. Such distinction as there is between operations in the second half of September and those of October springs rather from the big daylight attacks that were made against the aircraft industry during the former period (for only one comparable attack was launched in October) than from any radical change in the character of the attacks on London. It may well be, therefore, that more satisfactory chronological sub-divisions of the second half of the battle will be possible when more is known of German policy.

II. DISTRIBUTION OF THE GERMAN ATTACK: RELATION TO PLANS FOR IMMEDIATE INVASION

According to German records, some nine thousand tons of bombs were dropped during the month, of which approximately one tenth was dropped in daytime. On no night was London free of bombing and only on six nights was the weight of attack less than one hundred tons. Over six thousand tons were aimed at the capital by night, which was ten times as much as was dropped in the fighter-bomber attacks by day. Elsewhere, Birmingham and Coventry were most heavily attacked, over five hundred tons being dropped on the two cities, chiefly in the last ten days of the month. Liverpool was less of a target than in the two previous months and the weight of bombs dropped – two hundred tons at most – was less than half that which had been aimed at the area in August. Manchester, Hull and Glasgow were also attacked lightly; but the tonnage that was dropped on each place is hidden in the eight hundred tons that were dropped in dislocation raids and on alternative targets during the month. It is known, however, that some twelve tons of bombs were aimed at the Metrovickers works, Manchester, on the night of 9 October. The tonnage dropped on airfields was less even than the low figure for September. There was no sign of a renewed attempt to disorganise Fighter Command stations. If anything, Bomber Command stations were preferred for attacks. At dusk on the 27th, for example, nine Ju 88s of KG4 attacked three bomber stations in Yorkshire; which was the biggest single attack that was made on this type of target during the month. The only notable attacks on Fighter Command stations were carried out by small formations of Me 109 bombers against Hawkinge, North Weald and Martlesham; and in no case was there damage other than to the landing area.

The harassing attacks that were made in daylight by single aircraft were chiefly directed against important factories. De Havillands' works at Hatfield was accurately bombed by a single Ju 88 of KG77 shortly before noon on the 3rd. An assembly shed and the technical school received direct hits and the sheet metal shed was destroyed. The aircraft was brought down by the local ground defences. On the same day an attempt was made to hit the works of Phillips and Powis at Reading. Similar attacks, though none was as successful as that on de Havillands, were made on Hawkers at Slough, Fairey's at Hayes, Standard's at Coventry, the Royal Ordnance Factory at Pembrey and the BSA works at Redditch. Two attempts were made on the 21st and 30th to hit the Leyland Motor Company's works near Preston, but little damage was done. Rootes' aircraft works at Speke, near Liverpool, was unsuccessfully attacked on 8 October by a Ju 88 of KGr 806, which was shot down. Two days later three Do 17s of KGr 606 attempted another attack on the same target. The attack was timed to take place at dusk but No. 611 Squadron intercepted the German formation near Anglesey and destroyed it. The biggest daylight attack against a specific industrial target was carried out on the 7th by a dozen Ju 88s of KG 51, escorted, as usual, by Me 110s of ZG 26: their objective was the Westland works at Yeovil, which had escaped damaged in the much heavier attack of 30 September. The Germans were no more successful on this occasion, most of their bombs falling in the centre of the town. They were heavily engaged by squadrons of No. 10 Group on the return journey and five bombers and seven fighters were believed to have been destroyed. Two Ju 88s and five Me 110s crashed on land or were washed on shore after the battle.

It is fairly clear from the above summary that the enemy's bombing policy was, first, to continue the progressive destruction of London, chiefly by night attack; second, and on a much lower order of importance, to interfere with production in the great arms centres of the Midlands, again chiefly by night attack; and third, chiefly by means of attacks by single aircraft during the day, to damage plant and hamper production at some of the most important industrial key points in the country. The aircraft industry, in particular, had been selected for attack. Nearly thirty hits were recorded on aircraft factories during October compared to only eight in the period 7–30 September.

Now this was not the sort of bombardment that was expected to be a preliminary to invasion. It was, so to speak, an investment which would show small but growing dividends as damage to property, industrial and domestic, increased, and as communications weakened under constant attack. In this way it would, of course, assist invasion insofar as it succeeded in hampering production and distribution and lowering public morale. But it implied that no military operations were likely to be launched in the near future. In this connection, it was probably significant that the large forces of dive-bombers that had been assembled early in September in north-east France were as inactive during October as they had been in the previous month.

III. PREPARATIONS FOR INVASION

Preparations for invasion, however, were still being reported. During October the number of barges in the Channel ports and in the ports of the Scheldt decreased; on the other hand that of merchant ships had increased. No unit of the German Air Force was known to have moved to any other theatre of war, though as early as 15 September Ju 87s were reported in use against Malta. Further reports, and reliable ones, had been received of the conversion of barges for the carrying of tanks and guns. Embarkation exercises were also known to have taken place during the month. Altogether, the assemblies of shipping and barges remained sufficient to carry an expedition; and while one day substantial moves eastwards from the Channel ports indicated that the enterprise had been abandoned, two or three days later a move in the contrary direction would restore the threat. All that seemed to be certain was that the threat was not immediate.

IV. ENEMY ATTACKS BY DAY

a. Predominance of Fighters and Fighter-Bombers

The switch to night bombing, while it indicated that the Germans did not intend an early invasion, did not imply that the project had been abandoned. For the Germans were thus conserving their bomber strength, yet at the same time they were forcing difficult and strenuous battles upon one of the major obstacles to invasion, Fighter Command, by means of the fighter and fighter-bomber sweeps towards London. Moreover, while the absence of long-range bombers meant that only a light scale of day bombing was possible, it meant also that the German fighters could operate at a greater height and without the hampering responsibility of escort work.

The extent to which the Germans kept long-range bombers out of the fighting in the south-east is reflected in the claims of the No. 11 Group pilots and in the enemy aircraft that crashed on land or were recovered from the sea. Over one hundred and fifty fighters, including only nine Me 110s were believed to have been destroyed by pilots of the Group during the month, but only thirteen bombers, nearly all of which were found flying unescorted. These were out of a total for the whole Command of 171 fighters and forty bombers and other types. Correspondingly, seventy Me 109s and one Me 110 crashed in the No. 11 Group area, but only three bombers. Elsewhere, fifteen bombers and seven fighters crashed on land or were recovered from the sea; and of the twenty-six aircraft that were believed to have been shot down at night, only three of them by fighters, fifteen were found, all of them being bombers. It is interesting that there was a much closer agreement in October between the number of enemy aircraft positively identified as destroyed (153) and that claimed as destroyed (234). It may have been because most of the German losses were fighters which would not glide far before they finally crashed.

b. Character of the Attacks

Despatch, para 206

In his despatch on the battle Air Chief Marshal Dowding reported that of all the tactics employed by the Germans those of October were the most difficult to counter. On days of heavy activity – and on eleven days during the month Fighter Command made more than six hundred sorties – the sky over south-east England was rarely free of the enemy. At the beginning of the month formations of thirty and more fighters were encountered, and again for a short time towards its end; but for most of it the Germans operated in small formations, usually no more than nine fighters strong and frequently as small as two or three.

Whether large or small formations were used, the enemy fighters assembled over France and climbed to heights of 20,000 feet and more before they came across the coast of Kent. Herein lay the main obstacle to efficient defence; for RDF cover at these heights was incomplete and more than once British squadrons met formations that had escaped observation. It is very doubtful whether the Germans intended to avoid RDF observation; the probability is that they intended to give their fighters an advantage in combat. But their tactics meant that defending fighters found it the more difficult to reach a comparable height. Furthermore; if the RDF stations failed to locate an enemy force the chances were that it would escape detection altogether; for what with cloudy weather and the height at which the enemy flew the standard of tracking by the Observer Corps was understandably low.

The problem of interception was further complicated by the enemy's use of fighter-bombers, mostly Me 109s. The performance of the Me 109 fell away considerably when bomb-racks were fitted and bombs, usually one 250 or 500 kg, were carried. Its speed dropped by about 15 mph, its ceiling to 25,000 feet at most and manoeuvrability was seriously affected; and for this reason the bomb was usually jettisoned under attack. Nor could it bomb accurately from the heights at which it normally operated against London. But the Germans conceived it as much a bait to draw the defending fighters off the ground as a contribution to the bombardment of London. The fighter-bomber could well have become even the latter, however, if it had not been intercepted. There was nothing surprising, therefore, in the intelligence received during the month indicating that the Germans were contemplating, where they had not already begun, the conversion of one fighter *Staffel* in three to this type of aircraft.

Fighter-bombers were rarely, if ever, used during the month without a close escort of fighters. In addition, other fighter formations swept ahead at altitudes that not infrequently reached 30,000 feet. Below the combats that developed between the high fighter screen and the defending fighters and making use of cloud, the fighter-bombers would fly into the London area and drop their bombs, with seemingly little regard for specific targets. Their chance of penetrating successfully was not small; for their advance was much swifter than that of a long-range bomber formation. A not unusual interval between the first warning of attack and the fall of bombs in the London area was twenty minutes.

c. New Methods of Defence

In consequence, the new defensive methods which had been tentatively introduced in September were more extensively used. The special reconnaissance aircraft of No. 421 Flight began to operate regularly from Gravesend on 9 October. The pilots had strict orders to act as 'Jim Crows', i.e. to reconnoitre and shadow enemy formations, reporting by VHF R/T to No. 11 Group Headquarters, and to avoid combat. This proved to be difficult; for although the flight was equipped with Mk II Spitfires, and for a short time with Mk II Hurricanes, both of which had a higher ceiling than earlier models, enemy fighters were frequently met high over the Straits. In the first ten days of such patrols seven combats took place and four of the flight's pilots were shot down. From 18 October, therefore, a proportion of their patrols were made in pairs; and on 24 October this became the usual practice. Changes of equipment and changes of station hampered the work of the flight; but Air Vice-Marshal Park reported that invaluable reports of the height and strength of enemy raids – information that was not being obtained by the RDF stations or the Observer Corps – were frequently supplied. There was a good deal of evidence that the Germans were using He 113s for similar work; and the pilots of No. 421 Flight occasionally saw and engaged this type. Air Vice-Marshal Park therefore recommended that the flight should be strengthened to a squadron so that the enemy's reconnaissance could be interfered with more frequently and that the flight's own reconnaissance work could be extended. This was agreed to, but the expansion did not take place until January 1941 when the flight became No. 91 Squadron.

These reconnaissance aircraft were not intended to take the place of RDF stations, nor could they: and as the warning of attack was still insufficient to enable the defending squadrons to reach the enemy's height before the target area was reached a system of standing patrols was introduced on 7 October. These were at first limited to one Spitfire squadron which patrolled Biggin Hill–Maidstone–Gravesend at 15,000 feet, climbing to 30,000 whenever an enemy attack developed across the coast of Kent. Then on 16 October Air Vice-Marshal Park decided to augment this by a Hurricane squadron which would carry out a similar patrol, once in the morning and again early in the afternoon, if a raid was threatened at those times. The function of these squadrons was not to intercept as soon as possible but to cover the squadrons from the London sector stations as they were gaining height. Later still, controllers were ordered to maintain *continuous* patrols of two squadrons, if possible from the same station, whenever weather conditions were suitable for high-flying raids.

No. 11 Group Instructions to Controllers, No. 29

Ibid., No. 26, 9 October

Ibid., No. 34, 24 October

There was some improvement in the ratio of sorties to interceptions as a result of these measures. On the first day of the month only three out of thirty squadrons intercepted the enemy during the three sweeps which were made over Kent. On the 14th, a day of comparable activity, six squadrons intercepted out of twenty-four despatched. On the 27th the ratio was eight to twenty-six. The 29th was the best day of the month: thirty-four squadrons were despatched to meet four attacks; fifteen of them sighted and ten engaged the enemy. Generally, however, only squadrons that were airborne when an attack developed, and occasionally one or two of the squadrons that had been at 'Stand-By', succeeded in closing with the enemy.

d. Difficulties of the Fighting

The advantage in these circumstances was with the Germans, who were usually in a position to open a combat by diving down on the British fighters. Yet they seemed to the RAF pilots not to take advantage of this superiority as often as they might have done. This may well have been because the German pilots wished to fight as high as possible; for above 25,000 feet the Me 109 in service at this date was a better aircraft than either of the British fighters, thanks to the two-stage superchargers with which their engines were fitted compared to the single-stage superchargers of the Merlin engine. Towards the end of the month Mk II Hurricanes and Spitfires were being issued to the Command but neither type promised to be a satisfactory aircraft at over 25,000 feet.

The fighting itself was different from anything that had been experienced before. Loose groups of Me 109s were encountered rather than the rigidly disciplined formations of bombers and fighters of the earlier attacks. Consequently, surprise attacks by small forces of enemy fighters were more frequent than when most of the fighters taking part in an operation were chiefly concerned to protect the bombers. Correspondingly flexible formations were adopted by our own squadrons, who were also less strictly controlled from the ground than hitherto.[1] Other minor tactical changes were instituted to give greater security from surprise and facilitate speedier turns and changes of formation: sections of four aircraft rather than three were used so that pilots could work in pairs: squadrons patrolled on a wider front in sub-units of two instead of in sections of three in line astern, which was the normal patrolling formation earlier in the battle: an above-guard of a pair of fighters was usually maintained even when the enemy were below and no others could be seen above.

V. PILOT POSITION IN FIGHTER COMMAND

a. Effect of the Day Fighting

All things considered it was surprising that British casualties were not heavier. During October fifty three pilots of No. 11 Group were killed or missing and twenty-four wounded. These losses were exceeded by the *identifiable* German losses (the final figure would be even higher) in the Group area, which were between eighty and ninety aircraft; and to have destroyed more than they had lost was not the least remarkable achievement of the No. 11 Group pilots during the whole battle. In the whole Command one hundred pilots were killed and sixty-five wounded during the month, which represented only a little more than half the casualty rate for September; and by the end of the month the pilot strength of the Command had reached an average of twenty-six in each squadron. But not all of them were fit to fight; and even though casualties had been relatively light it had still been necessary to replace three of the 'A' squadrons, leaving only two 'B' squadrons to take the place of any squadrons in

1 It is interesting that whereas earlier in the battle captured German pilots had contrasted the rigidity of the ground control of British squadrons with what seemed to them to be their own greater freedom, these criticisms were not heard during the October fighting. British pilots remarked a similar difference between German fighter tactics in August and early September, when time after time defensive circles of forty and fifty aircraft were automatically formed, and those of October, when small and loosely knit formations were the rule.

the south and south-east that needed a rest. Nor had it been possible to build up any 'C' squadrons to full operational strength.

b. *Withdrawal of Day Squadrons for Night Fighting*

AC (40) 46

S.6287, Air Council – Dowding, 25 September

Moreover, amongst the many changes and new devices that were agreed upon during the months to combat the German night attacks was the transference of a number of single-seater fighter squadrons to night fighting. Such a move had been suggested after the night attack of London had begun by a committee on night interception of which Marshal of the Royal Air Force Sir John Salmond was chairman; but the Air Council supported the view of Air Chief Marshal Dowding that it must not be made until the scale of the day attack had fallen considerably. In the third week in October, however, two 'C' squadrons, Nos 73 and 151, which were equipped with Hurricanes, were instructed to train for night fighting; and the necessary postings to give each a minimum of twelve fully trained pilots were made during the next fortnight. No. 422 Flight was also formed at this time for the same sort of work; and early in November No. 73 Squadron was ordered to the Middle East and No. 85 took its place in the night fighter line. These changes meant some diminution of the strength of the day fighter force but that they were made was significant not only of the growing power of the night offensive but of the decline in intensity of the enemy's daylight operations.

VI. COMMENTARY

The daylight attacks of October were difficult to counter. Furthermore, they were the more dangerous in that they followed two months of bitter fighting which had weakened the overall strength of Fighter Command. Nevertheless, it is obvious enough that they meant that the crisis had been passed successfully. November was to see something of a return to the attack of coastal towns and shipping that had opened the battle: the wheel had come full circle. From the end of October the most important operational function of Fighter Command was to develop a system of night interception as effective as that which it practised by day. Otherwise the energies of the Command were chiefly taken up in repairing the effects of the summer and autumn fighting; in particular, in reorganising and expanding operational training, putting in hand the overdue expansion of front-line strength, improving the quality of its training and remedying the deficiencies of equipment and armament that had been revealed by the battle. As far as the day fighting squadrons were concerned the emphasis was on preparing for a renewal of the battle when the invasion season of the spring came round and preparing also for beginning its own offensive operations against enemy territory. They were, indeed, to operate throughout November and the winter but the fighting bears no comparison with the great battles of August and September. Nor, after the end of September, possibly as early as 15 September, were the objects of the German offensive the same. For while there is much that is not yet known of German policy this much is certain, that from the middle of August to the middle of September the German Air Force engaged

Fighter Command in an encounter battle which, if the issue had gone against the Command, would have meant at least the maintenance of daylight attacks on London comparable to those of 7 September, and at worst an early attempt at invasion. The battle which went on throughout the winter, however, insofar as it took place at night, was one of attrition against the British war economy. Insofar as it was fought by day, the aim was preparation for the battles of the spring. In either case the fruits of victory would only be gathered well in the future.

VII

A SURVEY OF THE BATTLE

I. THE DEVELOPMENT OF THE GERMAN OFFENSIVE

The main phases of the Battle of Britain have now been fairly clearly established. During the last three weeks of July and the first of August the Germans were probing and testing the air defences of the country, particularly in the south. Their attacks by day were chiefly directed against fringe targets – coastal shipping and ports in the east and south – and such attacks as were made against targets well inland were carried out by single aircraft or very small formations. By night small numbers of bombers were attacking widely dispersed targets, chiefly in the west and Wales and in coastal districts in the east. The second and third weeks of August saw a notable increase in the scale of attack by day; but the majority of the German targets were on or near the coast. Similarly, the night attacks during the same period, while they were stronger than before, followed the same pattern of widely dispersed effort. But during the third phase – the last week in August and the first in September – the German attacks not only grew in intensity but they were concentrated on a few types of target. By day the effort was almost exclusively against airfields in the No. 11 Group area: by night Merseyside, the Midlands and, during the first week in September, London itself were the targets for the heaviest attacks the Germans had so far launched. The development of the battle to a further stage commenced on 7 September with the attack on London. But then the rhythm faltered. For while the capital continued to be the enemy's prime objective at night throughout the rest of September and during the whole of October, by day the German effort was not so tidily applied. Attacks continued to be made against London but only on 15 September was an important bomber force despatched; and towards the end of the month the heaviest daylight bombing raids were made against aircraft factories in the south and south-west. Altogether, after 7 September the scale of the daylight offensive died away, a process which was registered by the fighter and fighter-bomber sweeps of late September and October, which for all that they posed a difficult problem of interception were no substitute for the type of attack that had been launched during the third phase and on 7 September. In short, and speaking of daylight attacks only, the German Air Force commenced to attack with what we must presume to have been its maximum available strength during the second week in August and maintained the attack for almost exactly a month, though only from 30 August were strong attacks carried out daily. And since, as far as Fighter Command was concerned, it was the attacks by day that held the greatest threat to the country, two questions immediately spring to mind: Why did the Germans start so late? Why did they stop so soon?

II. CONDITION OF THE GERMAN AIR FORCE

Only the Germans can answer these questions authoritatively. As far as the first is concerned the directly relevant evidence in British hands is very scanty and unreliable. Intelligence reports throughout July and early August indicated that the German Air Force had neither fully recovered after it exertions in the campaign of May and June nor had the problems of maintaining and supplying it in its new positions been satisfactorily overcome. We know, for example, that the process of re-equipment often entailed the withdrawal of a unit to Germany. We know also that many of the airfields in northern and north-western France were not suitable for the larger German aircraft; and the Germans began a big programme of extension and construction of airfields during the summer months. It may well be the case, therefore, that although the majority of the German squadrons had taken up by July the positions that they were to occupy during the rest of the summer, logistical factors forbade the mounting of any large-scale attack until the second half of August. Indeed, it was not until the first week in September, when extra dive-bomber and long-range bomber units were moved to northern France and Belgium, that the Germans appeared to be preparing to make full use of their greatly superior numbers. This at least is fairly certain: that the actual strength of the two *Luftflotten* in France and the Low Countries was smaller than the established first-line strength, especially in the long-range bomber units. Until 7 September the Germans rarely used more than one hundred and fifty long-range bombers in a single day and a similar number at night, while on 7/8 September itself, when they appear to have made a special effort, only six hundred bombers were employed, which were less than half of the forces nominally available in France, Belgium and Holland. It is doubtful whether the German fighter units were below strength, though judging from reports from prisoners individual squadrons seem to have been at least as hard worked as our own. On the other hand, it seems fairly clear that the German dive-bomber units could not continue to accept the losses that they suffered during the first three weeks of August; and they were withdrawn from the battle after 18 August.

Thus, a possible answer to the first of the two questions with which this section was introduced may also be the answer to the second. The Germans may have been forced to delay their offensive in the air because of difficulties of supply and maintenance; and those same difficulties, still operative, may have forced them to reduce the scale of the daylight attack and increase the weight of their attack by night even though they must have known that in so doing their chances of immobilising Fighter Command virtually disappeared. The hypothesis, of course, rests on what we believe to be a valid assumption: that the Germans would have continued their daylight attacks by long-range bombers if they had been able.

III. RELATION OF THE BATTLE TO A PROJECTED INVASION

It has generally been held that the defeat of Fighter Command was the most important single object that the Germans had in view, as a preliminary – possibly an indispensable one – to the invasion that they were believed to be preparing. On this view of the battle the operations of the German Air Force were closely linked with a projected invasion and governed by a timed programme.

If that is the case then the attacks on shipping and coastal towns during the first phase of the battle are to be interpreted rather as preliminary to a decisive encounter with Fighter Command than as an attempt to put out of action port facilities on the south coast and prohibit the Channel to Allied shipping. The detailed account of operations during this phase should have shown that while on a few days the Germans mounted serious attacks the effort over the period as a whole was inadequate for the purpose of blockade. It may well be that Channel shipping was not high on the list of German targets. Certainly, during late August and September, when the biggest battles were being fought, the Germans paid little or no attention to shipping in the south. Only when the daylight offensive was petering out did they renew their interest in shipping in this area. Moreover, what we know of the German mine-laying during the battle indicates that it fell away during August and September from the high level of effort in July; which also implies that when they were making their biggest attacks the Germans allowed their offensive against shipping to decline.

On the other hand, if the Germans wanted to bring the defending fighter squadrons to battle under circumstances as favourable to themselves as possible then these early attacks across the Channel were well conceived. For the shipping using the Channel, and the coastal towns on its shores, especially Dover, were sufficiently important to demand an effective defence, yet the problem of defending them was peculiarly difficult. Warning of attack was frequently short, particularly in the Straits of Dover; the small formations of fighters, which were all that could be afforded for the protection of convoy, were insufficient to deal with a serious attack and were occasionally overwhelmed before reinforcements could arrive; and even the latter, which usually arrived one squadron at a time, were often outweighed by the enemy formations. Nor had defending pilots that advantage of fighting overland which was to be the saving of so many lives in the later battles. Altogether, although shipping losses and damage to south coast ports were small, the phase clearly showed that it would be difficult, first, to maintain Channel traffic, and, second, to maintain Dover as a destroyer base, if the Germans made a wholehearted effort in the Channel.

But when the Germans did begin to operate daily in great strength it was against targets on land. Beginning on 12 August there was a week of strong attacks chiefly against coastal airfields in the south and south-east. A five days lull followed. Then on the 24th the offensive began again. This time airfields in the south-east were very obviously the main German target; and the attack was maintained until 6 September.

The first part of this period – what has been called in the narrative the second phase of the battle – is not so easily linked with the later operations as is the second. For it is difficult to see what policy of target selection governed the German attacks. Indeed, in default of any evidence to the contrary, we are entitled to say that if there was a coherent policy it was either a bad one or it was ill-executed. If it was the German aim to immobilise coastal airfields preparatory to invasion, then they should have attacked that type of target more consistently than they did. If, however, it was their aim to destroy Fighter Command (and the diversionary attack in the north-east on 15 August can be more easily squared with that purpose than any other) then they were ill-advised to spend so much effort attacking targets not vital to the Command. The heavy attack of RDF stations in the south and south-east on the 12th can also be squared with such a policy. Why, then, was the attack not maintained? The only thing that is certain is that the operations forced an intensive defensive effort upon Fighter Command, and resulted in a steep rise in the casualty rate of pilots and aircraft before the Command had fully recovered from the effects of the fighting in France and Flanders.

It may be that one purpose the Germans had in mind was to train their pilots and crews for the series of attacks which began on 24 August and continued with few breaks for a fortnight, and which represent quite the most critical phase of the whole battle, as the narrative has sought to make clear. Their object during this phase was obviously to destroy No. 11 Group, especially in the sectors guarding London, partly by attacking its communications and airfields, partly by forcing it to give battle to superior numbers almost daily. If they had succeeded, the defending squadrons would have been prevented from intervening effectively over south-east England.

But it is not certain by what date this situation was to have been brought about or what use the Germans intended to make of it. In view of what happened on 7 September it would appear to follow that No. 11 Group was to have been broken by that date and that the pounding of the capital could then have gone on without any interruption; and this, the obvious explanation, may well contain the truth of the matter. But the packing of dive-bombers and long-range bombers into the northern corner of France and the movement of barges and shipping into French ports opposite the coasts of Kent and Sussex – all this during the first week in September strongly indicated that invasion was timed for the very near future; in which case the purpose of the assault on the south-eastern airfields may have been to clear the air over Kent and Sussex and thus simplify the establishing of a bridgehead in that area.

What happened in fact was that the attacks on airfields were broken off just as they seemed likely to show a considerable dividend – though it is doubtful if the Germans knew this – and on 7 September the bombardment of London began with a heavy attack in the evening followed by one equally heavy the same night. Of itself this switch to the attack of London proved nothing regarding either the imminence or even the likelihood of invasion. A powerful blow at the capital was worthwhile politically and psychologically whether invasion was intended or not. On the other hand, it was not ill-conceived if its main purpose was to hamper the transport of troops and supplies to the south-east as well as to interfere with the ordinary processes of government. As to this, however, it should not be forgotten that such evidence as there is of aimed bombing indicates that the dock areas rather than the main railway terminals or the administrative districts were the chief German target; and it was damage to the latter types of target rather than the former which would have hindered counter-measures to an invasion.

And on the whole the available evidence best bears the interpretation that invasion was not the Germans' immediate intention at any time in September. For after 7 September the main weight of the attack on London was applied at night; and while in that way the Germans reduced their losses they could neither achieve the precision of bombardment which could be expected from a similar effort by day nor could they hope to inflict important losses on the far from beaten Fighter Command. This change to night attack was the more remarkable in that the evening attack of the 7th was – so it appears to us – much the most successful that the Germans has yet launched. Yet thenceforwards, except for the attacks of the 15th, no major raids were launched against the capital by day.

Indeed, it may be the case that the whole of the German air offensive of August and September was as much independent of any immediately projected military movements as, for example, was the offensive conducted by Bomber Command in 1942. For if it is true that the Germans reckoned the elimination of Fighter Command an essential preliminary measure to invasion it is noteworthy that preparations for an expedition seemed still to be going ahead during the second half of September and even in October, although by that time the scale of daylight attack had fallen away considerably from the peak of intensity that was reached during the first week in September. If the Germans had had any limited period earmarked for invasion their air offensive would surely have reached its peak at or shortly before the expedition sailed, as did our own air offensive during the spring and early summer of 1944.

There are two main alternative interpretations, therefore, of the German offensive: first, that it was part of a programme of invasion; second, that it was intended so to weaken Britain that the government would have been forced to negotiate even though the country had not been invaded. On either understanding the Germans failed. If the second was their aim they failed – to state the obvious – because their attack was neither sufficiently strong nor sufficiently accurate; in which case the victory of Fighter Command consisted principally in inflicting such losses on the Germans that they were forced to attack at night. If invasion was the end to which the Germans were working they may have cancelled the project partly for military and naval reasons; but it remains true that Fighter Command defeated what must have been an essential part of the German programme – if programme there was: an intensive air offensive by day.

IV. STRENGTH AND DEPLOYMENT OF FIGHTER COMMAND DURING THE BATTLE

Introduction, p. 6

This victory was the more remarkable in that the Command was so heavily outnumbered. It has already been pointed out that under an estimate drawn up on the same basis as had governed the size of the pre-war fighter force the new conditions of the summer of 1940 were reckoned to demand a maximum force of one hundred and twenty squadrons. It may be that the size of the German Air Force, which was an important factor in this calculation, was overestimated; but there is no doubt at all that the sixty squadrons, including the Blenheim squadrons, which were all that the Command could call upon throughout most of the battle, were a force far smaller than a reasonable security demanded. For the standards that had been adopted before the war applied no longer when German fighters and dive-bombers has to be met as well as long-range bombers; and the battle was only a tax upon Fighter Command because the German fighters were present: otherwise any bomber attacks by day could have been fought off without much difficulty. Indeed, the Germans would no more have been able to despatch large unescorted bomber formations against this country by day than could Bomber Command against Germany.

Not only was the offensive only possible to the Germans because their fighters could be utilised but its geographical scope was largely dictated by the operational range of the enemy fighters, especially the Me 109. Some success attended attacks that were made west of the Solent by long-range bombers and Me 110s; but it was in the south-east, where the Me 109 could operate, that the battle was necessarily fought. At the same time, the wide deployment of the German Air Force, threatening almost the whole of the United Kingdom, meant that defending fighters had to be stationed in parts of the country remote from the south-east, despite the fact that the main battle was being fought there and could only be fought there.

The Germans were clearly aware of their advantage; and by means of occasional attacks such as that of 15 August against the north-east coast and by daily sorties by single aircraft of small formations against widely scattered regions of the country they sought to ensure a measure of dispersion of the defenders' strength which could be ill afforded. Thus, from beginning to end of the battle there was no significant redistribution of fighter squadrons in order to strengthen No. 11 Group; which meant that the bulk of the German Air Force was opposed by little more than half of the squadrons in the Command. In short, the nominal strength of the three main fighter Groups varied little during the course of the battle.

The records of the battle, however, especially the minutes of conferences of sector commanders in No. 11 Group, show quite clearly that there was a feeling in the southern sectors that more squadrons ought to have been moved to that area. Yet Air Chief Marshal Dowding maintained an orthodox deployment for practically the whole of the battle. Indeed, the tendency was rather to move squadrons to the western half of the country (as witness the formation of No. 9 Group in September) than to the south-east. Now insofar as the main area of battle could only be in the south-east it is at least debatable whether the Commander-in-Chief's policy was correct. If, for example, he had packed additional squadrons into No. 11 Group early in the battle so powerful a blow might have been struck at the attacking forces that the daylight offensive might conceivably have been abandoned. At any rate, such a move would have made possible the earlier use of fighting formations larger than a single squadron and thus reduced the incidence of casualties in individual squadrons. This policy might have been successful against opponents less well trained, less numerous and less persistent than the Germans; but in the circumstances the risks involved in it were too great. Air Chief Marshal Dowding preferred to fight the battle for as long as he could with the force normally deployed in No. 11 Group and the flanking sectors, using the rest of his squadrons as replacements *in toto* for No. 11 Group squadrons, prior to which they carried out their usual defensive functions in the sectors in which they were stationed; and although this meant that units in the main area of battle were outnumbered, and often heavily outnumbered, it meant also that fresh squadrons could be called upon to take their places. If, on the other hand, more squadrons had been committed to the fight earlier in the battle, casualties and fatigue would have been spread so much more quickly and widely through the Command. Thus the supply of fresh squadrons would have been exhausted even earlier than it was; and this could not be accepted when there were no means of telling how long the offensive might last. Even so, such was the rate of casualties during August and the first week in September and so swift the shuttling back and forth of squadrons in

No. 11 Group and the other Groups that Air Chief Marshal Dowding was forced to alter his policy; and under the Stabilisation Scheme that was applied from 7 September the bulk of the squadrons outside No. 11 Group existed for little else but to serve its needs. In this way there was an effective reinforcement of the south-east at the expense of other regions even though the number of squadrons in the various Groups remained virtually unaltered. But the fact that the pressure of events forced the Commander-in-Chief to give specially preferential treatment to No. 11 Group does not mean that he was wrong in not doing so, at least not to the same extent, earlier in the battle.

V. THE WORKING OF THE FIGHTER COMMAND SYSTEM: DEFICIENCIES AND CHANGES

Moreover, to have reinforced in the south-east was not a simple matter of transferring a number of squadrons to that area. The system of controlled interception which had been built up prior to the war rested on a basis of three squadrons in one sector; and the signals equipment available in any sector was in most cases sufficient for only that number of squadrons to be controlled independently and simultaneously. To increase the size of the controllable force was not impossible; the No. 12 Group wing, for example, frequently operated five squadrons strong. But it could most easily be done by increasing the number of squadrons in the tactical formations employed against a big attack; and as we have seen there seemed both to Air Chief Marshal Dowding and Air Vice-Marshal Park to be good reasons for using fighting units of single squadrons until quite late in the battle. During the third phase – when airfields in the south-east were being regularly attacked – there was a further argument against increasing the number of squadrons in a sector: that to do so only meant increasing the number of potential casualties from bombing.

Altogether, it is the case that Fighter Command fought throughout most of the Battle without departing to any marked extent from the technique which had been conceived as early as 1936 and worked out during the intervening years. The principal features of the system are well known. They were, first, the initial location of an enemy formation by RDF and its subsequent tracking by the Observer Corps; second, the presentation of this information and that giving the position of defending fighters in an Operations Room; and, third, the control of the fighters from the Operations Room up to the time at which combat was about to be joined. At this point a number of standardised methods were applied for changing from a searching and cruising formation to a battle formation as well as a number of standardised attacks for opening the actual combat. The whole system was designed to allow an economical scale of effort. Thus, standing patrols were avoided if it was at all possible and single squadrons were employed. It represented without a doubt the most efficient scheme of air defence in the world at the time and during the battle it served well.

But, not surprisingly, deficiencies were revealed. They were of two sorts: those which arose from the way in which the system was operated and those which were unavoidable in the conditions under which the battle was fought. Those under the latter category were chiefly deficiencies of equipment. The

RDF stations occasionally failed to locate an enemy formation (though they never failed to detect a major attack); and the information they supplied was often imprecise, especially their height finding and estimations of numerical strength. There were similar deficiencies in the work of the Observer Corps, particularly during the fighting of late September and October when the height and speed of the enemy formations made visual tracking very difficult. Yet both these sources of intelligence were vital to the defence; and it is one of the mysteries of the battle that the Germans made so few and such small efforts to disrupt the RDF chain in the south and south-east.

The normal working of the technique of interception was also affected by the proximity of the German Air Force. The warning of attack was so short that often the defending squadrons could not reach the enemy's height in time to intercept before an objective was reached and bombed or they were themselves attacked while under an initial disadvantage in height. Even so, except for some convoy and sector patrols mostly by small formations, standing patrols were avoided during the most intense fighting; and it was only when the time and space problem was further aggravated by the fast fighter-bomber attacks towards the end of the battle that standing patrols in strength were introduced. In this way the Command was saved from an even higher and more fatiguing scale of effort than was actually employed.

This feature of the fighting is closely related to the question of the optimum size of tactical formation, which was indeed the one aspect of the way in which the Fighter Command system was operated which caused serious disagreement during the battle. Much has already been said on this subject; but insofar as it reflected the whole problem of repelling heavy daylight attacks it is worth considering again at some length.

It should first be appreciated that the problems confronting the two Groups most concerned in the controversy – Nos 11 and 12 – were different, primarily insofar as air defence is largely a problem in time. The battle was chiefly fought in the No. 11 Group area; and the squadrons there constantly faced the threat of a heavy and swiftly developed attack. No. 12 Group, however, while there was frequent activity within its area, had no comparable scale of attack to deal with; and any squadrons that were sent to the south-east could assemble with little or no risk of an attack being made upon them. In short, time was a problem for No. 11 Group which it never was for No. 12. In the circumstances, once granted the premise that the defenders' prime task was to protect objectives on the ground, there is little doubt that Air Vice-Marshal Park was justified in sending up individual squadrons as quickly as possible in order to impose some obstacle in the way of the attacking forces before they reached their objective. Nor should it be forgotten that if the German offensive diminished in strength after 7 September because of heavy casualties those casualties were largely suffered at the hands of No. 11 Group during the third phase of the battle, when orthodox methods of control and tactical employment were used.

But implicit in the tactics advocated by Air Vice-Marshal Leigh-Mallory was the notion that the chief task of the fighter force was to destroy enemy aircraft rather than to protect ground targets. It would be unfair and untrue to reduce this to the absurdity that objectives could well be left unprotected. The practical application of the policy of both Groups obviously resulted in enemy aircraft being destroyed and objectives of attack also being defended, or, what was more usually the case, some of the enemy being destroyed and ground targets being protected thereby from heavier and more accurate attack. But there was this difference between the two; that Air Vice-Marshal Leigh-Mallory was not as impressed as he would otherwise have been by the No. 11 Group claim, first, that the Duxford wing often came into action after the German formations had reached and bombed their objectives, and, second, that while the No. 11 Group forces were sent up as independent squadrons, and even by sections and single aircraft, they at least stood a better chance of intercepting and hampering the Germans on their way inland than if time was taken up in assembling larger fighting formations. For No. 12 Group could put forward the powerful argument that although their methods might not save a particular objective from attack on a particular day, the scale of the enemy's offensive would be the more reduced on future days through the heavier casualties which No. 12 Group inflicted. There is, it is true, no certainty concerning the relative efficiency of the two types of tactics as destructive of German aircraft: on the other hand, it is quite certainly the case that the casualties of the Duxford wing were lighter in all of their actions than those of an equal number of No. 11 Group squadrons operating independently against the same attack. Here again, however – and this illustrates how difficult it is to arrive at any final verdict – the No. 11 Group supporter would respond justifiably that the No. 12 Group record was the more impressive simply because the enemy had been previously harried and split up by those squadrons of No. 11 Group which had taken the first shock of the German advance.

This at least can be said: that the squadrons which No. 12 Group could spare for the battle in the south-east represented the only tactical reserve which could support No. 11 Group; and it was right, therefore, that they should have been used in the battle. The use to which they were put, for example on 7 and 15 September, was not the only one possible but it was an effective use and one which did no little harm to the enemy. That the intervention was not as disciplined and regulated as it might have been was unfortunate; and better arrangements for its control might well have been made not in October, when the battle was over, but in August, before it had properly opened. Finally, the pity is that a controversy was ever allowed to develop; for far from the two Group commanders representing two contrasting methods of solving one and the same tactical problem they really represented tactics complementary to each other, each of which had a valuable part to play in the common struggle, the more so as together the most economical use of the dangerously limited forces available would have been assured.

VI. CONCLUSION

For the battle only reached a critical stage because Fighter Command was not as strong numerically as the situation demanded. The Command was never outfought; it suffered no important disadvantages in equipment and none in skill and courage; and despite the deficiencies that have just been enumerated its technique of interception was sound and well organised. But there were neither enough operational squadrons nor sufficient reserves of pilots and aircraft to enable it to withstand the relatively heavy casualties of August and early September and still maintain its strength and efficiency; and although it is true that there were more squadrons in the Command at the end of October than at the beginning of July its fighting strength had fallen considerably. When the crisis came is clear enough. It was in what has been called in the narrative the third phase of the battle; for if the Command had continued to suffer the same casualties during the three weeks succeeding 7 September as in the previous fortnight there would have been no reserves of aircraft in the Aircraft Storage Units; and the pilot position, while we can attempt no accurate forecast, would certainly have been so bad that no effective defence could have been made against continuing attacks by day.

As it was, the battle was won and the daylight offensive petered out. We cannot say for certain that the German effort was reduced after 7 September because of the unacceptable casualties that had been inflicted on the German Air Force during the third and critical phase; but it will be surprising if the connection between the two is not firmly established when more evidence is to hand from the German side. It is, in any case, true beyond dispute that the decline in the German effort meant the checking of the disastrous rate at which the Command had been wasting away. And that this was accomplished by a force so small, facing one so large, was an achievement in air warfare that has never been equalled.

APPENDICES

APPENDIX 1: DISTRIBUTION OF GERMAN BOMBER AND FIGHTER UNITS 15 AUGUST 1940[1]

UNIT	*FUNCTION*	*MAIN AIRFIELDS*	*AIRCRAFT ESTABLISHMENT*[2] *IE*	*+*	*IR*	*Type*
		BREST–ST NAZAIRE–BOURGES–LE HAVRE				
I.II.III/KG27	Long-Range Bomber	Tours, Bourges, Rennes	99	+	27	He 111
I/KG 100		Vannes	30	+	9	
I/StKG1	Dive Bomber	Falaise	30	+	9	Ju 87
II/StKG2		Angers	30	+	9	Ju 87
I.II.III/StKG3		Dinard area	99	+	27	Ju 87
I.III/St KG77		La Coulanche, Argentan.	69	+	18	Ju 87
2/Ob DL	Bomber-Reconnaissance	Brest Poulmic	9	+	3	Do 17
4 (F) 14	Army Co-op	Cherbourg	9	+	3	Do 17
3 (F) 31	(Long-Range)	St Brieue	9	+	3	Do 17
I.II.III/JG27	Single-Engined	Plumetot, Crepon, Quettehou	99	+	27	Me 109
I.II.III/JG53	Fighter	Rennes, Dinan, Brest Guipavas	99	+	27	Me 109
I/ZG2	Twin-Engined Fighter	Caen Carpiquet	30	+	9	Me 110
II/ZG1		Laval	30	+	9	Me 110
II.III/ZG76		Lannion, Dinard Pleurtuit	69	+	18	Me 110
V/Lehr 1		Alencon	30	+	9	Me 110
		LE HAVRE–BOURGES–REIMS–ABBEVILLE				
I.II/KG1	Long-Range Bomber	Rosieres-en-Santerre	69	+	18	He 111
I.II.KG28		Chartres, Vreil	69	+	18	He 111
I.II.III/KG51		Melun, Villaroche	99	+	27	Ju 88
I.II/KG54		Evreux, St Andre	69	+	18	Ju 88
I.II.III/KG55		Villacoublay, Chartres	99	+	27	He 111
I.II.III/KG76		Beauvais, Creil, Cormeilles-en-Vexin	99	+	27	Ju 88/Do 215
I.II.III/Lehr 1		Orleans Bricy, Chateaudun	99	+	27	
I.II.III/StKG51	Dive-Bomber	not definitely known	99	+	27	Ju 87
I.II/StK76		Villenauxe	69	+	18	Ju 87
II/St77		Nevers	30	+	9	Ju 87
II/Lehr1		Soissons Doumies	30	+	9	FW 189
3,4/121	Bomber-321	Chateaudun, Villacoublay	18	+	6	Do 17
1/123	Reconnaissance	Buc	9	+	3	Do 17/Ju 88
2,4,5/221		Le Bourget, Villeneuve, St Mards	30	+	9	Do 17
2,3,4 (F) 11	Army Co-op.	Bernay area	30	+	9	Do 17
2 (F) 21	(Long-Range)	not definitely known	9	+	3	Do 17
1 (F) 31		not definitely known	9	+	3	Do 17

UNIT	*FUNCTION*	*MAIN AIRFIELDS*	*AIRCRAFT ESTABLISHMENT*[2] *IE + IR*	*Type*
I/JG1	Single-Engined	Soissons Saconin	30 + 9	Me 109
I.II.III/JG2	Fighter	Beaumont-le-Roger, Le Havre, Octeville	99 + 27	Me 109
I.II/JG3		Grandvillers, Brombos	69 + 18	Me 109
I/JG21		Octeville	30 + 9	Me 109
II/ZG2	Twin-Engined Fighter	Guyancourt	30 + 9	Me 110
I/ZG52		Guyancourt	30 + 9	Me 110
		NORTH EASTERN FRANCE		
I.II.III/KG2	Long-Range Bomber	St Leger, Cambrai	99 + 27	Do 215
I.II.III/KG53		Lille Nord, Lille Vendeville	99 + 27	He 111
II/StKG1	Dive-Bomber	Quoeux	30 + 9	Ju 87
IV/Lehr 1		Tramecourt	30 + 9	Ju 87
5/122	Bomber-Reconnaisance	Haute Fontaine	9 + 3	Do 17/Ju 88
Gruppe 210	Fighter-Bomber	Denain	30 + 9	Me 109/Me 110
II.III/JG1	Single-Engined	Laon, Chambry, Le Cateau	69 + 18	Me 109
III/JG3	Fighter	Guines	30 + 9	Me 109
I/JG20		St Omer	30 + 9	Me 109
I.II/JG26		Guines, St Inglevert	69 + 18	Me 109
I.II/JG51		St Omer, Longueness	69 + 18	Me 109
I/JG52		Laon Couvron	30 + 9	Me 109
I.II.III/ZG26	Twin-Engined Fighter	Yvrench, Crecy, Barly	99 + 27	Me 110
		HOLLAND AND BELGIUM		
I.II.III/KG3	Long-Range Bomber	Antwerp Deurne, St Trond	99 + 27	Do 215
I.III/KG4		Soesterberg, Amsterdam Schipol	69 + 18	He 111/Ju 88
1,2,3,4/122	Bomber-	Ursel, Brussels, Eindhoven	39 + 12	Do 17/Ju 88
2,3/123	Reconnaissance	Bruges, St Michael-en-Greve	18 + 6	Do 17/Ju 88
KG30	Fighter-Bomber	Amsterdam Schipol	9 + 3	Ju 88
I.II.III/JG54	Single-Engined	Soesterberg, Rotterdam	99 + 27	Me 109
I/Lehr 2	Fighter	Leeuwarden	30 + 9	Me 109
		GERMANY		
III/KG1	Long-Range Bomber	Giessen	30 + 9	He 111
II/KG4		Wittmundhafen	30 + 9	He 111
II/KG26		Lubeck	30 + 9	He 111
I/KG40		Marx	9 + 3	FW 200
I.II.III/KG77		Illesheim, Munich area	99 + 27	Do 215/Ju 88
K/Gr126		Marx	30 + 9	
1/121	Bomber-	Oldenburg	9 + 3	Do 17/Ju 88
3/221	Reconnaissance	Stade	9 + 3	Do 17
1,3/0bDL		Fritzlar, Oldenburg	21 + 6	Do 17/Ju 88
3,4 (F) 10	Army Co-op.	Cologne area	21 + 6	Do 17
4 (F) 13	(Long-Range)	Cologne area	9 + 3	Do 17
1,3 (F) 22		Frankfurt, Kassel	21 + 6	Do 17
III/Lehr 2		Wunstorf area	18 + 6	Do 17
I.II.JG70	Single-Engined	Boblingen area	69 + 18	Me 109
I.II/JG71	Fighter329	Wangerooge, Bremerhaven	69 + 18	Me 109
I/JG77		Doberitz	30 + 9	Me 109
I/ZG1	Twin-Engined Fighter	Dusseldorf area	30 + 9	Me 110

UNIT	*FUNCTION*	*MAIN AIRFIELDS*	*AIRCRAFT ESTABLISHMENT*[2] *IE*	*+*	*IR*	*Type*
		DENMARK AND NORWAY				
I/III/KG26	Long-Range Bomber	?	69	+	18	He 111
I/II.III/KG30		Aalborg area	99	+	27	Ju 88
III/KG100		?	30	+	9	He 111
I/StKG2	Dive-Bomber	Aalborg area	30	+	9	Ju 87
1/120	Bomber-	Stavanger	9	+	3	Do 17
2/121	Reconnaissance	Stavanger	9	+	3	Do 17/Ju 88
2 (F) 22	Army Co-op. (Long-Range)	Trondheim Vaernes	9	+	3	Do 17
I/JG76	Single-Engined	Stavanger	30	+	9	Me 109
II/JG77	Fighter	?	30	+	9	Me 109
I/ZG76	Twin-Engined Fighter	Stavanger	30	+	9	Me 110

Notes: [1] This table shows the German deployment as we knew it at the time. It has not yet been checked against German records, but is not anticipated that any important alterations will be necessary. It can also be taken as the basic deployment of the Germany Air Force from the middle of July to the end of September; any significant redispositions will be referred to in the body of the narrative. It does not include the ten Coastal *Gruppen*, which were chiefly stationed between the Stavanger and Rotterdam, and which continued during the Battle of Britain to carry out their normal anti-shipping operations in the North Sea. Nor does it include the nine Army Co-operation *Gruppen*, which were armed with the Henschel 126 short-range reconnaissance aircraft, and which took no part in the fighting.

[2] Each *Gruppe* HQ had a section (*Kette*) of three aircraft attached to it, and each *Geschwader* HQ a *Staffel* of nine aircraft. These units frequently took part in operations, and thus they have been included in the figures showing first-line establishment.

APPENDIX 2: FIGHTER COMMAND SECTOR ORGANISATION AND ORDER OF BATTLE, 7 JULY 1940 (0900 HOURS)

No 13 GROUP
Headquarters, Newcastle

WICK
No 3 (Hurricane) Wick
No 504 (Hurricane) Castletown

DYCE
No 603 (Spitfire) "A" Flight Dyce
"B" Flight Montrose

TURNHOUSE
No 602 (Spitfire) Drem
No 141 (Defiant) Turnhouse
No 243[1] (Hurricane) Turnhouse

USWORTH
No 152 (Spitfire) Acklington
No 72 (Spitfire) Acklington

CATTERICK
No 41 (Spitfire) Catterick
No 219 (Blenheim) Catterick

CHURCH FENTON
No 249[1] (Hurricane) Church Fenton
No 616 (Spitfire) Leconfield

No 12 GROUP
Headquarters Watnall

KIRTON-IN-LINDSEY
No 253 (Hurricane) Kirton-in-Lindsey
No 222 (Spitfire) Kirton-in-Lindsey

DIGBY
No 29 (Blenheim) Digby
No 611 (Spitfire) Digby
No 46 (Hurricane) Digby
No 266 (Spitfire) Digby

COLTISHALL
No 66 (Spitfire) Coltishall
No 242 (Hurricane) Coltishall

WITTERING
No 23 (Blenheim) Wittering
No 229 (Hurricane) Wittering

DUXFORD
No 19 (Spitfire) Duxford
No 264 (Defiant) Duxford

DEBDEN
No 17 (Hurricane) Debden
No 85 (Hurricane) Debden
("A" Flight at Martlesham)

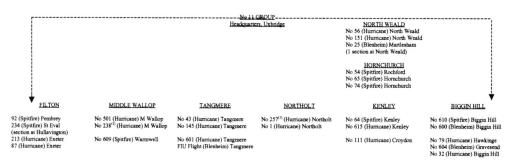

No 11 GROUP
Headquarters, Uxbridge

NORTH WEALD
No 56 (Hurricane) North Weald
No 151 (Hurricane) North Weald
No 25 (Blenheim) Martlesham
(1 section at North Weald)

HORNCHURCH
No 54 (Spitfire) Rochford
No 65 (Spitfire) Hornchurch
No 74 (Spitfire) Hornchurch

FILTON	MIDDLE WALLOP	TANGMERE	NORTHOLT	KENLEY	BIGGIN HILL
92 (Spitfire) Pembrey	No 501 (Hurricane) M Wallop	No 43 (Hurricane) Tangmere	No 257[1] (Hurricane) Northolt	No 64 (Spitfire) Kenley	No 610 (Spitfire) Biggin Hill
234 (Spitfire) St Eval (section at Hullavington)	No 238[1] (Hurricane) M Wallop	No 145 (Hurricane) Tangmere	No 1 (Hurricane) Northolt	No 615 (Hurricane) Kenley	No 600 (Blenheim) Biggin Hill
213 (Hurricane) Exeter	No 609 (Spitfire) Warmwell	No 601 (Hurricane) Tangmere		No 111 (Hurricane) Croydon	No 79 (Hurricane) Hawkinge
87 (Hurricane) Exeter		FIU Flight (Blenheim) Tangmere			No 604 (Blenheim) Gravesend
					No 32 (Hurricane) Biggin Hill

Note: [1]Operational by day only.

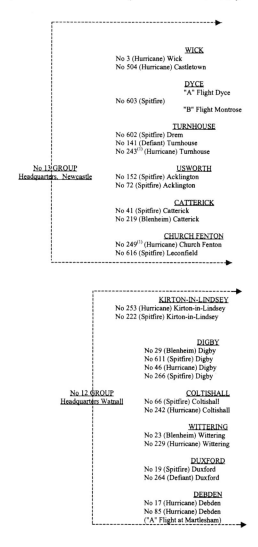

APPENDIX 3: BALLOON COMMAND ORDER OF BATTLE, 31 July 1940

STATION	*SQUADRON*	*LOCATION*	*EQUIPMENT*
No. 30 (Balloon Barrage) Group, London.			
Chigwell, No. 4 Balloon Centre	908	Metropolis	5 flights, 9 balloons
	909	East Ham	5 flights, 9 ballons
	910	Dagenham, Essex	5 flights, 9 balloons (Includes 3 waterborne sites.)
	928	Harwich	3 flights, 8 balloons (Includes 10 waterborne sites.)
Hook, No. 2 Balloon Centre	903	Forest Hill SE 23	5 flights, 9 balloons
	904	Clapham	5 flights, 9 balloons
	905	Kensington	5 flights, 9 balloons
Kidbrooke, No. 1 Balloon Centre	901	Abbey Wood, Kidbrooke, SE	5 flights, 9 balloons
	902	Kidbrooke	5 flights, 9 balloons
(Thames) (Convoy)	952	Sheerness	5 flights, 32 balloons all waterborne sites 1 flight, 8 balloons
	961	Dover	2 flights, 8 balloons, 1 flight, 8 balloons waterborne
Stanmore, No. 3 Balloon Centre	906	Hampstead NW3	5 flights, 9 balloons
	907	Woodberry Down, N4	5 flights, 9 balloons
	956	Colnbrook	3 flights, 8 balloons
No. 31 (Balloon Barrage) Group. Birmingham.			
Alvaston, Derby. No. 7 Balloon Centre	918	Alvaston, Derby	4 flights, 8 balloons
Fazakerley, Liverpool. No. 8 Balloon Centre	919	Birkenhead	5 flights, 8 balloons; 1 flight, 12 balloons waterborne
Manchester, No. 10 Balloon Centre	925	Manchester and Bowlee	5 flights, 8 balloons
	926	Bowlee, Manchester	5 flights, 8 balloons
Sutton Coldfield, No. 5 Balloon Centre	911	West Bromwich	6 flights, 8 balloons
	913	Sutton Coldfield	5 flights, 8 balloons
Barrington, No. 9 Balloon Centre	922	Cuerdley	4 flights, 8 balloons
	923	Runcorn	4 flights, 8 balloons
	949	Crewe	4 flights, 8 balloons
Wythall, No. 6 Balloon Centre	914	Groveley Hall, Northfield Birmingham 31	5 flights, 8 balloons
	915	Rowkeath, Birmingham	5 flights, 8 balloons
	916	Coventry	4 flights, 8 balloons
	917	Coventry	3 flights, 8 balloons

STATION	*SQUADRON*	*LOCATION*	*EQUIPMENT*
No. 32 (Balloon Barrage) Group. Romsey.			
Pucklechurch, Bristol, No. 11 Balloon Centre	912	Brockworth	3 flights, 8 balloons
	927	Bristol	4 flights, 8 balloons
	935	Filton	3 flights, 8 balloons
	951	3 Caledonia Place, Bristol	5 flights, 8 balloons
	957	Yeovil	3 flights, 8 balloons
Cardiff, No. 14 Balloon Centre	953	Cotterell	4 flight, 8 balloons; 1 flight, 7 balloons waterborne
Collaton Cross, Plymouth, No. 13 Balloon Centre	934	Beaumont House, Stoke, Plymouth	3 flights, 8 balloons
Titchfield, No. 12 Balloon Centre	924	Eastleigh	3 flights, 8 balloons
	930	Southampton	5 flights, 8 balloons; 1 flight, 10 balloons waterborne
	932	Portsmouth	4 flights, 8 balloons
	933	Gosport	3 flights, 8 balloons
No. 33 (Balloon Barrage) Group, Sheffield.			
Newcastle, No. 15 Balloon Centre	936	Benton	5 flights, 8 balloons (Includes 4 waterborne sites)
	937	South Tyne	4 flights, 8 balloons (includes 3 waterborne sites)
	938	Billingham-on-Tees	6 flights, 8 balloons
Sheffield, No. 16 Balloon Centre	939	Sheffield	5 flights, 8 balloons
	940	Rotherham	4 flights, 8 balloons
Sutton-on-Hull. No. 17 Balloon Centre	942	Hull	5 flights, total balloons 42 (Includes 24 waterborne sites.)
	943	Hull	4 flights, total balloons 32.
No. 34 (Balloon Barrage) Group Edinburgh.			
Bishopbriggs, No. 18 Balloon Centre (Firth of Forth)	929	South Queensferry, Midlothian	3 flights, 8 balloons (includes 7 waterborne sites.)
	945	Glasgow	5 flights, 8 balloons
	946	Renfrew	6 flights, 8 balloons
	947	Glasgow	4 flights, 8 balloons
(Firth of Forth)	948	Rosyth	3 flights, 8 balloons
Administered direct by 34 Group	920	Lochalsh	(1 flight, 5 balloons; 1 flight, 11 balloons (waterborne))
	950	Lyness	4 flights, 8 balloons

APPENDIX 4: TABLE OF OPERATIONS, 10 JULY–7 AUGUST

Date		*Fighter Losses*	*Claims*	*No. of Fighter Sorties*	*GAF Sorties (Estimated)*[a]		*Main Targets*
10 July	Day	6	11	609	–	Day:	Convoys off the North Foreland and DOVER.
	Night	0	0	19	C	Night:	The East coast: the Home Counties: West of Scotland.
11 July	Day	4	11	452	–	Day:	Convoys off Suffolk: PORTLAND HARBOUR.
	Night	0	0	27	–	Night:	South–West England: East Anglia and Yorkshire Coast.
12 July	Day	6	17	670	–	Day:	Convoy off Norfolk-Suffolk coast: shipping off the Isle of Wight: ABERDEEN.
	Night	0	0	32	–	Night:	South Wales and Bristol areas.
13 July	Day	1	6	449	–	Day:	Shipping off DOVER and PORTLAND
	Night	0	0	9	C	Night:	Suspected mine-laying in Thames Estuary.
14 July	Day	4	15	593	–	Day:	Shipping off DOVER and SWANAGE.
	Night	0	0	17	–	Night:	Bristol area, NW of Isle of Wight, Kent and Suffolk
15 July	Day	1	1	470	–	Day:	Shipping off Norfolk Coast.
	Night	0	0	14	C	Night:	Mostly minelaying.
16 July	Day	2	1	313	–	Day:	Very little activity.
	Night	0	0	0	C	Night:	Suspected minelaying off the North-East coast.
17 July	Day	1	2	253	–	Day:	Searched for shipping off Scottish, East and South coasts. Shipping attacked off DUNDEE and Beachy Head.
	Night	0	0	16	C	Night:	South-West England – including minelaying in the Bristol Channel: minelaying off the East coast.
18 July	Day	3	1	549	100	Day:	Shipping off South and East coasts.
	Night	0	0	41	C	Night:	Very little activity.
19 July	Day	8	12	701	150	Day:	DOVER.
	Night	0	1	13	C	Night:	Some activity west of the Isle of Wight as far as PLYMOUTH: also Thames Estuary – Harwich area.
20 July	Day	3	10	611	100	Day:	Convoys and shipping at DOVER.
	Night	0	1	34	C	Night:	Extensive minelaying operations in areas: NEEDLES to Lands End, Bristol Channel, Norfolk, Suffolk, Humber, Tees.

Date		Fighter Losses	Claims	No. of Fighter Sorties	GAF Sorties (Estimated)[a]		Main Targets
21 July	Day	6	13	571	–	Day:	Convoys in Channel and Straits of Dover.
	Night	0	0	24	C	Night:	Chiefly against Merseyside.
22 July	Day	0	1	611	100	Day:	Shipping off South coast.
	Night	0	1	23	A	Night:	Minelaying off whole of East coast.
23 July	Day	0	2	470	–	Day:	Shipping off East coast.
	Night	0	1	9	C	Night:	Minelaying off East coast from DOVER to the Tyne and Forth estuary.
24 July	Day	3	15	561	–	Day:	Convoys and shipping in the Channel.
	Night	0	0	0	C	Night:	Nil.
25 July	Day	7	13	641	–	Day:	Convoys and shipping in the Channel.
	Night	0	0	11	–	Night:	Minelaying in the Firth of Forth and Thames Estuary: reconnaissance over Bristol Channel area.
26 July	Day	2	12	581	–	Day:	Shipping off South coast.
	Night	0	0	4	C	Night:	Bristol area: Thames Estuary (suspected minelaying): Norfolk coast (suspected minelaying).
27 July	Day	1	2	496	–	Day:	Shipping and naval units in the Straits and in DOVER harbour.
	Night	0	0	19	C	Night:	Attacks in South-West England.
28 July	Day	5	10	794	–	Day:335	Shipping off DOVER: shipping and ports on the South coast.
	Night	0	0	29	C	Night:	Minelaying from Thames Estuary to the Humber: Overland raiding was scattered over whole of England and Wales.
29 July	Day	3	21	758	–	Day:	Convoy off DOVER.
	Night	0	0	15	C	Night:	Enemy activity on a reduced scale overland; minelaying in Dover Straits, Thames Estuary, HARWICH, coastline HARTLEPOOL, Firth of Forth.
30 July	Day	0	1	688	–	Day:	Convoys off ORFORDNESS, CLACTON, and HARWICH.
	Night	0	0	22	C	Night:	South Wales and the Midlands.
31 July	Day	3	1	395	–	Day:	Shipping off South, South-East and South-West coasts; DOVER balloon barrage.
	Night	0	0	29	C	Night:	South Wales and Thames area attacked.

Date		Fighter Losses	Claims	No. of Fighter Sorties	GAF Sorties (Estimated)[a]		Main Targets
1 August	Day	1	1	659	100	Day:	Shipping off South and East coasts.
	Night	0	0	61	C	Night:	Minelaying in Thames Estuary and off North-East and Scottish coasts. South Wales and Midlands.
2 August	Day	0	0	477	100	Day:	Shipping in the Channel and off East coast.
	Night	0	0	24	C	Night:	South Wales and Midlands.
3 August	Day	0	0	415	50	Day:	Reconnaissance of shipping off the South and South-East coast.
	Night	0	0	26	C	Night:	South Wales and some of those raids went North to CREWE, LIVERPOOL and BRADFORD areas.
4 August	Day	0	0	261	80	Day:	Reconnaissance along the South coast and Bristol Channel area.
	Night	0	0	4	C	Night:	Little activity.
5 August	Day	1	4	402	110	Day:	Shipping in the Straits.
	Night	0	0	26	C	Night:	Mine-laying between the Wash and the Tay.
6 August	Day	1	1	416	60	Day:	Little activity.
	Night	0	0	25	C	Night:	Minelaying off East and South-East coasts.
7 August	Day	0	0	393	70	Day:	Convoy reconnaissances: convoy off CROMER attacked.
	Night	0	0	20	C	Night:	Widespread raids from the Thames Estuary up to ABERDEEN and from POOLE to Lands End up to LIVERPOOL.

Note: [a]Until the end of July, British estimates of German sorties were rarely made, and when made are unreliable. They have therefore been omitted for the majority of days. German sorties at night are likewise not known to within fifty sorties, but as an approximation this simple key has been adopted:

A: Over 200 sorties.

B: Betwen 150 and 200 sorties.

C: Less than 150 sorties.

APPENDIX 5: FIGHTER COMMAND SECTOR ORGANISATION AND ORDER OF BATTLE, 8 AUGUST 1940 (0900 HOURS)

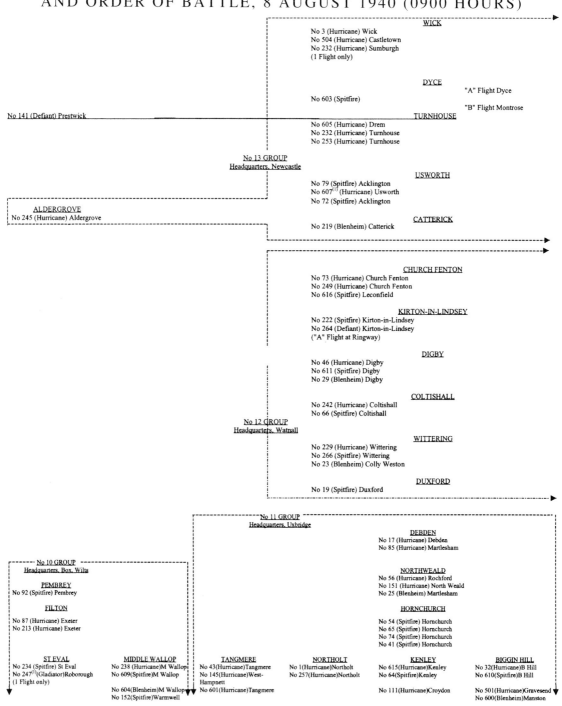

No 13 GROUP
Headquarters, Newcastle

WICK
No 3 (Hurricane) Wick
No 504 (Hurricane) Castletown
No 232 (Hurricane) Sumburgh
(1 Flight only)

DYCE
No 603 (Spitfire)
"A" Flight Dyce
"B" Flight Montrose

TURNHOUSE
No 141 (Defiant) Prestwick
No 605 (Hurricane) Drem
No 232 (Hurricane) Turnhouse
No 253 (Hurricane) Turnhouse

USWORTH
No 79 (Spitfire) Acklington
No 607[1] (Hurricane) Usworth
No 72 (Spitfire) Acklington

ALDERGROVE
No 245 (Hurricane) Aldergrove

CATTERICK
No 219 (Blenheim) Catterick

No 12 GROUP
Headquarters, Watnall

CHURCH FENTON
No 73 (Hurricane) Church Fenton
No 249 (Hurricane) Church Fenton
No 616 (Spitfire) Leconfield

KIRTON-IN-LINDSEY
No 222 (Spitfire) Kirton-in-Lindsey
No 264 (Defiant) Kirton-in-Lindsey
("A" Flight at Ringway)

DIGBY
No 46 (Hurricane) Digby
No 611 (Spitfire) Digby
No 29 (Blenheim) Digby

COLTISHALL
No 242 (Hurricane) Coltishall
No 66 (Spitfire) Coltishall

WITTERING
No 229 (Hurricane) Wittering
No 266 (Spitfire) Wittering
No 23 (Blenheim) Colly Weston

DUXFORD
No 19 (Spitfire) Duxford

No 11 GROUP
Headquarters, Uxbridge

DEBDEN
No 17 (Hurricane) Debden
No 85 (Hurricane) Martlesham

NORTHWEALD
No 56 (Hurricane) Rochford
No 151 (Hurricane) North Weald
No 25 (Blenheim) Martlesham

HORNCHURCH
No 54 (Spitfire) Hornchurch
No 65 (Spitfire) Hornchurch
No 74 (Spitfire) Hornchurch
No 41 (Spitfire) Hornchurch

TANGMERE
No 43(Hurricane)Tangmere
No 145(Hurricane)West-Hampnett
No 601(Hurricane)Tangmere

NORTHOLT
No 1(Hurricane)Northolt
No 257(Hurricane)Northolt

KENLEY
No 615(Hurricane)Kenley
No 64(Spitfire)Kenley
No 111(Hurricane)Croydon

BIGGIN HILL
No 32(Hurricane)B Hill
No 610(Spitfire)B Hill
No 501(Hurricane)Gravesend
No 600(Blenheim)Manston

No 10 GROUP
Headquarters, Box, Wilts

PEMBREY
No 92 (Spitfire) Pembrey

FILTON
No 87 (Hurricane) Exeter
No 213 (Hurricane) Exeter

ST EVAL
No 234 (Spitfire) St Eval
No 247[1](Gladiator)Roborough
(1 Flight only)

MIDDLE WALLOP
No 238 (Hurricane)M Wallop
No 609(Spitfire)M Wallop
No 604(Blenheim)M Wallop
No 152(Spitfire)Warmwell

Note: [1]Operational by day only.

APPENDIX 6: No. 11 GROUP INSTRUCTIONS TO CONTROLLERS No. 4

From: Air Officer Commanding, No. 11 Group, Royal Air Force

To: Group Controllers and Sector Commanders, for Sector Controllers

Date: 19 August 1940

The German Air Force has begun a new phase in air attacks, which have been switched from coastal shipping and ports on to inland objectives. The bombing attacks have for several days been concentrated against aerodromes, and especially fighter aerodromes, on the coast and inland. The following instructions are issued to meet the changed conditions:

a) Despatch fighters to engage large enemy formations over land or within gliding distance of the coast. During the next two or three weeks, we cannot afford to lose pilots through forced landings in the sea;

b) Avoid sending fighters out over the sea to chase reconnaissance aircraft or small formations of enemy fighters;

c) Despatch a pair of fighters to intercept single reconnaissance aircraft that come inland. If clouds are favourable, put a patrol of one or two fighters over an aerodrome which enemy aircraft are approaching in clouds;

d) Against mass attacks coming inland, despatch a minimum number of squadrons to engage enemy fighters. Our main object is to engage enemy bombers, particularly those approaching under the lowest cloud layer;

e) If all our Squadrons around London are off the ground engaging enemy mass attacks, ask No. 12 Group or Command controller to provide Squadrons to patrol aerodromes DEBDEN, NORTH WEALD, HORNCHURCH;

f) If heavy attacks have crossed the coast and are proceeding towards aerodromes, put a Squadron, or even the Sector Training Flight, to patrol under clouds over each Sector aerodrome;

g) No. 303 (Polish) Squadron can provide two sections for patrol of inland aerodromes, especially while the older Squadrons are on the ground refuelling, when enemy formations are flying over land;

h) No. 1 (Canadian) Squadron can be used in the same manner by day as other Fighter Squadrons.

(Sgd) K. R. Park
Air Vice-Marshal
Commanding No. 11 Group
Royal Air Force

Note: Protection of all convoys and shipping in the Thames Estuary are excluded from this instruction (paragraph (a))

APPENDIX 7: TABLE OF OPERATIONS, 8–23 AUGUST 1940

Date		*Fighter Losses*	*Claims*	*No. of Fighter Sorties*	*GAF Sorties*		*Main Targets*
8 August	Day:	19	53	621	280	Day:	Convoy off the Isle of Wight and off DOVER.
	Night:	1	0	33	C	Night:	Mine laying off South and East coasts: Overland, LIVERPOOL, LEEDS, BRISTOL and BIRMINGHAM.
9 August	Day:	3	1	409	110	Day:	East coast shipping reconnaissances: DOVER ballon barrage.
	Night:	1	0	14	C	Night:	Minelaying in Thames Estuary and off East coast. Convoys off AMBLE and HARTLEPOOL: East Anglia and N LONDON.
10 August	Day:	0	0	336	80	Day:	Shipping reconnaissances off East coast in the Channel.
	Night:	0	0	11	C	Night:	Minelaying off HARWICH, Bristol Channel and in the Thames Estuary.
11 August	Day:	32	33	679	370	Day:	Heavy attacks on PORTLAND: four attacks on the DOVER balloon barrage: Large formations attacked convoy in the Thames Estuary and off East Anglia.
	Night:	0	1	62	C	Night:	Bristol Channel area; Merseyside.
12 August	Day:	22	57	732	440	Day:	MANSTON: RDF stations in South and South-East England: convoy in Thames Estuary: DOVER: Solent area.
	Night:	0	0	50	–	Night:	Widespread raids in small numbers overland; Minelaying suspected off the North-East and East coasts, in the Thames Estuary and Bristol Channel.
13 August	Day:	13	76	700	450	Day:	SOUTHAMPTON: PORTLAND: Airfields at Detling, Andover.
	Night:	0	0	27	B	Night:	Light raids in many regions: BIRMINGHAM (Castle Bromwich).
14 August	Day:	8	23	494	600	Day:	South-East England: Manston: numerous airfields in West and South-West.
	Night:	0	0	15	C	Night:	Little activity.
15 August	Day:	34	158	974	650	Day:	North-East and Yorkshire coasts, airfields in South-East: PORTLAND and PORTSMOUTH areas.
	Night:	0	0	42	C	Night:	Little activity.
16 August	Day:	21	83	776	800	Day:	Airfields in Kent: Southern Hampshire and West Sussex: Essex and Suffolk.
	Night:	0	0	11	C	Night:	Bristol Channel area: East Anglia and the Home Counties.
17 August	Day:	0	0	288	50	Day:	Reconnaissance only.
	Night:	0	1	28	C	Night:	Midlands: Merseyside: South Wales.
18 August	Day:	27	125	766	560	Day:	Airfields in South and South-East: PORTSMOUTH.
	Night:	0	0	13	C	Night:	East Anglia, South Wales and Bristol areas: minelaying in Thames Estuary and Bristol Channel.

Date		Fighter Losses	Claims	No. of Fighter Sorties	GAF Sorties		Main Targets
19 August	Day:	3	5	383	400	Day:	Much reconnaissance at sea and overland: no large-scale attacks.
	Night:	0	0	57	B	Night:	Minelaying from Northumberland to the Thames Estuary: Midlands and East Anglia, Portsmouth, Bristol, South Wales and Hull areas were attacked by single a/c.
20 August	Day:	2	7	453	200	Day:	Single aircraft attacked targets in East Anglia. Reconnaissances in the Straits and the Thames Estuary: fighter sweeps in east Kent: Manston attacked.
	Night:	0	0	1	C	Night:	Enemy activity negligible: a few raids off the south-west coast.
21 August	Day:	1	13	589	170	Day:	Airfields in East Anglia, south and south-west lightly attacked.
	Night:	0	0	10	C	Night:	Slight enemy activity in the Southern counties, off Harwich the Humber estuary and the Firth of Forth.
22 August	Day:	5	7	509	220	Day:	Shipping reconnaissance off the South and East coasts: two convoys attacked in Straits of Dover.
	Night:	0	0	44	A	Night:	Aberdeen, West Riding, Hampshire, Bristol and South Wales and a convoy off Kinnaird's Head were attacked: Bristol aircraft company's works and Filton airfield were bombed: Minelaying in Thames Estuary up to Flamborough Head.
23 August	Day:	0	2	482	200 (70)	Day:	Reconnaissance off the East coast: Single raids crossed the South coast, chiefly on reconnaissance.
	Night:	0	0	24	B	Night:	Bristol and South Wales area, particularly CARDIFF.

APPENDIX 8: ATTACKS ON AIRFIELDS

I. ATTACK ON GOSPORT, 1430 HOURS, 18 AUGUST.

21 Junkers dive-bombers approached the aerodrome in three groups of 7. They were in no definite formation. The attack was made from a SW direction from the aerodrome at about 4,000 to 5,000 feet. On approaching the Station they broke into a wider formation (a rough line astern) and seemed to carry out a quick survey of the buildings as they flew round for one quick circuit before diving. They then peeled off and carried out very steep diving attacks out of the sun, the angle being from 70 to 80 degrees. They each attacked a separate place and followed each other down with only a short gap between each machine. After diving they pulled out at about 200 to 500 feet and quickly turned left inside the aerodrome boundaries and disappeared towards the SW again. Most of the bombs were dropped in the dive at about 800 feet. The salvoes consisted of one large and four small bombs.

After the dive attack 3 Me 109s were seen to dive from a Northerly direction and attack the balloons around the station. These machines were very persistent and continued to attack the balloons until most of these around the station were brought down. Heavy AA fire was concentrated on these aircraft but none was hit. The actual dive-bombing attacks on the Station lasted for only about 4–5 minutes, but the aircraft attacking the balloons continued for 15–20. Judging by a the deliberateness of the attack the squadron might well have been a veteran one with many dive-bombing attacks to its credit. No notice appeared to be taken of AA fire. All machine gun posts on the Station opened fire about 1,000 rounds being expended. The position of the bomb craters and unexploded bombs is as follows: 1. Salvo covering Grange Moat and Transport Section. 2. Salvo covering Main Stores and military road. 3. Salvo covering Torpedo Workshops. 4. Salvo covering No. 4 Hangar FAAMU. 5. Salvo covering No. 3 Hangar and Parachute Section. 6. Salvo covering Operations Room. 7. Salvo covering petrol dump area. 8. Salvo covering ramparts of Fort Rowner between Nos 1 and 3 warhead store.

The following buildings were demolished beyond repair: 34 Parachute Store. 40 Disinfector and Band Room. 56 MG Test Butt. 76 Articulated Trailer Shed. 152 Petrol Trailer Shed.

The following buildings received considerable structural damage but are repairable: 3 MT Shed. 17 United Board Chapel. 19 Station Headquarters Office. 24 Torpedo Workshop. 30 ARS and ERS. 175 Operations Room. 191 Bellman Hangar. 192 Bellman Hangar. 196 Flight Office. 197 Chemical latrines.

The following buildings received superficial damage: Rest Room for WAAF drivers. 24 Compressor Plant Buildings. 38 Bulk oil installation, No. 1. 94 Dining Room and Cook House, west end only. 95 Ration Store. 106 Barrack block.

Casualties to personnel: NIL.

The following percentage of estimated damage to various materials is as follows: Aircraft and engine spares 100%. Barrack equipment NIL. Clothing NIL. Tools, Torpedo and Armament spares 40%. Marine Craft and aerodrome equipment 20%. Wireless and electrical equipment 75%. Ration 5%. Petrol Nil. Oil 20%. Damage to aircraft. No. 2 AACU. Two recommended for repair by contractors 2 for repair at Unit by contractors. One burnt out. 2 for repair by Unit. One write off. Torpedo Development Flight Two write off. One for repair by Unit. Station Flight one write off. Mechanical transport: two completely destroyed 13 vehicles beyond unit repair.

II. ATTACK ON RAF STATION, KENLEY, 1310 HOURS, 18 AUGUST 1940.

1. The following report on the raid on this station on 18 August is submitted.

Type of Attack,

2. The station was attacked by two raids almost simultaneously, one high raid of 50 or more aircraft and a very low raid of 9 aircraft. (Bomber Do 17, Fighter escort of Me 109). The low raid developed first, although it appeared in the beginning that the high raid might be the more serious.

Aircraft detailed to Intercept.

3. No. 615 Squadron were detailed by Group to intercept a raid over Hawkinge.

4. No. 64 Squadron was ordered off on order of Sector Controller to patrol base to intercept high raid.

5. No. 111 Squadron was ordered off by Sector Controller to intercept the low raid.

6. Both raids were intercepted but the low flying raid could not be effectively dealt with by No. 111 Squadron for the following reasons:

(i) It was flying too low.

(ii) Squadron did not intercept it far enough away from the aerodrome.

Attack on Aerodrome.

7. Ample warning of attack and direction of approach was given to all ground defences.

8. The low flying raid approached at about 100 feet from South.

9. The approach was masked by trees and hangars and the AA guns were unable to open fire until the aircraft were over the camp.

10. The low bombing was extremely accurate and effective.

11. The combined effect of guns and PAC brought down 2 EA one on edge of aerodrome and another landed further afield.

12. The high raid bombed from 10,000 feet and was intercepted by both No. 64 and 615 Squadron. Twelve EA were claimed as destroyed.

13. Salvos from the high raid dropped on aerodrome buildings and aerodrome.

14. Approximately 100 bombs were dropped on the aerodrome and buildings and these were mainly high explosive and incendiary, but one petrol bomb was reported. Twenty-four bombs were either delayed action or duds.

15. Whilst bombing, the enemy aircraft attacked the gun post buildings and aircraft with their machine guns.

16. No poison gas was used.

Damage to Aerodrome

17. The damage was as stated in Form D mentioned in para 1 attached for ease of reference.

18. The aerodrome was temporarily out of action and No. 615 Squadron was ordered to land and refuel at Croydon and No. 64 Squadron to Redhill.

19. The craters were marked and runway was selected for landing in about one hour. Owing to insufficient crews at Redhill for refuelling, No. 64 Squadron were ordered to return to Kenley to refuel.

Operational Control

20. The cables to the transmitter were cut during the raid and R/T and electric supply failed.

21. Ground stripes were put out to instruct aircraft to land at Satellites.

22. R/T communication was broken at 1323 hours, the reserve transmitter was brought into action at 1337 hours.

23. The operation room itself was undamaged but communications were cut and transmitter and power were off during the above period.

24. All dispersal tie lines and outward lines were cut, with the exception of Ops line to No. 11 Group, Bromley, Biggin Hill and S/L lines.

Fire Services

25. The RAF Water Supply failed; the fires were, however, localised to buildings in which the fires started. This is being investigated.

26. Too many Civil Fire Brigades answered SOS and roads were congested; this has been discussed with Local ARP controllers and suitable arrangements made.

Medical Services

27. The hospital and reserve hospital were destroyed. One of the Medical Officers was killed in a shelter trench near hospital. The remaining Medical Staff, however, worked splendidly and with assistance of Civil doctors the situation was soon in hand.

Ground Defences

28. The ground defences were seriously hampered by firstly, the approach of raid being screened so that the low raid could not be engaged before it had released its bombs and the fact that smoke from low raid prevented the high raid being seen easily. Effective action was, however, taken by gun crews and two aircraft were brought down by AA fire and PAC combined. Many other aircraft must have been hit.

29. All ground defence crews remained at their posts and engaged the enemy under heavy fire.

Transport

30. The transport was fairly well dispersed in the transport yard and two roads under trees to the SW of the buildings. The transport dispersal area was heavily bombed and a large number of vehicles were put out of action.

RECOMMENDATIONS

31. The following recommendations are made as a result of experience gained from this raid:

(a) Immediate action to be taken to provide mountings and Bofors guns for the towers being built to defend the Southern approach to the aerodrome. These towers were commenced in May and are not completed yet.

(b) The Operations Room, which is unprotected against overhead attack should be scrapped and a new operations room fitted up away from the station in a concealed position. It is highly probable that in the next large scale raid the operations room and crew of 35–40 may be put out of action.

(c) Recommended that new VHF buildings (wood huts and towers) should be sited away from the main camp and camouflaged.

(d) The existing method of passing parachute alarm message would not work in large scale operations owing to congestion of lines, security of information, and damage to communication.

(e) Insufficient personnel at unoccupied satellites to refuel and rearm squadrons quickly; a definite establishment should be given for this.

(f) It is strongly recommended that the Station Sick Quarters be housed in a building some reasonable distance from the aerodrome. They are at present temporarily accommodated in a nearby house to the Station, but the distance from the danger area is not considered sufficient.

CASUALTIES RAF

Dead 9
Injured 10 (one WAAF)

OPERATIONAL AIRCRAFT

Hurricanes destroyed, 4.
Hurricanes damaged, 2.
Spitfires destroyed, Nil.
Spitfires damaged, 3.
Merlin Engines destroyed, 4.
Blenheims destroyed, 1.

NON-OPERATIONAL AIRCRAFT

Magisters destroyed, 2.
Master destroyed, 1.
Proctor destroyed, 1.
Magister damaged, 1.

TRANSPORT

Armadillos destroyed, 6.
Prime movers destroyed, 14.
Cooking trailers destroyed, 1.
Water trailer destroyed, 2.
Flat trailer destroyed, 6.
Tanker trailers destroyed, 3.

FIRE SECTION

Large numbers of extinguishers and buckets damaged and lost.
Other essential equipment intact.

BUILDINGS

11 Hangars except one totally destroyed.
Sick Quarters demolished.
Army Guard room damaged.
Married Quarters (2) destroyed.
Married Quarters (1) damaged.
Sergeants Quarters partly demolished.
Temporary Decontamination Centre demolished.
Sergeants Mess and Institute damaged.
Photographic section demolished.
Station Headquarters partly demolished.
Officers Mess badly damaged.
One dispersal hut wrecked.
One dispersal hut damaged.
"The Crest" requisitioned private property, completely demolished.

CABLES

Cables, telephones, lighting and Tannoy system temporarily out of action. Temporary measures taken and services now working.

Runways, Craters

Four craters on runways, immediately filled by REs.
Three craters on taxying track.
Three craters in dispersal pens.
Aerodrome was made serviceable in about two hours.

WIRELESS SECTION

No damage in section and OXX no operational equipment lost.

UNEXPLODED BOMBS

24 unexploded bombs dealt with.

SICK QUARTERS

All equipment destroyed.

RIFLES LOST

Approximately 25.

III. TABLE OF CHIEF ATTACKS ON AIRFIELDS AND RDF STATIONS 12 AUGUST–6 SEPTEMBER[a]

DATE	*PLACE*	*REMARKS*
12.8.40	*Lympne* No. 11 Group	Attack by enemy aircraft, dropping 141 bombs in a few seconds. Damage caused to hangars, offices and landing ground.
	Dunkirk (RDF) No. 60 Group	Two huts destroyed. 1,000 lb bomb dropped near Transmitting block. No vital damage.
	Dover (RDF) No. 60 Group	Considerable damage to huts inside the compound. Slight damage to aerial towers.
	Rye (RDF) No. 60 Group	All huts destroyed with the exception of the Transmitting and Receiving blocks and Watch Office. Normal working of essential services restored by noon.
	Ventnor (RDF) No. 60 Group	Dive-bombing attack by about 15 Ju 88s. Bombing continued until 1400 hours, although tailing off considerably. The local Fire Brigade rendered assistance, but owing to the lack of water on the site, all buildings were destroyed. *Casualties*: One soldier wounded.
	Manston No. 11 Group	Aerodrome bombed at low altitude. Some 150 HEs were dropped and aerodrome pitted with about 100 craters and rendered temporarily unserviceable. Night flying section operated from Hornchurch. Two hangars were damaged and workshops destroyed. Raid lasted about 5 minutes. *Casualties*: One civilian clerk. Aerodrome rendered serviceable by the 13th except for southern ridge where there were some unexploded bombs.
	Hawkinge No. 11 Group	Attack by Ju 88s. One hangar wrecked, another partially wrecked. Aerodrome and buildings machine-gunned. Main stores partially damaged by fire and clothing store almost completely destroyed. Station workshops destroyed. Twenty-eight craters made in landing ground, but not rendered completely unserviceable and by 9000 hours on the 13th it was completely serviceable. *Casualties*: 2 civilians and 3 airmen killed. 6 airmen severely injured. *Aircraft*: Two Spitfires seriously damaged. Others struck by splinters. Two non-operational aircraft damaged but repairable. Attack lasted approximately 10 minutes.
	Lympne No. 11 Group	Attack by two squadrons. 242 bombs dropped in two runs across aerodrome. Landing ground rendered unserviceable. *Casualties*: 1 airman killed. 2 airmen seriously injured.

Note: [a] Only attacks by twelve or more aircraft are given and such attacks by smaller formations as are worthy of mention for the damage that was caused

III. TABLE OF CHIEF ATTACKS ON AIRFIELDS AND RDF STATIONS 12 AUGUST–6 SEPTEMBER

DATE	*PLACE*	*REMARKS*
13.8.40	*Eastchurch* No. 16 Group	Attack by 2 waves of about 15 Dorniers in Vic formation. Over 100 HEs and incendiaries dropped. Duration of raid – 10 minutes. All hangars were hit. Damage caused to buildings, telephone and main petrol installations. All No. 266 Squadron's ammunition was destroyed. *Casualties*: 12 RAF and 2 Army – killed.
	Detling No. 16 Group	Heavy attack by Ju 87s and Me 109s. Severe damage. Direct hits on operations room. Numerous casualties. 5 Blenheims of No. 53 Squadron destroyed after being set on fire by incendiary machine-gun fire and two more seriously damaged by machine-gun fire,
14.8.40	*Middle Wallop* No. 10 Group	Dive-bombing attack by enemy aircraft. One hangar hit and set on fire. *Casualties*: 3 Airmen of No. 609 Squadron killed, and 1 airman wounded. 10 airmen of SHQ wounded. No. 609 Squadron ORB records raid by 3 twin-engined bombers. Direct hits on hangar, and offices were destroyed.
	Sealand No. 21 Group	He 111 approached station from West, flying below 1,000 feet. 8 HEs and 1 incendiary were dropped in a straight line on aerodrome. No serious damage. Enemy aircraft machine-gunned aerodrome. Only damage was bullet hole in wing of one Master aircraft and small piece of shrapnel in another. The other aircraft received slight damage to the 3-ply skin. Second attack by an He 111 approaching the Station from the South and flying at about 3,500 feet. Dropped 5 HEs and 1 incendiary within precincts of No. 30 MU. The Sergeants Mess was extensively damaged by direct hit and windows of other buildings broken. *Casualties*: One fatal casualty, and 9 injured. According to No. 30 MU ORB a full working day with 2 hours overtime was worked next day. The main HT cable was cut through and the water supply was in some danger of failing but the works Department had the power ready for work next morning by 8 o'clock and lighting and water were available.
15.8.40	*Lympne* No. 11 Group	Dive-bombing attack. Hangars damaged. Two wooden buildings used as paint stores burnt out. All power and water services cut. Direct hit on Station Sick Quarters. Accounts section, Orderly Room and Sick Quarters evacuated to houses near the aerodrome. Aerodrome according to Fighter Command ORB was serviceable in 48 hours.
	Hawkinge No. 11 Group	Attack by about 20 Dorniers, He 111s and Ju 87s. About 20 bombs were dropped, two of the heaviest hitting hangars and smaller ones falling on aerodrome surface. One small barrack block destroyed. Attack lasted about 10 minutes.

III. TABLE OF CHIEF ATTACKS ON AIRFIELDS AND RDF STATIONS 12 AUGUST–6 SEPTEMBER

DATE	*PLACE*	*REMARKS*
	Martlesham No. 12 Group	Attack by Ju 87s and Me 110s (Jaguar) dive-bombers with an above guard of Me 109s; Ju 87s concentrated on uncompleted Signal Station 2 miles to the West of the aerodrome and the Jaguars on the aerodrome. Signals Station suffered broken windows and burst water tank. The bombs were widely dispersed. Two craters were filled in by 1900 hours. Two bombs fell on the main camp road and wrecked the guardroom, coppersmiths and joiners shops, and burst the water main. Two bombs severely damaged the Officers' Mess. A visiting Fairey Battle, carrying 1,000 lb of bombs, was set on fire and blew up. The explosion rendered two hangars completely unserviceable and the Watch Office and Night Flying Equipment sheds were completely destroyed. The attack lasted approximately 5 minutes. On the 16th the station was engaged on repair work and by the end of the day, the telephone system was made 99% serviceable and water mains were re-connected.
	Hawkinge No. 11 Group	High level attack. Small bombs dropped on aerodrome surface. No serious damage. By the 16th the work of clearing away the debris was well in hand. The Station Administrative Staff moved to a house about half a mile from the aerodrome.
	Driffield No. 4 Group	30 enemy aircraft attacked in formation. Ten aircraft were destroyed by bombs and fire. Four hangars were considerably damaged. Over 100 bombs were dropped and attackers machine-gunned buildings and shelters. Nine enemy aircraft were shot down, 1 by anti-aircraft fire, and 8 by fighter patrols.
	Middle Wallop No. 11 Group	Attack by over 50 aircraft (Ju 88s escorted by Me 110s). War Room Summary gives damage as one hangar set on fire, but No 609 Squadron describes it as less damage than on previous day. No further details.
	West Malling No. 11 Group	High-level bombing attack by 38 enemy aircraft. New buildings damaged. Aerodrome cratered. Men's quarters damaged. *Casualties*: 2 airmen killed. Aerodrome unserviceable until 20th.
	Eastchurch No. 16 Group	Damage caused to landing area. Gas contamination centre rendered unserviceable.
16.8.40	*West Malling* No. 11 Group	Aerodrome still unserviceable from previous days attack. 18 enemy aircraft attacked on 16th with HEs and incendiaries; one aircraft 'C' Flight destroyed. No operational flying until 20th.
	Gosport No. 17 Group	Dive-bombing attack out of the sun was made by about 12 Ju 87s. Sky bright and cloudless. Duration of attack about 10 minutes. *Casualties:* Killed – 3 airmen and one civilian (no connection with Station). Seriously wounded – 1 airman and one civilian employee (both later died).

III. TABLE OF CHIEF ATTACKS ON AIRFIELDS AND RDF STATIONS 12 AUGUST–6 SEPTEMBER

DATE	*PLACE*	*REMARKS*
	Ventnor (RDF) No. 60 Group	A dive-bombing attack by about 5 Junkers 87s commenced at 1300 hours, and continued to 1306 hours. 7 (HE) bombs dropped. *Casualties*: Nil. As a result of the two raids, the only buildings habitable are the Diesel House, R Block, and underground buildings.
	Tangmere No. 11 Group	Attack by Ju 87s and Me 110s. All hangars, workshops, stores, sick quarters, pumping station, Officers' Mess and Salvation Army hut destroyed. The Tannoy broadcasting system, all lighting, power, water and sanitation temporarily out of action. 3 Blenheims completely destroyed, and 3 Blenheims, 7 Hurricanes and 1 Magister damaged. 6 Merlin engines damaged and 7 MT and 30 private cars damaged beyond repair. *Casualties*: 10 Service personnel and 3 civilians killed. 20 personnel injured. Attack lasted 20 minutes.
	Brize Norton No. 23 Group	Attack by 2 enemy aircraft. About 32 bombs dropped. 3 failed to explode. Damage to No 6 MU as follows: 3 petrol bowsers damaged; one tractor rendered unserviceable; Tutor aircraft superficially damaged by flying debris; bomb crater outside No 4 hangar filled in within an hour. Considerable damage done to No 2 SFTS Hangars Nos 1 and 3 gutted by fire. 46 aircraft destroyed. Roof of one barrack damaged and electricity and water supply damaged. *Casualties*: 1 civilian killed. 5 airmen and 4 civilians injured.
18.8.40	*Croydon* No. 11 Group	11 HEs and 8 delayed action bombs and incendiaries dropped. Hangar and buildings damaged. Two craters on edge of tarmac and a hut on roadway. *Casualties*: 1 soldier killed.
	Thorney Island No. 16 Group	Attack by about 25 Ju 87s and 6 Me 109s, which dived to 1000 feet and dropped about 35 HEs and incendiaries. Approximately 14 HEs did not explode. 2 hangars hit and damaged by fire. 3 aircraft destroyed and 1 slightly damaged. 5 civilians slightly wounded.
	Ford FAA Station	Station severely bombed, with heavy damage to buildings. One hangar was completely demolished, together with Equipment Stores, Workshops, and wooden huts used as Officers' and Men's sleeping quarters. 8 hangars remained intact, except for slight damage.
	Poling (RDF) No. 60 Group	Approximately 90 bombs dropped. Station badly damaged. Emergency equipment had to be installed.

III. TABLE OF CHIEF ATTACKS ON AIRFIELDS AND RDF STATIONS 12 AUGUST–6 SEPTEMBER

DATE	*PLACE*	*REMARKS*
24.8.40	*Manston* No. 11 Group	Very heavy bombing attack. Living quarters badly damaged and presence of a number of unexploded bombs made it necessary temporarily to vacate the area. Later it was decided to evacuate permanently to Westgate all administrative personnel and those not required for station defence and aircraft servicing. 600 Squadron ORB states that all communications were cut and remainder of the Squadron moved from Manston to Hornchurch.
	North Weald No. 11 Group	30 to 50 Do 215s attacked accompanied by He 111s and Me 110s. 150 to 200 bombs were dropped. Airmen's and officers' married quarters suffered severely. Power house was badly damaged. *Casualties*: 9 killed. 10 wounded.
25.8.40	*Driffield* No. 5 Group	12 bombs dropped, destroying Sergeants' Mess, damaging water and heating mains and electric light cables. One aircraft damaged. No personnel casualties. On 26th 102 Squadron moved from Driffield to Leeming. 77 Squadron moved on 28th and in September Driffield was reduced to a Care and Maintenance Party.
	Warmwell No. 10 Group	Approximately 20 bombs dropped. 2 hangars damaged. Sick Quarters burnt out. Nine unexploded bombs located in camp. As a result of attack communications were disorganised until approximately 1200 hours on 26th.
26.8.40	*Debden* No. 11 Group	Approximately 100 bombs, excluding incendiaries, dropped. Direct hits were scored on landing area, Sergeants' Mess, NAAFI, MT Yard and Equipment Section. Electricity and water mains were damaged. *Casualties*: 4 fatal RAF casualties, and one civilian driver.
	St Eval No. 15 Group	E/a set fire to false flare path and put bombs on it until early hours of the morning. 62 craters were made, but damage was mostly on the heath.
28.8.40	*Eastchurch* No. 16 Group	Damage caused to landing ground. 3 tents damaged. 2 Battles destroyed and 3 Battles damaged. Landing ground serviceable for restricted day flying. No casualties.
30.8.40	*Biggin Hill* No. 11 Group	High level bombing attack. Damage to aerodrome surface, but not rendered unserviceable. Aircraft continued to operate.
	Detling No. 16 Group	40-50 bombs dropped. Airfield rendered unserviceable. Camp main road hit and small oil storage tank fired. Electricity supply cable cut off and emergency unit in use. Airfield estimated repairable by 0800 hours on 31st. One Blenheim damaged. *Casualties*: One fatal casualty.

III. TABLE OF CHIEF ATTACKS ON AIRFIELDS AND RDF STATIONS 12 AUGUST–6 SEPTEMBER

DATE	*PLACE*	*REMARKS*
	Biggin Hill No. 11 Group	Low-level bombing attack. Very serious damage to buildings and equipment. 16 large HEs dropped rendering workshops, transport yard, stores, barrack stores, armoury guard, meteorological office and station institute completely useless. 'F' type hangar also badly damaged. All power, gas and water mains were severed and all telephone lines running North of the camp were cut in three places. *Casualties*: 39 fatal. 26 injured.
31.8.40	*Debden* No. 11 Group	Attack by Do 17s escorted by Me 110s. Bombs fell at south of aerodrome, straddling the target in a NW direction. About 100 HEs and incendiaries were dropped. The Sick Quarters and a barrack block received direct hits and other buildings were damaged, including a hangar. The operations side of the station functioned throughout and there was no failure of lighting or communications in the Operations Room. *Casualties*: One civilian and one airman killed and 12 RAF personnel injured.
	Eastchurch No. 16 Group	Some damage to aerodrome surface but still serviceable. Railway track outside NW corner of camp received 2 direct hits.
	Detling No. 16 Group	Aerodrome attacked by enemy dive-bombers. Camp machine-gunned, but no bombs dropped.
	Croydon No. 11 Group	Attack by about 12 e/a which bombed and machine-gunned at approximately 2,000 feet. Redwing hangar demolished. 'B' hangar – glass broken and walls pierced. A 30 cwt lorry was destroyed.
	Hornchurch No. 11 Group	Two attacks 30 Dorniers dropped about 100 bombs across the aerodrome. The power cable was cut and emergency power equipment was brought into operation. 3 a/c of 54 Squadron were destroyed. *Casualties*: 3 killed and 11 wounded. Second attack of the day was even less successful than the first. 2 Spitfires were destroyed. The aerodrome remained serviceable. *Casualties*: One killed.
	Biggin Hill No. 11 Group	High-level bombing attack. Extensive damage to buildings and hangars. The operations block received a direct hit and caught fire, while the temporary lash up of telephone lines and power cables was completely destroyed. The Officers' Married Quarters and Officers' Mess were also damaged.
1.9.40	*Debden* No. 11 Group	According to No. 257 Squadron ORB about 160 bombs were dropped on aerodrome and surrounding buildings. Aerodrome remained serviceable. This attack is not mentioned in the Station ORB.

III. TABLE OF CHIEF ATTACKS ON AIRFIELDS AND RDF STATIONS 12 AUGUST–6 SEPTEMBER

DATE	*PLACE*	*REMARKS*
	Biggin Hill No. 11 Group	High-level bombing attack. Bombs fell among the camp buildings without doing much further damage, but shaking buildings and making them unsafe. One aircraft was destroyed, but the aerodrome remained serviceable. Practically no buildings were left in a safe condition and the road running through the camp was blocked by 3 large craters. All main services and communications were destroyed. As a result, it was decided to disperse sections in the vicinity of Keston, chiefly because of the damaged buildings which made it necessary to salvage all equipment and transfer it elsewhere.
	Detling No. 16 Group	Attack by about 15 Me 109s and 3 bombers. 2 bombs fell at the back of the Operations Room, damaging the Teleprinter Room. One wireless mast was brought down, and the Guardroom was machine-gunned. Flying operations were not affected. *Casualties*: One fatal. 4 injured. No. 53 Squadron gives time of attack as 1600 hours.
	Detling No. 16 Group	Incendiaries and HEs dropped by enemy aircraft. Fires were started at the Officers' Mess and Dispersal Point, but were soon put out. An MT shed was hit. There were no casualties. Group was informed that Detling would be unserviceable until 0600 hours on the 2nd, when the aerodrome would be inspected. *Casualties*: There were no casualties.
2.9.40	*Gravesend* No. 11 Group	Bombs dropped on edge of aerodrome, but no material damage done. *Casualties*: 2 soldiers slightly injured.
	Lympne No. 11 Group	Returning formation of enemy aircraft dropped about 30 bombs around aerodrome. A few holes made in the landing field. Emergency landing still possible. No other damage. *Casualties*: No casualties.
	Eastchurch No. 16 Group	Attack by 18 aircraft in waves of 3, escorted by fighters. A dump of 350 x 250 lb bombs were exploded by a delayed-action bomb. E 1 hangar was further damaged by fire. Administrative buildings were wrecked and the hospital partially wrecked. The NAAFI was destroyed by fire and water mains cut and sewerage system broken. Most roads were hit. The teleprinter service was put out of action and most of the telephone communications cut. 5 aircraft were damaged beyond repair. *Casualties*: 3 fatal. 8 wounded.
	Detling No. 16 Group	30 enemy aircraft attacked aerodrome, severely damaging 'C' Flight hangar. Aerodrome reported by Station Commander unserviceable until 1630 hours.

III. TABLE OF CHIEF ATTACKS ON AIRFIELDS AND RDF STATIONS 12 AUGUST–6 SEPTEMBER

DATE	*PLACE*	*REMARKS*
	Eastchurch No. 16 Group	Bombing attack by 12 enemy aircraft in waves of 3 escorted by fighters. 8 large craters in landing ground. E 3 hangar completely wrecked. Further damage to roads. On the 3rd, GHQ and Accounts Section moved from Eastchurch Camp to Wymswold Warden. Station Sick Quarters moved from Eastchurch Camp to Eastchurch Village. *Casualties*: 1 fatal, 4 wounded.
	Hornchurch No. 11 Group	About 100 bombs dropped. Only 6 fell on landing field. No essential damage caused.
3.9.40	*North Weald* No. 11 Group	Station bombed by 25 to 30 Dorniers, escorted by Me 110s. Hangars Nos 151 and 25 were set on fire. The MT section yard was badly damaged and several lorries set on fire. There was damage to living quarters and buildings. The Tannoy system panel was destroyed and the loud speaker warning system rendered unserviceable. The new Operations Room received a direct hit on the roof, but stood up to it. Communication with the Observer Corps was severed except for Walford. HF relay system between receiver and transmitter was severed and the main stores was severely damaged. The aerodrome was not rendered unserviceable for day operations, although there were many craters and delayed-action bombs on the South and South West corners. *Casualties*: 2 fatal, 7 seriously wounded and 30 minor injuries.
4.9.40	*Eastchurch* No. 16 Group	Attack by 18 enemy aircraft. Immediate ration store demolished. Ration Store damaged. 6 small holes on end of runway. *Casualties*: No casualties. 2nd attack by about 30 enemy aircraft. 2 huts seriously damaged. 2 Battle aircraft damaged. A few small holes in landing ground. One wall of MT Shed blown in. *Casualties*: No casualties.
6.9.40	*Biggin Hill* No. 11 Group	High level bombing attack. Damage was done to some dispersal points and to the aerodrome surface; but most of the bombs overshot the aerodrome and fell on the Westerham road, again destroying telephone lines.

APPENDIX 9: No. 11 GROUP INSTRUCTIONS TO CONTROLLERS No. 6

From: Air Officer Commanding, No. 11 Group, Royal Air Force

To: Group Controllers

Date: 26 August 1940

Group Controllers, Instruction No. 6

The following signal, addressed today to all Sectors, is repeated for the information of each Control:-

> 'Our fighter squadrons are frequently engaging greatly superior numbers because other squadrons despatched to engage fail to intercept owing to accidents of cloud and inaccuracies of sound plotting by ground observers. To enable Group and Sector Controllers to put all squadrons in contact with the enemy formation leaders are to report approximate strength of enemy bombers and fighters, their height, course and approximate position immediately on sighting the enemy. A specimen R/T message would be, "Tally Ho! thirty bombers forty fighters Angels twenty proceeding North Guildford." These reports should enable us to engage the enemy on more equal terms and are to take effect from dawn 27 August. Acknowledge.'

(Sgd) K.R. Park

Air Vice-Marshal
Commanding No. 11 Group
Royal Air Force

APPENDIX 10: No. 11 GROUP INSTRUCTIONS TO CONTROLLERS No. 7

From: Air Officer Commanding, No. 11 Group, Royal Air Force

To: Group Controllers

Date: 27 August 1940

Group Controllers, Instruction No. 7

REINFORCEMENT from 10 and 12 GROUPS

1. Thanks to the friendly co-operation afforded by 10 Group, they are always prepared to detail two to four Squadrons to engage from the West mass attacks (100 or more) approaching the Portsmouth area.

2. The AOC 10 Group has agreed that once his Squadrons have been detailed to intercept a group of raids coming into Tangmere Sector, his Controllers will not withdraw them or divert them to some other task without firstly consulting us.

3. Because of the above, Controllers are clearly to understand that once they have detailed Tangmere Squadrons to intercept raids entering Middle Wallop Sector, they must not withdraw them without first informing 10 Group of the intention; to do otherwise might embarrass Middle Wallop Sector.

4. Up to date 12 Group, on the other hand, have not shown the same desire to co-operate by despatching their Squadrons to the places requested. The result of this attitude has been that on two occasions recently when 12 Group offered assistance and were requested by us to patrol our aerodromes, their Squadrons did not in fact patrol over our aerodromes. On both these occasions our aerodromes were heavily bombed, because our own patrols were not strong enough to turn all the enemy back before they reached their objective.

5. As acceptance of direct offers of assistance from 12 Group have not resulted in their Squadrons being placed where we had requested, Controllers are from now onwards immediately to put their requests to Controller, Fighter Command, stating clearly when and where reinforcing Squadrons from the North are required to patrol, eg, two Squadrons required to patrol North Weald-Hornchurch, 10,000 feet, immediately, to protect aerodromes in absence of our own Squadrons on forward patrol. These requests will only be submitted to Command when mass attacks are approaching in such strength (160 or more) that it appears that our own Squadrons are unlikely to prevent their reaching inland objectives.

6. Such requests via Command will be a little slower in obtaining assistance but they should ensure that the reinforcing Squadrons from the North are in fact placed where they can be of greatest assistance. Because of the delay in the arrival of these Squadron, their obvious task is to patrol aerodromes or other inland objectives to engage enemy formations that break through our fighter patrols, that normally engage well forward of our Sector aerodromes.

(Sgd) K.R. Park

Air Vice-Marshal
Commanding No. 11 Group
Royal Air Force

APPENDIX 11: No. 11 GROUP INSTRUCTIONS TO CONTROLLERS No. 10

From: Air Officer Commanding, No. 11 Group, Royal Air Force

To: Group Controllers and Sector Commanders, for Sector Controllers

Date: 5 September 1940

Instruction to Controllers No. 10

The Commander-in-Chief has directed that the following aircraft factories shall be given the maximum fighter cover, (not necessarily close patrols), during the next week:

Hawkers, Kingston-on-Thames
Langley,
Brooklands,
Southampton aircraft factories.

2. As the enemy bombing attacks on our fighter aerodromes during the past three weeks have not outwardly reduced the fighter defence, he is now directing some of his main attacks against aircraft factories, especially in the West and South-West of London. The only direct protection that we can at present afford is to obtain from 10 Group two Squadrons to patrol the lines, (a) Brooklands–Croydon, and (b) Brooklands–Windsor, whenever there is a heavy attack South of the Thames river. The task of these Squadrons is to intercept bomber formations that may elude 11 Group fighters that are despatched to engage the enemy well forward of the factories and Sector aerodromes.

3. The Southampton factories are of vital importance to the RAF, and 10 Group have agreed to reinforce the Tangmere Sector by up to three or four Squadrons whenever a mass attack approaches the Southampton–Portsmouth area from the South.

Hawkinge and Manston or Rochford Squadrons

4. Whenever time permits, these two Squadrons are to rendezvous over Canterbury, and then be detailed to engage the enemy.

The Main Attack

5. The enemy's main attack must be met in maximum strength between the coast and our line of Sector aerodromes. Whenever time permits, Squadrons are to be put into the battle in pairs. Some Spitfire Squadrons are to be detailed to engage the enemy fighter screen at 20,000 or more feet. The Hurricanes, because of their inferior performance, should normally be put in against the enemy bombers, which are rarely above 16,000 feet by day.

Aerodrome Protection

6. North of the Thames, 12 Group Squadrons are to be requested, via Command, to cover North Weald, Stapleford, Hornchurch, also Debden. Pending arrival of 12 Group Squadrons, the Group Controller should cover our Sector aerodromes by one or two Squadrons. These must, however, be sent forward into the main battle immediately 12 Group Squadrons arrive.
7. The aerodromes West and South-West of London can be covered by 10 Group Squadrons. Biggin Hill, Kenley and Croydon aerodromes can be covered by a maximum of two Squadrons; normally one flight should be adequate for each aerodrome, because the enemy should already have been engaged before he reaches the line of these Stations.

(Sgd) K.R. Park

Air Vice-Marshal
Commanding No. 11 Group
Royal Air Force

APPENDIX 12: No. 11 GROUP INSTRUCTIONS TO CONTROLLERS No. 12

From: Air Officer Commanding, No. 11 Group, Royal Air Force

To: Group Controllers, and all Sector Controllers

Date: 7 September 1940

Instruction to Controllers No. 12

Interception of Enemy BOMBER Formations:

1. From reports by RAF personnel at aerodromes, also from AA gun Stations, and lastly from our own fighter formations, it is evident that during the past week some enemy bomber formations have proceeded uninterrupted to their inland objectives. This has happened on numerous occasions when we have had from twelve to twenty Squadrons despatched to intercept and to cover aerodromes. The reason is mainly that our fighters are patrolling so high that they are normally becoming heavily engaged with the enemy fighter screen, flying above 20,000 feet.

2. On one occasion yesterday, only seven out of eighteen squadrons despatched, engaged the enemy. On another occasion on the same day, seven out of seventeen squadrons engaged the enemy.

3. It is obvious that some of our Controllers are ordering Squadrons intended to engage bombers to patrol too high. When Group order a Squadron to 16,000 feet, Sector Controller in his superior knowledge, adds on one or two thousand, and the Squadron adds on another two thousand in the vain hope that they will not have any enemy fighters above them. The nett result has been that daily some of the enemy bomber formations slip in under 15,000 feet, frequently without any fighter escort, and bomb their objectives, doing serious damage as at Brooklands. In fact, the majority of the enemy bomber formations have only been intercepted after they have dropped their bombs and are on the way out.

(Sgd) K.R. Park

Air Vice-Marshal
Commanding No. 11 Group
Royal Air Force

APPENDIX 13: BALLOON COMMAND ORDER OF BATTLE 31 AUGUST 1940

STATION	*SQUADRON*	*LOCATION*	*EQUIPMENT*
No. 30 (Balloon Barrage) Group, London			
Chigwell, No. 4 Balloon Centre	908	Metropolis	5 flights, 9 balloons
	909	East Ham	5 flights, 9 balloons
	910	Dagenham, Essex	5 flights, 9 balloons (includes 3 waterborne sites)
	928	Harwich	3 flights, 8 balloons (includes 10 waterborne sites)
Hook, No. 2 Balloon Centre	903	Forest Hill, SE23	5 flights, 9 balloons
	904	Clapham	5 flights, 9 balloons
	905	Kensington	5 flights, 9 balloons
No. 1 Balloon Centre	901	Abbey Wood, Kidbrooke, SE	5 flights, 9 balloons
	902	Kidbrooke	5 flights, 9 balloons
	952	Sheerness	5 flights, 32 balloons
(Thames)			(all waterborne sites).
(Convoy)			1 flight, 8 balloons
	961	Dover	2 flights, 8 balloons 1 flight, 8 balloons (waterborne)
Stanmore, No. 3 Balloon Centre	906	Hampstead NW3	5 flights, 9 balloons
	907	Woodberry Down, N4	5 flights, 9 balloons
	956	Colnbrook	3 flights, 8 balloons
No. 31 (Balloon Barrage) Group, Birmingham			
Alvaston, Derby No. 7 Balloon Centre	918	Alvaston, Derby	4 flights, 8 balloons
Fazakerley, Liverpool, No. 8 Balloon Centre	919	Birkenhead	5 flights, 8 balloons 1 flight, 12 balloons (waterborne)
	921	Fazakerley, Liverpool	6 flights, 8 balloons
Manchester, No. 10 Balloon Centre	925	Manchester and Bowlee	5 flights, 8 balloons
	926	Bowlee, Manchester	5 flights, 8 balloons
Sutton Coldfield No. 5 Balloon Centre	911	West Bromwich	6 flights, 8 balloons
	913	Sutton Coldfield	5 flights, 8 balloons
	962	Milford Haven	1 flight, 8 balloons 1 flight, 7 balloons 1 flight, 9 balloons (waterborne)
Warrington No. 9 Balloon Centre	922	Cuerdley	4 flights, 8 balloons
	923	Runcorn	4 flights, 8 balloons
	949	Crewe	4 flights, 8 balloons

STATION	*SQUADRON*	*LOCATION*	*EQUIPMENT*
Wythall, No. 6 Balloon Centre	914	Croveley Hall, Northfield Birmingham 31	5 flights, 8 balloons
	915	Rowkeath, Birmingham	5 flights, 8 balloons
	916	Coventry	4 flights, 8 balloons
	917	Coventry	3 flights, 8 balloons
No. 32 (Balloon Barrage) Group Ramsey			
Pucklechurch, Bristol No. 11 Balloon Centre	912	Brockworth	3 flights, 8 balloons
	927	Bristol	4 flights, 8 balloons
	935	Filton	3 flights, 8 balloons
	951	Bristol	5 flights, 8 balloons
	957	Yeovil	3 flights, 8 balloons
	953	Cardiff	4 flights, 8 balloons 1 flight, 7 balloons (waterborne)
	958	Swansea	(3 flights, 8 balloons 1 flight, 11 balloons (3 waterborne)
	965	Port Talbot	2 flights, 8 balloons
	966	Newport	5 flights, 8 balloons
	969	Barry	2 flights, 8 balloons
Collaton Cross, Plymouth, No 13 Balloon Centre	934	Plymouth	3 flights, 8 balloons
	959	Falmouth	2 flights, 8 balloons 1 flight, 8 balloons (waterborne)
	964	Torpoint	2 flights, 8 balloons 1 flight, 8 balloons (6 waterborne)
Titchfield No. 12 Balloon Centre	924	Eastleigh	3 flights, 8 balloons
	930	Southampton	5 flights, 8 balloons 1 flight, 10 balloons (waterborne)
	932	Portsmouth	4 flights, 8 balloons
	933	Gosport	3 flights, 8 balloons
No. 33 (Balloon Barrage) Group, Sheffield			
Newcastle, No. 15 Balloon Centre	936	Benton	5 flights, 8 balloons (includes 4 waterborne sites)
	937	South Tyne	4 flights, 8 balloons (includes 3 waterborne sites)
	938	Billingham-on-Tees	6 flights, 8 balloons
Sheffield No. 16 Balloon Centre	939	Sheffield	5 flights, 8 balloons
	940	Rotherham	4 flights, 8 balloons
Sutton-on-Hull No. 17 Balloon Centre	942	Hull	5 flights, total balloons 42 (includes 24 waterborne sites)
	943	Hull	4 flights total balloons 32

STATION	*SQUADRON*	*LOCATION*	*EQUIPMENT*
No. 34 (Balloon Barrage) Group, Edinburgh			
Bishopbriggs No. 18 Balloon Centre (Firth of Forth)	929	South Queensferry Mid Lothian	3 flights, 8 balloons (includes 7 waterborne sites)
	945	Glasgow	5 flights, 8 balloons
	946	Renfrew	6 flights, 8 balloons
	947	Glasgow	4 flights, 8 balloons
(Firth of Forth)	948	Rosyth	3 flights, 8 balloons
	967	Ardrossan	6 flights, 8 balloons
	968	Bishopbriggs (in process of formation, moved to Belfast 12.9.40)	5 flights, 8 balloons (includes 8 waterborne sites)
Lyness No. 20 Balloon Centre	950	Lyness	4 flights, 8 balloons
	960	Lyness	2 flights, 8 balloons (waterborne) 1 flight, 8 balloons
administered direct by 34 Group	920	Lochalsh	1 flight, 5 balloons 1 flight, 11 balloons (waterborne)

APPENDIX 14: FIGHTER COMMAND SECTOR ORGANISATION AND ORDER OF BATTLE, 7 SEPTEMBER 1940 (0900 HOURS)

WICK
No. 3 (Hurricane) Castletown
No. 232 (Hurricane) Sumburgh
(1 Flight only)

DYCE
No. 145 (Hurricane) "A" Flight Dyce
"B" Flight Montrose

No. 615 (Hurricane) Prestwick

TURNHOUSE
No. 605 (Hurricane) Drem
No. 65 (Spitfire) Turnhouse
No. 141 (Defiant) Turnhouse

No. 13 GROUP
Headquarters, Newcastle

USWORTH
No. 607 (Hurricane) Usworth
No. 610 (Spitfire) Acklington
No. 32 (Hurricane) Acklington

ALDERGROVE
No. 245 (Hurricane) Aldergrove

CATTERICK
No. 54 (Spitfire) Catterick
No. 219 (Blenheim) Catterick

No. 12 GROUP
Headquarters, Watnall

KIRTON-IN-LINDSEY
No. 74(Spitfire) Kirton-in-Lindsey
No. 264 (Defiant) Kirton-in-Lindsey

CHURCH FENTON
No. 85 (Hurricane) Church Fenton
No. 302 (Polish) (Hurricane) Church Fenton
No. 64 (Spitfire) Church Fenton
("B" Flight at Ringway)

DIGBY
No. 611 (Spitfire) Digby
No. 151 (Hurricane) Digby
No. 29 (Blenheim) Digby

COLTISHALL
No. 616 (Spitfire) Coltishall
No. 242 (Hurricane) Coltishall
No. 266 (Spitfire) Coltishall
("A" Flight at Wittering)

WITTERING
No. 23 (Blenheim) Wittering
No. 229 (Hurricane) Wittering
("B" Flight at Bircham Newton)

DUXFORD
No. 19 (Spitfire) Duxford
No. 310 (Czech) (Hurricane) Duxford

No. 11 GROUP
Headquarters, Uxbridge

DEBDEN
No. 17 (Hurricane) Debden
No. 73 (Hurricane) Castle Camps
No. 257 (Hurricane) Martlesham
("B" Flight at North Weald)

NORTH WEALD
No. 249 (Hurricane) North Weald
No. 46 (Hurricane) Stapleford

HORNCHURCH
No. 222 (Spitfire) Hornchurch
No. 603 (Spitfire) Hornchurch
No. 600 (Blenheim) Hornchurch
No 41 (Spitfire) Rochford

TANGMERE
No. 601 (Hurricane)Tangmere
No. 43 (Hurricane)Tangmere
No. 602(Spitfire) Westhampnett

NORTHOLT
No. 1 (Hurr) Heathrow
No. IRCAF (Hurr) Northolt
No. 303 Polish (Hurr) Northolt
No. 504 (Hurr) Northolt

KENLEY
No. 111 (Hurr)Croydon
No. 72 (Spit)Croydon
No. 66(Spit) Kenley
No. 253(Hurr) Kenley

BIGGIN HILL
No. 79(Spitfire) B. Hill
No. 501(Hurr) Gravesend

No. 10 GROUP
Headquarters, Box, Wilts

PEMBREY
No. 92 (Hurricane) Pembrey

FILTON
No. 213 (Hurricane) Filton
No. 87 (Hurricane) Exeter
("B" Flight at Bibury)

ST EVAL
No. 238 (Hurricane) St Eval
No. 247 (Gladiator) Roborough
(1 Flight only)

MIDDLE WALLOP
No. 234 (Spitfire) M Wallop
No. 609 (Spitfire) M Wallop
No. 604 (Blenheim) M Wallop
No. 56 (Hurricane) Boscombe Down
No. 152 (Spitfire) Warmwell

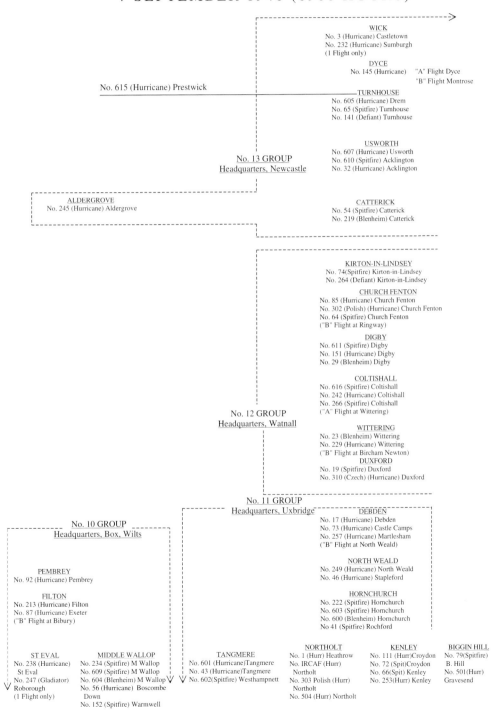

APPENDIX 15: TABLE OF OPERATIONS, 24 AUGUST–6 SEPTEMBER

Date		Fighter Losses	Claims	No. of Fighter Sorties	GAF Sorties		Main Targets
24 August	Day:	22	42	936	550	Day:	Dover and Airfields in South-East: PORTSMOUTH.
	Night:	0	1	45	A	Night:	South Wales: BIRMINGHAM: North east coast: London area. Minelaying off East coast.
25 August	Day:	16	49	481	325	Day:	Scattered activity chiefly in South-West, South and Kent.
	Night:	0	0	43	A	Night:	As on previous night.
26 August	Day:	31	49	787	440	Day:	DOVER and FOLKESTONE: airfields in Kent and Essex: Solent area.
	Night:	0	0	42	A	Night:	Widespread activity: some concentration against BIRMINGHAM and COVENTRY.
27 August	Day:	1	3	288	50	Day:	Reconnaissance activity chiefly in the Portsmouth–Southampton area.
	Night:	0	0	47	A	Night:	Airfields and Industrial areas in the Midlands, East Anglia, Kent and Surrey, Lincolnshire, Norfolk, South Wales, Middlesborough, Chatham and Portsmouth.
28 August	Day:	20	27	739	400	Day:	Airfields in Kent.
	Night:	0	0	22	B	Night:	Activity chiefly against Merseyside and Midlands: North-East coast.
29 August	Day:	9	9	498	390	Day:	Airfields in South and South-East.
	Night:	0	0	28	A	Night:	As on previous night.
30 August	Day:	26	59	1054	600	Day:	Airfields in South and South-East: LUTON.
	Night:	0	0	–	A	Night:	As on previous night with addition of West Riding
31 August	Day:	39	72	978	800	Day:	Airfields in Kent, Essex and Suffolk.
	Night:	0	0	29	A	Night:	MERSEYSIDE and Midlands: North-East coast.
1 September	Day:	15	25	661	490	Day:	Airfields in South-East: CHATHAM.
	Night:	0	0	29	B	Night:	MERSEYSIDE: SOUTH WALES: Midlands
2 September	Day:	22	43	751	750	Day:	Airfields in East Kent–Thames Estuary area.
	Night:	0	0	29	B	Night:	Midlands: Merseyside: Manchester and Sheffield.
3 September	Day:	16	25	711	550	Day:	As on previous day.
	Night:	0	0	34	B	Night:	Merseyside: South Wales and South-East England.
4 September	Day:	17	52	678	550	Day:	As on previous day.
	Night:	0	0	20	A	Night:	As on previous night.
5 September	Day:	20	39	662	460	Day:	As on previous day,
	Night:	0	0	50	B	Night:	As on previous night but with more attention to London area.
6 September	Day:	23	46	987	730	Day:	Airfields in South-East: oil targets in Thames Estuary.
	Night:	0	0	44	C	Night:	Reduced activity, chiefly against London and Merseyside.

APPENDIX 16: INVASION: TASKS OF FIGHTER COMMAND

(Memorandum compiled by Air Staff, Fighter Command)

(A) PRELIMINARY STRUGGLE FOR AIR SUPERIORITY

1. The main feature of this phase is likely to be heavy enemy bomber and fighter attacks directed against aerodromes and aircraft factories and other objectives, designed to destroy the fighter squadrons on the ground and to draw them in the air into engagements against superior numbers.

2. This attack will be met by Fighter Command in accordance with the general principles on which it has been organised and trained for the interception and destruction of the enemy bomber and fighter forces.

3. An important responsibility of Fighter Command in this phase is the protection of our Naval Forces and their bases against enemy attack.

(B) AIR-BORNE INVASION

4. The enemy may be expected to make attempts to land troops, light artillery, and possibly small tanks by air. Any large scale attempt of this sort might be expected to take place in conjunction with sea-borne invasion.

5. The primary aim of Fighter Command operating against air-borne invasion will be to destroy the enemy tank and troop carriers.

(C) SEA-BORNE INVASION

6. The sea-borne invasion may be regarded in three phases:-

(i) Assembly and embarkation at Continental ports.
(ii) The voyage.
(iii) The approach and landing.

7. These three phases will merge, and there may be a number of independent operations. The enemy, if he is to meet with any material success, must also continue shipments to maintain his forces where they have gained footing. The phase can, however, be considered separately.

Assembly and Embarkation

8. Enemy activities in this phase will be the object of attack by both Bomber and Coastal Commands, and Fighter Command is required to do what is practicable to cover their operations. As the Command, however, will no doubt be engaged in intensive operations under (a) above, and as fighter ranges are so limited, it will normally be practicable only to cover the assembly and return of our bombers.

The voyage

9. The enemy may choose the shortest routes and make the initial voyage under cover of darkness, or screened by weather or smoke. There will be areas and times, however, in which enemy transports will be engaged by our Naval Forces under circumstances in which enemy bombers may be directed against our ships.

10. The primary responsibility of Fighter Command in this connection will be protection of our Naval Forces against enemy bomber - particularly dive-bomber attack, wherever this is within fighter range of our coast. Similarly, the Command must do what is practicable to support the operations of our bomber aircraft attacking enemy convoys.

Approach and Landing

11. This will become temporarily the focus of the air battle, with the enemy probably endeavouring to land troops by air as well as by sea, covered by intensive bomber attacks against our defences with strong fighter support. There may well be more than one landing and therefore more than one battle, becoming main or subsidiary operations according to the scale of the enemy attack at each point.

12. The primary aim of Fighter Command in such operations must be to destroy the enemy troop and tank carrying aircraft.

13. This aim must be subject, however, to the continued protection of our Naval Forces against enemy bomber attack within fighter range of the coast, since the enemy is unlikely to be able to consolidate any landing if our Naval Forces can continue to operate freely against his sea lines of communication.

14. Further tasks which Fighter Command must be prepared to undertake in connection with such operations will be, in order of their importance, as follows:-

(i) Fighter cover to be given to the Bomber and 'Banquet' aircraft which will be attacking enemy's convoys and landing craft.
(ii) Attacks by Cannon Fighters, wherever these can be made available, to be directed against the enemy's barges and landing craft, particularly those containing armoured fighting vehicles or guns.
(iii) Cannon fighters, if available, to be prepared to engage enemy tanks wherever these may succeed in making a successful landing from either air or sea transport.
(iv) Finally, fighter protection may have to be afforded to our own troops against the attack of enemy dive-bombers, which may be operating in conjunction with a landing or covering a lodgment against our counter offensive.

14 September 1940

APPENDIX 17: GERMAN ESTIMATE OF TONNAGE (METRIC) DROPPED IN ATTACKS ON LONDON, SEPTEMBER 1940

Date	*HE Tons (Metric)*	*No. of Incendiaries*[a]	*Date*	*HE Tons*	*No. of Incendiaries*
Sep 7[(b)]	316	356	Sep 19/20	312	603
Sep 7/8	333	378	Sep 20/21	154	79
Sep 8/9	202	257	Sep 21/22	162	329
Sep 9/10	259	315	Sep 22/23	140	361
Sep 10/11	175	1018	Sep 23/24	310	601
Sep 11/12	208	328	Sep 24/25	256	384
Sep 13/14	125	200	Sep 25/26	260	441
Sep 15[(b)]	133	108	Sep 26/27	270	239
Sep 15/16	234	279	Sep 27/28	167	437
Sep 16/17	207	308	Sep 28/29	325	305
Sep 17/18	317	651	Sep 29/30	311	136
Sep 18/19	339	628	Sep 30/1	295	106

Dropped in Attacks of under 100 tons	– 691 tons: 685 incendiaries.
Gross Total for September	– 6501 tons: 9540 incendiaries.
August	– 12 tons: 12 incendiaries
October	– 7242 tons: 4869 incendiaries

Notes: [a] No. of incendiaries is given in terms of incendiary containers, each holding 36 1Kg incendiary bombs.
[b] Day Attacks

APPENDIX 18: FIGHTER COMMAND SECTOR ORGANISATION AND ORDER OF BATTLE, 30 SEPTEMBER 1940 (0900 HOURS)

No. 13 GROUP
Headquarters, Newcastle

WICK
No. 232 (Hurricane) Castletown
(1 Flight only)

DYCE
No. 145 (Hurricane) "A" Flight Dyce
"B" Flight Montrose

TURNHOUSE
No. 65 (Spitfire) Turnhouse
No. 3 (Hurricane) Turnhouse
No. 141 (Defiant) Turnhouse
("A" Flight only)
No. 111 (Hurricane) Drem
No. 263 (Hurricane) Drem
(1 Flight only)

USWORTH
No. 43 (Hurricane) Usworth
No. 32 (Hurricane) Acklington
No. 610 (Spitfire) Acklington

CATTERICK
No. 54 (Spitfire) Catterick
No. 219 (Blenheim) Catterick
("B" Flight at Acklington

ALDERGROVE
No. 245 (Hurricane) Aldergrove

No. 12 GROUP
Headquarters, Watnall

KIRTON-IN-LINDSEY
No. 616 (Spitfire) Kirton-in-Lindsey
No. 264 (Defiant) Kirton-in-Lindsey
("B" Flight at Acklington

CHURCH FENTON
No. 85 (Hurricane) Church Fenton
No. 302 (Polish) (Hurricane) Leconfield
No. 64 (Spitfire) Leconfield
("A" Flight only)

No. 64 "B" Flight, Ringway (Cheshire)

DIGBY
No. 151 (Hurricane) Digby
No. 29 (Blenheim) Digby
No. 611 (Spitfire) Digby
("A" Flight only)

No. 611 "B" Flight, Ternhill (Salop)

COLTISHALL
No. 74 (Spitfire) Coltishall
No. 242 (Hurricane) Coltishall

WITTERING
No. 266 (Spitfire) Wittering
No. 1 (Hurricane) Wittering

DUXFORD
No. 19 (Spitfire) Duxford
No. 310 (Czech) (Hurricane) Duxford

No. 11 GROUP
Headquarters, Uxbridge

DEBDEN
No. 17 (Hurricane) Debden
No. 73 (Hurricane) Castle Camps
No. 257 (Hurricane) Castle Camps

NORTH WEALD
No. 249 (Hurricane) North Weald
No. 46 (Hurricane) Stapleford
No. 25 (Blenheim) North Weald
(1 Flight at Martlesham re-equipping with Beaufighters)

HORNCHURCH
No. 41 (Spitfire) Hornchurch
No. 603 (Spitfire) Hornchurch
No. 222 (Spitfire) Rochford

TANGMERE
No. 607 (Hurricane)Tangmere
No. 613 (Hurricane)Tangmere
No. 602(Spitfire) Westhampnett
No. 23(Blenheim) Ford
(1 Flight at Middle Wallop)

NORTHOLT
No. 1 (RCAF)(Hurr)Northolt
No. 303(Polish)(Hurr)Northolt
No. 229(Hurr) Heathrow
No. 264(Defiant) Luton
("A" Flight only)
No. 241 (Defiant) Gatwick
("B" Flight only)

KENLEY
No. 233 (Hurr)Kenley
No. 501 (Hurr)Kenley
No. 605(Hurr)Croydon

BIGGIN HILL
No. 72(Spitfire) B. Hill
No. 92(Spitfire) B. Hill
No. 66(Spitfire) Gravesend

No. 10 GROUP
Headquarters, Box, Wilts

PEMBREY
No. 79 (Hurricane) Pembrey

FILTON
No. 504 (Hurricane) Filton
No. 601 (Hurricane) Exeter
No. 87 (Hurricane) Exeter
("B" Flight at Bibury)

ST EVAL
No. 234 (Spitfire) St Eval
No. 247 (Gladiator) Roborough
(1 Flight only)

MIDDLE WALLOP
No. 238 (Hurricane) M Wallop
No. 609 (Spitfire) M Wallop
No. 604 (Blenheim) M Wallop
No. 152 (Spitfire) Warmwell
No. 56 (Hurricane) Boscombe Down

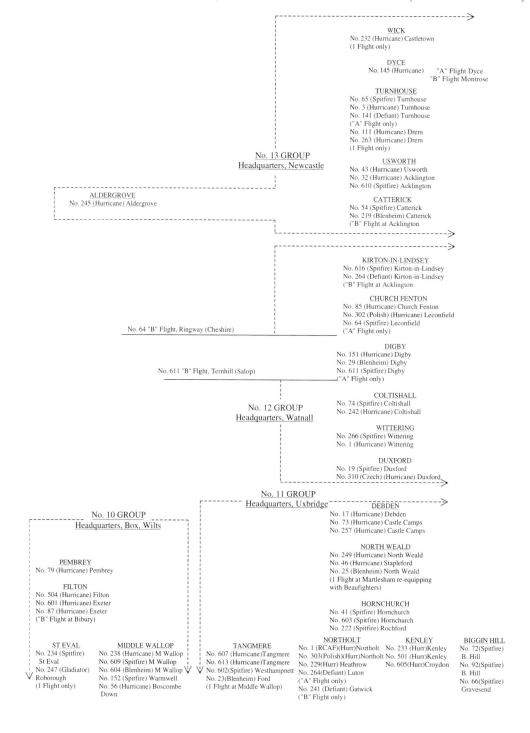

APPENDIX 19: No. 11 GROUP, INSTRUCTIONS TO CONTROLLERS, No. 16

From: Air Officer Commanding, No. 11 Group, Royal Air Force.

To: Group Controllers and Sector Commanders, for Sector Controllers.

Date: 11 September 1940.

Engagement of Mass Attacks

The enemy has recently dropped his plan of making two or three separate attacks by two or three hundred aircraft in one day. Recent attacks in the 11 Group area have been made by three or four hundred aircraft in two or three waves following in quick succession, the whole engagement covering about 45 to 60 minutes.

The object of the following instruction is to ensure that we meet the enemy in maximum strength, employing our fighters Squadrons in pairs of the same type where possible.

READINESS SQUADRONS: Despatch in pairs to engage first wave of enemy. Spitfires against fighter screen, and Hurricanes against bombers and close escort.

AVAILABLE 15 SQUADRONS:
a) Bring to Readiness in pairs;
b) Despatch in pairs to engage second wave.

AVAILABLE 30 SQUADRONS:
a) Bring to Readiness;
b) Despatch singly to protect aircraft factories or sector aerodromes, or to reinforce Squadrons already in the air.

If there is a third wave and it is necessary to despatch these Squadrons, they should be sent in pairs as follows:

DEBDEN and NORTH WEALD Squadrons together;
HORNCHURCH and BIGGIN HILL Squadrons together;
KENLEY and NORTHOLT Squadrons together.

TANGMERE SQUADRONS: When not required to protect the Portsmouth–Southampton area in conjunction with 10 Group Squadrons, the Tangmere Squadrons should be employed within the Kenley or back Tangmere Sector to engage enemy formations that approach London from the South, or endeavour to pass round the South of London to attack aircraft factories at Kingston, Brooklands and Langley.

Whenever time permits, the Readiness Squadron and the Available 15 Squadron should be despatched to work as a pair after having rendezvoused at base.

RENDEZVOUS OF SQUADRONS: The Group Controller must name the base over which pairs of Squadrons are to rendezvous, as they normally occupy separate aerodromes within a Sector. Sector Controllers should inform Group Controllers immediately a pair of Squadrons have rendezvoused over any given point. Group Controller should then detail those Squadrons to a raid and leave the rest to Sector.

SELECTION OF SQUADRON TO LEAD A PAIR OF SQUADRONS: The detailing of the directing Squadron should be done by Sector Controller, who should know which Squadron is best suited to lead. Sector Controllers must also repeat to the Squadron being led all orders issued to the directing Squadron in case those units become separated by clouds. Sector Commanders must impress on Squadron Commanders the importance of leading Squadrons in a pair joining up and maintaining contact with the Squadron being led.

(Sgd.) K. R. Park,

Air Vice-Marshal,
Commanding No. 11 Group,
Royal Air Force.

APPENDIX 20: No. 11 GROUP, INSTRUCTIONS TO CONTROLLERS, No. 18

From: Air Officer Commanding, No. 11 Group, Royal Air Force.

To: Group Controllers and Sector Commanders, for Sector Controllers.

Date: 16 September 1940.

Engagement of Mass Attacks

During the air fighting of the last week, I have noticed the following deficiencies in our control by Group and Sectors:

A) Individual Squadrons failing to rendezvous as detailed;

B) Individual Squadrons being detailed to big raids;

C) Pairs of Squadrons being placed on patrol too far forward, too low, resulting in their being attacked by German high fighter screen;

D) Individual Squadrons being given a rendezvous so far forward as to become engaged before meeting their paired Squadron;

E) Very high raids of between 100 and 150 fighters being allowed to draw up nearly all the Group prematurely – the bomb raids then approaching about 45 minutes later when a number of our Squadrons are on the ground refuelling;

F) A persistent tendency of Group Controllers to delay in detailing pairs of Squadrons that have reached their height and rendezvous on to individual raids or on to a suitable patrol line across the line of approach;

G) Failing to check Sectors when they report in error less pilots and aircraft effective than are reported on the evening state of Squadrons.

FRESH INSTRUCTIONS

Very High Enemy Fighters:

2. The Spitfire Squadrons of Hornchurch and Biggin Hill are, in clear weather, to be detailed in pairs to attack the high fighter screen which is normally between 25,000 and 30,000 feet.

Rendezvous:

3. When the sky is almost completely overcast, Squadrons should rendezvous over an aerodrome below cloud base, otherwise they should rendezvous high over an aerodrome or point well in advance of the enemy's raids, in order not to be dived on while still climbing.

Patrol Lines:

4. Whenever it is not possible to get fairly reliable information about the strength, height and composition of strong incoming raids, fighter Squadrons must be detailed to short patrol lines, if necessary two Squadrons very high and two Squadrons between 15,000 and 20,000 ft.

Diversions by Enemy Fighters:

5. If it appears that the first wave of raids are high flying fighters, act as follows:

(i) Detail not less than several pairs of Spitfires to fighter screen;

(ii) Get ample Hurricane Squadrons rendezvoused in pairs in the region of Sector aerodromes;

(iii) Get Northolt and Tangmere Squadrons to Readiness to despatch as wings of three Squadrons to intercept the enemy's second or third wave, which normally contains bombers.

State of Preparedness:

6. During the coming months there will be a few days in which cloud conditions are suitable for the enemy to assemble mass attacks covered by high fighter screen. Whenever these conditions obtain, we must maintain a higher State of Preparedness, and fresh instructions to this end have been issued.

(Sgd.) K. R. Park.

Air Vice-Marshal,
Commanding, No. 11 Group,
Royal Air Force.

APPENDIX 21: No. 11 GROUP, INSTRUCTIONS TO CONTROLLERS, No. 31

From: Air Officer Commanding, No. 11 Group, Royal Air Force.

To: Group Controllers.

Date: 17 October 1940.

Engagement of Mass Bomber Attacks on the London Area.

General Plan:

To engage enemy high FIGHTER SCREEN with Spitfire Squadrons from Hornchurch and Biggin Hill half-way between London and the coast, and so enable Hurricane Squadrons from North Weald, Kenley and Northolt to attack bomber formations plus close escort before they reach the line of fighter aerodromes East and South of London. The remaining Squadrons around London that cannot be got up in time to intercept the first wave, to provide a rear screen by climbing over the line of aerodromes East and South of London.

2. The Squadrons from Debden and Tangmere (if disengaged), to be despatched and employed in Wings or pairs, so as to form a screen East and South-East of London to intercept third or fourth wave coming inland, also the retreating earlier waves.

Spitfire Sqaudrons:

3. Assembled at height in pairs on back patrol lines, then detailed to engage high fighter screen at 30,00 feet.

Role: To protect pairs or Wings of Hurricane Squadrons whilst climbing up, also while attacking bombers plus escort. If the high fighter screen withdraws to the coast, a proportion of the Spitfires may be detailed to attack the escorts to incoming bomb raids.

Hurricane Squadrons:

4. Squadrons at Readiness to be despatched in pairs to back patrol lines covering line of aerodromes. Immediately pairs have reached operating height, detail to bomb raids or to forward patrol lines under Spitfires. Squadrons at Available to be brought to Readiness and assembled in pairs at operating height on back patrol lines covering Sector aerodromes, and detailed to second wave of bomb raids.

5. Whilst gaining height the latter Squadrons may have to be detailed to split raids by bombers that attempt to attack vital points on the flank of the mass of bombers plus escort.

Hurricane Squadrons from Flank Sectors (Debden, Tangmere, and possibly Northolt):

6. Despatch in pairs or Wings, according to the clouds, to patrol mid-Kent patrol lines at 20,000 to 25,000 feet, to engage

(i) Third or fourth wave attacks of bombers plus escort;

(ii) Retreating bomb raids of first and second wave;

(iii) To protect fighter aerodromes whilst the earlier Hurricane and Spitfire Squadrons are refuelling.

Reinforcement from other Groups:

7. Immediately the enemy numbers appear to be more than 150, request two to three Squadrons to cover the Northern approaches to London, or the South-Western Group of vital points near London, as directed in Controllers Instructions No. 7, dated August 27th 1940.

(Sgd.) K. R. Park,

Air Vice-Marshal,
Commanding, No. 11 Group,
Royal Air Force.

APPENDIX 22: No. 11 GROUP, INSTRUCTIONS TO CONTROLLERS, No. 35

From: Air Officer Commanding, No. 11 Group, Royal Air Force.

To: Group Controllers and Sector Commanders, for Sector Comtrollers.

Date: 26 October 1940.

Group Reinforcement by No. 12 Group Wing from Duxford

The following arrangements have been made for the operation of the No. 12 Group Wing from Duxford in No. 11 Group area.

(i) The No. 12 Group Controller will advise the AOC, or the Duty Controller of the hours between which the Duxford Wing will be at "Readiness". This information will if possible, be given by 09.00 hours daily, in order to fit the Duxford Wing into the programme for the day.

(ii) As soon as the Group Controller gets a clear indication of raids building up over the French Coast, he is to request No. 12 Group Controller to despatch the Duxford Wing to patrol East of London on an approximate line North and South through Hornchurch. The arrival of the Wing on the Patrol Line will be communicated to No. 11 Group Controller who will indicate to the No. 12 Group Controller the best position in the Estuary or Northern Kent to which the Wing should be directed to effect an interception.

(iii) The No. 12 Group Controller will inform No. 11 Group immediately the Duxford Wing has left ground.

(iv) No. 11 Group Controller is then to inform Sector Controller, Hornchurch, who is to fix the position of the Duxford Wing. This will be possible as two aircraft of the VHF Squadron in the Duxford Wing are fitted with the Hornchurch fixer crystals (one working, one in reserve).

(v) On arrival on the Patrol Line, Hornchurch will give Zero to the Duxford Wing on its operational frequency. Hornchurch will hold a crystal of the leading Squadron's frequency in the Duxford Wing and set up a channel on their frequency. With R/T facilities as indicated, Hornchurch Controller will be able to fix the Duxford Wing and inform the Observer Corps via the Group Observer Corps Liaison Officer, flank Sectors and Group Operations, of the position of the Duxford Wing, at frequent intervals.

(Sgd.) G Harcourt-Smith, G/C

for Air Vice-Marshal,

Commanding, No. 11 Group,

Royal Air Force.

APPENDIX 23: TABLE OF OPERATIONS, 7 SEPTEMBER–30 SEPTEMBER

Date		*Fighter Losses*	*Claims*	*No. of Fighter Sorties*	*GAF Sorties*		*Main Targets*
7 September	Day	28	74	817	700	Day:	LONDON.
	Night	0	0	23	A	Night:	LONDON.
8 September	Day	2	4	305	200	Day:	Slight activity.
	Night	0	0	25	A	Night:	LONDON.
9 September	Day	19	48	466	430	Day:	Thames Estuary and South LONDON: Southampton.
	Night	0	0	41	A	Night:	LONDON.
10 September	Day	1	2	224	50	Day:	Slight activity.
	Night	0	0	41	A	Night:	LONDON: South Wales and Merseyside.
11 September	Day	29	80	678	500	Day:	London area and Southampton.
	Night	0	0	58	A	Night:	LONDON: Merseyside.
12 September	Day	0	1	247	80	Day:	Slight activity.
	Night	0	0	5	B	Night:	Chiefly LONDON: South Wales: Midlands: Merseyside.
13 September	Day	1	1	209	130	Day:	Series of small raids, chiefly against London area.
	Night	0	0	55	A	Night:	LONDON.
14 September	Day	14	15	860	400	Day:	London area.
	Night	0	1	28	B	Night:	Reduced activity: London: South Wales.
15 September	Day	26	174	705	600	Day:	LONDON: Portland: Southampton.
	Night	0	0	68	A	Night:	LONDON: Midlands.
16 September	Day	1	0	428	250	Day:	Slight activity chiefly in South-East and East Anglia.
	Night	0	2	0	A	Night:	LONDON: Midlands and Merseyside.
17 September	Day	5	5	544	350	Day:	As on previous day, but with one large fighter sweep in the afternoon.
	Night	0	0	45	A	Night:	LONDON: Merseyside.
18 September	Day	12	45	1165	800	Day:	Oil targets in Thames Estuary.
	Night	0	1	65	A	Night:	LONDON: Merseyside.
19 September	Day	0	4	237	75	Day:	Reduced activity, chiefly over Thames Estuary and East London.
	Night	0	0	16	A	Night:	LONDON: Merseyside.
20 September	Day	7	4	540	150	Day:	One large fighter sweep towards London: Otherwise reconnaissance only.
	Night	0	0	46	B	Night:	LONDON:
21 September	Day	0	2	563	260	Day:	Slight activity: some fighter sweeps in east Kent.
	Night	0	0	46	A	Night:	LONDON: Merseyside.
22 September	Day	0	1	158	140	Day:	Slight activity.
	Night	0	0	50	A	Night:	LONDON.
23 September	Day	11	11	710	300	Day:	Fighter sweeps towards London.
	Night	0	0	70	A	Night:	LONDON: Merseyside.

Date		Fighter Losses	Claims	No. of Fighter Sorties	GAF Sorties		Main Targets
24 September	Day	4	7	880	500	Day:	Tilbury: Southampton.
	Night	0	0	50	A	Night:	LONDON: Merseyside.
25 September	Day	4	23	668	290	Day:	BRISTOL: Plymouth.
	Night	0	0	39	A	Night:	LONDON: South Wales: Lancashire.
26 September	Day	9	32	417	220	Day:	SOUTHAMPTON.
	Night	0	0	34	A	Night:	LONDON: Merseyside.
27 September	Day	28	131	939	850	Day:	LONDON: Bristol.
	Night	0	0	27	A	Night:	LONDON: Merseyside: Midlands.
28 September	Day	16	6	770	300	Day:	London: Solent area.
	Night	0	0	65	A	Night:	LONDON.
29 September	Day	5	3	441	180	Day:	Reduced activity in South-East and East Anglia.
	Night	0	0	25	A	Night:	LONDON: Merseyside.
30 September	Day	20	46	1173	650	Day:	Fighter sweeps towards London: few bombs dropped.
	Night	0	0	50	A	Night:	LONDON.

APPENDIX 24: FIGHTER COMMAND SECTOR ORGANISATION AND ORDER OF BATTLE, 3 NOVEMBER 1940

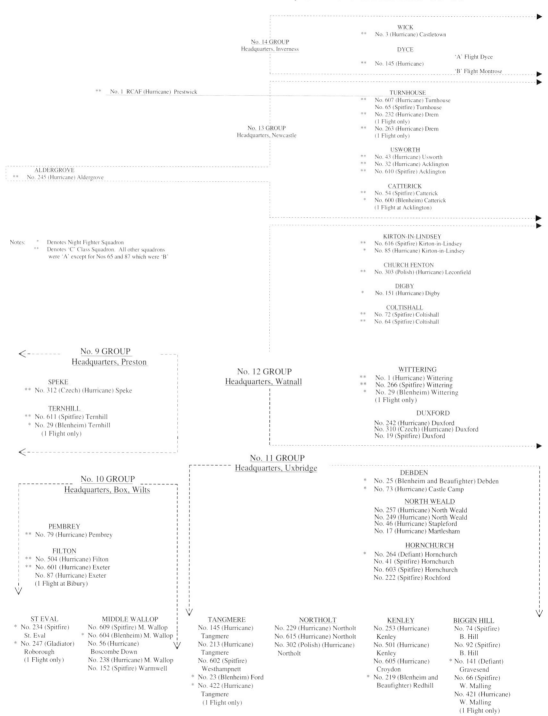

No. 14 GROUP
Headquarters, Inverness

WICK
** No. 3 (Hurricane) Castletown

DYCE
** No. 145 (Hurricane) 'A' Flight Dyce
'B' Flight Montrose

No. 13 GROUP
Headquarters, Newcastle

** No. 1 RCAF (Hurricane) Prestwick

TURNHOUSE
** No. 607 (Hurricane) Turnhouse
No. 65 (Spitfire) Turnhouse
** No. 232 (Hurricane) Drem
(1 Flight only)
** No. 263 (Hurricane) Drem
(1 Flight only)

USWORTH
** No. 43 (Hurricane) Usworth
** No. 32 (Hurricane) Acklington
** No. 610 (Spitfire) Acklington

ALDERGROVE
** No. 245 (Hurricane) Aldergrove

CATTERICK
** No. 54 (Spitfire) Catterick
* No. 600 (Blenheim) Catterick
(1 Flight at Acklington)

Notes: * Denotes Night Fighter Squadron
** Denotes 'C' Class Squadron. All other squadrons were 'A' except for Nos 65 and 87 which were 'B'

No. 12 GROUP
Headquarters, Watnall

KIRTON-IN-LINDSEY
** No. 616 (Spitfire) Kirton-in-Lindsey
* No. 85 (Hurricane) Kirton-in-Lindsey

CHURCH FENTON
** No. 303 (Polish) (Hurricane) Leconfield

DIGBY
* No. 151 (Hurricane) Digby

COLTISHALL
** No. 72 (Spitfire) Coltishall
** No. 64 (Spitfire) Coltishall

WITTERING
** No. 1 (Hurricane) Wittering
** No. 266 (Spitfire) Wittering
* No. 29 (Blenheim) Wittering
(1 Flight only)

DUXFORD
No. 242 (Hurricane) Duxford
No. 310 (Czech) (Hurricane) Duxford
No. 19 (Spitfire) Duxford

No. 9 GROUP
Headquarters, Preston

SPEKE
** No. 312 (Czech) (Hurricane) Speke

TERNHILL
** No. 611 (Spitfire) Ternhill
* No. 29 (Blenheim) Ternhill
(1 Flight only)

No. 10 GROUP
Headquarters, Box, Wilts

PEMBREY
** No. 79 (Hurricane) Pembrey

FILTON
** No. 504 (Hurricane) Filton
** No. 601 (Hurricane) Exeter
No. 87 (Hurricane) Exeter
(1 Flight at Bibury)

ST EVAL
* No. 234 (Spitfire) St. Eval
* No. 247 (Gladiator) Roborough
(1 Flight only)

MIDDLE WALLOP
No. 609 (Spitfire) M. Wallop
* No. 604 (Blenheim) M. Wallop
No. 56 (Hurricane) Boscombe Down
No. 238 (Hurricane) M. Wallop
No. 152 (Spitfire) Warmwell

No. 11 GROUP
Headquarters, Uxbridge

DEBDEN
* No. 25 (Blenheim and Beaufighter) Debden
* No. 73 (Hurricane) Castle Camp

NORTH WEALD
No. 257 (Hurricane) North Weald
No. 249 (Hurricane) North Weald
No. 46 (Hurricane) Stapleford
No. 17 (Hurricane) Martlesham

HORNCHURCH
* No. 264 (Defiant) Hornchurch
No. 41 (Spitfire) Hornchurch
No. 603 (Spitfire) Hornchurch
No. 222 (Spitfire) Rochford

TANGMERE
No. 145 (Hurricane) Tangmere
No. 213 (Hurricane) Tangmere
No. 602 (Spitfire) Westhampnett
* No. 23 (Blenheim) Ford
* No. 422 (Hurricane) Tangmere
(1 Flight only)

NORTHOLT
No. 229 (Hurricane) Northolt
No. 615 (Hurricane) Northolt
No. 302 (Polish) (Hurricane) Northolt

KENLEY
No. 253 (Hurricane) Kenley
No. 501 (Hurricane) Kenley
No. 605 (Hurricane) Croydon
* No. 219 (Blenheim and Beaufighter) Redhill

BIGGIN HILL
No. 74 (Spitfire) B. Hill
No. 92 (Spitfire) B. Hill
* No. 141 (Defiant) Gravesend
No. 66 (Spitfire) W. Malling
No. 421 (Hurricane) W. Malling
(1 Flight only)

APPENDIX 25: No. 11 GROUP, INSTRUCTIONS TO CONTROLLERS, No. 20

From: Air Officer Commanding, No. 11 Group, Royal Air Force.

To: Group Controllers and Sector Commanders, for Sector Controllers.

Date: 28 September 1940.

Engagement of Daylight Raids:

1. Attention is called to Instruction to Controllers No. 18, which deals with enemy heavy attacks covered by high flying fighter screen.

2. Enemy attacks during the past three days along the South coast have shown that he is reverting to bomb raids covered by close escort. Owing to difficult cloud conditions that will probably obtain on most days, future bombing attacks in the 11 Group area will probably be made without the cover of a very high fighter screen.

Wing Formations:

3. To counter enemy mass attacks, it had been hoped to develop patrols by wings of three fighter Squadrons. Experience has shown, however, that even with quite a small amount of cloud, Squadrons take a long time to form up, and also have great difficulty in maintaining contact on patrol. Moreover, the time taken to get three Squadrons to a point seems to be double the time required for a pair of Squadrons. With the RDF giving us shorter warning than during mid-Summer, we cannot afford to waste from five to fifteen minutes while Squadrons are assembling and sorting themselves out in wings of three. Therefore unless the sky is clear of cloud layers and the Group Controller gets ample warning of a heavy scale attack forming up over the French coast, he will despatch pairs of fighter Squadrons as described in Instruction to Controllers No. 16, during the Winter months. This does not mean that wings of three Squadrons will not be required on occasion in the Winter, and frequently in the coming Spring, when it is hoped we shall be permitted to take a more offensive role and attack the enemy before he reaches the Kentish coast.

State of Preparedness:

4. Controllers should note that the NORMAL STATE fits in more readily with the employment of pairs of Squadrons than of wings of three. Nevertheless, when the Group is at ADVANCED STATE, it does not follow that Controllers are to detail wings of three unless they get ample warning from the RDF, and weather is clear of clouds.

(Sgd.) K. R. Park.

Air Vice-Marshal,
Commanding, No. 11 Group,
Royal Air Force.

APPENDIX 26: No. 11 GROUP, INSTRUCTIONS TO CONTROLLERS, No. 24

From: Air Officer Commanding, No. 11 Group, Royal Air Force.

To: Group Controllers and Sector Commanders, for Sector Controllers.

Date: 4 October 1940.

Height of Fighter Patrols

With the prevailing cloudy skies and inaccurate heights given by the RDF, the Group Controller's most difficult problem is to know the height of incoming enemy raids. Occasionally reconnaissance Spitfires from Hornchurch or Biggin Hill are able to sight and report the height and other particulars of enemy formations. Moreover, the special fighter reconnaissance flight is now being formed at Gravesend (attached to No. 66 Squadron) for the purpose of getting information about approaching enemy raids.

2. Because of the above-mentioned lack of height reports and the delay in receipt of RDF and Observer Corps reports at Group, plus longer times recently taken by Squadrons to take off, pairs and Wings of Squadrons are meeting enemy formations above, before they get to the height ordered by Group.

3. 'Tip-and-run' raids across Kent by Me110s carrying bombs, or small formations of long-range bombers escorted by fighters, give such short notice that the Group Controller is sometimes compelled to detail even single fighter Squadrons that happen to be in the air to intercept the enemy bombers before they attack aircraft factories, Sector aerodromes, or other vital points such as the Docks, Woolwich, etc. Normally, however, Group Controller has sufficient time to detail from one to three pairs (two to six Squadrons) to intercept raids heading for bombing targets in the vicinity of London.

4. Whenever time permits, I wish Group Controllers to get the Readiness Squadrons in company over Sector aerodromes, Spitfires 25,000 feet, Hurricanes 20,000 feet, and wait till they report they are in position before sending them to patrol lines or to intercept raids having a good track in fairly clear weather.

5. This does not mean that the Controller is to allow raids reported as bombers to approach our Sector aerodromes or other bombing targets unengaged because pairs or Wings of Squadrons have not reported that they have reached the height ordered in the vicinity of Sector aerodrome or other rendezvous.

6. I am sending a copy of this Instruction to all Sector Commanders and Controllers, also Squadron Commanders, in order that they may understand why their Squadrons have sometimes to be sent off to intercept approaching bombers before they have reached the height originally ordered or perhaps have joined up with the other Squadron or a pair or Squadrons of a Wing. Our constant aim is to detail one or more pairs of Squadrons against incoming bomb raids, but the warning received at Group is sometimes

not sufficient and our first and primary task is to intercept and break up the bombers before they can deliver a bombing attack against aircraft factories, Sector aerodromes, Docks, etc.

7. Circumstances beyond the control of Group or Sector Controllers sometimes demand that Squadrons engage enemy bomber formations before they have gained height advantage and got comfortably set with the other Squadrons detailed by Group.

8. I wish the Squadron Commanders and Sector Controllers to know that everything humanly possible is being done by Group to increase the warning received of incoming enemy raids. Meanwhile, Squadrons can help by shortening the time of take-off, assembly and rendezvous with other Squadrons to which they are detailed as pairs or Wings.

(Sgd.) K. R. Park.

Air Vice-Marshal,
Commanding, No. 11 Group,
Royal Air Force.

APPENDIX 27: No. 11 GROUP, INSTRUCTIONS TO CONTROLLERS, No. 26

From: Air Officer Commanding, No. 11 Group, Royal Air Force.

To: Group Controllers and Sector Commanders, for Sector Controllers.

Date: 8 October 1940.

Height of our Fighter Patrols

The following instruction is issued in amplification of para 3 of Instructions to Controllers No. 25.

2. When a Spitfire Squadron is ordered to Readiness Patrol on the Maidstone Line, it's function is to cover the area Biggin Hill–Maidstone–Gravesend, while the other Squadrons are gaining their height, and protect them from the enemy high Fighter Screen. The form of attack which should be adopted on the high enemy fighters is to dive repeatedly on them and climb up again each time to regain height.

3. The Squadron is not to be ordered to intercept a Raid during the early stages of the engagement, but the Sector Controller must keep the Squadron Commander informed as to the height and direction of approaching raids.

4. The object of ordering the Squadron to patrol at 15,000 feet while waiting on the Patrol Line for Raids to come inland, is to conserve oxygen, and to keep the pilots at a comfortable height. Pilots must watch this point most carefully, so that they have ample in hand when they are subsequently ordered to 30,000 feet which is to be done immediately enemy raids appear to be about to cross our coast.

5. When other Squadrons have gained their height and the course of the engagement is clear, the Group Controllers will take a suitable opportunity to put this Spitfire Squadron on to enemy raids where its height can be used to advantage.

(Sgd.) K. R. Park.

Air Vice-Marshal,
Commanding, No. 11 Group,
Royal Air Force.

APPENDIX 28: No. 11 GROUP, INSTRUCTIONS TO CONTROLLERS, No. 28

From: Air Officer Commanding, No. 11 Group, Royal Air Force.

To: Group Controllers and Sector Commanders, for Sector Controllers.

Date: 14 October 1940.

Rate of Climb of Fighter Formations

Owing to the very short warning given nowadays by the RDF Stations, enemy fighter formations (some carrying bombs), can be over London within twenty minutes of the first RDF plot, and have on occasion dropped bombs on South-East London seventeen minutes after the first RDF plots.

2. Under these circumstances, the only Squadrons that can intercept the enemy fighters before they reach London or Sector aerodromes are the Squadrons in the air on Readiness patrol, or remaining in the air after an attack, plus one or two Squadrons at Stand-By at Sectors on the East and South-East of London.

3. In these circumstances, it is vitally important for Group Controllers, also Sector Controllers, to keep clearly in mind the time taken for Squadrons and other formations to climb from ground level to operating height. The following times are those for a good average Squadron of the types stated:

(A)	Spitfire (Mark I)	13 minutes to 20,000 feet.
		18 minutes to 25,000 feet.
		27 minutes to 30,000 feet.
(B)	Hurricane (Mark I)	16 minutes to 20,000 feet.
		21 minutes to 25,000 feet.

Pairs: The rate of climb for a pair of Squadrons in company will be 10% to 12% greater than the time given above.

Wings: The rate of climb of Wings of three Squadrons is between 15% and 18% greater than the times given above.

Rendezvous

4. In view of the above, Controllers will see the importance of ordering pairs of Wings to rendezvous over a point at operating height in order that they can climb quickly, singly, and not hold one another back by trying to climb in an unwieldy mass. Bitter experience has proved time and again that it is better to intercept the enemy with one Squadron above him than by a whole Wing crawling up below, probably after the enemy has dropped his bombs.

(Sgd.) K. R. Park.

Air Vice-Marshal,
Commanding, No. 11 Group,
Royal Air Force.

APPENDIX 29: No. 11 GROUP, INSTRUCTIONS TO CONTROLLERS, No. 30

From: Air Officer Commanding, No. 11 Group, Royal Air Force.

To: Group Controllers and Sector Commanders, for Sector Controllers.

Date: 17 October 1940.

Engagement of High Fighter Raids

The general plan is to get one or two Spitfire Squadrons to engage enemy fighters from above about mid-Kent, in order to cover other Spitfire and Hurricane Squadrons whilst climbing to operating height at back patrol lines East and South of London.

Preparation:

2. Whenever the cloud conditions are favourable for high raids by fighters the following preparations will be made:

(1) *Reconnaissance Aircraft*: One or two reconnaissance aircraft to be kept on patrol near the Kentish coast, height depending on cloud layers.

(2) *Readiness Patrol*: A patrol by one or two Squadrons to be maintained on Maidstone Patrol Line at 15,000 feet, between 0800 hours and 1800 hours.

(3) *Stand-By Squadron*: One Squadron at Sector providing patrol at (2) to be at Stand-By during the peak periods, - breakfast, noon and early tea-time.

(4) *London & Debden Squadrons*: State of Readiness of Hurricane Squadrons to be *advanced state* whenever cloud conditions are suitable for very high fighter raids.

Attack:

3. Immediately enemy formations are plotted over the French coast or Dover Straits, the following action will be initiated:-

(1) *Reconnaissance Aircraft*: Despatched to the area enemy raids are plotted, to locate, shadow and report.

(2) *Readiness Patrol*: Ordered to climb to 30,000 on the Maidstone patrol line to cover other Squadrons whilst climbing over base patrol lines.

(3) *Stand-By Squadrons*: Despatched to operating height over base, and then to join the Readiness Squadrons at 30,000 feet.

(4) *Readiness Squadrons* Despatched to rendezvous over base at 20,000 to 27,000 feet, and when assembled, detailed to raids or forward patrol lines.

(5) *Squadrons at Available, Spitfires*: To be brought to Readiness, and if necessary despatched to assemble in pairs on back patrol lines at 25,000 to 30,000 feet, and then detailed to raids.

(6) *Squadrons at Available, Hurricanes*: Brought to Readiness, and if there is a second or third wave, assembled in pairs over back patrol lines so as to protect Sector aerodromes and London area whilst climbing.

(7) *Hurricane Squadrons from Tangmere and Debden*: Despatch in Wings or pairs at 20,000 to 27,000 feet, according to time and weather conditions, for one of the following purposes:

(a) To reinforce London Sectors if there is a second or third wave of enemy raids;

(b) To protect Sector aerodromes and London area whilst the earlier Squadrons are refuelling.

(8) *Close Defence of Important Bombing Objectives*; If enemy raids are approaching aircraft factories, London area, Sector aerodromes, etc., single Hurricane Squadrons that have not been included in pairs or Wings should be detailed to protective patrols between 15,000 and 18,000 feet, depending on clouds.

(Sgd.) K. R. Park
Air Vice-Marshal
Commanding, No. 11 Group
Royal Air Force

APPENDIX 30: No. 11 GROUP, INSTRUCTIONS TO CONTROLLERS, No. 34

From: Air Officer Commanding, No. 11 Group, Royal Air Force.

To: Group Controllers and Sector Commanders, for Sector Controllers.

Date: 24 October 1940

Readiness Patrols Against High Flying Fighter Raids

Experience gained during these attacks confirm that the only sure method of countering a series of raids by bomb carrying *fighters* is to keep a pair of Hurricane or a pair of Spitfire Squadrons, from the same Station if possible, continuously on patrol in clear weather and to relieve them in ample time, keeping them at 15,000/18,000 feet until raids appear imminent, when they should be ordered to full operational height. Though less economical in flying hours this method is far more effective and economical in lives than our long established method of intercepting from ground level, which was most successful against bomber formations. Those Squadrons should be on a common R/T Frequency whenever possible.

2. During the present short days and when weather conditions are suitable for heavy high flying fighter raids, Controllers should maintain standing patrols as indicated.

3. Such standing patrols should only be maintained during the full light period of the day, i.e. at present between 08.00 and 17.00 hours, and when the base of clouds is above 2,000 feet. Group and Sector Controllers must be on the alert to withdraw Standing Patrols before new cloud or thick ground mist closes down on the parent and adjacent aerodromes. These patrols must be relieved while they retain adequate petrol to allow for delays in finding a clear-weather fighter aerodrome.

4. Squadrons proceeding to Readiness Patrol are normally to gain height over base before going forward to relieve the Squadrons on patrol.

(Sgd) G. Harcourt-Smith, G/C
for Air Vice-Marshal
Commanding, No. 11 Group
Royal Air Force

APPENDIX 31: TABLE ILLUSTRATING DAMAGE TO INDUSTRIAL AND COMMERCIAL KEY POINTS, 1 JUNE–30 SEPTEMBER

Type of Key Point	*1st June to 9th August*			*10th August to 6th September*			*7th September to 30th September*		
	Slight	*Substantial*	*Total*	*Slight*	*Substantial*	*Total*	*Slight*	*Substantial*	*Total*
Factories									
Aircraft	2	1	3	18	7	25	5	3	8
ROF*	1	–	1	4	1	5	10	1	11
Shipbuilding Yards	4	1	5	9	–	9	6	–	6
Steel Work	7	1	8	9	–	9	6	–	6
Other	2	1	3	29	6	35	132	–	132
Total	16	4	20	69	14	83	159	4	163
Utilities –									
Electricity	–	–	–	1	–	1	12	3	15
Water	1	–	1	2	–	2	4	–	4
Gas (i) Works	3	–	3	7	1	8	15	1	16
(ii) Coke Ovens	–	–	–	–	–	–	3	–	3
Total	4	–	4	10	1	11	34	4	38
Oil									
Commerical	2	–	2	8	6	14	9	7	16
RAF	–	–	–	–	–	–	1	–	1
RN	2	–	2	1	1	2	–	–	–
Total	4	–	4	9	7	16	10	7	17
Telecommunication									
PO Telephone Exchanges	–	–	–	–	–	–	3	–	3
Wk Stations	–	–	–	1	–	1	1	–	1
Commercial W/T Station	–	–	–	–	–	–	1	–	1
Cable Huts	–	–	–	–	–	–	–	–	–
BBC Stations	–	–	–	–	–	–	–	–	–
Total	–	–	–	1	–	1	5	–	5
Storage									
Raw Materials	–	–	–	–	–	–	1	–	1
Service Depots	2	–	2	–	–	–	3	–	3
Total	2	–	2	–	–	–	4	–	4
Food	–	1	1	7	2	9	11	5	16
Docks and Harbours	12	2	14	30	3	33	46	6	52
Grand Total	38	7	45	126	27	153	269	26	295

Note: *Royal Ordnance Factories

APPENDIX 32: TABLE SHOWING GERMAN ESTIMATE OF BOMBS DROPPED ON BRITISH TARGETS – AUGUST–OCTOBER 1940[1]

Target	*Type of Bomb*	*August*		*September*		*October*	
London	HE Bombs (Metric tons)	12	(12)	6501	(691)	7242	(1118)
	Incendiary[2]	12	(12)	9540	(685)	4869	(305)
Liverpool	HE Bombs	454	(94)	326	(326)	210	(210)
	Incendiary	1029	(301)	787	(787)	300	(300)
Birmingham	HE Bombs	94	(94)	14	(14)	339	(339)
	Incendiary	204	(204)	7	(7)	864	(864)
Coventry	HE Bombs	89	(89)	19	(19)	163	(163)
	Incendiary	277	(277)	18	(18)	536	(536)
Manchester	HE Bombs	6	(6)	12	(12)	–	–
	Incendiary	–	–	10	(10)	–	–
Southampton	HE Bombs	–	–	117	(117)	6	(6)
	Incendiary	–	–	77	(77)	–	–
Plymouth	HE Bombs	–	–	49	(49)	14	(14)
	Incendiary	–	–	12	(12)	62	(62)
Bristol	HE Bombs	–	–	110	(110)	25	(25)
	Incendiary	–	–	68	(68)	58	(58)
	HE Bombs	406	(406)	292	(292)	77	(77)
Zerstörungziele[3]	Incendiary	261	(261)	83	(83)	88	(88)
Ausweichziele[4]	HE Bombs	397	(397)	1112	(1112)	769	(769)
	Incendiary	2492	(2492)	1202	(1202)	188	(188)
Ships	HE Bombs	86	(86)	24	(24)	30	(30)
	Incendiary	–	–	–	–	–	–
Airfields	HE Bombs	1004	(1004)	333	(333)	182	(182)
	Incendiary	321	(321)	122	(122)	56	(56)
Total	HE Bombs	2548	(2188)	8909	(3099)	9057	(2933)
	Incendiary	4596	(3868)	11926	(3071)	7021	(2457)

Notes:

1. These figures have been abstracted from reliable German documents, but they cannot be accepted as authoritative for the weight of bombs that actually fell on the different categories of target. They are of interest as showing how the Germans intended that their bombing effort should be distributed.
2. The number of incendiaries is given in terms of incendiary containers, each of which held 36 1 Kilogramme incendiary bombs.
3. *Zerstörgziele*: Targets attacked in dislocation raids (*Störangriffe*). In this type of operation specific industrial targets, especially aircraft and aero engine works, were attacked.
4. *Ausweichziele*: Alternative and secondary targets. Railway communications were the chief objectives in this category.
5. Figures in brackets denote amount dropped in attacks of under 100 tons of HE Bombs.

APPENDIX 33: BRITISH AND GERMAN AIRCRAFT CASUALTIES

TABLE 1: WEEKLY HURRICANE AND SPITFIRE PRODUCTION AND WASTAGE[1] 27 July–26 October 1940

		Output			*Wastage*						
					Operational Flying Casualties		*Accidents*				
Week Ending	*Type*	*Contractors Gross Output*	*Cat. 2 repaired*[2]	*Total*	*Cat 2*	*Cat 3*	*Cat 2*	*Cat 3*	*Exports*	*Total*	*Immediate*[3] *Issue Aircraft*
27 July	H	65	23	137	4	5	13	8	24	87	177
	S	37	12		10	12	10	1	–		95
3 Aug	H	58	23	134	4	5	9	6	–	56	164
	S	41	12		8	15	7	2	–		99
10 Aug	H	58	19	130	2	14	9	3	–	64	160
	S	37	16		11	14	8	3	–		129
17 Aug	H	45	20	102	50	84	11	2	6	247	109
	S	31	6		37	44	11	2	–		126
24 Aug	H	73	16	145	38	45	10	5	30	178	86
	S	44	12		25	21	4	–	–		75
31 Aug	H	63	21	134	23	95	8	4	9	236	78
	S	37	13		26	62	5	4	–		81
7 Sept	H	54	25	135	57	81	8	5	7	270	86
	S	36	20			45	53	10	4		39
14 Sept	H	57	48	168	19	45	10	1	–	124	80
	S	38	25		16	24	8	1	–		51
21 Sept	H	57	45	182	22	37	7	3	–	113	99
	S	40	40		18	19	7	–	–		40
28 Sept	H	58	45	171	27	45	17	3	8	172	116
	S	34	34		28	34	11	–	–		43
5 Oct	H	60	31	148	23	30	7	7	–	102	111
	S	32	25		12	10	8	5	–		51
12 Oct	H	55	41	157	17	27	9	5	–	120	119
	S	31	30		16	31	10	5	–		52
19 Oct	H	55	38	140	29	20	13	6	–	101	137
	S	25	22		9	12	11	1	–		71
26 Oct	H	70	37	173	11	17	16	8	12	95	158
	S	42	24		11	11	6	3	–		62

Notes: 1. Excludes aircraft destroyed on the ground by enemy action (see Table II).
2. Cat 2: Wrecked beyond unit capacity to repair. Cat 3: Missing or wrecked beyond repair.
3. As at last day of week for which Output and Wastage figures are given. These aircraft were held in Aircraft Storage Units.

APPENDIX 34: FIGHTER PILOT CASUALTIES

TABLE I: GROSS MONTHLY CASUALTIES – July–October 1940
(Number of pilots made casualties in the air and on the ground by enemy action and flying accidents in all squadrons of Fighter Command)

	Killed, POW, Missing	*Wounded and Injured*
July	74	49
August	148	156
September	159	152
October	100	65
Total	481	422

TABLE II: CASUALTY RATES – August–October 1940

	August	*September*	*October*
Casualties per 100 miles flown	6.5	6.6	3.9
Casualties as percentage of pilot strength	22.4	24.4	10.5
Actual casualties as percentage of postulated	172.1	163.3	84.7

TABLE III: FIGHTER COMMAND AIRCRAFT[1] DESTROYED OR BADLY DAMAGED ON GROUND BY ENEMY ACTION – 15th August–25 September 1940

	Hurricane		*Spitfire*		*Blenheim*		
Week ending	*Cat 2*	*Cat 3*	*Cat 2*	*Cat 3*	*Cat 2*	*Cat 3*	*Total*
21 August	8	12	9	3	5	5	42
28 August	2	2	Nil	1	Nil	5	7
4 September	1	2	1	2	Nil		6
11 September	Nil		Nil		Nil		Nil
18 September	Nil		Nil		Nil		Nil
25 September	Nil		Nil	1	Nil		1
Total	11	16	10	7	5	7	56

Note: [1]Operational types only.

APPENDIX 35: ANTI-AIRCRAFT COMMAND GUN DISPOSITIONS, 11 JULY–9 OCTOBER

AA Division	*HAA Gun Zones*	*11 July*	*21 Aug*	*11 Sept*	*9 Oct*
2nd	LEIGHTON BUZZARD	4	4	4	4
	NORWICH	–	–	4	4
	NOTTINGHAM	16	16	16	16
	DERBY	40	40	32	32
	SHEFFIELD	23	27	27	28
	SCUNTHORPE	–	24	–	–
	HUMBER	38	38	26	26
	Mobile Battery	8	8	–	–
RAF Stations	Duxford	2	2	2	2
	Watton	2	2	2	2
	Marham	2	2	2	2
	Feltwell	2	2	2	2
	Daventry	4	4	4	4
	Wattisham	4	4	4	4
	Grantham	4	4	4	4
	Horsham St Faith	–	2	2	2
	LAA GUNS	82	78	82	82
	AALMGs	788	765	835	839
7th	LEEDS	20	20	20	22
	TEES	30	30	30	30
	TYNE	54	50	50	46
	Mobile Guns	–	4	–	–
RAF Stations	Linton	4	4	4	4
	Driffield	4	4	–	–
	Topcliffe	–	–	2	2
	Dishforth	–	–	2	2
	Thornaby	4	4	4	–
	Acklington	2	2	2	2
	LAA GUNS	50	62	55	55
	AALMGs	321	270	277	263
3rd	BELFAST	7	7	7	12
	LONDONDERRY	–	–	4	4
	CLYDE	28	27	34	40
	ARDEER	4	8	8	8
	KYLE OF LOCHALSH	4	4	4	4
	ABERDEEN	4	4	4	4
	SCAPA	88	88	88	88
	SHETLANDS	12	12	12	12

AA Division	*HAA Gun Zones*	*11 July*	*21 Aug*	*11 Sept*	*9 Oct*
RAF Stations	Kinloss	2	2	2	2
	Lossiemouth	2	2	2	2
	Wick	4	2	2	2
	Castletown	–	2	2	2
	LAA GUNS	119	122	132	132
	AALMGs	368	378	367	375
4th	BARROW	–	–	8	9
	LIVERPOOL	52	56	58	76
	MANCHESTER	20	20	20	20
	CREWE	8	16	8	8
	DONNINGTON	–	–	–	4
	BIRMINGHAM	64	71	64	64
	COVENTRY	44	32	24	24
RAF Stations	Ringway	4	4	4	4
	LAA GUNS[1]	52	80	84	92
	AALMGs[2]	376	389	397	411
5th	MILFORD HAVEN	–	–	4	4
	SWANSEA	–	16	24	24
	CARDIFF	12	26	26	30
	NEWPORT	4	16	20	22
	BROCKWORTH	36	24	24	24
	BRISTOL	36	32	32	32
	FALMOUTH	8	12	8	8
	PLYMOUTH	18	46	26	24
	YEOVIL	–	4	4	4
	PORTLAND	6	14	14	16
	HOLTON HEATH	8	8	8	8
	SOUTHAMPTON	43	39	31	32
	PORTSMOUTH	44	44	40	40
	BRAMLEY	8	8	8	8
RAF Stations	Tangmere	4	4	4	4
	Farnborough	–	–	4	4
	Brooklands	16	16	16	16
	LAA GUNS	136	181	190	184
	AALMGs	560	547	553	521
6th	DOVER	18	18	14	14
	THAMES & MEDWAY (S)	70	72	72	72
	THAMES & MEDWAY (N)	46	48	48	48
	HARWICH	17	15	8	8

AA Division	*HAA Gun Zones*	*11 July*	*21 Aug*	*11 Sept*	*9 Oct*
RAF Stations	Biggin Hill	4	4	8	8
	Hawkinge	7	7	7	7
	Manston	8	8	8	8
	West Malling	2	2	2	2
	Rochford	4	4	4	4
	North Weald	4	4	8	8
	Martlesham	4	4	4	4
	Ipswich	4	2	2	2
	LAA GUNS	101	133	141	145
	AALMGs	437	415	396	443
1st	LANGLEY	28	28	28	28
	HOUNSLOW	4	4	4	4
	STANMORE	4	4	4	4
	IAZ	92	92	199	199
	LAA GUNS	34	38	44	60
	AALMGs	183	167	161	161

Notes: [1] Bofors, Vickers 2-pdr. (Mk VIII) and 3" (Case 1) guns: deployed for the defence of industrial and communication VPs, RAF stations and RDF stations.

[2] Lewis and Hispano guns: deployed chiefly at searchlight sites and RAF stations.

APPENDIX 36: NOTE ON CLAIMS AND CASUALTIES DURING THE BATTLE OF BRITAIN

The discrepancy between the number of German aircraft claimed as destroyed during the Battle of Britain and that of which concrete and indisputable evidence of destruction was obtained, was so large that no account of the operations would be complete unless it described, first the rules that governed our pilots' claims, and second the attempts that were made during the battle to calculate on other bases than pilots' claims what casualties the Germans were incurring.

During the whole of the campaign in France and during July the principles that were followed when claims were registered were as follows:

For a confirmed loss:

a. the enemy aircraft had to be seen on the ground or in the sea by a member of a crew or formation, or confirmed as destroyed from other sources, eg ships at sea, coastguards, the Observer Corps and police.

b. the enemy aircraft had to be seen to descend with flames issuing. It was not sufficient if only smoke was seen.

c. the enemy aircraft must be seen to break up in the air.

For an unconfirmed loss:the enemy aircraft had to be seen to break off the combat in circumstances which led our pilot or crew to believe that it would be a loss.

In short, the two main categories were 'Destroyed Confirmed' and 'Destroyed Unconfirmed'; and the onus of deciding into which category a particular claim fell lay with Fighter Command Headquarters.

During July a number of arguments were advanced against the existing categorisation. The number of combats was so large that a great burden of checking pilots' and witnesses statements was imposed on intelligence officers who were already overworked. Even more important was the effect on the pilots; for their understandable desire to follow a stricken opponent down and mark the precise location of its crash might well expose them to attack from above. It would certainly mean that they would lose height and thus frequently miss any further action. These arguments gained acceptance rather than the one maintained by Air Vice-Marshal Park, that to retain the unconfirmed category would act as a brake on over-eagerness.

Consequently, the following revised categories were applied from midnight on 13 August:

Category I – Destroyed: to cover all cases in which the enemy aircraft was positively reported to have been seen to hit the ground or sea, to break up in the air, or to descend in flames, whether or not confirmation by a second source was available. This term also covered cases in which the enemy aircraft was forced to descend and was captured.

Category II – Probably Destroyed: to be applied to those cases in which the enemy aircraft was seen to break off combat in circumstances which led to the conclusion that it must be a loss.

Category III – Damaged: to be applied to those cases in which the enemy aircraft was obviously considerably damaged when under attack, such as undercarriage dropped or aircraft parts shot away.

The new system undoubtedly simplified the making of claims by the pilots of the Command; but it was soon apparent that in solving the pilots' problem, a problem had been set on all officers whose duty it was to assess at what rate German air strength was being affected by the battle. For whereas 279 enemy aircraft were claimed as destroyed in the week following 8 August, wreckage or prisoners were only recovered from 51. It was estimated that up to eighty per cent of combats and destructions had occurred over the sea; and of most of these there was no record. But as this could not be confirmed nobody could be sure what precise ratio existed between claims and actual casualties. Nor was there any means of checking how many of the 147 German aircraft that were claimed as probably destroyed during the same period, had crashed into the sea or in Europe, and so been lost. Obviously another and more satisfactory assessment of enemy casualties was required, not in order to put on trial the honesty and reliability of the fighter pilots but so that some trustworthy estimate of German air strength could be formed. Simply to have returned to the old categories would perhaps have added to the value of the pilots' claims. Such a reversion, however, with its implication that a number of claims, if not all, were exaggerated, would not perhaps have been happily received by the pilots, who were indeed convinced that their claims could be accepted as they were made.

Furthermore, by the middle of August, the Air Ministry were almost irrevocably committed to maintaining not only the existing standards for assessing casualties, but also the methods whereby claims were passed on to the press and the general public. The fact was that the consolidated initial claims of pilots and AA guncrews, after no more than a cursory check by the Fighter Command intelligence section, were passed to the press and the BBC by the Air Ministry News Service in such a form that they were generally understood as a verified figure of German losses; and this they never were nor could be, so short was the interval between the end of a day's operations and the publication of figures. It is not surprising that there was no lack of newspapermen – amongst whom a number of American papers were represented – to agitate for facilities to visit Fighter Command stations, talk with pilots, attend interrogations of pilots by squadron intelligence officers, and so have the chance of making up their own minds whether the Air Ministry figures were to be relied upon. The Prime Minister and Air Chief Marshal Dowding were not in favour of granting such facilities: both of them felt that only the issue of the battle could convince the world that for the first time the German Air Force was being checked; and, moreover, to allow civilians, including other nationals than British, to carry out what was virtually an inquest into the probity of the fighter pilots seemed to them undignified and cheap. However, as might have been expected, those journalists who did obtain permission to visit fighter stations were so impressed by the patent honesty and confidence of the pilots that no harm came from this somewhat dubious precedent.

But as the Air Ministry was at such pains early in the battle to convince the press, and through the press the public, that the claims were accurate, it would have been next to impossible to have introduced a conditional or disclaiming element into their casualty figures, even though it became increasingly obvious that the published claims were at best only a guide to what the Germans had actually lost. Air Chief Marshal Dowding himself deplored to the Secretary of State for Air the impression that was being formed in the public mind. He did not claim exact accuracy for the total claims of the

Command: he did maintain, however, that the assessments were genuine and based on the best evidence available.[1]

During the first month of the battle the problem continued to cause concern; and early in September a section (A I 3(b)) of Air Intelligence was instructed to collate all possible evidence of certain destruction to see how far our claims could be substantiated. The results were disappointing. The officers of the section could only say that 843 German aircraft had been certainly destroyed between 8 August and 2 October, ie during the weeks when the battle was most intense. This was made up of 437 aircraft found on land, 67 in the sea (from prisoners' of war reports), another 267 in the sea (from interceptions of wireless messages from and to the German air/sea rescue organisation), and 73 in the sea or land abroad reported through various secret channels.[2] Over the same period the total claimed as "Destroyed" by fighters or AA guns was 2,091.

It is beyond doubt that there were some German losses that were not covered by the various sorts of evidence that served as a basis for this investigation. In the first place, the interception of wireless messages when enemy aircraft were about to come down in the sea, was not comprehensive; nor was every German pilot in difficulties over the sea able to despatch a call for help. Secondly, missing German airmen, of whom we had no record, were for a time enquired after by aero clubs in Europe, the request being transmitted by the Royal Aero Club: German prisoners also asked frequently after other airmen who had not returned to their base but whose deaths were unknown to us. Also, it is unlikely that there was anything approaching complete cover of all cases of German aircraft crashing in France or Belgium on their return journey. Finally, there was the small number of aircraft totally destroyed in the air when machine gun or anti-aircraft fire detonated the bombs they were carrying. For all these reasons the A I (3)(b) figures are to be reckoned only a proportion of the German losses.

What these were exactly is not known at the time of writing (January 1945) any more than in the autumn of 1940. Late in the battle Air Chief Marshal Dowding expressed his personal views in a letter to the Vice-Chief of the Air Staff that the claims were probably a twenty five per cent overestimate; and the narrator would venture his own opinion that they were at least that. If this proves to be so, there is likely to be a sense of deflation and disappointment amongst those who fought the battle and amongst the public at large. For it is true to say that the success that Fighter Command undoubtedly achieved has largely been measured by the casualties suffered by the German Air Force. Nor has this criticism been given any less validity by the Air Ministry's continuing policy of claiming to publish the precise losses in battle of the enemy, as well as of the Royal Air Force.

---

1 In a letter to Sir Archibald Sinclair on 16 August Air Chief Marshal Dowding stated: 'Where the claims run into three figures it is quite impossible to arrive at anything more than an approximation of the actual numbers; not only because there is no time for detailed enquiry, but also because the pilots themselves have only a general idea of what had happened to the aircraft at which they have fired in the heat of a general engagement. A pilot may be morally certain that he has destroyed an opponent at 15,000 feet, but before the latter has had time to do more than go into an uncontrolled spin our pilot is engaged with two or three more of the enemy. Any attempt, therefore, to prove that the figures are exact can only result in proving the contrary. The main safeguard against exaggerated claims is the care with which each pilot's unofficial score is kept in a squadron; and any pilot who made unsubstantiated claims would soon be "bowled out" by others who had been in the fight with him.' The Commander-in-Chief did not say what is demonstrably the case, that in the confusion of combat more than one pilot has honestly claimed the destruction of one and the same opponent.

2 The first of the AI 3(b) weekly summaries was circulated on 19 September to a small number of the Air Staff: it was retrospective to the beginning of the second phase of the battle. The following table gives a digest of the findings from the beginning of August to the end of October. It must not be considered an authority for German losses: its interest lies rather in giving those casualties that could possibly be identified at the time.

As to this, an important question of policy emerges. During the Battle of Britain the Germans were daily made a present of more exact and detailed information of the casualties in Fighter Command than the Air Staff had available concerning German losses. The Germans, therefore, if they chose to take advantage of it, had reliable knowledge of the position in Fighter Command; and that they either did not realise how serious was the fighter pilot position or that, if they did, they were unable to press their advantage owing to their own losses, does not alter the fact. On the other hand, the Air Ministry's claims of German aircraft destroyed seemed to the public at large to be the more reliable because British casualties were given with such precision; and it is the case that the profit and loss account of the battle was a notable factor in stimulating public morale at the time.

If indeed the Germans ceased their attacks because of casualties it would be interesting, to say the least, to know exactly what these were. For it would show at what point the Germans considered that the losses of their air force were insufficiently backed by the prospective production of supplies and aircrews, and that future operations were being jeopardised.

In the very nature of things the success of fighting in the air cannot be judged by the amount or importance of ground lost or won, which is a standard that can usually be applied to military operations on land. For this reason casualties incurred in the air have a significance perhaps greater than in any other form of warfare. But the significance lies not in the simple ratio of relative losses but in the relationship between casualties and reserves and production of men and aircraft, and the importance of the objectives that are being attacked or defended. In short, there are many factors in the algebra of air warfare. But until evidence to the contrary becomes available, we are at least entitled to say this, that the German commanders probably called off the heavy attacks by day because they were being punished beyond an acceptable scale of casualties.

	Number Claimed			*Number Identified*					
					In Sea				
Week	*Des*	*Prob*	*Dam*	*On Land*	*Prisoners*	*W/T*	*Other Sources*	*Total Identified*	*German Admissions*
8–14 Aug	279	147	95	39	12	25	15	91	98
15–21 Aug	396	117	115	74	14	26	7	121	111
22–28 Aug	193	64	70	43	8	39	14	104	75
29 Aug–4 Sept	303	123	156	76	6	54	5	141	132
5–11 Sept	330	126	141	73	15	52	13	153	94
12–18 Sept	263	71	113	57	2	22	7	88	70
19–25 Sept	63	30	45	16	4	18	7	45	23
26 Sept–2 Oct	244	86	94	59	6	30	5	100	89
3–9 Oct	72	20	45	28	13	8	–	49	36
10–16 Oct	48	25	29	17	2	7	–	26	22
17–30 Oct	108	58	84	47	15	8	6	76	70

APPENDIX 37: GERMAN VIEWS ON THE BATTLE OF BRITAIN

On 7 June 1945 the Senior Narrator, Air Historical Branch, addressed a lengthy questionnaire on the subject of the Battle of Britain to Generalfeldmarschall Milch and Generalleutenant Galland. For most of the war the former was Inspector-General of the *Luftwaffe* and Secretary of State for Air. The latter commanded JG 26 during the Battle of Britain and afterwards rose to be Inspector of Fighters. There is no reason to doubt the honesty of their replies. Insofar as these were phrased in general terms this was due to the lapse of time and the absence of documents that would doubtless have refreshed their memories. The substance of the interview is embodied below.

REASONS FOR THE INTERVAL BETWEEN THE FALL OF FRANCE AND THE BATTLE OF BRITAIN

Pt VII, p. 317

In Part VII of the narrative the point was made that, in all, the intensive offensive by day lasted almost exactly a month, from 8 August to 7 September, which prompted the questions, why did the Germans start so late? Why did they stop so soon? All that could be said in answer to the first was that such information as was available indicated that the German Air Force was re-equipping and resting after its exertions in May and June and that the problems of supplying and maintaining it in its new positions had not been properly solved for some weeks. The magnanimous offer of peace by Hitler and its obtuse and criminal spurning by the British Government – the theme of German propaganda – were, it must be confessed, disdained as explanations of the delay in launching the air offensive.

Yet Milch sincerely believes that these were actually the reasons. He said that he strongly deprecated the delay. The *Luftwaffe* was ready to begin operations after the fall of France and he urged that immediate action should be taken. Hitler, however, was not anxious to fight England and the offensive had to wait until it was clear that his overture of 19 July would not lead to anything. Galland added the detail that on the day, as commander of JG 26, he was engaged in supplying fighter protection for the *Reichstag* instead of escorting bombers against Great Britain as Milch would have wished.

RELATION OF THE BATTLE TO INVASION

Both Milch and Galland were quite definite that the air attacks were designed as a preliminary to invasion and that a plan of invasion was prepared under the codename of "Operation Sealion"; but they were equally definite that the plan had no particular date of launching assigned to it. It depended essentially on obtaining air superiority over the Channel and the South of England, which would bring in its train some degree of ascendancy over British naval forces. Thus, they went on, the whole object of the Battle of Britain was to wear down the British fighter force. Whether the objectives were convoys in the Channel, or airfields inland, or London, the object was always the same – to bring the defending squadrons to battle and to weaken them.

About the plan that was to have governed the projected expedition Milch said he was not clear. He did say, however, that the barges that were assembled at Channel ports were genuinely intended for the transport of invading troops; and his observations in general implied that landings would have taken place between the Solent and the North Foreland.

GERMAN INTENTIONS DURING THE BATTLE

Such a view of the battle implies that the targets that were attacked were of secondary importance compared to combat with Fighter Command. It implies also – and this has been stressed in the narrative – that the scope of the battle was largely dictated by the range of the German fighters, especially the Me 109. Both Milch and Galland confirm this. The progressive extension of the offensive – first, the Channel convoys, second, coastal airfields, third, airfields near London, finally, London itself – was intended to force Fighter Command into increasingly intensive battle for the defence of increasingly important objectives. Galland said indeed that attacks had to be extended further inland in order to get the British pilots to fight. The implication can be ignored – it was not infrequently an accusation on the part of our own men that the Germans were timorous; perhaps all spirited fighter pilots get the same impression – but the observation has the merit of underlining what were the chief ends the Germans had in view.

Galland, however, was a fighter commander; and his views, though Milch confirmed them, must not be taken to mean that the Germans were not especially interested in the targets that they attacked. Some of them were obviously well chosen, notably fighter airfields; for in their attacks on this type of target the Germans furthered their main object in two ways, first by taking toll of the defending fighters in the air, second by damaging airfields facilities on the ground. The attack of London by day had also the advantage, from the German standpoint, that our fighters would come up in the utmost strength to defend the capital.

On the other hand, neither officer had appreciated to what extent the coastal airfields that were attacked in the period 8–23 August were important to Fighter Command; and to the extent that this was the case they considered that German Intelligence was at fault. As for RDF stations, the prisoners agreed that they thought that serious damage had been done to one or two – which was so – but that in general they were considered difficult targets to damage effectively. This also is true; but the fact remains that neither seemed to realise how important were the RDF stations to the Fighter Command technique of interception or how embarrassing sustained attacks upon them would have been.

THE INFLUENCE OF THE ME 109

The narrative has emphasised to what extent the location of the battle was dictated by the range of the Me 109. Indeed, the battle could hardly have been

Pt VII, p. 322 ibid.

fought at all if the Me 109 had not been able to reach this country and stay over it for long enough to accept combat. It is doubtful, however, whether anyone in this country has appreciated to what extent the Germans may view the battle as one fought out between fighter forces. This is certainly the view of Galland. In it, as in his emphasis in general on the fighting in the air rather than on bombing, some allowance must be made for his bias as a fighter pilot. But it explains more satisfactorily than any theory that has been advanced in the narrative what has been hitherto one of the most puzzling features of the battle: the low scale of the German bomber effort compared to the total strength of the bomber force. The substance of his views, with which Milch was in agreement, is as follows:

Bombers were an essential component of the German offensive as a means of ensuring that the British fighters came up to give battle; but the majority of the bomber force would only have been employed when air supremacy had been won, or almost won, and invasion was at hand. Early in the battle some attacks were made by unescorted bombers but they suffered unacceptably heavy losses. (To the best of our knowledge such attacks were very few.) Henceforth all bombers were strongly escorted. These operations were not too expensive in themselves: the trouble was that they were difficult to organise. The root fault of the German equipment was the short range of the Me 109, especially as the Me 110, which was a disappointing aircraft, was no substitute for it. This meant that an escort of Me 109s had to link up quickly with the bomber component if they were to have enough fuel to penetrate inland and fight effectively. Milch here pointed the contrast of the ability of American fighters to spend some time over the East Anglian coast simply getting into formation. This was not too difficult for the Germans during 1940 if the weather was good; but in cloudy weather the chances were not good, particularly as the German bombers had no suitable radio equipment for communicating with the attendant fighters. Milch maintained that on several occasions whole operations were given up because the bombers had not found the fighters: Galland contradicted this and said that he knew of no complete operation that was abandoned but that often a considerable part of the bombers taking part failed to make contact with the escort. This last observation is certainly borne out by events as they appeared to us. It is particularly applicable to September when the weather was much more cloudy than in the previous month; and during that month the proportion of bombers destroyed rose sharply.

REASONS FOR ABANDONING HEAVY DAYLIGHT ATTACK

This difficulty of providing deep fighter escort was an important factor, according to the two officers, in the abandoning of the heavy daylight attacks and the concentration upon attacks by night; and the emphasis that the narrative has placed upon the significance of the latter appears to be justified. Daylight attacks did continue, of course, after the switch to night attacks had taken place; but the German commanders were aware that the chance of destroying Fighter Command had disappeared. Galland could not recollect a specific date for this change of policy: it is unlikely, however, to have been later than the middle of

September, by which time by far the greater weight of the German effort was being applied at night.

THE SWITCH TO THE ATTACK OF LONDON

It was also being applied against London, which led to the question of why the attack of airfields was discontinued in favour of that against London. Both Milch and Galland professed to know nothing. Asked why, in view of the success of the daylight attack of 7 September, no comparable attacks were later launched, Galland referred again to the difficulty of providing escorts of Me 109s for attacks against targets well inland.

THE FAILURE OF THE JU 87

There is certainly no doubt that the Germans were convinced by the operations during the first half of August that Ju 87s could not be used where they would meet fighter opposition. After 18 August they were withdrawn from the battle, the intention being to use them against Channel shipping when an invasion expedition was launched. This accounts at once for the concentration of dive-bombers in the Pas de Calais during the first days of September and their complete inactivity during that and the following months.

STRENGTH OF BRITISH FIGHTER OPPOSITION: GERMAN CASUALTIES

Galland indicated that British fighter opposition was stronger than anticipated. He said he was continually being assured that only a hundred or so fighters would be met in any operation over the south-east; but in his experience anything from two hundred to three hundred might be found. Comment is unnecessary beyond this, that even including the squadrons from Middle Wallop and Duxford there were rarely more than three hundred British fighters available in the south-east at any time; and it would be surprising if Galland ever saw all of them in the air at once.

More important was his statement that up to a certain date, he could not remember exactly when, the German pilots felt that the British air opposition was weakening, but from that date on the defence seemed to pass its crisis and became stronger and more effective. (The most likely, in our view, would be sometime during the second week in September). At this stage, taking into account the difficulty of providing fighter escorts, it became clear that no real progress was being made; and thenceforth the Germans concentrated on night attacks.

It was not to be expected that either officer would recollect what were the German casualties. Milch had in mind the figure of an average daily loss of twenty-eight bombers, but he was obviously not sure. They confirmed, however, that the scale of casualties was heavy, in view of the other factors that have been mentioned, for heavy daylight attacks to be continued.

CONCLUSION

Without regarding the views of Milch and Galland as authoritative – obviously we need to see documentary evidence – their answers do permit certain generalisations about the battle that are unlikely to be shaken in future. They are simple enough. First, the Battle of Britain was indeed a battle that decided the fate of the projected invasion: that no specific date was assigned to the expedition is unimportant. Second, its object, from the German point of view, was to obtain supremacy in the air over south-east England. German eyes were firmly fixed on this part of England and the fighter squadrons there; and it is noteworthy that neither Milch nor Galland remembered anything of the attack on 15 August against the north-east coast. Thirdly, the German Air Force was not properly equipped for the sort of operations demanded by their object. The offensive depended on fighters and the fighters that the Germans had were not satisfactory. Fourthly, the attack was called off, and with it the invasion, not so much because of losses as such as because there was no apparent return for them and progressively less prospect of one.

More justifying detail is necessary on this last point as it is for a fifth generalisation arising out of the interview: that the Germans did not "throw in all that they had got". Yet even if this is the case it does not detract in the slightest from the magnitude of the British victory. For the Germans used all the aircraft that could be effectively employed to attain the object that they had in view. One complete category of aircraft, the dive-bomber, was demonstrated to be ineffective simply because our pilots handled it so roughly. For the rest, it appears that all the German fighters were employed and just so many bombers as could be escorted. Certainly there were bombers available for the night attacks even when the day fighting, on which the Germans pinned their best hopes, was most intense.

None of this adds much to what had already been appreciated. But it emphasises the success of the measures that were taken during the battle to maintain the fighting strength of the Command in the south-east, even at the expense of other areas. In fact, it seems to be the case that from 7 September onwards the Germans got the impression that opposition was stronger than ever; and it will be recalled that it was about the time that larger fighting formations began to be employed by Fighter Command. However, this does not mean that the tactics of September would have been successful in August. The switch to the attack on London was to the defenders' advantage; for it allowed more time for interception and for assembling of pairs and wings of squadrons than did the previous attacks on airfields.

One final point is worth making. If Milch is to be believed, the Germans used all that they could for this battle yet failed to win it. They were certainly not restrained from using more aircraft because of the campaigns that they were to engage in during 1941. He says that the daylight offensive was abandoned some time before the decision was taken to turn against the Balkans and Russia. His particular offices during the war give the observation no little authority; and while in this case, as in others, proof would be welcomed, it is hard to discover any motive for misleading us.

INDEX